THE OXFORD HANDBOOK OF

MANAGEMENT

Adrian Wilkinson is Professor and Director of the Centre for Work, Organisation and Wellbeing at Griffith University. He holds Visiting Professorships at Loughborough University, Sheffield University and the University of Durham, and is an Academic Fellow at the Centre for International Human Resource Management at the Judge Institute, University of Cambridge. Adrian has authored/co-authored/edited thirty books and over one hundred and fifty articles in academic journals. He was elected as an Academician (Fellow) of the Academy of Social Sciences in the UK as well as a Fellow of the Academy of Social Sciences in Australia.

Steven J. Armstrong is Emeritus Professor at Hull University Business School and Professor of Organizational Behaviour at the University of Lincoln International Business School in the UK. He is also past president of the Management Education & Development Division of the Academy of Management. He has presented more than 50 conference papers, edited 4 books, and authored more than 50 articles/book chapters. He previously spent 15 years at the leading edge of research, design and development within the electronics industry and became an R&D manager responsible for new product developments involving multi-million pound projects.

Professor Michael Lounsbury is the Canada Research Chair in Entrepreneurship and Innovation at the University of Alberta School of Business. His research focuses on the relationship between organizational and institutional change, entrepreneurial dynamics, and the emergence of new industries and practices. Professor Lounsbury serves on a number of editorial board and is the series editor of *Research in the Sociology of Organizations*. Previously, he served as Chair of the Organization and Management Theory Division of the Academy of Management.

THE OXFORD HANDBOOK OF
MANAGEMENT

Edited by
ADRIAN WILKINSON, STEVEN J. ARMSTRONG,
and
MICHAEL LOUNSBURY

OXFORD
UNIVERSITY PRESS

OXFORD
UNIVERSITY PRESS

Great Clarendon Street, Oxford, OX2 6DP,
United Kingdom

Oxford University Press is a department of the University of Oxford.
It furthers the University's objective of excellence in research, scholarship,
and education by publishing worldwide. Oxford is a registered trade mark of
Oxford University Press in the UK and in certain other countries

© Oxford University Press 2017

The moral rights of the authors have been asserted

First published 2017
First published in paperback 2018

All rights reserved. No part of this publication may be reproduced, stored in
a retrieval system, or transmitted, in any form or by any means, without the
prior permission in writing of Oxford University Press, or as expressly permitted
by law, by licence or under terms agreed with the appropriate reprographics
rights organization. Enquiries concerning reproduction outside the scope of the
above should be sent to the Rights Department, Oxford University Press, at the
address above

You must not circulate this work in any other form
and you must impose this same condition on any acquirer

Published in the United States of America by Oxford University Press
198 Madison Avenue, New York, NY 10016, United States of America

British Library Cataloguing in Publication Data

Data available

Library of Congress Cataloging in Publication Data

Data available

ISBN 978-0-19-870861-2 (Hbk.)
ISBN 978-0-19-882800-6 (Pbk.)

Links to third party websites are provided by Oxford in good faith and
for information only. Oxford disclaims any responsibility for the materials
contained in any third party website referenced in this work.

Acknowledgements

We are grateful to our editor David Musson for his ideas and support as well as Clare Kennedy for steering the book safely through to production.

Contents

List of Figures xi
List of Tables xiii
List of Contributors xv

1. Introduction and Theoretical Overview: Management—
Past, Present, and Future 1
ADRIAN WILKINSON, STEVE J. ARMSTRONG, AND MICHAEL LOUNSBURY

PART I MAIN HISTORIC MODELS

2. Scientific Management 19
LUCY TAKSA

3. Human Relations 39
KYLE BRUCE AND CHRIS NYLAND

4. Operations Management 57
MARTIN SPRING

5. Peter F. Drucker's Management by Objectives and Self-Control 81
PETER STARBUCK

6. Studying Culture in Organizations: Not Taking for Granted
the Taken-for-Granted 103
MATS ALVESSON, DAN KÄRREMAN, AND SIERK YBEMA

7. The Opening Up of Organization Theory: Open Systems,
Contingency Theory, and Organizational Design 127
C. R. (BOB) HININGS AND ROYSTON GREENWOOD

8. Future in the Past: A Philosophical Reflection on the Prospects
of Management 145
STEWART CLEGG, MARCO BERTI, AND WALTER P. JARVIS

PART II THE DOING/FUNCTIONS OF MANAGEMENTS

9. Managing People: Understanding the Theory and Practice of Human Resources Management — 179
   ANDY CHARLWOOD AND KIM HOQUE

10. Managing Operations — 200
    NICOLA BATEMAN AND ZOE RADNOR

11. Managing Projects — 219
    JEFFREY K. PINTO AND PEERASIT PATANAKUL

12. Managing Data, Information, and Knowledge — 237
    WENDY L. CURRIE

13. Managing Meaning—Culture — 256
    VIOLINA P. RINDOVA AND SANTOSH SRINIVAS

14. Management and Leadership — 276
    RONALD E. RIGGIO

15. Fragmentation in Strategic Management: Process and Agency Issues — 293
    MARK SHANLEY

16. Management Practice—and the Doing of Management — 325
    STEFAN TENGBLAD

17. Managing Change — 343
    DAVID A. BUCHANAN

PART III THEMES

18. Management as a Practice of Power — 367
    DAVID COURPASSON

19. Management and Morality/Ethics—The Elusive Corporate Morals — 386
    MICHEL ANTEBY AND CAITLIN ANDERSON

20. Management and Modernity — 400
    GRAHAM SEWELL

PART IV MANAGEMENT IN SOCIETY AND MANAGEMENT ORGANIZATIONS/INSTITUTIONS

21. Evidence-Based Management 419
    KEVIN MORRELL AND MARK LEARMONTH

22. Management Education in Business Schools 437
    KENNETH G. BROWN AND ROBERT S. RUBIN

23. Management as an Academic Discipline? 461
    DAMIAN O'DOHERTY AND CHRISTIAN DE COCK

24. Culture, Context, and Managerial Behaviour 481
    LUCIARA NARDON

25. International Management 497
    MIKE GEPPERT AND GRAHAM HOLLINSHEAD

26. Management and Consultancy: Ambivalence, Complexity, and Change 518
    ANDREW STURDY, CHRISTOPHER WRIGHT, AND NICK WYLIE

Author Index 539
Subject Index 557

List of Figures

4.1	Incidence of 'Operations Management' and Related Terms	58
4.2	The Refinement of New Problems into Policies and Automatic Decision Rules	72
4.3	Scope of Management Decisions	72
10.1	Analysis of Research Approaches by Year	202
10.2	Comparison of Research Methods, 1980–2014	203
10.3	Number of Publications by Region	204
11.1	Project Life Cycle	221
11.2	Traditional Execution-based Approach to Project Delivery	226
11.3	The Management of Projects	227
12.1	The Trilogy of Data, Information, and Knowledge	240
12.2	Unpacking Financialization, Finance, and Technology	246
17.1	Assessing Depth of Change	345
17.2	The Institute for Healthcare Improvement Large-scale Change Framework	347
17.3	The Stace-Dunphy Contingency Model of Change Implementation	349
17.4	The Processual Framework	350
21.1	A Simple Hierarchy of the Sciences	424
22.1	GMAT Test Scores Sent to Programs Worldwide by Program Type	441
22.2	An Open Systems Model of Program Quality	445
24.1	Context and Managerial Behaviour	483
24.2	Context, Cognition, and Behaviour	484
26.1	Images of the Passive and Active Managerial Client	529

List of Tables

4.1	Indication of the Rise of 'Theory' in OM	68
14.1	The Components of Transformational Leadership Theory	281
17.1	Managing Change on Google	346
17.2	The McKinsey & Co. Recipe for Successful Transformational Change	348
17.3	Change Management Institute Competency Model	356
22.1	Most-cited Articles in Business and Management Education, 1970–2013	447
24.1	Managers' Influence on Context	488
25.1	Largest MNCs, Sectors, and Headquarter Locality	500
25.2	Reasons for Corporate Internationalization	502
25.3	Dunning's Resource-, Market-, Strategic Resource-, and Efficiency-Seeking Behaviours	503
25.4	(box) Bartlett and Ghoshal's Transnational Typology	507

List of Contributors

Editors

Adrian Wilkinson is Professor and Director of the Centre for Work, Organisation and Wellbeing at Griffith University, Australia. He holds Visiting Professorships at Loughborough University, Sheffield University, and the University of Durham, and is an Academic Fellow at the Centre for International Human Resource Management at the Judge Institute, University of Cambridge. Adrian is author, co-author, or editor of twenty-five books, over 150 articles in refereed journals, and numerous book chapters. Adrian was appointed as a British Academy of Management Fellow in 2010. He is an Academician of the Academy of Social Sciences and a Fellow of the Australian Acdemy of Social Sciences. He has been shortlisted by HR magazine for the award of HR (Human resources) Most Influential International Thinker.

Steven J. Armstrong is Emeritus Professor at Hull University Business School and Professor of Organizational Behaviour at the University of Lincoln International Business School in the UK. He is also past president of the Management Education & Development Division of the Academy of Management. He has presented more than 50 conference papers, edited 4 books, and authored more than 50 articles/book chapters. He previously spent 15 years at the leading edge of research, design, and development within the electronics industry and became an R&D manager responsible for new product developments involving multi-million pound projects.

Michael Lounsbury is Professor, Thornton A. Graham Chair, and Associate Dean of Research at the University of Alberta School of Business, and a Principal Investigator at the Canadian National Institute of Nanotechnology. His research focuses on the relationship between organizational and institutional change, entrepreneurial dynamics, and the emergence of new industries and practices. In addition to serving on a number of editorial boards, Professor Lounsbury is the series editor of Research in the Sociology of Organizations, Co-Editor of *Organization Studies*, and Associate Editor of the *Academy of Management Annals*. He is also the Chair Elect of the Organization and Management Theory Division of the Academy of Management.

The Contributors

Mats Alvesson Professor of Business Administration at University of Lund, University of Queensland, and Cass Business School, City University London

Caitlin Anderson Research Associate, Harvard University

Michel Anteby Associate Professor of Organizational Behavior, Boston University

Nicola Bateman Associate Professor, University of Leicester

Marco Berti Lecturer, University of Technology Sydney (UTS) Business School

Rob Briner Professor of Organisational Psychology, School of Management, University of Bath

Ken Brown Professor of Management and Organisations, Tippie College of Business, University of Iowa

Kyle Bruce Senior Lecturer in Management, Macquarie University

David A. Buchanan Emeritus Professor of Organizational Behaviour, School of Management, Cranfield University

Andy Charlwood Professor of Human Resource Management, Leeds University Business School

Stewart Clegg Professor of Management, University of Technology Sydney (UTS) Business School, Visiting Professor at Nova School of Business and Economics, Lisbon, Portugal, and a Strategic Research Advisor, Newcastle University Business School, Newcastle

David Courpasson Professor of Sociology at EMLYON business school, Professor at Cardiff University

Wendy Currie Professor of Information Systems, Audencia School of Management Nantes

Christian De Cock Professor, Copenhagen Business School

Mike Geppert Professor of Strategic and International Management, School of Economics and Business Administration, Friedrich Schiller University Jena

Royston Greenwood Telus Professor of Strategic Management, University of Alberta

Bob Hinings Professor Emeritus, Department of Strategic Management and Organisation, University of Alberta

Graham Hollinshead Reader in International and Comparative Human Resource Management, Hertfordshire Business School, University of Hertfordshire

Kim Hoque Professor of Human Resource Management Warwick University

LIST OF CONTRIBUTORS

Walter P. Jarvis Lecturer, University of Technology Sydney (UTS) Business School

Dan Kärreman Professor, Copenhagen Business School

Mark Learmonth Professor of Organization Studies, Durham University

Kevin Morrell Professor of Strategy, Durham University

Luciara Nardon Associate Professor of International Business, Sprott School of Business

Chris Nyland Professor of International Business, Monash University

Peerasit Patanakul Associate Professor of Management, Penn State University

Damian O'Doherty Professor, Manchester Business School, University of Manchester

Jeffrey Pinto Professor of Management, Penn State University

Zoe Radnor Dean, School of Business, and Professor of Service Operations Management, University of Leicester

Ronald E. Riggio Kravis Professor of Leadership and Organizational Psychology, Claremont McKenna College

Violina Rindova Professor of Management, University of Texas

Robert S. Rubin Associate Professor, Driehaus College of Business, DePaul University

Graham Sewell Professor, Department of Management and Marketing, University of Melbourne

Mark Shanley Professor of Management, University of Illinois at Chicago

Martin Spring Professor of Management Science, Lancaster University

Peter Starbuck Visiting Professor University of Chester; Founding Visiting Professor at University Centre Shrewsbury

Santosh Srinivas, McCombs School of Business, The University of Texas at Austin

Andrew Sturdy Professor of Management, University of Bristol

Lucy Taksa Professor, Department of Marketing and Management, Macquarie University

Stefan Tengblad Professor of Business, University of Skovde

Christopher Wright Professor of Organisational Studies, University of Sydney, Australia

Nick Wylie Principal Lecturer in HRM, University of Coventry

Sierk Ybema Associate Professor, Department of Organization Sciences, VU University Amsterdam

CHAPTER 1

INTRODUCTION AND THEORETICAL OVERVIEW
Management—Past, Present, and Future

ADRIAN WILKINSON, STEVEN J. ARMSTRONG, AND MICHAEL LOUNSBURY

> Managers are the dinosaurs of our modern organizational ecology. The Age of Management is finally coming to a close ... (Cloke and Goldsmith, 2002)
>
> 'The End of Management' (title of *Wall Street* article, 21 August 2010)

MANAGEMENT, commonly referred to as the pursuit of objectives through the organization and coordination of people, remains a core feature, and function, of modern society. Some 'classic' forms of corporate and bureaucratic management may come to be seen as a prevalent form of organization and organizing in the twentieth century (Weber, 1978), and in the post-Fordist, global, knowledge-driven contemporary world we are seeing different patterns, principles, and styles of management as old models are increasingly questioned (Diefenbach and By, 2012; du Gay and Morgan, 2013; Holmqvist and Spicer, 2012).

The functions, ideologies, practices, and theories of management have changed over time, as recorded by many scholars (e.g. Barley and Kunda, 1992) and may vary according to different models of organization (Morgan, 1986) and between different cultures and societies (Bendix, 1956; Guillén, 1994). Whilst the administrative, corporate, or factory manager may be a figure on the wane, management as an ethos, organizing principle, culture, and field of academic teaching and research has increased dramatically in the last half century, and spread throughout the world not least through the influence of university business schools from which many of our contributors are based. And to the extent that we live in a society of organizations, managerial ideas and practices have become prevalent not only in for-profit firms, but also non-profits, cooperatives, state agencies, and any aspect of society that requires organizing and organization (Hwang and Powell, 2009; Perrow, 1991; Scott and Davis, 2015).

The purpose of this handbook is to analyse and explore the evolution of management: the core functions and how they may have changed; its position in the culture/zeitgeist of modern society; the institutions and ideologies that support it; and likely challenges and changes in the future. In doing so, we provide a broad overview of management—its history, development, context, changing function in organization and society, key elements and functions, and contemporary and future challenges. We then ask whether the twentieth century was the 'golden age' of the corporate, bureaucratic manager and if so what might we expect in the future? And if this was indeed a 'golden age' why has there been such an upsurge in interest in management in the last fifty years—with a huge growth in management education, and management and business cultures?

The handbook provides both an overview and detailed analyses of the main functions and how these may have changed over time. It comprises original chapters by leading international scholars in the field from around the globe. A key dynamic of the handbook is a retrospective and prospective overview of the discipline, with a critical assessment of past and present theory that also looks to the future. The handbook emphasizes the theoretical diversity within management by examining the integrity and intellectual coherence of the field while also looking at resonances within and between its key components.

The interdisciplinary nature of the field is reflected in the contributions whose aims are to analyse, promote, and critique the role of management. Each chapter offers a comprehensive, critical overview of aspects of the field, a discussion of key debates and research, and a review of the emerging agenda in the topic area.

Historical Context

According to Bowden and Lamond (2015: viii), despite:

> the proliferation of business schools throughout the world and the vast amount of management research that has been conducted in recent years, there remains considerable confusion as to what constitutes 'management'. There is also misunderstanding as to when, where, and how management emerged as a practical system of organizing work and of creating wealth. It is, for example, commonly stated both in academia and the wider business community that management has been around for millennia.

They note that historians generally take a dim view of management predating the industrial revolution by hundreds, if not thousands, of years and stories of pyramid building as early examples of management given that Pollard (1965) notes that—unlike pyramid builders—modern managers have to not just show absolute results but relate them to costs and see them competitively. Drawing from both Pollard and Wren, they identify the industrial revolution as the crucible for the creation of modern management, although not with the steam engine as the driver; they argue that it had much more to do with the new modes of thought that accompanied the industrial revolution. In this sense we can regard management as a response to solve the problem created by the growth of the firm (Fligstein, 1990; Willman, 2014) and that the industrial revolution and competitive pressures led to specific responses which led to a broad universal management model. Taylorism invented management as we know it today with managers taking responsibility and skills previously held by workers, plus also systematically taking responsibility for taking those responsibilities (Salaman, 1995: 9). Of course much depends on what we mean by management. Management as someone getting things done through other people, the classic Rosemary Stewart (1967) argument, establishes management as a universal activity as old as the hills, but this is management as a human activity rather than as a distinct occupation—as humans we all have to manage. Management is the art of getting things done through people but not all take on the occupation of management. Our ordinary (normal) requirements of life are provided by organizations which require managers to run them and managers hence play a major role in modern society.

From the industrial revolution, organizations grew simply too large to be properly controlled by their owners, so managers became responsible for them. As Reed explains:

> Effective corporate control was seen to pass out of the hands of private owners into the laps of managerial technocracy that was forced to attend to the impact of their policies on a diverse, and often bewildering, array of interest groups which had to be molded into a coherent and sustainable public constituency. The dominance of the capitalist class was giving way to the increasing power of a managerial technocracy. (Reed, 1992: 13)

That is not to say everything was new. Willman (2014) and others point out that good parts of the *management armoury* were available before the industrial revolution, given that all large organizations have to deal with issues of coordination and control, which in themselves raise issues of agency and accountability and point to the example of the Arsenal of the Venetian merchants in the Italian Renaissance.

However, management is not only technical but also social. As a result, the managerial task becomes one that involves establishing control over the meaning of work as much as execution of tasks. That is, the managerial task is to inspire and enthuse, not simply to provide orders (Grugulis et al., 2000). As Watson puts it:

> To shape human activity requires systems rules and procedures but people working in organizations who have common interests also have divergent interests and rules themselves are not sufficient to bring people together. (Watson, 1994: 33)

Reed describes a shift from 'control by repression to control by seduction' with work redefined in emotional, rather than productive, terms.

The rise of management as a response to business developments and external events also helped shape those developments (Willman, 2014: 4), and has been accompanied by dramatic growth in the provision of management education programmes over the past century. Although there have also been increasing doubts over the relevance (Pfeffer and Fong, 2002) and effectiveness (Mintzberg, 2004) of management education, Engwall (2007) shows early attempts to introduce economic disciplines into universities in Europe in the eighteenth century (e.g. Frankfurt-an-der-Oder, Rinteln, and Halle in Germany, 1727 and Uppsala, Sweden, 1741). The first notable institutions for academic business education began to appear in the middle of the nineteenth century. Business colleges were also being founded in other parts of the world around this time, for example in Tokyo (1887), Osaka (1901), and Kobe (1902) in Japan and also in India (1913). In the UK, it was not until the British Institute of Management (founded in 1948) assembled a committee to address aspects of management education (Ivory et al., 2006) that interests began to accelerate (Tiratsoo, 1998). However, business education really began to gain momentum in the UK in the early 1960s following the Robbins Report in 1963 which called for two postgraduate business schools to be established. Shortly afterwards, a centre for business education was created at Warwick University and then two new business schools were founded within the universities of Manchester and London in 1965. By the 1970s, management education was being provided by 237 different institutions in the UK (Tiratsoo, 1998), and by the 1990s UK business schools brought in more than £400 million a year (Crainer and Dearlove, 1999) to the nation's economy. Engwall (2007) reports a similar proliferation of business schools across northern, central, and eastern Europe and notes that the American model has played a dominant role in their developments.

The roots of many of these business schools—despite others appearing in Europe at the same time, such as HEC (école des Hautes Etudes Commerciales de Paris) and Handelshochschulen in Germany—can be traced back to the United States and in particular to the Wharton School at the University of Pennsylvania when a Bachelor's degree in Business was initiated in 1881 by Joseph Wharton, an American businessman. Believed to be the first of the prominent business schools, it was founded, somewhat ironically, as we will demonstrate later in the book, on the basis of his criticisms of the 'learning by doing' approach common in colleges at that time. Wharton favoured a structured and theoretical approach to management education (Sass, 1982). His criticisms were to be echoed nearly eighty years later in two landmark studies that were to change the face of management education. The first Master's degree in Business Administration (MBA) appeared at Dartmouth College's Tuck School of Business in the USA in 1902. This school was established in 1900 by Edward Tuck, an international financier and philanthropist (Friga, Bettis, and Sullivan, 2003), at a time when there was explosive growth in commerce and industry. In 1908, the Harvard Business School launched its first MBA and Stanford followed suit in 1925. By 1915, there were approximately forty business schools in the USA and a year later the American Association of Collegiate Schools of Business, otherwise known as the AACSB, became the accrediting agency. The number of business schools then increased in the USA fivefold to nearly 200 by 1925. Interestingly, most business professors at that time were either practising or retired corporate managers who focused on sharing lessons learned in the workplace.

The earlier 'trade school' approach to management education came to an abrupt end following massive reforms driven by two landmark studies by the Ford Foundation and the Carnegie Corporation, commissioned in North America during the 1950s. These were aimed at making business schools more academic and research based, in line with academic programmes at other universities. The professionalization of management teaching that ensued brought about the domination of business functions such as finance, marketing, law, management science, and so on, but interestingly, not *management* per se. These reforms encouraged a scientific model of management education (Bennis and O'Toole, 2005). The strategies and structures of business schools today, both in the USA (Mintzberg, 2004) and in Europe (Ivory et al., 2006), are similar to those established in the 1950s.

Bennis and O'Toole argue that this scientific model is predicated on the false assumption that management is an academic discipline like chemistry or physics when they would be better seen as a profession like medicine or law. In their view, business school professors know a lot about academic publishing, but few have ever worked in a real business. This contrasts sharply with medical schools, for example, where members of teaching faculty are often practising doctors. This controversy over academic rigour versus practical relevance of the learning attained in business schools has been widely discussed over the past two decades. Mintzberg (2004: 32) observes that, 'As businesses work valiantly to bust down the walls between their silos, business schools work valiantly to reinforce them.'

However, many suggest that management is not a profession. Sociologists have identified four common aspects across professions: a common body of knowledge; a system for certifying that individuals possess such knowledge before being licensed or allowed to practise; a commitment to use specialized knowledge for the public good; and a code of ethics with provisions for monitoring individual compliance with the code and a system of sanctions for enforcing it (Khurana et al., 2005). When we compare business management with more traditional professions, such as medicine or engineering, and apply these four aspects, we can see that management is found wanting. There is no solid common body of knowledge able to account for much of the social environment of business. There is neither a formal educational requirement nor a system of examination and licensing for aspiring members. An MBA is not a requirement for becoming a manager. Business managers are not universally committed to the public good, and finally, are not governed by a shared normative code (Khurana et al., 2005).

Management is more art than a science, and effective managing happens where art (emphasizing insight), science (emphasizing analysis), and craft (emphasizing experience) meet (Mintzberg, 2004). It involves 'becoming aware, attending to, sorting out, and prioritizing an inherently messy, fluxing, chaotic world of competing demands that are placed on a manager's attention' (Chia, 2005: 1092). Managing is more an acquired coping capability than a science; more a set of skilled practices than a profession; more a phenomenon of method than a field of study. Ironically, scientific management might have been all too successful with too much of a scientific approach to problem-solving and managing (Mintzberg, 2004; see Armstrong and Fukami, 2009).

Overall, we follow Willman (2014: 4) in seeing management as an applied social science. Willman identifies three characteristics: first it is derivative, eclectic, and fragmented; second it has emerged over a relatively short period of time with most business theory from the 1890s; and third it has almost all emerged in English and English-speaking countries even if it did not all originate there.

With that said, we offer this handbook as a state of the current affairs of this discipline. It is our hope that others will find these collected chapters compelling, and will set out to address the many needs that are outlined for the future.

Chapter Summaries

This book provides perspectives from leading scholars in the field of management, with consideration of the past, present, and future. The book is organized into four parts and contains twenty-six chapters. In the first part, we discuss the main historic models of management, beginning with the scientific model of management. Lucy Taksa in Chapter 2 discusses how the scientific model developed by F. W. Taylor, known as Taylorism, represents a hegemonic ideology which continues to be relevant to contemporary management philosophies and practices. She outlines how Taylor's philosophy, principles, and methods came to represent a reform agenda during the early decades of the twentieth century, which promoted social harmony within the context of an era seeking high productivity and experiencing high consumption. Taksa concludes that the influence of Taylor has been immense and that his scientific management principles, based on unitary ideals and vision, continue to influence the design and operation of work organizations, particularly in the field of knowledge, work, and education.

In Chapter 3, Kyle Bruce and Chris Nyland discuss the Human Relations School of Management, which arose during 1924–1932 when Elton Mayo and his Harvard Business School colleagues investigated the role of human association in the workplace at the Hawthorne plant of Western Electric. The chapter begins with a narrative on Mayo's background and how he came to develop his theories based on the Hawthorne studies. In contrast to the scientific model of management, which urged improved wages and conditions and workplace democracy, Mayo contested that employee psychosocial maladjustment was responsible for reduced productivity and increased turnover. However, as Bruce and Nyland proffer, Mayo's theories and methodologies have since been questioned by other scholars, who argue that Mayo did not discover anything new. Rather, Mayo advocated an elitist management system that was the antithesis of workplace democracy—a paradigm shift that was attractive to employers who were eager to reduce union influence and to offer psychological counselling, rather than increased wages. The chapter goes on to discuss this paradigm shift and the differences between Taylorism and the Human Relations School of thought, before demonstrating how Mayo and his Harvard colleagues pioneered the field of organizational psychology, which continues to influence contemporary human resource management.

The evolution of operations management is charted by Martin Spring in Chapter 4. Spring explores the emergence of Operations Management during the 1950s and 1960s, as the field developed its terminology and evolved from production management studies and attempts to develop a 'science of management'. Next, he discusses how during the decades since, the field has been dominated by various terminologies and theories, including materials requirements planning, which arose as mainframe computers were increasingly used by manufacturing firms to plan and control production, and Japanese manufacturing models, such as Just In Time and Total Quality Management. He argues that the field of Operations Management as a research area has lacked specific theories and often been accused of being detached from practice. He concludes that the operations manager plays a vital role in applying management to the field and linking technologies and people, thus maintaining Operations Management as a model of management.

Peter Starbuck explores the influence of Drucker's model, Management by Objectives and Self-Control, in Chapter 5, detailing the model which was put forward by Drucker (1954) in *The Practice of Management*. At the heart of this model was the notion of self-control, whereby organizational members were considered to be responsible workers, working towards agreed objectives without the need for continual reminders from management. He discusses how Drucker's approach of integrating the mechanical components of management with human performance, meant that the planning and doing of work did not need to be separated, as previously modelled by Taylor. Next, he details its adoption in US, UK, and Japanese contexts. He concludes by arguing that Management by Objectives is not a fad and has played a significant role in influencing management and scholars across various country domains.

Chapter 6 by Mats Alvesson, Dan Kärreman, and Sierk Ybema examines how organizational culture and image has been used as a management tool. They begin by providing an historical overview of the literature on organizational culture, which, like many of the management models detailed in this book, originated in Japan. They note that organizations initially embraced the application of culture as a tool of management, as scholars identified culture as a new paradigm that could be used to analyse and interpret organizations. However, interest in organizational culture waned in the late 1980s, as organizations found it could not be used as a practical tool for management and scholars found that the cultures within organizations were often fragmented and fluid. Soon after, a 'second wave' of organizational culture studies emerged reinvigorated through Swindler's (1986) culture toolkit framework and studies on organizational identity, neo-normative control, and discourse. The authors suggest that to further reinvigorate the field of study, future research on organizational culture studies should consider drawing close and immersion; defamiliarization and lending strangeness; and critical questioning and problematization.

Chapter 7 examines another management model that arose in the 1950s, the open systems theory, which considers the organization as an internally cooperative system that has to relate and adjust to external environments. The chapter begins with a discussion on the history of the open systems approach and the application of contingency theory to this model. Bob Hinings and Royston Greenwood examine three variants of open systems theory: general systems theory, specific systems thinking, and contingency theory. They then discuss how open systems theory contributed to our understanding of managing organizations, particularly the functioning of organizations, organizational variety, and the development of bureaucracy. The authors conclude that in contemporary studies, the theory has become generic and, as argued in the previous chapter, the theory needs revitalizing in order to shed new light on organizational and institutional design.

In the final chapter of this part, Stewart Clegg, Marco Berti, and Walter P. Jarvis suggest that in order to understand organizations better and create high impact research in management studies, scholars should adopt a philosophical standpoint and critically question the basic assumptions and prejudices of the descriptions and theories devised from the 'technical' and the 'scientific' orientation. They argue that, in the past, scholars have played 'language games' with respect to organizational discourse, and that implicit statements become normalized as part of the discourse on organizations, thus limiting organizational capacities for innovation. Discussing the role of power in organizations, they argue that while power is eternal, its forms are not essential, and thus power relations can be reshaped using a philosophically grounded perspective.

In the second part of this book, we look at the actual doing of management and its functions. Chapter 9 begins by looking at one of the critical functions of management, managing people. In this chapter, Andy Charlwood and Kim Hoque consider the human resource management (HRM) function and how it can move from a 'handmaiden' or administrative role to one which is more strategic and centred on high commitment management. They begin by discussing the HRM–performance relationship and the concepts of path dependency and institutional isomorphism. They argue that normative models of HRM have not been widely adopted due to continued scepticism over HRM's performance effects and that high commitment HRM is rarely put into practice. Some of the reasons cited for this include the expectations, skills, and competencies of HR professionals that are influenced by historical models of HRM; the impact of competing narratives such as lean manufacturing and Ulrich's model of the HR function; the impact of globalization and financialization logics; and societal rules and norms. In conclusion, the authors argue that by considering HR analytics, the HR function could become more strategic and consequently enhance its ability to lobby for the adoption of high commitment models of HRM.

In Chapter 10 Bateman and Radnor reflect on the past and present move of operations management (OM) from manufacturing to service before considering in more depth the future of OM in terms of the 'fit' for public services. This chapter also presents an analysis of 'lean' in public services which is often heralded as a new philosophy and methodology with which to manage operations effectively. The authors argue that uncritically applying manufacturing ideas to public service is flawed. In conclusion, the chapter suggests that managing operations across all sectors in the future should draw on a range of disciplines, theory, and concepts.

In Chapter 11, Jeffrey K. Pinto and Peerasit Patanakul examine project management and how the increasing adoption of project-based work has had a significant impact upon the need for project management skills. In this chapter, Pinto argues that project performance across many industries is unsatisfactory and that there are a number of challenges in managing projects, including the project lifecycle, the indeterminate nature of authority and composition of teams, planning and optimism bias, project leaders being tasked with multiple projects, and the challenges of communicating and interacting with virtual project teams. He argues that a lack of training for project managers and an incomplete model of required skills have exacerbated these challenges. After outlining the traditional 'execution-based' project management model and the more comprehensive 'management of projects' paradigm, he argues that the latter model provides project managers and scholars with a far richer and more inclusive synthesis of the challenges faced in managing projects to successful completion.

In Chapter 12, Wendy Currie discusses managing data, information, and knowledge. She begins by examining these three concepts in relation to the three eras of computerization: the data-processing era, management information systems phase, and the strategic information systems era. In this chapter, she argues that it is important for management research to consider the relationships between these stages and how they have each presented new data and information challenges and the growth of knowledge work. An understanding of these relationships is particularly important within the context of the finance trading sector, which has a long history of using information technology and computerization. Currie discusses one aspect of financialization, high frequency trading, and discusses how this has changed the nature of work for traders, reducing human intervention and increasing the extent to which computerized algorithms make trading decisions. This has implications on transparency and how traders use data, information, and knowledge. She suggests that in order to understand the impacts of high frequency trading on the public, media and regulatory fields, future research should adopt an interdisciplinary approach and draw on studies related to the sociology of finance, IT artefacts, and social studies of technology.

In Chapter 13, Violina Rindova and Santosh Srinivas explore the concept of managing meaning as a core managerial task. They begin by discussing the definitions and scholarly debates concerning the field of managing meaning, which began with the seminal paper titled 'Management as Symbolic Action' by Pfeffer (1981). Next they examine some of the key themes related to the management of meaning, including organizational culture and identity, strategic change, innovation, environmental enactment, and the use of communication for external stakeholder audiences. Drawing on Pfeffer's seminal work regarding symbolic and substantial aspects of organizational activity and subsequent scholarly research, they argue that both symbolic and substantive actions enhance the mobilization of action inside and outside organizations. They conclude by offering some suggestions for future research, including theory building concerning the resources and capabilities organizations need in order to manage meanings strategically; and an examination of meaning co-construction, which explores the exchanges of meanings between and within the various communities in which organizations are embedded.

In Chapter 14, Ronald E. Riggio looks at management and leadership, noting that, while there is an important distinction between the two, they are also intertwined. In this chapter, he provides an historical overview of the literature on leadership and discusses some of the key foundational leadership theories, including the Situational Leadership Model, Decision-making Model, and Contingency Model of Leadership. Next he turns to contemporary models, which consider that leadership effectiveness is dependent upon the relationship between leaders and followers. The role of the follower is an integral part of the Leader–Member Exchange Theory, which stipulates that leaders will value and treat certain followers differently. Contingency Theory is another theory with a focus on the follower, whereby leaders must gain the respect and admiration of followers. Moving beyond charisma alone, the Transformational Leadership Theory focuses on the leader's ability to motivate and stimulate follower creativity and to empower them. Models related to ethics are discussed next, including Authentic Leadership Theory and Ethical Leadership. Given organizations' desire to attract leaders who display the behaviours identified in these theories, there has been significant research undertaken to develop ways of selecting leaders and to measure their effectiveness, including 360-degree feedback. The chapter concludes with suggestions for future research which focus on the follower's role in leadership and how they co-construct leadership, along with the competencies required for leaders, and leadership diversity.

In Chapter 15, the importance of strategy and management is discussed, a theme which arises throughout many of the chapters in this book. Despite the interest in strategic management, or perhaps because of it, Mark Shanley argues that it does not represent a distinct field and consequently research on strategic management is fragmented. In this chapter, he outlines several of the reasons for this intellectual fragmentation, including undertheorized aspects of decision and implementation processes, and undertheorized assumptions of action behind strategy theories, especially concerning how top managers make decisions in multiple temporal frames, complex organizational settings, prior experiences, and conflicting environmental demands. He suggests that in order to improve the conceptualization of strategic management, process issues concerning interconnected linkages, intertemporal linkages, and inter relational linkages should be examined, along with a craft approach to organizational agency.

Stefan Tengblad considers everyday management and explores management from a practice perspective in Chapter 16. In his historical overview of the topic, he discusses the two main streams of research that have been undertaken on management practice, namely the functionalist stream, that emphasizes the classic conceptualizations and analyses of managerial work behaviour; and the ethnographic stream, which emphasizes the study of managerial culture and knowledge. As new trends have developed regarding work, the research on management practices has expanded, with the term 'post-bureaucracy' coined to describe this contemporary era in managerial practices. However, he argues that managers are often so busy that there is little time to reflect. Consequently, management practices, and in particular work supervision, are slow to change. In his conclusion, he provides a summary of Tengblad's (2012) ten theses on management practice, which culminates sixty years of studies on management work practices.

In the final chapter of this part, Chapter 17, David A. Buchanan examines managing change. He notes that there is often resistance to organizational change but argues that resistance can be positive for organizations and its managers, halting inappropriate ideas from being implemented. He details a number of change management strategies, including those developed by scholars and management consultants, many of whom are influenced by Kurt Lewin's 'unfreeze–move–refreeze' model. Next he argues the importance of processual perspectives, which help change leaders to manage the unpredictable nature of change and to intervene in the politics of the organization. Consequently, change agents need to engage in the 'management of meaning', a concept discussed in Chapter 13. Buchanan also warns against implementing change at an accelerated pace, recommending that organizations implement large- and smaller-scale changes at appropriate intervals. While numerous actors may be involved in the change process, a change leader needs to provide the vision and direction for major change initiatives. Competency models have been developed to articulate the skills required of the change leader; however, Buchanan argues that these models typically relate to any management role, and do not recognize the political skill required of the change leader. In summary, he offers suggestions for future research, including an examination of how different economic conditions impact on change management; the multifaceted nature of transformational change; building change management capability; using the concept of path dependence to explain why change initiatives may be successful; and a consideration of post-crisis change management.

Part II of this book explores themes of management. Chapter 18 by David Courpasson explores the theme of management as a practice of power, considering it as a means for managers to encourage people to act and engage in activities that they would not have done otherwise. In this regard, structural relationships may create networks of dependencies between non-equivocal actors where obedience is sought, while also recognizing that conflict and resistance may also occur. However, changes to the structures within contemporary organizations and evolving technologies means that the typical bureaucratic formal reporting relationships may no longer exist, creating new forms of power and resistance within organizations. This theme is explored following Courpasson's discussion of several contemporary theories of power, along with several historical models that allude to the political nature of management. He begins by discussing Fleming and Spicer's (2007) four dimensions of power, that is, power as coercion, manipulation, domination, and subjectification. Next, he provides a brief genealogy of managing power and the infrastructures of power by looking at Taylorist's disciplinary infrastructure, the Fordist moral infrastructure, the human relations infrastructure, and corporate culturalism epitomized by Google. He then addresses how power is reshaped in new organizations, suggesting that these neo-bureaucracies have transformed power relationships between central authorities and peripheral actors, with those employees peripheral to the central structure exercising greater power through new forms of resistance, while managerial power at the centre is obscured. He then poses questions regarding the ways technology and violence in organizations may reshape power relations within this new era of managing power.

Management and morality is examined in Chapter 19, with Michel Anteby and Caitlin Anderson discussing whether morals can exist within the corporate context. They begin the chapter with a review of the literature on corporate morals from the middle of the twentieth century through to recent developments and demonstrate that, while historical perspectives by authors such as Durkheim (1961) claimed that professional business morals were non-existent, there is sufficient empirical evidence that exists to suggest that corporate morals do indeed exist, but perhaps not always within the normative view of ethics. Using a sociological perspective, they suggest that while the corporate morals held within organizations may not be considered ethical to outsiders, they indeed represent an internally coherent code of conduct for the organization's members to follow and adhere to. The apparent elusiveness of corporate morals may be a manifestation of the difficulties of gaining access to study morals within organizations, and therefore scholars have had to infer corporate morals through observation. To better understand corporate morals, the authors suggest that there should be a consideration of meta-ethical content, which shows there is value in corporations accommodating multiple moral viewpoints at once.

The part on Themes ends with the chapter on Modernity and management by Graham Sewell. Sewell begins with a discussion on how to define Modernity in management, noting that management is the conscious act of trying to shore up unstable labour in order to reconcile the opposing forces of change and stability that are part of the modern culture. Therefore, Modernity can be perceived as a condition of ambivalence borne from these conditions. Sewell then examines perspectives and critiques of Modernity portrayed by three authors, Gibson Burrell, Stewart Clegg, and Paul du Gay, who draw on Continental theorists to build on the insights of the key thinkers of the Modernist project such as Marx, Durkheim, and Weber. This then forms the basis for a comparison with 'new' institutional theory and the way it deals with the relationship between management and Modernity. Finally, he discusses Lash's notion of 'another modernity' to critique Weber's concept of *Stahlhartes Gehäuse* as a personal disposition, rather than an iron cage.

The final part of this book looks at management in society and management organizations/institutions. This part begins with a chapter on evidence-based management by Kevin Morrell and Mark Learmouth. The authors adopt a critical perspective and focus on the management-as-medicine-motif (MAMM), which is used by evidence-based advocates in two ways. First, they suggest following the same model of knowledge production and science in management studies as in medicine, for example in promoting systematic reviews. Second, they rely on comparisons between management and medicine as professional practices. Highlighting these two aspects to MAMM allows the authors to consider questions such as 'to what extent is management a profession?' and 'what kind of knowledge do managers need?' In identifying the limitations of MAMM, they caution against a wider medicalization of management—a tendency for social phenomena to be studied through the clinician's lens. 'Evidence' in the evidence-based approach is a particular form of evidence allied to positivism and reductionism. They conclude by examining a case where medicalization leads to distortions of the phenomenon studied and even to incoherence.

In Chapter 22, Kenneth G. Brown and Robert S. Rubin explore how business schools operate and educate our future managers, noting the need for business schools to become more innovative and to balance their emphasis on theoretical, disciplinary research and technically oriented training, with practical research and blended soft- and hard-skills training. The authors discuss the emerging literature since the Porter and McKibbin (1988) report, with a focus on foundational research that has either created new research domains, fundamentally changed the direction of prior work, or provided a basis for future work. They begin with a discussion on the contested concept of management education, choosing a definition that encompasses the whole range of knowledge and skills that would help prepare students for management work.

Next, they discuss the forces pushing for changes in management education, such as financial pressures, student characteristics, programme demand, and technology. They then provide an overview of scholarly management education literature, noting changes in journals and pinpointing highly cited studies. Next they review research in online learning, which has shown tremendous growth in recent years and is likely to be a trend that will continue, and MBA curricula. Finally, they discuss two emerging areas of research, including engagement and the informal curriculum, and teaching with problems and the interaction of real-life learning.

In Chapter 23, Damian O'Doherty and Christian De Cock investigate how management, as a discipline, has been haunted by aporia and incoherence. The authors discuss how the practice and discipline of management has been ill-defined in historical scholarship, complicated by ideological and historical differences concerning management as mere agents of capital, versus the role of management to mediate and reconcile the contradictory or antagonistic relation between capital and labour. It is argued that labour process study represents one of the most significant bodies of research to have taken management as a discipline seriously, with its focus on the policies and practices of management. The authors suggest that the work of Foucault shows the importance of a vigilant and permanent questioning of discipline. However, the labelling of management as a discipline may require a post-disciplinary method of study that includes daring and innovation so that we are not delimited by those disciplinary features which ensnare us in a restrictive form of management. To achieve this, the authors suggest moving beyond an intra-disciplinary focus and human mindset to resituate management within a post-human ecology.

In Chapter 24, Luciara Nardon examines cross-cultural management and argues that the literature has under-emphasized the role of context. Reviewing the literature, she demonstrates that, while there is growing recognition that contextual variables mediate the influence of culture on behaviour, context is seldom articulated. The author draws on a perspective of situated cognition, which considers the role of context in shaping cognition and behaviour. She proposes that a manager's cognitive process and actions result from the interaction between an individual's cognitive schemas and institutional, organizational, and situational layers of context. Furthermore, the actions taken may influence or modify contextual characteristics as well as reinforce or modify existing schemas. Nardon concludes that the context of global management is not static and independent of the manager, but, rather, it is shaped by the manager and his or her interactions with other actors. To better understand the role of context, the author suggests rethinking expatriate adaptation to the host environment, the role of cultural differences in global management, the relationship between culture and behaviour, and the role of global managers and their required skills.

International management, which concerns the study of multinational corporations (MNCs), is the focus of Chapter 25 by Mike Geppert and Graham Hollinshead. The chapter begins with a discussion on the internationalization of organizations as a precursor to the international division of labour, demonstrating how post-Fordist 'high-tech' MNCs now search for locations where expert knowledge and low labour costs are available. Literature concerning the organization of the MNC and the relationship between the parent and its subsidiaries is explored next, and the authors suggest that existing theories are based upon ideal typologies which do not always fit organizational reality. Using an institutionalist approach, they argue that subsidiary units are 'embedded' in distinctive and diverse socio-economic contexts and are prone to manifest organizational disparity as well as unity. Furthermore, they find that human relations within the MNC are often characterized by contestation and 'power playing'. Consequently, there is a need to better understand local embeddedness, whether local managers identify with the host company or parent, and the issue of 'identity work' and identity politics within the local subsidiary.

The final chapter in this book examines management and consultancy. The historical scholarly literature demonstrates an ambivalent relationship between the two, but also provides evidence of an inter-relationship. The chapter's authors, Andrew Sturdy, Christopher Wright, and Nick Wylie review the dominant image of consulting, which is that it is distinct from management in terms of knowledge, relationships, work and career patterns, and personal characteristics. However, they also note the influence consultancy has had on management practice and suggest that managers may be synonymous with management consultants, requiring skills in change management, and the use of formal tools, project working, and facilitation. They suggest that consultancy has been heavily involved in spreading management ideas to organizations, including those based around critiques of bureaucracy, and the internalization of consultancy practices. Consultancy has also served their managerial clients through their expertise and legitimizing and provided a role model and career trajectory for managers. In this regard, consultancy can be perceived as an extreme case of management spanning organizational boundaries.

The purpose of developing this handbook has been to explore the evolution of management and its position in the zeitgeist of modern society as well as the institutions and ideologies that support it. In doing so, we have provided a broad overview of management—its history, development, context, changing function in organization and society, key elements and functions, and contemporary and future challenges. Our aim is to introduce the reader to the pluralism of management research and the nature of management science and practice that continues to be played out and indeed contested. The chapters in this collection embrace different kinds of theory and we stress the need to engage with various disciplinary lenses in order to more fully understand management processes.

References

Armstrong, S. and Fukami, C. (2009). *The Sage Handbook of Management Learning Education and Development*. London: SAGE.

Barley, Stephen R. and Kunda, G. (1992). 'Design and Devotion: Surges of Rational and Normative Ideologies of Control in Managerial Discourse'. *Administrative Science Quarterly*, 37: 363–99.

Bendix, R. (1956). *Work and Authority in Industry: Ideologies of Management in the Course of Industrialization*. New York: Wiley.

Bennis, W. G. and O'Toole, J. (2005). 'How Business Schools Lost Their Way'. *Harvard Business Review*, 83: 96–104.

Bowden, B. and Lamond, D. (2015). *Management History: Its Global Past and Present*. Charlotte, NC: IAP.

Chia, R. (2005). 'The Aim of Management Education: Reflections on Mintzberg's Managers Not MBAs'. *Organization Studies*, 26(7): 1090–2.

Cloke, K. and Goldsmith, J. (2002). *The End of Management and the Rise of Organizational Democracy*. New York: Wiley.

Crainer, S. and Dearlove, D. (1999). *Gravy Training: Inside the Business of Business Schools*. San Francisco, CA: Jossey-Bass.

Diefenbach, T. and By, R. T. (eds.) (2012). *Reinventing Hierarchy and Bureaucracy—from the Bureau to Network Organizations*. Research in the Sociology of Organizations, vol. 35. Bradford: Emerald.

Drucker, P. (1954). *The Practice of Management*. New York: Harper and Row.

du Gay, Paul and Morgan, G. (eds.) (2013). *New Spirits of Capitalism: Crises, Justifications, and Dynamics*. Oxford: Oxford University Press.

Durkheim, E. (1961). *Moral Education: A Study in the Theory and Application of the Sociology of Education*. Trans. E. K. Wilson and H. Schnurer. New York: The Free Press.

Engwall, L. (2007). 'The Anatomy of Management Education'. *Scandinavian Journal of Management*, 23(1): 4–35.

Fligstein, N. (1990). *The Transformation of Corporate Control*. Cambridge, MA: Harvard University Press.

Fleming, P. and Spicer, A. (2007). *Contesting the Corporation*. Cambridge: Cambridge University Press.

Fligstein, N. (1990). *The Transformation of Corporate Control*. Cambridge, MA: Harvard University Press.

Friga, P., Bettis, R., and Sullivan, R. (2003). 'Changes in Graduate Management Education and New Business School Strategies for the 21st century'. *Academy of Management Learning & Education*, 2(3): 233–49.

Grugulis, I., Dundon, T., and Wilkinson, A. (2000). 'Cultural Control and the 'Culture Manager': Employment Practices in a Consultancy'. *Work, Employment and Society*, 14(1): 97–116.

Guillén, M. F. (1994) *Models of Management: Work, Authority, and Organization in a Comparative Perspective*. Chicago, IL: University of Chicago Press.

Holmqvist, M. and Spicer, A. (eds.) (2012). *Managing 'Human Resources' by Exploiting and Exploring People's Potentials*. Research in the Sociology of Organizations, vol. 37. Bradford: Emerald.

Hwang, H. and Powell, W. W. (2009). 'The Rationalization of Charity: The Influences of Professionalism in the Non-Profit Sector'. *Administrative Science Quarterly*, 54: 268–98.

Ivory, C., Miskell, P., Shipton, H., White, A., Moeslein, K., and Neely, A. (2006). 'UK Business Schools: Historical Contexts and Future Scenarios', Summary Report from an EBK/AIM Management Research Forum, Advanced Institute of Management Research, London.

Khurana, R., Nohria, N., and Penrice, D. (2005). 'Management as a Profession', in J. W. Lorsch, L. Berlowitz, and A. Zelleke (eds.), *Restoring Trust in American Business*. Cambridge, MA: MIT Press (Produced by the American Academy of Arts & Sciences), 43–60.

Mintzberg, H. (2004). *Managers Not MBAs: A Hard Look at the Soft Practice of Managing and Management Development*. San Francisco, CA: Berrett-Koehler.

Morgan, G. (1986). *Images of Organization*. Newbury Park, CA: SAGE.

Murray, A. (2010). 'The End of Management'. *The Wall Street Journal*, 21 August: 84.

Perrow C. (1991). 'A Society of Organizations'. *Theory and Society*, 20: 725–62.

Pfeffer, J. and Fong, C. (2002). 'The End of Business Schools? Less Success Than Meets the Eye'. *Academy of Management Learning & Education*, 1(1): 78–95.

Pollard, S. (1965). *The Genesis of Modern Management: A Study of the Industrial Revolution in Great Britain*. Cambridge, MA: Harvard University Press.

Porter, L. and McKibbin, L. E. (1988). *Management Education and Development: Drift or Thrust in the 21st Century?* New York: McGraw-Hill.

Reed, M. (1992). *The Sociology of Organizations: Themes, Perspectives and Prospects*. London: Harvester Wheatsheaf.

Salaman, G. (1995). *Managing*. Milton Keynes: Open University Press.

Sass, S. A. (1982). *The Pragmatic Imagination: A History of the Wharton School, 1881–1981*. Philadelphia, PA: University of Pennsylvania Press.

Scott, W. R. and Davis, G. F. (2015). *Organizations and Organizing: Rational, Natural and Open Systems Perspectives*. New York: Taylor and Francis.

Stewart, R. (1967). *Managers and Their Jobs*. London: Macmillan.

Swidler, A. (1986). 'Culture in Action: Symbols and Strategies'. *American Sociological Review*, 51: 273–86.

Tengblad, S. (2012). *The Work of Managers: Towards a Practice Theory of Management*. Oxford: Oxford University Press.

Tiratsoo, N. (1998). 'What You Need Is a Harvard: The American Influence on British Management Education', in T. Gourvish and N. Tiratsoo (eds.), *Missionaries and Managers: American Influences on European Management Education, 1945–1960*. Manchester: Manchester University Press, 140–56.

Watson, T. J. (1994). *In Search of Management: Culture, Chaos and Control in Managerial Work*. London: Routledge.

Weber, M. (1978). *Economy and Society*. Berkeley, CA: University of California Press.

Willman, P. (2014). *Understanding Management*. Cambridge: Cambridge University Press.

PART I
MAIN HISTORIC MODELS

CHAPTER 2

SCIENTIFIC MANAGEMENT

LUCY TAKSA

Introduction

The continuing impact of F. W. Taylor and his system of scientific management is indisputable as scholars have repeatedly stressed. Drucker (1974: 181) called Taylor 'the Isaac Newton (or perhaps the Archimedes) of the science of work' and Kanigel (1997: 503) concluded that 'Taylor helped make modern life what it is—not only in the factory or even in the broader workplace but also everywhere.' Similarly, Wren (2011: 19) argued that Taylor's 'ideas shaped how we live and think today'. In a special issue of the *Journal of Business and Management*, commemorating the hundredth anniversary of the publication of Taylor's *The Principles of Scientific Management*, editors Giannantonio and Hurley-Hanson (2011: 7) noted: 'The merits of Taylor's work can certainly be debated, but what cannot be argued is that Taylor changed the way people worked in the 20th century'; he has consistently topped lists of most significant 'contributors to American management thought and practice'.

Yet despite extensive recognition of the impact of Taylor's ideas and methods, it can be argued that the ideological implications of scientific management (SM) have been underestimated (Littler, 1982: 55; Merkle, 1980: 3). As Tsutsui (2001: 10) commented, 'even revisionist scholars have been inclined to' conceive Taylorism narrowly 'as a technique rather than an ideology, as an interwar phenomenon rather than a transwar one, as the idiom of the assembly line rather than an expansive language of political, economic, and social reform'. What then can be made of conclusions such as expressed by Dunford (1992: 56) that 'the spirit of scientific management' has remained 'a significant influence on the design and operation of work organisations even if its mortal form (the set of practices and techniques advocated by Taylor)' is absent?

This question is addressed here in order to explore the precise impact of these ideas and this spirit on 'how we live and think today' (Wren, 2011: 19). The chapter begins with an outline of the system's nature and a consideration of the way SM has been represented by Taylor's contemporaries and by scholars. It then extends the gaze beyond the 'classical' focus on SM methods, their impact on the labour process and capacity to deskill labour (Braverman, 1974) and the related mechanistic perspective (Clegg and Dunkerley, 2013: 96). By framing SM as a hegemonic ideology, the treatment presented here supports Merkle's interpretation of SM as one of 'the most pervasive and invisible of the forces that have shaped modern society' (Merkle, 1980: 3) and it agrees with Kanigel (1997), who argued that SM 'was always much more than a bundle of tools and techniques'. In short, I stress that the synthesis of Taylor's philosophy, principles, and methods was pivotal to Taylor's vision and to those who promoted and adopted it. As Taylor (1911: 140) put it, SM 'is no single element, but rather this whole combination (…) which may be summarized as: Science, not rule of thumb. Harmony, not discord. Cooperation, not individualism. Maximum output, in place of restricted output'. He therefore told the Special House of Representatives Inquiry into his and other systems of management that SM should not be presented as 'any bunch or group of efficiency devices' (Taylor, 1947b/1912: 26–7). Of far greater importance to him was the system's underlying philosophy, the 'conviction that the true interests' of employers and employees were the same (Taylor, 1911: 10). To give effect to this philosophy Taylor promoted 'a complete mental revolution' on the part of the workers and on the part of foremen, superintendents, business owners and boards 'toward all of their daily problems' because he believed that 'without this complete mental revolution on both sides Scientific Management' did 'not exist' (Taylor, 1947b/1912: 27, 29, 150). According to Kaufman (2008: 119) the 'mental revolution in which all stakeholders submerge their selfish, short-term interests and co-operate as a united team to maximize production' provides the 'fulcrum upon which successful SM rests'. Does this mean that SM is best seen as 'a vision and a hope' (Kanigel, 1997: 502) and if so what precisely has been the long-term impact of this vision?

The advocacy of the mental revolution was an integral part of Taylor's ideological arsenal, which heralded a conflict free society (Merkle, 1980: 15). As numerous scholars have pointed out, this consensus ideology ensured its long-term influence. The earliest exponent of this view was Gramsci, who saw 'Taylorism as a hegemonic ideological force' and a harbinger 'of the most sophisticated mode of capitalist domination in which the workers would be totally subordinated to machine specialization and the cult of efficiency' (Boggs, 1976: 46–7). Another was Bendix (1974), who argued that Taylor's 'social philosophy rather than his techniques became a part of prevailing managerial ideology'. For Merkle (1980: 3, 86–7, 93, 97) it was 'an ideology about management and for managers' which had a profound influence on 'the ideology of the modern state and its industrial and business enterprises'. For Stark (1980: 102, 117), SM functioned as an ideology of technical expertise, which assisted professionalization, most conspicuously but not exclusively in the engineering sector. As Doray (1988: 131) commented, 'Taylorism's effect upon industrial life extends far beyond its immediate and explicit applications'. Indeed, he argued that 'Taylorization of factories' included 'ideological labour', which was manifested in the journals of various French firms where Taylor's ideas were adapted, and which raised political issues, such as '(t)he organization of consent, cultural expropriation, the legitimization of managerial power, and the subordination of the labour process to the process of valorization'. Other scholars arrived at similar conclusions (Littler, 1978, 1990: 52; Noble, 1977; Taksa, 1992, 1995; Witt, 2004).

This chapter builds on these interpretations of SM. However, as Littler (1978, 1982) pointed out, the impact of SM ideology on the structuring of work was not adequately addressed by either the 'classical' technical approach nor the ideological perspective. Efforts were made to address this issue (Taksa, 1997, 1998). Here, however, attention is given to SM's operation as a hegemonic ideology, reaching beyond the management of work to the management of meaning at the time of its early development and ever since.

If, as Adamson (1980: 174, cited in Lears, 1985: 571) argued, 'hegemony is a process of continuous creation', what are the cultural contexts in which it is created and what is its cultural trajectory? In addressing these questions I explore how SM philosophy, principles, and methods operated as a 'general conception of life' and as a 'scholastic programme' (Boggs, 1976: 39) in two fields—the workplace and education. Partly this will illustrate how Taylor and his followers were involved in shaping the values and attitudes of the society they inhabited and partly it will provide a basis for considering the scholarly claims of its continuing influence.

Framing Scientific Management as a Hegemonic Ideology

Merkle's definition of ideology as 'the shared beliefs of a group about the proper goals of society and the appropriate distribution of power and benefits within that society' provides a useful starting point (Merkle, 1980: 3). Also important is her argument that while 'most ideologies are transmitted with a large proportion of words and a small proportion of objects', SM was transmitted 'with a large number of objects and a relatively small proportion of words' in order 'to symbolize (…) the appropriate relations of the individual to the hierarchies of specialization, to authority, and to other people, as well as the correct attitude toward work and the reward for work' (Merkle, 1980: 3–4).

Gramsci's concept of hegemony is particularly helpful in exploring the cultural trajectory of this ideological transmission, from the factory to the office (Haigh, 2012) and the educational sphere (Brooks and Miles, 2008; Cooke, 1910; Callahan, 1962; Hunter and Sanderson, 2001; Taksa, 2007) and from there to broader assumptions, norms, and practices that still affect us today. According to Williams (1960: 587) when Gramsci used the term 'hegemony', he seemed 'to mean (…) a "moment" in which the philosophy and practice of a society fuse (….); an order in which a certain way of life and thought is dominant, in which one concept of reality is diffused throughout society in all its institutional and private manifestations (…) and all social relations'. Implicit in this concept is the 'element of direction and control', which is 'not necessarily conscious' and the socialization of an 'organizing principle (...) into every area of daily life' (Boggs, 1976: 39).

Gramsci's theories also provide an extremely useful paradigm for considering how the socialization of 'discoveries' made by intellectuals become 'the basis of vital action' (Hoare and Smith, 1971: 325). As Gramsci argued 'philosophical activity' should not 'be conceived solely as the "individual" elaboration of systematically coherent concepts, but also (...) as a cultural battle to transform the popular "mentality" and to diffuse philosophical innovations' in such a way that they come to 'demonstrate themselves to be (...) historically and socially—universal' (Hoare and Smith, 1971: 348). From this perspective, hegemony operates as 'an educational relationship (...) between intellectual and non-intellectual (...), between (...) elites and their followers, leaders (dirigenti) and led' and internationally 'between complexes of national and continental civilisations' (Hoare and Smith, 1971: 350). Further, for a hegemonic ideology to be successfully translated into practice 'it must operate in a dualistic manner: as a "general conception of life" for the masses, and as a "scholastic programme" or set of principles which is advanced by a sector of the intellectuals' (Boggs, 1976: 39). This conceptual framework provides a means of considering the cultural trajectory of SM philosophy, principles, and practices, and how they created new modes of control over attitudes, behaviour, and social interaction that sought to replace the 'collective effect' of workers' formal and informal relations with 'a collection of separated individualities' (Foucault, 1995: 201).

While Taylor's all-encompassing aims were not accomplished exactly in accordance with his aspirations, nevertheless, I suggest that SM has operated as a hegemonic ideology, which is still influencing organizational cultures today through a range of different management strategies. Included among them are, as Petter Øgland (2013: 45) pointed out citing the work of Churchman (1968: 17–18), Ishikawa (1985) and Shingo (1987), echoing Warner (1994) and Taneja et al. (2011) and foreshadowing Mortenson et al. (2015): total quality management, 'operations research, management science and systems analysis'. For Box and Marshall (2006), 'Taylor's legacy remains firmly in place today not only in his view of worker–management relations but also in the form of systems from managerial accounting, organizational form and function, artificial intelligence applications, and many other organizational systems.' Some have even referred to ' "Digital Taylorism"—a new form of deskilling', which is being applied to managerial and professional work by 'translating knowledge work into working knowledge through extraction, certification and digitisation of knowledge into software prescripts that can be transmitted and manipulated by others regardless of location' (Brown et al., 2008: 139, cited in Grugulis and Lloyd, 2010: 105). As Evans and Holmes (2013: 1) commented, the 'ghost of Taylor is still very much alive in "high value" (so high skill) knowledge and service sector organisations, highlighting how contemporary knowledge workers are just as constrained by the principles of scientific management as the industrial workers Taylor studied in the early twentieth century'.

These management strategies rely on the hegemonic diffusion of SM and they continue to influence culture in a myriad of ways. Their impact on higher education provides one notable example, as Payne, Youngcourt, and Watrous (2006) pointed out in their analysis of portrayals of Taylor and his system in college textbooks in management, organizational behaviour, human resource management, and psychology and as Kemp (2013: 350) noted in relation to the activities of the Association to Advance Collegiate Schools of Business (AACSB). It would therefore appear to be difficult to sustain the notion that SM has been a failed management ideology as Fox (1974) and Rose (1975) claimed so many years ago. According to Hales (2013), Taylor's principles can be likened to a 'stem cell' that has shaped subsequent approaches to management in that Taylor's philosophy has continued to influence general assumptions about management and more importantly the culture of work.

SCIENTIFIC MANAGEMENT: PHILOSOPHY

The term 'scientific management' was coined in 1910 by the reformist lawyer Louis D. Brandeis and Taylor's followers as 'the likeliest eye-and-ear catcher' (Copley, 1969b: 320, 366, 1969a: 6–7) in the proceedings of the United States (US) Eastern Rate Case in which the north-eastern railroad companies sought an increase in freight charges from the Interstate Commerce Commission to offset growing costs, particularly associated with wage increases. Opposing the increases on behalf of the shipping companies, Brandeis argued that railroad costs could be reduced with improved efficiency through the adoption of SM. As the journalist Ray Stannard Baker noted at the time, the 'extraordinary fervour and enthusiasm' presented in the testimonies from Taylor's followers reflected 'the firm faith of apostles: it was a philosophy which worked and they had the figures to show this' (Callahan, 1962: 20). According to Merkle (1980: 58), this case transformed Taylorism 'overnight from an obscure obsession of certain middle-class engineers to an amazing and highly publicized nostrum for the evils of society'. The cultural value implicit in the word 'science' invested the system 'with an aura of impartiality' and therefore increased the likelihood of greater acceptance of the strategy itself (Zerzan, 1984: 141).

This language of science infused the philosophy, principles, and methods through which Taylor sought to increase the degree of coordination and control over the production process. Only Taylor's synthesis simultaneously presented solutions for technical problems and the growing social conflict between workers and employers (Merkle, 1980). The foundation of SM, according to Taylor (1911: 10), was 'the firm conviction (…) that it is possible to give the workman what he most wants—high wages—and the employer what he wants—a low labor cost—for his manufactures'. Scientific managers promoted this 'harmony of interests' gospel and its practical 'scientific' manifestations, through their consultancies and popular literature, and in the process ensured popular acceptance of Taylor's ideas (Callahan, 1962: 42). Social workers, educators, and government employees all flocked to Taylor's home to hear him talk on the subject. Professor Wallace C. Sabine, Dean of Harvard's Graduate School of Applied Science told Taylor: 'I am persuaded that you are on the track of the only reasonable solution of a great sociological problem' (Copley, 1969b: 283–4, 288).

Yet SM was not new. Taylor's ideas about rationalization basically codified and restated in coherent form a range of planning, coordination, and control practices which had been evolving since the inception of the industrial revolution (Cadbury, 1914; Renold, 1914; Urwick, 1957: 7; Doray, 1988: 184). Taylor himself recognized that SM did not involve 'the discovery of new or startling facts' (Taylor, 1911: 139–40). As James M. Dodge commented, 'we were impressed that Mr. Taylor in formulating his system had taken good points of management from various sources and had skilfully combined them in a harmonized whole' (Dodge, 1905–6: 723). For his contemporaries, Taylor's significance rested on the combination of a 'unifying philosophy' with 'scientific methodology' (Urwick, 1957: 8–9, 217), which centred on his argument that 'one best way' could be discovered for the performance of any task, given sufficient investigation (Taylor, 1911: 25, 106, 122, 1912: 62, 104–5, 143, 196, 199, Taylor, 1947a: 21, 101, 177).

The reduction of Taylor's advocated 'one best way' to a popular slogan has obscured the importance he and his followers placed on the need for constant improvement through investigation, experimentation and rationalization (Gilbreth, 1980: 6). As Taylor (1972: 54) told a conference on SM in 1911, scientific managers usually approached workers by saying:

> We do not know the best (…) but what we know is the result of a long series of experiments (…) these standards that lie before you are the results of these studies (…) the moment any man sees an improved standard (…) come to us with it; your suggestion will not only be welcome but we will join you in making a carefully tried experiment (…) If that experiment shows that your method is better (…) every one of us will adopt that method until somebody gets a better one.

This, coupled with Taylor's insistence on the documentation of experiments and their results, served to extend the impact of SM to the culture of work. As Hollis Godfrey remarked in 1924, before Taylor introduced a new emphasis on the need to record industrial processes, written records had not been used as guides for the future (Godfrey, cited in Cooke, 1924: 35).

The claim that SM could 'be applied with equal force to all social activities' (Taylor, 1911: 8), including to the management of homes, farms, churches, philanthropic institutions, universities, and government departments, according to Haber (1964: 26–7), broadened the scope of Taylor's 'proposals to an extent unimagined by most systematizers and (…) industrial betterment advocates'. Haber's view that this enabled Taylor's philosophical orientation to reach 'out to the society as a whole' was echoed by Sydney University academic, R. F. Irvine (1915: 15–16) to an Australian audience in 1915. In effect, Taylor's proposals for social and national efficiency gained widespread political support because middle-class reformers believed his assertion that SM would lead 'to the day when the working people' would be able to 'live as well and have the same luxuries, the same opportunities for leisure, for culture, and for education' as were 'possessed by the average businessmen of this country' (Taylor, 1947b/1912: 209). In fact, President Roosevelt stated that SM was 'the application of the conservation principle to production'. As he saw it:

> When the right way has been worked out in every detail, Scientific Management sets it up as a standard for that job; then instructs and trains the workman until he can accomplish this standard. And so on with all other workmen and all other jobs. From these efficient units is built up an efficient organization. And when we get efficiency in all our industries and commercial ventures, national efficiency will be a fact (Roosevelt, cited in Gilbreth, 1973: 2–3).

SCIENTIFIC MANAGEMENT: METHODS AND PRINCIPLES

Taylor devised numerous methods to fulfil his vision. The most renowned was a system of timing and measuring work, which allegedly applied science to the definition of a 'fair day's work'. Others entailed procedures for organizing and supervising work performance, new approaches to accounting and book keeping, planning, recruitment, and marketing. His methods included: functional foremanship; standardization of workers' movements, and also of tools and centralized storage systems; mnemonic symbols for the classification of tools and products; a routing system; the creation of a planning department; use of slide-rules for the production of mathematical formulae; instruction cards; and a new 'differential' pay scheme. Yet, Taylor warned his readers that the mechanisms of SM 'must not be mistaken for its essence, or underlying philosophy' because if they were introduced without the philosophy, the results would be disastrous (Taylor, 1911: 129–30).

Both Taylor's philosophy and his methods were underpinned by the assumption that traditional ways of doing things, as well as ways of thinking about the world, had to be discarded (Thompson, 1917: 244). Urwick and Brech (1957: 9) stressed that basically SM meant 'thinking scientifically instead of traditionally or customarily about the processes involved in the control of social groups who co-operate in production and distribution'. His four principles reflected this modern way of thinking by advocating that management should assume new duties by: 1) management gathering together of the traditional 'rule-of-thumb' knowledge previously possessed by craft workers, classifying it and reducing it 'to rules, laws and formulae'; 2) scientific selection; 3) scientific education; and 4) ensuring the intimate friendly cooperation between management and labour (Taylor, 1911: 36, 128–30, 1947b: 40–5). Together with SM methods, these principles fostered a greater division of labour than had previously existed. Time and motion studies enabled tasks to be broken up and standardized into their elementary components (Taylor 1911: 77–80, 117, 1947a: 58–60) and the 'planning department' where 'experts' coordinated the information before passing it on in the form of written instructions to workers enabled separation of planning from execution. This, in turn, extended the numbers, importance, and power of supervisory, engineering, and clerical staff and changed the way employees were recruited. By redefining power relations, the planning department operated like the panopticon; it was a laboratory which 'could be used as a machine to carry out experiments, to alter behaviour, to train or correct individuals' (Foucault, 1995: 203). Taylor maintained that these technical alterations would eliminate waste, increase profit, and so secure higher pay, shorter hours, and improved working conditions. Not only would the potential for industrial efficiency and national prosperity increase, he also claimed that personal, friendly contact between workers and managers was sure to follow (Taylor, 1911: 34, 39, 142–3, 1947a: 95).

Although Taylor promoted his system as an entire package, it was rare for even the majority of his methods to be adopted by any one enterprise. When asked in 1912 how many establishments had implemented his system in its entirety, Taylor answered: 'None; not one' (Taylor, 1947b: 280). And in 1914, Frank B. Gilbreth (1973: 37) commented that the system could never be totally installed 'because there is no end to it'. The following year, in his report for the US Federal Commission on Industrial Relations, Professor Robert Franklin Hoxie wrote: 'Scientific management in practice is never fully installed' and 'never wholly conformable with the ideals and principles laid down by the leaders'. Nevertheless, Hoxie did not think that this necessarily invalidated Taylor's ideals (Hoxie, 1915: 26, 113). Indeed, many of Taylor's followers who adopted his system stressed that they did not deviate from his philosophy even though they varied some of his methods (Drury, 1922: 188). In other words, SM was not a monolithic entity. Its implementation and diffusion involved a creative process or perhaps more akin to what Schumpeter (1994: 83–4) referred to as 'creative destruction'.

Why then did many later interpretations concentrate on its technical features? In part the answer can be found in the industrial conflict which occurred when attempts were made to implement SM at various US Government arsenals between 1909 and 1910. The subsequent insertion of amendments into various Congressional Acts prohibiting the use of time study and bonus payment systems in American Government shops (Aitkin, 1960: 135–85; Copley, 1969b: 348–51) and their annual renewal until 1949 (Aitkin, 1960: 170–3; Nadworny, 1955: 101–3) reinforced this narrow representation. As Merkle pointed out (1980: 48–9), the prohibition of Taylor's more prominent methods forced their application 'underground' from where SM developed a flexibility which not only helped it to survive but also to 'gain universality'.

In addition, the hostility of workers to the system led various contemporary management practitioners and writers to distinguish their strategies from SM, usually by renaming it, as was demonstrated by Sydney University academic Bernard Muscio's (1917) book *Lectures on Industrial Psychology*, which was basically an account of SM although its title concealed this fact. By 1920, even Taylor's American colleagues began to construe SM narrowly, in terms of its most contentious technical features. Frank and

Lillian Gilbreth attacked 'the unscientific pretensions of the proponents and advocates of the stop watch', while simultaneously emphasizing the 'human element' and the 'psychology of management' (Nadworny, 1955: 108–11). By this stage many of Taylor's early followers were involved in accommodating the more acceptable findings of the rapidly professionalizing industrial psychologists, who nevertheless acknowledged their debt to Taylor (Munsterberg, 1913). This broadening of SM's 'armory of techniques' enabled it to survive when 'the anti-Taylor reaction set in', but did nothing to change the central elements of its philosophy (Merkle, 1980: 48–9). At the same time, the narrower, politically inspired representations of SM gave rise to a discourse which profoundly circumscribed later accounts in popular texts (Mukhi, Hampton, and Barnwell, 1988: 37–9; Pugh, 1984: 133).

An astounding range of scholars have explored SM's broader impact on a range of different fields, including, for example, on the professions generally (Larson, 1977) and on the legal, medical, and engineering professions more specifically (Callahan, 1962: 46; Kanigel, 1997: 489), on the management of the home and child-rearing (Reiger, 1985) and on education (Brooks and Miles, 2008). And while this work has been fragmented along disciplinary lines, a critical point that unites it is the recognition that SM justified 'managerial authority by rooting it in depersonalised, rational rules of conduct' (Khurana, 2007: 94). This 'idea of management domination' was, according to Witt (2003: 3) the lynchpin of Taylor's system and informed the ideology and 'the principle of enterprise liability for industrial injuries'. He therefore described 'scientific management ideas as a cause of the enterprise liability revolution' (Witt, 2003: 38) and the 'dramatic changes in American Tort law in the second half of the twentieth century' (Witt, 2003: 40). While Khurana (2007: 95) may be right that SM did not bring about a 'mental revolution (…) along the lines envisaged by its creator', as he notes, 'it did help to achieve (…) the triumph of management (…) providing ideological and cultural justification for that control'. In what follows, I outline some of the critical dimensions of hegemony to frame my subsequent account of how Taylor's synthesis of philosophy, principles and methods were socialized in the workplace and in education.

Interpreting the Cultural Trajectory of a Hegemonic Ideology

Writing in the context of Taylor's growing influence on Olivetti and Fiat industrialists in Italy (Clegg and Dunkerley, 2013: 110, 121), Gramsci suggested that American 'rationalisation' focused on 'psycho-physical adaptation to the new industrial structure' and sought the elaboration of 'a new type of man suited to the new type of work and productive process' (Hoare and Nowell Smith, 1971: 286). Gramsci not only realized that Taylorist theory 'had practical consequences such as the division of mental and manual labour, the separation and isolation of workers as individuals, and so on, but that it also' concentrated 'their consciousness on (…) their individual output, their individual productivity and their individual wage' (Clegg and Dunkerley, 2013: 111). Implicit here is the notion of domination, not in the sense of manipulation but rather legitimation and consent; that is, the validation of 'the ideas, values and experiences of dominant groups (…) in the public discourse (Lears, 1985: 568, 574). And while 'Gramsci's writings contain no precise definition of cultural hegemony' (Lears, 1985: 568) Lears notes that Gramsci identified 'values, norms, perceptions, beliefs, sentiments, prejudices', as being those 'components of a dominant culture' that require the consent of subordinates' (1985: 569). For Gramsci, culture was 'the stuff of which power is made and by which it is maintained' (Dombroski, 1989: 132, cited in Ives, 2004: 162). Not only did he emphasize 'the political importance of cultural matters', he also conceived of 'language as a political issue' and expressed concern about 'everyday language practices', as well as the standardization of language (Ives, 2004: 4–5) and the link between language and 'hegemonic formations' (Ives, 2004: 9). In this sense, Lears (1985: 569) argued that 'Gramsci anticipated Michel Foucault's emphasis on the role of "discursive practice" in reinforcing domination' to the extent 'that "every language contains the elements of a conception of the world"'.

These dimensions of cultural hegemony, generally and the language of science, efficiency and rationality, more specifically, provide the leitmotif connecting the diffusion of SM in the workplace and education. Of course, many scholars have acknowledged that culture is complex and nuanced both in practice and in scholarship and the field of organizational culture is in itself a minefield, as Parker (2000) comprehensively showed. For present purposes, I draw on the definition outlined by Raymond Williams, who noted that 'culture' can be used in two senses: to refer to 'a whole way of life' as this entails common meanings which people ascribe to and/ or to the arts and learning (Gable: 1989: 4). Both senses denote interwoven processes that together shape common experiences, habits of thought, language, symbols, perceptions of social relationships, morals, values, rituals, and patterns of behaviour (Williams, 1979: 312–14). In organizational contexts, these cultural variables underpin and are reinforced by artefacts such as formal structures, rules, policies, goals, job descriptions, and standardized operating procedures, which as Morgan (1986: 132) pointed out, perform an important interpretative function as to a given social reality. In a similar vein, Williams (1961: 145–6) commented that the way education is organized 'can be seen to express, consciously and unconsciously, the wider organization of a culture and a society' and the way that culture has been actively shaped to particular social ends. What is conceived of as an 'education' is 'in fact a particular selection, a particular set of emphases and omissions'. From this perspective the aim of the industrial training reforms introduced in most industrializing countries, during the late nineteenth and early twentieth centuries, were not simply designed to extend literacy and the range of technical skill. More significantly, they sought to inculcate a 'pattern of culture' and of power relations through the diffusion of particular values, morals, and discipline concerning group loyalty, authority, justice, and lifestyle (Graff, 1981: 258–9). This dual cultural trajectory will now be explored in relation to Taylor's advocated reforms to the organization of work and education.

The Locus of Diffusion: Reforming the Workplace

The first pivotal 'site' for the socialization of SM and the internalization of its advocated power relations was, of course, the workplace. Here, SM was used to institutionalize new forms of communication through a formal system of information exchange based on written instructions. This feature sought to eliminate the informal oral communication through which workers articulated their common experiences and interests and sustained what Montgomery (1979: 14–17) called a 'mutualistic ethical code', which enabled them to control output and support each other in a myriad of ways, including teaching 'newcomers (…) covert forms of collective resistance'. For Taylor, this ethos sustained 'rule of thumb' knowledge and opposition to management (Taylor, 1911: 30–2). As part of his effort to institutionalize new forms of communication, Taylor denigrated the way craft skills were learned as they had been 'in the Middle Ages', not from books but 'by word of mouth'. And he devised many systematic methods for preventing workers from talking to each other, including a range of literary artefacts and mnemonic and mathematical devices all of which were meant to be integrated into written instructions (Taksa, 1992). Books, he argued, would help to eradicate 'rule-of-thumb' knowledge, which he distinguished from that provided in schools and colleges (Taylor, 1895: 875–6, 1911: 30–2, 1947b: 35–6), particularly if used in conjunction with supplementary training in scientific principles, in line with his third principle. These literary devices enhanced the disciplinary power of the new, technical personnel or 'functional foremen' and their capacity for surveillance. At the same time, these instructions gave a new type of power over the individual body of the worker. They provided an additional method of domination through their ability to individualize. Much like Bentham's Panopticon, the planning room and its instructions constituted 'the individual as a describable, analysable object (…) under the gaze of a permanent corpus of knowledge' (Foucault, 1995: 190) and reduced her/him to an 'object of information' rather than 'a subject in communication' (Foucault, 1995: 200).

Taylor's ideas on written instructions and training were widely disseminated by H. L. Gantt, F. B. Gilbreth, M. L. Cooke, C. B. Thompson, and F. A. Parkhurst, amongst others (Drury, 1922: 153). It was through them that Taylor's 'gospel' was spread internationally. In 1914, Cooke coordinated lectures on the application of SM to government administration for Philadelphia's public employees and during the First World War, he 'fathered the building up of courses in the handling of stores in some ten American colleges' (Drury, 1922: 188). Meanwhile, Gantt extended Taylor's ideas on vocational education by promoting 'a different training' that used the instruction card method as 'a system of education with prizes for those who learn' (Gantt, 1919: 111–12, 256). In his and Taylor's bonus pay schemes, rewards were given to those workers who cooperated with management by following instructions and he argued that the methods associated with SM could 'never be utilized properly until the rank and file have been trained to operate them' (Gantt, 1919: 8). 'To my mind', he wrote, 'the training of workmen (...) is one of the most important functions of the management' and 'the only method which holds out any hope of producing even a partial solution of our present industrial problems'. If these methods were introduced extensively, he argued, 'the habit of the shop would influence that of the community, and there would be a general increase in efficiency', fulfilling the 'dream of the millennium' (Gantt, 1919: 148, 220–1).

This focus on training provided a critically important channel for the cultural diffusion of SM and indeed its marketing. The evident connection between it and incentive pay schemes calls into question the claims made by scholars about Taylor's simplistic assumptions about economic motivations (Brody, 1980: 13). Taylor consistently stressed that bonus payments were offered as an exchange for continued effort, as compensation for increased monotony and to ensure submission 'to the new terms of work' (Taylor, 1911: 74; Hobson, 1913: 200, 209). Through the promotion of technical and professional training reforms, Taylor, his followers and educational administrators challenged the verbal and behavioural transmission of traditional values, norms and rituals among workers through traditional modes of training and socialized SM philosophy, principles, and methods. Taylor's claim that SM constituted a 'practical system of vocational guidance and training' impressed Hoxie, who suggested that if SM could 'show the way through practical vocational adaption', it deserved the support of all classes, regardless of 'its limitations and shortcomings' (Hoxie, 1915: 34–7).

Clearly, SM involved both a 'set of principles' and a 'scholastic programme' that legitimated 'a general conception of life' by directly attacking the norms of prevailing work cultures. The instruction cards, mathematic formulae, and mnemonic symbols created a new language which reinforced new meanings, values, norms, and behaviours. As Matthew Stewart (2006), the retired founding partner of a consulting firm, noted, 'I can confirm on the basis of personal experience that management consulting continues to worship at the shrine of numerology where Taylor made his first offering'. This specialized language helped to sustain patterns of communication which legitimated SM and a new rational and standardized culture of work focused on production and output. The planning and centralized tool rooms and the new routing system operated as cultural variables insofar as they created new spatial boundaries which circumscribed social interaction. However, it was the diffusion of the 'scholastic programme' in the educational field that had the greatest impact on modern life and continues to have the greatest influence over postmodern life in the twenty first century.

The Locus of Diffusion: Reforming the Educational Field

As President of the American Society of Mechanical Engineers in 1906, Taylor actively pursued links with educational institutions. When he was awarded an honorary doctorate from the University of Pennsylvania, his address, 'A Comparison of University and Industrial Methods and Discipline', criticized existing educational methods and his proposals for the reform of industrial and professional education attracted extensive attention in academic circles. In 1907, Professor Ira N. Hollis from Harvard University's Division of Engineering wrote that his 'ideas on the subject of education were well worth spreading' and invited him to serve on Harvard's Visiting Committee for Engineering (Copley, 1969b: 265–6). Taylor later also promoted his proposals for reform of university administration to Richard C. Maclaurin, President of the Massachusetts Institute of Technology, Henry Thompson, one of Princeton University's trustees and other university administrators (Copley, 1969b: 269). Taylor's criticisms had far-reaching consequences. In 1909, Henry S. Pritchett, the President of the Carnegie Foundation for the Advancement of Teaching, initiated an 'economic study of (...) the administration of educational work', which was undertaken by Cooke whose report, *Academic and Industrial Efficiency*, was published in 1910 as the Foundation's Fifth Bulletin, heralding the spread of Taylor's ideas to university education and administration (Copley, 1969b: 267–9; Cooke, 1910). Through his prosthelatizing on educational reform Taylor continued to promote his mental revolution, as did Professor John Price Jackson's paper on 'College and Apprentice Training' (Jackson, 1907: 499–500), W. B. Russell (1907), who advocated formal instruction classes during working hours to ensure organizations would be 'replete with cooperation and efficiency' and Gantt, whose paper 'Training Workmen in Habits of Industry and Cooperation' was described by Professor William Kent as 'in harmony with humanitarian ideals (Kent cited in Gantt, 1908: 1061). From here, SM spread rapidly to the American school system, as was thoroughly outlined by Callahan (1962), and the administration of public education (Brooks and Miles, 2008). This reorganization of teaching provided scope for increased surveillance and discipline similar to that exercised in the workshop. Taylor appears to have recognized that these 'disciplinary institutions' simultaneously differentiated individuals in a hierarchical manner, homogenized them, and punished or excluded those who were unwilling or unable to conform (Foucault, 1995: 182). The adoption of SM philosophy and principles by educational administrators in schools and universities effectively enabled students to be 'described, judged, measured, compared with others', selected, individualized, 'trained or corrected, classified' and 'normalized' (Foucault, 1995: 191) This process of normalization served to distribute 'pupils according to their aptitudes and their conduct, that is, according to the use that could be made of them' after 'they left the school' (Foucault, 1995: 182).

According to English (2002: 110, cited in Brooks and Miles, 2008) infatuation 'with the rhetoric and publicity surrounding' Taylor's ideas, led education colleges to develop a 'new mission (...) to scientifically prepare educational leaders' and their adoption of 'administrative goals and functions' were aligned with SM's 'penchant for efficiency, control, and effectiveness'. Brooks and Miles (2008) argue that during the 1920s, principals were increasingly depicted as scientific managers or business managers 'responsible for devising standardized methods of pupil accounting and introducing sound business administration practices in budgeting, planning, maintenance, and finance'. In this context, 'business values' and an emphasis on 'expertise and efficiency' gained credence in school systems. The 'supervision of employees' also became an important aspect 'of educational leadership' and 'University-based educators contributed to the development of educational leadership as a professional occupation by creating degree programs and special courses of study' in 'finance, business administration, organization and administration' to prepare such leaders.

According to Bouie (2012: 2), today, American public education is dominated 'by a focus on standards-based reform and high-stakes accountability systems' that revolve around 'student performance standards, standardized-testing', rewards in terms of 'financial and positive recognition' for schools and 'promotion to the next grade' for students 'who demonstrate satisfactory achievement'. Bouie (2012: 7), like Brooks and Miles, highlights the 'No Child Left Behind Act' of 2002, which reinforced the emphasis on accountability and 'on increasing student achievement'. For some scholars, 'the new accountability is a Clarion call for a Second Wave of Scientific Management' that 'favors a business management, market driven, and high stakes outcome-oriented model of educational leadership' and 'business-style efficiency', which 'bears an uncanny resemblance to the Frederick Taylor-inspired traditions' of earlier eras (Brooks and Miles, 2008). In fact, Bouie (2012: 6) argues that '(t)he logic of standards-based reform is firmly rooted in' Taylor's principles, which:

> are operationalized through (...) scientifically-determined best practices, teacher and administrator evaluation systems designed to focus on observing (...) efficient standards of behavior by trained supervisors, teacher pay-for-performance and sanctions against teachers, administrators, schools, and students for failure to achieve predetermined standards of performance. (Bouie, 2012: 7)

Similar developments are evident in tertiary education generally and in business education more specifically. According to Thomas, Lorange, and Sheth (2013: 29), the standardization of business education started with the establishment of the AACSB in 1916. Designed to bring 'scientific rigour to the study of business' (Thomas, Lorange, and Sheth, 2013: 7), this organization included among its founding members Columbia University, where prominent Taylorite Drury (1915: 114) read for his PhD, and Harvard University and Dartmouth College, where courses on SM principles had been launched in 1910 (Callahan, 1962; Copley, 1969b: 277). Indeed, a conference at Dartmouth on SM in 1911 included a paper on 'Academic Efficiency' by the first Dean of the Harvard Business School (Gay, 1972). As noted previously, Taylor was on intimate terms with Harvard's leading professors, who were ardent supporters. Not surprisingly then the AACSB 'provided a significant building block for (...) institutional standardisation of business education' and gave rise to 'the focus in the US on a single, somewhat insular educational model' (Thomas, Lorange, and Sheth, 2013: 29). The advent and 'market acceptance of the MBA' provides the best example of this trend 'towards similarity, homogeneity and mass production in business education' (Thomas, Lorange, and Sheth, 2013: 29). As Kemp (2013: 350) notes 'formulas to measure academic production are now arrived at in a similar manner to the "standard operating procedure" of the modern industrial era'. Now a range of electronic software is used to create standardized curriculum vitae in line with AACSB metric requirements and software programs that measure 'publications through author/journal impact'. Kemp argues that the ranking of journals applies 'the principles of SM' and concludes that 'Taylor's ghost haunts Higher Education as attempts continue to measure efficiency in academic performance through "performativity"'; are embedded in increasing demands for accountability that involve 'the application and monitoring of compliance with *legitimate* standards' (my emphasis).

Conclusion

In this treatment, which has construed SM as a hegemonic ideology, I have argued that Taylor's philosophy, principles, and methods were legitimated and socialized in the workplace and in education during the early decades of the twentieth century through a range of cultural practices combined with a language of science and efficiency. What made SM much more than the sum of all its component parts was the combination of 'scientific' methodology with a consensus ideology which promoted social harmony and a vision of a new era of high productivity and high consumption.

Taylor's reform agenda was not limited to production but extended to changing the way people think, communicate, and learn. As Gramsci pointed out, hegemony not only operates as 'an educational relationship (…) throughout society as a whole' and between individuals but also internationally 'between complexes of national and continental civilisations' (Hoare and Nowell Smith, 1971: 350), as the global influence of the AACSB cogently indicates. In the neo-liberal era, the spread of Taylor's spirit and the resurgence of his principles and methods, particularly in schools and universities, through the medium of a range of regulatory and disciplinary mechanisms, has shown how SM has, and continues to, operate as a 'general conception of life' and a 'scholastic programme' (Boggs, 1976: 39). There can be no doubt that Taylor's impact has been immense. But the 'spirit of scientific management' has not simply remained 'a significant influence on the design and operation of work organisations'. Nor has 'its mortal form'—its practices and techniques— disappeared, as was suggested earlier (Dunford, 1992: 56). On the contrary, it has continued to exert a legitimating force and has succeeded in uniting and dominating knowledge work and the field of education in a way hitherto unimagined. In this sense, its cultural trajectory has gone a long way towards fulfilling Taylor's unitary ideals and vision.

References

Aitkin, H. G. J. (1960). *Taylorism at Watertown Arsenal.* Melbourne: Oxford University Press.
Bendix, R. (1974). *Work and Authority in Industry: Ideologies of Management in the Course of Industrialization.* Berkeley, CA: University of California Press.

Boggs, C. (1976). *Gramsci's Marxism*. London: Pluto Press.
Bouie, Jr., E. L. (2012). 'The Impact of Bureaucratic Structure, Scientific Management, and Institutionalism on Standards'. *Mercer Journal of Educational Leadership*, 1(1): 1–21.
Box, R. C. and Marshall, G. (2006). 'Democracy and Public Administration'. *Faculty Books and Monographs*, Book 249, available at: <http://digitalcommons.unomaha.edu/facultybooks/249> (accessed 10 June 2015).
Braverman, H. (1974). *Labor and Monopoly Capitalism: The Degradation of Work in the Twentieth Century*. New York: Monthly Review Press.
Brody, B. (1980). *Workers in Industrial America: Essays on the Twentieth Century Struggle*. New York: Oxford University Press.
Brooks, J. S. and Miles, M. T. (2008). 'From Scientific Management to Social Justice ... and Back Again? Pedagogical Shifts in the Study and Practice of Educational Leadership', in A. H. Normore (ed.), *Leadership for Social Justice: Promoting Equity and Excellence Through Enquiry and Reflective Practice*. Charlotte, NC: Information Age Publishing Inc., 99–114.
Cadbury, E. (1914). 'Some Principles of Industrial Organisation: The Case For and Against Scientific Management'. *Sociological Review*, 7(2): 99–117.
Callahan, R. E. (1962). *Education and the Cult of Efficiency*. Chicago, IL: The University of Chicago Press.
Clegg, S. and Dunkerley, D. (2013). *Organisation, Class and Control*. Abingdon: Routledge & Kegan Paul.
Cooke, M. L. (1910). '*Academic and Industrial Efficiency: A Report to the Carnegie Foundation for the Advancement of Teaching*', Bulletin 5 (New York: Carnegie Foundation for the Advancement of Teaching).
Cooke, M. L. (1914). 'Some Factors in Municipal Engineering'. *Transactions, American Society of Mechanical Engineers (ASME)*, 36: 605–18.
Cooke, M. L. (1924). 'The Influence of Scientific Management upon Government—Federal, State and Municipal'. *Bulletin of the Taylor Society*, 9(1): 31–8.
Copley, F. B. (1969a). *F. W. Taylor: Father of Scientific Management*, vol. 1. New York: Augustus M. Kelley Publishers.
Copley, F. B. (1969b). *F. W. Taylor: Father of Scientific Management*, vol. 2. New York: Augustus M. Kelley Publishers.
Dodge, J. M. (1905–1906). 'A History of the Introduction of a System of Shop Management'. *Transactions, ASME*, 27(1115): 720–9.
Dombroski, R. (1989) *Antonio Gramsci*. Boston, MA: Twayne.
Doray, B. (1988). *From Taylorism to Fordism: A Rational Madness*. London: Free Association Books.
Drucker, P. F. (1974). *Management: Tasks, Responsibilities, Practices*. New York: Harper & Row.
Drury, H. B. (1922). *Scientific Management: A History and Criticism*. New York: Columbia University Press (revised version; originally published 1915).
Dunford, R. W. (1992). *Organisational Behaviour*. Sydney: Addison-Wesley.
Evans, C. and Holmes, L. (2013). 'Introduction', in C. Evans and L. Holmes (eds.), *Re Tayloring Management: Scientific Management a Century On*. Farnham: Gower Publishing.
Foucault, M. (1995). *Discipline and Punish: The Birth of the Prison*. New York: Vintage Books.
Fox, A. (1974). *Beyond Contract: Work Power and Trust Relations*. London: Faber and Faber.
Gable, R. (1989). *Raymond Williams, Resources of Hope Culture, Democracy, Socialism*. London: Verso.

Gantt, H. L. (1908). 'Training Workmen in Habits of Industry and Cooperation'. *Transactions, ASME*, 30: 1037–48.

Gantt, H. L. (1919). *Work, Wages and Profits*. New York: The Engineering Magazine Co.

Gay, E. F. (1972). 'Academic Efficiency', in *Dartmouth College Conferences, First Tuck School Conference—Addresses and Discussions at the Conference on Scientific Management Held October 12, 13, 14, Nineteen Hundred and Eleven*. Easton: Hive Publishing Company.

Giannantonio, C. M. and Hurley-Hanson, A. E. (2011). 'Frederick Winslow Taylor: Reflections on the Relevance of the Principles of Scientific Management 100 Years Later'. *Journal of Business and Management*, 17: 7–10.

Gilbreth, F. B. (1973). *Primer of Scientific Management*. Easton: Hive Publishing Company (facsimile edition originally published 1914).

Gilbreth, F. B. (1980). 'Introduction', in F. B. Gilbreth and Young Men's Christian Association (Worcester, MA) (eds.), *Scientific Management Course: A Landmark Series of Lectures Given at the Y.M.C.A., Worcester, Massachusetts*. Easton: Hive Publishing Co. (facsimile edition originally published 1912).

Graff, H. J. (1981). 'Literacy, Jobs and Industrialization', in H. G. Graff (ed.), *Literacy and Social Development in the West: A Reader*. Cambridge: Cambridge University Press.

Grugulis, I. and Lloyd, C. (2010). 'Skill and the Labour Process: The Conditions and Consequences of Change', in P. Thompson and C. Smith (eds.), *Working Life: Renewing labour Process Analysis*. Basingstoke: Palgrave Macmillan.

Haber, S. (1964). *Efficiency and Uplift: Scientific Management in the Progressive Era 1890-1920*. Chicago, IL: University of Chicago Press.

Haigh, G. (2012). *The Office: A Hardworking History*. Carlton: Miegunyah Press.

Hales, C. (2013). 'Stem Cell, Pathogen or Fatal Remedy? The Relationship of Taylor's Principles of Management to the Wider Management Movement', in C. Evans and L. Holmes (eds.), *Re-Tayloring Management: Scientific Management a Century On*. Farnham: Gower Publishing, 15–40.

Hoare, Q. and Nowell Smith, G. (1971). *Selections from the Prison Notebooks of Antonio Gramsci*. London: Lawrence & Wisehart.

Hobson, J. A. (1913). 'Scientific Management'. *Sociological Review*, 6(3): 197–212.

Hoxie, R. F. (1915). *Scientific Management and Labor*. New York: D. Appleton and Co.

Hunter, J. and Sanderson, G. (2001). 'Training Packages: The Scientific Management of Education', Australian Vocational Education and Training Research Association Conference Paper, available at: <http://www.avetra.org.au/abstracts_and_papers_2001/Hunter_full.pdf> (accessed 12 June 2015).

Irvine, R. F. (1915). *National Efficiency*. Melbourne: Victorian Railways Printing Branch.

Ives, P. (2004). *Language and Hegemony in Gramsci*. London: Pluto Press.

Jackson, J. P. (1907). 'College and Apprentice Training', *Transactions, ASME*, 29: 473–90.

Kanigel, R. (1997). *The One Best Way: Frederick Winslow Taylor and the Enigma of Efficiency*. London: Little, Brown and Company.

Kaufman, B. E. (2008). *Managing the Human Factor: The Early Years of Human Resource Management in American Industry*. Ithaca, NY: ILR Press an imprint of Cornell University Press.

Kemp, L. J. (2013). 'Modern to Postmodern Management: Developments in Scientific Management'. *Journal of Management History*, 19(3): 345–61.

Khurana, R. (2007). *From Higher Aims to Hired Hands: The Social Transformation of American Business Schools and the Unfulfilled Promise of Management as a Profession*. Princeton, NJ: Princeton University Press.
Larson, S. M. (1977). *The Rise of Professionalism: A Sociological Analysis*. Berkeley, CA: University of California Press.
Lears, T. J. (1985). 'The Concept of Cultural Hegemony: Problems and Possibilities'. *American Historical Review*, 90(3): 567–93.
Littler, C. R. (1978). 'Understanding Taylorism'. *British Journal of Sociology*, 29(2): 185–202.
Littler, C. R. (1982). *The Development of the Labour Process in Capitalist Societies*. London: Heinemann.
Littler, C. (1990). 'The Labour Process Debate: A Theoretical Review 1974–1988', in D. Knights and H. Willmott (eds.), *Labour Process Theory*. London: Macmillan, 46.
Merkle, J. A. (1980). *Management and Ideology: The Legacy of the International Scientific Management Movement*. Berkeley, CA: University of California Press.
Montgomery, D. (1979). *Workers' Control in America: Studies in the History of Work, Technology and Labor Struggles*. Cambridge: Cambridge University Press.
Morgan, G. (1986). *Images of Organizations*. Beverly Hills, CA: SAGE.
Mortenson, M. J., Doherty, N. F., and Robinson, S. (2015). 'Operational Research from Taylorism to Terabytes: A Research Agenda for the Analytics Age'. *European Journal of Operational Research*, 241(3): 583–95.
Mukhi, S., Hampton, D., and Barnwell, N. (1988). *Australian Management*. Sydney: McGraw-Hill.
Munsterberg, H. (1913). *Psychology and Industrial Efficiency*. Boston, MA: Houghton Mifflin Co.
Muscio, B. (1917). *Lectures on Industrial Psychology*. Sydney: Angus & Robertson Ltd.
Nadworny, M. (1955). *Scientific Management and the Unions 1900–1932: A Historical Analysis*. Cambridge, MA: Harvard University Press.
Noble, D. F. (1977). *America by Design: Science Technology and the Rise of Corporate Capitalism*. New York: Alfred A. Knopf.
Øgland, P. (2013). 'Mechanism Design for Total Quality Management: Using the Bootstrap Algorithm for Changing the Control Game', unpublished PhD thesis, Faculty of Mathematics and Natural Sciences, University of Oslo.
Parker, M. (2000). *Organizational Culture and Identity: Unity and Division at Work*. London: SAGE.
Payne, S. C., Youngcourt, S. S., and Watrous, K. M. (2006). 'Portrayals of F. W. Taylor across Textbooks'. *Journal of Management History*, 12(4): 385–407.
Pugh, D. S. (1984). *Organization Theory*. Harmondsworth: Penguin.
Reiger, K. M. (1985). *The Disenchantment of the Home: Modernizing the Australian Family 1880–1940*. Melbourne: Oxford University Press.
Renold, C. G. (1914). 'Comment on Cadbury's Paper', *Sociological Review*, 7(2): 122–4.
Rose, M. (1975). *Industrial Behaviour*. London: Allen Lane.
Russell, W. B. (1907). 'Industrial Education'. *Transactions, ASME*, 29: 121–43.
Schumpeter, J. A. (1994). *Capitalism, Socialism, and Democracy*. London: Routledge.
Stark, D. (1980). 'Class Struggle and the Transformation of the Labor Process'. *Theory and Society*, 9: 89–130.
Stewart, M. (2006). 'The Management Myth', *The Atlantic*, available at: <http://www.theatlantic.com/magazine/archive/2006/06/the-management-myth/304883/> (accessed 24 May 2015).

Taksa, L. (1992). 'Scientific Management: Technique or Cultural Ideology?' *Journal of Industrial Relations*, 34(3): 365–95.

Taksa, L. (1995). 'The Cultural Diffusion of Scientific Management: The United States and New South Wales'. *Journal of Industrial Relations*, 37(3): 427–61.

Taksa, L. (1997). 'Scientific Management and the General Strike of 1917: Workplace Restructuring in the New South Wales Railways and Tramways Department'. *Historical Studies in Industrial Relations*, 4: 37–64.

Taksa, L. (1998) 'All a Matter of Timing: Managerial Innovation and Workplace Culture in the New South Wales Railways and Tramways prior to 1921'. *Australian Historical Studies*, 110: 1–26.

Taksa, L. (2007). 'Uniting Management and Education in Pursuit of Efficiency: F. W. Taylor's Training Reform Legacy'. *Economic and Labour Relations Review*, 17(2): 129–56.

Taksa, L. (2009). 'Intended or Unintended Consequences? A Critical Reappraisal of the Safety First Movement and Its Non-Union Safety Committees'. *Economic and Industrial Democracy*, 30(1): 9–36.

Taneja, S., Pryor, M. G., and Leslie A. (2011). 'Frederick W. Taylor's Scientific Management Principles: Relevance and Validity'. *Journal of Applied Management and Entrepreneurship*, 16(3): 60–87.

Taylor, F. W. (1895). 'A Piece-Rate System Being a Step toward Partial Solution of the Labor Problem'. *Transactions, ASME*, 16: 865–903.

Taylor, F. W. (1911). *The Principles of Scientific Management*. New York: Harper & Bros.

Taylor, F. W. (1947a). 'Shop Management', in *Scientific Management*. New York: Harper & Brothers Publishers (originally published as F. W. Taylor (1903) 'Shop Management'. *Transactions, ASME*, 24: 1337–1480).

Taylor, F. W. (1947b). 'Taylor's Testimony Before the Special House Committee', in *Scientific Management*. New York: Harper & Brothers Publishers (originally published as United States Congress House Committee on Labor. Special committee to investigate the Taylor and other systems of shop management (1912). *The Taylor and Other Systems of Shop Management: Hearings before Special Committee of the House of Representatives to Investigate the Taylor and other Systems of Shop Management under Authority of House of Representatives. 90 ... [Oct. 4, 1911–Feb. 12, 1912]*. Washington, DC: Government Printing Office. 62nd Congress, Second Session, House Report 403, 1912.

Taylor, F. W. (1972). 'The Principles of Scientific Management', in Dartmouth College Conferences, First Tuck School Conference—*Address and Discussions at the Conference on Scientific Management Held October 12, 13, 14, Nineteen Hundred and Eleven*. Easton: Hive Publishing Company (reprint, originally published 1911).

Thomas, H., Lorange, P., and Sheth, J. (2013). *The Business School in the Twenty-First Century: Emergent Challenges and New and New Business Models*. Cambridge: Cambridge University Press.

Thompson, C. B. (1917). *The Theory and Practice of Scientific Management*. Boston, MA: Houghton Mifflin Company.

Tsutsui, W. M. (2001). *Manufacturing Ideology: Scientific Management in Twentieth Century Japan*. Princeton, NJ: Princeton University Press.

Urwick, L. (1957). *The Making of Scientific Management*, vol. 2. London: Sir Isaac Pitman & Sons.

Urwick, L. and Brech, E. F. L. (1957). *The Making of Scientific Management*, vol. 1. London: Sir Isaac Pitman & Sons Ltd.

Warner, M. (1994). 'Japanese Culture, Western Management: Taylorism and Human Resources in Japan'. *Organization Studies*, 15(4): 509–33.

Williams, G. A. (1960). 'The Concept of "Egemonia" in the Thought of Antonio Gramsci: Some Notes on Interpretation'. *Journal of the History of Ideas*, 21(4): 586–99.

Williams, R. (1961). *The Long Revolution*. London: Penguin.

Williams, R. (1979). *Culture and Society 1780–1950*. Harmondsworth: Penguin.

Witt, J. F. (2003). 'Speedy Fred Taylor and the Ironies of Enterprise Liability'. *Columbia Law Review*, 103(1): 1–49.

Witt, J. F. (2004). *The Accidental Republic: Crippled Workingmen, Destitute Widows, and the Remaking of American Law*. Cambridge, MA: Harvard University Press.

Wren, D. A. (2011). 'The Centennial of Frederick W. Taylor's *The Principles of Scientific Management*: A Retrospective Commentary'. *Journal of Business and Management*, 17: 11–22.

Zerzan, J. (1984). 'Taylorism and Unionism: The Origins of Partnership', *Telos*, 60: 140–5.

CHAPTER 3

HUMAN RELATIONS

KYLE BRUCE AND CHRIS NYLAND

As ritualistically conveyed in the 'habitual revelatory narrative' in management and organization studies textbooks (Hassard, 2012), the Human Relations 'School' or model of management (HRS hereafter) is understood to have emerged from the investigations into human association in the workplace by Elton Mayo and his Harvard Business School associates between 1924 and 1932 at the Hawthorne plant of Western Electric. Mayo and members of HRS are construed to be humanists who developed a model of management based on the assumption that workers are complex psycho-social beings who are at once individuals with diverse ('high-level') needs and members of social groups where congregation modifies their individualistic impulses to make collective action possible. HRS is said to have brought people's social needs into the limelight and thereby increased their capacity for 'spontaneous collaboration' at work. Employees, exponents of the human relations' model argued, obtain identity, stability, and satisfaction if managed in ways that provide for these needs thus rendering them more willing to cooperate with each other and management and contribute their efforts towards accomplishing organizational goals (Wren, 2005; Duncan, 1999; Wren and Greenwood, 1998; Kaufman, 2004, 2008).

This favourable perspective, however, has been challenged by a growing body of scholars (O'Connor, 1999a; Bruce and Nyland, 2011; Nyland and Bruce, 2012) who have demonstrated that Mayo's model was far more sinister than the conventional wisdom concedes and spoke directly to conservative business concerns. In short, it is charged that HRS provided employers with a management model that held employees are irrational, agitation-prone individuals whose demand for increased wages and improved working conditions was symptomatic of a deep psychosocial maladjustment, and so, unfit for 'voice' in the workplace. This situation precluded the need for employers to bargain with workers; however, it did necessitate that they draw on behavioural and social psychology to 'scientifically' determine how employee maladjustment might be managed to ease workers' 'non-logical' concerns and abet them to work in ways that benefited themselves and organizations. In this context, the purpose of this chapter is to provide a steadied account of HRS. We begin by providing contextual background to

Mayo and the Hawthorne investigations and then proceed to problematize the received wisdom. We conclude with an assessment of the significance of HRS for contemporary organizational behaviour and human resource management theory and practice.

Mayo, Hawthorne, and HRS

Born in Adelaide, the capital of South Australia, on 26 December 1880, George Elton Mayo failed to complete medical school and only found his niche as a mature-age student studying philosophy at the University of Adelaide, graduating in 1911.[1] Thereafter, he lectured in philosophy at the University of Queensland but subsequently sought to gain the work experience in England that he deemed requisite for a senior academic position in Australia. Accordingly, he set sail for England in July 1922, travelling via the west coast of the USA where he had been led to believe he would be able to generate the funds needed to remain in England for an extended period. This was not to be, for even though he had procured 'official' documents that falsely claimed he was a professor of psychology and physiology at the University of Queensland, he was unable to gain a visiting position at the University of California, Berkeley, which he understood had been arranged. Following some rather desperate networking with leading social scientists and grant and philanthropy officials, Mayo landed what initially was a six-month research fellowship at the Wharton School in Philadelphia in 1923 (Trahair, 1984).

What made Mayo's Wharton appointment possible was the fact that numerous employers and intellectuals were attracted to his claim that much 'abnormal' industrial behaviour was a consequence of unhealthy 'reveries'. This conviction enabled him to attract public attention when he first arrived in the USA because he told reporters that this factor explained the 'flapper' phenomenon. Shrouding his beliefs in the language of medical psychoanalysis and applied psychology he likewise insisted that workers' daily experiences, domestic life, and employment conditions caused them to experience pessimistic or obsessional reveries and reduced them to the equivalent of 'shell shocked' soldiers in need of serious psychological/psychiatric attention. Mayo postulated that workers' mental health problems were not innate but rather were the product of the industrialization process and hence a cost that society and working people had to bear if they were to realize the benefits made possible by modern production methods. Even before leaving Australia he had dismissed suggestions that workers might be dissatisfied with their work experience because of poor wages, employment conditions, and lack of voice suggesting such claims were manifestations of 'socialistic radicalism' and symptomatic of deep psychosocial maladjustment.

Mayo's position at Wharton enabled him to undertake studies in Philadelphia factories that sought to address excessively high labour turnover (Bulmer and Bulmer, 1981).

---

[1] Readers are urged to consult the definitive biography of Mayo by Trahair (1984), but see also Bruce (2013).

These studies involved in-depth interviews with workers and marked his initial effort at counselling employees to determine what needed to be done to resolve their concerns. His major recommendation was not improved wages and conditions and workplace democracy, as was being urged by progressive members of the scientific management movement, but to address unhealthy reveries induced by excessive fatigue, the solution for which was increased rest pauses, a proposal that that was reportedly effective in reducing turnover and increasing output (Trahair, 1984; O'Connor, 1999a, 1999b).

'Discovering' a correlation between workers' productivity and their mental health won Mayo the enthusiasm of John D. Rockefeller Jr. (JDR Jr. hereafter) and coalesced with the latter's concern with improving industrial relations following the infamous 1914 Ludlow massacre in which striking miners and their families were killed at the Rockefeller-owned Colorado Fuel and Iron company (Gitelman, 1988; Rees, 2010). JDR Jr. became Mayo's financial and professional benefactor, underwriting Mayo's salary initially at Wharton and subsequently at Harvard, arranging access to companies for his research (including Hawthorne), and assuring him a receptive audience for his ideas (Bulmer and Bulmer, 1981; Fisher, 1983; Trahair, 1984; Harvey, 1982; Gillespie, 1991; Magat, 1999; O'Connor, 1999a). Mayo arrived at Harvard in 1926 and remained there until his retirement in 1947. During this time he utilized his Rockefeller connections to hire young acolytes who collectively became famous as the 'Harvard human relations group'.

In October 1927, Arthur H. Young, the head of Rockefeller-backed, conservative think-tank, Industrial Relations Counselors, arranged for Mayo to address a group of industrialists at to what his variant of industrial psychology might offer them. In his address Mayo spoke directly to the concerns of his audience explaining that his research had revealed how to calm the irrational, agitation-prone mind of the worker and how a curriculum could be developed to train managers in the required techniques. He advised those gathered to approach him directly if they wished to discuss the possibility of having the Harvard HRS researchers provide their firms with advice and/or training. Auspiciously, the personnel director of Western Electric was in the audience and invited Mayo to become involved in ongoing studies that were being undertaken at the firm's Hawthorne plant, thus precipitating the most public and enduring aspect of the diffusion of his knowledge-claims. His involvement with the Hawthorne studies was attractive to many industrialists because this research promised 'a technology of social control that could confront problems of industrial unrest and individual maladjustments among workers' (Gillespie, 1991: 112–13). It was also attractive to HBS because it raised its reputation from its initial 'low status as a trainer of money grabbers into a high-prestige educator of socially conscientious administrators' (Hoopes, 2003: 141; O'Connor, 1999a).

Conducted between 1924 and 1932, the Hawthorne studies are 'the largest, best known and most influential investigations in the history of organizational research' and 'synonymous with stimulating the most notable "paradigm-shift" in the history of organizational research: scientific management to human relations' (Hassard, 2012: 1432–3). In brief,[2] the studies consisted of the Illumination Tests (commencing in

---

[2] For an in-depth history and analysis of the studies, see Landsberger (1958) and also Gillespie (1991).

1924 investigating whether workplace lighting and labour productivity were correlated), the Relay-Assembly Tests (commencing in 1927 designed to evaluate the impact of rest periods and hours of work), and finally, the Bank Wiring Tests (commencing in 1931 designed to observe and study social relationships and social structures within work groups). The results of these investigations were so inconclusive and confusing to management at Western Electric that outside assistance was sought from HBS researchers (Gillespie, 1991). Mayo first visited Hawthorne for two days in April 1928, then for four days in 1929, and then began a deeper involvement in the ongoing experiments in 1930 (Trahair, 1984).

Mayo's interpretation of the data purported to demonstrate that once the irrationalities of workers are removed, or ameliorated, they will respond positively to non-economic incentives and be motivated to increase their productivity. Though there were several sets of independent 'experiments', this finding was actually based entirely on the study of six women (two of whom were replaced) at a workbench—the Relay-Assembly studies—over some five years. In November 1928 Mayo reported his interpretation of the preliminary findings of the Relay-Assembly studies to members of the Special Conference Committee, another Rockefeller-backed think-tank. They were very impressed, especially now that his theories were cloaked in facts and figures and emphasized that changes in supervision could solve worker maladjustment and improved productivity and enhance the firm's objective of keeping trade unions out of plants (Trahair, 1984; Gillespie, 1991). The study of six unrepresentative staff whose numbers had been purged when this was deemed necessary was sufficient for big business to accept Mayo's theory and be 'enrolled' in his research programme: such was business desire for an explanation of worker behaviour that exonerated management for any blame for workers' dissatisfaction and that promised a means of control that did not require improved wages and employment conditions (Bruce and Nyland, 2011).

In 1933 Mayo published his *Human Problems of an Industrial Civilization* (Mayo, 1933) and in 1939 used Rockefeller funding to have Roethlisberger and Dickson's *Management and the Worker* published by Harvard University Press. The latter work argued that the employees studied in the bank wiring room 'possessed an intricate social organization in terms of which much of their conduct was determined'. It was this social code rather than individual malady that resulted in output restriction, the code serving as a 'protective mechanism' insulating the group from outside changes in work conditions and personal relations (Roethlisberger and Dickson, 1939: 525). In sum, and in a much cited stanza,

> (t)he study of the bank wiremen showed that their behavior at work could not be understood without considering the *informal organization* of the group and the relation of this informal organization to the total social organization of the company. The work activities of this group, together with their satisfactions and dissatisfactions, had to be viewed as manifestations of a complex pattern of interrelations. In short, the work situation of the bank wiring group had to be treated as a *social system*;

moreover, the industrial organization of which this group was a part also had to be treated as a social system (Roethlisberger and Dickson, 1939: 551).

So it was, that organizations came to be viewed as social systems wherein we find a number of individuals working towards common goals but each bringing to the work situation different, personally and socially conditioned goals or aspirations (Roethlisberger and Dickson, 1939). The aim of the organization, or more realistically its management with the assistance of industrial psychologists, is to temper these individual goals so that they become congruent with those of the organization. These notions, along with an embryonic discussion of organizational or corporate culture, can be found in *Management and the Worker* and they infuse any meaningful contemporary discussion of OB and HRM, a point to which we will return in the final section of this chapter.

Problematizing the Received Wisdom Regarding HRS

There are several problems with the orthodox understanding of HRS. First, Mayo's precise place in the evolution of HRS is the subject of significant debate. His role in the Hawthorne investigations has been variously conceived, with substantial contention both as to his function and his scientific credibility. There is doubt, for instance, as to whether Mayo's interpretation of the Hawthorne experiments was more reflective of his preconceived personal views than of the actual empirical results, and whether this shaped Roethlisberger and Dickson's 'official' 1939 account (Carey, 1967; Gillespie, 1991; Smith, 1998; Wren and Greenwood, 1998). In this context, Mayo's personal contribution to the Hawthorne studies has been construed as little more than a scientific populariser for Western Electric, particularly given the main series of experiments were well under way when he arrived in 1928 (Smith, 1976, 1998). Indeed, Trahair (2001) maintains, 'Mayo was never responsible for doing any research as such at the Western Electric works, all he did was make the magic run, others did the work.' Sofer (1973) similarly has maintained that Mayo's main contribution was handling the relationships between the research team and the company and assisting with the design of research projects, whilst O'Connor (1999a) argues his major function in the investigations was that of legitimizing the academic rigour and the practical industrial relevance of the Harvard Business School. Above all else, it is charged that Mayo's theory of human relations was based almost entirely on his personal political interpretation of worker motivation and that the tests were fabricated in ways that were consciously designed to hide the fact that the primary influence motivating the workers studied to increase their work effort was the promise of increased wages. Highlighting this last point at the Academy of Management a few days before his death, Charles Wrege (2014) summarized a lifetime of research on HRS when he unequivocally declared there was no 'Hawthorne Effect' and that what motivated the workers at Hawthorne was not the salving of their social needs by psychologists or the welfare capitalism of the firm. Rather it was the fact that they were offered the change to increase their income, in short" 'It was the money!'

The second problem with the received wisdom is that many thinkers preceded Mayo and his associates in discussing 'the human problem in industry', and not all exponents or writers on scientific management ignored the human element. These points are well understood in the history of management thought, though seldom so in management or organizational behaviour textbooks. Indeed, the term 'human relations' was used frequently before the Hawthorne investigations, both by academic and practitioner writers on personnel management (Kaufman, 1993, 2001) and it has been said that Mayo and his HBS colleagues did not actually 'discover' anything that was not already widely known by Western Electric officials or in American industry more broadly (Gilson, 1940). In this context, Wren (2005) has chronicled the contributions of pivotal figures in the progressive faction of the Taylor Society—Ordway Tead, Henry Dennison, Mary Parker Follett, Mary van Kleeck, and Whiting Williams—as laying the path for the development of human relations. Similarly, Bruce (2006) has demonstrated that Mayo's perceived contributions to HR, namely a critique of the conventional, individualistic, and hedonistic view of human nature, and the importance of the informal work group and its impact on worker performance, were actually ideas forwarded by Boston businessman and scientific manager, Henry S. Dennison, long before Mayo and his followers arrived at Harvard. In fact, both Boddewyn (1961) and Locke (1982) have argued that much of the Hawthorne conclusions regarding informal norms and output restriction were identified by F. W. Taylor several decades before the Hawthorne studies. In a similar vein, Duncan (1970) has noted that many of the early scientific management engineers appreciated human and social elements in industry. This would make sense, for as Wren and Greenwood (1998) have argued, Taylor himself did not provide solely for economic incentives, but made important contributions to modern thinking about human motivation and inspired Hugo Munsterberg to found the discipline of industrial psychology.

The third problem with the conventional wisdom is that Hawthorne and Western Electric have been treated as an 'anonymous actor' in a 'closed system'. In other words, little is known of the socio-political context shaping Hawthorne and its workers. In fact, Hawthorne was long a role-model for 'welfare capitalism' (albeit as part of hard-edged paternalism and tough-minded anti-unionism) and its 'family' and 'home' culture and positive work relationships predated the Hawthorne studies and were founded largely if not entirely on both innate ethnic and gender bases, as well as the ensuing social bonding that emerged from the collective trauma following the sinking of *SS Eastland* in January 1915 in which 841 Hawthorne employees and/or family members drowned (Hassard, 2012).

Finally, the real motivation behind Mayo's theory was arguably that of psychological control over workers. As we will demonstrate below, while Taylor and his followers were supportive of improvements in workers' pay and conditions and was eager to enable them to gain a 'voice; in managerial decision-making, Mayo and HRS promised to eliminate such calls entirely. Mayo's conceptualization of managers as a natural elite, possessing the ability and so the right to rule workplaces (and indeed, the nation), is especially problematic. Mayo and HRS accorded this elite vastly enhanced potential for authoritarianism than any alleged Taylorist ideas or measures. In brief, the school offered a new model for inducing workers to accept less while claiming that they needed the psychological counselling that only managers and their technicians could administer (Bruce and Nyland, 2011). We will explore these ideas in greater depth in the following two sections.

Puncturing the Popular Historical Myth of HRS: Taylor, Mayo, and Workplace Democracy

That Mayo was an advocate of elitist management systems went understated for many years, even by scholars who recognized his antipathy to workplace democracy. However, O'Connor (1999a, 1999b) and Bruce and Nyland (2011) have documented both Mayo's conviction that 'therapy' could substitute for workplace democracy and his efforts to promote this message to the 'rulers' of society. Critical to this line of argument is Mayo's claim that workers do not have the mental capacity to participate in management activity and consequently must be managed by those whose background and training has provided them with the emotional and mental capacities required to address the complexity of management processes. Mayo's portrayal of workers as individuals with minds that are unsophisticated and motivated primarily by custom and emotion and who consequently need to be managed by elites was very attractive to corporate America. It was attractive, not least, because it was a powerful counterweight to the growing popularity of claims being promoted by the trade unions and scientific managers which insisted workers do have the mental and emotional capacity to comprehend and apply scientific laws participate in management activity (Taylor, 1914; McKelvey, 1952).

That the interwar Taylorist movement rejected the HRS claim that workers could not and should not participate in management is well captured by Jacoby (1985a: 103), who notes that Morris Cooke of the Taylor Society and Phillip Murray of the miners' union together 'advocated "tapping labor's brains" by which they meant making organized labour an active participant in determining production procedures and administrative policies designed to increase the output and distribution of goods and services'. Similarly, Nyland, Bruce and Burns (2014) demonstrate that the Taylor Society sustained an ongoing collaboration with the ILO through the interwar years that aimed to globalize industrial democracy. The latter argue that rather than supporting employer hegemony, the Society shared with the ILO a commitment to codetermination, both in the workplace and in wider society more broadly.

The overt hostility that surfaced between the Taylorist democrats and members of the HRS because of their divergent views is reflected in Mary Gilson's 1940 review of Roethlisberger and Dickson's *Management and the Worker*. Gilson came to this task with twenty-seven years' experience as practitioner and scholar and an abiding commitment to the principles advocated by the Taylor Society. She began her commentary by noting that the work was the product of extensive funding by the Rockefeller Foundation and, not mincing her words, proceeded to make clear her disdain for the volume. Her contempt was based partly on her conviction that what the HRS researchers claimed they had determined would have been clear at the outset to any individual with knowledge of the relevant literature or practical experience of the industrial workplace. She noted, for example, that the notion that employees' practices and beliefs at work are influenced by what happens in their wider world she personally had documented as early as 1916. As for the 'science' that allegedly underpinned the work she observed that all the paraphernalia and statistical tools utilized had not produced anything as sophisticated as what was already available to any intelligent person who had worked on a factory floor. Accordingly, she advised that rather than generating information that anyone in the 'kindergarten stage of industrial knowledge' knew already, the researchers might have better utilized their time training foremen on how to elicit and handle complaints from workers and that they should have embraced Taylor's advice that before seeking to modify workers' practices and beliefs the scholar-practitioner should first do everything possible to improve plant and work practices.

Warming to her message, Gilson proceeded to note that in his preface Mayo had asked how humanity's capacity for spontaneous cooperation could be restored. She advised that the answer was not to be found in *Management and the Worker* and suggested that if Mayo really wanted an answer to this question, he would be wise to look to a book that pointed far more significantly to what should be the way forward:

> It is organized *Labor and Production* by an industrial engineer, Morris Llewellyn Cooke, and a labor organizer, Philip Murray, and it spells out simply and clearly the effects of union-management co-operation. It does not stop with 'two-way communication' from management to worker and worker to management as does this book, but it shows what can be done by management taking labor into its confidence and working shoulder to shoulder on operational processes and industrial policies at every level of production and supervision. (Gilson, 1940: 100)

Drawing her review to a close, Gilson noted that in *Management and the Worker* almost no reference is made to organized labour, this omission being justified on the grounds that interviewed workers had made no reference to unions. Why this would be, she pondered, might possibly have something to do with the fact that Western Electric workers were aware the firm was spending tens of thousands of dollars on espionage aimed to identify union sympathizers and added that the existence of industrial spies might also help explain why in 20,000 interviews the workers are reported to have 'criticized the company in no instance'. Finally, Gilson advised that she was willing to make one concession to the authors, for she fully agreed with one of their observations:

> Someday a study should be made of 'researches in the Obvious, financed by Big Business.' But maybe that too will turn out to be a set of tables and charts and mathematical formulas to prove what we already know. In any case the originator of the Western Electric experiment, Elton Mayo, modestly states that the authors of *Management and the Worker* do not claim that the enlightenment the many collaborators of the scheme got from their researches was 'either very extensive or very profound.' With this I am in complete agreement. (Gilson, 1940: 101)

Mayo responded to Gilson's review by advising his collaborators that she was insane. However, the ability of the HRS theorists to dismiss their Taylorist critics in such a cavalier manner was almost immediately undermined when, in mid-1940, Roosevelt appointed Sidney Hillman, the leader of the Amalgamated Clothing Workers of America as commissioner of employment on the Council of National Defence. This was a critical development for as Fraser (1991) has documented, Hillman had maintained a close working relationship with the Taylor Society from before the First World War. Roosevelt charged Hillman with the task of building the workforce that was needed to support the allies in Europe and prepare America for possible entry into the war against fascism. To further this objective, the latter sounded out industrialists and the American Federation of Labor and the Congress of Industrial Organization, and subsequently appointed Channing R. Dooley, a personnel manager with Socony-Vacuum, as Director of the Training within Industry (TWI) organization and appointed Walter Dietz of Western Electric as his assistant. These twin appointments reflected the views of the trade unions and corporate heads respectively. Dooley had the support of the trade unions largely because he was endorsed by the Taylor Society of which he was long-term member while Dietz had the support of corporate heads who were attracted to the ideas of Mayo and his colleagues at Harvard with whom he had collaborated when employed at Western Electric (Nyland and Bruce, 2012).

In this context, Breen (2002) has provided a detailed study of how Dooley and Dietz interacted through the years they remained with the TWI, noting in particular how initially the Taylorists dominated the training effort. Aware that there was an acute shortage of skilled craftsmen, these technicians focused on job redesign, expanding the number of tradesmen but with the latter being trained to undertake tasks that required long-term training and removing tasks that were relatively unskilled and that could be undertaken by workers with relatively little training. To ensure this did not become an exercise in deskilling, the scientific managers insisted that unions must actively participate in making all decisions relating to policy and practice. By incorporating the unions into the management process in this manner, the Taylorists were able to achieve a great increase in the quality of the training available to both the trades and workers who were formerly unskilled. They were also able to gain union support in this effort (only a very small minority of craftsmen resisted and their resistance was based not on a fear of deskilling but on fear that increasing the number of skilled workers would undermine their bargaining position). Employers, by contrast, found the Taylorist job training programme very much to their distaste both because unions were intimately involved in the management of the process and because it involved a great increase in the resources they had to commit to training.

If the training programme reflected the dominant influence of the Taylorists within the TWI, the existence of Dietz's commitment to the HRS became increasingly influential over time. Reflecting the suspicion if not hostility of the unions and the Taylorists, those trying to develop an HRS input into the training agenda found progress difficult. This was despite the fact that employers were much more supportive of the notion that foremen should be trained as counsellors than they were of enhancing the skills of workers. Important in overcoming the Taylorist-union resistance was the great influx of women with no experience of industrial life into the nation's workplaces. Also of significance was the fact that Roethlisberger began to distance himself from Mayo from 1940 (Trahair, 1984). This was a process that involved an attempt by Roethlisberger to build a positive relationship with the trade unions and the Taylorists, as is evidenced by a positive, if not enthusiastic, review of Cooke and Murray's *Organized Labor and Production* (Roethlisberger, 1940).

With these developments, the advocates of the HRS were able to convince both the scientific managers and the trade unions that the techniques they advocated need not necessarily be mere tools for consolidating elite control of the workforce. This enabled the two groupings to collaborate in implementing a joint programme of personnel training and industrial democracy in over 5,000 workplaces (Jacoby, 1985a). Jacoby (1985b: 274) has observed that the programme developed by the TWI was the last spasm of the continuing campaign that Taylorist democrats had sustained over many years as they strove to build management as a science rather than as a tool for promoting elite interests. This effort, he adds, had embodied the best attributes of the 'scientific, neutral approach to personnel management [and the] independent profession that Brandeis and the Taylorists had hoped it might prove to be'. The war years revealed on a mass scale that 'science and the democratic way of life' can flourish within industry and the wider community. Reflecting the appreciation of what was achieved, in 1945 the Taylorists awarded Dooley and Dietz the Taylor Key, the highest award given by the Taylor Society (by now renamed the Society for the Advancement of Management) for their work in promoting human relations in the TWI programme. This was, however, a pinnacle that having been scaled was compelled to be abandoned in the immediate post-war years once corporate America mobilized to win back the gains won by labour and those who had dare to hope that management might be developed as a science and not merely as a tool available to the rulers to whom Mayo had successfully appealed for support.

The Taylorists' unrelenting efforts to combat business insistence that profit accumulation must be the primary driver in both industry and society made them aware that the war years were extraordinary times and that eventually the corporate rulers of America would seek to restore what they saw as their 'right to manage' (Harris, 1982; Fones-Wolf, 1994; Phillips-Fein, 2006, 2009). Similarly, they were aware that when this period of reaction came the commitment of the industrial psychologist and the personnel administrator to science would be seriously tested. In an effort that harked back to Taylor's attempts to convince the engineering profession that knowledge should trump profit in industry and wider society, they prepared for the post-war years by urging personnel professionals to embrace a code of conduct that maintained that their field must be ruled by knowledge and not by the whims of employers. As Ordway Tead, the long-time editor of the *Bulletin of the Taylor Society*, observed in 1943 when seeking to further this position in an extended discussion on employee counselling:

> In a democracy it is peculiarly true that those responsible for the labor and laboring welfare of other self-respecting individuals should gladly hold themselves to standards of dealing which reflect the rights of persons as such along with the recognition of their responsibilities to the organization for which they work. (Tead, 1943: 103)

Promotion of this perspective, however, proved to be in vain. For corporate America simply refused to allow the industrial psychologist and the personnel administrator the freedom to prioritize knowledge over profit accumulation. If the Taylorist-union alliance was able to at least partly overcome employer hostility to the Cooke-Murray programme, it was largely due to the fact that it had gained support from the military, which, unlike private firms, prioritized the needs of war even where this meant according workers a voice in the management of the production process (Breen, 2002). The ability of the Taylorist-union alliance to enlist military support diminished dramatically, however, with the end of hostilities. In this new context, Taylor Society progressives and the unions were left exposed, and employers seized their chance to launch a major offensive to restore their 'right to manage' (Harris, 1982; Fraser, 1991; Fones-Wolf, 1994; Phillips-Fein, 2006, 2009). This offensive enabled the employers to take back many of the gains that had been won through the New Deal years, and ended only when the unions agreed to abandon codetermination and settle for the right to negotiate over a small range of employment conditions.

Very few scholars within management and organization studies are aware of even the more outrageous cases of intellectual 'cleansing' that occurred in the immediate post-war years as part of the process of redefining what constitutes a 'scientific business education'. Indeed, in the hands of the victors and their scribes, the Taylorist democrats came to be perceived as mechanistic, anti-union authoritarians while Mayo was deified, and the elitist HRS model he advocated was successfully marketed as a manifestation of corporate humanism (Nyland and Bruce, 2012).

In this reactionary environment, the liberal centre failed to hold and the HRS was able to flourish. Those committed to management as a participatory practice and a science informed by high ideals retreated. Gathering the spoils, the victors began to rewrite management history, beginning with the lauding of Mayo and the HRS as the advocates of 'high performance' personnel management. In this way, the business community was able to gain access to a body of intellectual 'servants of power' willing to help suppress the notion that management activity and theory should be democratized while concomitantly deifying themselves as humanists who should be applauded for expelling the 'demon' of Taylorism from the workplace.

HRS, Organizational Behaviour, and Human Resource Management

After Mayo's death, Roethlisberger carried the HRS torch in Harvard's burgeoning MBA programme ensuring that Human Relations was taught to all first-year MBA students in the 1950s in the guise of his 'Administrative Practices' course. He also created a new subject in the Business School's doctoral programme, 'Organizational Behaviour', and as a consequence 'the Harvard OB program graduated doctoral students who became professors elsewhere, [and] tough-minded psychological realism became part of the business-school ethos' (Hoopes, 2003: 159). This is an important point for it marks the beginning of the virtual domination of organizational or occupational psychology—and the concomitant marginalization of sociology—in the disciplines of Organizational Behaviour and HRM which would have disastrous consequences for workplace democracy. Namely, it marked the rise of 'neo-normative control' wherein employees would become regulated 'by way of their self-image and existential aspirations rather than through bureaucratic roles' (Ekman, 2013: 1161). In this way, the evolution of HRS signifies what Deetz (2003: 35) describes as 'focused on the management of the employees' insides—their values, commitment and motivation—and less on the supervision of their behaviour'.

By rendering the intersubjective space of the factory more 'governable' and by redefining the identity of the worker, HRS established a nexus between the government of production and the government of the social field. Mayo, the master publicist, problematized production at the junction of the concern with the regulation of 'the social' and a concern with the government of 'the self'. As noted above, he established a correlation between poor work performance and all manner of social ills/pathologies construed as a threat to good order and social tranquillity while systematically understating the importance of pay and working conditions that might impose costs on employers. Work was accorded a crucial role in responsible selfhood upon which free society depends: if an elite of socially skilled managers gave due regard to workers' psychological state and their relations with others in the workplace, then anomie and social disintegration might be averted and harmony and profitability would be enhanced (Rose, 1978; Miller and Rose, 1995).

In this context, HRS represented a new alliance between psychology, political thought and the government of the workplace which justified managerial authority in corporations as the natural order of things, reconciling it with democratic ideals by asserting that the individual was the fundamental unit on which all legitimate cooperative organization was founded. The same social contract melding citizens in the polity provided the model for the bond between the individual and the business firm. The corporation, together with the managerial authority it necessitated, could be thus represented as the perfect embodiment of the democratic ideal of the complex individuality that allegedly constitutes the distinctly American way of life. Managerial authority did not hold society down; rather, it held it together: the agitation-prone masses were unfit for leadership and had to be manipulated and controlled by an elite leadership nurturing vital non-logical impulses amongst work-groups in order to stabilize their emotions and be rendered willing to accept the authority of their controllers and of the psychologists who acted as the servants of power to those who paid the piper (Rose, 1978; Miller and O'Leary, 1989; Miller and Rose, 1995; O'Connor, 1999a, 1999b).

Regarding this privileged position, two important points should be made. First, as Deetz (2003) has highlighted, there is nothing 'natural' about the privileged place of capitalist ownership and attendant management authority. Rather, it is produced and reproduced via discursive practices ranging from lexical choice producing and distinguishing people and events in specific ways, to telling stories and giving instructions and orders. Second, Mayo and HRS accorded this managerial elite with vastly greater potential for authoritarianism—'corporate fascism with a human face' (Rose, 1978: 121)—than any Taylorist ideas or measures, a point seemingly lost on many critics of SM, past and present. While Taylorism (notwithstanding Taylor's own exhortations for a great 'Mental Revolution') presented managers with the potential to exert power physically over the human body spatially and temporally, Mayoism offered a more a subtle and efficient means of exercising this power mentally, via workers' cognition and emotions. As Townley (1993: 538) has observed:

> Traditionally, the concept of personnel has been viewed as stressing the rights of labor and the importance of the human side of the organization. But the discourse of welfare and the human relations' school clouds HRM's role in providing a nexus of disciplinary practices aimed at making employees' behaviour and performance predictable and calculable—in a word, manageable.

HRM, with its foundations in the 'science' of organizational psychology and psychiatry, presented the potential for greatly restricting workplace democracy and participation. Deetz (2003) makes a similar point, highlighting that the same controllers of discourse in Foucault's conception of disciplinary power—psychiatrists, doctors, wardens, teachers, and so on—who arbitrarily deem certain ways of life 'normal' and others pathological, provide the same privileged knowledge/power of HRM. As he observes:

> In the modern corporation, disciplinary power exists largely in the new 'social technologies of control'. HRM experts and specialists operate to create 'normalized' knowledge, operating procedures, and methods of enquiry, and to suppress competitive practices. (Deetz, 2003: 36)

In sum then, freedom, both in society and in the workplace, is enacted only at the price of relying upon the opinions of 'experts of the soul'; though we might be free from arbitrary prescriptions of political authorities, we are bound into new relationships with new authorities that are more profoundly subjectifying, as they appear to emanate from our individual desires for self-fulfilment (Rose, 1998). And further,

> (t)he legitimacy and neutrality of management were to depend not only on its basis in practical experience, but also on a scientific knowledge that would cast this experience within the framework of technical rationality. And to manage rationally, one now required a knowledge of the individual and social psychology of the worker. The language and techniques of human relations allowed management to reconcile the apparently opposing realities of the bosses' imperative of efficiency with the intelligibility of the workers' resistance to it, and to claim the capacity to transform the subjectivity of the worker from an obstacle to an ally in the quest for productivity and profit. (Rose, 1998: 140)

This desire for self-fulfilment is critical for disciplinary power in the workplace, that is, for organizational psychology and HRM to play on the insecurity about the value of the 'self', and so, exercise the requisite self-regulation (actually self-exploitation) that systematically restricts workplace democracy and participation.

Inspired by the HRS model, generations of HRS researchers including Abraham Maslow, Carl Rogers, Victor Frankl, Eric Fromm, Frederick Herzberg, Kurt Lewin, Victor Vroom, and others, painted a psychological picture of workers as self-actualizing egos whose personal strivings to make something of themselves through work could be steered towards pursuit of organizational goals. Work was constructed not as deferred gratification, but as the means of producing, discovering, and experiencing our 'selves' (Rose, 1990). Branded as 'behaviouralist' management theorists, in the 1950s and 1960s this incarnation of HRS theory argued that human motivation operates via our personal craving to fix and secure the very sense we have of ourselves as mirrored in the attitudes and opinions that (significant) others—for instance, managers or bosses—have towards us. We are constantly striving for this sense of self; it is never 'actualized' or realized (contra Maslow), so we have a strong innate desire to know, fix, and secure the 'self'. Our sense of 'who we are' is always vulnerable to the responses of others: a mirror in which we see ourselves. This vulnerability of the 'self' means we constantly compare ourselves to others and are alert to how they see us—in the 'mirror' of others' responses, we look both for confirmation/recognition, and feel ourselves exposed to possible rejection or attack. In this way, managers are able to shape the very ideals which we use to judge our own and others' actions (Roberts, 2007).

Accordingly, the central architecture and techniques of HRS, and the behavioural approach founded on same which focused on the human need for belonging, for love, for status, for recognition, and so on, became a powerful lever for conduct. Indeed, the relationship between manager and employee echoes earlier (infantile) relationships, such that workers strive for recognition from their bosses. Hierarchy serves as a mirror of the value of the 'self', and promotion in organizations is construed as 'making something of myself'. Further, performance appraisals and other auditing techniques make workers 'visible', and so, susceptible to praise and criticism, as well as shaping their success or failure. In sum, desired recognition and/or feared blame renders workers self-governing; as an employee, I strive to actualize/recognize the real or best me (Roberts, 2007). As Rose (1990: 117–18) notes:

> In the psychologies of human relations, work itself could become the privileged place for the satisfaction of the social needs of individuals. In the psychologies of self-actualization, work is no longer necessarily a constraint upon the freedom of the individual to fulfil his or her potential (…). Work is an essential element in the path to self-fulfilment. There is no longer any barrier between the economic, the psychological, and the social (…). The government of work now passes through the psychological strivings of each and every one of us for what we want.

Further developed in the UK in the 1960s in the guise of the Tavistock Institute of Human Relations and its key researchers, Fred Emory and Eric Trist, workers were envisaged as searching for meaning, responsibility, achievement, and 'quality of life' through work. Workers should not be emancipated from work, but rather fulfilled in work (Rose, 1990). This line of management theory spawned notions of job enrichment, job rotation, autonomous work groups, participation, and self-management:

> Finding meaning and dignity in work, workers would identify with the product, assume responsibility for production, and find their own self-worth embedded, reflected and enhanced in the quality of work as a product and an experience. (Rose, 1990: 105–6)

Trist went as far as to propose that people are resources to be developed, regulating themselves because they were committed and involved, and so arguably set in motion notions inextricably linked to contemporary HRM strategies. Such is the legacy of Mayo, the HRS, and the behaviouralist approach currently informing the contemporary study of organizational behaviour and HRM.

References

Boddewyn, J. (1961). 'Frederick Winslow Taylor Revisited'. *Journal of the Academy of Management*, 4: 100–7.
Breen, W. J. (2002). 'Social Science and State Policy in World War II: Human Relations, Pedagogy, and Industrial Training, 1940–1945'. *Business History Review*, 76: 233–66.
Bruce, K. (2006). 'Henry S. Dennison, Elton Mayo and Human Relations Historiography'. *Management and Organisational History*, 1(2): 177–99.
Bruce, K. (2013). 'G. Elton Mayo', in M. Witzel and M. Warner (eds.), *The Oxford Handbook of Management Theorists*. Oxford: Oxford University Press, 94–112.
Bruce, K. and Nyland, C. (2011). 'Elton Mayo and the Deification of Human Relations'. *Organization Studies*, 32(3): 383–405.
Bulmer, M. and Bulmer, J. (1981). 'Philanthropy and Social Science in the 1920s: Beardsley Ruml and the Laura Spelman Rockefeller Memorial, 1922–1929'. *Minerva*, 19(3): 347–407.

Carey, A. (1967), 'The Hawthorne Studies: A Radical Criticism'. *American Sociological Review*, 32: 403–16.

Deetz, S. (2003). 'Disciplinary Power, Conflict Suppression and HRM', in M. Alvesson and H. Willmott (eds.), *Studying Management Critically*. London: SAGE, 23–46.

Duncan, W. J. (1970). 'Engineers and Psychologists of the Scientific Management Period: An Overdue Exercise in the Notion of Similarities'. *Southern Journal of Business*, 5: 30–40.

Duncan, W. J. (1999). *Management: Ideas and Actions*. New York: Oxford University Press.

Ekman, S. (2013). 'Fantasies about Work as Limitless Potential: How Managers and Employees Seduce Each Other through Dynamics of Mutual Recognition'. *Human Relations*, 66(9): 1159–1181.

Fisher, D. (1983). 'The Role of Philanthropic Foundations in the Reproduction of and Production of Hegemony: Rockefeller Foundations and the Social Sciences'. *Sociology*, 17(2): 206–33.

Fones-Wolf, E. (1994). *Selling Free Enterprise: The Business Assault on Labor and Liberalism, 1945–1960*. Champaign, IL: University of Illinois Press.

Fraser, S. (1991). *Labor Will Rule: Sidney Hillman and the Rise of American Labor*. Ithaca, NY: Cornell University Press.

Gillespie, R. (1991). *Manufacturing Knowledge: A History of the Hawthorne Experiments*. Cambridge: Cambridge University Press.

Gilson, M. (1940). 'Review of M. L. Cooke and P. Murray Organized Labor and Production'. *Journal of Political Economy*, 49(1): 142–4.

Gitelman, H. (1988). *Legacy of the Ludlow Massacre: A Chapter in American Industrial Relations*. Philadelphia, PA: University of Pennsylvania Press.

Harris, H. J. (1982). *The Right to Manage: Industrial Relations Policies of American Business in the 1940s*. Madison, WI: University of Wisconsin Press.

Harvey, C. E. (1982). 'John D. Rockefeller, Jr, and the Social Sciences: An Introduction'. *Journal of the History of Sociology*, 4: 1–31.

Hassard, J. (2012). 'Rethinking the Hawthorne Studies: The Western Electric Research in Its Social, Political, and Historical Context'. *Human Relations*, 65(11): 1431–61.

Hoopes, J. (2003). *False Prophets: The Gurus Who Created Modern Management and Why Their Ideas are bad for Business Today*. Cambridge, MA: Perseus.

Jacoby, S. M. (1985a). 'Union-Management Cooperation in the United States During the Second World War', in M. Dubofsky (ed.), *Technological Change and Workers' Movements*. Beverly Hills, CA: SAGE, 100–129.

Jacoby, S. (1985b). *Employing Bureaucracy: Managers, Unions, and the Transformation of Work in American Industry, 1900–1945*. New York: Columbia University Press.

Kaufman, B. (1993). *The Origins and Evolution of the Field of Industrial Relations in the United States*. Ithaca, NY: ILR Press.

Kaufman, B. (2001). 'The Theory and Practice of Strategic HRM and Participative Management: Antecedents in Early Industrial Relations'. *Human Resource Management Review*, 11: 505–33.

Kaufman, B. (2004). *The Global Evolution of Industrial Relations*. Geneva: ILO.

Kaufman, B. (2008). *Managing the Human Factor: The Early Years of HRM in American Industry*. Ithaca, NY: ILR Press.

Landsberger, H. A. (1958). *Hawthorne Revisited*. New York: W.F. Humphrey Press.

Locke, E. (1982). 'The Ideas of Frederick Winslow Taylor: An Evaluation'. *Academy of Management Review*, 7(1): 14–24.

McKelvey, J. T. (1952). *AFL Attitudes Toward Production, 1900–1932*, Cornell Studies in Industrial and Labor Relations. Ithaca, NY: Cornell University Press.

Magat, R. (1999). *Unlikely Partners: Philanthropic Foundations and the Labor Movement*. Ithaca, NY: ILR Press.

Mayo, E. (1924). 'The Basis of Industrial Psychology'. *Bulletin of the Taylor Society*, 9: 249–59.

Mayo, E. (1933). *The Human Problems of an Industrial Civilization*. New York: Macmillan.

Miller, P. and O'Leary, T. (1989). 'Hierarchies and American Ideals, 1900–1940'. *Academy of Management Review*, 14(2): 250–65.

Miller, P. and Rose, N. (1990). 'Governing Economic Life'. *Economy and Society*, 19(1): 1–31.

Miller, P. and Rose, N. (1995). 'Production, Identity, and Democracy'. *Theory and Society*, 24(3): 427–67.

Nyland, C. (1998). 'Taylorism and the Mutual Gains Strategy'. *Industrial Relations*, 37(4): 519–42.

Nyland, C. and Bruce, K. (2012). 'Democracy or Seduction? The Demonization of Scientific Management and the Deification of Human Relations', in N. Lichtenstein and E. Shermer (eds.), *The Right and Labor in America: Politics, Ideology, and Imagination*. Philadelphia, PA: University of Pennsylvania Press, 42–76.

Nyland, C., Bruce, K., and Burns, P. (2014). 'Taylorism, the International Labour Organization and the Diffusion of Codetermination'. *Organization Studies*, 35(8): 1149–69.

O'Connor, E. S. (1999a). 'The Politics of Management Thought: A Case Study of the Harvard Business School and the Human Relations School'. *Academy of Management Review*, 24(1): 117–31.

O'Connor, E. S. (1999b). 'Minding the Workers: the Meaning of "Human" and "Human Relations" in Elton Mayo'. *Organization*, 6(2): 223–46.

Phillips-Fein, K. (2006). 'Top-Down Revolution: Businessmen Intellectuals and Politicians Against the New Deal 1945–1964'. *Enterprise and Society*, 74: 686–94.

Phillips-Fein, K. (2009). *Invisible Hands: The Making of the Conservative Movement from the New Deal to Reagan*. New York: W. W. Norton.

Rees, J. (2010). *Representation and Rebellion: The Rockefeller Plan at the Colorado Fuel and Iron Company 1914–1942*. Boulder, CO: University of Colorado Press.

Roberts, J. (2007). 'Motivation and the Self', in D. Knights and H. Willmott (eds.), *Introducing Organizational Behaviour and Management*. London: Thomson, 42–73.

Roethlisberger, F. J. (1940). 'Review of Organized Labor and Production'. *Annals of the American Academy of Political and Social Science*, 211: 230.

Roethlisberger, F. J. and Dickson, W. J. (1939). *Management and the Worker*. Cambridge, MA: HBS Press.

Rose, M. (1978). *Industrial Behaviour: Theoretical Developments since Taylor*. Harmondsworth: Penguin.

Rose, N. (1990). *Governing the Soul: The Shaping of the Private Self*. London: Routledge.

Rose, N. (1998). *Inventing Ourselves: Psychology, Power, and Personhood*. Cambridge: Cambridge University Press.

Smith, J. H. (1976). 'The Significance of Elton Mayo'. Foreword in Elton Mayo, *The Social Problems of an Industrial Civilization*. London: Routledge.

Smith, J. H. (1998). 'The Enduring Legacy of Elton Mayo'. *Human Relations*, 51: 221–49.

Sofer, C. (1973). *Organizations in Theory and Practice*. London: Heinemann.

Taylor, F. W. (1914). 'Scientific Management and Labor Unions'. *Bulletin of the Society to Promote the Science of Management*, 1: 3.

Tead, O. (1943). 'Employee Counseling: A New Personnel Assignment—Its Status and Its Standards'. *Advanced Management*, 8: 97–103.

Townley, B. (1993). 'Foucault Power/Knowledge and its Relevance for Human Resource Management'. *Academy of Management Review*, 183: 518–45.

Trahair, R. (1984). *The Humanist Temper: The Life and Work of Elton Mayo*. New Brunswick: Transaction Publishers.

Trahair, R. (2001). Personal Conversation with Authors, 12 October.

Wrege, C. (2014). 'A Conversation with Dr. Charles D. Wrege', Academy of Management annual meeting, Philadelphia', available at: <http://youtu.be/diRTCgFNNBM> (accessed 29 June 2016).

Wren, D. (2005). *The Evolution of Management Thought*. New Jersey: John Wiley, 5th edn.

Wren, D. and Greenwood, R. G. (1998). *Management Innovators: The People Who Have Shaped Modern Business*. New York: Oxford University Press.

CHAPTER 4

OPERATIONS MANAGEMENT

MARTIN SPRING

Introduction

OPERATIONS management (OM) is, according to one widely used textbook, 'the activity of managing the resources that produce and deliver products and services' (Slack, Chambers, and Johnston, 2010: 2). This chapter charts the emergence and evolution of OM, the major stages and themes in its development, some of the controversies and major shifts in areas of investigation and concern, the role of theory and changes in methods and, briefly, its relationship to the wider domain and practice of management as such.

In doing this, it follows in the footsteps of others in OM who have examined the discipline (including Sprague, 2007; Meredith, 2001, 2002; Meredith et al., 1989; Buffa, 1980; Chase, 1980; Slack, Lewis, and Bates, 2004). In what follows, I make specific reference to these studies, as appropriate, but also want to acknowledge their general influence on my approach. Furthermore, whereas those surveys were written for an OM audience, this chapter is written for a more general one, and I have attempted to explain OM concepts accordingly, while hopefully still conveying the specific points that are important to the argument.

Defining the Field

OM began to emerge as a term, and as an area of academic enquiry, in the early 1960s.[1] Figure 4.1 shows a Google nGram plot of the incidence of the term 'operations management', along with those for several related terms, over the period 1900–2008. Meredith

---
[1] Singhal, Singhal, and Starr (2007: 310) credit Elwood Buffa with first using the term.

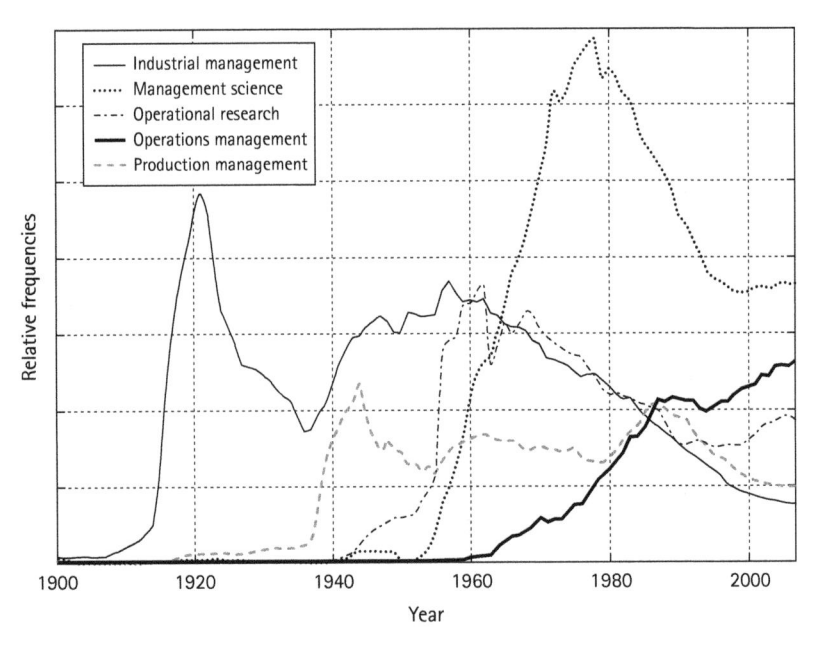

FIGURE 4.1 Incidence of 'Operations Management' and Related Terms.

(2001) identifies OM's predecessors as including 'industrial management' which, as Figure 4.1 shows, was the dominant term until the 1960s. OM's most immediate forebear was 'production management': Figure 4.1 shows that it co-existed with OM for a couple of decades before going into relative decline.

In university departments, OM is often combined with operational research (OR) and management science. Figure 4.1 shows that OR grew rapidly in the 1950s,[2] following its development and extensive use in the Second World War.[3] Although OR is an approach and a set of mathematically oriented techniques that has more general applicability, it has found its most widespread application in OM contexts (Meredith et al., 1989: 298). This relationship between OR and OM is one to which I will return. OR and 'management science' are often used interchangeably or, at least, like conjoined twins in the form 'OR/MS'. Stafford Beer (1966) is among those who suggested that management science is the managerial application of OR techniques; elsewhere, 'management science' refers to a much broader application of science(s) to the field of management. In any case, usage of the term 'management science' follows a similar trajectory to that of 'operational research', with a time-lag of about ten years (Figure 4.1).

---

[2] In the US, the term 'operations research' is used; in the UK, 'operational research'. The graph uses the latter, partly because it conveniently happens to provide a plot of similar amplitude. The profiles of the plots for the two terms are very similar, but the US variant dwarfs the UK one—and hence those of all the other terms, too—by virtue of the volume of publication in the US.

[3] The history of the development of OR is beyond the scope of this chapter, but this has been extensively chronicled, for example Mccloskey (1987), Kirby (2000).

The Emergence of OM and a 'Science of Management'

The period 1953–63 is the 'primeval swamp' from which OM emerged. Some notable landmarks include the founding of the Institute of Management Sciences (1953) and the first issue of its journal *Management Science* (1954); the founding of the American Production and Inventory Control Society (APICS) and of its UK chapter (BPICS) (1957 and 1963 respectively); the first issue of the *International Journal of Production Research* (1961); the publication of a number of notable books, including Brown's *Statistical Forecasting for Inventory Control* (1959), Holt et al.'s *Planning Production, Inventory and Workforce* (known after its authors' initials as 'HMMS' (Holt et al., 1960)), Forrester's *Industrial Dynamics* (1961), and Buffa's textbook *Models for Production and Operations Management* (1963).

There were several common ingredients in many of these developments. First of all was an intent to develop a 'science of management': for example, the title of the first article in Volume 1, Issue 1 of *Management Science* was 'Evolution of a "Science of Managing" in America' (Smiddy and Naum, 1954); the first chapter of Buffa's book was entitled 'Science in Management'; and the Introduction to Forrester's book was entitled 'Management and Management Science'. This prospect of a science of management was, in many of these sources, set against the notion of management as an art, where management was learned from direct experience and could not be codified to be used in 'different companies in different industries, managed by different men [sic]' (Buffa, 1963: 5).

A second feature, part of the process of developing the science, was the development and use of models, mostly mathematical models. This drew on the advances made in OR during and after the Second World War (see footnote 3), and the technical capabilities of those who were now working in the management field: for instance, Buffa and Forrester were both originally trained as engineers, and the HMMS foursome included two Nobel laureates in Economics (Modigliani and Simon). Singhal and Singhal (2007: 301) quote Muth (one of the 'M's in HMMS) commenting on the state of OM in the 1950s: 'Textbooks at the time focussed on the EOQ formula,[4] Gantt chart displays, punched card systems, moving average forecast, and that's about it.' Buffa (1980) describes MS/OR as the saviour of OM, as it provided 'the scientific methodology that allowed us to develop something akin to the "natural science" or physics of operating systems': he places the moment of salvation at 1961.

Buffa's texts are a telling indication of the shift from production management to operations management and all the more important because, at least initially, they dominated the OM textbook market (Singhal, Singhal, and Starr, 2007). In his 1961 book,

---

[4] Economic Order Quantity, originally developed by Harris (1913).

Modern Production Management (Buffa, 1961), there are a few chapters that deal with analytical methods, but these are of a fairly rudimentary nature, and include some now rather quaint techniques such as using cardboard cut-out models of machines to help in designing shop-floor layouts, and the 'SCHED-U-GRAPH' manual machine scheduling tool. Other chapters included a great deal of descriptive material, for example about particular production (mostly metal-working) processes, ergonomic and safety factors in job design, and even designs for the roofs of factory buildings. These echo much earlier descriptive texts such as Mitchell's (1931), which included advice on how to design boiler-room equipment and railway tracks serving factory sites. *Models for Production and Operations Management* (Buffa, 1963) retains a little of the material on schematic models (such as the cut-out layout design tools), but mainly comprises much more general, mathematical models: sections include 'Waiting Line Models', 'Programming Models', 'Models of Investment Policy', and 'Inventory Models'. By the second edition (1968), the title had changed to 'Operations Management', the cut-out models had disappeared, and chapter 2, previously 'Models and the Production Function', was entitled, simply, 'Costs'. Operations management has become much more explicitly about using analytical models to arrive at cost-optimizing decisions, decisions concerning such issues as how big production batches should be, how often machines should be maintained, how much capacity to allocate at which stage of the process, what level of defects to accept, and how much inventory to hold to achieve acceptable levels of product availability.

Later texts (e.g. the first OM book I ever used, Terry Hill's 1983 *Production/Operations Management* (Hill, 1983)) and, indeed, Sprague's review of the OM field (Sprague, 2007) reason that the term 'operations management' rather than 'production management' is used to make the discipline inclusive of services as well as of manufacturing. However, that is certainly not the shift that is evident in the Buffa books. They all *claim* to be about both products and services but the application and examples used are relentlessly about manufacturing; the 'operations' comes from operations research, and signals the incorporation of OR-type techniques into production management. As Buffa underlines, 'From an academic point of view, the formal models we have discussed represent the development of a theory of operational systems where none existed only a few years ago. We are witnessing the healthy growth of an applied science' (Buffa, 1963: 591).

A third strand, in Forrester especially, was the systems approach. Buffa conceptualized production as an input-conversion-output system; Forrester developed dynamic systems models of production processes, firms and even entire industries, drawing on concepts from engineering control systems. In part drawing on Forrester, Buffa's third edition (1972) included a new, final substantive chapter on 'Large Scale System Simulation', attempting to address the tendency of the analytical methods treated elsewhere in the text to deal with only parts of the whole problem—inventory, perhaps, or maintenance. Although there had been a realization in principle that these subsystems interacted with one another, the techniques and tools to deal with the whole system had not existed. The next generation took this as their main theme: for example, the preface to the second edition of Martin Starr's 1972 *Production Management: Systems and Synthesis* included the following:

> The first edition of this book [1964] took an uncertain stand, attempting to straddle the mathematical and the systems-oriented approaches to production management. This second edition avoids such hedging. This is a *systems book*. (Starr, 1972: v, emphasis in the original)

Starr's perspective is important in emphasizing the *management* in operations management: his text is written for the management student, and he argues that 'management is a synthesizing function' (Starr, 1972: vi), in contrast to the *analysing* that characterizes the models and techniques that had been developed in the first decade of OM. As such, 'mathematical analysis is used, not produced, by the manager' (Starr, 1972: vi).

Subsequent Developments

This section identifies and discusses some of the major developments and themes over the next three or four decades.

Materials Requirements Planning

The digital computer was an important influence on the subsequent development of OM practice and research. This was reflected in the creation in 1969 of the American Institute for Decision Sciences, subsequently the Decision Sciences Institute. The Institute and its journal, *Decision Sciences*, inaugurated in 1970, originally extended across multiple functional areas and included mathematical and behavioural approaches to the 'science of decision-making'. It addressed the overlap between OM and the newly emerging field of Management Information Systems.[5] The big story in manufacturing practice during the 1970s and 1980s was the diffusion of Materials Requirements Planning (MRP) (Orlicky, 1975; Vollmann, Berry, and Whybark, 1984), a system of production planning and control that utilized the increasing capabilities of mainframe computers. To some extent, this delivered on the hope in the early OM texts that routine decisions on, for example, production planning and ordering of materials could be automated. MRP became the dominant research area in OM during the 1980s (Pilkington and Meredith, 2008), presenting new challenges in terms of inventory modelling and, from an organizational perspective, challenges regarding the management of change (see Section 'So, where is the Management in Operations Management?').

---

[5] At the time of writing, the strapline of *Decision Sciences* was 'Information Systems, Operations and Supply Chain Management'.

Japanese Manufacturing, Manufacturing Strategy, and the Quality 'Revolution'

The first journals more explicitly embracing OM rather than production management came along in 1980: the *Journal of Operations Management* (APICS) in the US and the *International Journal of Operations and Production Management* (*IJOPM*) in the UK. While MRP was a dominant research theme during the 1980s, two new themes also emerged: Japanese manufacturing techniques and manufacturing strategy, the latter of which was the subject of Terry Hill's opening article in Volume 1, Issue 1 (p. 3) of *IJOPM*. Japan was the rising power in manufacturing and the US and European sectors came under threat. The early 1980s saw the first publications on Japanese production management (Schonberger, 1982; Wheelwright, 1981; Shingo, 1981). Then, in 1984, Hayes and Wheelwright published *Restoring Our Competitive Edge: Competing through Manufacturing*, which was intended as a response to the Japanese (and German) threat, and developed the concept of manufacturing strategy, originally set out by Wickham Skinner (1969). Skinner argued that manufacturing (a) was potentially an important source of competitive advantage and should therefore be managed strategically and (b) needed to be designed and managed to support a specific competitive task, such as quality, flexibility, or cost, rather than trying to be good at everything. Hayes and Wheelwright (1984) was the most cited source in OM as at 2007, and dominated the field during the 1990s and into the 2000s (Pilkington and Meredith, 2008). These two developments were in many ways the very reverse of what had gone before: Japanese production planning methods tried to *remove* the complexity from the task, whereas MRP had tried to *mirror* the complexity of the production task by devising complex, computer-based systems for planning and controlling it; and whereas many OM techniques had been about optimizing the sub-system (e.g., a particular machine shop) in terms of cost, manufacturing strategy was about (a) considering the whole production function and (b) aligning it with the competitive strategy of the business, which might be focussed on criteria other than cost, for example exceptionally high quality.

Quality management also gained in importance, with two texts being particularly influential during the 1980s and 1990s: Crosby's *Quality Is Free* and Deming's *Out of the Crisis* (Crosby, 1979; Deming, 1986; Pilkington and Meredith, 2008). Whereas the planning and control innovations such as JIT that arose from Japanese manufacturing could to some extent be incorporated into the OM modelling worldview, quality management, and especially Total Quality Management (TQM) (Dale, 2003) took OM into completely new territory because it brought organizational culture and basic assumptions about managerial roles into OM teaching and research. This was perhaps the first time that OM research considered the operations manager's role in, and the effect of, pervasive organizational change programmes.

Japanese approaches and TQM turned many basic OM assumptions on their head: there is no 'optimum' level of quality—zero defects is the aim; there is no optimum 'economic order quantity'—a batch size of one is the aim; processes are not just designed by 'staff specialists' and then run unquestioningly by shop-floor employees, but are subject to 'continuous improvement' based on bottom-up shop-floor teamwork and quality circle activities. And so on. In the wake of this, the trade-off argument, which was, on the grand scale central to Skinner's manufacturing strategy approach (Skinner, 1974) and, on the micro-scale the basic assumption of many of the models in, say, Buffa (1963), came under fire (e.g., Schonberger (1986), but see also Colin New (1992)). However, order was restored in OM as, in various ways, the trade-off concept was revised. Clark (1996) explained this accommodation in terms of 'performance frontiers': most operations could improve on various parameters simultaneously by eliminating bad practice in relation to quality problems, poor inventory management and so on—but only up to a point. In the end, they would reach a 'frontier' of performance, where they had maximized the potential of a particular configuration of processes, staff skills, capacity, technology, and so on, and could then only trade off one parameter against another, unless they invested in structural change—adding capacity or developing new technology, for example. This revision of the trade-off concept coincided with and was informed by the emergence of the resource-based view and its incorporation into manufacturing strategy (Hayes and Pisano, 1996).

Supply Chain Management

Manufacturing strategy continued to dominate research activity during the 1990s, but another theme was emerging. 'Supply chain management' was a term first used in the early 1980s, as logistics and purchasing scholars and consultants advocated that their domains, like manufacturing itself, should become more 'strategic' (Houlihan, 1984; Kraljic, 1983). Initially, supply chain management was concerned with the more effective linking together of operations *within* the firm—manufacturing, sales, stores, production, distribution—but was quickly extended beyond the firm to encompass relationships with suppliers and customers (Harland, 1996). There were several factors at work. More advanced forms of MRP allowed activities beyond the firm—scheduling orders on suppliers, for example—to be more effectively coordinated using computer systems. Japanese manufacturing approaches often involved close, long-term relationships with suppliers, in contrast to the arm's length, short-term trading that had prevailed in the West (Lamming, 1993). Conceptually, Forrester (1961) had demonstrated that decisions that seemingly rational decisions at the sub-system level could have disastrous consequences in their cumulative, emergent effect on the whole. All this pointed to managing the bigger system—the supply chain—in a strategic manner.

The first papers in the leading OM journals, the *Journal of Operations Management* and *International Journal of Operations and Production Management* including 'supply chain' in their titles were published in 1996 (Choi and Hartley, 1996; Lamming, 1996): at the time of writing, supply chain management had become the dominant overarching concept in OM. Indeed, in many ways the two are inseparable—journals routinely refer to the discipline as 'operations and supply chain management' and, in 2014, APICS announced its merger with the Supply Chain Council in the US.

Despite its inclusiveness, supply chain management is based on a few core concepts. Integration, which has carried through from the early definitions, is one of these. 'Managing the system as a whole', as advocated by, for example, Houlihan (1984), meant more tightly coordinating activities (a) between functions such as purchasing, production and distribution *within* the firm and then came to mean (b) coordinating activities *between firms*—between the producing firm, its suppliers, and its customers, and maybe beyond that into successive 'links' in the chain. Following the Japanese model, and perhaps based on the insights of Forrester, Western firms, consultants and academics argued that it was beneficial to coordinate operations with supply chain counterparts, for example by sharing information that had hitherto been treated as commercially confidential about sales forecasts and new products; this happened in longer-term 'partnerships' rather than adversarial 'arm's length' relationships. One widely cited empirical examination of this claim (Frohlich and Westbrook, 2001) suggests that it does indeed have beneficial consequences for firm performance. This kind of insight has led some to claim that 'the real competition is not company against company, but rather supply chain against supply chain' (Christopher, 2011: 15 and in previous editions from 1992).

While more integration is almost taken for granted as an essential part of supply chain management, a secondary part of this particular story is to determine how much integration, of what sort, is appropriate to a given circumstance. Fisher (1997) asks, 'What is the right supply chain for your product?', and reduces the answer to ideal types: one best suited to supplying predictable end-markets with relatively standard, low-margin products, and the other aligned with volatile, unpredictable markets for short-lived, high-margin products. These have been characterized by others as 'lean' and 'agile', respectively (Christopher, 2011), and the choice has implications for many key operations decisions: location, sourcing, inventory, capacity, information systems, process technology to name some of the more obvious. In many ways, this is a parallel, contingency-type argument to the classic manufacturing strategy 'process choice' approach, but applied to the wider supply chain rather than merely the plant or process.

Reflecting this emergence of supply chain management as a practice and then as a discipline in its own right, the *International Journal of Purchasing and Materials Management* became, in 1999, the *Journal of Supply Chain Management*. Then in 2007, it was radically re-positioned to shift it from a practitioner-oriented to a more scholarly publication. Likewise, the European-based *Supply Chain Management: An International Journal* was inaugurated in 1996.

Service Operations

Buffa's classic text provides the following definition: 'Production is the process by which goods *and services* are created' (Buffa, 1963: 14, emphasis added). 'Production', then, was not specific to manufacturing—at least in theory. Buffa's text, however, is relentlessly concerned with manufacturing. Even in the chapters on queuing theory, where service processes are mentioned, the examples given are of maintenance services provided by in-house maintenance staff within a manufacturing facility. In a contemporaneous text, Mayer (1962) also defines 'production' as including both manufacturing and services. But, in order to simplify the treatment in his book, he chooses to omit services, arguing as follows:

> The firm we shall consider is a manufacturing firm. The decision is not an arbitrary one. You will find that the most complex production problems are to be associated with this type of organization. Also if you become familiar with the nature of the production management function in an environment such as this, you will experience little difficulty in applying this knowledge to the analysis of the production management function in other types of firms. (Mayer, 1962: 2–3)

Such a view would cause the hackles to rise in most contemporary researchers and practitioners in service operations. And yet for a while, influential voices were arguing that services ought to be treated more like production-line operations in order to improve their productivity (Levitt, 1972, 1976). However, the Harvard Business School introduced its first course on Managing Service Operations in 1972, 'operating on the hypothesis that the tasks of managing service firms differ significantly enough from those of manufacturing firms to justify separate (or at least special) treatment' (Sasser, Olsen and Wyckoff, 1978: ix). The defining characteristics of services that Sasser and his colleagues identified were: intangibility, heterogeneity, simultaneity and perishability, and these were considered to 'make the management tasks of service executives different from their counterparts in manufacturing firms' (Sasser, Olsen, and Wyckoff, 1978: 15). In most subsequent formulations, 'simultaneity' has become 'inseparability', and the set of characteristics hence known as 'IHIP'. These endured until recent years as fundamental precepts of service OM teaching (Nie and Kellogg, 1999). Richard Chase, one of the most influential service OM researchers, introduced the concept of 'customer contact' as a critical ingredient of service OM (Chase, 1978, 1981), arguing that, while customer contact was in some ways the defining characteristic of services, it was also potentially a source of inefficiency, and so processes should be designed to minimize its occurrence and maximize the use of standardized 'back-office' processes to improve the productivity of those elements not requiring customer contact.

Despite this attempt to delineate services as somehow 'different', and the growing realization elsewhere of the growing importance of the service economy (e.g., Gershuny and Miles, 1983), the position of services within OM research has continued to be a contentious subject. For example, Slack, Lewis, and Bates (2004) pointed out a huge disparity between the importance of the service sector to developed economies and the proportions of empirical OM work devoted to services. In 1980, Buffa had argued that services were wide open as a research domain: 'service systems are virgin territory and virtually everything needs to be done' (Buffa, 1980: 6). Service research increased during the 1980s and 1990s. Johnston (1999) characterizes three phases up to his vantage-point in 1998:

'service awakening'; 'breaking free from product-based roots'; and then 'service management', each representing, in his view, more convergence and integration from the three functions of OM, marketing and human resource management. Empirical research typically focussed on classic 'service sectors' (e.g., Voss et al., 1985)—for example, banking and insurance, professional services, education, health, and hospitality management. More recently, stimulated by influential work in marketing (Grönroos, 2008; Vargo and Lusch, 2004), as well as the increased blurring in industry between manufacturing and service, there has been a shift to studying 'service' as such, recognizing that service processes and relationships occur in manufacturing sectors and that the IHIP characteristics are not a useful way to identify a 'difference' between manufacturing and services (Spring and Araujo, 2009). This shift is also reflected in the re-naming, in 2009, of *The International Journal of Service Industry Management* as *The Journal of Service Management*.[6]

THEORY AND METHOD IN OPERATIONS MANAGEMENT

As discussed, before the 1960s, OM writing was largely descriptive. The 'revolution' then arising from the introduction of OR techniques provided a technical underpinning for the study of some types of production problems, typically narrowly defined ones. Systems approaches (e.g., Starr, 1972) then broadened the scope of OM, beyond optimization of each small part of the operation, to the consideration of the whole operation. However, despite these developments, there was no overarching *theory* of OM. Meanwhile, in other branches of management research, original, pervasive theories such as contingency theory (e.g., Woodward, 1958; Hickson, Pugh, and Pheysey, 1969) and institutional theory (e.g., Scott, 1995) were being developed.

In OM, the twin shocks of Japanese manufacturing and manufacturing strategy called into question, even more strongly, the value of narrowly defined technical optimization techniques for the challenges that operations managers faced. New technologies and new initiatives, some deriving from the Japanese models, were being adopted in operations practice: MRP, Computer-Integrated Manufacturing (CIM), Just-in-Time (JIT), TQM, and so on. These stimulated new streams of research, often driven by a series of questions such as: (a) 'What is TQM/CIM etc?'; (b) 'How is TQM/CIM implemented?'; (c) 'Does TQM/CIM work?'. Representative papers along these lines relating to one of these initiatives, MRP, are: Salmon (1981), White et al. (1982), Bitran et al. (1985), Schroeder et al. (1981) and Sum et al. (1995). Initiatives related to production planning and control (MRP, JIT) also provided grist to the mill of OR-inclined OM researchers. For MRP, this was an important part of improving the algorithms that underlay its function (although the number of papers in this vein greatly outnumbered those that

---

[6] For a fuller discussion of these developments, see Spring (2014).

considered any management issues). However, for JIT, modelling the effects of different numbers of kanbans rather missed the point of JIT and the Toyota Production System on which it was based (New, 2007),[7] as the underlying philosophy was to use devices such as kanbans to drive continuous improvement in the process rather than to arrive at some 'optimum' level of inventory.

Some of the more managerially oriented OM studies had the makings of rudimentary theories. They pointed to 'critical success factors' in implementation; they identified links between the extent of use a particular initiative and the performance of the operation. But they did not have the extensive explanatory power of theories found in some other management disciplines or in underlying social science disciplines. On manufacturing strategy, Anderson, Cleveland, and Schroeder (1989) bemoaned the lack of consistent definitions and theory, arguing that most of the work in that area had been conceptual or exploratory. Their own early empirical work (Schroeder, Anderson and Cleveland, 1986) was itself a very basic survey of thirty-nine firms, presenting simple descriptive statistics. All that was to change, however, as empirical science arrived in OM. Ebert (1989), as incoming Editor of *JOM*, published an announcement encouraging submissions based on 'empirical/field-based methodologies'. Flynn et al. (1990) and Swamidass (1991) set out a charter for empirical research as the 'new frontier' in OM.[8] To some extent, it worked. Again, using *JOM* as a rough indication of the state of affairs predominantly in the US, a trickle of formal survey-based papers turned into a more sustained flow by about 1998.[9] Meredith et al. (1989) reviewed the methods used in three leading US-based OM journals in 1977 and 1987 and, combining these two periods, found that only 7% of papers had any empirical content; in a follow-up study using the same approach, Craighead and Meredith (2008) show that, by 2003, over 50% of papers in the same three journals were empirically based, the vast majority being survey-based papers. It is striking that a book on psychometric methods (Nunnally, 1978) is the fifth most cited source in OM in the period 1980–2006 (Pilkington and Meredith, 2008); furthermore, this first appears only in 1990, coming to dominate citations by the 2000s. By 2008, OM had its first handbook of empirical measurement scales for survey research (Roth et al., 2008), something that was already an established part of the methodological furniture in other disciplines, such as marketing (e.g., Bearden and Netemeyer, 1999).[10]

---

[7] The visual method used in JIT processes to regulate the amount of product to be produced.

[8] Flynn et al. were only able (despite casting the net very widely) to list about sixty published empirical papers in OM, of which well over two-thirds had used basic descriptive statistics; the rest used cases and an assortment of simple statistical methods.

[9] A simple search within JOM for 'Cronbach' was used as a rough guide here: fifteen papers *in total* were published in the period up to and including 1997 (i.e., seventeen years); subsequently, around fifteen papers *per year* were published, up to 2013 (the last full year for which data were available).

[10] However, also in 2008, at least one prominent OM author and editor wrote with his colleagues about the 'threat' of another methodological revolution in supply chain management (and, by implication, OM as well), namely the rise of econometric methods based on secondary data (Carter, Sanders, and Dong, 2008). Their concerns were based on a comparison with the field of marketing, which had indeed shifted towards these types of methods.

Alongside this development of empirical research and increasingly sophisticated analysis of survey-based data came growing use of theory from outside OM. This was partly driven by the emerging research issues: researchers of supplier relationships (Lamming, 1993; Macbeth and Ferguson, 1994) turned to transaction cost economics (Williamson, 1985); manufacturing strategy researchers (e.g., Hayes and Pisano, 1996) drew on the resource-based view of the firm (Barney, 1991; Wernerfelt, 1984). But the methodological shift also served to *draw in* theory: researchers needed theory from which to develop hypotheses for formal testing but, because they mostly lacked rich empirical OM case study research from which to develop OM theory, they resorted to using theory from other fields. As a rough indication of this phenomenon, I have counted, in the leading journal, *JOM*, the incidence of references to 'Williamson' (as a proxy for the use of TCE) and to 'Barney' (for RBV): the results (Table 4.1) tell their own story (the number of papers published per year is roughly the same throughout this period). In IJOPM, from the European perspective, the first papers to cite Williamson and Barney were in 1994 and 1995 respectively. Building on the calls for empirical research in the early 1990s, a special issue of *JOM* was devoted to 'theory-driven' empirical research in 1998; a special issue of IJOPM was devoted to research methods in 2002. By 2011, in a review paper devoted to case-study research in leading OM journals, Barratt, Choi, and Li (2011: 336) used the presence of such theories as an indicator of a paper's quality: 'An existing theory (i.e., transaction cost economics, resource based view, etc.) adds validity to the conclusions one may draw from the data whether inductive or deductive.'

Schmenner and Swink (1998) saw things rather differently. Characterizing the OM field as having 'theory envy' towards other disciplines, they argued that OM had developed insights that, if appropriately organized and expressed, could constitute a body of 'home-grown' OM theory. They propose the 'Theory of Swift, Even Flow': 'the more swift and even the flow of materials through a process, the more productive that process is' (Schmenner and Swink, 1998: 102). And, ten years later, Schmenner suggested that there was 'too much theory and not enough explanation', a state of affairs arising from the widespread use of sophisticated data analysis methods such as structural equation

Table 4.1 Indication of the Rise of 'Theory' in OM

Period	JOM papers citing Williamson (TCE)	JOM papers citing Barney (RBV)
1990–1994	3	1
1995–1999	8	7
2000–2004	15	17
2005–2009	48	45
2010–2014	57	44

modelling and the appropriation of theories from 'one social science or another', leading to a proliferation of at best weakly explanatory theories that 'shamelessly escape[s] [testing] to be cited another day' (Schmenner et al., 2009: 340).

Nevertheless, theories from 'one social science or another' continue to be drawn into the OM fold: TCE (Ellram, Tate, and Billington, 2008), RBV (Mills, Platts, and Bourne, 2003), stakeholder theory (Tate, Ellram, and Brown, 2009), institutional theory (Bhakoo and Choi, 2013), complexity theory (Pathak et al., 2007) and so on. As Amundson (1998) argued in the early days of this trend, such theories can act as lenses through which to see OM phenomena in a different way. But, not surprisingly, the versions of these theories that are deployed by OM specialists who only have so much time to devote to reading about theory from other fields, are often rather reductive caricatures of the nuanced and contested sets of ideas that these theories' specialist adherents (and enemies) spend their whole working lives elaborating and exploring. To turn the tables, it is a useful experience for an OM scholar to read, say, an economic geographer's rough and ready account of an OM practice such as JIT? one has to assume that the uninitiated OM researcher who appropriates 'theory' most likely does the same kind of disservice to its finer points as the geographer does to the concepts dear to OM hearts. As such, OM people need to proceed with caution and not become completely detached from their roots (cf. Johnston (1999) on service OM's 'roots').

Relationship between Academic OM and Practice

Academic OM has had a complicated relationship with the practice of factory, industrial, production, operations, and, latterly, supply chain managers. It is often said that OM is by its nature an inherently practical domain. However, it has often been accused of becoming detached from the practical concerns of managers. Readers currently preoccupied with publishing in top-level academic OM journals for promotion, tenure, or research assessment exercises may be comforted (or dismayed) by this comment from Elwood Buffa in 1963:

> The problem is presented here as mainly one of translation. But more often, 'Too often, the management scientist feels that his task has been completed when a paper (often exhibiting mathematical elegance) has been published in an academically-oriented journal (which the practicing manager does not, and cannot read, because it is written in a language that is foreign to him). Usually the same ideas and results can be translated into the English language with the help of charts and graphs, but there is an apparent hesitancy to do this because such a paper may be misjudged by academic colleagues as work of "low power." We face a breakdown of communications. (Buffa, 1963: 5)

As? Meredith et al. put it, 'Managers looked at this research and found that they could neither understand the solutions being proposed nor the problems OM researchers thought they were addressing' (Meredith et al., 1989: 299).

This gulf between a good deal of published OM research and what was seen as relevant to practice endured and widened. This was the main reason for the inauguration, in 1980, of the *Journal of Operations Management* (*JOM*). In his introductory comments, editor Lee Krajewski (under the heading 'Return to Reality') argued:

> we must never lose sight of the purpose of theory and technique development—to enable the analysis of *meaningful* problems faced by operations managers in *practice*. The concept of *management* should be brought back into research studies in operations management. (Krajewski, 1980: vi, italics in original)

Writing twenty years later in an invited retrospective commentary on the development of the discipline, the same theme (and the same concern) is still there:

> As we develop our field, let us not lose sight of our roots. We need to provide answers when a manager asks 'What should I do?' (Krajewski cited in Meredith, 2002: 5)

In 1992, Kalyan Singhal, in his editorial introduction to the first edition of *Production and Operations Management* (*POM*) wrote, 'Our objective in publishing this journal is to improve practice' (Singhal, 1992: 1).

There are at least two dimensions to the relevance question. One is the extent to which the research is evidently related to practice—by being grounded in empirical research, perhaps or, as Meredith et al. (1989) suggest, addressing questions that practitioners can at least understand. A second dimension is the extent to which research leads practice rather than lagging behind it. Arthur V. Hill, second editor of *JOM*, writing in 2002, is particularly critical here: 'When I consider the seminal developments in the operations management field in the last 25 years, I cannot think of a single one that came out of academia' (Hill cited in Meredith, 2002: 6): one assumes he is referring to such developments as MRP and supply chain management (both developed by consultants), lean manufacturing and TQM (both developed in (Japanese) industry) and so on. Moreover, Krajewski links this tendency to follow behind practice to the methods used, arguing that empirical research is doomed always to be limited to understanding what is currently happening rather than developing insights into what could happen. (In doing so he perhaps underestimates the potential of theory to enable us to project forward from current practice.)

Part of the source of the tension between research and practice is the question of whether operations management is first and foremost an academic discipline, or an organizational function. For Buffa, operations management was an 'applied science', applying the techniques of OR to production problems. Later on, we see calls for academic research in OM to be 'concerned with real problems, with all their messiness and nuances' (Krajewski, 1980: vi); and (although rarely evident in the mix of papers actually published in the *POM* Journal) there was at least an *intent* in the inaugural issue to incorporate perspectives from a variety of disciplines: '[OM] involves several areas, among them behavioral science, operations research, statistical analysis, decision support systems, strategic planning, economics and engineering' (Singhal, 1992: 2). This multi-faceted nature of the operations *function* has led, in some instances, the empirical tail to wag the disciplinary dog. For example, the influence of Japanese manufacturing on the management of suppliers saw OM researchers theorizing and collecting data about notions such as trust, which is a long way from the traditional conceptual territory of OR and industrial engineering. More recently, research on sustainability in supply chains in the OM field seems to have been 'occupied' as OM territory mainly because the phenomenon of interest occurs in what can be construed as supply chains, not because the core concepts of OM have much to do with sustainability (or, rather, those that *could* be used to study sustainability are actually used less than imported conceptualizations such as TCE, institutional theory, etc.)

Clearly, the theory–practice debate has been present since OM was born. Furthermore, this phenomenon is not unique to the OM discipline (Wensley, 2007), and is not going to go away any time soon. But perhaps it does have a particular resonance and characteristics peculiar to OM in that, in practice and in academic contexts, OM people are often seen as the ones who know how to get things done and make things happen 'in the real world'.

So, Where Is the Management in Operations Management?

As we have seen, in the first issue of *JOM*, editor Lee Krajewski expressed a hope that, amongst other things, the new journal would 'put the word *management* back into operations management' (Krajewski, 1980: vi, emphasis in original). The perceived problem was that other journals 'either tend to prefer sophisticated mathematical model building or have a prejudice against it' (Krajewski, 1980: v). So, the vision here was that the technical models would be judged in terms of their contribution to operations management, rather than simply in terms of their technical sophistication per se. Such concerns have already been touched on in the previous section. But here my emphasis is slightly different. If there is a set of operations management knowledge, captured in models, contingency theories, conceptual frameworks, improvement methods and the like, what is it that is left for the human beings called operations managers to do when they go to work on a Monday morning?

As discussed, the early decades of the emergence of OM were couched in terms of the 'science of management'. Buffa and Forrester both represented this 'science' as providing varying degrees of support for managerial decision-making (Figures 4.2 and 4.3), ranging from completely specified, automated decision rules to completely new problems with no existing decision guides at all. The job of academic OM, this suggests, is to provide ever greater support for managerial decision-making: according to Buffa (see Figure 4.2):

> We wish to expand progressively the relative size and scope of each of the areas representing the application of management science at the expense of any of the areas representing a lesser application of scientific methodology. (Buffa, 1963: 7)

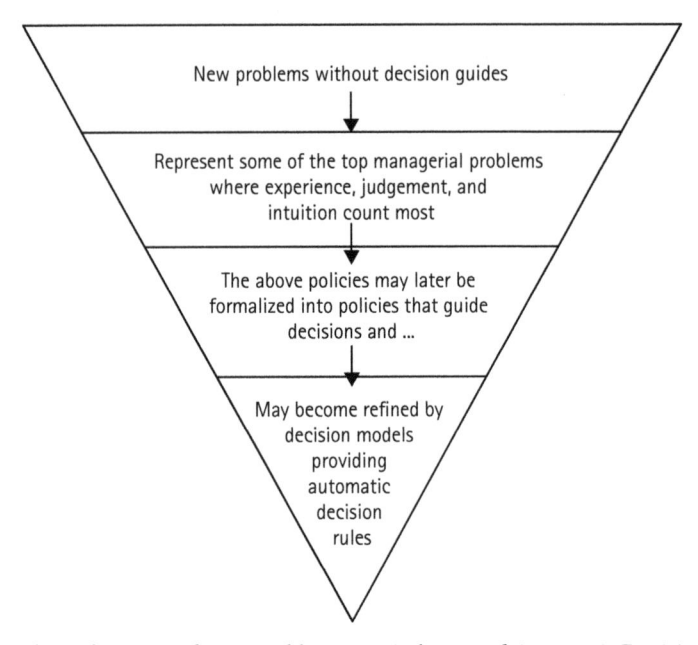

FIGURE 4.2 The Refinement of New Problems into Policies and Automatic Decision Rules.

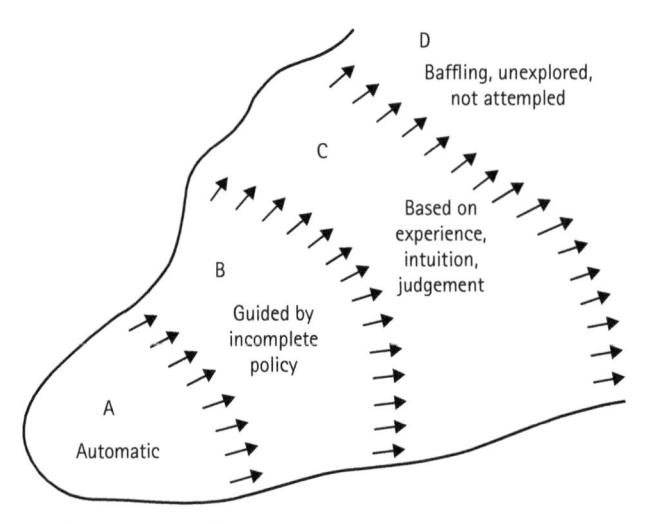

FIGURE 4.3 Scope of Management Decisions.

The role for managers here can be seen in several different ways. Certainly there is a role for intuitive decision-making in those areas that are not (yet) susceptible to automated decision rules—on this view, managers are managers because they have experience and can exercise judgement and use intuition under conditions of novelty and uncertainty. Buffa also writes that his text's objective (being directed at management students) is to 'develop a comprehension of these new methods so that in operations situations one can make intelligent decisions based on the results of analysis by staff specialists' (Buffa, 1963: vii). So, managers are also managers because they exercise ('intelligent') judgement about when to allow automated decision rules to hold sway, and when not to. But on what basis? It is not clear—but one possibility is that, while decision rules can provide solutions to isolated operations issues, it is only the manager who has responsibility for and a view of the whole system, and must take account of how the outcome of the decision rule on one issue interacts with that on a second and third issue. This seems to be the view of Starr (1972), who, as we have seen, sees management as a synthesizing function: 'The executive is expected to understand in logical (not mathematical) terms what analytic tools are available and how he [sic] can relate them to the performance of the total system with which he [sic] must deal' (Starr, 1972: vi).

During the late 1960s, Skinner was expounding his notion of manufacturing strategy, and also arguing that operations managers needed to think about the much bigger system—the whole production plant or process (Skinner, 1969). Twenty-odd years later, reflecting on why the manufacturing strategy concept had not taken hold as well as it might have, Skinner commented:

> We say that manufacturing policy decisions must be made such that the system designed meets the manufacturing task. But the manager is left to figure out how to get from task to structure without much specific guidance.... In my own and others' defence we have not been prescriptive because it is more art than science and there are 999 variables and 998 equations, so to speak. (Skinner, 1992: 22)

The implication here is ambiguous: in part there is an admission that 'art'—judgement, intuition, experience—is an inevitable part of OM, at least at a strategic level; but there is also a suggestion that, if only we could solve the set of 998 simultaneous equations, then operations strategy analysis, too, could be automated. One way to simplify the simultaneous consideration of multiple elements of the system is to adopt an 'integrated solution' and, arguably, that is the attraction of many of the various improvement methods, such as TQM, 'lean', and six sigma, that have emerged in practice and in the OM literature. The management decision reduces to 'should we adopt TQM/lean/BPR/six sigma? (delete as appropriate)'. Skinner (1996) is critical of such methods, arguing that, while the improvements that they entailed might have some value, they did not serve to provide a lasting differentiation to a manufacturing firm—when everyone has 'done' TQM, we are back to the competitive square one. Similarly, Slack and Lewis (2011) describe these methods as 'substitutes for strategy'.

Another possible role for managers is also inspired by one of Buffa's conceptualizations. Framing the science of management as very much centred on *decision-making*, he contends that 'In decision-making, management selects from a set of alternatives what is considered to be the best course of action' (Buffa, 1963: 7). However, there is no consideration of where these alternatives come from (This rather parallels the 'design school' approach to the corporate strategy process (Andrews, 1965), which typically includes a stage labelling something like 'create strategy', followed by 'evaluate and choose strategy' (Mintzberg, 1990). So, there is an interesting and largely unexplored aspect of OM, which concerns the 'imagining' of alternative courses of action, rooted in an understanding of operations and related issues and current and past practice in particular situations. The overlap between this 'entrepreneurial' aspect of management and OM is only just being explored (Kickul et al., 2011; Spring and Araujo, 2013).

TQM in particular emphasized the role of operations managers in managing change. Of course, operations managers have always had to manage change, but the treatment of this in OM texts and maybe, often, in practice too, centred on the technical at the expense of the human. For example, when redesigning a plant layout, various schematic and mathematical models exist for analysing alternative layouts, and project planning techniques are available for planning and controlling the implementation process. Furthermore, job changes that might be associated with such a change effort can also be reduced to the scientific methods of time and motion study (e.g., see Buffa, 1963: chapters 4 and 5). Quality management initiatives—TQM in its day and, more recently, 'Six sigma' (e.g., Nonthaleerak and Hendry, 2008)—often require huge, pervasive change programmes that challenge many fundamental OM assumptions (as discussed earlier). They also include a philosophy of continuous, often bottom-up improvement. Similarly, the widespread adoption of enterprise systems has also given rise to massive change programmes centred on the operations and supply chain functions (Snider, Silveira, and Balakrishnan, 2009). So if, as argued earlier, adopting such 'solutions' in some ways simplifies the management decision-making task, it, on the other hand, presents change management challenges of an entirely different order. In this sense, OM in practice can sometimes appear to consist mainly of assimilating and implementing a succession of externally imposed (and typically unwelcome) improvement initiatives (e.g., see Salmon (1981) for an early example in relation to MRP).

A final possible way to think about the relationship between OM models and the activity of operations management is that managers are managers because they can translate general models and concepts into (their) specific contexts. Someone who has been on an OM course, read Hayes and Wheelwright (1984) and maybe even bought a copy for their office shelf is not necessarily an operations manager. But if they can take Hayes and Wheelwright's general idea that certain aspects of the design of an operation should be aligned with the requirements of the customer groups that are being served, and then make judgements about appropriate levels of aggregation and precision with which to translate (inevitably inaccurate) sales forecasts, costings, and other data into feasible activity and investments in machines or staff training and recruitment, given the realities of the particular production processes current and emerging, and of the labour market, and handle the internal politics of making that all happen—well, maybe then we have an operations manager.

The manager in the scenario just sketched out is trying to bring about action in the world—making products, delivering services to customers, installing new machines, influencing what his/her staff do, and so on. They may well also be drawing on insights from areas of management theory and practice other than OM, such as human resource management, marketing, and management accounting. According to Czarniawska and Mouritsen (2009), managers seek to distance themselves from 'unrulable' technology and complex human beings by using 'managerial technologies' to make 'manageable objects'. For example, a physical machine is given an asset number and added to an asset register in an enterprise system to make it, in respect of certain activities, susceptible to management manipulation, comparison, and control; an employee is made into a manageable object by being framed, for certain purposes, as a certain grade of employee who has been trained to operate certain processes. This is what our OM models and frameworks do in many and varied ways: machines are treated as units of capacity to be incorporated into production planning calculations; products are treated as existing in some stage or another in the product life-cycle, hence allowing us to position them in the Hayes and Wheelwright product-process matrix. Always, we abstract, of course. But the claim of Czarniawska and Mouritsen is that there is always an 'excess of reality' (2009: 172); or, as Callon (1998) would put it, whenever we 'frame' something, there is always overflowing, and aspects of it defeat the attempt to bound it, to make it calculable and (in our context) manageable. As such, it is perhaps in this process of using managerial technologies—in particular, the managerial technologies of OM—and in the interplay between them and the manager on one hand, and the concrete reality of technologies and people on the other, that the study of operations management *as management* can best be conducted.

Acknowledgements

I would like to acknowledge comments on earlier drafts from Luis Araujo, Tom Choi, Jack Meredith, Chris Voss, and Finn Wynstra. All remaining errors and shortcomings are my responsibility alone.

References

Amundson, S. D. (1998). 'Relationships between Theory-Driven Empirical Research in Operations Management and Other Disciplines'. *Journal of Operations Management*, 16(4): 341–59.

Anderson, J. C., Cleveland, G., and Schroeder, R. G. (1989). 'Operations Strategy: A Literature Review'. *Journal of Operations Management*, 8(2): 133–58.

Andrews, K. R. (1965). *The Concept of Corporate Strategy*. Homewood, IL: Irwin.

Barney, J. B. (1991). 'Firm Resources and Sustained Competitive Advantage'. *Journal of Management*, 17: 99–120.

Barratt, M., Choi, T. Y., and Li, M. (2011). 'Qualitative Case Studies in Operations Management: Trends, Research Outcomes, and Future Research Implications'. *Journal of Operations Management*, 29(4): 329–42.

Bearden, W. O. and Netemeyer, R. G. (1999). *Handbook of Marketing Scales: Multi-Item Measures for Marketing and Consumer Behavior Research*. Thousand Oaks, CA: SAGE.

Beer, S. (1966). *Decision and Control: The Meaning of Operational Research and Management Cybernetics*. Chichester: John Wiley.

Bhakoo, V. and Choi, T. (2013). 'The Iron Cage Exposed: Institutional Pressures and Heterogeneity across the Healthcare Supply Chain'. *Journal of Operations Management*, 31(6): 432–49.

Bitran, G. R., Marieni, D. M., Matsuo, H., and Noonan, J. W. (1985). 'Multiplant MRP'. *Journal of Operations Management*, 5(2): 183–203.

Buffa, E. (1961). *Modern Production Management*. New York: John Wiley.

Buffa, E. (1963). *Models for Production and Operations Management*. New York: Wiley.

Buffa, E. (1968). *Operations Management: Problems and Models*. New York: John Wiley.

Buffa, E. S. (1980). 'Research in Operations Management'. *Journal of Operations Management*, 1(1): 1–7.

Callon, M. (1998). 'An Essay on Framing and Overflowing: Economic Externalities Revisited by Sociology'. *The Sociological Review*, 46(S1): 244–69.

Carter, C. R., Sanders, N. R., and Dong, Y. (2008). 'Paradigms, Revolutions, and Tipping Points: The Need for Using Multiple Methodologies within the Field of Supply Chain Management'. *Journal of Operations Management—OSM Forum*.

Chase, R. B. (1978). 'Where Does the Customer Fit in a Service Operation?' *Harvard Business Review*, 56(6): 137–42.

Chase, R. B. (1980). 'A Classification and Evaluation of Research in Operations Management'. *Journal of Operations Management*, 1(1): 9–14.

Chase, R. B. (1981). 'The Customer Contact Approach to Services: Theoretical Bases and Practical Extensions'. *Operations Research*, 29(4): 698–706.

Choi, T. Y. and Hartley, J. L. (1996). 'An Exploration of Supplier Selection Practices across the Supply Chain'. *Journal of Operations Management*, 14(4): 333–43.

Christopher, M. (2011). *Logistics and Supply Chain Management*. Harlow: Pearson Education Ltd.

Clark, K. B. (1996). 'Competing through Manufacturing and the New Manufacturing Paradigm: Is Manufacturing Strategy Passé?' *Production and Operations Management*, 5(1): 42–58.

Craighead, C. W. and Meredith, J. (2008). 'Operations Management Research: Evolution and Alternative Future Paths'. *International Journal of Operations & Production Management*, 28(7/8): 710–26.

Crosby, P. B. (1979). *Quality Is Free: The Art of Making Quality Certain*. New York: McGraw-Hill.

Czarniawska, B. and Mouritsen, J. (2009). 'What Is the Object of Management?: How Management Technologies Help to Create Manageable Objects', in C. S. Chapman, D. J. Cooper, and P. B. Miller (eds.), *Accounting, Organizations, and Institutions: Essays in Honour of Anthony Hopwood*. Oxford: Oxford University Press, 157–74.

Dale, B. (2003). 'The Received Wisdom on TQM', in B. G. Dale (ed.), *Managing Quality*. Oxford: Blackwell, 58–73.

Deming, W. E. (1986). *Out of the Crisis*. Cambridge, MA: Massachusetts Institute of Technology.

Ebert, R. J. (1989). 'Empirical/Field-Based Methodologies in JOM'. *Journal of Operations Management*, 8(4): 294–6.

Ellram, L. M., Tate, W. L. and Billington, C. (2008). 'Offshore Outsourcing of Professional Services: A Transaction Cost Economics Perspective'. *Journal of Operations Management*, 26(2): 148–63.

Fisher, M. (1997). 'What Is the Right Supply Chain for Your Product?' *Harvard Business Review*, March/April: 105–16.

Flynn, B. B., Sakakibara, S., Schroeder, R. G., Bates, K. A. and Flynn, E. J. (1990). 'Empirical Research Methods in Operations Management'. *Journal of Operations Management*, 9(2): 250–84.

Forrester, J. (1961). *Industrial Dynamics*. Boston, MA: MIT Press.

Frohlich, M. and Westbrook, R. (2001). 'Arcs of Integration: An International Study of Supply Chain Strategies'. *Journal of Operations Management*, 19: 185–200.

Gershuny, J. and Miles, I. (1983). *The New Service Economy: The Transformation of Employment in Industrial Societies*. London: F. Pinter.

Grönroos, C. (2008). 'Service Logic Revisited: Who Creates Value? And Who Co-Creates?' *European Business Review*, 20(4): 298–314.

Harland, C. (1996). 'Supply-Chain Management: Relationships, Chains and Networks'. *British Journal of Management*, 7: S63–S80.

Harris, F. (1913). 'How Much Stock to Keep on Hand'. *Factory, The Magazine of Management*, 10: 240–1.

Hayes, R. H. and Pisano, G. P. (1996). 'Manufacturing Strategy: At the Intersection of Two Paradigm Shifts'. *Production and Operations Management*, 5(1): 25–41.

Hayes, R. H. and Wheelwright, S. C. (1984). *Restoring Our Competitive Edge: Competing through Manufacturing*. New York: John Wiley.

Hickson, D. J., Pugh, D. S., and Pheysey, D. C. (1969). 'Operations Technology and Organisation Structure: An Empirical Reappraisal'. *Administrative Science Quarterly*, 14: 378–97.

Hill, T. (1983). *Production/Operations Management*. London: Prentice-Hall International.

Holt, C., Modigliani, F., Muth, J. and Simon, H. (1960). *Planning Production, Inventories, and Work Force*. Englewood Cliffs, NJ: Prentice-Hall

Houlihan, J. (1984). 'Supply Chain Management'. *Proceedings of 19th International Technical Conference, BPICS*, 101–110.

Johnston, R. (1999). 'Service Operations Management: Return to Roots'. *International Journal of Operations and Production Management*, 19(2): 104–24.

Kickul, J. R., Griffiths, M. D., Jayaram, J. and Wagner, S. M. (2011). 'Operations Management, Entrepreneurship, and Value Creation: Emerging Opportunities in a Cross-Disciplinary Context'. *Journal of Operations Management*, 29(1): 78–85.

Kirby, M. W. (2000). 'Operations Research Trajectories: The Anglo-American Experience from the 1940s to the 1990s'. *Operations Research*, 48(5): 661–70.

Krajewski, L. (1980). 'The Inauguration of a Journal'. *Journal of Operations Management*, 1(1): v–vi.

Kraljic, P. (1983). 'Purchasing Must Become Supply Management'. *Harvard Business Review*, September/October: 109–17.

Lamming, R. (1993). *Beyond Partnership: Strategies for Innovation and Lean Supply*. Hemel Hempstead: Prentice-Hall.

Lamming, R. (1996). 'Squaring Lean Supply with Supply Chain Management'. *International Journal of Operations and Production Management*, 16(2): 183–96.

Levitt, T. (1972). 'Production-Line Approach to Service'. *Harvard Business Review*, September/October: 41–52.

Levitt, T. (1976). 'The Industrialization of Service'. *Harvard Business Review*, 54: 63–74.

Macbeth, D. and Ferguson, N. (1994). *Partnership Sourcing: An Integrated Supply-Chain Approach*. London: Financial Times/Pitman.

Mccloskey, J. F. (1987) OR Forum. 'The Beginnings of Operations Research: 1934–1941'. *Operations Research*, 35(1): 143–52.

Mayer, R. R. (1962). *Production Management*. New York: McGraw-Hill.

Meredith, J. (2002). '20th Anniversary of JOM: An Editorial Retrospective and Prospective'. *Journal of Operations Management*, 20(1): 1–18.

Meredith, J. R. (2001). 'Hopes for the Future of Operations Management'. *Journal of Operations Management*, 19: 397–402.

Meredith, J. R., Raturi, A., Amoako-Gyampah, K. and Kaplan, B. (1989). 'Alternative Research Paradigms in Operations'. *Journal of Operations Management*, 8(4): 297–326.

Mills, J., Platts, K. and Bourne, M. (2003). 'Applying Resource-Based Theory: Methods, Outcomes and Utility for Managers'. *International Journal of Operations and Production Management*, 23(2): 148–66.

Mintzberg, H. (1990). 'The Design School: Reconsidering the Basic Premises of Strategic Management'. *Strategic Management Journal*, 11: 171–95.

Mitchell, W. N. (1931). *Production Management*. Chicago, IL: The University of Chicago Press.

New, C. (1992). 'World-Class Manufacturing versus Strategic Trade-Offs'. *International Journal of Operations & Production Management*, 12(4): 19–31.

New, S. J. (2007). 'Celebrating the Enigma: The Continuing Puzzle of the Toyota Production System'. *International Journal of Production Research*, 45: 3545–54.

Nie, W. and Kellogg, D. (1999). 'How Professors of Operations Management View Service Operations'. *Production and Operations Management*, 8(3): 339–55.

Nonthaleerak, P. and Hendry, L. (2008). 'Exploring the Six Sigma Phenomenon Using Multiple Case Study Evidence'. *International Journal of Operations & Production Management*, 28(3): 279–303.

Nunnally, J. (1978). *Psychometric Theory*. New York: McGraw-Hill.

Orlicky, J. (1975). *MRP: Material Requirements Planning: The New Way of Life in Production and Inventory Management*. New York: McGraw-Hill.

Pathak, S. D., Day, J. M., Nair, A., Sawaya, W. J. and Kristal, M. M. (2007). 'Complexity and Adaptivity in Supply Networks: Building Supply Network Theory Using a Complex Adaptive Systems Perspective'. *Decision Sciences*, 38(4): 547–80.

Pilkington, A. and Meredith, J. R. (2008). 'The Evolution of the Intellectual Structure of Operations Management—1980–2006: A Citation/Co-Citation Analysis'. *Journal of Operations Management*, 27(3): 185–202.

Roth, A. V., Schroeder, R., Huang, X. and Kristal, M. M. (2008). *Handbook of Metrics for Research in Operations Management: Multi-Item Measurement Scales and Objective Items*. Thousand Oaks, CA: SAGE.

Salmon, M. A. (1981). 'Senior Management Paper Section: What Is the Relevance of MRP to You?' *International Journal of Operations & Production Management*, 1(3): 180–3.

Sasser, W. E., Olsen, R. and Wyckoff, D. (1978). *Management of Service Operations: Text, Cases and Readings*. Boston, MA: Allyn and Bacon.

Schmenner, R. W. and Swink, M. L. (1998). 'On Theory in Operations Management'. *Journal of Operations Management*, 17(1): 97–113.

Schmenner, R. W., Wassenhove, L. V., Ketokivi, M., Heyl, J. and Lusch, R. F. (2009). 'Too Much Theory, Not Enough Understanding'. *Journal of Operations Management*, 27(5): 339–43.

Schonberger, R. J. (1982). 'Some Observations on the Advantages and Implementation Issues of Just-in-Time Production Systems'. *Journal of Operations Management*, 3(1): 1–11.

Schonberger, R. J. (1986). *World Class Manufacturing*. New York: Free Press.

Schroeder, R. G., Anderson, J. C. and Cleveland, G. (1986). 'The Content of Manufacturing Strategy: An Empirical Study'. *Journal of Operations Management*, 6(4); 405–15.

Schroeder, R. G., Anderson, J. C., Tupy, S. E. and White, E. M. (1981). 'A Study of MRP Benefits and Costs'. *Journal of Operations Management*, 2(1): 1–9.

Scott, W. R. (1995). *Institutions and Organizations*. Thousand Oaks, CA: SAGE.

Shingo, S. (1981). *Study of Toyota Production System from Industrial Engineering View-Point*. Japan Management Association.

Singhal, J. and Singhal, K. (2007). 'Holt, Modigliani, Muth, and Simon's Work and Its Role in the Renaissance and Evolution of Operations Management'. *Journal of Operations Management*, 25(2): 300–9.

Singhal, K. (1992). 'Introduction: Shaping the Future of Manufacturing and Service Operations'. *Production and Operations Management*, 1(1): 1–4.

Singhal, K., Singhal, J., and Starr, M. K. (2007). 'The Domain of Production and Operations Management and the Role of Elwood Buffa in Its Delineation'. *Journal of Operations Management*, 25(2): 310–27.

Skinner, W. (1969). 'Manufacturing—Missing Link in Corporate Strategy'. *Harvard Business Review*, May/June: 136–145.

Skinner, W. (1974). 'The Focussed Factory'. *Harvard Business Review*, May/June: 113–21.

Skinner, W. (1992). 'Missing the Links in Manufacturing Strategy', in C. A. Voss (ed.), *Manufacturing Strategy: Process and Content*. London: Chapman and Hall, 13–25.

Skinner, W. (1996). 'Three Yards and a Cloud of Dust: Industrial Management at Century End'. *Production and Operations Management*, 5(1): 15–24.

Slack, N., Chambers, S. and Johnston, R. (2010). *Operations Management*. London: FT Prentice-Hall.

Slack, N. and Lewis, M. (2011). *Operations Strategy*. Harlow: FT Prentice-Hall.

Slack, N., Lewis, M. and Bates, H. (2004). 'The Two Worlds of Operations Management Research and Practice: Can They Meet, Should They Meet?' *International Journal of Operations & Production Management*, 24(4): 372–87.

Smiddy, H. F. and Naum, L. (1954). 'Evolution of a "Science of Managing" in America'. *Management Science*, 1(1): 1–31.

Snider, B., Silveira, G. J. C. D. and Balakrishnan, J. (2009). 'ERP Implementation at SMEs: Analysis of Five Canadian Cases'. *International Journal of Operations & Production Management*, 29(1): 4–29.

Sprague, L. G. (2007). 'Evolution of the Field of Operations Management'. *Journal of Operations Management*, 25(2): 219–38.

Spring, M. (2014). 'The Shifting Terrain of Service Operations Management', in K. Haynes and I. Grugulis (eds.), *Managing Services: Challenges and Innovation*. Oxford: Oxford University Press, 21–47.

Spring, M. and Araujo, L. (2009). 'Service, Services and Products: Re-Thinking Operations Strategy'. *International Journal of Operations & Production Management*, 29(5): 444–67.

Spring, M. and Araujo, L. (2013). 'Beyond the Service Factory: Service Innovation in Manufacturing Supply Networks'. *Industrial Marketing Management*, 42(1): 59–70.

Starr, M. K. (1972). *Production Management: Systems and Synthesis*. Englewood Cliffs, NJ: Prentice-Hall.

Sum, C.-C., Yang, K.-K., Ang, J. S. K. and Quek, S.-A. (1995). 'An Analysis of Material Requirements Planning (MRP) Benefits Using Alternating Conditional Expectation (ACE)'. *Journal of Operations Management*, 13(1): 35–58.

Swamidass, P. M. (1991). 'Empirical Science: New Frontier in Operations Management Research'. *Academy of Management Review*, 16(4): 793–814.

Tate, W. L., Ellram, L. M. and Brown, S. W. (2009). 'Offshore Outsourcing of Services: A Stakeholder Perspective'. *Journal of Service Research*, 12(1): 56–72.

Vargo, S. and Lusch, R. (2004). 'The Four Service Marketing Myths: Remnants of a Goods-Based, Manufacturing Model'. *Journal of Service Research*, 6(4): 324–35.

Vollmann, T., Berry, W., and Whybark, D. (1984). *Manufacturing Planning and Control Systems*. Homewood: Dow Jones-Irwin.

Voss, C. A., Armistead, C., Johnston, R., and Morris, B. (1985). *Operations Management in Service Industries and the Public Sector: Texts and Cases*. Chichester: Wiley.

Wensley, R. (2007). 'Beyond Rigour and Relevance: The Underlying Nature of both Business Schools and Management Research'. AIM Research Working Paper Series. London: The Advanced Institute of Management Research.

Wernerfelt, B. (1984). 'A Resource-Based View of the Firm'. *Strategic Management Journal*, 5: 171–80.

Wheelwright, S. C. (1981). 'Japan—Where Operations Really Are Strategic'. *Harvard Business Review*, July/August: 67–74.

White, E. M., Anderson, J. C., Schroeder, R. G., and Tupy, S. E. (1982). 'A Study of the MRP Implementation Process'. *Journal of Operations Management*, 2(3): 145–53.

Williamson, O. E. (1985). *The Economic Instituitons of Capitalism: Firms, Markets, Relational Contracting*. New York: The Free Press.

Woodward, J. (1958). *Management and Technology*. London: HMSO.

CHAPTER 5

PETER F. DRUCKER'S MANAGEMENT BY OBJECTIVES AND SELF-CONTROL

PETER STARBUCK

INTRODUCTION

In this chapter I examine the influence of Drucker's 'Management by Objectives (MbO) and Self-Control' since it was first introduced in his book *The Practice of Management* (1954) over sixty years ago.

Drucker defined MbO as an all-encompassing philosophy of management that *integrates* all of the functions and activities of the manager into one holistic whole, and commences with the top management team of the organization determining organizational objectives by asking the simple question: What is our business? Although this was a simple question Drucker stated that the answer was not as always obvious. However, once answered the structure of the organization should evolve and be determined by the requirements of the organization and not imposed indeterminately. From this framework MbO embodies a democratic process, providing members freedom under the law, with all of the other basic requirements of a free-market economy's status and function.

In Drucker's view when Management by Objectives (MbO) is properly applied, the members of the organization agree upon their purpose and make their contribution to the organization's requirements with confidence, and without continual reminders of what the objectives are. Drucker termed this 'Self-Control', and the enabler for a just and workable industrial society to be met.

This chapter defines the basics of Drucker's MbO; its reception, application, and outcomes. It also provides an overview of what has happened to MbO in terms of its adoption within US, UK, and Japanese contexts.

Management by Objectives was the key idea put forward by Drucker (1954) in *The Practice of Management*. MbO was viewed as the essential integrator of all the functions of management emphasizing 'Self-Control', in the knowledge that managers are responsible workers and are capable with performing to plan without receiving continual reminders from their supervisors.

The Practice of Management (hereafter titled *Practice*) has been described as Drucker's seminal work, influencing and changing the way we manage. It is considered to be one of the most complete management books ever written, being in continual print since it was first published. Drucker described the book as being written from experience, with the aim of improving the performance of the average manager. Further, the book aimed to initiate new management recruits and inform 'the citizen' about what business management means and what the levels of expectation around performance were. Although the book was practice-based, it was not concerned with techniques but rather emphasized rational decision-making, with Drucker declaring that the days of management by intuition were over (Drucker, 1954: 9). What made the book important was that it was the first to describe how managers should set about making the decisions needed to manage a business in a manner that would produce the results essential for survival.

Drucker gave credit to two other writers, Knauth and Dean. They had been the only authors to explore the area and understood what was required in managing a business (see Knauth, 1948; Dean, 1951). Their work, however, was incomplete, as was the work of Holden, Fish and Smith, whose twelve editions of *Top-Management Organisation and Control* (from 1941 to 1951), reputedly America's best selling management book for a decade, was still describing what top management's job was, without indicating specifically what had to be done (O'Donnell, 1952).

It was Drucker who then provided the answer to the question of 'What has to be done?' with his MbO. It was this milestone in management practice that gave *Practice* its rating.

MbO has three basic parts:

1. The setting of objectives and their constant monitoring;
2. The agreement and adaptation of the specific objectives with, and for, the individual members of the enterprise. All made relevant by frequent feed-back of results; and
3. That all functions and activities of the business must be *integrated* into a whole. It is this *integration* that is the basis for the claim of Drucker that MbO should be regarded as a 'philosophy of management'.

Setting Objectives

Who sets the objectives? Drucker stated that MbO commenced with top management, whose responsibility was to define the organization's policies (the objectives).

This he identified in his book *Concept of the Corporation* (1946) (hereafter *Concept*). The starting point was for the Chief Executive Officer (CEO) to ask the question 'What is our business?' (as posed by Drucker in *The New Society* (1950) (hereafter *Society*) to which in his following book, *Practice*, he added the further question—'What should it be?' (1954: 46)). He pointed out that the question was not asked often enough and when it was asked, it was more difficult to answer than it appeared. It was from this starting point that top management in the organization could proceed to organize their work.

Drucker's view was that the CEO no longer worked alone, but was responsible as leader of a small team of two or three people. The executive team had to set the objectives for the business and recognize their practical limits as they should never be seen as a railroad timetable or 'a compass by which a ship navigates' (Drucker, 1954: 58). Drucker also noted that regardless of the type of business, these objectives would be primarily the same but have a different emphasis depending on what the business is concerned with (e.g., market standing, innovation, productivity, etc. (Drucker, 1954: 60)). In setting the objectives Drucker acknowledged that it was a difficult and risky part of the manager's job, while many others saw it as an obvious function (Greenwood, 1981).

Having established that objectives were in principle the same for every business, illustrations were highlighted to indicate the differences between areas and emphasis. One of these areas was 'time-span' in relation to the objective of production. For example, a steam turbine would have a time-span of six years in production, whereas trees for wood pulp would take fifty years to mature (Drucker, 1954: 81). If a long-term view did not prevail within the enterprise, then when 'the first cloud appears' sudden cuts in the production process could destroy in one day, what took years to build (this was a warning against short-termism (Drucker, 1954: 82)). Although the emphasis of the objectives must be balanced against each other, this balance may also change from time to time, as explained in *The Balanced Scorecard* (Kaplan and Norton, 1996), and so importantly, objectives need to have regard for the future when obtaining results for today. Further, it was not a mechanical job of staying within budget, but one requiring judgement that could only be achieved upon a 'social analysis of the business' (Drucker, 1954: 83–4).

To determine the objectives, Drucker recommended that the manager must make balanced decisions upon an extensive examination of the facts, using the appropriate methods established for decision-making. He drew attention to the 'new tools' of management grouped under the heading of 'Operations Research', including 'the tools of systematic, logical and mathematical analysis and synthesis'. While being important tools, Drucker emphasized that they were options where each could be used to examine developing alternatives and underlying patterns. However, he argued that these tools alone could not ask the right questions, set objectives, or make decisions; only managers could do that. The great advantage of MbO was that it made it possible for managers to control their own performance (Drucker, 1954: 128). To do so, the manager needed to know his/her own goals and then have the necessary information to measure them (Drucker, 1954: 129). MbO was dependent on the manager being able to identify and measure *all* functions of the business including those considered impossible to measure, such as worker morale, as MbO was seen as an aid towards lifting performance.

As an illustration of the proper use of measurement, Drucker made reference to General Electric's (GE) travelling audit team, which visited every management unit at least once a year. A report was developed and then sent to unit managers. The report's function was to act as an aid in assisting self-control, as opposed to being a form of control from above. In Drucker's opinion the system engendered trust and was evident in GE managers' response. This was in contrast to an unidentified business, which operated an audit unit (the 'president's Gestapo') that reported to the president, and the report was used as a tool of confrontation. The outcome was that management objectives were then directed at 'passing' the audit rather than achieving best performance.

While Drucker did not oppose the view that managers should be held accountable for the results of their performance he argued that by using measurements to aid MbO and self-control, better results could be obtained (Drucker, 1954: 130). In addition, he warned against isolating one objective, as this had a danger of destroying other objectives if the overall effect of the action of one objective was not taken into account in terms of its impact on another (as later endorsed by Kaplan and Norton, 1996). Therefore, results would be harmed rather than improved if an integrated approach was not taken.

For Drucker, MbO gave genuine freedom under the law by providing freedom, function, and status. In doing so it gave workers and managers what was missing in the social part of the industrial society: a workable social society that complemented the mechanical one. Drucker also recommended an idea put forward by Harold Smiddy in a case study, whereby subordinates wrote to their manager twice a year. In the letter subordinates defined theirs and their manager's job, setting out what was required from their manager in order for them to achieve their goals. The letter also recorded the support they expected from others within the organization. Once agreed it became 'the charter' under which they could operate (Drucker, 1954: 126–8). This provided an environment of mutual commitment between the subordinate and their manager and is considered to be one of the cornerstones of MbO.

Humble (1972) also reminded us that to make MbO work required 'relevant and timely feed-back information'. Drucker also added that '*a manager—makes a team out of people—through constant communication*' (Drucker, 1954: 338); not just on a two-way basis, but also through multiple channels (Drucker, 1954: 139).

Total Integration

Drucker's position was that enterprises are social organizations and while there was a mechanical component to management, this had to be integrated with human performance to produce results. He had moved away from Taylor's idea of separating the planning of work and its doing, to the new method of working, thus progressing from the conveyor track towards that of 'Automation, the new integrating method'. This meant that Taylor's planning and doing could be put together and performed, not always by different people but by the same person who could carry out both of these essential operations. This made work more complete, and workers would be motivated to make their own contributions, without which nothing would happen as Drucker described in his 'Human Organisation for Peak Performance': '*When it comes to the job itself, however, the problem is not to dissect it into parts or motions but to put together an integrated whole. This is the new task.*' (Drucker, 1954: 289).

Drucker offered several explanations for what needed to be integrated. However, he also stated that while we could attempt to list them all, there are others that are still yet to be discovered, as businesses in different sectors may not have the common relationships that others have in relation to all of the common objectives. Drucker also made further discoveries during this period when working as a consultant at GE, illustrated in the book *Control Your Own Destiny or Someone Else Will* (Tichy and Sherman, 1993: 37). In 1951 Ralph Cordiner (CEO at GE) assembled an intelligent team of GE top management, consultants and professors, including Harold Smiddy and then later, Peter Drucker, to look into ways of improving GE's management. 'Two years later, they emerged with the Blue Books, a five-volume, 3,463-page management bible. This included such powerful concepts as management by objectives—as well as some of the most revolutionary ideas that Welch would later espouse' (Tichy and Sherman, 1993: 37). What should also be remembered was that the book *Practice* was written while Drucker was working as a management consultant during the time of the massive reorganization and decentralization of GE.

The Outcome of MbO

In their article 'A Dissenting View of MbO' Halpern and Osofsky (2005) reject the relevance of Drucker's MbO as being an equally participating management practice, referring to it as 'pseudo participation' as its application was providing a different control mechanism of an organization's management and its people. I turn now to the reception, application, and outcome of MbO in the American, UK, and Japanese contexts.

American View

In America MbO was welcomed in its home market as a way of improving 'how we manage'. Odiorne (1965, 1978) and Greenwood (1981), two of Drucker's close followers, were among the best American exponents of his work in terms of assessing the meaning of MbO, its perception and acceptance.

Odiorne in *Management by Objectives: A System of Managerial Leadership* examined MbO in detail, offering the following description of MbO: 'management by objectives is essentially a system of incorporating into a more logical and effective pattern to the things many people are already doing' (Odiorne, 1965: 56). 'MbO is a system of managing, not an additional managers job' (Odiorne, 1965: 77).

Odiorne then followed this 1965 book with an article published in *Business Horizons* (October 1978) recording that a *'popular pastime amongst academics is uncovering the origins of MbO'*, which he cites as including Abraham and God, The Koran, and the philosophers ranging from Plato through to Marx. More objectively, Arthur Moxham is recorded as the earliest tutor on MbO with Pierre du Pont as his student at the turn of the twentieth century. He was followed by Frank Donaldson Brown, initially at du Pont, who joined Alfred Pritchard Sloan Jr at General Motors, who themselves were followed by later adherents.

Odiorne had moved Drucker to centre stage and wrote:

> Drucker was undoubtedly forced into paying attention to MbO as a natural product of decentralization by the response of his audience in lectures and books. For Drucker MbO was necessitated by the need for political changes in the corporation. His belief was that structural changes were necessary from within the organisation to enable them and the capitalist system to survive. (1978: 18)

While Odiorne recorded the impact of Drucker's ideas in *Concept* and *Practice* and the work on MbO by a school of competent contributors, he acknowledged that there were 'haters' of the concept, who were vociferous rather than large in numbers. Some were employees of businesses where MbO was incorrectly used as a threat where 'employment will be terminated by cause' unless performance targets were met. The malpracticers of MbO were 'the anti-planner [who] are a common type in both business and government'. His considered conclusion was that 'MbO is a philosophy that reacts to the remoteness of bureaucracy and isolation from the leadership of the corporation.' It was a response to what top management demanded and how people at work could meet the demands.

> It depends on human commitment self development and responsibility to produce results. It is based upon the creation of the future and forward planning rather than reacting to problems. It is about opportunities.
>
> MbO is based upon logic and is therefore easily proven to be job-related rather than related to caste, class, or personality. (Odiorne, 1978:24)

Odiorne further concluded that it helped resolve some chronic areas of management failure. It was a catalyst for correcting some of the long outstanding retarders to advancement by helping to determine performance, effectiveness, training, and rewards.

Greenwood's analysis of MbO was in his work 'Management by Objectives: As Developed by Peter Drucker, Assisted by Harold Smiddy' (1981).

For Drucker the setting of objectives was the real work of management which thirty years later had not yet been understood.

> For Sloan and Smiddy objectives were obvious; for Drucker they were anything but obvious. Drucker, found setting objectives to be the difficult, highly risk-taking aspect of the manager's job. Drucker built management as a discipline and managing as a practice around the high risk taking decisions on objectives—something few others understood. (Greenwood, 1981: 229)

The earlier systematic writers on management had focused on process, whereas for Drucker setting objectives was an intellectual exercise based upon conceptualism and analysis 'from which the process of management would flow' (William J. Greenwood/Ronald G. Greenwood, personal communication, 22 November 1979). In answer to the question, 'Did you know anybody who practiced MbO before you wrote about it?' Drucker replied, 'A good many people in earlier times managed by objectives as Sloan.(...) with probably Pierre du Pont, before him and—no doubt—Donaldson Brown.'

For Greenwood, 'Peter Drucker put objectives onto centre stage and made them the core of the structure of a discipline of managing. Many other managers probably "invented" and used an MbO concept before 1954, but it took Drucker to put it all together, [to] think through its underlying philosophy, and then explain and advocate it in a form others could use' (Greenwood, 1981: 230).

In a later reflection Greenwood was more definite about Drucker's contribution. 'Drucker did develop the concept there is no doubt about that.' 'MbO as it is understood today was conceptualized by Drucker and first put into practice by Harold Smiddy and his staff at GE' (Wren and Greenwood, 1998: 230–1).

Greenwood also cleared up a misunderstanding that Sloan was the first to use the term 'MbO'. Tarrant, in his book on Drucker, *Drucker: The Man who Invented the Corporate Society* (1976), quoted Drucker as saying, 'I didn't invent the term 'management by objectives' actually, Alfred Sloan used it in the 1950s' (Tarrant, 1976). 'Tarrant now says that he misconstrued what Drucker said about Sloan using objectives as a key to his management style to mean he used the term; in fact Sloan used neither the term nor the MbO philosophy' (Greenwood, 1981: 226).

Following on from Odiorne and Greenwood, for Drucker objectives had to be decided upon longer-term predictions, which are always difficult. Predictions of between five to fifteen years in the future are always going to be 'guesses'—a gamble or a 'hunch'. This was Sloan's philosophy. However, what business needed was not a 'business forecast' in the usual sense but some better tools that would enable the business to continue without the fear of unpredictable business cycles neutralizing their thinking.

Drucker provided three useful tools:

1. Test the assumptions against the sharpest set-back that our experience could lead us to expect;
2. Use Bedrock Analysis, which is based upon events that have already happened and tries to find 'the why' of future events. However, nothing was inevitable, and Bedrock Analysis should not be used on its own (1954: 89–91). This saw the start of Drucker's use of demographics, being included in the analysis;

As well as being used with:

3. Trend Analysis to limit risks. Trend Analysis attempted to analyse 'how likely' or 'how fast'. Drucker also referred to a new set of decision-making tools as 'Operations Research', which he identified as important. For Drucker, this was not as new as most managers thought, as the tool was used by the 'medieval symbolical logicians such as St Bonaventure'.

Drucker continued by saying that now these new tools had been brought into everybody's reach, and despite the fact that mathematical information theory was in its infancy, they would potentially enable the identification of deviations and action patterns (Drucker, 1954: 360–1). On the decision-making process Drucker refers to his own wide ranging advice on the difficulties of making decisions. He describes the process of requiring an integrated approach that can never be achieved by a *single* objective. It was a rational activity based on 'definite assumptions' and 'calculated assumptions' in his article 'Management Science and the Manager' (1955b: 119).

Drucker stated that once the executive team had determined the objectives of the business these could then be set in all of the identified key functions. What was also important was how these decisions were made, to enable the business to obtain the desired results for five to fifteen years hence. Drucker suggested a further three methods to be used in order to make the primary decisions: namely, Activity Analysis, Decision Analysis, and Relation Analysis. By using these methods the business can be analysed and the question of 'What is our business' and 'What should it be' could be answered in a practical manner. Only then could the structure of an organization be determined. This was Drucker's idea, that structure must follow the business not the business following the structure, as the latter was a flawed strategy (Drucker, 1955a: 190–8), and predated Alfred Chandler Jr, who is generally acknowledged as the originator of this idea (see Chandler, 1962).

While others had practised MbO prior to Drucker, he combined these ideas and identified the flaws in the previous methods of setting objectives and created something new which made it possible for MbO to be applied as a discipline. In this respect Drucker had a substantial role in originating MbO, not just in coining the name, but it was Drucker's 'total integration' that made it different.

'Total integration' practised in successful enterprises, was self-evident, otherwise they would fail to survive. This is illustrated by the fact that concentration of manufacturing, which produces large inventories without sales and payments, would mean that the enterprise would run out of cash and would be unable to pay its bills. The outcome was insolvency and resulted in failure. Although Drucker wrote that previously, Harry Hopf saw the need for integration and Lyndall Urwick expressed it; however, Urwick never pressed home his initial emphasis. It was Drucker that made it a central necessity followed closely by Smiddy in his 1955 essay, 'Integration and Motivating for Effective Performance'. Drucker's clear message in *Practice* was a that MbO was total integration of all the functions of an enterprise that were not set in a static pattern, as the order and emphasis would change over time.

With MbO, Drucker now had a workable system of management, 'a philosophy'. In *Concept* he had identified decentralization as the structure of the enterprise and its method. In *Society* he then refined and honed his ideas on decentralization and with *Practice*, for the large corporation or enterprise, he had identified a complete management system. However, he also foresaw when decentralization would not always be the appropriate structure for all businesses, as he perceived that more responsive hybrid forms of structure were yet to emerge. Even so, MbO in these new structures would still be considered an appropriate method of management.

Other reactions from America to MbO are the responses of a cross-section of academics, management writers, and practising businessmen. The following four PhD theses are such examples:

A. Faramarz Nazerzadeh (1979), Claremont Graduate School: 'Central Theses in Peter F. Drucker's contribution to the Study of Administration'.

An interesting coincidence is that this submission was made to Claremont, where Drucker was the Professor of Management. The thesis covers the ideas in his work, books, papers, and articles up to 1976. For Nazerzadeh, Drucker's approach was holistic as he worked towards a unified theory of business enterprise based on Theory 'Y' with an emphasis on entrepreneurship and objectives, all dependent upon a market-oriented society. With a total emphasis on integrating MbO, despite its critics, there was 'no end in sight', a conclusion that was apparent from the abundant literary support.

B. Robert Louis Olcese (1980), University of Loyala: 'An Analysis of the Application of Management by Objectives in Selected School Systems of Cook County, Illinois. Based upon Six Principles Established by Peter Drucker for the Management of Service Institutions for Performance'.

This thesis differed from Nazerzadeh's as it sets out to establish Drucker's applicability to extending the knowledge of management and its practised contribution in live situations. It did not question Drucker's utility but applied it, using the teaching of MbO to determine management teaching performance of twelve school districts in Cook County, Illinois.

C. Joseph Gardner Ormsby (1980), The University of Arkansas: 'Management by Objectives: Management's Perception of Organisation Objectives'.

This thesis was in response to the criticism of MbO during the last twenty-five years and was intended to test the validity of these accusations. It concluded that MbO was not a failed philosophy in itself, but that it did fail in practice where the objectives remained at the top of an organization and were not communicated down to middle management and the workers, although Drucker's protests about lack of communications were not noted.

D. Sandford Apfelroth (1983), School of Education, Health, Nursing and Arts Professions, New York University: 'Peter F Drucker's Contribution to Management Education: An Analysis of Selected Introductory College Management Text Books'.

This research analysed seventy-four colleges to test the influence of Drucker's ideas on the teaching of management. It confirms his considerable impact and correctly concluded that his target audience was the active practitioner and that in effect Drucker was providing insights and tools, which would not be used until the manager has gained some practical experience.

Of the four theses, Olcese and Apfelroth's analysis of the application of MbO were in the public sector in general, and in education in particular. The involvement of MbO's use in the public sector is an extension of MbO's utilization outside that of a free market enterprise.

Henry L. Tosi and Stephen J. Carroll (1968) reported that interest in MbO had been growing since 1954, but their results were patchy. For them, communication of the progress of the objectives must be maintained, and the failure to communicate this progress is the common cause for why MbO would not achieve its potential. Tosi and Carroll continued that they were optimistic about MbO and summarized that a 'constant review is needed to ensure that the programme fills a legitimate need in the organisation, a need which operation managers sense exists. The objective approach cannot be sold in books, meetings or theory. It can only be sold in practice' (1968: 426).

This optimism is supported later by Wren and Greenwood:

Management by Objectives and Self-Control.
Most fads die a quick death after much fanfare. Management by Objectives (MbO) was a fad in the 1960s, though it developed a number of problems, mainly because the concept was improperly used. Today the concept is even more popular, but with far less fanfare—perhaps the secret to its current success. (Wren and Greenwood, 1998: 230)

James Hoopes' later contribution accurately epitomizes the social aim of MbO in a manner that was a model for a mission statement:

To liberate employees from the workplace's new psychological tyranny, Drucker proposed 'Management by Objectives'. By articulating goals based on 'the objective requirements of the enterprise,' managers enable subordinates to work with autonomy and 'self-control' rather than as irrational neurotics manipulated from above False Prophets. (Hoopes, 2003: 253)

Of the practitioners, two of America's most successful businesses confirm the applicability of MbO. First Andrew Groves, the founder of Intel writes:

> The idea behind MbO is extremely simple. But the MbO system cannot be run mechanically by a computer. The system requires judgment and common sense to set the hierarchy of objectives and the key results that support them. Both judgment and common sense are also required when using MbO to guide you in your work from one day to the next. (Groves, 1983: 103, 106)

In explaining the applicability of Drucker's MbO to the management of the enterprise, Groves used the organization of Christopher Columbus' voyage of discovery of the New World as a case study (1983: 104). He reflects his day's work related to Drucker's demand for responsibility by managers. In his own case Groves said that he deals with things in a random pattern much as his wife as a housewife, depicting that where day ends is when she is tired. 'Like a housewife's, a manager's work is never done. There is always more to be done, more that should be done, always more than can be done' (Groves, 1983: 104).

Jack Welch, former CEO of GE (which alternated with Microsoft as the world's most valuable) was quoted as being influenced by Drucker: 'I began reading Peter's work in the late 1970s' as he prepared for his 'transition to CEO', where he inherited GE's adaptation of MbO that had been integrated into GE's management method by Drucker and the team in the early 1950s. Welch continued: 'If there was ever a genuine management sage, it is Peter. He always dropped a few unique management pearls into his many management books' (Welch and Byrne, 2001: 108). The evidence of what the team left for Welch is referenced previously, but is best summarized by Greenwood from this unpublished 1952 draft of *Professional Management in General Electric Book III*, are interesting because they portray MbO and the self-control side of that concept—the most overlooked aspect of the Drucker philosophy.'

> Dynamic Management Organisation explains: Effective control of every Operating Component depends on the establishment of definite goals in terms of specific dates and figures for the measurement of performances, as a stimulus toward complete achievement of stated objectives. This is a simple requirement for a manager to set objectives, time periods, costs, and standards against which to be measured.

It was during this period that Drucker wrote *The Practice of Management*, including the now classic chapter 'Management by Objectives and Self-Control'. Drucker comments:

> I wrote the draft of Practice of Management, and especially of the parts that deal with objectives and with the manager's work in 1951/52.(…) when I finished the first draft of that book.(…) [it] was finished at Cape Cod in the summer of 1953. (Greenwood, 1981)

Conclusion of American Use

The foregoing has illustrated the acceptance of MbO as a working philosophy in business initially, and then in the public sector. The evidence is that the academics whose work has been to sustain and give understanding to the intention of MbO made the ideas more explicit for the American market. That MbO is still used by two of the world's most successful businesses, GE and Intel, whose methods are embedded in the management of much of corporate America, is testament to the applicability and longevity of Drucker's work.

UK View

MbO was not a slogan or a 'magic wand' that, when waved, would sort out management problems. It was seen as an all-embracing philosophy that covered all and every aspect of management. For MbO to succeed it needed two basic actions. The first was a considerable effort to understand what MbO was about. Initially this was an intellectual challenge that required study and thought rather than 'picking it up' through casual reading. The second was the continual communication, negotiation, and team care in order to prevent *fade away*.

The initial evidence was that for most British managers, although they needed MbO, the demands of the necessary changes were too great. Most top management could not or would not clear the first essential obstacle of commitment and continual evolvement from the CEO and their team. Rather than make the commitment, the British lacked detailed application due to the common feeling was that 'it won't work, [as] it wasn't invented here'.

Even while Tosi and Carroll (in Appleby, 1991) stated that 'Research has shown that participation of employees will lead to "greater employee acceptance of performance goals and managerial decisions" and improvements in communications and understanding, among managers and their subordinates', Appleby highlights that there are both disadvantages and advantages to MbO. First, the disadvantages were that MbO was seen as a catalogue of what should not be done if it were to succeed within a firm. As such, there was a British reluctance to change in general, and for management to change in particular. The outcome was that for the British, MbO was a problem, rather than an opportunity. Appleby concluded, 'MbO is not yet practiced on a very large scale although it has been widely talked and written about. Larger companies, as may be expected, use it to a greater extent than smaller companies' (1968: 350). He also writes that 'less than 10 per cent of firms in a recent survey regard its effectiveness and its effect as "very successful". Some applications, though, have been successful' (1968: 92). However, no further details were given of the survey, thus preventing verification.

A further academic view of the British interpretation of MbO came from Tennant and Roberts of the Warwick Manufacturing Group, University of Warwick, who have written about why MbO failed in its original form in Japan. They stated that MbO was based upon 'the short term', 'top-down', 'trouble-shooting', 'targets', 'incentives', 'job evaluation', 'failure', and 'tending to focus on profit', which was incorrect. In their five papers, which were considered later, they only reference Drucker twice and incorrectly reported that his MbO was launched in his *Managing for Results* (Drucker, 1964). The British work at Urwick, Orr and Partners by Humble and his colleagues was not mentioned although Kaplan and Norton's book *The Balanced Scorecard* (1996) is correctly included as an extrapolation of MbO.

In an extensive paper entitled 'Urwick, Orr & Partners: Management by Objectives: A Case Study. The Origin, Evolution and Gestation of Management Consultancy within Britain, in the 20th Century' (1996), Michael Ferguson studied the archives of Urwick, Orr and Partners, who were the premier British Management Consultants for fifty years from the mid-1930s. His objective was to identify their commitment and success in making MbO work from their British base. He confirmed the effort and application, and in his summation found that although it was applied to their client organizations from 1963 until 1984, it was too expensive to introduce and was therefore resisted by many top management teams. By 1984, MbO had become out of fashion. However, Ferguson's paper did describe that the Urwick, Orr and Partners' British version of MbO did align with Drucker's ideas and that MbO had been successful for them for over three decades. This contradicts McDonald's view, of Cranfield School, Milton Keynes, that the life cycle of a management 'fad' from inception to being discredited was eleven to thirteen years (Kennedy, 2001: xvi–xvii); thus MbO was seen to be something more serious than a fad.

From the examination of Ferguson's paper the significance of Humble's work also became apparent. In the tradition of Urwick, Brech and Drucker I interviewed John Humble at his home on 28 April 2005 and again on 17 December 2009 to obtain first-hand knowledge. What became clear very quickly at the first interview was that Humble's relationship was unique as he was the only Briton who had worked extensively with Drucker since the early 1960s. Humble recalled, 'I was privileged to have Peter as my friend and mentor for over thirty years. We ran conferences and workshops in Europe and the USA and made films together.'

Following Humble's introduction to Drucker he wrote *A Dynamic Approach to Management by Objectives* (1965), which was the first book on MbO by a British writer. This was the first in a series of books that Humble wrote during the 1960s–1970s, which included:

Management by Objectives in Action (Humble, 1970a);
Management by Objectives in Banking (Humble, 1970b);
The Effective Computer: A Management by Objectives Approach (Grindley and Humble, 1971);
Improving Business Results (Humble, 1967, paperback 1972);

How to Manage by Objectives (Humble, 1972);
Improving the Performance of the Experienced Manager (Humble, 1973b);
Social Responsibility Audit: A Management Tool for Survival (Humble, 1973a), and
The Responsible Multinational Enterprise (Humble, 1975).

These became the textbooks that enabled Drucker's concepts of MbO to be applied in detail to the workings of organizations in Britain. They were translated into seventeen languages, and were copied illicitly by the Russian Communist Government and their satellite countries.

For Humble, the ideas expressed in *Practice* were the most important management ideas of the last forty years. His job was to make Drucker's concepts work. Humble stressed that Drucker was the first to realize that as production caught up with demand following the vacuum of supply left after the Second World War, the only way for business to survive was when their customers had choices and would provide the service the customer wanted. Theodore Levitt, who became the Harvard Doyen of Marketing, supports this contention:

> Practice of Management introduced me to what is now called the marketing concept when I was a practicing economist but one who was badly dissatisfied with the confining rhetoric of the formal sophistries of PhD level economics. Drucker's view of economic effort—its character and purposes—liberated me from the frustrations of what classical economics failed to explain, Schumpeter being the nearest who rigorously suggested but did not conclude Levitt's The Living Legacy of Peter Drucker in Peter Drucker Contributions to Business Enterprise. (Bonaparte and Flaherty, 1970)

Humble also showed that Drucker used demographics to tell us who tomorrow's customers were; indeed, they had already been born.[1] He continued that Drucker highlighted the need for corporate values, social responsibility, and integrity within and outside organizations; however, Drucker emphasized that management was the *integration* of all of these activities.

Further, there was the conclusion drawn by some that MbO was a passing fad and would not work in Britain. This is not supported by the evidence. The cross-section of users who form the case studies in Humble's *Management by Objectives in Action* (1970a) confirm this. Those organizations that successfully used MbO included, in the public sector, the Ministry of Defence and the Transport Commission. In manufacturing,

---

[1] It is interesting that Humble mentions Drucker's use of demographics as a forecasting tool. In late 2002 I discussed with David Coleman (a longtime colleague on a social housing programme), Professor of Demography, Oxford University, that Drucker had used demography in one of his now least mentioned books *America's Next Twenty Years* (1955). Of Drucker's book Coleman wrote, 'It was extraordinarily prescient over measures concerning pensions and retirement and surely one of the few forecasts over 20 years, which have stood the test of time to any reasonable degree. Where it could not foresee is of course—migration, which thanks in part to legislation in 1965 took off in a most unexpected way in the US and now accounts for a high proportion of population and workforce growth' (David Coleman, email 6 January 2003).

industries included Colt Heating and Ventilation, Rolls Royce and Smith Industries. In the consumer industries, John Player and Imperial Tobacco, all of which experienced success. MbO became so successful for Urwick, Orr and Partners that at its peak, it produced one-third of the consultancy's revenues. The demand from managers to know about MbO was so great that Humble presented his internationally acclaimed six film series on MbO at the end of 1960s and early 1970s. The films were shown in major cities in Britain to packed houses. These were the first box office management films in Britain, and they were remade in five languages. Due to their overwhelming success, Humble made further films on the same topic, two being with Peter Drucker and two with Theodore (Ted) Levitt, and were presented by Humble during their showing in America and Europe.

In our interview, Humble recalled that the rewards for Urwick, Orr and Partners, where they originally termed MbO 'Improving Management Results', were not only from the British market. They had clients in most South American countries such as Venezuela, Argentina, Chile, Peru, and Brazil. The geographic spread also included Australia and New Zealand, South Africa, India, and most of free Europe. During one of Humble's trips, a Russian told him that they had unofficially copied his books and that they were the 'Training Manuals for Senior Engineers'. Poland followed the Russian example. He recalled that on 20 May 2005 'MbO was used in central and local government in the UK together with manufacturing and service businesses. It was also used, with appropriate variations, in religious and voluntary organisations.'[2]

Conclusions of UK Use

My conclusion is that MbO is not a passing fad. It is the basis for the contributions that must be made individually and collectively if organizations are to exist and succeed. I agree with John Humble's synopsis that the problem that academic researchers had was the absence of a response through 'internet searches' for references to MbO. This, however, does not prove that it has stopped. That it has not stopped cannot be proven from a laptop but instead by applying one of the oldest management lessons of 'walking the job' to find out what is happening in practising management; this is because people aren't told that they are MbO-ing, but it does not mean they are not. As Humble says, 'It became the way of life.'[3]

I also agree with Humble and his conclusion that it may be the most important aspect of this chapter. Simon London in an article, 'Why are the Fads Fading Away', records that sales of management books have fallen by 30% since the late 1990s. He bemoans the fact that there are neither new ideas nor fads making big impacts. To support this contention, Professor Evie Abrahamson of Columbia Business School is quoted, 'When one fad

---

[2] Interesting is the inclusion of central and local government, religious and volunteer organizations, shows that Drucker's 1954 intention as a 'business solution' had extended to include all organizations.

[3] Similarly to the previously referenced Operations Research, which Drucker contends is integrated into MbO.

fades it usually creates a void that gets filled with a lot of new ideas. Right now I'm not sure what comes next' (*Financial Times*, 12 June 2003). Drucker has offered an explanation for why the next big idea is elusive—'Management skills have advanced so far'—and the 'big' discoveries have been made (Interview: Pollack, *New York Times*, 14 November 1999; Flaherty, 1999: 113). Of Drucker's 'big' discoveries, MbO arrived over half a century ago and still works. Arguably, providing it is fully understood and applied in whole rather than in part, it is the most successful management foundation used in the UK.

Japanese View

As part of the US Government policy for the recovery of Japan, Post the Second World War, General MacArthur, the Supreme Commander of South-East Asia, invited the statistical analyst of Quality Management, William Edwards Deming, to visit Japan in 1947 to aid their individual recovery. By 1954 a second management advisor, Joseph Moses Juran, was also invited to give his ideas on Quality Management. The reports are that it needed Juran to explain to the Japanese how to apply Deming's theory in practice.

In the book *Peter F. Drucker: Critical Evaluation in Business and Management* (Wood and Wood, 2005) there is a collection of twenty-seven papers on Drucker. Seven are repeated from Bonaparte and Flaherty (1970) including 'Peter Drucker and Japanese Management' (Takamiya, 1970). Drucker's influences on Japanese management were first recorded in his visit to Japan in 1959. Takamiya's analysis was that Drucker had an impact on the changes in Japanese management post-Second World War, which at the time were difficult to pin-point in the Japanese context because 'tradition and innovation are thus inevitably linked as a process'. He concluded, 'Drucker has played an influential role in welding the links in the chain of progress of management in Japan' (1970: 263). That MbO had been amalgamated into *Hoshin Kanri*, which was a Japanese evolved process, places Takamiya's paper as a harbinger of things to come, and was further confirmation of Drucker's impact on Japanese management.

Tennant and Roberts (2000), of the Warwick Manufacturing Group, University of Warwick, claimed that the Japanese dropped MbO in the 1960s because it did not work as it was a 'top down' imposed system. Regrettably this is a misinterpretation; not only for the general development of MbO into *Hoshin Kanri* but also on the specific point of 'top down'. For Drucker, communications and agreements should be neither 'top down' nor 'bottom up', but 'multi directional', which are essential in all successful management practices, although the vocabulary may be different.

> If only for aesthetic reasons, I am not over-fond of the term 'Bottom-up Management' [New York: Harper & Brothers, 1949] coined by William B. Given, Jr., of the American Brake Shoe Company.
> It is not top-down or bottom-up. It has three dimensions: a relationship up from the lower to the higher manager; a relationship of every manager to the enterprise; and a relationship down from the higher to the lower manager.

Following an interview with Dr Roger Hargreaves (the long-serving principal British Director of Ricoh UK Products, Telford, Shropshire, 4 August 2004) I further disagreed with Tennant and Roberts' second contention that Japanese strategic decisions or objectives are bottom-up. Dr Hargreaves made it clear that the top management in Japan set the objectives for the business and need to do so: this is common practice in a free economy, if the enterprise is to survive. Once Japanese 'Top Management' has determined the objectives, the implementation of the detail to achieve these objectives is agreed incrementally, from the bottom upward through the structure of the organization. The objective of this process is to ensure that by the time it reaches the top of the structure, everyone is in agreement. This is compatible with Drucker's MbO and self-control concepts, and therefore is a Japanese cultural adaptation of MbO. What Tennant and Roberts recorded is important for what the Japanese did with MbO. They adapted it to their own management philosophy, 'Hoshin Kanri', which means 'pointing the direction of management'. *Hoshin Kanri* is described in:

> *Using Hoshin Kanri for Strategy Deployment* (Tennant and Roberts, 2000);
> *Hoshin Kanri: A Tool for Strategic Policy Deployment* (Tennant and Roberts, 2001a);
> *Hoshin Kanri: Implementing the Catchball Process* (Tennant and Roberts, 2001b);
> *Application of the Hoshin Kanri Methodology at the Higher Education Establishment in the UK* (Tennant and Roberts, 2003a), and
> *Managing Knowledge through Hoshin Kanri* (Tennant and Roberts, 2003b).

It is a description of the amalgamation of Juran's Total Quality Management and the Japanese adaptation of Drucker's MbO.

Conclusion of Japanese View

Credit is due to the Japanese for amalgamating the two best American management ideas of the second half of the twentieth century and to the authors for their identification.

There is evidence that the Japanese treated *Kaizen* similarly. Peter Drucker and Joseph Juran had both identified that IBM had been practising *Kaizen* before the Japanese in the mid-1930s is consequential. In *Practice* Drucker describes IBM as practising continual improvements (Drucker, 1954: 251–6), while three years earlier Juran, in an anonymous entry in his *Total Quality Management* (Juran et al., 1951: section 9) from IBM, details their Quality Control sheets showing *Kaizen* in practice.

It is recorded that *Kaizen* evolved in Japan in 1937, and was applied by the founding family of Toyoda (Toyota). The background shows that Toyoda's loom-making business was responding to the Japanese Government's request, that they make motor vehicles for the war effort. The incentive for Toyoda was to conserve scarce raw materials but not to save on labour.

In his 1986 book, *The Frontiers of Management*, I believe Drucker contradicted this when he wrote of Thomas Watson Snr:

> Fifty years ago or more he also invented and put into practice what in this country is now known, studied and imitated as Japanese management—needless to say, he did so without the slightest knowledge of Japan and without owing anything to the then-nonexistent Japanese practices. (Drucker, 1986: 276)

Drucker continued:

> Again and again I have been laughed at in Japan when I talk about Japan's management embodying Japanese values. "Don't you realize' my Japanese friends ask, 'that we are simply adapting what IBM has done all along?" (Drucker, 1986: 284)

The fact that the American Auto Industry ignored Juran's explicit message and those of Deming to their detriment is now history, as was their neglect of MbO as a total *integrated* philosophy which also contributed to their problems.

Of the attraction of MbO from a business owner's point of view, is that it requires all members of the organization to be self-responsible to perform effectively. Much is written about employers acting responsibly towards their employees. It is the expectation in a democracy that people should be treated well to uphold their dignity and democratic rights. Sometimes this becomes an over emphasis that eclipses the engagement within the organization where there should be equality in all directions not only from the promoter/owners to employees but also from the employed to the promoter/owners. As the promoter/owners/CEO, their responsibility is to meet the payroll every payday, and this requires that all team members contribute more than their net costs. For those responsible for the economic survival of the organization the danger from within are the sub-performers, who sub-perform at say 80% of required output and cancel out the efforts and contributions of the 110% plus performers. To put the situation simply, customers will not volunteer to pay the cost of 80% effort.

What was clear to Drucker in *Practice* was that for personal performance, communication had to be multi-directional to enable MbO to achieve its practical objective as 'It ensures performance by converting objective needs into personal goals. And this is genuine freedom, freedom under the law' (Drucker, 1954: 134).

Drucker is credited as the most famous proponent of MbO: 'In Japan, MbO did develop as Drucker and others had seen it, as an important component of Hoshin Kanri'. Drucker believed that MbO was a philosophy of management that could and must be added to and adjusted and has been borne out by its most successful practitioners such as Welch, Groves, and Humble. It was Sloan, Drucker's first management mentor, in his *My Years with General Motors* (1964: 443), who said: 'In describing the General Motors organisation I hope I have not left an impression that I think it is a finished product. No company ever stops changing.' For Drucker the process of management change is continuous because 'management theory' is 'an unfinished business always in need of constant repairs and rejuvenation' (Interview: Pollack, *New York Times*, 14 November 1999; Flaherty, 1999: 113).

More recently, MbO has come to life through the vehicle of *Hoshin Kanri* (Hutchins, 2008) and Witcher and colleagues at Norwich Business School University of East Anglia have explored the application of *Hoshin Kanri* at Hewlett-Packard and Japanese-owned British subsidiaries. Witcher and Butterworth (2000) see Kaplan and Norton's *Balanced Scorecard* as an extrapolation of MbO, and suggest that *Hoshin Kanri* is the amalgamation of Drucker's MbO and Self Control with Edwards Deming's Quality Management (QM), although they do not mention Joseph Juran.

However, Deming listed among his fourteen points to transform business in America and top management Japan to 'Eliminate management by objectives. Eliminate management by numbers, minimise goals. Substitute leadership.' This raised two issues: the first is that Deming is using the term 'management by objectives' pre-Drucker 1954 and more importantly it questions whether *Hoshin Kanri* is an amalgamation of MbO and Deming's QM.

Overall Summary

From the evidence presented, MbO has become a part of the way that we manage. It is similar to Taylor's Scientific Management, which started with 'A Piece Rate System' described over a century ago in 1895. If we look at Odiorne, then Arthur Moxham's use of MbO at du Pont, we see that they are as old as Taylor's Scientific Management. This does seem to support that neither Scientific Management nor MbO are fads if judged by Hugh McDonald's definition of the eleven to thirteen life span.

What is interesting is that Kaplan and Norton's Balanced Scorecard is an adjunct of MbO, while also a further developed management practice based on the Japanese-initiated *Hoshin Kanri*, which integrated Drucker's MbO and Juran's Total Quality Management.

Acknowledgements

I wish to record my thanks to editor Brian C. Jones.

References

Anonymous (21 March 2005). Rick Warren, founder of Saddlebach Church and author of *The Purpose-Driven Life Regularly sit at the feet of Peter Drucker*, Fortune, USA.

Apfelfroth, S. (1983). 'Peter F. Drucker's Contribution to Management Education: An Analysis of Selected Introductory College Management Text Books', PhD Thesis, New York University.

Appleby, R. (1968). *Modern Business Administration*. London: Pitman.

Bonaparte, T. H. and Flaherty, J. E. (1970). *Peter Drucker: Contributions to Business Enterprise*. New York: New York University Press.

Chandler Jr, A. D. (1962). *Strategy and Structure: Chapters in the History of the American Industrial Enterprise.* Boston, MA: MIT Press.
Dean, J. (1951). *Managerial Economics.* Englewood Cliffs, NJ: Prentice-Hall Inc.
Drucker, P. F. (1946). *Concept of the Corporation.* New York: The John Day Corporation.
Drucker, P. F. (1950). *The New Society.* London: William Heinemann.
Drucker, P. F. (1954). *The Practice of Management.* London: Heron Books Ltd.
Drucker, P. F. (1955a). *America's Next Twenty Years.* New York: Harper Brothers.
Drucker, P. F. (1955b). 'Management Science and the Manager'. *Management Science,* 1(1) (January).
Drucker, P. F. (1964). *Managing for Results.* London: William Heinemann.
Drucker, P. F. (1986). *The Frontiers of Management.* London: William Heinemann.
Ferguson, M. (21 September 1996). 'Urwick, Orr & Partners: Management by Objectives: A Case Study. The Origin, Evolution and Gestation of Management Consultancy within Britain, in the 20th Century'.
Flaherty (1999). 'Interview: Pollack.' *New York Times,* 14th November 1999.
Givens Jr, W. B. (1949). *Bottom-Up Management.* New York: Harper Brothers.
Greenwood, R. G. (1981). 'Management by Objectives: As Developed by Peter Drucker, Assisted by Harold Smiddy'. *Academy of Management Review,* 6(2): 225–30.
Grindley, K. and Humble, J. W. (1971). *The Effective Computer: A Management by Objectives Approach.* London: McGraw-Hill Book Company (UK) Limited.
Groves, A. (1983). *High Output Management.* New York: Random House.
Halpern, D. and Osofsky, S. (1990). 'A Dissenting View of MbO'. *Public Personnel Management,* 19(3): 321–30.
Holden, P., Fish, L., and Smith, H. (1941–1951). *Top-Management Organisations and Control.* New York: McGraw-Hill.
Hoopes, J. (2003). *False Prophets: The Gurus Who Created Modern Management and Why Their Ideas Are Bad for Business Today.* Cambridge, MA: Perseus.
Humble, J. W. (1965). *A Dynamic Approach to Management by Objectives.* London: Management Publications Ltd, British Institute of Management.
Humble, J. W. (1967, paperback 1972). *Improving Business Results.* London: McGraw-Hill—Pan Books Ltd for Management Centre Europe.
Humble, J. W. (1970a). *Management by Objectives in Action.* London: McGraw-Hill.
Humble, J. W. (ed.) (1970b). *Management by Objectives in Banking.* London: Institute of Banks.
Humble, J. W. (1972). *How to Manage by Objectives.* New York: AMACOM.
Humble, J. W. (1973a). *Social Responsibility Audit: A Management Tool for Survival.* London: McGraw-Hill.
Humble, J. W. (ed.) (1973b). *Improving the Performance of the Experienced Manager.* London: McGraw-Hill.
Humble, J. W. (1974). *The Responsible Multinational Enterprise.* London: Foundation for Business Representatives.
Humble, J. W. (1976). *Social Responsibility: The Heart of Business.* Unilever Magazine.
Humble, J. W. (1992). Service *The New Competitive Edge: What Europe's Managers Really Think of the Service Ethics in their Organisations* (the research being repeated in Japan, America, Canada, Australia and Portugal) the European Headquarters of the American Management Association International Management Counsel in association with John Humble.
Hutchins, D. (2008) *Hoshin Kanri: The Strategic Approach to Continuous Improvement.* Aldershot: Gower Publishing Company.

Juran, J. (et al.) (1951 [1962]). *Quality Control Handbook*. McGraw-Hill.
Kaplan, R. S. and Norton, D. P. (1996). *The Balanced Scorecard: Translating Strategy into Action*. Boston, MA: Harvard Business School Press.
Kennedy, C. (2001). *The Next Big Idea*. London: Random House Business Books.
Knauth, O. (1948). *Managerial Enterprise*. New York: W. W. Norton.
Levitt, T. (1970). 'The Living Legacy of Peter Drucker', in T. H. Bonaparte and J. E. Flaherty, *Peter Drucker Contributions to Business Enterprise*. New York: New York University Press, 8.
London, S. (2003). 'Why Are the Fads Fading Away?'. *Financial Times* (12 June).
Micklethwaite, J. and Wooldridge, A. (2009). *God Is Back*. London: Allen Lane Penguin Group.
Nazerzedeh, F. (1970). 'Central Theses in Peter F. Drucker's Contribution to the Study of Administration', Claremont Graduate School, Claremont California.
O'Donnell, C. (1952). 'Review of Top-Management Organization and Control by Paul E. Holden, Lounsbury S. Fish, Hubert L. Smith', *The Journal of Marketing*, 16(4): 487–89. Available at: http://www.jstor.org/stable/1246997.
Odiorne, G. S. (1965). *Management by Objectives: A System of Managerial Leadership* London: Pitman Publishing.
Odiorne, G. S. (1978). 'MBO: A Backward Glance'. *Business Horizons*, 21(5): 14–24.
Olcese, R. (1980). 'An Analysis of the Adoption of Management by Objectives in Selected School Systems of Cork County Illinois. Based upon Six Principles Established by Peter Drucker for the Management of Service Industries for Performance', University of Loyola, University of Chicago.
Ormsby, J. G. (1980). 'Management by Objectives: Management's Perception of Organisation Objectives', University of Arkansas.
Pollock (1999). 'Management Skills Have Advanced so Far', *New York Times* (14 November).
Sloan, A. Jr, J. McDonald, and C. Stevens (1964). *My Years with General Motors*. New York: Doubleday & Company Inc.
Smiddy, H. (1955/1979). 'Integration and Motivating for Effective Performance', in M. Zimet and R. G. Greenwood (eds.), *The Evolving Science of Management*. New York: AMACOM.
Takamiya, S. (1970). 'Peter Drucker and Japanese Management', in T. H. Bonaparte and J. E. Flaherty (eds.), *Peter Drucker Contributions to Business Enterprise*. New York: New York University Press.
Tarrant, J. J. (1976). *Drucker: The Man who Invented the Corporate Society*. New York: Warner Books.
Tennant, C. and Roberts, P. (2000). 'Using Hoshin Kanri For Strategy Deployment'. *International Journal Manufacturing Technology and Management*, 2(1–7): 517–31.
Tennant, C. and Roberts, P. (2001a). *Hoshin Kanri: A Tool for Strategic Policy Deployment*. New York: John Wiley & Sons Ltd.
Tennant, C. and Roberts, P. (2001b). *Hoshin Kanri: Implementing the Catchball Process*. Elsevier Science Ltd.
Tennant, C. and Roberts, P. (2003a). 'Application of the Hoshin Kanri Methodology at a Higher Education Establishment in the UK'. *The TQM Magazine* 15(2), MCB UP Limited.
Tennant, C. and Roberts, P. (2003b). *Managing Knowledge through Hoshin Kanri Industry and Higher Education*. London: IP Publishing Ltd.
Tichy, N. M. and Sherman, S. (1993). *Control Your Destiny or Someone Else Will*. London: Harper Collins.
Tosi, H. L. and Carroll, S. J. (1968). 'Managerial Reaction to Management by Objectives'. *Academy of Management Journal*, 2 (4 December): 415–26.

Warren, R. (2005). 'Founder of Saddleback Church'. *Fortune* (21 March), USA.
Welch, J. and Byrne J. (2001). *Jack—What I've Learned Leading a Great Company and Great People*. London: Hendhouse Book Publishing.
Witcher, B. J. and Butterworth, R. (2000). 'Hoshin Kanri at Hewlett-Packard', *Journal of General Management*, 25(4): 70–85.
Wood, J. C. and Wood, M. C. (eds.) (2005). *Peter F. Drucker: Critical Evaluations in Business and Management*. London and New York: Routledge.
Wren, D. and Greenwood, R. G. (1998). *Management Innovators: The People and Ideas that Have Shaped Modern Business*. Oxford: Oxford University Press.
Zahra, S. (2003). 'Introduction: Peter F. Drucker's "The Practice of Management"', *Academy of Management Perspectives*, 17(3): 7–8. Available at: <http://www.jstor.org/stable/4165973>.

CHAPTER 6

STUDYING CULTURE IN ORGANIZATIONS

Not Taking for Granted the Taken-for-Granted

MATS ALVESSON, DAN KÄRREMAN, AND SIERK YBEMA

AT the beginning of the 1980s the publication of several key books and special issues of journals in the field of organization and management studies heralded the arrival of a new field known today as 'organizational culture'. For academics the concept of culture served as a vehicle to renew their interest in the symbolic dimensions of organizational life and processes of meaning-making in organizations (Yanow and Ybema, 2009). For practitioners, it provided the promise of a most welcome toolkit for creating commitment in times of economic recession. However, after more than a decade of being a dominant management fashion, slowly scholarly and managerial interest in 'culture' started to wane, diminishing culture to a standard chapter in organization theory (OT) and organization behaviour (OB) textbooks. Recently, however, some scholars claim to be witnessing a renaissance of interest in culture and culture management (Fine and Hallett, 2014; Weber and Dacin, 2011). Some claim that the characteristics of this 'second wave' of culture interest are different from the first in its attribution of agency to individuals and organizations and its increased attention to 'public culture' and outside appearances (Weber and Dacin, 2011: 287–8). Although we warmly welcome renewed interest and we see merit in analysing culture as strategically drawn on by organizational actors in their self-presentation to an outside audience, we also believe it is worth critically discussing this renewed interest by going back to the original inspiration for studying culture in organizations. We may lose some of culture's strengths as a root metaphor in the second wave's movement away from studying 'internalized taken-for-granted beliefs' and 'private culture'. Specifically, culture as a concept used to have the capacity to elicit interest in more implicit processes of meaning-making and covert power processes and backstage politics, as well as dedication to provide thickly described analyses of everyday organizational life.

In this chapter we first briefly revisit the earlier literature on organizational culture and culture management by offering a short historical overview. We then discuss the renewed interest in culture and compare its characteristics to the original interest. Nostalgically embracing the original ambitions of culture as a root metaphor then provides us with a viewpoint from which to critically assess the current interest in culture's offsprings in organizational research as well as a foundation for offering an alternative. We claim that the zeal for providing layered interpretation and thick description typical of the original approach deserves to be revitalized in contemporary accounts of, and approaches to, cultural life in organizing. The movement in academic interest in culture and culture management from substance to image, from taken-for-granted beliefs to branding, deserves critical scrutiny. Rather than scratching the surfaces of public culture and actors' strategies of self-presentation, we suggest that organizational research needs to focus on critically examining outward appearances, puncturing its myths by demasking its symbolic and staged qualities, and probing into the not-readily observable, the silent and silenced, backstage and off-stage worlds in the organizational dungeons, rekindling its fascination for what might be under the skin, beneath the surface, behind the scenes, and between the lines.

Organizational Culture: A Brief History

The Rise of Organizational Culture

There is a case to be made that the concept of culture and culture management entered organization studies via Japan. The stagnation of the US economy in the mid-1970s, the story goes, in combination with the unprecedented economic success of Japanese companies in the 1970s and 1980s fuelled an explosive interest in culture among practitioners and management scholars (Barley and Kunda, 1992; Handel, 2004; Parker, 2000). Japanese management was assumed to be built around a clever use of cultural factors. In this narrative, culture was thought to improve product and service quality, to increase worker loyalty and commitment, and to spur economic performance. 'Strong' cultures, the argument went, supported consensus across the organization, consistency between espoused values and actual behaviour, a committed workforce that could be governed flexibly, and clarity of strategic goals.

Companies were suddenly not only sites for the manufacturing of goods and services. They were home to a host of myths, rituals, and stories that demonstrated and reinforced the core values of the organization. Strong organizational cultures were not only at the heart of employee commitment and organizational efficiency. More importantly, influential scholars argued (e.g., Deal and Kennedy, 1982), strong cultures could be designed and manipulated. Given the right tools, management could infuse emotions and values beneficial to the organization into the workforce. In management theory and practice, 'culture' no longer referred to the occasional painting on the wall in the company's boardroom, but came to stand for organizational members' presumed values and persistent practices, as well as management's use of a 'soft' armantarium to change or control these.

Alongside the explosion in managerialist understandings of culture, organizational culture and symbolism also burst onto the academic scene of organizational studies in roughly the same period with the publication of several key books and special issues of journals (Barley, Meyer, and Gash, 1988). Rather than embracing culture as a tool of management, organizational scholars heralded culture as a new paradigm in organization studies. For them, the notion of culture constituted, not a 'variable' that could be measured and managed, but a 'root metaphor' for interpreting and analyzing organizations (Smircich, 1983). It served as a vehicle to renew their interest in processes of meaning-making in organizations and subjective dimensions of organizational life (Alvesson, 2013; Yanow and Ybema, 2011). Despite earlier symbol-sensitive studies of, for instance, bureaucracy in the 1950s and 1960s (e.g., Gouldner, 1954), culture was being proclaimed as a 'new' way of seeing and understanding organizations. Enabled by the concept of culture (Martin and Frost, 1996) the tired tropes of systems and structures could be replaced with the study of ideational and symbolic aspects. Influenced by anthropology and symbolic interactionism (Barley and Kunda, 1992), these scholars sought a paradigm for organizational analysis that allowed them to study values, meanings, symbolism, and emotions, topics that had thus far been largely neglected in organizational research.

The Fall of Organizational Culture

For a short period of time around the end of the 1980s, cultural perspectives almost dominated management research. This is hardly the case today. Whatever happened? A telling clue can be found in an article by Calas and Smircich from 1987. The title itself is revealing: 'Post-culture: Is the Organizational Culture Literature Dominant but Dead?' Organizational culture did not fully live up to its promise as a new, paradigm-shifting metaphor in the field of organizational studies, because, as Calas and Smirchich point out, the culture-as-variable view was the predominant approach to culture during this time, crowding out of the culture-as-root metaphor. Notwithstanding some solid new work, objectivist and managerial ways of thinking thus showed to be persistent and, in a critical sense, organizational culture as a new concept proved to be intellectually dead.

If not intellectually dead, managerial interest in culture was also bound to die. It was clear from relatively early on that cultures were difficult to control and design from a management point of view, which ultimately undermined the culture perspective's claim to be a practical tool for management. The fall of Japanese management styles further discredited this claim. While American business was perceived to be in crisis in the early 1980s and Japanese management was understood as the difference between American stagnation and Japanese success, by the end of the 1980s, the roles had been reversed. American business was experiencing a revival, centered on Silicon Valley, and Japanese business was starting to stagnate; a stagnation that to some extent was blamed on the Japanese management style and the rigidity of 'strong' corporate cultures.

However, the most important explanation, perhaps, is that it became clear that most organizations do not develop strong and distinctive cultures at all. On the contrary, most organizational cultures were perceived to be generic and derivative (Martin et al., 1983). Scholarly work showed that culture in organizations was not necessarily a force that knit things together, but as much a force that was dynamic and potentially disintegrating, as organizations were themselves destabilized through various changes not necessarily aligned with cultural patterns. Organizations were disrupted and downsized, and increasingly organized in more fluid patterns through outsourcing and offshoring.

This does not mean that organizations lack culture. It means that they are more like sites where different cultural elements, for example functional, occupational, national, and locally emerging cultures, intermingle. Culture researchers developed understandings that accounted for the fragmentation and fluidity by exploring, for example, cultural ambiguities (Young, 1989) and paradoxes (Ybema, 1996), and the occurrence of subcultures (Van Maanen and Barley, 1985) and countercultures (Martin and Siehl, 1983). Such work contributed to an increasing awareness among practitioners of cultural processes being complicated which, for them, took the shine of 'culture' as a potentially uniting force in organizations and as a promising tool of management. The variable view on culture, or the view that cultures could be designed and engineered, became much more complicated, turning culture into an impractical instrument, since management now needed to engage with several culture variables, and not just one, some of which were outside its control, for example educational, professional, industrial, and national cultures.

A Note of Caution: A Moderate Fall

Our narrative of organizational culture's presumed fall from grace should not be overinterpreted. Organizational culture as a central concept may have retired to a standard chapter in organization studies textbooks, its legacy, whether the academics' or the practitioners' version, has certainly not vanished from the scene. In management practice, culture management is still a central part of many organizations' agenda, albeit perhaps more implicitly. Values, understandings, beliefs, ideas, and meanings are key elements of what corporate management and leadership address. The great interest in transformational leadership concerns itself with the management of meaning and emphasizes the cultural dimension more than conventional management and leadership which focused on behaviours and outcomes and the exchange relationship, thus caring less about values, emotions, and other ideational elements. Many organizations actively cultivate the symbolic significance of shared meanings, a common history, a golden age, idiosyncratic founders and dramatic developments, which, they claim, make up a quite distinct organization with a unique or strongly guiding organizational culture. Often, the promotion of such a joint culture parallels, and aims to 'supplement' or bridge, internal variation.

Not only leadership practice is suffused with cultural themes. There is also continued interest in the role of culture in, for instance, international management and cross-cultural collaboration, as well as in processes of organizational change. Some focus on cultural change per se (Alvesson and Sveningsson, 2015), while others acknowledge that change includes a strong cultural element or that culture filters, obstructs, or revises the process (Canato, Ravasi, and Phillips, 2013). So, despite organizational culture having become much less the object of attention, inspiration and hope since the 1980s and probably having become addressed in much more realistic ways, it is still an important theme in organizational practice.

In a similar vein, the academic interest in organizational culture also started to live a more retired life behind the scenes, but only after it inspired the emergence of a variety of new perspectives. Organizational scholars open to an interpretivist approach and sensitive to meaning-making processes sailed off in different directions, no longer studying 'organizational culture', focusing instead on, for instance, storytelling and discourse, institutions and institutional work, individual and collective identities, control and resistance, practices of strategizing, cultural change, cross-cultural collaboration, sociomaterial dimensions of organizational life, leadership or sensemaking. Even though the rise and domination of approaches such as discourse, organizational identity, and institutional theory have squeezed out serious attention to organizational culture, these fields are to some extent endebted to (without explicitly building on) the 1980s and 1990s studies of organizational culture. This may be explained by changes in fashion and, perhaps, by an apparent preference for easier-to-observe, more surface-focused phenomena at the expense of interpreting meanings, symbolism, and taken-for-granted ideas associated with organizational culture studies (Alvesson and Kärreman, 2011; Alvesson and Robertson, 2016). In this sense post-culture orientations have been a move in the wrong direction.

Re-Turn of Organizational Culture?

Research into the cultural dimension has thus redirected attention away from studying organizational cultures per se and towards an interest in elements that are shaped by cultural processes. Throwing out a wide net (including, e.g., studies of 'institutions' and institutional work as studies of 'culture'), Weber and Dacin (2011) speak of a second wave of cultural analysis. This wave, they maintain, is characterized by a move away from the idea of stable and shared cultural elements that operated as constraints on organizational activity. Instead, the second wave emphasizes the idea that culture might be a resource, or a repository of resources, for action, rather than a constraint.

Relatedly, cultural analysis increasingly views cultural elements as constructs, as outcomes of construction processes, and not as givens, handed down over time by tradition. In this way culture has become more of a perspective on social reality, rather than the object of study. Key notions in the second wave of cultural analysis, according to Weber and Dacin (2011), are the cultural toolkit approach (Swidler, 1986; Harrison and Corley, 2011; Howard-Grenville et al., 2011; Kellogg, 2011; Leonardi, 2011; Rindova, Dalpiaz, and Ravasi, 2011) and organizational sensemaking (Weick, 1993, 1995). In the following sections, we want to sketch some of the central tenets of contemporary thinking about culture, building on Swidler's ideas, and explain how these ideas relate to the field of identity studies.

The Culture Toolkit and Identity Formation

Culture as Toolkit

Swidler's framework assumes that there are not only different cultures, but also different ways to mobilize and use culture. She introduces the metaphor of a 'toolkit', or 'repertoire' (Swidler, 1986), to describe culture. This helps her to debunk the idea that culture is simply a 'unified system that pushes action in a consistent direction' (Swidler, 1986: 277). Individuals are assumed to possess a repertoire of diverse cultural resources that can be either tacit cultural elements such as attitudes and styles or explicit cultural material such as rituals and beliefs (Swidler, 1986: 281). The toolkit represents the available cultural capabilities of a given person at a given time that can be used to construct strategies for actions. Culture is something that provides skills and capacities that can be exploited. People draw on their available set of cultural resources to put together, and shape, strategies of action when facing different types of situation. In short, the toolkit view understands culture as a way of engaging with and solving concrete and specific problems at hand.

As indicated above, Swidler suggest that this is accomplished through strategies of action. Strategies of action depend on culture because culture provides and sustains the strategies of action that are possible to pursue. Over time, individuals may learn new, or refine existing, skills and capabilities through the culture they inhabit. The use of a set of particular cultured capabilities, and not others, constitutes the repertoire of strategies of action available for use.

The toolkit view recognizes that although culture influence action, it may not do that in a static and predictable way. Swidler highlights two main models for how culture may frame action, settled lives, and unsettled lives. Within settled lives, cultural experiences reinforce, or refine, the skills, habits, and attitudes of one's repertoire at hand. Here actions and behaviours do not depend upon immediate cultural experiences. This means that strategies of action do not compete with alternative models of arranging life experiences. The 'undisputed authority of habit, normality and common sense' (Swidler, 1986) are the guiding forces behind people's behaviours. However, these forces do not provide commanding unique patterns or strategies of action by imposing cultured capabilities. They rather constrain action by providing a limited set of resources out of which individuals can construct strategies of action. As a consequence, when living the settled life people can live with major discrepancies and contradictions between what they claim, and how they act, as demonstrated by the sometimes striking differences between espoused values and values in use in organizational settings (Argyris and Schön, 1995).

In unsettled periods, the strain of finding appropriate templates for action through existing culture lacking moves people to develop more overt and elaborate templates for strategies of action. Here Swidler borrows a page from Geertz (1973) and labels these overt templates ideologies, who establishes new symbolic resources that facilitates the emergence of new strategies of actions. Ideology is a somewhat unfortunate choice of concept because of the many connotations attached. It has many uses and meanings in social science, with two dominant framings: a) it is used to refer to false beliefs covering up a dominant social order, and b) it is viewed more neutrally as a system of ideas and values (Hartley, 1983). Ideology also offers avenues for decontestation (Freeden, 2003)—making essentially contestable concepts less contentious. In this sense, ideology can be viewed as a device to cope with ambiguity and the indeterminacy of meaning. Ideology orders, patterns, and suppresses surplus meaning. Geertz (1973) distinguishes between an interest and a strain theory of ideology, where the interest theory uses the concept of ideology to explain a group's search for power, while the strain view considers ideology as a means to reduce stress and anxiety due to lack of cultural resources (see also Kunda, 1992). Swidler adheres to the strain theory of ideology.

Because of the strain of lacking sufficient and readily available cultural resources, people are moved to align their life experiences with their cultural understanding. Thus, cultural resources, in the shape of ideologies, have more visible influence over action than in settled lives. The culture becomes more visible and consistent with values in use because this type of period is characterized by the development of new strategies of action due to the fact that actors are actively using and making sense of the cultural experiences they are encountering. The ideologies actors embrace have a strong direct influence on them. They provide them with new symbolic resources that allow new strategies of action to compete with existing ones. People that find themselves in unsettled periods actively engage with their actions and behaviours to make them coherent with their beliefs.

Identity Work

Organizational identity and identity work in organizations are perhaps the most frequently studied cultural resources and processes in organizational analysis. Arguably, identity regulation is the most studied way of engaging in ideology in Swidler's sense: as a way of providing a template for strategies of action. Hence, research into organization culture has continued mostly due to an interest in how identities are shaped and played out in organizations, sometimes with explicit reference to organizational actors' active deployment of culture as a resource to establish, maintain, or alter an individual or collective identity (e.g., Ailon-Souday and Kunda, 2003; Ybema and Byun, 2011). Identity offers the possibility to continue probing the cultural dimension, but without having to assume that the organization is or has a culture.

Perhaps the most common way of understanding identity today is viewing it as a construction and as a performance that is constituted through linguistic acts and practices (Broms and Gahmberg, 1983; Turner, 1984; Butler, 1988; Giddens, 1991; Shotter, 1993; Alvesson, 1994; Somers, 1994; Dunne, 1996; Antaki and Widdicombe, 1998; Gioia, Schulz and Corley, 2000; Sveningsson and Alvesson, 2003; Collinson, 2003; Alvesson, Ashcraft, and Thomas, 2008; Ybema et al., 2009a)—or to be more specific, focusing on the social and interactive co-construction and performance of a shared identity within a work community. All interactions potentially have identity effects, but more specific processes regulate actual impact. In this sense, identities are developed, maintained, and reconfigured through accounts and interactions. They may take on the form of narration—a more or less coherent story—or the form of conversation—a more interactive, and potentially disruptive form for the production of accounts about one's self. Sometimes, narratives are salient in a conversation, sometimes the latter are less story-like. Life-events build into life-stories, build into identities—episode by episode—telling people who they are. Identities thus stem from people's attempts to construct selves that accord with present circumstances and previous life-stories. From this perspective, social identities are knitted together through the various accounts people tell about the events and circumstances of their lives—informing others as well as themselves about who they are and, perhaps, equally importantly, about who they want to be(come).

The notion of identity as a construction has the advantage of offering a way of understanding how people preserve their sense of self without losing their capacity to act as they believe necessary according to particular circumstances. The same identity material can thus be crafted into different life stories, and can have a different impact on people's social identity, depending on how it is related to other identity material. Since identity is an accomplishment, the way identity is accomplished is in itself an important question. In a sense, this means that the accomplishment—the identity produced—becomes less important to study. It is, rather, the ways and means people deploy in constructing their identities that becomes important. Such processes of identity work are not only more important but also more accessible to study than narratives as fixed texts or frozen states of subjectivity (identity as a set of traits).

Perhaps organizational actors' present preoccupation with identity can be understood as their way of dealing with the increasingly unsettled—in Swidler's sense—character of organizational life. Working life in contemporary organizations is frequently portrayed as unstable, ambiguous, and conflicted (Watson, 1994; Sennett, 1998). Workers as well as managers frequently encounter ethical problems, stress, a sense of lack of meaning, and feelings of insufficiencies (Jackall, 1988; Sennett, 1998; Thomas and Linstead,

2002)—experiences that are often laden with the perceived threat of the risk for and effects of down-sizing (Scarbrough and Burrell, 1996; Watson, 1994). They are also frequently affected by ambiguous and contradictory expectations and demand, and exposed to incoherent organizational discourses—for example, they are targets for discourses on strategic leadership, while simultaneously responsible for carrying out standard operations procedures, and administrative and sometimes non-managerial work (Alvesson and Sveningsson, 2003).

Culture Management and Identity Regulation

Organizations and organizational realities can be said to have become messier. They are more loosely structured, more difficult to control, and more prone to break down. As a result, alternate ways of exercising organizational control have emerged, including efforts that target occupational and organizational identities. Such attempts include corporate culture engineering, management seminars and feedback sessions, and other attempts to influence and regulate organizational members' identities and sense of self (Kunda, 1992; Alvesson and Willmott, 2002).

As in the field of organizational culture a large portion of management research into identity is motivated from an organizational control point of view. Management in general, and perhaps even more so in complex organizations, is partly about trying to control identity (Alvesson and Willmott, 2002). Identity becomes an anchoring point for management control and regulation. This is not the same thing as to claim that identity regulation and culture management always have impact. Most, if not all, empirical studies show how identity regulation and other forms of culture management can be complicated, creating unintended and complex social dynamics.

Kunda's (1992) inspirational study on how strong cultures or ideologies, in Kunda's vocabulary, may interfere with the development of a sense of self provides an instructive example. In Kunda's study, the intense efforts to streamline the organizational membership role, and the scripts to identify with the role, increased the levels of ambiguity in a workplace already rife with ambiguity. On balance, Kunda's study highlights the problem with high-intensity identity regulation through enforced ideology: on the one hand, this kind of identity regulation has some positive coordinating effects; on the other it also leads to cynical and opportunistic conduct that distorts and disrupts social relations. From a critical stance, it may undermine organizational members' capacity to craft selves that are not colonized or co-opted by organizational ideology.

Kunda's account is vivid and persuasive, but it is important to remember that most complex organizations do not engage in creating the kind of idiosyncratic and intense ideology at display in Kunda's study. Complex organizations are more likely to exploit collective identities already at hand, rather than create them wholesale. Or they might not engage in identity regulation at all. Kunda and Ailon-Souday (2005) argue that there was a shift away from culture management and normative control during the decades after the heydays of the 1980s and early 1990s. They claim that a new managerial model—market rationality—closely aligned with downsizing, outsourcing, and distributed work emerged in US industry and increasingly elsewhere during neo-liberalism's 'hegemonic' phase, which undermined the interest in culture management of the 1980s and 1990s. Kunda and Ailon-Souday don't mince words: 'market rationalists seem to have little patience for culture, no matter how strong' (2005: 203).

Kunda and Ailon-Souday have a point, but the turn towards market-rationalism is perhaps better understood as a force that unsettles organizations and organizing, in Swidler's sense, as argued above, than as a wholesale repudiation of culture management, normative control, and identity regulation. Indeed, market ratonalism itself could be seen as a form of identity regulation as it sets forth an implicit identity template— that of the entrepreneur. The continued interest in identity in organizational analysis and the recent renaissance in the interest of cultural analysis and forms of culture management supports this interpretation. For example, recent research has revealed how branding initiatives can be used to stabilize and maintain a particular organizational identity that has become unsettled though corporate growth and expansion (Kärreman and Rylander, 2008) and how elite claims (Alvesson and Robertson, 2006; Thornborrow and Brown, 2009), human resources management (HRM) practices (Alvesson and Kärreman, 2007) and CSR initiatives (Costas and Kärreman, 2013) can be mobilized for identity regulation.

A Return to Culture Management?

More support for continued managerial interest in (new forms of) culture management and identity regulation can be found in the emergence of more critical studies. Fleming and Sturdy (2009) introduce the concept of neo-normative control. This type of culture management draws on the observation that corporations today are more likely to mobilize identity aspects already expressed by individuals, rather than to mould them wholesale for organization members, as suggested by normative control. In this sense, neo-normative control is about co-opting identities already in play, and to encourage organizational members to align their 'authentic' selves to corporate realities: 'neo-normative control aims to enhance the enjoyment of the job via the freedom of identity and emotional expression surrounding the work performance rather than through it' (Fleming and Sturdy, 2009: 572).

Land and Taylor (2010) provide a vivid example of how neo-normative control may operate. Drawing on a case of a boutique brand for clothing associated with outdoor sports, they show how employee lifestyle is mobilized to articulate and specify the brand. Employees, who are all expected to embrace and participate in outdoor sports, are offered vouchers for 'Too Nice to Work Day' which can be used to take a day off—although, as Land and Taylor point out, the subtext is that it is expected that the experience is shared on the company blog and in promotion materials. Narratives and anecdotes from employee's own active lifestyle, retold from their own experiences of canoeing or surfing, are extensively used in promotion materials. To prove the edge of the brand, the firm, for example, playfully charts one employee's sick leave days and correlates it with height of surf in one catalogue feature, on one hand emphasizing that life is more important than work, on the other hand using life as an example of what work is about at the firm, implying that life is work and vice versa. Although the company comes off as alternative and accommodating to employees' needs and wants, Land and Taylor show that this is a two-way street, where the employees' lifestyles are mined for providing brand meaning and value. In this sense, 'branding functions as a form of identity management that extends beyond the workplace to govern the performance of labour—understood as value productive activity—in work and life (Land and Taylor, 2010: 408).

Fleming (2014) and Cederström and Fleming (2012) push the idea of neo-normative control in even bleaker directions. Cederström and Fleming speak about the boss-function, which explains how decentralized and flexible work schemes, with 'flat' hierarchies and no formal supervisor, are nonetheless directed and governed by managerialist preconceptions: 'hierarchies of regulation have been horizontalized. Most of us still have a boss above us giving orders. But we have also partially internalized this "boss function". Whereas under Fordism workers could mentally tell the boss to "fuck off" as they left the factory, now they take it home with them. Turning-off is no longer an available option' (Cederström and Fleming, 2012: 13).

Fleming (2014) fleshes out the development towards co-opting the life, rather than the behaviour or the norms, of the organization member by drawing on the notion of biocracy. Under biocracy, the members' subjectivity, non-work activities, private time, and unpaid labour is put to work. The members' subjectivity is put to work by recruiting and selecting individuals that volunteer to sub-ordinate themselves to the corporate logic. This can be observed, for example, in how management consultancy firms and law firms explicitly tell recruitment prospects that they are expected to work very long hours as junior consultants and associates, and only hire individuals that willingly accept this condition; and in how these firms exploit the socialization provided by higher education to facilitate coordination and control. Non-work activities are co-opted according to the logic described in the Land and Taylor (2010) vignette above. Private time is put to work through more and less systematic blurring of the lines between work and life, often pushed through well-intended work schemes such as telecommuting and flex-time, which shifts the responsibility to do the blurring to the individuals themselves. Unpaid labour, finally, has made its mark in the increasingly commercialized use of crowd-sourcing, open software, and social media. Here work is harvested through enabling users, consumers, and hobbyists to provide 'content', develop code, and produce data points that are monetized by commercial behemoths such as Facebook, Google, Amazon, and Apple, to only mention a few.

Neo-normative control, the boss function, and biocracy are useful additions to the organization analysis toolbox, but they clearly build and extend rather than substitute for more established understandings of culture management. Fleming and Sturdy

(2009) are explicit about this and claim that neo-normative control is more of an extension of normative control than a replacement. They also emphasize that neo-normative control is likely to operate in hybrid arrangements that interface and align to other complementary forms of control (see Gabriel, 2005; Kärreman and Alvesson, 2004).

Grandiosity and Organizational Cultures

A standard tool in the culture management toolkit tends to be the inclination to boost the organization's reputation and to polish up its outward appearance to make it look good to an outside world of clients, competitors, controllers, and so on, as well as to create a strong 'brand' for employees' orientation and identification. Again, we see organizational culture then being used as a symbolic resource for managers, communicators, and marketeers to make claims of being unique, excellent, and superior. Modern society, business, and organizations are characterized by grandiose self-personifications and claims on a large scale (Alvesson, 2013). One could argue that we live an organizational 'mega-culture' of grandiosity. There is a strong desire to be labelled in the most attractive and pretentious terms. This applies to individuals, occupations, organizations, and various elites. A problem is that the struggle for the most coveted sugar plums—high professional status, conspicuous consumption, 'world-class education', 'excellence', and so on—involves a zero-sum contest. This means that a benefit for a specific individual or group is gained at the expense of another. Not everybody can be excellent or afford high-status goods or get a degree from a high-status university or be the leader in a field. Superiority calls for inferiority, so the competiton to be above others is fierce. Grandiose projects occupy an ever-increasing proportion of the time, commitments, and resources of various elite groups, such as politicians, media people, corporate executives, union leaders, and other representatives of organizations and professional groups. But also the lives of common people increasingly circle around grandiosity. There is a strong emphasis on illusionary tricks to back this up: CV improvement, title and grade inflation, organizations exhibiting impressive window-dressing through policy formulation and executive development programmes, and occupations re-launched as professions (Alvesson, 2013).

Grandiosity means attempts to give yourself, your occupational group/organization, or even the society in which you live a positive—if somewhat superficial—well-polished and status-enhancing image. As much as possible is fused with positive labels and meanings. Many organizational elements are targeted for symbolic upgrading. They are made remarkable and impressive, adding to status and self-esteem. Issues of substance (practices or tangible results) are marginalized. Representations that privilege sounding good are preferred to possibly more precise and insightful descriptions.

In other words, grandiosity does not necessarily mean delusions of grandeur or something that is obviously mad. It does not primarily illuminate the obsession of chief executive officers (CEOs) and other business people suffering from hybris, active in the construction of monuments to commemorate themselves, or in the recognition of the value of major achievements, such as the Nobel Prize or Olympic championships or impressive corporate achievements. Contemporary grandiosity—at least in open, relatively equality-oriented societies and organizations—is socially controlled, semi-realistic, and confined to loading an increasing number of phenomena with strongly positive, exaggerated meaning that generate attractiveness, success, and distance from the paltriness and mediocrity of everyday life. Grandiosity is being democratized. Everybody wants it and feels entitled to it. It is typically camouflaged and represented as a favourable, but not obviously misleading representation of a phenomenon. Grandiosity gilds the lily by lending a golden haze to various phenomena. Since this involves considerable doctoring of a world that is not always beautiful, it also involves the application of smokescreens. Grandiosity is linked with an increasingly widespread 'narcissism' and a desire to enhance self-esteem. We want to be in the public eye, confirmed, associated with something prestigious, and to distance ourselves from what is trivial. The desire to be fascinating is not just an individual, but also very much a collective phenomenon, characterizing contemporary cultural meanings in organizations. It applies to various institutions and groups that acquire labels to provide a boost in terms of meaning, sophistication, and status. Let us give some examples of this phenomenon.

Most Western (and some other) societies have rapidly moved from being seen as industry- and service-oriented to one of information (during the 1970s) and, in the absence of more rapid upgrading, have wound up being identified as 'knowledge' societies. A similar, perhaps even more grandiose idea is the one of the rise and domination of 'the creative class' and 'the creative economy' (Florida, 2001). All this sounds great and is very popular to communicate. Thompson et al. (2000: 122) write: 'Policy-makers and academics alike (…) endlessly repeat the mantra that knowledge work offers a rationale for the development of capital in the workplace, a blueprint for the creation of "world class" firms, and a way of preventing advanced economies restructuring away their sunset industries from becoming peripheral low-wage, low skill national economies.'

In working life, bureaucracy and mass production have had to make way for so-called knowledge-intensive companies, dynamic networks, and flexible, customer-steered operations. And people are employed for 'value creation processes' rather than for the production of goods and services. Managers and supervisors are increasingly labelled as 'leaders'. Strategic visions and empowerment have pushed aside organizational management of a more conventional, more boring, nature. In the universities a sluggish collegial spirit has been surplanted by academic leadership. Organizations are supposed to work with creativity, competence, and innovation, not mainly hard work, reliability, and product modification. Personnel administration has been replaced by HRM and 'talent management'. More and more work is supposed to be 'strategic': HRM, communication, marketing, branding, purchasing, and so on. Many studies on strategy in practice seem to be upbeated versions of managerial work (Blom and Alvesson, 2015).

There is considerable inflation of job titles: more and more people have become 'managers' and 'executives', and it is not particularly exclusive to have 'vice president' on your business card these days.

And this is not exclusive to individual titles. Groups have become teams, and when senior managers meet they become 'executive teams'. Rationalization is now termed 'business process engineering'. Plans have become 'strategies'. Management training now takes the form of 'executive development programmes'. Giving advice is referred to as 'coaching', which has become a booming industry, supposedly helping a world in increasing need of expert advice. Expressions like 'world class' and 'excellence' are increasingly used, often without much back-up in terms of demonstrated qualities or accomplishments.

Institutional theory claims that most organizations nonetheless adopt such ideas and recipes, at least at the formal structural level. They introduce, for example, techniques, practices, and structures, establish new departments, initiate projects, and programmes and employ certain terms. Such actions are implemented not because they have a proven positive effect on operations but in order to reduce cognitive uncertainty and/or to establish legitimacy. People might, for example, be uncertain about what should be done. Is it essential to have a budget? Would quality circles lead to improvements? Is it a good idea to employ consultants? Would gender equality perhaps result in better managerial recruitment? It is not easy to disperse uncertainty. In the absence of self-confidence, time to think, and critical reflection, people tend to imitate others.

One advantage of doing what others do is that you gain legitimacy. If you do not have a gender equality policy, a training programme for 'leaders', strategic plans and visions, you may on the contrary appear to be out-of-date, irresponsible, sloppy, or unprofessional in some other respect. As a result, in order to avoid this and give the impression you are rational, ethical, up to date, or simply like everyone else, you adopt various well-established and new ideas and recipes, even though it is difficult to demonstrate any gains in efficiency or any other substantial advantages. All these tend increasingly to be not just about adaptation to myths/external expectations or being as everyone else, but often lead to strong claims of scoring high in terms of appearing impressive and ahead of everybody else. Legitimacy is then being supplemented and often replaced by grandiosity. Visions, values, and branding aim to signal superiority; cultural meanings are geared to back up these.

As we have seen, an exaggerated interest in change—or at least the initiation of more or less well-considered projects—is closely linked to a high degree of sensitivity for what people think others are doing. Appearing dynamic and progressive in a fantastic world, full of turbulence and pressure to be adaptive and on top of things. As there are frequent mass media reports about the strong need for change and organizations are often engaged in various change activities, it is vital to keep up—both with the general norm and with the signalled moves of others. The risk of deviating and, in particular, falling behind is a major motive force. A key factor here is the surface—what seems to be visible from a distance and without much deeper knowledge—in an organizational and management context. This chapter focuses on the links between these aspects, in which imitations and fashions have a particularly high impact at the shop-window level (i.e., the illusion level), and where an increasing emphasis on the shop-window factor encourages imitations and fashion-following behaviour.

Isomorphism largely takes place at a superficial level, even though it can go deeper. Plans and models that attract the attention of managers can often be interpreted and applied in different ways. Hence organizations with similar formal structures and/or using certain labels to display what they are or do often turn out to be quite different in practice. For example, local dynamics, traditions, and ways of working are important and can rarely be imitated. Thus, outsiders find it hard to understand the deeper insights obtained from long-term participation that are required for adopting specific ways of operating. As a result, these modes of operation are difficult to copy. Hence, companies imitate and develop what they believe are particularly advanced structures, as described by the media, but which actually only bear a superficial resemblance. Genuine, 'in-depth' imitation is another matter, and more difficult (Rövik, 2011). Although many organizations have corporate social responsibility (CSR) in the form of a policy and certain activities, and hence appear to be similar, considerable variation exists at the practical level, that is, to the extent that anything at all goes on there. Sometimes, they only have the label in common, and certain buzzwords in their policy documents.

Overall, there is an expansion of operations involving 'the corporate beauty industry'. An aesthetic and decorative surface—architecture, premises, letterhead design, elegant brochures, posters, PowerPoint presentations, company uniforms, beautiful and attractive employees, and so on—are becoming increasingly important (Hancock, 2003). This applies to both physical and verbal symbolism.

As beauty is something relative, the more aesthetically appealing competitors or colleagues become, the more ugly a company may discover itself to be (in the eyes of others or in its own). This aestheticization affects organizational cultures in a variety of ways. One extreme is a low 'culture effect', surface is viewed as surface. There is a disconnect between impression management and cultural orientations guiding understandings and actions in 'normal', operative work. This is sometimes what culture as resource authors have in mind, emphasizing the instrumental use of cultural resources, addressed above.

This overall cultural trend towards grandiosity affects organizations in different ways. Some—small, manufacturing or routine service oriented—probably are affected less. Large organizations working with complicated products or intangible services are probably affected much more. But also here there is large variation. Parts of organizations may work very much influenced by grandiosity fantasies and ambitions. Branding people try to frame their work in line with highly symbolic, successful brands. HRM people dream about working with strategies and being the left-hand and speaking partner of the CEO. Senior people often live in the idealized, clean world of discourse: plans, PowerPoint presentation and persuasive talk are key elements of their workplace reality. All these live to a considerable degree in grandiosity-fused cultures, although the inevitable imperfections of corporate life also put their imprints. So grandiosity meanings compete with other elements. Many people in organizations we have studied fluctuate between rather different meanings. Branding is fusing products and consumers with a higher purpose, creating value—and struggling for name recognition and supporting sales and market shares through fighting for space in shops and offering discount prices. HRM is about developing human capital, increasing competence, and creating cultures of excellence—but mainly a lot of routine service work and administration. Leadership is about developing people and creating committed, loyal employees seeing the higher purpose through vision—but sitting in meetings, listening to other managers, and doing administration and operative work making the organizational machinary function is a more significant experience. Cultures are then in a variety of ways characterized by the ideals, representations, experiences, and fantasies that people develop and communicate in various work groups and organizational units. Positive meaning and uplifted identities are created—but also confusion, cynicism, and depression. A mix of these, often with a strong element of ambiguity—a key quality in many contemporary organizations (Alvesson, 2013; Martin, 2002; Martin and Meyerson, 1988).

Let us illustrate this trend towards investment in attractive superficial structures by discussing a case where there is a clear signal value to the outside as well as to junior employees but with an ambigious, even negative, connection with 'core' operations.

An Illustration: The Business Concept of an IT Consultancy Firm

The business concept of a corporation may be seen as a cultural phenomenon—a symbol summarizing certain shared meanings. The business concept is supposed to provide an overall indication of what the company does and summarize its core competence and market offerings (Normann, 1977). The IT consultancy firm studied by Alvesson (2000) promised a combination of strategic and IT expertise (i.e., management). IT issues were put in a wider, business-oriented perspective and, it was claimed, involved much more than programming. Many managers and employees proudly referred to the company's business concept and considered that the company's strength was precisely a combination of management and IT skills. Strategy and management gave an attractive picture of operations, compared to being 'only' into programming. It was a source of pride and community. Many managers and other employees emphasized the progressive and sophisticated nature of the firm, their ability to create close contacts with client top management, work with communication and getting the assignments 'right' also in a business sense. People claimed that the business concept guided their work.

However, the extent to which people complied with this was highly doubtful. The relationship between the ideals laid down in the business concept and the actual operations in day-to-day work was ambiguous. This was to some extent dealt with through broad meanings of 'strategy', 'business', and 'management' ('project management is also management'), but also through pointing at the future and developments. The business concept alternated between being realized and the principle and an ambition and hope. So the business concept worked as a key symbol and had an integrating and uplifting function. But the selective and status-enhancing way of representing the firm and its people meant that it illustrated grandiosity as defined above. This is to some extent camouflaged and buried under ambiguity of meanings when we did the study in 'real time', but comes out much more clearly when doing a number of follow-up interviews with people asked to comment retrospectively about the firm.

This is how one subsidiary manager expressed himself in an interview a few years later after he had left the company:

> This is often the way it goes with companies in this industry, it is one thing to profile yourself, but matching the profile is something else.

Another former subsidiary manager put it more crudely:

> What we live off in the consultancy world is actually resources and volume. We depend on sales and the middle level, not the brilliant analysts out front. System analysts and programmers are what counts. And that's what we lived off. We packaged and disguised that we were working in projects at Datakonsultus, but we rarely needed to take any major project risks. It was on cost-plus basis, and a packaging of volume consulting. But that's not the way they worked in England (i.e., at the British subsidiary). They believed in 'now the new view of management and IT is on the way', and we talked about this in Sweden but didn't do very much about it, but they believed in it wholeheartedly, and everything went to pot. [laughs] Volume was what it was all about! That's bulk! What we were good at was IT, that's the whole story, and that's what we earned money on too.

The interviewee referred to the business concept as a sales trick and a myth, and said that the business concept was rarely mentioned in discussions among senior managers.

> We didn't have that kind of competence. It was a cleverly dreamed-up and skilfully maintained myth, I might say, rather meanly. But I think it is true too.
>
> But nonetheless I wouldn't say it was wrong because that myth held up all through the 1980s. [laughs] And that's not a bad rating at all. If people thought we were good at combining management and IT—fine. And they were happy with that, worked on their projects and made money out of programming, because that was what it was all about, really.

The impression, based on two rounds of interviews with the company's managers and others, during and some years after the phase in which the myth was fostered so strongly, was that the mixture of naïvety and cynicism was crucial. Doubts and uncertainty often evaporate in an atmosphere of enthusiasm, wishful thinking, and rationalization pressures. Naïve faith is sometimes an asset (Alvesson and Spicer, 2012). At the same time, some degree of business thinking and clear-sightedness is required if the grandiose aspects are not to be taken too seriously. Ambivalence and oscillation between naïve faith in the gilt-edged and an instrumental and pragmatic approach seem to characterize many of the participants. There is a mixture or smooth alternation, on the one hand, between a somewhat naïve view of future expectations and attempts to allow practices to be interpreted and depicted in 'myth-friendly' terms and, on the other hand, more strategic, even cynical thinking about what is involved and pragmatic behaviour, paired with sales and morale-enhancing talk that makes people happy. These somewhat complex meanings indicate the workings of organizational culture and culture management in an age of grandiosity. Genuine beliefs and values—held also by managers, but often with some ambivalance and caution—overlaps with a managerial-instrumental interest in creating a favourable image, thereby impressing clients and making the employees feeling more committed to a firm with, it was claimed, an impressive business concept and a clear identity.

Immersion, De-Familiarization, and Problematization

The contemporary interest in (neo-)normative control, organizational identity and discourse as well as the turn to a culture-as-toolkit view (emphasizing cultural resources forming elements in constraining but primarily facilitating certain types of action) is quite diverse, but all tend to have a focus on the agentic use of culture. This captures important aspects of management and control and is thus valuable. It also means an avoidance of ambitious ethnographic work that aims to dig into the taken-for-granted, implicit, and fine-grained layers of meanings making up organizational life-worlds. Given the importance of frontstage presentation in, and the instability and non-homogenous nature of many contemporary organizations, this may appear as reasonable. Yet, perhaps the tendency to shy away from layered interpretation and thick description in the research practice of organizational scholars is another manifestation of the increasing preoccupation in Western societies with outward appearances at the expense of substance. As indicated earlier, some of the key advantages of a cultural approach to the understanding of organizations are here at risk of being lost: the interest in illuminating the taken-for-grantedness of corporate reality and working life. What is 'behind' or what are the 'deeper' or non-explicit workings of discourse, identity claims, and other forms of (neo-)normative control—where the possible constitutive effects may be less about spoken or written words and more about unspoken scripts and implicit acts and the cultural context in which they are played out.

A related theme concerns the focus of attention. Management and organization is about much more than explicit action, use of discourse, the instrumental employment of cultural objects and resources, and other 'attention-attracting' features. The domains and aspects of the not so obvious are significant and worthy of attention and 'in-depth' exploration. This calls for 'thick description', serious efforts to learn about and describe (or portray) layers of meaning difficult to verbalize in straightforward ways, for example on gender, age, authority, community, obligations, values, selfhood, work, competence, politics, and so on. Some of the better cultural studies score high in this regard.

Exemplary here is Jackall (1988), who explores the cultural understandings of morality and politics in corporate life, an extraordinary rich and insightful study.

This type of cultural study is quite independent of the possibility and existence of stable, homogeneous, and integrated organizational cultures being targeted for culture management. The use of a cultural theoretical perspective and the ambition to do thick description is not in any way dependent on organizational cultures as fixed objects. Organizations represent a wealth of cultural phenomena important to be unpacked also—and perhaps in particular—regardless of what is being aired in organizational discourse. We may study such phenomena in the absence of corporate actors who engage in attempts to manage, engineer, change, resist, or market these phenomena. In fact, what is most interesting for scholars doing in-depth cultural research may lie well outside organizational actors' conscious deliberations and agentic reach. As Alvesson and Sveningsson (2015) show in an in-depth study following a 'cultural change' programme at close range (longitudual observations and interviews with actors across organizational levels and subsites), what was targeted for cultural change did not affect or reflect any of the taken-for-granted understandings that actually framed interpretations and guided (in-)action. Such cultural analyses thus bring into view what is otherwise overlooked, ignored, uncritically accepted, or silently assumed.

We suggest that the lack of layered interpretations in culture research can, at least partially, be remedied with immersive study, defamiliarization, and radical problematization. We understand *immersive study* as open-ended ethnography which involves drawing close to subjects and situations and allows to thickly describe the various layers of meaning of the topic under study (Ybema et al., 2009b). The idea with immersive study is to break away from the standard idea that an organization, group, or phenomenon necessarily constitutes a bounded and stable phenomenon. Rather, the point is to treat such phenomena as an entry point and then follow the flow, so to speak (van Hulst, Ybema, and Yanow, forthcoming). As pointed out above, there are good reasons to at least consider the idea that organizations and work life arrangements have been destabilized. However, it is unlikely that meanings and understandings have been eliminated or completely destabilized. They are likely to operate in a different manner and under different forms of stability. The issue here is to relax a priori understandings about what constitutes a 'culture' (a profession, an organization, a community) and look for emergent meanings and patterns. It is not only about 'following the animal' but also about deciding which animals are present and who to follow. Key here is to be particularly sensitive to breakdowns in understanding and mysteries (Alvesson and Kärreman, 2011). Immersive study is similar to ethnomethodology in the sense that it focuses on local practice. It is different from ethnomethodology in drawing more strongly on the cultural conceptual apparatus: meanings, rituals, and understandings.

While immersion elicits knowledge 'from within', it also blinds the researcher's eye to alternative viewpoints stemming from outsider positions which may generate equally interesting insight (Ybema and Kamsteeg, 2009). Alongside 'closeness' to the field, social, emotional, and analytical detachment is thus equally important. A key rationale for organizational culture studies, in particular those with a critical edge, is thus the ability to contribute to *de-familarization*, for example turning the seemingly well-known, natural, reasonable, and familiar into remarkable phenomena, and encouraging rethinking and reflection (Alvesson and Deetz, 2000). Part of the problem is that over-familiarity is rarely viewed as a problem in anthropology, apart from the routine advice to 'not go native'. The main methodological issue here is, however, not just 'making the familiar strange', but rather the opposite, making 'the strange familiar (Van Maanen, 1995: 20). The ethnographic toolkit is rather empty when it comes to questioning the familiar. Key elements of defamiliarization are to highlight what is strange, odd, and weird about the reality at hand (Ybema and Kamsteeg, 2009). For example, when studying higher education, there might be more mileage in viewing universities as training camps for the administered society, or parking places for hedonistic expression, rather than semi-sacred places for learning. Or, when studying modern work places, to view them as places for idle and pointless activities (Paulsen, 2014), rather than spaces for production of products, services, and modern beings.

Finally, *radical problematization* highlights that although it is important to uncover hidden meanings and tacit understandings a truly critical project also needs to critically assess and question meanings and understandings. There needs to be an element of wonderment and doubt about meanings and understandings at use—in Habermas' terms, an engagement in the hermeneutics of suspicion. What are the key assumptions and ideas that underlie meanings, understandings and cultural toolkits? What are the root metaphors? How does it connect to access to resources and other forms of power? Who benefits?

Utlimately, a radical problematization leads to a systematic questioning of dominant patterns of meaning and how it relates to social stratification and the mobilization and exercise of power. However, the point here is not to provide critique only. In radical problematization critique is not an end in itself; it is a means through which researchers come to a re-imagining of the cultural order. The point is not to develop blueprints for radical social change, but rather to point to entry points for the discussion and development of socially progressive ideas. Radical problematization is not about fantasizing about the revolution, it is about probing the weak spots in spaces marked by hegemonic practices and social domination. It is a search for the crack in the system, where the light comes in.

Conclusion

In this chapter we have argued that, with the waning of interest in 'organizational culture', the research ambition to puncture surface symbolism and to critically probe the taken-for-granted layers of organizational life also seems to have gone out of vogue. The baby got washed away with the bathwater as research attention shifted towards outside appearances and agentic display of culture. This is why this chapter has argued for research that explicitly aims to move beyond or behind surface appearances, to explore the minutiae of silent, less-visible, overlooked, neglected, or silenced realities, and to thickly describe the 'layeredness' of organizational life. To remedy the paucity of layered interpretation in cultural research we suggested to draw on three strategies, objectives, or ideals for doing cultural research: drawing close and immersion; defamiliarization and lending strangeness; and critical questioning and problematization. These seem to hold an important promise for invigorating culture research in the field of organization and management studies as they allow researchers to ground understanding in both intimate familiarity with, and detached and critical analysis of, processes of meaning-making in organizational settings.

REFERENCES

Ailon-Souday, G. and Kunda, G. (2003). 'The Local Selves of Global Workers: The Social Construction of National Identity in the Face of Organizational Globalization'. *Organization Studies*, 24(7): 1073–96.

Alvesson, M. (1994). 'Talking in Organizations: Managing Identity and Image in an Advertising Agency'. *Organization Studies*, 15(4): 535–63.

Alvesson, M. (2000). *Ledning av kunskapsföretag*, 3rd edn. Stockholm: Norstedts.

Alvesson, M. (2013). *Understanding Organizational Culture*, 2nd edn. London: SAGE.

Alvesson, M. and Deetz, S. (2000). *Doing Critical Management Research*. London: SAGE.

Alvesson, M. and Kärreman, D. (2007). 'Unraveling HRM: Identity, Ceremony, and Control in a Management Consultancy Firm'. *Organization Science*, 18: 711–23.

Alvesson, M. and Kärreman, D. (2011). 'Decolonializing Discourse: Critical Reflections on Organizational Discourse Analysis'. *Human Relations*, 64(9): 1121–46.

Alvesson, M. and Robertson, M. (2006). 'The Best and the Brightest: The Construction, Significance and Effects of Elite Identities in Consultancy Firms'. *Organization*, 13(2): 195–224.

Alvesson, M. and Robertson, M. (2016). 'Organizational Identity: A Critique', in M. Pratt, M. Schulz, B. Ashforth, and D. Ravasi. (eds.), *Oxford Handbook of Organizational Identity*. Oxford: Oxford University Press, 160–80.

Alvesson, M. and Spicer, A. (2012). 'A Stupidity Based Theory of the Organization'. *Journal of Management Studies*, 49(7): 1194–220.

Alvesson, M. and Sveningsson, S. (2003). 'The Good Visions, the Bad Micro- Management and the Ugly Ambiguity: Contradictions of (Non-)Leadership in a Knowledge-Intensive Company'. *Organization Studies*, 24(6): 961–88.

Alvesson, M. and Sveningsson, S. (2015). *Changing Organizational Culture*, 2nd edn. London: Routledge.

Alvesson, M. and Willmott, H. (2002). 'Identity Regulation as Organizational Control: Producing the Appropriate Individual'. *Journal of Management Studies*, 39(5): 619–44.

Alvesson, M., Ashcraft, K. and Thomas, R. (2008). 'Identity Matters: Reflections on the Construction of Identity Scholarship in Organization Studies'. *Organization*, 15(1): 5–28.

Antaki, C. and Widdicombe, S. (ed.) (1998). *Identities in Talk*. London: SAGE.

Argyris, C. and Schön, D. (1995). *Organizational Learning: A Theory of Action Perspective, 1978*. Reading, MA: Addison-Wesley Publishing Company.

Barley, S. R. and Kunda, G. (1992). 'Design and Devotion: Surges of Rational and Normative Ideologies of Control in Managerial Discourse'. *Administrative Science Quarterly*, 37: 363–99.

Barley, S. R., Meyer, G.W. and Gash, D. C. (1988). 'Cultures of Culture: Academics, Practitioners and the Pragmatics of Normative Control'. *Administrative Science Quarterly*, 33: 24–60.

Blom, M. and Alvesson, M. (2015). 'A Critical Perspective on Strategy-as-Practice', in D. Golsorkhi, L. Rouleau, D. Seidl, and E. Vaara (eds.), *Cambridge Handbook of Strategy-as-Practice*. Cambridge: Cambridge University Press.

Broms, H. and Gahmberg, H. (1983). 'Communication to Self in Organizations and Cultures'. *Administrative Science Quarterly*, 28: 482–95.

Butler, J. (1988). 'Performative Acts and Gender Constitution: An Essay in Phenomenology and Feminist Theory'. *Theatre Journal*, 519–31.

Calas and Smircich (1987). 'Post-Culture: Is the Organizational Culture Literature Dominant but Dead?' Paper, Dept of Management, Univ. of Massachusetts.

Canato, A., Ravasi, D. and Phillips, N. (2013). 'Coerced Practice Implementation in Cases of Low Cultural Fit'. *Academy of Management Journal*, 56: 1724–53.

Cederström, C. and Fleming P. (2012). *Dead Man Working*. Winchester: Zero Books.

Collinson, D. L. (2003). 'Identities and Insecurities: Selves at Work'. *Organization*, 10(3), 527–47.

Costas, J. and Kärreman, D. (2013). 'Conscience as Control–Managing Employees through CSR'. *Organization*, 20(3): 394–415.

Deal, T. E. and Kennedy, A. A. (1982) *Corporate Cultures: The Rites and Rituals of Corporate Life*. Reading, MA: Addison-Wesley.

Dunne, J. (1996). 'Beyond Sovereignty and Deconstruction: The Storied Self', in R. Kearney (ed.), *Paul Ricoeur: The Hermeneutics of Action*. London: SAGE.

Fine, G. and Hallett, T. (2014). 'Group Cultures and the Everyday Life of Organizations: Interaction Orders and Meso-Analysis'. *Organization Studies*, 35(12): 1773–92.

Fleming, P. (2014). 'Review Article: When "Life Itself" Goes to Work: Reviewing Shifts in Organizational Life through the Lens of Biopower'. *Human Relations*, 67(7): 875–901.

Fleming, P. and Sturdy, A. (2009). '"Just Be Yourself!": Towards Neonormative Control in Organizations?'. *Employee Relations*, 31(6): 569–83.

Florida, R. (2001). *The Rise of the Creative Class: And How It's Transforming Work, Leisure, Community and Everyday Life*. New York: Basic Books.

Freeden, M. (2003). *Ideology: A Very Short Introduction*. Oxford: Oxford University Press.

Gabriel, Y. (2005). 'Class Cages and Glass Palaces: Images of Organizations in Image-Conscious Times'. *Organization*, 12(1): 9–27.

Geertz, C. (1973). *The Interpretation of Culture*. New York: Basic Books.

Giddens, A. (1991). *Modernity and Self Identity: Self and Society in the Late Modern Age*. Stanford, CA: Stanford University Press.

Gioia, D., Schulz, M., and Corley, K. (2000). 'Organizational Identity, Image, and Adaptive Instability'. *Academy of Management Review*, 25(1): 63–81.

Gouldner, A. W. (1954). *Patterns of Industrial Bureaucracy*. Glencoe, IL: Free Press.

Hancock, P. (2003). 'Uncovering the Semiotic in Organizational Aestethics'. *Organization*, 12: 29–50.

Handel, M. (ed.) (2004). *The Sociology of Organizations: Classic, Contemporary, and Critical Readings*. Thousand Oaks, CA: SAGE.

Harrison, S. H. and Corley, K. G. (2011). 'Clean Climbing, Carabiners, and Cultural Cultivation: Developing an Open-Systems Perspective of Culture'. *Organization Science*, 22(2): 391–412.

Hartley, J. F. (1983). 'Ideology and Organizational Behavior'. *International Studies of Management & Organization*, 13(3): 7–34.

Howard-Grenville, J., Golden-Biddle, K., Irwin, J., and Mao, J. (2011). 'Liminality as Cultural Process for Cultural Change'. *Organization Science*, 22(2): 522–39.

Jackall, R. (1988). *Moral Mazes: The World of Corporate Managers*. New York: Oxford University Press.

Kärreman, D. and Alvesson, M. (2004). 'Cages in Tandem: Management Control, Social Identity, and Identification in a Knowledge-Intensive Firm'. *Organization*, 11(1): 149–75.

Kärreman, D. and Rylander, A. (2008). 'Managing Meaning through Branding: The Case of a Consulting Firm'. *Organization Studies*, 29(1): 103–25.

Kellogg, K. C. (2011). 'Hot Lights and Cold Steel: Cultural and Political Toolkits for Practice Change in Surgery'. *Organization Science*, 22(2), 482–502.

Kunda, G. (1992). *Engineering Culture: Control and Commitment in a High-Tech Corporation*. Philadelphia, PA: Temple University Press.

Kunda, G. and Ailon-Souday, G. (2005). 'Managers, Markets, and Ideologies', in S. Ackroyd, R. Batt, P. Thompson, and P. Tolbert (eds.), *The Oxford Handbook of Work and Organization*. Oxford: Oxford University Press, 200–19.

Land, C. and Taylor, S. (2010). 'Surf's Up: Work, Life, Balance and Brand in a New Age Capitalist Organization'. *Sociology*, 44(3): 395–413.

Leonardi, P. M. (2011). 'Innovation Blindness: Culture, Frames, and Cross-Boundary Problem Construction in the Development of New Technology Concepts'. *Organization Science*, 22(2): 347–69.

Martin, J. (2002). *Organizational Culture: Mapping the Terrain*. Thousand Oaks, CA: SAGE.

Martin, J. and Frost, P. (1996). 'The Organizational Culture War Games: A Struggle for Intellectual Dominance', in S. R. Clegg, C. Hardy, and W. Nord (eds), *Handbook of Organization Studies*. London: SAGE, 599–621.

Martin, J., Feldman, M. S., Hatch, M. J. and Sitkin, S. B. (1983). 'The Uniqueness Paradox in Organizational Stories'. *Administrative Science Quarterly*, 28: 438–53.

Martin, J. and Frost, P. (1996). 'The Organizational Culture War Games: A Struggle for Intellectual Dominance', in S. R. Clegg, C. Hardy, and W. Nord (eds.), *Handbook of Organization Studies*. London: SAGE, 599–621.

Martin, J. and Meyerson, D. (1988). 'Organizational Cultures and the Denial, Channelling, and Acknowledgment of Ambiguity', in L. Pondy, R. Boland, and H. Thomas (eds.), *Managing Ambiguity and Change*. New York: Wiley, 93–125.

Martin, J. and Siehl, C. (1983). 'Organizational Culture and Counterculture: An Uneasy Symbiosis'. *Organizational Dynamics*, 12(2): 52–64.

Normann, R. (1977). *Management for Growth*. London: Wiley.

Parker, M. (2000). *Organizational Culture and Identity*. London: SAGE.

Paulsen, R. (2014). *Empty Labour*. Cambridge: Cambridge University Press.

Rindova, V., Dalpiaz, E., and Ravasi, D. (2011). 'A Cultural Quest: A Study of Organizational Use of New Cultural Resources in Strategy Formation'. *Organization Science*, 22: 413–31.

Rövik, K. A. (2011). 'From Fashion to Virus: An Alternative Theory of Organizations' Handling of Management Ideas'. *Organization Studies*, 32(5): 631–53.

Scarbrough, H. and Burrell G. (1996). 'The Axeman Cometh', in S. Clegg and G. Palmer (eds.), *The Politics of Management Knowledge*. Thousand Oaks, CA: SAGE.

Sennett, R. (1998). *The Corrosion of Character*. New York: Norton.

Shotter, J. (1993). *Conversational Realities: Constructing Life through Language*. London: SAGE.

Smircich, L. (1983). 'Concepts of Culture and Organizational Analysis'. *Administrative Science Quarterly*, 28: 339–58.

Somers, M. R. (1994). 'The Narrative Constitution of Identity: A Relational and Network Approach'. *Theory and Society*, 23(5): 605–49.

Sveningsson, S. and Alvesson, M. (2003). 'Managing Managerial Identities: Organisational Fragmentation, Discourse and Identity Struggle'. *Human Relations*, 56(10): 1163–93.

Swidler, A. (1986). 'Culture in Action: Symbols and Strategies'. *American Sociological Review*, 51: 273–86.

Thomas, R. and Linstead, A. (2002). 'Losing the Plot? Middle Managers and Identity'. *Organization*, 9(1): 71–93.
Thompson, P. et al. (2000). 'Human Capital or Capitalizing on Humanity? Knowledge, Skills and Competences in Interactive Service Work', in C. Prichard et al. (eds.), *Managing Knowledge*. Basingstoke: MacMillan.
Thornborrow, T. and Brown, A. D. (2009). 'Being " Regimented": Aspiration, Discipline and Identity Work in the British Parachute Regiment'. *Organization Studies*, 30(4): 355–76.
Turner, V. (1984). 'Liminality and the Performative Genres', in J. J. MacAloon (ed.), *Rite, Drama, Festival, Spectacle: Rehearsals toward a Theory of Cultural Performance*. Philadelphia, PA: Institute for the Study of Human Issues, 19–41.
Van Hulst, M., Ybema, S., and Yanow, D. (forthcoming). 'Ethnography and Organizational Processes', in A. Langley and H. Tsoukas (eds.), *Handbook of Process Studies of Organizations*. Oxford: Oxford University Press
Van Maanen, J. (1995). 'An End to Innocence: The Ethnography of Ethnography', in J. Van Maanen (ed.), *Representation in Ethnography*. Thousand Oaks, CA: SAGE, 1–35.
Van Maanen, J. and Barley, S. R. (1985). 'Cultural Organization: Fragments of a Theory', in P. J. Frost et al. (eds.), *Organizational Culture*. Beverly Hills, CA: SAGE, 31–53.
Watson, T. (1994). *In Search of Management*. London: Routledge.
Weber, K. and Dacin, M. T. (2011). 'The Cultural Construction of Organizational Life: Introduction to the Special Issue'. *Organization Science*, 22(2): 287–98.
Weick, K. E. (1993). 'The Collapse of Sensemaking in Organizations: The Mann Gulch Disaster'. *Administrative Science Quarterly*, 38: 628–52.
Weick, K. E. (1995). *Sensemaking in Organizations*. Thousand Oaks, CA: SAGE.
Yanow, D. and Ybema, S. (2009). 'Interpretivism in Organizational Research: On Elephants and Blind Researchers', in D. A. Buchanan and A. Bryman (eds.), *The Sage Handbook of Organizational Research Methods*. London: SAGE, 39–60.
Yanow, D. and Ybema (2011). 'Introduction', in D. Yanow, S. Ybema, and I. Sabelis (eds.), *Organizational Culture*. Cheltenham: Edward Elgar, xi–xxxii.
Ybema, S. (1996). 'A Duckbilled Platypus in the Theory and Analysis of Organisations: Combinations of Consensus and Dissensus', in W. Koot, I. Sabelis, and S. Ybema (eds.), *Contradictions in Context: Puzzling over Paradoxes in Contemporary Organizations*. Amsterdam: VU University Press, 39–61.
Ybema, S. and Byun, H. (2011). 'Unequal Power Relations, Identity Discourse and Cultural Distinction Drawing in MNCs', in C. Dörrenbächer and M. Geppert (eds.), *Politics and Power in the Multinational Corporation: The Role of Interests, Identities, and Institutions*. Cambridge: Cambridge University Press, 315–45.
Ybema, S. and Kamsteeg, F. (2009). 'Making the Familiar Strange: A Case for Disengaged Organizational Ethnography', in S. Ybema, D. Yanow, F. Kamsteeg, and H. Wels (eds.), *Organizational Ethnography: Studying the Complexities of Everyday Life*. London: SAGE, 101–19.
Ybema, S., Keenoy, T., Oswick, C., Beverungen, A., Ellis, N., and Sabelis, I. (2009a). 'Articulating Identities'. *Human Relations*, 62(3): 299–322.
Ybema, S., Yanow, D., Wels, H. and Kamsteeg, F. (2009b). 'Studying Everyday Organizational Life', in S. Ybema, D. Yanow, H. Wels, and F. Kamsteeg (eds.), *Organizational Ethnography: Studying the Complexity of Everyday Life*. London: SAGE,. 1–20.
Young, E. (1989). 'On the Naming of the Rose: Interests and Multiple Meanings as Elements of Organizational Culture'. *Organization Studies*, 10(2): 187–206.

CHAPTER 7

THE OPENING UP OF ORGANIZATION THEORY

Open Systems, Contingency Theory, and Organizational Design

C. R. (BOB) HININGS
AND ROYSTON GREENWOOD

Introduction

THIS chapter explores the history of an open-systems approach in the study of management and organizations and reviews its current status. There is a sense in which open-systems theory has moved from a specific approach to thinking about organizations, internally and externally, to becoming a taken-for-granted, institutionalized part of the organizational lexicon. But when it was introduced into organization theory in the 1960s it pushed our understanding of organizations forward in a major way. Until then, the focus for both academics and practitioner scholars had been on the internal management and organization of activities. Thus, open-systems theory marked a move from a concern with the organization per se to a concern with the organization in its environment. Central to this movement towards an open-systems approach was contingency theory. Hence, in tracing the development of open-systems theory we also review how, for a time, contingency theory became a dominant approach within organization theory.

In doing so, we examine three variants of open-systems theory: *general-systems theory* specifically (Von Bertalanffy, 1956), which argues that there are general ideas that can be applied to all systems, biological, ecological, organizations, and so on; *specific-systems thinking* where the concept of interdependent parts is accepted without necessarily accepting that all systems exhibit similar functions and processes, for example, organizations are systems but not of the same kind as a biological system; and approaches that theorize the organization as within and transacting with its environment but without any specific use of systems concepts and metaphors. Contingency theory fits this latter variant.

In tracing the sequence of ideas and the streams of thought that embraced these systems ways of thinking we argue that this generic approach is now taken for granted but without the specific language of systems theory.

Before the 1960s

There are three streams of thought within this time period that expressed the foundations of an open-systems approach: an interest in the overall functioning of organizations using a self-consciously systems-oriented framework; work on bureaucracy; and a concern with how to manage organizations. Although we treat these streams as separate there are connections and crossovers between them.

The Overall Functioning of Organizations

General systems theory arose after the Second World War. It was not concerned with organizations in particular. Instead, exponents such as Von Bertalanffy (1956) argued that all systems—whether biological, ecological, social, political, organizational—have similar characteristics. That is, 'all systems are characterized by an assemblage or combination of parts whose relations make them interdependent' (Scott, 1992). Systems can vary from simple to complex, depending on the number and types of parts that are interdependent. Moreover, Wiener (1956) stated that interdependence between parts is a matter of degree; it can be very tight, or somewhat looser.

Nevertheless, the central theme of general systems thinking was to conceptualize organizations as systems because of the interdependence between their parts. The parts can be 'activities', 'processes', and 'structures'. A concentration on the interdependence of organizational parts alone treats the organization as a closed system. An open-systems perspective emphasizes the systems nature of the relationship between an organization and its environment. There is a throughput of resources from the environment to the organization and vice versa (Boulding, 1956). A particular expression of this approach, by Ashby (1952), elaborates the idea of requisite variety that, in essence, says that variety in an organizational system should be the same as the variety in its environment, and no more. (There are hints here of the later work by Lawrence and Lorsch, 1967.)

A sociological variation of the systems approach by Parsons (1956, 1958), conceptualized organizations as made up of various subsystems embedded within wider social systems (Mouzelis, 1967). Systems *within* organizations were essentially the units or building blocks of organizations—such as departments, work groups, and so on. Systems within which an organization is embedded were local communities, wider society, and so on. The whole approach was one of nested, embedded, and interlocking systems. Congruent with most of sociology at the time, Parsons' theorizing was highly functionalist in that it assumed that there are basic functional requirements that must be solved by any system in order for the system to survive. Parsons proposed four such requirements—*goal achievement* (the mobilizing of resources), *adaptation* (the acquiring of resources), *integration* (the design of internal system relationships), and *latency* (tension management). The open-systems nature of this approach is seen in two assumptions: that all organizations have the same system requirements; and, that those requirements cover both internal system interdependence and the external relationship between an organization and its environment.

It was not only academics who drew upon systems theory as they sought to understand organizations. Fayol (1949), a French mining engineer, writing before systems language was current, outlined six generic activities that all organizations have to undertake—technical, commercial, financial, security, accounting, and managerial—and five key managerial roles, which became famous and widely adopted: forecasting and planning, organizing, commanding, coordinating and controlling. Barnard (1938), a US business executive, was another early proponent of the idea that organizations should be seen as systems of activities: 'A cooperative system is incessantly dynamic, a process of continual readjustment to physical, biological and social environments as a whole' (Barnard, 1938: 23). This is an archetypal open-systems statement, defining an organization as an internally cooperative system that has to relate and adjust to external environments. At its heart is the idea that organizations carry out a range of activities in a collective fashion (Scott and Davis, 2007). Barnard's (1938) key message was that organizations are cooperative systems and the role of management is to ensure cooperation in pursuit of organizational ends.

The aim of these analyses—whether by academics or practitioners—was to conceptualize the role of management as the design and ongoing coordination of inter-related activities and functions—for example, planning, goal setting, performance management. It was through the management of activities in concert and cooperation that superior performance would be achieved. These analyses, however, were highly abstract and functional in form. A much more grounded approach was carried out at the Tavistock Institute of Human Relations in the UK. Studying technical change in a British coalmine, Trist and Bamforth (1951) conceived of organizations as comprised of social and technical elements—that is, as 'socio-technical systems'. A later study, of an Indian textile mill (Rice, 1958), elaborated this idea, showing how the socio-technical system at the supervisory level was nested within other organizational systems of control and communication. Indeed, for Rice, a key element of any supervisory role is managing the 'boundary conditions' between the technical and social systems of an organization because of their interdependence.

Common to all of the above studies is an emerging interest in understanding large-scale organizations that were appearing across all societal sectors, partly because of the increasing pace of technical change, but underpinned in Europe by the massive rebuilding of states post Second World War. The common assumption was the idea of organizations as systems, which lead to the notion that change or disturbance in one element affects the other elements. A system is open when it obtains resources from its environment and uses them for maintenance and development. It was not until the 1960s, though, that such general systems thinking began to impact the study of organizations in a significant way.

How to Manage Organizations

The 1930s to the 1950s saw the development of what became known as 'classical management theory'. Initially, through the work of Taylor (1947), it was known as 'scientific management' and focused upon how to achieve efficiencies in the arrangement of work at the shop floor level. But those concerned with how better to manage organizations went further and sought to identify the functions of management and to establish principles of how they could be best performed. There was much interest in the design of organizational structures, which were seen as especially problematical and significant (Follett, 1942; Mooney, 1937; Gulick and Urwick, 1936; Urwick, 1943). As Van de Ven, Ganco, and Hinings (2013: 399) put it, 'A generation of scholar practitioners attempted to outline the principles of management and administration (…) Their aim was to understand the management of organizations through a set of generic principles, always looking for the ingredients of better management.'

These 'scholar practitioners' sought to distil theirs and others' experience to produce principles of how to design and manage organizations. They wished to improve the practice of management. Their focus was on what later became conceptualized as the elements of organizational design—such as lines of hierarchy, spans of control, the bases of specialization, line and staff arrangements, standardization, centralization-decentralization, hierarchy, policies, and procedures. Their approach has been generically referred to as searching for 'the one best way'. There was an insistence, for example, upon a unified line of control in which supervisors should have limited spans of control. (Graicunas (1937), for example, showed mathematically that six was the optimal number of subordinates that should report to a superordinate!).

Mouzelis (1967), referring to them as the 'universalist' school, highlights that they portrayed the organization as a set of formal structures, systems and processes. Rather like Weber's analysis of bureaucracy, the emphasis was placed upon patterns of responsibility and prescribed relationships. Thus, good management was a matter of sound organizational design with supporting policies and rules. Organization charts and manuals of policies and rules were important organizational components. In this sense, the organization was seen as a closed system of interdependent structural features.

The Study of Bureaucracy

The early days of the academic study of organizations were dominated by Weber's (1947) concept of bureaucracy (Gouldner, 1954; Gerth and Mills, 1958; Mouzelis, 1967).

Weber strode the sociology of organizations like a colossus with his huge intellectual sweep of the historical development of civilizations. Integral to his theory was the idea of authority systems—that is, the reason why those in subordinate positions accept the right (legitimacy) of those in superordinate positions to give direction and issue commands. Weber suggested three bases of authority and identified the organizational forms associated with each one.

The first basis of authority is *charisma*. Authority is based on the personal qualities of a leader who is seen as different from, or set apart from, ordinary mortals. The implicated organizational form is a leader and disciples; the latter have the task of mediating between the leader and the masses. Typical examples are small-scale, revolutionary political and religious movements, although many organizations have charismatic founders, such as Steve Jobs at Apple. Because authority embodied within an individual is inherently unstable, Weber pointed to the routinization of charisma into families or particular roles, as with the Pope in the Catholic Church.

A second reason why subordinates accept the exercise of authority is *tradition*. Precedent, usage, inherited status, and custom are the sources of legitimacy. Weber wrote of feudal and patrimonial systems with their attendant traditional organization. Later scholars have identified the family firm as an example of an organization with an inherited status authority system (Miller and Le Breton-Miller, 2005; Miller, Le Breton-Miller, and Lester, 2011). Similarly, religious organizations are examples based on custom and precedent, often with roles that represent the routinization of charisma (Hinings and Raynard, 2014).

Interestingly, there has been very little analysis of charismatic and traditional authority systems in organization theory. Instead emphasis has been on organizations based on Weber's third basis of authority: *rational-legal authority*. Rationality, according to Weber, comes from the attempt to align means with organizational goals, to carry out rational analysis to achieve organizational purposes. To do so, office-holding is based on expertise and offices have legal authority defined and constrained by policies, rules, and procedures. The form of organization associated with this basis of authority is the bureaucracy. The central components of bureaucracy, according to Weber, are: specialized, technically qualified, office holders; a distinct hierarchy of authority; policies, rules, and procedures formalizing duties and authority; written records and files (in the 'bureau'); and the separation of personal and business affairs.

Weber (1947: 217) states that bureaucracy is technically the most 'efficient' form of organization: 'Precision, speed, unambiguity, knowledge of files, continuity, discretion, unity, strict subordination, reduction of friction and of material and personal costs— these are raised to the optimum point in the strictly bureaucratic administration.' Further, he portrayed this type of organization as the dominant institution of modern society, something echoed by Boulding (1953) and Whyte (1956). While not formulated in systems theory terms, and certainly not open systems, Weber's presentation of the components of a bureaucracy clearly portrays them as a complete system; all necessary and all interdependent. There is an internal coherence between the elements of the system.

Essentially, the sociology of organizations (from which organization and management theory primarily developed) accepted the basic bureaucratic thesis, that this form of organization was indicative of the modern world as it moved to larger-scale production and the depersonalization of society (Scott and Davis, 2007). And the initial analysis of the phenomenon was focused on understanding the internal organization and dynamics of bureaucracy. Key works (Selznick, 1949; Merton et al., 1952; Gouldner, 1954; and Blau, 1955) accepted the central theme of bureaucratization whilst developing critiques that were important in leading to a more open-systems approach. Details of the various critiques can be found elsewhere (e.g., Mouzelis, 1967; Scott, 1992). What is important for us is that the study of bureaucracy provided the basis for the later development of contingency theory.

THE 1960S AND 1970S

Essentially, studies in these two decades were elaborations of the ideas of the 1950s, but with a considerable convergence around systems thinking in a more direct sense, or indirectly by recognizing the relationship between an organization and its context. These decades also saw the flowering of the comparative study of organizations (King, Felin, and Whetten, 2009).

The Overall Functioning of Organizations

Studies examining the functioning or organizations diverged into two distinct streams. One was the continuing work of the Tavistock Institute that sought to systematize and theorize the idea of organizations as socio-technical systems. The other, in North America (Katz and Kahn, 1966; Thompson, 1967) was more theoretical and arose more directly from general systems theory and structural functionalism.

Emery and Trist (1965) continued to focus on the relationship between the social and the technical within organizations, portraying an organization as taking resources from its environment, converting those resources through the internal socio-technical system into outputs that were then exported back into the environment. They saw these relationships between internal and external systems as dynamic with continual interchange taking place across organizational and environmental boundaries. They argued that environments were becoming more turbulent with increasing interconnection between actors in the organization and the environment. The organization, *conceptualized as a system*, interacts with the environment, *also conceptualized as a system*.

In North America, Katz and Kahn (1966) and Thompson (1967) made significant contributions to open-systems theory. Katz and Kahn articulated the idea that organizations are made up of five interrelated sub-systems: production, external monitoring, boundary-spanning, control, and managerial. Production involves activities that create products and services; external monitoring concerns scanning and monitoring the environment; boundary-spanning deals with connections with external organizations; control is internal monitoring; and management is about direction, control, and coordination of these other sub-systems. There is a strong functionalist tone to this formulation, in that, and echoing studies of biological systems, all organizations have to address the same set of issues, such as linking with the environment, ensuring efficient performance, and so on. For systems theorists this emphasis upon functionality derives from the goal-directed nature of organizations. However, a generic critique of functionalist theory developed in the 1970s and remains dominant today.

Katz and Kahn articulated the *open* nature of the system, emphasizing the importance of the environment or context in which an organization is located. As we noted above, the theory of bureaucracy and classical management theory gave little or only modest attention to organizational externalities. Open-systems theory changed that way of thinking forever. So important and wide ranging was this change that today it is difficult to imagine that there was a time in our theorizing when the environmental context of organizations was not taken into account! Attention was drawn to understanding that environment, in systems terms.

It is necessary within any systems theory to specify how the components of a system and the activities that comprise them, are related to each other (Von Bertalanffy, 1956). Thompson (1967), who adopted an open-systems perspective, paid more attention to these specifics than did Katz and Kahn. Indeed, Thompson's is the seminal contribution, utilizing the ideas of open-systems theory but grounded in organizations. Essentially he was examining the appropriateness of organization design strategies under conditions of environmental uncertainty and heterogeneity and, as with many writers in the 1960s (Perrow, 1967; Woodward, 1965; Pugh et al., 1969; Hage and Aiken, 1969), Thompson saw technology as playing a central role in determining the appropriateness of organization design arrangements. In particular, he emphasized how technologies are associated with different forms of interdependence between organizational sub-units. His framework consists of three types of technologies—*mediating, long-linked,* and *intensive*—and analysed their association with distinctive patterns of interdependences.

A mediating technology derives from *pooled interdependence*. Pooled interdependence is where organizational sub-units are not directly linked but rely on, and contribute to, a common pool of resources (Lorsch and Allen, 1973)—conglomerates and highly diversified corporations are examples. Long-linked technology occurs where there is *sequential interdependence*—as in an assembly line where one task or activity leads directly to another (Lorsch and Allen, 1973). In this arrangement, activities are directly connected in a workflow, horizontally or vertically, or both; outputs from one unit are inputs for the next. For sequential interdependence to work there has to be a planning system. Finally, Thompson associates an 'intensive' technology with *reciprocal interdependence*. It is intensive because the connections between sub-units, tasks, activities and systems are essentially two-way, in that inputs and outputs move backwards and forwards between the units. Classic examples are team-based organizations, and the relationship between research and development and production departments.

Thompson is important for the way in which he opened up the idea of a technical core and analysed how it could differ in terms of system relationships. But he took another important step. Building upon his own work from the previous decade (Thompson and Bates, 1956; Thompson and Tuden, 1959), Thompson suggests that organizations have to take account of two aspects of the environment—its uncertainty, and its complexity—and organizations have to design internal systems that appropriately address them. Environmental uncertainty refers to the rate of change *and* the degree of predictability. Complexity refers to the homogeneity or heterogeneity of the organizations or systems with which the focal organization interacts. Are they similar or dissimilar to that organization and/or different from each other? For Thompson, and all later organization design scholars, the nature of the environments is critical for the design of an organization's internal systems. As we will see, these ideas became central to contingency theory.

How to Manage Organizations

The formulation of principles by the classical management school and the idea of a 'one best way' was soon discredited (e.g., Simon, 1947) but the implicit theme—that the component elements of organizational structures are interrelated (i.e., the idea of an internal system)—was retained and led to structural-contingency theory, which became the dominant theory of organizations in the 1960s and 1970s. Underpinning it was the notion of organizations as open systems—exemplified in the works of Woodward, Burns and Stalker, and Lawrence and Lorsch. From their approaches came the three critical components of contingency theory: 'an analytical description of organizations; the external circumstances that produce particular organizational designs; and the idea that there is an appropriate linkage between the external, the internal, and performance' (Van de Ven, Ganco, and Hinings (2013).

Joan Woodward's initial work was published in the 1950s (Woodward, 1958), but was systematized in the 1960s (Woodward, 1965). Her work certainly began as a critique of the one best way. For her, 'the danger lies in the tendency to teach the principles of administration as though they were scientific laws, when they are really little more than administrative expedients found to work well in certain circumstances but never tested in any systematic way' (quoted in Pugh and Hickson, 2007: 13). Clearly she was 'attacking' the idea of there being one best way. To do so, in her early work she conceptualized and measured organizational elements such as levels in the authority chain, spans of control, and various management ratios (Woodward, 1958) and in her later work systematized them as 'systems of management control' using terms such as 'personal/impersonal' and 'fragmented/unified'. For Woodward, the prime 'circumstance' (this is Van de Ven, Ganco, and Hinings's term) that determined the appropriateness of different systems of management control was the technology used. She analysed the technologies found in manufacturing organizations and, using a sophisticated measurement procedure, ranked them along a continuum from the least to most complex. An underlying dimension, as with Thompson, was that of predictability or uncertainty

Woodward's research suggested that achieving a 'fit' between the technology being used by an organization and the organization's systems of management control was critical for successful performance. However, although Woodward's focus on this fit meant that her emphasis was primarily internal—she explicitly acknowledged the importance of the environment. In her later studies (Woodward, 1970) she emphasized how changes in markets led to product innovation which then led to changes in technology and subsequently organization structures. In this sense, organizations are open systems.

Unlike Woodward, Burns and Stalker (1961) were explicitly concerned with both internal and external systems, but especially with the importance of achieving an appropriate alignment with the environment. Their argument stressed the implications of environmental and task uncertainty. As Donaldson (2001: 37) puts it, Burns and Stalker offer 'an elegant theory that has proved to be compelling for many subsequent scholars'—perhaps because they produced a simplified typology of internal organizational systems. Based on their empirical work, organizations were classified into 'mechanistic' and 'organic'. The mechanistic organization is very similar to a bureaucracy in that it exhibits a clear hierarchy, uses a specified division of labour in order to gain specialization, and is underpinned by detailed and clear rules and procedures. Roles are carefully specified and communication systems are based on formal position. Organic organizations, in contrast, have little specification of roles, a relative absence of formal control systems, and an emphasis upon expertise—not position—as the basis of authority. Unlike the highly programmed, almost machine-like mechanistic organization, the organic organization relies upon a continual high levels of interactions between units and individuals not through the hierarchy, but according to ability to assist and a willingness to experiment and adjust.

Burns and Stalker, in other words, provide an analytical description of two sets of internal systems, arranged in typological rather than continuous terms. This distinction between mechanistic and organic systems continues to resonate through organization theory (e.g., see Sine, Mitsuhashi, and Kirsch, 2006). But the really critical contribution of Burns and Stalker was to elaborate the conditions under which these two types or organization could operate and, indeed, successfully survive. The mechanistic organization performs well under conditions of both environmental and task certainty. Stable conditions, where markets and products are either not changing or do so in predictable ways, enable the specification of activities and control systems; the organization can be programmed and operate like a machine. The organic organization, on the other hand, thrives in conditions where there are high levels of uncertainty and unpredictability, both in the environment and in the nature of the tasks being performed. It can deal with new and unfamiliar issues in markets and products through its systems of adjustment and mutuality. Critically, neither the organic nor the mechanistic organization can successfully operate in both types of environments.

While not using the concept, per se, 'fit' is central to the Burns and Stalker argument and they recognized the inherent stability of systems once in place. They resist change. As Pugh and Hickson (2007: 33) point out, Burns and Stalker were at pains to demonstrate the difficulty of organizational change: 'The almost complete failure of the traditional Scottish firms to absorb electronics research and development engineers into their organizations lead Burns to doubt whether a mechanistic firm can consciously change into an organismic one.' In fact, in their efforts to change, mechanistic organizations exhibit 'pathological systems'. That is, in facing new problems and uncertainty of how to do so, they typically add more bureaucratic elements. In further development of this work, and in distinct contrast to other early contributions to the systems approach, Burns introduced a conceptualization of organizations as comprising three interacting and self-reinforcing social systems—the formal authority system, the career system, and the political system (Burns, 1966, 1977). The latter pair of these systems contributes to the inability of a mechanistic organization to move towards the organic form.

It was Lawrence and Lorsch (1967a, 1967b) who first used the notion of contingency theory. As with Woodward and Burns and Stalker, Lawrence and Lorsch (1967a, 1967b) directly challenged the idea of the 'one best way'. They examined two basic design processes, 'differentiation' and 'integration' and suggested that the ways that organizations manage these processes vary according to the environmental and task uncertainty that they faced. Hence, although they did not label themselves as systems theorist per se, Lawrence and Lorsch clearly exhibit an open-systems view of organizations.

For Lawrence and Lorsch, organizations are made up of three basic and generic sub-systems: production, sales, and research and development. Organizations are structured around these sub-systems and can be examined in terms of the extent of differentiation across the sub-systems (in terms of the relative formalization of their structures, differences in their time orientations, etc.) and the implication it has for achieving integration. Such attempts to define generic organizational activities are very much at the heart of systems theory. The central theme of Lawrence and Lorsch's analysis was that the greater the extent of differentiation, the greater the need for integration. Integration deals with the possibility of high levels of differentiation leading to conflict. This emphasis on sub-unit differences is taken up in current concerns with institutional logics and hybrid organizations (e.g., Battilana and Lee, 2014).

The existence of a range of organizational designs raises the question of why these differences between subunits arise—that is, why are units designed and managed differently, and why does that differentiation vary across organizations? Here the idea of an open system is critical. For Lawrence and Lorsch, as with Burns and Stalker, the link was with the environment in which an organization was located. In particular, sub-units (departments) and their associated structures were related to the extent of environmental uncertainty that *they* faced. Unlike Burns and Stalker, Lawrence and Lorsch recognized that an organization's environment is not an amorphous, undivided category—on the contrary, each subunit faces its own environment and those environments could vary in their degree of uncertainty. Lawrence and Lorsch (1967a: 5) were very clear about this,

> In this division of tasks, the organization is also ordering its environment into three sectors: the market sub-environment, the technical-economic sub-environment,

and the scientific sub-environment. It is readily apparent that each of these environments can range from highly dynamic to extremely stable. The importance of this variability can easily be obscured by the usual approach of thinking of an organization's environment as a single entity.

Thus, the critical environmental features were the different degrees of uncertainty (stability/dynamism) in markets, technologies and innovation. An organization facing *different* levels of uncertainty in these *different* environments have to be *more* internally differentiated if they are to be appropriately aligned; *and*, this greater differentiation will require more integrative effort (in the form of coordinating structures) if the organization is to function effectively. Lawrence and Lorsch were an important and definitive application of the open-systems approach to organizational design and performance.

The Study of Bureaucracy

In the 1960s and 1970s a fine-grained analysis of Weber's notion of bureaucracy came to dominate comparative organizational research with an emphasis on explaining organizational differences 'as a function of environmental, technological, and task-related variation' (King, Felin, and Whetten, 2009: 7). Similar to contingency theory, at the heart of this approach was the idea of fit.

Bureaucracy scholars questioned the idea of bureaucracy as one unitary type of organization (Hall, 1963; Hage and Aiken, 1967; Pugh et al., 1968; Blau and Schoenherr, 1971; Child, 1972a). Instead, bureaucracy was conceptualized as a set of organizational elements (in particular, of structures), which raised questions of causation for the differences in structures that were being found. An important implication was a growing interest in using this approach to derive typologies of bureaucracy as the basis for comparative organizational analysis. Admittedly, as King, Felin, and Whetten (2009: 7) put it, 'comparative analysis by the late 1960s was primarily interested in explaining *static* (emphasis added) differences between organizations as a function of environmental, technological, and task-related variation'. Nevertheless, such an approach does show an open-systems approach to organizational analysis.

As we noted earlier, Weber's ideal type of bureaucracy is a systems type model in the sense that the elements of the ideal type were conceptualized as systematically related. This is the nature of an ideal type. There is also the idea of an open system as the bureaucratic organization is a result of societal trends of rationalism and industrialization. However, the starting point for studies of bureaucracy in the 1960s and 1970s was that these internal system elements could be combined in different ways. The 'Aston' school, for example, was ordered around the concepts of specialization, standardization, formalization, and centralization (Pugh et al., 1968) and each of these elements of bureaucracy was treated as a 'dimension' (i.e., organizations could vary in the degree of its standardization, centralization, etc.). Empirically, patterns were observed in the way that elements came together, thus forming a typology of bureaucracies.

Studies producing typologies of bureaucracy contributed to the development of contingency theory—first, by systematizing the empirical study of organizations in order to capture their internal coherence; and second, by exploring the relationship between patterns of bureaucracy and aspects of the organization (e.g., its size and/or its technology) and the environment (Donaldson, 2001; Van de Ven, Ganco, and Hinings, 2013). These studies, in other words, increasingly reflected an open-systems theory approach. There was an explicit theorization of an organization as made up of interrelated elements. The components of a bureaucracy hang together. (In this respect, there is a distinctly 'structural functional' undertone in the assumption that the way an organization is structured derives from the goals and associated activities that it embraces.) Further, the theme that organizational form is related to the environment in which it is set, the idea of an open system, was taken for granted.

Typologies and taxonomies were an important part of theorizing about contingencies and organizational design in the 1960s and 1970s. Typologies, as with Weber, are theoretically derived, with the underlying idea that organizational elements are systemically related (Meyer, Tsui, and Hinings, 1993). Taxonomies are empirically derived through multivariate classification of organizational elements (Pugh, Hickson, and Hinings, 1969; McKelvey, 1982). Indeed, Miller and Friesen (1984) took the typology/taxonomy argument further with the idea of configurations. Organizations strive for coherence through the internal consistency of structures and systems. Such consistency produces systematic configurations of organizational elements. Miller and Friesen imply that there are a limited number of configurations and that the configurations are related to organizational size and technology, and to environmental uncertainty and complexity.

Mintzberg (1979, 1983) produced a typology of five organizational designs that, for him, synthesized all of the research on organizational structure and functioning and the relationship to organizational characteristics and environmental features: the simple structure, the machine bureaucracy, the professional bureaucracy, the divisionalized form, and the adhocracy. This classification was based on differences in coordinating mechanisms such as supervision and standardization, the type and degree of centralization, and which organizational group is dominant. In addition, an organization's age, size, and the extent of environmental and technological complexity and stability were included to produce the five types. As with Weber on bureaucracy and other typologies, Mintzberg adopts the contingency thesis that it is closeness to one of these ideal types that produces effectiveness.

All of these scholars, whether concerned with the functioning of organizations, their management, or the empirical analysis of bureaucracy, converge around the two ideas central to contingency theory: that organizations strive for internal coherence in their structures and systems *and* external coherence with the environmental demands. Internal and external coherence produces organizational effectiveness. Essentially, in other words, for contingency theory organization design is a constrained optimization problem: 'At the organization level, this entails maximizing performance outcomes by minimizing the misfit between diverse environmental demands and internal organizational arrangements, which in turn requires maximizing the benefits of organizational differentiation and minimizing the costs of integration' (Van de Ven, Ganco, and Hinings, 2013).

This contingency and typological view dominated throughout the 1960s and 1970s before the emergence of resource dependency theory, population ecology, and institutional theory. In part, these new theories arose because of the narrow definition of both the organization and its environment that contingency theory adopted, and also its static nature. There was, too, a strong move away from a structural functionalist analysis of organizations.

BEYOND THE 1970S

King, Felin, and Whetten (2009: 7) summarize the 'post-contingency theory' decline of interest in the issues of the 1960s and 1970s, 'the limited scope of the project—to explain fit between organizational structures and task or environmental requirements—brought on the radical transformation of organizational sociology in the late 1970s. Declining interest in organizational structure as a phenomenon was accompanied by a sudden move to higher levels of analysis.' In one sense, open-systems theory and its expression in contingency theory had done what they set out to do, dealing with issues that were historically significant. Scholars had demonstrated that there was no 'one best way'. They had shown that bureaucracy was a more complicated concept than had been suggested previously. They had shown that organizational designs were systematically related to environmental issues. And in doing these things they had established an organization-in-context, open-systems approach. So, as King, Felin, and Whetten (2009) suggest, there was a kind of 'where to next' '*mood to*' theorizing.

Essentially, four new paths were developed during the 1970s, three of which became the most important theoretical directions for the study of organizations over the next several decades. The three theories, each illustrating King, Felin, and Whetten's point about a move to higher levels of analysis, were resource dependence (Pfeffer and Salancik, 1978), population ecology (Hannan and Freeman, 1977), and institutional theory (Meyer and Rowan, 1977). All three are rooted in the organization-environment relationship. The fourth approach derives from Child's (1972b) concept of 'strategic choice', which is related to resource dependency, but is mainly a direct critique of contingency theory and an attempt to add to it and make it more amenable to analysis of internal processes.

In addition, there is also the behavioural theory (BTH) of the firm (Cyert and March, 1963). BTH was developed as a counter to the theory of the firm in neo-classical economics; as such it was very internally focused. 'Cyert and March saw goals within the firm emerging and changing over time as coalitions formed and shifted among organizational members' (Barney and Hesterley, 2006: 121). Gavetti et al. (2012) argue that the behavioural theory of the firm is itself an open, theoretical system and so its ideas, such as bounded rationality and a focus on decision-making, have been highly influential in strategy and organization theory, but it is not directly concerned with the issues that we raise here.

These developments signalled some key points that had, on the one hand, been established by systems and contingency theory, and, on the other hand, pointed clearly at new developments in order to develop the issues raised by these theories. By the end of the 1970s it was taken-for-granted that organizations were systems, even if the specific language of systems theory was not used; that there were a variety of designs of those organizational systems; and that they were open systems with that variety being related to external circumstances. But the new theorizing dealt with two issues facing contingency theory. One issue (Child, 1972b; Pfeffer and Salancik, 1978) was a concern with internal processes of adaptation and change, emphasizing, through concepts such as strategic choice and power, the ways in which organizations responded to environmental pressures. There was no assumption that organizations would respond uniformly to the same pressures, because of internal differences. A second issue was that of the ways in which organizations changed the contexts in which they were located (Pfeffer and Salancik, 1978). Thus, organizations would have influence over their environments. The emphasis is on understanding the relationship between the internal dynamics of organizations and their external context (Greenwood and Hinings, 1996).

Population ecology and institutional theory took up the contextual concerns of open-systems theory and contingency theory but either asked questions about the ecological structure of populations of organizations, or elements of the environment that were socio-cultural rather than economic and technological. Both of these approaches opened up a whole new series of questions around broad patterns of organizational adaptation and change rather than organizational stasis.

Conclusions

We have outlined the development of open-systems theory and contingency theory in the 1950s, 1960s, and 1970s, from its roots in how to understand the functioning of organizations, organizational variety, and the development of bureaucracy. As a result of all this work, the notion of organizations as set in environments and adapting to, and changing those environments is taken-for-granted in organizational theory. However, the specific approach through the language of systems theory, in its biological form, is not really part of the lexicon of organization theory although an evolutionary, biological approach is found in population ecology and its developments (Aldrich, 1979, 1999).

A number of scholars have pointed to the loss of attention to organizations, per se, in contemporary organization theory (Gavetti, Levinthal, and Ocasio, 2007; King, Felin, and Whetten, 2009; Greenwood, Hinings, and Whetten, 2014). For these authors, the concern with collectives of organizations, with the structures of environments, and with internal processes of decision-making and choice (Langley, 2007), has led to a lack of focus on the organization, leading Van de Ven, Ganco, and Hinings (2013) to suggest that contingency theory could usefully be revitalized in ways that would 'shed new light on the fundamental questions of organizational and institutional design'. Moreover, as King, Felin, and Whetten (2009: 12) conclude, 'the bottom line is that the organization needs to be theorized as a unique kind of context and social actor'. Open-systems theory and contingency theory, revisited, would give us that possibility.

References

Aldrich, H. E. (1979). *Organizations and Environments*. Englewood Cliffs, NJ: Prentice Hall.
Aldrich, H. (1999). *Organizations Evolving*. Thousand Oaks, CA: SAGE.
Ashby, W. R. (1952). *Design for a Brain*. New York: Wiley.
Barnard, C. (1938). *Functions of the Executive*. Cambridge, MA: Harvard University Press.
Barney, J. and Hesterley, W. (2006). 'Organizational Economics: Understanding the Relationship between Organizations and Economic Analysis', in S. Clegg, C. Hardy, T. Lawrence, and W. Nord, *The SAGE Handbook of Organization Studies*. London: SAGE.
Battilana, J. and Lee, M. (2014). 'Advancing Research on Hybrid Organizing: Insights from the Study of Social Enterprises'. *Annals of the Academy of Management*, 8.
Blau, P. (1955). *The Dynamics of Bureaucracy*. Chicago, IL: University of Chicago Press.
Blau, P., and Schoenherr, P. (1971). *The Structure of Organizations*. New York: Basic Books.
Boulding, K. (1953). *The Organizational Revolution*. New York: Harper.
Boulding, K. (1956). 'General Systems Theory: The Skeleton of Science'. *Management Science*, 2: 197–208.
Burns, T. (1966). 'On the Plurality of Social Systems', in J. R. Lawrence (ed.), *Operational Research and the Social Sciences*. London: Tavistock.
Burns, T. (1977). *The BBC: Public Institution and Private World*. London: Macmillan.
Burns, T. and Stalker, G. M. (1961). *The Management of Innovation*. London: Tavistock.
Child, J. (1972a). 'Organization Structure and Strategies of Control: A Replication of the Aston Study'. *Administrative Science Quarterly*, 17: 163–77.
Child, J. (1972b). 'Organizational Structure, Environment and Performance: The Role of Strategic Choice'. *Sociology*, 6: 1–22.
Cyert, R. and March, J. (1963). *A Behavioral Theory of the Firm*. Englewood Cliffs, NJ: Prentice-Hall.
Donaldson, L.(2001). *The Contingency Theory of Organizations*. Thousand Oaks, CA: SAGE.
Emery, F. and Trist, E. (1965). 'The Causal Texture of Organizational Environments'. *Human Relations*, 18: 21–32.
Fayol, H. (1949). *General and Industrial Management*. London: Pitman.
Follett, M. P. (1942). *Dynamic Administration*. New York: Harper.
Gavetti, G., Greve, H., Levinthal, D., and Ocasio, W. (2012). 'The Behavioral Theory of the Firm: Assessments and Prospects'. *Annals of the Academy of Management*, 6: 1–40.
Gavetti, G., Levinthal, D., and Ocasio, W. (2007). 'Neo-Carnegie: The Carnegie School's Past, Present and Reconstructing the Future'. *Organization Science*, 18: 523–36.
Gerth, H. H. and Mills, C. W. (ed.) (1958). *From Max Weber: Essays in Sociology*. New York: Galaxy.

Gouldner, A. W. (1954). *Patterns of Industrial Bureaucracy*. Glencoe, IL: The Free Press.
Graicunas, V. A. (1937). 'Relationship in Organization', in G. Luther and L. F. Urwick (eds.), *Papers on the Science of Administration*. New York: Institute of Public Administration, Columbia University.
Greenwood, R. and Hinings, C. R. (1996). 'Understanding Radical Organizational Change: Bringing Together the Old and New Institutionalism'. *Academy of Management Review*, 21: 1022–55.
Greenwood, R., Hinings, C. R., and Whetten, D. (2014). 'Rethinking Institutions and Organizations'. *Journal of Management Studies*, 51(7): 1206–20.
Gulick, L. and Urwick, L. (1936). *Papers on the Science of Administration*. New York: Institute of Public Administration.
Hage, J. and Aiken, M. (1969). 'Routine Technology, Social Structure and Organizational Goals'. *Administrative Science Quarterly*, 14: 366–76.
Hall, R. H. (1963). 'The Concept of Bureaucracy: An Empirical Assessment'. *Administrative Science Quarterly*, 8: 32–40.
Hannan, M. and Freeman, J. (1977). 'The Population Ecology of Organizations'. *American Journal of Sociology*, 82: 929–64.
Hinings, C. R. (2010). 'The Contribution of Joan Woodward: A Personal Reflection'. *Research in the Sociology of Organizations*, 29: 41–5.
Hinings, C. R., Pugh, D. S., Hickson, D. J., and Turner, C. (1967). 'An Approach to the Study of Bureaucracy'. *Sociology*, 1: 61–72.
Hinings, C. R. and Raynard, M. (2014). 'Organizational Form, Structure and Religious Organizations'. *Religion and Organization Theory, Research in the Sociology of Organizations*, 41: 159–86.
Katz, D. and Kahn, R. (1966). *The Social Psychology of Organizations*. New York: John Wiley.
King, B., Felin, T., and Whetten, D. (2009). 'Comparative Organizational Analysis: An Introduction', in B. King, T. Felin, and D. Whetten (eds.), *Studying Differences between Organizations: Comparative Approaches to Organizational Research. Research in the Sociology of Organizations*, vol. 26. Bingley: Emerald Publishing Group Ltd, 3–20.
Langley, A. (2007). 'Process Thinking in Strategic Organization'. *Strategic Organization*, 5: 271–82.
Lawrence, P. and Lorsch, J. (1967a). *Organization and Environment*. Cambridge, MA: Harvard University Graduate School of Business Administration.
Lawrence, P. R. and Lorsch, J. W. (1967b). 'Differentiation and Integration in Complex Organizations'. *Administrative Science Quarterly*, 12(1): 1–47.
Lorsch, J. and Allen, S. (1973). *Managing Diversity and Inter-Dependence: An Organizational Study of Multidivisional Firms*. Boston, MA: Harvard University Press.
Lorsch, J. and Lawrence, P. (1972). 'Environmental Factors and Organization Integration', in J. Lorsch and P. Lawrence (eds.), *Organizational Planning: Cases and Concepts*. Homewood, IL: Irwin Dorsey.
McKelvey, W. (1982). *Organizational Systematics: Taxonomy, Evolution and Classification*. Berkeley, CA: University of California Press.
Merton, R. K., Gray, A., Hockey, B., and Selvin, H. (ed.) (1952). *Reader in Bureaucracy*. Glencoe, IL: Free Press.
Meyer, J. and Rowan, B. (1977). 'Institutionalized Organizations: Formal Structure as Myth and Ceremony'. *American Journal of Sociology*, 83: 340–63.
Meyer, A., Tsui, A., and Hinings, C. R. (1993). 'Configurational Approaches to Organizational Analysis'. *Academy of Management Journal*, 36: 1175–95.

Miller, D. and Friesen, P. (1984). *Organizations: A Quantum View*. Englewood Cliffs, NJ: Prentice Hall.

Miller, D. and Le Breton-Miller, I. (2005). *Managing for the Long Run*. Boston, MA: Harvard Business School Press.

Miller, D., Le Breton-Miller, I., and Lester, R. H. (2011). 'Family and Lone Founder Ownership and Strategic Behavior: Social Context, Identity and Institutional Logics'. *Journal of Management Studies*, 48: 1–25.

Mintzberg H. (1979). *The Structuring of Organizations: A Synthesis of the Research*. Englewood Cliffs, NJ: Prentice Hall.

Mintzberg, H. (1983). *Structure in Fives: Designing Effective Organizations*. Englewood Cliffs, NJ: Prentice-Hall.

Mooney, J. (1937). *The Principles of Organization*. New York: Harper.

Mouzelis, N. P. (1967). *Organization and Bureaucracy*. London: Routledge and Kegan Paul.

Parsons, T. (1956). 'Suggestions for a Sociological Approach to the Theory of Organizations, I and II'. *Administrative Science Quarterly*, 1: 63–85, 224–39.

Parsons, T. (1958). 'Some Ingredients of a General Theory of Formal Organization', in A. W. Halpin (ed.), *Administrative Theory in Education*. Chicago, IL: University of Chicago Press.

Perrow, C. (1967). 'A Framework for the Comparative Analysis of Organizations'. *American Sociological Review*, 32: 194–208.

Pfeffer, J. and Salancik, G. (1978). *The External Control of Organizations: A Resource Dependence Perspective*. New York: Harper and Row.

Pugh, D. S. and Hickson, D. J. (2007). *Writers on Organizations*, 6th edn. London: SAGE.

Pugh, D. S., Hickson, D. J., and Hinings, C. R. (1969). 'An Empirical Taxonomy of Structures of Work Organizations'. *Administrative Science Quarterly*, 14: 115–26.

Pugh, D. S., Hickson, D. J., Hinings, C. R. and Turner, C. (1968). 'Dimensions of Organization Structure'. *Administrative Science Quarterly*, 13: 65–105.

Pugh, D. S., Hickson, D. J., Hinings, C. R. and Turner, C. (1969). 'The Context of Organization Structures'. *Administrative Science Quarterly*, 14: 91–114.

Rice, A. M. (1958). *Productivity and Social Organization*. London: Tavistock.

Scott, W. R. (1992). *Organizations: Rational, Natural and Open Systems*. Englewood Cliffs, NJ: Prentice Hall.

Scott, W. R. and Davis, G. (2007). *Organizations and Organizing: Rational, Natural and Open System Perspectives*. Englewood Cliffs, NJ: Prentice Hall.

Selznick, P. (1949). *TVA and the Grass Roots*. Berkeley, CA: University of California Press.

Simon, H. (1947). *Administrative Behavior*. New York: Macmillan.

Sine, W., Mitsuhashi, H., and Kirsch, D. (2006). 'Revisiting Burns and Stalker: Formal Structure and New Venture Performance in Emerging Economic Sectors'. *Administrative Science Quarterly*, 49(1): 121–32.

Taylor, F. W. (1947). *Scientific Management*. New York: Harper and Row.

Thompson, J. D. (1967). *Organizations in Action*. New York: McGraw-Hill.

Thompson, J. D. and Bates, F. L. (1956). 'Technology, Organization and Administration'. *Administrative Science Quarterly*, 2: 325–42.

Thompson, J. D. and Tuden, A. (1959). 'Strategies, Structures, and Processes of Organizational Decision', in J. D. Thompson (ed.), *Comparative Studies in Administration*. Pittsburgh, PA: University of Pittsburgh Press.

Trist, E. and Bamforth, K. (1951). 'Some Social and Psychological Consequences of the Longwall Method of Coal Getting'. *Human Relations*, 4: 3–38.

Urwick, L. F. (1943). *The Elements of Business Administration*. London: Pitman.

Van de Ven, A., Ganco, M. and Hinings, C. R. (2013). 'Returning to the Frontier of Contingency Theory of Organizational and Institutional Design'. *Annals of the Academy of Management*, 7: 393–440.
Von Bertalanffy, L. (1956). 'General Systems Theory', in L. Von Bertalanffy and A. Rapoport (eds.), *General Systems: Yearbook of the Society for the Advancement of General Systems Theory*, vol 1.
Weber, M. (1947). *The Theory of Economic and Social Organization*. Glencoe, IL: The Free Press.
Wiener, N. (1956). *I am a Mathematician*. New York: Doubleday.
Woodward, J. (1958). *Management and Technology. Problems of Progress in Industry*, vol. 3. London: HMSO.
Woodward, J. (1965). *Industrial Organization: Theory and Practice*. New York: Oxford University Press.
Woodward, J. (ed.) (1970). *Industrial Organization: Behaviour and Control*. New York: Oxford University Press.
Whyte, W. H. (1956). *The Organization Man*. New York: Simon and Schuster.

CHAPTER 8

FUTURE IN THE PAST

A Philosophical Reflection on the Prospects of Management

STEWART CLEGG, MARCO BERTI, AND WALTER P. JARVIS

We are ignorant of the meaning of the dragon in the same way that we are ignorant of the meaning of the universe; but there is something in the dragon's image that fits man's imagination, and this accounts for the dragon's appearance in different places and periods.

Jorge Luis Borges, *The Book of Imaginary Beings* (1957)

INTRODUCTION: IS ORGANIZING THE FUTURE OF ORGANIZATION?

WHAT will be the *next big thing* in management and organization? Both practitioners and theorists have been outpouring words and ideas in attempts to be at the forefront of innovation in the design of work and business activities. In the last century, structures were first designed according to scientific principles (Taylor, 1911), then corrected to allow for presumed psychological needs (Mayo, 1949), and afterwards aligned with technological and environmental contingencies (Donaldson, 2001). More recently, a flurry of disparate structural forms have been hailed as breakthrough innovations destined to revolutionize the production of goods and services: lean manufacturing (Jones, Roos, and Womack, 1990), hierarchies, matrix structures (Galbraith, 2008), process-driven systems (Hammer and Champy, 1993), learning organizations (Senge, 1994), boundaryless organizations (Ashkenas et al., 1998), virtual organizations (Hedberg, Dahlgren, and Olve, 1997) are just some of the many. Organizational scholars, for some time, have been busy debating how the bureaucratic forms that dominated the world between the nineteenth and the twentieth centuries were on the verge of being displaced, or at least supplemented by 'something else', producing a more diverse organizational ecology. Ideal models describing these alternate forms include culture driven clans (Ouchi, 1979); organically developed, informal adhocracies (Mintzberg, 1983); highly integrated 'post-modern' organizations (Clegg, 1990); post-bureaucracies based on dialogue and soft-management tools (Donnellon and Heckscher, 1994), and hybrid forms that merge bureaucratic and post-bureaucratic elements (Josserand, Teo, and Clegg, 2006).

All models and approaches to organization structuring tend to be based on the same tacit assumption, the idea that organizations can be represented as 'solid' entities, possessing discrete and objectively appraisable attributes. These objects can be fabricated out of a blueprint, modified and shaped according to the desires of their designers. As such they can be represented in the forms of static models, made of boxes and connecting lines, their activities represented by regular flows and predictable cycles. The capacity and authority to bring to life and direct the operations of these machines rests on a small group of individuals, endowed with special skills and ability, the managers. As a consequence management scholars have the role of understanding the principles that regulate the functioning of these apparatuses, and to instruct their makers and masterminds on how best to extract performances from their functioning.

Various commentators lament, however, that management studies 'lost its way', either because of their incapacity to produce 'high-impact research' (Lorsch, 2009; Alvesson and Sandberg, 2013) or because they fail to address both the ethical and practical implications of lived realities of management (Mintzberg, 2004; Bennis and O'Toole, 2005). A possible way for the discipline to regain lost relevance, and to provide added value to practitioners resides not in focusing on objects (organizations, institutions, structures) but on processes of organizing, investigating the multiple different ways in which individuals build an inter-subjective 'order' out of a muddle of possibilities, and how organizations emerge out of particular temporary arrangements of different modes of organizing. In this sense 'organization' is not the opposite of chaos but only one possible way to arrange bodies, activities, and things, aligning them in relation to specific objectives. Concrete organizations are therefore not the expression of 'optimal' ordering models, as a long stream of studies, ranging from Taylor to the Aston school, from transaction cost theory to system theory, assumes. On the contrary, they are the outcome of a political struggle between different modes of organizing.

These different modes are discursively constituted in more or less implicit, and sometimes explicit, theories of organization. The instrumentality of organization is a concept long discussed (Selznick, 1949). Specific combinations of organizing modes serve as tools at the same time for different purposes: efficiently and effectively performing a specific task; guaranteeing the continuity to a structure of domination; even surviving and self-reproducing. Focusing on organization as an effect of discursive struggles between protagonists of more or less explicit theories requires abandoning, at least momentarily, both the 'technical' and the 'scientific' orientation that have typically characterized organization studies. A philosophical standpoint is required, one that enables critical questioning of the basic assumptions and prejudices on which descriptions and theories are based (Tsoukas and Chia, 2011a). In this regard, perhaps, the search for the future (of management studies) should begin in the past (the tradition of philosophical enquiry).

A philosophical lens prepared by Wittgenstein (1958) allows (or even imposes) doubt and uncertainty: the will not to claim the intrinsic 'superiority' or truthfulness of a particular 'organizing' of language games but a willingness to dwell within them. Today, the use of information technology has enabled forms of interaction that collapse space and time, remodulating the relevance of certain physical aspects pivotal to 'modern' bureaucracies. As such, the centrality of organizing to a century of management and organization studies language games has become just another rusted-on prejudice. Prejudice, of course, should not be denigrated, since these prejudices incorporate our historical context as a precondition for understanding in social sciences (Gadamer, 2004: 277–89).

WHAT GIVES SUBSTANCE TO ORGANIZATIONS? THE IMPLICATIONS OF ESSENTIALIST VIEWS

The 'traditional' discourses that focus on the essential nature of organizations, assuming their 'ontological solidity', give life and substance to an otherwise precarious object, a sense of solidity rooted in the languages of everyday life. They deploy power/knowledge effects constructing a socially acknowledged subject. This happens through a multitude of symbolic and material acts that produce their truths: legal 'incorporation' (a very fitting term) formally attributes social existence to this subject; the production of a set of texts (statutes, mission, vision, brand, strategic statements, etc.) gives symbolic presence to the entity; the attribution of borders and finalities provides shape and legitimation, as instruments of technical rationality (Weber, 1978). Scholars of organizations have been actively engaged in this reification of organizations, by taking them for granted as empirical objects (Czarniawska, 2008) and neglecting the role that they were playing in (re)producing them, since 'there is no giveness of the object which is not given within the interpretative field' (Butler, 2004: 274, cited in Borgerson, 2005: 64).

It is undoubted that the social constructions of these objects as central elements in the language games of management and organization theory can display a remarkable permanence and that, while utilized to pursue objectives, their instrumental role is in time replaced by an institutional character, so that the tool often acquires 'a life of its own' (Selznick, 1949: 10). Nothing that assumes life remains unquestioningly the same—accepting the fixity of the organizational phenomenon and privileging the institutionalized features of organizations present two major dangers.

The first problem is that, by concentrating on the construction of an ideal type out of the language games of any moment in history risks becoming blind to the variety of naturally emerging forms of organizing, imposing an idiosyncratic social construction as a universal phenomenon. The use of ideal types to describe organizational forms in general, and the bureaucratic model in particular was legitimated by Weber (1978). His intent in using these abstract representations was neither to describe the utopian prototype of a supremely desirable form of work organization nor to catalogue empirically observable phenomena. The purpose of his ideal types was to 'give a precise meaning to (…) forms of action which in each case involve the highest possible degree of logical integration (…) it is probably seldom if ever that a real phenomenon can be found which corresponds exactly to one of these ideally constructed pure types' (Weber, 1978: 20). Ideal types were useful benchmarks with which to understand and recognize characteristics of an observed phenomenon deemed theoretically fundamental at a significant moment in their emergence: a convenient methodological instrument with troubling power/knowledge effects.

On the one hand, as reasoned by Schütz (1932), it is not clear whether Weberian ideal types should be seen as a construct belonging to the social scientist or a category actually employed by the organization's members to interpret and categorize their experiences. Clearly, these types stand at the intersection of two distinct language games—constructed out of lay conceptions of their enterprise they passed into the technical sphere of formal analysis with Weber's formulation. The distinction between these two sites for the language games is not only relevant from an epistemological perspective but has serious practical implications, because of the double hermeneutic effect (Giddens, 1984). Theorizations of social phenomenon that draw from lay conceptions are assimilated into theoretical practices by academic agents who then recursively translate them back into practice that changes in consequence of the eternal mutability of all translation. Ideal constructions become taken-for-granted 'facts', which are taught and promoted as correct interpretations, inducing an un-reflexive reification of the phenomenon. As a consequence, academic practice in management and organization studies contributes to the diffusion of a form of fetishism in which lay actors function both as subjects of anxiety, worried about their organizations being insufficiently 'lean', 'process centric' or 'networked', a concern that can lead to unwarranted and harmful restructuring decisions, and as privileged respondents to translations as yet unrecorded. Neo-institutional studies (DiMaggio and Powell, 1983; Powell and DiMaggio, 1991) have demonstrated the pervasiveness of mimetic phenomena and their homogenizing effects.

On the other hand, concentrating attention on the common, easily recognizable aspects of social interactions, those everyday phenomena that can be made to 'fit the model' can lead to overlooking and downplaying the variety and the importance of forms of goal oriented collaborative action emerging from other, less familiar language games to those that, almost by historical accidents, became institutionalized in the academy.

The chief accident was considering organizations as well defined 'organisms' (or machines) with a clear identity, a permanent and always coherent structure, with their members considered as cells (or gears). Narratives that focused on the strategic decisions of leaders to design and redesign organizations were privileged; the necessity of taming individual creativity and initiative by running it through the gauntlet of standardized routines and impersonal norms became legitimated as normal; bottom-up social innovations were instead deviance, resistance, or anarchy. Multiple 'organizing principles' are at play in organizations and the multifarious language games surrounding and contesting them. Hierarchy and the use of formal norms are only two among many of the principles that animate these games. Mutual adjustment, co-determination, technology enabled collaboration, shared values and beliefs, could be equally or even more powerful points of reference.

The second peril that derives from the a-critical acceptance of the centrality of forms given by language over action is the ease with which such paradigms give way to an unbridled form of managerialism (Knights and Willmott, 1997; Parker, 2002). In fact the separation between theory (as represented by the legitimated ideal types) and practice (the embodied and emerging reality of organized action) is based on the postulation of subject–object separation (Sandberg and Tsoukas, 2011), the idea that an observing subject can know an external object (the 'organization'). The production of an absolute and dispassionate form of knowledge on which action can be based is assumed, one that leads to separating the thinking minds (management) and the working bodies (the subordinates). The manager is represented as 'a morally neutral technician' (Roberts, 1996: 55), oriented not 'toward the realization of practical goals but toward the solution of technical problems' (Habermas, 1987: 103). This creed is typically reproduced by the language games of business education, behooven to the stories that circulate in the executive language games. Students are socialized through the routine application of these discursive techniques, through the use of case study analysis, that privileges technical rationality over critical reflection on goals (Roberts, 1996), effectively making 'hired hands' of managers (Khurana, 2007), albeit with the brain of the management consultancy industry, loosely coupled to these hands, spewing out ever more language games of formal reasoning. Consequently, the reification of organizations and institutional attention buttress an ideology based on 'performativity (work until you drop), efficiency (people defined as expendable resources), and commitment to short term, bottom line decision criteria' (Boje and Al Arkoubi, 2009: 104). Another 'commonsensical' concept resonates with and further supports the idea that the purpose of organizations is to produce 'value' in financial terms, guaranteeing a handsome return on investment to those who provided capital for their operation.

The social rift that these mutually reinforcing discourses produce is not only morally and politically questionable but, paradoxically, does not even best serve the purpose of 'extracting value'. Contemporary developed economies, within their territories, are not the domain of manufacturing and the exploitation of surplus value from proletarian labour but of service and knowledge intensive industries. The crude exploitation is off-shored and housed in new mega-manufactories into which new proletarians are recruited and the old proletariat from the heartlands of industrial society either escapes the old manufactories, now largely derelict, the old industrial towns, now more shuttered than not, into service jobs, narcotics, and other escape attempts to fill lives made poorer. What is happening in southern Europe is that the 'orphans' of manufacturing are struggling to find any job (not even in the de-qualified service industry) and in addition to escapism there is also recruitment in the underworld of organized crime, the only thriving industry. Finally, all this drives casualization, creating a new class that needs a new label. These are definitely not 'proletarian' (they are educated enough to understand they cannot afford to have children); since the only assets they possess are their mind and flexibility, they could be labelled 'intellectuarians', rich in ideas, appreciation, and aesthetics but poor in pocket, if not in spirit.

Elsewhere, in the service economy, in the longer and less standardized value chains typical of this context, creativity and exploration capabilities are essential for organizational performances and subjectivities, emotions, and cognitions become objects of control rather than the labouring time and intensity of yore (Alvesson and Deetz, 2006). Employees whose identities, rather than hand and bodies, must be regulated (Alvesson and Willmott, 2002), who are asked to perform emotion work (Hochschild, 1979), are no longer confined by bureaucratic 'iron cages'. Hence, asking what is the purpose of considering the design of such cages becomes a most legitimate object of discussion and reflection.

The reification of organizational phenomena produces static expressions of objects.[1] If we consider them as phenomena 'in a constant state of becoming (…) rather than "existing", what we think of as an organization is the momentary apprehension of an ongoing process of organizing that never results in an actual entity' (Clegg, Kornberger, and Rhodes, 2005: 158). As with the river described by Heraclitus, organizations are not really always there: they change and flow constantly and we need to understand what in the collective conscience gives coherence and shape to their flow. Instead of taking for granted the persistence of institutions and corporations, looking at them as if they were made of solid rock, we should highlight how their coherence can only be maintained thanks to the constant emotional, intellectual, creative, and cognitive work of their members, who are performing a 'chronic rebuilding' effort (Weick, 1979: 44).

We should not consider organizations as mere containers in which processes occur but regard these processes and those organizations as emergent accomplishments (Feldman, 2000), 'emerging from the reflective application of (…) rules in local contexts over time' (Tsoukas and Chia, 2002: 570) redirecting our attention to the ways in which coherence and uniformity can be achieved. Rather than ontology, the practical accomplishment of process view of organization is an alternative epistemological focus that enables a richer ontological understanding, allowing *both* the investigation of organizing (the processes and the practices) *and* of organizations (the lasting configurations

---

[1] A perfect metaphorical illustration of the concept of the static organization as a work in process can be found in the Uffington White Horse, a stylized figure about 100 metres long, carved on a hillside in Oxfordshire, England. Formed by a deep trench filled with chalk, it dates back to the Bronze Age, which makes it between 2,500 and 3,500 years old. Since vegetation tends to overgrow and rains wash away the chalk, the persistence of this figure has been made possible only by a constant work of scrubbing and cleaning of the site, which has been performed at least once every generation over the last three millennia (Schwyzer 1999). This probably makes this figure one of the most durable example of continuing organized efforts in the history of humanity, and it clearly demonstrates that even structures that have become part of the 'natural landscape' are the fruit of an unceasing toil.

and narrative reconstructions of acts). By considering the aspects of organizing and the (temporary but persistent) effects of these organizing efforts it is possible to examine different and mutually constituting facets of the phenomenon. Such an approach would be aligned with the attempt to consider both episodic and systemic expressions of power (Clegg, 1989) and to consider the interplay of agency and structure (Giddens, 1984).

Consequently, organizing (verb) and organization (noun) must be considered in conjunction. The former produces the latter, while at the same time the attribution of identity to the systematic disposition of expectations, relationships, and exchanges that characterize organization as a thing, as an empirical object, is not just a descriptive act. It is a form of *poiesis*, a generative act, turning ephemeral networks of repeated actions into 'conceptually-stabilized abstractions: "islands" of fabricated coherence in a sea of chaos and change' (Chia, 2002: 866). The symbolic and discursive dimension of organizations (Chia, 2000; Grant et al., 2004; Alvesson and Kärreman, 2011) necessarily looms large in such a conceptualization. Organizational students become as the mythical Gorgon Medusa, who petrified onlookers with her gaze; caught in the gaze organizations only gain stability and persistence by inter-subjective agreements that fix them with a series of coherent narratives, which have both an ostensive (ideal, conjectural, notional) and a performative (producing action, thinking, and feeling) quality (Latour, 1986).

A phenomenological view, incorporating social, techno-material, and symbolic aspects, is necessary to apprehend these 'post', liquid, organizations (Clegg and Baumeler, 2014). While recognizing the relevance of formal structures at a minimum, because of the power/knowledge effects of enforceable design, the phenomenological view enables analysis to transcend artificially set boundaries to focus on the inscription of these within wider action nets (Latour, 2005) and institutional fields (Bourdieu, 1990). As such, a phenomenological view of this type is more aligned with the 'lifeworlds' (Husserl, 1965) of more liquid, less structurally rigid, postmodern economies. Many contemporary organizations seek transcendence of their bureaucratic imprint, leaching the artificial limits imposed by vertical hierarchies and formal departmental and corporate boundaries. Simultaneously, these 'post-bureaucracies' are transforming control regimes in order to provide sufficient freedom of action for creativity to be properly tapped while inducing continuing roosting through use of moral controls and emotional ties (Illouz, 2007; Baumeler, 2010). Almost paradoxically, the same forces aiming at overcoming structural strictures reinforce institutional grip of core organizational members, while surrounding them, at home and away, with a vastly expended and subcontracted contingent labour force.

The brave new world has, as noted before, very old origins—organizations have always been the object of constant reproduction. Even the Weberian bureaucracy was based on the formation of a particular type of moral character, of a 'bureaucratic individual' characterized by an emotionally strong sense of duty as a vocation (Clegg, 1990). However, the contemporary 'network society' (Castells, 2000) and the unfolding 'third industrial revolution', characterized by an increase in horizontal connections rather than vertical integration (Dosi and Galambos, 2013) brings to the fore the necessity to shift the main focus of attention of organization studies and of business education.

Views of the empirical object typical of classic approaches such as 'contingency' 'theory', championed by the Aston school are largely irrelevant. It is now necessary to take into account the multiple modalities by which 'organizing' happens in practice. Modern corporations are going through a profound *crisis* (in the etymological meaning of 'point of transformation'). The collapse of the traditional form of large bureaucratic public corporations which characterized the twentieth-century economy, as they morph into less concentrated, less durable, less integrated, and more liquid entities is having negative social effects, reducing opportunities for individual security, in the form of long-term employment, healthcare, retirement security (Davis, 2013). The technological and social 'ingredients' necessary to build an alternative, more democratic model of interaction, capable of replacing the 'vertically integrated communities' that traditional corporation were providing, are already available (Davis, 2013). However, a mode of thinking that privileges institutional stability and consolidated structures over processes and practices is ill equipped to understand or support this transformation.

Parker (2008) proposes a bold idea that could turn business education around, from a bastion of conservatism to a champion of social and economic innovation: transforming management schools from schools *for* managers into *schools for organizing*. This means shifting the accent to one of exploring the multiple opportunities for arranging activities and pursuing common goals that human beings have been autonomously developing throughout history, including in this dialogue not just the 'strategic heads' but also the humble hands that give life to corporations, in order to ensure greater polyphony (Kornberger, Clegg, and Carter, 2006). Doing so is not just a matter of re-aligning research interests or adjusting the discipline vocabulary or the teaching syllabus. It rather requires assuming a different intellectual stance, performing a new revolution in the approach to business studies.

The 'first revolution' of business education took place in the mid-twentieth century (Khurana, 2007) when American business schools repudiated their origins as trade schools in an attempt to gain respectability and stature by more properly assuming the character of academic institutions devoted to scientific study (Bailey and Ford, 1996: 8), responding to incentives and pressures from both large foundations and the federal government (Ghoshal, 2005: 77; Khurana, 2007: 210–22). This scientific process of 'rationalization of society [was] linked to the institutionalization of scientific and technical development' (Habermas, 1987: 81) and founded on two main ideas: first, teaching had to be informed by positivistic scientific research and second, to be organized along disciplinary lines inspired by the functional areas of business administration (Clegg and Ross-Smith, 2003: 88). The normal science paradigm (Kuhn, 1962) at the basis of this approach was focused on systems theory, a theoretically informed and abstract corpus of knowledge that could be applied to all organizations, anywhere (Parsons, 1951).

A second revolution, capable of overthrowing the stifling effect of a system-centric perspective requires letting go of the desire to ape natural sciences, accepting that the highly contextual and situated nature of human activity hinders the possibility of identifying absolute laws governing the behaviour of social agents (Flyvbjerg, 2001). Why don't we try to turn to a time-honoured discipline that for a century has pondered the ineffable complexity of becoming? Such a discipline is *philosophy*. However, before looking into how a philosophical outlook can be used to expand our thinking on organizations it is important to expose the negative consequences that derive from a lack of reflexive consideration of the nature of the 'organizational being'.

Reification as a Limit to Innovation: A Case Study

The story of the attempts of the US Department of Energy (DOE) to solve problems connected with the long-term management of a nuclear waste site in New Mexico can demonstrate how 'reifying' prejudices can limit the performative potential of organizing. The case can be read as a parable on how implicit statements that are normalized as part of the discourse on organization end up 'boxing' organizational capacities for innovation, highlighting the necessity to look at the issue of organizational issues from a different standpoint. What is taken for granted needs to be revealed and questioned, order deconstructed and doubt created, starting from the idea that 'wisdom is to see the borders of our knowledge' (Kaulingfreks, 2007: 43). All the characteristics of an 'extreme' case study (Flyvbjerg, 2006a) are present in this example because it shows how reification and objectification of organizing can impair innovation capacities, even in an organization that had the institutional mandate to be uniquely imaginative and forward thinking.

Located in a salt basin near the town of Carlsbad, the *Waste Isolation Pilot Plant* is a deep geological repository where wastes resulting from the production of nuclear weapons are buried. The site will eventually be sealed in 2030 in order to segregate the radioactive material for 10,000 years (van Wyck, 2005). One of the major challenges for DOE is the design of a set of markers capable of minimizing the risk of 'inadvertent human intrusion' (van Wyck, 2005: 69) in a site that will remain dangerously radioactive for thousands of years. Apart from the difficulties of producing something that can endure for that long, the problem of semiotic endurance seems daunting. The mandate for DOE is to produce warnings that could remain understandable for at least 300 generations. Languages change rapidly—one just has to think about the difficulties for a contemporary reader in interpreting Chaucerian English, even if only thirty generations separate us from Chaucer, not to mention the fact that in the fourteenth century Navajo (not English) was the dominant idiom in New Mexico.

In order to cope with this challenge, the organization summoned panels of experts, tasking them to imagine a variety of possible future scenarios. They also commissioned studies to semiologists, designers, and artists attempting to devise some 'universal' warning signs, symbolising danger. They even devised an action plan aimed at testing the durability of markers that spans one century. While these steps might appear bold and creative when compared with run-of-the-mill strategic planning problems faced by ordinary organizations, they instead reveal how any organization can remain entangled in a net of tacit assumptions.

The problem DOE had to deal with was a time scale that is orders of magnitude removed from the usual planning practices of modern organizations. In this regard it is emblematic of the contrast between the industrial timescape of modernity, focused on short-term action and results, and the timescape of the physical environment, which moves at a much slower pace (Adam, 1998). Environmental degradation as a consequence of production happens in a matter of years but environmental forces require millennia to restore balance.

Among the various experts consulted by DOE, the semiologist Thomas Sebeok proposed a truly revolutionary solution. He reasoned that, since knowledge is context-bound, any message produced today is likely to become unintelligible to a culture in the far future. Those who will try to decode such messages will interpret it in the framework of a completely different, and currently unpredictable, context of reference (Sebeok, 1986). Building redundancy (multiple messages, signs and modes of communications) can only mitigate the inescapable increase in entropy caused by the second law of Thermodynamics. As any other form of constructed 'order', information will spontaneously tend to lose coherence over time, evolving towards a state of entropy.

To counter this unavoidable decaying of information Sebeok suggested developing a 'relay system' whereby information should be transmitted 'with the supplementary aid of folkloristic devices, in particular a combination of an artificially created and nurtured ritual-and-legend' (Sebeok, 1986: 460). His idea was to start disseminating a myth similar to that of Pandora's box in the local population, even to create a 'priesthood' supporting replication of rituals that will ensure the avoidance of the site. Essentially, the proposal is to produce a new language game and associated practices that tap into the universality of myth in human culture.

While this strategy might sound far-fetched, the abovementioned case of the Uffington White Horse is a tangible proof of the fact that apparently ephemeral ritual 'organizing acts' can be more durable than any edifice. This is not a unique example—the Aboriginal Australian practice of repainting or retouching rock-art (O'Connor, Barham, and Woolagoodja, 2008) is another case of a plurimillenary tradition being kept alive through ritual acts. In this regard, the idea of purposefully creating language games of religious ritual and practice to convey information over centuries seems a more 'grounded' solution than the untried attempts to build a landmark the meaning of which will probably become unintelligible. In fact, considering this solution could be considered as a form of 'reference class forecasting', a predicting technique based on using the knowledge of similar past situations and their outcomes. Such an approach has been demonstrated to be a more effective means of predicting the future than speculation or classic project planning, since it avoids optimism bias (Flyvbjerg, 2006b).

Despite this, the idea of resorting to processes, rather than structures, to guarantee the durability of meaning was completely abandoned by DOE decision makers. While this could be attributed to their lack of imagination or desire to experiment the fact that

DOE planners managed to produce and approve a century-long plan seems to bear witness to their capacity to make novel and bold moves. The problem—more likely—is connected with the fact that the DOE's choices were constrained by the discursive forces in which they are enveloped. Discourse is constituted by a mesh of statements, practices, norms that act as sensemaking devices, typifying reality and enabling a 'regime of truth' (Foucault, 1980: 131). As a result, 'power and discourse are mutually constitutive' (Hardy and Phillips, 2004: 299) since power relations impose particular worldviews, which in turn enable specific relations of power, constantly reconfiguring circuits of power and domination (Clegg, 1989).

The planners were expected to dream up and explore new scenarios, and to project their action into an unpredictable future; at the same time they were held back by a set of discursive pressures, entangling them in the past. Institutional forces demanded that they comply with standardized rules and expectations, delivering quantifiable and immediate results. These constraining forces became embodied in the requirements formulated by the US government, via its Environmental Protection Agency (EPA):

> In October 1996, the EPA received the DOE's impossibly huge 'Compliance Certification Application' (some 84,000 pages) (...). The task of the EPA was to decide whether or not the DOE had met with the criteria as previously set out.
>
> The DOE—at least as far as this document was concerned—opted for a lowest common denominator solution of compromise. By making simpler arguments for simpler designs, the DOE attempted to ensure the project would be granted approval. (van Wyck, 2005: 93)

The mundane requirements of present-day organizational design for 'ticking boxes' and filling forms appears to have provoked a classic example of bureaucratic goal displacement (Merton, 1940). DOE members became more concerned with their contemporary audience (their EPA counterpart) than with their future one (the posterities who must be warned of the dangers of tampering with nuclear waste). As a consequence, 'the discussion of the question of meaning had been successfully shifted to a concern about the durability of materials' (van Wyck, 2005: 98). Discussing something tangible such as icons, texts, designs, and material supports was certainly more intelligible (and less controversial), in the frame of reference of the late twentieth-century US bureaucracy, than proposing long-term socio-cultural engineering. In this sense power operates both at systemic level (the use of a compliance certification model) and a relational one (the relationship between the two government agencies), producing knowledge by drawing the borders of what is a meaningful, 'productive' contribution to the planning exercise.

This case is exemplary of how *Zweckrationalität*, the instrumental rationality that is the foundation of modern bureaucracies (Weber, 1978) acts also as a rationalizing device, silencing alternatives (albeit evidence based), interpretations and models of action, paradoxically producing less 'intelligent' solutions to problems. Contemporary organizational discourse, with its structure-centric bias ends up silencing alternative possibilities.

In order to overcome these limitations, freeing up organizing and creative potential, it is necessary to reconsider the way in which organizations are discussed and studied, starting from first principles. This requires adopting a *philosophical* outlook.

Philosophy as a Guide to Expand and Renew the Views of Organizational Studies

The opportunity of considering management issues in the light of a philosophical perspective has been the object of a number of works in the last decade (Jones and ten Bos, 2007b; Spoelstra, 2007b; Koslowski, 2010; Tsoukas and Chia, 2011b). Most of these contributions concur on an important point: using a philosophical perspective to approach the problem of how to expand the reach of organization studies and business education should not be limited to using the ideas of great philosophers to interpret organizational phenomena. This would mean treating philosophy as an 'under-labourer', employed to clear 'the path of scientific progress by removing some of the obstacles, rectifying linguistic confusion or resolving logical contradictions' (Spoelstra, 2007b: 58), an ancillary use of philosophy in the management studies field that is an established tradition. The often cited work by Burrell and Morgan (1979), which identified the basic paradigms underlying alternative discourses on management, does exactly this (Spoelstra, 2007b). In fact, waxing philosophical has become a normalized part of management and organization studies academic practice, usually circumscribed within a methodological section in which, typically, at least in qualitative studies, ontological (what is reality?), epistemological (how do we know things?) and praxeological (how can we transform knowledge in action?) issues are succinctly addressed.

Jones and ten Bos (2007a) introduce us to a much broader understanding of the potential of philosophy. Referring to the works of Plato, Aristotles, and Descartes, they affirm that the purpose of philosophy is to 'wonder' which entails asking basic, naïve questions, questioning what usually remains unquestioned, taken for granted, embracing the component of *aporia* (puzzlement, doubt, non-decidability). Oddly, despite its presumed rationality a similar condition often characterizes the living experience of organizing when events confound routines (Deroy and Clegg, 2011). Spoelstra (2007a) is even more explicit, stating that the purpose of philosophical inquiry is to challenge common sense, the shared layer of socially constructed assumptions that buttress our thinking and acting. The problem with common sense is that it is 'abstracted from the social reality it creates' (Spoelstra, 2007a: 17) and this abstraction makes it indifferent to the consequences that it produces, both in term of limiting our capacity to innovate and in becoming insensible to oppression and suffering. In this regard social science (such as organization studies) and philosophy must go hand in hand in order to be able to consider the implication of the set of assumptions used to anchor observation and analysis, especially to reflect on the moral, practical, political implications of different ways of arranging ideas, bodies, and technologies.

Deconstruction of 'common sense' entails considering production of knowledge in a Socratic perspective: as something that does not reduce but increases our ignorance of reality. This oxymoron signifies that, as we increase our understanding, we become more aware of the complexity and extension of what we don't know (Kaulingfreks, 2007). As a consequence, the pursuit of knowledge as a 'gap spotting' or 'gap filling' exercise is not only scarcely relevant but increasingly inane. It is better replaced by organizational research that acts as a means to problematize issues (Alvesson and Sandberg, 2013), questioning taken-for-granted and established beliefs. Problematization means creating a breakdown (Koschmann, Kuutti, and Hickman, 1998; Sandberg and Tsoukas, 2011), an interruption in the flow of practice that enables us to become aware of what we do unthinkingly. 'Philosophy is a matter of interruption, of breaking open familiar universes of understanding and practice' (Jones and ten Bos, 2007a: 14).

One way of doing research that embodies this attitude, marrying a sociological, technical, and philosophical investigation, is the phronetic social science approach championed by Bent Flyvbjerg (Flyvbjerg, 1998, 2001; Flyvbjerg, Landman, and Schram, 2012; Clegg, Flyvbjerg, and Haugaard, 2014). The approach, which empirically explores the way in which truth is produced through power relations, allows challenging dominant perspectives, critiquing decision-makers and proposing alternative modes of action. Doing this is not simply an intellectual exercise. The research conducted on megaprojects and the botched decision-making processes underlying their costly failures (Flyvbjerg, Rothengatter, and Bruzelius, 2003; Van Marrewijk et al., 2008) is exemplary of how such a philosophically imbued mode of research can produce very practical, evidence-based, and relevant results.

Organizational researchers who choose to incorporate a philosophical understanding in their enquiry will have to accept that incompleteness, imperfection, and transformation are positive traits (rather than limitations) of their production. Management academics, used to being asked for solutions and tools by their clients and students, need to develop a greater degree of humility, accepting that their brand of knowledge is not necessarily better than that of other actors.

In sum, philosophical reflection makes it possible to discuss the common sense that dominates our social reality. The most 'commonsensical' view about organizations is that organizations are *real and stable objects, containers of action, accomplished events*. The alternative view sees the 'stuff' of which these objects are made, the routines, procedures, structures, and so on as *enactments*. In this perspective organizations can be conceived of as 'a field of practices, which are constantly practised' (Gherardi, 2006: 227), neither as empirical objects nor as pure abstractions but as virtual objects or *action nets*, sets of 'connections between and among actions [that], when stabilized, are used to construct the identities of actors' (Czarniawska, 2008: 18). The issue of the contextuality of organizational phenomena, a factor that limits the possibility to discover universal regularities, is thus brought to the foreground. Tsoukas and Chia (2011a) suggest that a concern with contextuality is a problem only if we embrace an *instrumental praxeology*, one that assumes that theory and practice are separated and that the function of the former is to inform the latter. If instead we use a *poetic praxeology*, theory and practice become intertwined, the former providing identity and interpretation value for the latter. Hence, the purpose of management research is not so much one of devising theory-based management technologies but one of reflexively, recursively, and critically refining a common vocabulary for language games in which the implications of our choices are discussed and examined.

These two praxeologies can be bridged if the focus of business research and education is not just on the epiphenomena (organizational structures and arrangements) but also on the organizing acts and recursive language games underpinning the creation and maintenance of these disciplinary objects. Doing so would make management and organization studies truly critical, that is, reflexively and recursively attuned to the consequences of its and others' practices. Moreover, this phenomenological investigation should be aimed not only at describing local contexts but should also aim at identifying regularities, in the form of organizing principles employed by human actors. It should be possible to describe how specific arrangements of different modes of organizing become stabilized in institutionally sanctioned norms and practices, assuming the discursive status of a generalized 'normal', ideal type (e.g., 'bureaucratic organization'), the conformation of an institutionalized organization (e.g., Microsoft) or the unstable and yet consequential network of relationships (e.g., the members of a virtual community, such as *Second Life*). The specificity and context-bound nature of these emergent 'concretions of social acts' would be considered. In the last section we define a research agenda to develop this approach, taking inspiration both from theoretical and practical experiences that emphasize *participation* over control.

Participation and Organizing as Constitutive Elements of Organizations

Human beings are well versed in the art of organizing. We constantly order, catalogue, arrange, box, separate, categorize things, time, activities. Since the time of Fayol (1949) few systematic attempts have been made to identify whatever basic principles characterize 'managing' as a form of organizing. The strength of Fayol's fourteen administration principles is their grounding in practice (he developed them on the basis of his experience as a mine director); however, this is at the same time their major flaw, since they are far too embedded in a modernist, bureaucratic, proto-industrial reality to assume any character of universality. The criticism is of Fayol but it could be of any attempt at transcendence and universal principles that can only ever be of their moment. A few decades later Simon (1996) reflected on the value of hierarchy as an organizing principle—his reflections have a much stronger epistemic strength but they refer to only one of many possible modes of ordering. In all the contemporary literature on the process of organizing, the phenomenological stance assumed by authors seems to preclude any attempt at investigating regularities in the observed processes. Yet the same authors who protect the epistemological purity of their works by avoiding the risk of positivistic drifts have no qualms in labelling the organizations they study according to general types (e.g., as bureaucratic, post-bureaucratic, etc.).

The silence in research on the general modes of organizing is echoed by a silence in education on these issues. Mintzberg (2004) famously accused hyper specialized business schools of not educating MBA students in the practice of managing. This strong *j'accuse* has provoked defensive reactions (Tyson, 2005) but also induced a necessary reflection on the nature of the knowledge taught in business education. Chia and Holt (2008: 484) summarize the essence of the problem: 'what is crucially important is not so much the production, transmission, and application of representational knowledge but how the representations connect with and evoke businesslike experiences in ways that enhance the specific habituated predispositions, sensitivities, and personal awareness of business school students'. Understanding and discussing the ways in which individuals and groups unreflexively arrange and organize their activities would constitute a foundational exercise for management students but this practice is remarkably absent from curricula.

Such neglect of basic reflexivity reflects and supports a dominant discourse dating back to the time of Fayol and Taylor that sees employees of an organization as passive receivers of organizing instructions, entrusting the possibility of devising and implementing a blueprint for creating and maintaining order to managers. Paradoxically, this model is so pervasive that even managers become inert recipients of pre-set models, despite all the rhetoric on innovation that conventional business academics and consultant produce. Contrariwise, considering the multiple ways in which actions and resources can be ordered and given continuity, consistence, and shared meaning, and how this constant organizing activity is performed by each individual, would allow better exploration and understanding of the rich ecosystem of organizing modes that characterize every organization and that can be imaginatively constructed from other narratives, other places, other times.

At this point we pause to consider what, as management scholars and practitioners, we have learned about managing and organizing in the wake of the global financial crisis (GFC). Taylor, Ladkin, and Statler (2015), Nonaka et al. (2014), together with Shotter and Tsoukas (2014) argue that most management academics and practitioners alike seemed to have learned very little, if anything, from the GFC. So, what kinds of questions should we be asking? Where to start? Our argument is that we need to step back a little in order to ask broader, more philosophical questions—along the lines of what it is we seek though organizing and managing and why? What are we striving to accomplish, for whom, for what purpose? To what extent and how do answers to these questions shape ideas about theory and practice in managing and organizing?

Through posing philosophical questions we wish to rediscover, first, the coherence and prescient relevance of Mary Parker Follett's pragmatic-idealist answers—not just for enterprises as entities but as ideas that have significant potential for communities more broadly; second, we will find a practical applications of Follett's visionary teachings in the North European experiences of codetermination; third, we will argue that those similar questions and answers retain profound implications for business school curriculum and pedagogy.

Our questions are derived from focusing on two prominent and related socio-economic issues seen before but accentuated since the GFC: the concentration of wealth, causing an increase in power inequities and the unquestioned primacy of shareholder value. There has been renewed concern about massive and growing income inequalities (Stockhammer, 2013; Wisman, 2013). Both deregulation and concentration of wealth are not the outcome of unavoidable natural courses but consequences of contested social processes. On the one hand, they can be seen as a consequence of an unchecked liberal market and relatively unregulated capitalism which ends up favouring financial and patrimonial gains over investment in the 'material economy', which seems to be taking the world back to an era in which society was dominated by an oligarchy based on inherited wealth (Piketty, 2014). From this perspective, the brief post-war interlude of social democratic ascendancy in a limited number of European countries is an abnormality rather than the normal basis for political economy.

The massive asymmetry of power has created a new class of 'precarious' workers not only suffering job and income insecurity but also identity insecurity (Standing, 2011). Organizations can be openly evil (Jurkiewicz, 2012) but they can also practice subtle forms of evil: lack of permanent employment in a society in which labour is a commodity is profoundly immoral, wicked even, when there are ways of ensuring full employment (Clegg, Boreham, and Dow, 2014). Davis (2013) provides ample evidence of how large corporations increasingly shirk past roles as pillars of the US economy and society as they hollow out employment, subcontract, and outsource. New financially agile and less materially integrated structures controlled by a relatively small number of financial institutions now employ fewer people whilst being, in terms of shareholder value, the profitable titans of late modern times. A single multinational investment management corporation, Blackrock, is the single largest shareholder of one in five corporations in the United States, with a portfolio of managed assets (over 3.5 *trillion* dollars) as large as Germany's GDP (Davis, 2013: 289).

The increasing domination of shareholders capitalism and its negative consequences both in economic and social terms has been engaged in a rich debate that goes beyond critiques and exposes of Wall Street. One consequence is that as research interests shift from historical economic analysis of the present (Kelly, 2012; Stout, 2012; Mayer, 2013; Tyler, 2013; Block and Somers, 2014; Laloux, 2014) to considering alternative forms of enterprise ownership and governance for the future, some discarded history, unincorporated in the business school curricula, offers opportunities for imagining better realities than recent histories have unfolded.

The political responsibility for increased inequities and the shift of power balance from 'doers' (people working in material production of use values) to 'moneylenders' (financial investors) falls not only on greedy plutocrats but also on the political quiescence of social democrats to 'growing inequality of wealth and opportunity; injustices of class and caste; economical exploitation (…) corruption, money and privilege occluding the arteries of democracy' (Judt, 2011: 7). Redressing the issue of the wider social and economic wellbeing of the broader population requires a 'return to an ethically informed public conversation' (Judt, 2011: 8) about, inter alia, the role of the state.

Despite the relevance of the US economy and its hegemonic influence on economic and organizational discourse, especially by means of business education models (Clegg and Ross-Smith, 2003) different nations have dealt differently with the challenge of balancing capitalist economy and pluralistic society. Thelen (2014) highlights major institutional differences between varieties of capitalism, describing the ways in which three institutional realms (industrial relations, labour markets, and vocational education and training (VET)) have served to preserve social solidarity in some nations despite neo-liberal pressures. Her sophisticated analysis highlights major institutional tensions between employers, labour, and the state that need to be faced if there is to be redress of the erosions in social solidarity in neo-liberal times rather than a race to the populist pits of blaming almost everything on the erosion of ethnic solidarity through large-scale migration. Such analysis shows that alternative, ameliorative approaches to laissez-faire neo-liberalism are already in place in different parts of the developed world that could provide alternative contributions to the managerial challenge of mounting global economic insecurity and power inequities.

Before looking at these alternatives, notably drawn from northern Europe, almost always from Germany or Scandinavian countries such as Sweden, it is useful to put them in a theoretical frame which allows us to consider them not simply as 'technical fixes' but as exemplary of a different managerial paradigm. This framework is provided by a regrettably under-recognized approach to philosophical perspectives in organizing, the work of Mary Parker Follett.

Alternatives that positively and realistically address the issues caused by unbridled neo-liberalism are sorely required. Such neo-economic liberalism is characterised by a self-interested (i.e., not other-regarding) individualism that postulates the supremacy of the maximization of selfish desires, preferences, and utility (conveniently reduced as 'rational' self-interest—meaning that anything less would be irrational). The consumer has eclipsed the citizen in this neo-economic liberalism and the preservation of the liberty of the individual as the ultimate goal of society and government has come to be expressed in nothing nobler than a spurious 'freedom of choice' as to how one will be exploited as a consumer. Markets, as the central institutional device of society, are considered only as spheres of voluntary exchange between individuals (Cahill, 2014).

Contemporary management scholars, by and large, have made little or no productive contribution to countering these tendencies. Given the future orientation of this chapter such an approach could draw on Clegg, Courpasson, and Phillips's (2006) considerations of frameworks with which to think about the futures of power. In that regard these authors point to increasingly reflexive structures, 'collegial niches', fusions of political and moral power that are politically soft (Clegg, Courpasson, and Phillips, 2006: 383). One such alternative derives from reconsidering the philosophy of organizing advanced by Mary Parker Follett (1868–1933), in particular what Ansell (2011) describes as Follett's pragmatic-idealist philosophy.

The life work of Follett can be summed as a campaign for cooperative forms of power and democratic corporate governance, where management, owners, and labour, could work together in a theory of co-active or co-power (Boje and Rosile, 2001; Melé, 2011). More than twenty years of civic work in Boston shaped insights into the influence of community life on learning democracy (Tonn, 2008), ideas Follett developed and applied in organizing, leading, and managing across multiple sectors. Those ideas cohere in ways that enable a distinctive philosophical approach to practices that can provide a model of coordinated action not reliant on autocratic, unaccountable leaders that are free to demonstrate crass irresponsibility (Child, 2013: 91).

The questions under Follett's consideration relate to material and ethical-moral perspectives about the future role of managing and leading, along with some major pedagogical implications.[2] In his reading of Follett's work, Child (2013) identifies four key themes in her thinking on coordination that are particularly relevant to organizing and management:

1. *Coordination by direct contact*: The responsible person must be in direct contact regardless of their positions in the organization. 'Horizontal' communication is as important as 'vertical' chains of command in achieving coordination. This is due to what Follett valued in learning together through groups where 'the vital relationship for the individual to the world is through groups' (Follett, 1918/1998, cited in Child, 2013: 79). Central for Follett is *integration*, 'interlocking, inter-relating (…) a working unit, not a congerie of separate pieces' (Follett, 1949: 61).
2. *Constructive conflict*: While she considered dissensus as normal she saw the absence of integration as dysfunctional. Follett emphasizes that conflict that ends in compromise is sub-optimal and thus to be avoided. What is needed again is integration, seeking ways to satisfy responsibilities for functions while taking into account the needs and expert advice of others.
3. *Core processes of management*: Follett focused on a wider range of core processes than is customary today. Her key concepts—coordination, constructive conflict, integration, and power—are all grounded in human relationships and for her, fundamental to democracy. Questions of authority and the 'sharing of the whole enterprise' (Follett, 1949: 73), were central, raising the need for clarity regarding leadership, coordination, and control by 'interweaving, a matter of reciprocal modification (…) of integration' (Follett, 1949: 75).
4. *Business and society*: Follett envisaged management as a traditional profession, serving public needs while delivering enterprise requirements. But she also saw in business management the potential to engage more directly in cultivating core

---

[2] See Maciariello and Linkletter (2011: 324–5) for how Follett's work on power and conflict, particularly with regard to the functioning society of organizations, shaped thinking on organizations and management practice, where she is referred to as the 'prophet of management' (see also Ansell, 2011).

social processes as themes for more effective integration and collaboration within groups and communities—and in doing so strengthening democracy and society. It should be noted that Child's final theme is aligned with mounting calls for representation in work organizations (and the wider polity through community groups)—not just through unions, whose representational role is diminishing almost everywhere but more conspicuously through other forms of civil society engagement and non-union employee representation (NER) (Kaufman and Taras, 2010; Wilkinson, Wood, and Deeg, 2014).

The ideas of Mary Parker Follett remain uncannily prescient, both in the light of the socio-economic challenges posed by the GFC but also with the strategic needs of more liquid organizations. Following the 'third industrial revolution' (Jensen, 1993) many organizations cannot simply buffer uncertainty by means of layers of control and formalization but need instead to respond to it by delegating power and becoming less structured (Child and McGrath, 2001). This poses new issues of governance and corporate social responsibility but also increases the need for trust in the active and intelligent collaboration of organizational members. Follett anticipated the needs of companies operating in the creative industries and in the digital economy when she called for working peoples' experience to be added to that of the experts (Follett, 1924: 20). To understand the practical relevance and implications of her alternative organizing paradigm better we can examine two contexts in which some of her ideas and principles seem to have found a concrete application: the co-determination management models of Germany and Sweden.

The German rights-based,[3] democratic framework of *Mitbestimmung* (Codetermination) (Addison, 2009) is unjustly neglected in business education's modal models normatively based on US free market enterprise. The German human rights-based, legislated stakeholder framework (Schulz and Wasmeier, 2012) is still largely neglected in contemporary Anglo-US university-based management education.[4] In contrast to neo-liberal or free market economies Germany is a social/coordinated-market economy (Nicholls, 2000; Spicka, 2007; Glossner, 2010; Meyer and Rutherford, 2011; Zacher, 2012). There is a telling history behind *Mitbestimmung* (Logue et al., 2015). Under the law of co-determination there are two boards in German business, a supervisory board and a management board. What is distinctive, however, is that this *Mitbestimmung* legislation ensures substantial employee/worker representation on the supervisory board overseeing enterprise management. These employee representatives are elected from Works Councils, and depending on the industry sector, make up at least one-third, and up to half the number of board membership. The rights of employee representation in

---

[3] Dembour (2006) argues that there are four 'schools' of human rights—natural, deliberative, protest, and discourse. She argues that understanding human rights in terms of these constructions challenges the unquestioned metaphysical standing attributed to rights and enables a more critical evaluation of human rights outcomes.

[4] Two rare exceptions are Steers, Nardon, and Sanchez-Runde (2013) and Silvia (2013).

codetermination are associated with the right to veto management decisions (Budd and Zagelmeyer, 2010: 495), relating to 'matters that are of material importance to employees and their working condition (...) to the activities of the enterprise, such as: substantial investments, changes in systems and methods of production, quality, product development, plans for expansion, reductions, or restructuring' (Budd and Zagelmeyer, 2010). Indeed, 'decisions of this kind are submitted to Works Councils for its opinion before any decision is made' decisions (Carley, Baradel, and Wälz, 2005, cited in Budd and Zagelmeyer, 2010). For Silvia, co-determination is not merely 'the pillar of post-war German industrial relations' (2013: 43) but central to Germany's economic success through a distinctive 'social partnership', in that

> industrial action is rare (...) the [co-determination] law does not favour one side over the other, and co-determination legislation facilitates peaceful and productive exchanges between managers and their employees in the workplace and the boardroom. Co-determination has its critics, but it retains widespread support in German society (...) where organized labour and management understand themselves to be social partners in a "conflictual partnership" rather than enemies (...) social partnership has helped German firms to become some of the most successful in the world and German employees to rank among the most affluent (...) making possible the deliberation, coordination and shared sacrifice that helped Germany to weather the GFC better than any other high-income country. (Silvia, 2013: 221–6)

Germany displays a complex though coherent mix of reasons, historical, cultural values (Walker, 1971; Kocka, 1999; Blackbourn, 2003) embodied in political philosophy and customs, the distinctive 1947 Constitution (Currie, 1994; Eberle, 2002; Kommers, Miller, and Ginsburg, 2012), government policies re multilateralism (Fioretos, 2011), alongside the broadly supported industrial relations and workplace legislation (Silvia, 2013; Pontusson, 2005; Streeck, 2009). It is notable that, under Allied occupation and reconstruction in the post-war era American business interests were bitterly and fiercely opposed to the framework of co-determination (Locke and Spender, 2011). It is equally as notable, surveying the carnage of the GFC, that Locke and Spender recommend the adoption of something similar to the German codetermination model as the governance structure of non-financial firms with limited voting rights attached to institutional shareholders in which all stakeholders should have power over the appointment of chief executie officers (CEOs) and boards as well as remuneration strategies. These reforms, they suggest, should be accompanied in business schools made more responsive and responsible to all stakeholders, not just business, including trade unions and non-management employees. The alternative, they suggest, is to shut them down because their impact has been so pernicious in promoting failed models of neo-liberalism.

Not only in Germany are there alternative traditions opposed to the rationality of unregulated neo-liberalism. There are strong traditions of political economy and social democracy shaping business enterprises and the welfare state in Scandinavia, especially Sweden. Unlike almost any other country, Sweden has a high concentration of trade union membership—mostly through the public sector. In orthodox terms this would be a recipe for stagnation, stasis, lack of innovation, and entrenched anti-business interests, yet, paradoxically, Sweden presents an enigma. Along with high taxes and an egalitarian income distribution and policies that stood in contrast with almost all that constitutes neo-economic liberalism, Sweden 'demonstrated from the mid 1990s to 2008 that is was possible to improve competitiveness, secure macroeconomic balances, lower unemployment, and engage a high proportion of women, youngsters, and senior people in economic activity, while state institutions played a large role in the economy' (Kristensen and Lilja, 2011: vii).

What made the Swedish enigma possible? Higgins and Dow (2013) argue that it was a coherent and practical programme of social democracy that made the largest inroads and consolidations against the ravages of liberal capitalism in Sweden, in particular through the ideas promoted by Ernst Wigforss (1881–1977), the architect of the achievements sketched in Kristensen and Lilja (2011). These theoretical and programmatic ideas about combining economic efficiency and social equity warrant revisiting in the wake of the GFC, argue Higgins and Dow. 'Economic liberalism places these two values in an antagonistic relationship, such that one must be bought at the expense of the other (…) [in essence] Wigforss demonstrated a politics that married equity to efficiency, thus redefining progress' (Higgins and Dow, 2013: 16). Sejersted and Adams' (2011) account of Wigforss positions him as an ' "action ideologue" who combined political positions with a reflective ideological engagement' (Sejersted and Adams, 2011: 167), but as Berman (2006: 169–72) suggests, Sweden's distinctive social democracy was forged through long political struggles that combined democracy with communitarianism—a marriage not without serious tensions.[5] In particular Berman attributes Sweden's developments to inter-war strategic decisions by the social democrats that were taken in the belief that 'the state could and should control markets without destroying them' (Berman, 2006: 17) in a rejection of both Marxism and liberalism. What emerged was 'the reconciliation of things long viewed as incompatible: a well-functioning capitalist system, democracy, and social stability' (Berman, 2006: 17).

Allied to this reconciliation are questions about rights and ownership issues—which were specifically addressed by Abrahamsson, Broström, and McCune (1980). For these authors, the principle of the rights of labour is the principle for the reunification of decision-making *and* executive power over production—a reunification that is a necessary part of economic democracy. That is where the rights of labour are defined as 'mandators' (Abrahamsson, Broström, and McCune, 1980: 24–8); in other words, being in a power relation in which they share the power to appoint the executive who would act on behalf of *all* 'with a stake/interest' in production, which returns us to the issue of co-ownership as well as restoring the place of production (Chang, 2014). However, before drawing these threads together we pause to briefly recap the narrative so far.

We started this section with concerns about what academics and practitioners have learned about managing and organizing in the wake of the GFC—with the neo-liberal frame clearly discredited but with seemingly little attention being given to alternatives.

---

[5] See Berman (2006: 207–8).

Somewhat counter-intuitively we are arguing for a more philosophical orientation that we regard, despite its auspices, as inherently more practical. We started by outlining unjust insecurity and inequities when seen from the grounds of human rights to co-power, in Follett, which we illustrated through the broadly community supported success of codetermination in Germany and the imaginative integration of capitalism and welfare through social democracy in Sweden. The perspective offers a degree of coherence underpinned by an explicit framework infused with concerns for shared, joint power, articulated in response to philosophical questions of rights and responsibilities for democratic/co-active governance that reconceives managing and organizing as functions of joint stewardship, not as something defined by positions in an organization chart and the usurpation of legitimacy claims based on these positions rather than the actions that flow from them. There are evident lessons for what we teach in business schools.

Business School Curriculum

We conclude with reflecting on what the foregoing suggests for business school curricula and pedagogy. Starting with a philosophical outlook has, we believe, been a liberating opportunity to consider wider questions about the purposes and directions of managing and organizing, in particular from the perspective of higher education, with the implicit assumption of education that it is both a component of and in the public good (Nixon, 2011). Mary Parker Follett's pragmatic idealism provides a valuable framework for presenting a coherent focus on what such an education would need to address. Those can be summed as a range of core managing and organizing capabilities and dispositions considered not as typical standard OB textbook topics but as expanded *and specifically integrated* with Follett's distinctive ambition to cultivate soft, political and moral capabilities (Clegg, Courpasson, and Phillips, 2006), essential for shared responsibility of the enterprise.

The emerging structures ('organizations') can be seen as the result of a combination of different modes, as cocktails of organizing principles and doings. All organizations in this sense are hybrids, because they incorporate different forms of organizing. Also these dynamics are constantly at work, even if they are not part of the dominant model—in this regard non-mainstream forms of organizing can be seen as forms of resistance or dis-organization. For instance, attempts to develop cross-functional, horizontal networks can be found in classic bureaucracies even if these will be usually considered as forms of individual 'disorderedly behaviour'. Conversely, in a contemporary 'post-bureaucratic' setting these actions are not only sanctioned but also actively promoted by the organization.

A scholar who only looks at the 'solid' and 'durable' manifestations of organization, such as organizational charts, formal procedures, strategic plans, corporate headquarters, plants, balance sheets, and so on, ignoring the manifold ways in which individuals strive to create order and sense, risks becoming analogous to a marine biologist who wants to examine corals but whom, instead of observing the colonies of tiny polyps that produce them, only pays attention to the hard corals that form when colonies of coral polyps produce limestone skeletons to support themselves. In organization theory, we have mistaken the dead skeleton for the living self-organization of the polyps while, analogically, with respect to process we have focused too much on processes' beautiful effects, the sway, flow, and motion, akin to looking at the reproduction of soft corals, without paying attention to the tiny structures (spicules) that support them. Humans differ in significant ways from polyps; they do more than react and adapt to the threats and opportunities offered by their immediate environment: they creatively arrange the available materials, strategizing, manipulating, resisting pressures. This determines a complex sets of constantly evolving conditions that are shaping the environment itself, that lattice of interdependences on which organization are based; a latticework that can be identified with the concept of *power relations*.

In Conclusion: Power as the Latticework of Organizing

Whoever specifies organization fixes power relations—or at least attempts to do so. Most organizational fixity of power is an amalgam of custom, habit, law, tradition, and privilege. We have suggested some ways of undoing these, of deconstructing power, of imagining new futures. For the future, power in organizations is likely to revolve around overcoming two major issues. First, how can organizations preserve and enhance individual freedom and initiative and develop new managerial institutions that do not strengthen narrow circles of powerful individuals monitoring the organization from the top? How will they combine a structural and a minimalist agenda? How will organizational leadership embody increasing societal and political dimensions? Put differently, the transformation of leadership from a set of managerial practices and rules to a set of institutional capacities implies thinking about power as a means to educate, socialize individuals, to create and sustain identities and to consider how institutions are governed as well as managed. The role of political power is to invent and engineer powerful institutions that create the necessary obedience-generative constraints and legitimacies inside organizations and societies. One of the most pressing questions posed by a perspective based on a political agenda is that of moral disagreement: citizens that have become consumers made poorer by austerity and unnecessary unemployment and under-employment are increasingly unlikely to agree with the fate that the elites hold out for them.

The ideological signification of democracy in the organizational world is not only related to a kind of moral utterance. It is also the work of power, since democracy in economic institutions is antagonistic to oligarchic and bureaucratic practices and values.

It is power not only in the mechanical sense of 'force applied to a people by external government in the pursuit of its own objectives, but power regarded as arising from the people, transmitted by libertarian, egalitarian and rationalist ends so that it becomes, in effect, not power but only the exercise of the people's own will' (Nisbet, 1993: 40). The question arising from this quotation is not merely how far organizations can be truly democratic but concerns the peculiar interconnections between democracy, power, and morality. As Nisbet (1993) puts it, while power without morality is despotism, morality without power is sterile.

Today's organizations are characterized by the fact that power is, so to speak, *not* fused in the wider society. Deference is no longer given or expected to elders and betters. Organizations cannot simply rely on staffing their ranks with high-status males and expecting the subaltern ranks to obey unquestioningly. The social order is no more mediated by clear-cut figures and organizational institutions supporting masculinity, authority, religious or ethnic supremacy. It is wavering from one individual to another, from endogenous actors and groups to external constraints and thus, power is not generating individual security and beliefs in the relative unity of organizations as centres of power. Simultaneously, while the idea of power is dislocated, organizations relentlessly produce alternative managerial instrumentations of, and discourses about, performance, that play the role of political devices of control, mediating the invisible power of the invisible centre, reshaping the body politic. All the past's seeming social solidity has melted into air, and where, once, there was the illusion of an order that few questioned, now we can see only the effects of repressive tolerance—as long as the elites were mimicked, obeyed, and reproduced in the masses' behaviour they would be tolerated. Acceptance was contingent on obedience. Obedience is always contingent, provisional, an uncertain legitimation.

Power *is* moral life, because it is through 'the practice of moral values we develop the capacity to govern' (Durkheim, 1961: 46). But power is also plural, by definition, according to Durkheim; it is manifested in the diverse spheres of social life, communities, webs of kinship, professions, school, unions, and so on. Organizations endeavour to restore the consistency of a powerful social group, by gripping more firmly the individuals, by generating constantly new reasons to bind them to the corporate future, to make them believe they act for the sake of a socially useful and fruitful entity, to give a greater significance to individual actions, as Durkheim put it.

Power was always a reciprocal matter; not only of its relations and its exercise but also its anticipation and normative shaping on the part of those subject to it. Today it is a much more instrumentally mediated relationship rather than one of face-to-face imperative coordination. With the restatement of social democracy, of rights, of co-active power, these instrumentally mediated relations may be changed although organizations are not an easy place in which to develop and implement democratic principles and practices. Organizations, and specifically, business organizations, are among the least democratic institutions of modern times. Their attachment to hierarchy as an organizing principle is remarkable. Such proclivities do not mean that most organizations are coercion-based regimes but that they are not designed to distribute power equally among members, their power holders are not elected by members, their crucial decisions are made in small circles of power without necessarily seeking members' opinions. Even at their best they are oligarchies based, sometimes, on some notions of merit. We would argue that the common good could never be captured in a mode of domination, in a vision imposed on the others, in a claim based on any pretext of managerial fiat or real ownership over and above those of the managed and non-owning. Whosoever says organization must imply power—but there is huge variability and creativity in how the relations implied may be socially constructed. The crucial question is how power is embedded in relations of domination. Power cannot not be: relations between people are unthinkable without power, because all social relations are relations of various shades of domination, seduction, manipulation, coercion, authority, and so on. Power is inescapable even as its specific relations, forms, practices, processes, structures, identities, and meanings change. Power may be eternal but its forms are not essential. In this chapter we have sought to suggest some philosophically grounded and practically demonstrable ways of reshaping power relations for the better.

REFERENCES

Abrahamsson, B., Broström, A. and McCune, D. (1980). *The Rights of Labor*. London: SAGE.

Adam, B. (1998). *Timescapes of Modernity: The Environment and Invisible Hazards*. New York: Routledge.

Addison, J. T. (2009). *The Economics of Codetermination: Lessons from the German Experience*. New York: Palgrave Macmillan.

Alvesson, M. and Deetz, S. (2006). 'Critical Theory and Postmodernism Approaches to Organizational Studies', in S. R. Clegg, C. Hardy, T. B. Lawrence, and W. R. Nord (eds.), *The SAGE Handbook of Organization Studies*, 2nd edn. London: SAGE, 255–84.

Alvesson, M. and Kärreman, D. (2011). 'Decolonializing Discourse: Critical Reflections on Organizational Discourse Analysis'. *Human Relations*, 64: 1121–46.

Alvesson, M. and Sandberg, J. (2013). 'Has Management Studies Lost Its Way? Ideas for More Imaginative and Innovative Research'. *Journal of Management Studies*, 50(1): 128–52.

Alvesson, M. and Willmott, H. (2002). 'Identity Regulation as Organizational Control: Producing the Appropriate Individual'. *Journal of Management Studies*, 39: 619–44.

Ansell, C. K. (2011). *Pragmatist Democracy: Evolutionary Learning as Public Philosophy*. Oxford: Oxford University Press.

Ashkenas, R. N., Ulrich, D., Jick, T., Kerr, S., Prahalad, C. and Bossidy, L. A. (1998). *The Boundaryless Organization: Breaking the Chains of Organizational Structure*, 1st edn. San Francisco, CA: Jossey-Bass Publishers.

Bailey, J. and Ford, C. (1996). 'Management as Science versus Management as Practice in Postgraduate Business Education'. *Business Strategy Review*, 7: 7–12.

Baumeler, C. (2010). 'Organizational Regimes of Emotional Conduct', in B. Sieben and A. Wettergren (eds.), *Emotionalizing Organizations and Organizing Emotions*. Basingstoke: Palgrave Macmillan, 272–92.

Bennis, W. G. and O'Toole, J. (2005). 'How Business Schools Lost Their Way'. *Harvard Business Review*, 83: 96–104.

Berman, S. (2006). *The Primacy of Politics: Social Democracy and the Making of Europe's Twentieth Century*. New York: Cambridge University Press.

Blackbourn, D. (2003). *History of Germany 1780–1918: The Long Nineteenth Century*. New York, NY: Avalon Publishing Group.

Block, F. and Somers, M. R. (2014). *The Power of Market Fundamentalism: Karl Polanyi's Critique*. Boston, MA: Harvard University Press.

Boje, D. M. and Al Arkoubi, K. (2009). 'Critical Management Education beyond the Siege', in S. Armstrong and C. Fukami (eds.), *The SAGE Handbook of Management Learning, Education and Development*. London: SAGE, 104–23.

Boje, D. M. and Rosile, G. A. (2001). 'Where's the Power in Empowerment? Answers from Follett and Clegg'. *The Journal of Applied Behavioral Science*, 37(1): 90–117.

Borgerson, J. (2005). 'Judith Butler: On Organizing Subjectivities', in C. Jones and R. Munro (eds.), *Contemporary Organization Theory*. Malden, MA: Blackwell, 63–79.

Bourdieu, P. (1990). *The Logic of Practice*. Cambridge: B. Blackwell.

Budd, J. W. and Zagelmeyer, S. (2010). 'Public Policy and Employee Participation', in A. Wilkinson, P. J. Gollan, M. Marchington, and D. Lewin (eds.), *The Oxford Handbook of Participation in Organizations*. Oxford: Oxford University Press, 476–503.

Burrell, G. and Morgan, G. (1979). *Sociological Paradigms and Organisational Analysis*. London: Heinemann.

Butler, J. (2004). 'Changing the Subject: Judith Butler's Politics of Radical Resignification', in Sara Salih (ed.), *The Judith Butler Reader*. Oxford: Blackwell, 325–56.

Cahill, D. (2014). *The End of Laissez-Faire?: On the Durability of Embedded Neoliberalism*. Cheltenham: Edward Elgar Publishing.

Carley, M., Baradel, A., and Wälz, C. (2005). 'Works Councils: Workplace Representation and Participation Structures'. Dublin: European Foundation for the Improvement of Living and Working Conditions.

Castells, M. (2000). *The Rise of the Network Society*, vol. 1. Malden, MA: Blackwell Publishers.

Chang, Y.-C. (2014). 'An Economic and Comparative Analysis of *Specificatio* (the Accession Doctrine)'. *European Journal of Law and Economics*, 39(2): 225–43.

Chia, R. (2000). 'Discourse Analysis as Organizational Analysis'. *Organization*, 7(3): 513–18.

Chia, R. (2002). 'Essai: Time, Duration and Simultaneity: Rethinking Process and Change in Organizational Analysis'. *Organization Studies*, 23: 863–8.

Chia, R. and Holt, R. (2008). 'The Nature of Knowledge in Business Schools'. *Academy of Management Learning & Education*, 7: 471.

Child, J. (2013). 'Mary Parker Follett', in M. Witzel and M. Warner (eds.), *The Oxford Handbook of Management Theorists*. Oxford: Oxford University Press, 74–93.

Child, J. and McGrath, R. G. (2001). 'Organizations Unfettered: Organizational Form in an Information-Intensive Economy'. *Academy of Management Journal*, 44(6): 1135–48.

Clegg, S. R. (1989). *Frameworks of Power*. London: SAGE.

Clegg, S. R. (1990). *Modern Organizations: Organization Studies in the Postmodern World*. San Francisco, CA: SAGE.

Clegg, S. R. and Baumeler, C. (2014). 'Liquid Modernity, the Owl of Minerva, and Technologies of the Emotional Self', in J. Kociatkiewicz and M. Kostera (eds.), *Liquid Organization: Zygmunt Bauman and Organization Theory*. London: Routledge, 35–57.

Clegg, S. R., Boreham, P. and Dow, G. (2014[1986]). *Class, Politics and the Economy*. London: Routledge.

Clegg, S. R., Courpasson, D., and Phillips, N. (2006). *Power and Organizations*. London: SAGE.

Clegg, S. R., Flyvbjerg, B., and Haugaard, M. (2014). 'Reflections on Phronetic Social Science: A Dialogue between Stewart Clegg, Bent Flyvbjerg and Mark Haugaard'. *Journal of Political Power*, 7(2): 275–306.

Clegg, S. R., Kornberger, M. and Rhodes, C. (2005). 'Learning/Becoming/Organizing'. *Organization*, 12: 147–67.

Clegg, S. R. and Ross-Smith, A. (2003). 'Revising the Boundaries: Management Education and Learning in a Postpositivist World'. *Academy of Management Learning & Education*, 2: 85.

Currie, D. P. (1994). *The Constitution of the Federal Republic of Germany*. Chicago, IL: University of Chicago Press.

Czarniawska, B. (2008). 'Organizations as Obstacles to Organizing', paper presented to the 'Nobel Symposium Foundations of Organization, 28–30 August 2008 Stockholm', available at: <http://bit.ly/Zo2fcx> (accessed 1 March 2012).

Davis, G. F. (2013). 'After the Corporation'. *Politics & Society*, 2(41): 283–308.

Dembour, M.-B. (2006). *Who Believes in Human Rights?: Reflections on the European Convention*. Cambridge: Cambridge University Press.

Deroy, X. and Clegg, S. (2011). 'When Events Interact with Business Ethics'. *Organization*, 18(5): 637–53.

DiMaggio, P. J. and Powell, W. W. (1983). 'The Iron Cage Revisited: Institutional Isomorphism and Collective Rationality in Organizational Fields'. *American Sociological Review*, 48: 147–60.

Donaldson, L. (2001). *The Contingency Theory of Organizations*. Thousand Oaks, CA: SAGE.

Donnellon, A. and Heckscher, C. C. (1994). *The Post-Bureaucratic Organization: New Perspectives on Organizational Change*. Thousand Oaks, CA: SAGE.

Dosi, G. and Galambos, L. (2013). *The Third Industrial Revolution in Global Business*. Cambridge: Cambridge University Press.

Durkheim, É. (1961). *Moral Education: A Study in the Theory and Application of the Sociology of Education*. New York: Free Press.

Eberle, E. J. (2002). *Dignity and Liberty: Constitutional Visions in Germany and the United States*. Santa Barbara, CA: Praeger.

Fayol, H. (1949[1916]). *General and Industrial Management*. London: Pitman.

Feldman, M. S. (2000). 'Organizational Routines as a Source of Continuous Change'. *Organization Science*, 11: 611–29.

Fioretos, K. O. (2011). *Creative Reconstructions: Multilateralism and European Varieties of Capitalism after 1950*. Ithaca, NY: Cornell University Press.

Flyvbjerg, B. (1998). *Rationality and Power: Democracy in Practice*. Chicago, IL: University of Chicago Press.

Flyvbjerg, B. (2001). *Making Social Science Matter: Why Social Inquiry Fails and How It Can Succeed Again*. Cambridge: Cambridge University Press.

Flyvbjerg, B. (2006a). 'Five Misunderstandings about Case-Study Research'. *Qualitative Inquiry*, 12: 219–45.

Flyvbjerg, B. (2006b). 'From Nobel Prize to Project Management: Getting Risks Right'. *Project Management Journal*, 37(3): 5.

Flyvbjerg, B., Landman, T. and Schram, S. (2012). *Real Social Science: Applied Phronesis*. Cambridge: Cambridge University Press.

Flyvbjerg, B., Rothengatter, W. and Bruzelius, N. (2003). *Megaprojects and Risk: An Anatomy of Ambition*. Cambridge: Cambridge University Press.

Follett, M. P. (1924). *Creative Experience*. London: Longmans, Green and Co.

Follett, M. P. (1918/1998). *The New State: Group Organisation, the Solution of Popular Government*. New York: Longmans, Green.
Follett, M. P. (1949). 'Coordination', in M. P. Follett (ed.), *Freedom and Coordination, Lectures in Business Administration by Mary Parker Follett*. London: Management Publications Trust, 61–76.
Foucault, M. (1980). *Power/Knowledge: Selected Interviews and Other Writings, 1972–1977*. New York: Harvester Wheatsheaf.
Gadamer, H.-G. (2004[1960]). *Truth and Method*, trans. J. Weinsheimer and D. G. Marshall. New York: Continuum.
Galbraith, J. R. (2008). *Designing Matrix Organizations That Actually Work: How IBM, Proctor & Gamble and Others Design for Success*. San Francisco, CA: John Wiley & Sons.
Gherardi, S. (2006). *Organizational Knowledge: The Texture of Workplace Learning*. London: Blackwell.
Ghoshal, S. (2005). 'Bad Management Theories Are Destroying Good Management Practices'. *Academy of Management Learning & Education* 4: 75.
Giddens, A. (1984). *Constitution of Society: Outline of the Theory of Structuration*. Cambridge: Polity Press.
Glossner, C. L. (2010). *Making of the German Post-War Economy: Political Communication and Public Reception of the Social Market Economy after World War Two*. London: IB Tauris.
Grant, D., Hardy, C., Oswick, C., and Putnam, L. L. (eds.) (2004). *The SAGE Handbook of Organizational Discourse*. London: SAGE.
Habermas, J. (1987). *Toward a Rational Society*. Cambridge: Polity Press.
Hammer, M. and Champy, J. (1993). *Reengineering the Corporation: A Manifesto for Business Revolution*. London: Nicholas Brealey Publishing.
Hardy, C. and Phillips, N. (2004). 'Discourse and Power', in D. Grant, C. Hardy, C. Oswick, and L. L. Putnam (eds.), *The SAGE Handbook of Organizational Discourse*. London: SAGE, 299–315.
Hedberg, B., Dahlgren, G. and Olve, N.-G. (1997). *Virtual Organizations and beyond: Discover Imaginary Systems*. San Francisco, CA: John Wiley & Sons.
Higgins, W. and Dow, G. (2013). *Politics against Pessimism: Social Democratic Possibilities since Ernst Wigforss*. Bern: Peter Lang.
Hochschild, A. R. (1979). 'Emotion Work, Feeling Rules, and Social Structure'. *The American Journal of Sociology*, 85: 551–75.
Husserl, E. (1965[1935]). *The Crisis of European Sciences and Transcendental Phenomenology: An Introduction to Phenomenological Philosophy*, trans. Q. Lauer. New York: Harper & Row.
Illouz, E. (2007). *Cold Intimacies: The Making of Emotional Capitalism*. Malden, MA: Polity Press.
Jensen, M. C. (1993). 'The Modern Industrial Revolution, Exit, and the Failure of Internal Control Systems'. *Journal of Finance*, 48(3): 831–80.
Jones, C. and ten Bos, R. (2007a). 'Introduction', in C. Jones and R. ten Bos (eds.), *Philosophy and Organisation*. New York: Routledge, 1–17.
Jones, C. and ten Bos, R. (eds) (2007b). *Philosophy and Organisation*. New York: Routledge.
Jones, D. T., Roos, D. and Womack, J. P. (1990). *The Machine That Changed the World*. New York: Simon and Schuster.
Josserand, E., Teo, S. and Clegg, S. (2006). 'From Bureaucratic to Post-Bureaucratic: The Difficulties of Transition'. *Journal of Organizational Change Management*, 19(1): 54–64.
Judt, T. (2011). *Ill Fares the Land: A Treatise on our Present Discontents*. London: Penguin UK.

Jurkiewicz, C. L. (ed.) (2012). *The Foundations of Organizational Evil*. London: ME Sharpe.

Kaufman, B. E. and Taras, D. G. (2010). 'Employee Participation through Non-Union Forms of Employee Representation', in A. Wilkinson, P. J. Gollan, M. Marchington, and D. Lewin (eds.), *The Oxford Handbook of Participation in Organizations*. Oxford: Oxford University Press.

Kaulingfreks, R. (2007). 'The Uselesness of Philosophy', in C. Jones and R. ten Bos (eds.), *Philosophy and Organisation*. New York: Routledge, 39–54.

Kelly, M. (2012). *Owning Our Future: The Emerging Ownership Revolution*. San Francisco, CA: Berrett-Koehler Publishers.

Khurana, R. (2007). *From Higher Aims to Hired Hands: The Social Transformation of American Business Schools and the Unfulfilled Promise of Management as a Profession*. Princeton, NJ: Princeton University Press.

Knights, D. and Willmott, H. (1997). 'The Hype and Hope of Interdisciplinary Management Studies'. *British Journal of Management*, 8: 9–22.

Kocka, J. (1999). *Industrial Culture and Bourgeois Society: Business, Labor, and Bureaucracy in Modern Germany*. New York: Berghahn Books.

Kommers, D. P., Miller, R. A., and Ginsburg, R. B. (2012). *The Constitutional Jurisprudence of the Federal Republic of Germany*, 3rd edn, revised and expanded. Durham, NC: Duke University Press.

Kornberger, M., Clegg, S. R., and Carter, C. (2006). 'Rethinking the Polyphonic Organization: Managing as Discursive Practice'. *Scandinavian Journal of Management*, 22(1): 3–30.

Koschmann, T., Kuutti, K., and Hickman, L. (1998). 'The Concept of Breakdown in Heidegger, Leont'ev, and Dewey and Its Implications for Education'. *Mind, Culture, and Activity*, 5: 25–41.

Koslowski, P. (ed.) (2010). *Elements of a Philosophy of Management and Organization*. Berlin: Springer.

Kristensen, P. H. and Lilja, K. (2011). *Nordic Capitalisms and Globalization: New Forms of Economic Organization and Welfare Institutions*. Oxford: Oxford University Press.

Kuhn, T. S. (1962). *The Structure of Scientific Revolutions*. Chicago, IL: University of Chicago Press.

Laloux, F. (2014). *Reinventing Organizations*. Brussels: Nelson Parker.

Latour, B. (1986). 'The Powers of Association', in J. Law (ed.), *Power, Action and Belief*. London: Routledge and Kegan Paul, 264–80.

Latour, B. (2005). *Reassembling the Social: An Introduction to Actor-Network-Theory*. Oxford: Clarendon.

Locke, R. R. and Spender, J. C. (2011). *Confronting Managerialism: How the Business Elite and Their Schools Threw Our Lives Out of Balance*. London: Zed Books.

Logue, D., Jarvis, W. P., Clegg, S. R., and Hermens, A. (2015). 'Translating Models of Organization: Can the Mittelstand Move from Bavaria to Geelong?'. *Journal of Management and Organisation*, 21(1): 17–36.

Lorsch, J. W. (2009). 'Regaining Lost Relevance'. *Journal of Management Inquiry*, 18: 108–17.

Maciariello, J. A. and Linkletter, K. (2011). *Drucker's Lost Art of Management: Peter Drucker's Timeless Vision for Building Effective Organizations*. New York: McGraw-Hill Education.

Mayer, C. (2013). *Firm Commitment: Why the Corporation Is Failing Us and How to Restore Trust in It*. Oxford: Oxford University Press.

Mayo, E. (1949). *The Social Problems of an Industrial Civilization: With an Appendix on the Political Problem*. London: Routledge & Kegan Paul.

Melé, D. (2011). *Management Ethics: Placing Ethics at the Core of Good Management*, Basingstoke: Palgrave Macmillan.

Merton, R. K. (1940). 'Bureaucratic Structure and Personality'. *Social Forces*, 18: 560–8.

Meyer, H. and Rutherford, J. (2011). *The Future of European Social Democracy: Building the Good Society*. Basingstoke: Palgrave Macmillan.

Mintzberg, H. (1983). *Power in and Around Organizations*. Englewood Cliffs, NJ: Prentice-Hall.

Mintzberg, H. (2004). *Managers Not MBAs: A Hard Look at the Soft Practice of Managing and Management Development*. San Francisco, CA: Berrett-Koehler.

Nicholls, A. J. (2000). *Freedom with Responsibility: The Social Market Economy in Germany 1918–1963*. Oxford: Oxford University Press.

Nisbet, R. A. (1993). *The Sociological Tradition*. New Brunswick, NJ: Transaction Publishers.

Nixon, J. (2011). *Higher Education and the Public Good: Imagining the University*. London: Bloomsbury Publishing.

Nonaka, I., Chia, R., Holt, R. and Peltokorpi, V. (2014). 'Wisdom, Management and Organization'. *Management Learning*, 45(4): 365–76.

O'Connor, S., Barham, A., and Woolagoodja, D. (2008). 'Painting and Repainting in the West Kimberley'. *Australian Aboriginal Studies*, 1: 22–38.

Ouchi, W. G. (1979). 'A Conceptual Framework for the Design of Organizational Control Mechanisms'. *Management Science*, 25(9): 833–48.

Parker, M. (2002). *Against Management: Organization in the Age of Managerialism*, Cambridge: Polity Press in association with Blackwell.

Parker, M. (2008). 'Schools for Organizing', in D. Barry and H. Hansen (eds.), *The SAGE Handbook of New Approaches in Management and Organization*. Thousand Oaks, CA: SAGE, 213–14.

Parsons, T. (1951). *The Social System*. London: Routledge & K. Paul.

Piketty, T. (2014). *Capital in the Twenty-First Century*. Boston, MA: Harvard University Press.

Pontusson, J. (2005). *Inequality and Prosperity: Social Europe vs. Liberal America*. Ithaca, NY: Cornell University Press.

Powell, W. W. and DiMaggio, P. J. (1991). *The New Institutionalism in Organizational Analysis*. Chicago, IL: University of Chicago Press.

Roberts, J. (1996). 'Management Education and the Limits of Technical Rationality: The Conditions and Consequences of Management Practice?', in R. French and C. Grey (eds.), *Rethinking Management Education*. London: SAGE, 54–75.

Sandberg, J. and Tsoukas, H. (2011). 'Grasping the Logic of Practice: Theorizing through Practical Rationality'. *Academy of Management Review*, 36: 338.

Schulz, M. and Wasmeier, O. (2012). *The Law of Business Organisations: A Concise Overview of German Corporate Law*. Berlin: Springer.

Schütz, A. (1932). *The Phenomenology of the Social World*. Evanston, IL: Northwestern University Press.

Schwyzer, P. (1999). 'The Scouring of the White Horse: Archaeology, Identity, and "Heritage"'. *Representations*, 65: 42–62.

Sebeok, T. A. (1986). 'Pandora's Box: How and Why to Communicate 10,000 Years into the Future', in M. Blonsky (ed.), *I Think I am a Verb: More Contributions to the Doctrine of Signs*. New York: Plenum Press, 448–66.

Sejersted, F. and Adams, M. B. (2011). *The Age of Social Democracy: Norway and Sweden in the Twentieth Century*. Princeton, NJ: Princeton University Press.

Selznick, P. (1949). *TVA and the Grass Roots: A Study in the Sociology of Formal Organization.* Berkeley, CA: University of California Press.

Senge, P. M. (1994). *The Fifth Discipline: The Art and Practice of the Learning Organization.* New York: Doubleday/Currency.

Shotter, J. and Tsoukas, H. (2014). 'In Search of Phronesis: Leadership and the Art of Coming to Judgement'. *Academy of Management Learning & Education*, 13(2): 224–43. Also available at: <http://amle.aom.org/content/13/2/224> (accessed 16 August 2016).

Silvia, S. J. (2013). *Holding the Shop Together: German Industrial Relations in the Postwar Era.* Ithaca, NY: Cornell University Press.

Simon, H. A. (1996[1969]). *The Sciences of the Artificial.* Cambridge, MA: MIT Press.

Spicka, M. E. (2007). *Selling the Economic Miracle: Economic Reconstruction and Politics in West Germany, 1949–1957.* New York: Berghahn Books.

Spoelstra, S. (2007a). *What Is Organization?* Lund: Lund Business Press.

Spoelstra, S. (2007b). 'What Is Philosophy of Organization?'. *Philosophy and Organization*, 19 (April): 55–67.

Standing, G. (2011). *The Precariat: The New Dangerous Class.* London: Bloomsbury Publishing.

Steers, R. M., Nardon, L. and Sanchez-Runde, C. J. (2013). *Management across Cultures: Developing Global Competencies.* Cambridge: Cambridge University Press.

Stockhammer, E. (2013). 'Rising Inequality as a Cause of the Present Crisis'. *Cambridge Journal of Economics*, 39(3): 935–58.

Stout, L. A. (2012). *The Shareholder Value Myth: How Putting Shareholders First Harms Investors, Corporations, and the Public.* San Francisco, CA: Berrett-Koehler Publishers.

Streeck, W. (2009). *Re-Forming Capitalism: Institutional Change in the German Political Economy.* New York: Oxford University Press.

Taylor, F. W. (1911). *The Principles of Scientific Management.* New Haven, CT: Student Computing, Yale ITS Academic Media & Technology.

Taylor, S., Ladkin, D., and Statler, M. (2015). 'Caring Orientations: The Normative Foundations of the Craft of Management'. *Journal of Business Ethics*, 128(3): 575–84.

Thelen, K. (2014). *Varieties of Liberalization and the New Politics of Social Solidarity.* Cambridge: Cambridge University Press.

Tonn, J. C. (2008). *Mary P. Follett: Creating Democracy, Transforming Management.* New Haven, CT: Yale University Press.

Tsoukas, H. and Chia, R. (2002). 'On Organizational Becoming: Rethinking Organizational Change'. *Organization Science*, 13: 567–82.

Tsoukas, H. and Chia, R. (2011a). 'Introduction: Why Philosophy Matters to Organization Theory', in H. Tsoukas and R. Chia (eds.), *Philosophy and Organization Theory.* Bradford: Emerald Group Publishing Ltd, 1–21.

Tsoukas, H. and Chia, R. (eds.) (2011b), *Philosophy and Organization Theory.* Bradford: Emerald Group Publishing Ltd.

Tyler, G. R. (2013). *What Went Wrong: How the 1% Hijacked the American Middle Class ... and What Other Countries Got Right.* Dallas, TX: BenBella Books, Inc.

Tyson, L. D. A. (2005). 'On Managers Not MBAs', *Academy of Management Learning & Education.* 4(2): 235–6.

Van Marrewijk, A., Clegg, S. R., Pitsis, T. S., and Veenswijk, M. (2008). 'Managing Public–Private Megaprojects: Paradoxes, Complexity, and Project Design'. *International Journal of Project Management*, 26(6): 591–600.

van Wyck, P. (2005). *Signs of Danger: Waste Trauma, and Nuclear Threat*. Minneapolis, MN: University of Minnesota Press.

Walker, M. (1971). *German Home Towns*. Ithaca, NY: Cornell University Press.

Weber, M. (1978[1922]). *Economy and Society: An Outline of Interpretive Sociology*. Berkeley, CA: University of California Press.

Weick, K. E. (1979[1969]). *The Social Psychology of Organizing*, 2nd edn. Reading, MA: Addison-Wesley.

Wilkinson, A., Wood, G., and Deeg, R. (2014). *The Oxford Handbook of Employment Relations: Comparative Employment Systems*. Oxford: Oxford University Press.

Wisman, J. D. (2013). 'Wage Stagnation, Rising Inequality and the Financial Crisis of 2008'. *Cambridge Journal of Economics*, 37(4): 921–45.

Wittgenstein, L. (1958). *Philosophical Investigations*, trans. G. E. M. Anscombe. Oxford: Blackwell.

Zacher, H. F. (2012). *Social Policy in the Federal Republic of Germany: The Constitution of the Social*. Berlin: Springer.

PART II
THE DOING/ FUNCTIONS OF MANAGEMENTS

CHAPTER 9

MANAGING PEOPLE

Understanding the Theory and Practice of Human Resources Management

ANDY CHARLWOOD AND KIM HOQUE

INTRODUCTION

HUMAN resources management (HRM) comprises of a set of activities related to: attracting and selecting suitable workers; ensuring that those workers have the competencies to do the job; designing and administering payment systems, and systems to monitor and encourage effort and performance; designing and monitoring systems and processes to manage employees who are failing to meet performance standards; dealing with employee complaints and grievances; managing compliance with legal regulations related to employment; and overseeing systems and processes for making workers redundant if they are surplus to the organization's requirements. It is often taken as axiomatic that, as people are a key source of competitive advantage, such activities should be seen as central to organizational success. Despite this, HRM as it is typically practised in the advanced industrial economies that are the focus of this chapter, occupies a paradoxical position within the management pantheon. The human resources (HR) function often occupies a handmaiden role (Storey, 1992), portrayed as an overhead to be minimized, essentially administrative in character and lacking strategic influence. Despite evidence that the role of HR professionals is changing in response to more complex demands (Caldwell, 2003), the character of the HR function remains largely administrative and service orientated, fragmented, ad hoc, and marginal to business decision-making (Caldwell and Storey, 2007). In addition, in most organizations most of the time, normative 'high commitment' models of HRM (outlined below) have not been widely adopted in practice. This chapter seeks to explain why this is. Drawing on debates over the HRM–performance relationship and on new institutional theory (specifically the concepts of path dependency and institutional isomorphism; Di Maggio and Powell, 1983) it argues that the normative models have not been widely adopted because of five powerful forces: continued scepticism over their performance effects when put into practice; the history of the HR function and the expectations, skills, and competencies of HR professionals that follow from that history; the impact of competing narratives such as 'lean' and Ulrich's model of the HR function; the impact of globalization and financialization logics; and societal rules and norms. Finally, the chapter turns to the developing field of HR analytics, arguing that this has the potential to raise the strategic profile of the HR function (and hence its ability to lobby for the adoption of the normative models of HRM), but that there is nothing inevitable about this process.

What Are the Normative Models of HRM, and How Widely Adopted Are They?

Before the early 1980s, HRM did not have a central place in business school curricula. Courses in what was then often termed personnel management reflected the largely administrative character of the personnel function. However, this began to change from the mid-1980s onwards, most notably following the development of a number of new theoretical models of High Commitment Management, High Involvement Management and High Performance Work Systems (e.g., Beer et al., 1984; Walton, 1985; Lawler, 1986; Pfeffer, 1994; Applebaum and Batt, 1994).[1] These new models were inspired by examples of (mainly US) companies and plants which had achieved extraordinary levels of productivity and performance. Theoretically, they were informed by the quality of working life (QWL) movement, which emerged in the USA in the 1960s and 1970s in an attempt to deal with problems of low morale, high turnover, and poor labour relations associated with Fordism and scientific management. In particular, the models proposed specific approaches to HRM to support a high commitment/involvement approach to work design. For example, Beer et al. (1984: 170) advocated: greater employee influence in selection, promotion and training; pay related to competency and team involvement; and a facilitative, coaching approach to team leadership. Pfeffer (1994, 1998) put forward a list of specific human resource policies including employment security, selective hiring, self-managed teams, extensive training, reduced status differentials, extensive information sharing, and high compensation contingent on performance. These specific combinations of practices were held to lead to superior performance because firms would be able to attract higher quality employees. Those employees would be better able to do their jobs because of extensive training and development. They would also be better motivated to remain with the organization and to perform at a high level given

---

[1] For the sake of consistency we adopt the generic term 'high commitment HRM' to refer to all of these theoretical approaches unless discussing a study which makes explicit use of another term.

the synergistic interaction of pay and performance management systems and the provision of more interesting work tasks over which they would enjoy more autonomy and control. In addition, they would feel more involved in the company because they would have a greater say in how it was run, while employment security would allow the development of trust and cooperation between workers and management, encouraging employees to contribute cost-saving ideas without concerns that management would exploit these ideas to workers' detriment.

At the time of their inception, the new models were widely viewed as a panacea to the problems faced by organizations in advanced industrial countries, particularly in relation to competitive threats from the newly industrializing countries of the Pacific Rim and Japan (Legge, 1995). To counter these threats, companies in advanced industrial nations would no longer be able to compete on the basis of cost, but instead would need to refocus their activities on the provision of hi-tech, high quality and high value added products and services, and on ensuring organizational flexibility to enable them to compete on the leading edge of innovation. This would only become possible if they adopted the sort of 'high commitment' approaches to HRM outlined above in order to encourage workers to buy into organizational goals of flexibility and innovation, and to go the 'extra mile' for the company (Appelbaum et al., 2000). Therefore, it was widely held that the adoption of the high commitment model would be a logical and inevitable consequence of competitive and market pressures.

Despite this, however, the uptake of the high commitment model has been surprisingly limited. While it is common to see versions of it widely adopted in specific industries, it is rare for the whole package of measures laid out by theorists such as Lawler, Pfeffer, Beer, and colleagues to be implemented in full. For example, in the case of Britain—which has exceptionally good data on the adoption of HRM practices owing to the British Workplace Employment Relations Survey (WERS)—while there is some evidence of the increasing adoption of individual HR practices (performance appraisal, for example, has been increasingly widely adopted in recent years) (van Wanrooy et al., 2013), estimates have suggested that at best only 16% of workplaces have adopted the full high commitment package. Guest and Conway (1999) argue that instead, Britain has seen a growth in 'black hole' or 'bleak house' employment relations. This refers to the growing number of non-union workplaces that, at a time of union decline, have not adopted HRM practices as a substitute for union voice. Such workplaces, Guest and Conway argue, are likely to be characterized by authoritarian top-down management, low job satisfaction, low pay, limited training, and high levels of quit and dismissal rates. Elsewhere, Appelbaum and Batt (1994) argue that there have been two patterns of adoption of the normative models of HRM: 'lean' and 'team'. HR practices associated with 'lean' and 'just-in-time' methods of production constitute one system, while practices that facilitate high levels of employee autonomy and involvement in decision-making constitute the team approach. The two rarely co-exist (De Menezes and Wood, 2006). Moreover, the type of long term employment security advocated by Pfeffer (1998) is increasingly rare under either approach. Overall, therefore, the evidence suggests that the normative models of high commitment HRM presented by Beer et al. (1984), Walton

(1985), Lawler (1986), Pfeffer (1994, 1998) and Appelbaum and Batt (1994) have not been widely adopted in practice. The following sections of the chapter turn to the explanations for this, exploring first scepticism over the models' performance effects.

The HRM and Performance Debate

The publication of work outlining the new 'high commitment' models of HRM was followed by a flurry of academic research seeking to test how far the models, when implemented in practice, impacted positively on organizational performance. A series of influential studies established evidence of a cross-sectional correlation between the use of HR practices associated with a high commitment approach and organizational performance in the steel industry (Arthur, 1994; Ichniowski, Shaw, and Prennushi, 1997), the automotive industry (MacDuffie, 1995), metal-working plants (Youndt et al., 1996), banking (Delery and Doty, 1996), and across US companies as a whole (Huselid, 1995). These early studies triggered a swarm of imitators seeking to replicate the results in other contexts. Indeed, a meta-analysis of ninety-two such studies published in the mid-2000s found support for the existence of a cross-sectional correlation between extensive HR practices and better organizational performance (Combs et al., 2006).

However, there are a number of limitations common to all of these studies, which raise questions about how far they genuinely demonstrate a causal HR–performance relationship. It is not clear that the studies are able to measure HR systems and organizational performance accurately or consistently. The extent to which important contextual variables that are likely to interact with HR systems (such as organizational strategy and particularly organizational culture and management quality) can be measured adequately in surveys is questionable. Therefore, it may be these omitted variables rather than the HR practices themselves that are the cause of higher performance (see Purcell and Kinnie, 2007, and Guest, 2011, for more detailed reviews of these issues). These concerns are magnified by the fact that longitudinal studies, which are able to control for time invariant omitted variables, tend not to find evidence of an HR–performance link (e.g., Cappelli and Neumark, 2001). In addition, while Bloom and colleagues' experimental study set in the Indian textile industry (2013) finds strong causal evidence that the adoption of some of the HR practices associated with a high commitment approach results in higher performance, their results undermine the theoretical argument that the normative models need to be implemented in their entirety, as they show that a relatively narrow set of HR practices combined with a fairly traditional approach to job design and management control systems are capable of engendering large performance improvements without the full paraphernalia of high commitment HRM. Looking at evidence from the small and medium-sized enterprise (SME) literature, there is significant doubt as to whether even a correlational relationship exists between HRM and performance. While some studies have found HR to be associated with higher labour productivity, lower voluntary turnover, and increased sales growth in SMEs (Messersmith and

Guthrie, 2010; Patel and Conklin, 2012; Sels et al., 2006; Way, 2002), other studies have failed to identify a relationship between HR and financial performance, arguing instead that within SMEs, the costs associated with the introduction and operation of such practices cancel out the benefits stemming from their productivity-enhancing effects (Faems et al., 2005; Way, 2002).

A possible explanation, therefore, in explaining the lack of adoption of the high commitment models of HRM is that question-marks remain over how far such models really impact on organizational performance. If HR professionals judge the evidence on the HR–performance relationship to be insufficiently convincing, and if this concurs with their real-life experiences in their managerial roles within their own organizations, it is unlikely that they will be inspired by the research to pursue the adoption of a high commitment approach. They will also not be sufficiently trusting of the research to mobilize it within their organizations to attempt to persuade other management functions (finance managers in particular) of the need invest in potentially highly costly HR practices. In view of this, it is perhaps unsurprising that scepticism remains within the HR profession over the claims and arguments made in support of the high commitment HRM.

Institutional Theory and Path Dependency: A Short History of the Personnel/HR Function

This section explores whether a further explanation for the lack of adoption of the high commitment models of HRM relates to the organizational status of the HR function. This is in itself a product of history, or from an institutional theory perspective, a consequence of path dependency (DiMaggio and Powell, 1983). The emergence of the HR function in a form that is visibly recognizable in the approaches to people management seen in contemporary organizations began in the late nineteenth century at more or less the same time in Britain, France, Germany, and the USA (Kaufman, 2007: 20). This emergence can be related to the requirements of the new, capital-intensive industries (e.g., iron and steel, engineering and chemicals), which needed to find more efficient ways of managing their workforce in order to secure a financial return on considerable capital investments. Prior to this period, workers were employed indirectly through gang masters and subcontractors (Grey, 2013), so owners of factories and industrial enterprises had little direct control over the labour process. However, the introduction of 'scientific management' (Taylor, 1911) brought an end to this traditional approach.

At the heart of Taylor's ideas was the systematic and scientific study of work tasks to identify the most efficient way of doing a job. To support this approach, Taylor advocated a specific set of HR practices, including 'scientific' selection methods to identify the best workers for each particular role, training of workers in how to perform tasks in the most efficient way, piece rate payment systems that incentivized maximum effort and close surveillance and supervision to ensure worker compliance. These ideas were often resisted by workers because they resented the loss of control and autonomy and the requirement to expend maximum effort. A number of refinements emerged in response to these problems and criticisms, but Taylor's key ideas nevertheless became central to management orthodoxy in the twentieth century. Taylor's ideas provided the basis for further radical developments in the organization of manufacturing work, pioneered by US automotive manufacturer Henry Ford, who developed the moving assembly line to mechanize the flow of objects between workers, taking the scientific design of work from the individual work task to the whole system of manufacturing.

From the 1890s it is possible to discern two distinct developments that emerged in parallel with scientific management and Fordism, which would eventually evolve into the modern HRM function: first, the development in a number of large industrial enterprises of 'employment offices' to centralize and standardize employment related activities such as hiring, payroll, and record-keeping; and second, the introduction of welfare services, including works canteens, medical care, adult education and social activities, and the appointment of staff to manage these activities. The First World War (1914–18) provided impetus to both developments. The expansion of production to meet almost unlimited demands for the materiel of war, combined with a labour shortage as men joined the armed forces, created a need for the expansion of employment offices. At the same time, the need to preserve industrial order at a time of full employment created an increased demand for welfare services. Some companies, particularly in the USA, began to bring these two functions together into a single department. Over the course of the 1920s, inspired by the 'welfare capitalism' movement, these nascent personnel departments were given the strategic task of promoting cooperation and unity of interest between workforce and management (Kaufman, 2007).

However, the major international economic depression that followed the Wall Street Crash of 1929 led to the demise of many of these emergent personnel departments, as they came to be seen as an unnecessary luxury to businesses fighting for survival. Nevertheless, one of the political consequences of the depression was a significant realignment of politics in the USA, heralded by the election of Franklin D. Roosevelt in 1932. One consequence of this realignment was the widespread adoption of collective bargaining between employers and workers' unions as the key method of regulating the employment relationship over the course of the 1930s. This revitalized prospects for the personnel function in the USA, as specialist industrial relations managers were needed to lead and conduct collective bargaining, while personnel administrators were needed to implement and manage the resulting contracts and procedural rules.

Variations on this approach to the regulation of the employment relationship spread throughout most advanced industrial economies in the years after 1945. In the United Kingdom, the economic demands of the Second World War resulted in the wartime coalition government giving a much greater role to trade unions and collective bargaining in order to maintain industrial peace. After the war, the Labour government elected in 1945 continued to support collective bargaining through a range of non-statutory methods, while the commitment to full employment that was pursued by all UK governments until 1979 gave unions unprecedented bargaining power. Elsewhere, in the years immediately after 1945, the USA realized it would need to assume economic and political leadership or see Western Europe and Japan fall under communist political control. In response, it was generous in providing (via the Marshall Plan) low-cost loans to finance economic reconstruction. At the same time, non-communist trade unions and collective bargaining were given support and encouragement, as a way of institutionalizing industrial conflict to head off the threat of unregulated industrial unrest leading to political unrest and communist revolutionary activity, and to create strong civil society institutions that would act as a buttress against authoritarian politics of both the far left and the far right. Consequently, collective bargaining was to rise in importance in most of Western Europe, Japan, and Korea (Western, 1999).

At the same time as collective bargaining rose to global prominence, in the USA and to a lesser extent the UK, a small number of large companies sought to avoid or contain collective bargaining and the constraints and costs it was perceived to engender through the use of sophisticated human resource strategies, thus providing further impetus for the development of personnel departments. While the roots of this approach can be traced back to the welfare capitalism movement of the 1920s, it also derived intellectual inspiration from the Human Relations movement (Kaufman, 2007: 29). At its core, the Human Relations movement was based on two related beliefs: first, that unions were a sign of pathological dysfunction in the relationship between worker and manager that could be 'healed' through the more humane treatment of workers; and second, that there was a positive correlation between employee morale and the productive efficiency of the firm. In organizations seeking to encapsulate this philosophy (IBM was perhaps the most heralded example), the personnel function enjoyed considerable status and strategic involvement. Such organizations were, however, relatively rare.

From the early 1970s, however, a number of factors combined to create pressure for change that had a deleterious effect on the organizational status of the personnel function. At the heart of this change was a decline in union bargaining power, which had a number of causes. New technologies that replaced people with automated processes undermined ability of unions to control the supply of skilled workers. In addition, the global economic consequences of wars in Vietnam and the Middle-East made it harder for governments to maintain full employment through Keynesian economic policies, so higher levels of unemployment and the associated threat of job loss made workers more cautious in challenging employers. Furthermore, political mobilization by employers and those sympathetic to them led to legal restrictions on some union activities, particularly in the USA and UK. Beyond this, a sustained period of prosperity and generational change undermined the class identifications that once been a bedrock of worker support for unions.

As a result, collective bargaining coverage declined, initially in the USA and then in many Western European countries (Schmitt and Mitukiewicz, 2012: 267). By the late 1990s, collective bargaining covered less than 10% of the US private sector workforce, down from 25% in 1973 (Farber and Western, 2001). In Europe, collective bargaining coverage declined in Germany, Italy, Portugal, the UK, and Ireland. In other countries, statutory regulation preserved the status of collective bargaining, but declining union membership levels signalled a weakening of union power (Schmitt and Mitukiewicz, 2012: 267; Western, 1999). While the decline of trade union power and/ or collective bargaining opened up opportunities for employers to recast the employment relationship in a manner more to their liking, it also undermined the importance of the personnel function in those firms and industries where collective bargaining had previously been important, given that the status of the personnel function had stemmed largely from its role in leading collective bargaining and promoting unity. With this role no longer being so necessary, personnel departments were left as an essentially administrative function. This is demonstrated perhaps most forcefully by evidence of how far the function lost ground in the boardroom from the 1990s onwards, with data from the British Workplace Employment Relations survey showing that there was a fall in the proportion of organizations with a director on the board with responsibility for personnel or HR issues from 69% in 1990 to 61% in 2004 (Kersley et al., 2006).

Hence, although the demands facing HR professionals have intensified in recent times in response to some of the challenges discussed below (e.g., Hope Hailey, Farndale, and Truss, 2005), the HR function has become increasingly fragmented and removed from strategic decision-making (Caldwell and Storey, 2007). As such, it might be viewed as paradoxical that while the decline in union power and collective bargaining provided greater scope for managers to innovate with new approaches to managing the workforce (such as the introduction of high commitment HRM), it simultaneously weakened the strategic importance of the HR function, so in the years following the inception of the high commitment models in the 1980s and early 1990s, the HR function found itself increasingly poorly placed to lobby for their introduction. Added to this, as sophisticated HR policies were seen in part as an antidote to or inoculation against powerful trade unionism, when the perceived threat that unions posed to businesses declined, the case for high commitment models of HR was also weakened.

Institutional Isomorphism: Competing Narratives, Globalization, Financialization, and the Impact of National Employment Systems

This section of the chapter turns to arguments concerning institutional isomorphism (DiMaggio and Powell, 1983). Isomorphism is a constraining process that forces organizations to adopt similar structures, systems, policies, and practices. Coercive isomorphism occurs when national rules, institutions, and cultural norms force organizations to adopt a particular approach to managing people in order to comply with these rules and norms so as to secure the goal of social legitimacy. Mimetic isomorphism is a process of modelling supposed 'best practice' management practices (typically those followed by organizations perceived to be the most successful in their field) in response to environmental uncertainty and competitive pressures. Normative isomorphism operates through the development and spread of professional norms across and between organizations. Such institutional isomorphism may provide a further explanation for the lack of uptake of high commitment HRM. Isomorphic pressures on HRM have stemmed from a number of different sources, including: the appeal of alternative best practice models and the logics of globalization and financialization (both of which are underpinned by rapid and wide-ranging developments in technology and by political and ideological change); and the impact of national employment systems on HR practice. The discussion below addresses these pressures in turn.

How Competing Narratives Have Shaped HR Practice: Lean Principles and the Ulrich Model

While it might be expected that the high commitment models of HRM would themselves exert considerable normative and mimetic isomorphic effects, other powerful competing narratives may have proved equally, if not more influential. Two such narratives might be deemed particularly important here: the growing influence of 'lean' principles; and the attention paid to Dave Ulrich's model of the HR function. Both developments have arguably been important in influencing the approach organizations take to HRM.

Turning first to 'lean' principles, changes in management practice since the late 1970s have been driven by the need to reduce costs and to increase productivity and profits in the face of intensifying product market competition and greater demands from shareholders and financial markets (see below). A key early driver of change was the success of Japanese manufacturing firms. This challenge inspired firms in other advanced industrial economies to attempt to emulate Japanese manufacturing methods. As a result, traditional scientific and Fordist management has now been largely replaced by 'lean production', an approach to manufacturing originated by and closely associated with the Japanese automotive manufacturer Toyota (Bloom et al., 2014).

Lean principles are most widespread in industries with higher levels of product market competition and among multinationals, that are typically subject to higher levels demands from shareholders and capital markets than are smaller domestic firms (Bloom et al., 2014). Although lean originated in the manufacturing sector, its principles have also been applied in many areas of the services and public sector (McCann et al., 2015). The related idea of business process re-engineering (BPR) has seen the information technology-driven redesign of jobs and work organization to reduce costs, including labour costs, in many service organizations (Batt, 2007). There is evidence from a variety of sectors that firms adopting a lean approach secure significant performance advantages (Bloom et al., 2014; Appleyard and Brown, 2001; Appelbaum et al., 2000; Ichniowski, Shaw, and Prennushi, 1997; MacDuffie, 1995; Arthur, 1994).

Lean has a number of potential implications for HRM. At the heart of the lean approach is the systematic integration of market demand, technical and operational management, and work organization, supported by appropriate HR practices (Delbridge, 2007; MacDuffie, 1995). It is underpinned by a continuous improvement philosophy which strives to make constant incremental improvements to productivity and quality. It does this by involving employees in process improvements, seeking to elicit employee suggestions and then testing these suggestions rigorously to see if they bring about improved performance. Improved methods and processes are then incorporated into standard operating procedures (as per scientific management). Lean principles also require HR practices such as careful recruitment and selection, and investments in training, particularly from the point of view of equipping workers with the skills they need to engage in continuous improvement and take responsibility for their own work targets. Identifying and developing supervisory and managerial talent is also prioritized, with qualitative studies suggesting that the success of lean initiatives is critically dependent on line managers successfully adopting the role of teachers, coaches, and mentors (Sparrow, Hird, and Cooper, 2015). As such, a particular set of HRM policies and practices go hand-in-hand with lean systems, and appear to be integral to its effectiveness. The lean narrative might therefore be seen as encouraging the adoption of practices synonymous with the high commitment HRM models.

It is important, however, to exercise caution in reaching this conclusion too readily. For example, in relation to the empowerment concept that is held to be central to the lean philosophy, is it often argued that the limits to this are tightly drawn, with employees enjoying only limited autonomy, control, and work variety. Indeed, qualitative case study research has shown that the day-to-day realities of lean may fail to live up to the normative model (Delbridge, 2007), with production workers' day-to-day experiences of work being little different than under Fordist systems (Sparrow, Hird, and Cooper, 2015: 100; Delbridge, Lowe, and Oliver, 2000; Parker and Slaughter, 1988). Employees within lean systems may not, therefore, enjoy the level of autonomy, control, or variety that the normative theories of high commitment HRM prescribe. In addition, survey research (Bloom et al., 2014) suggests that the adoption of lean principles tends to engender a 'hard' focus on quantitative measures of performance. As such, firms adopting lean production methods tend to have extensive monitoring and measurement of employee performance through key performance indicators and targets (KPIs), alongside systems for redeploying, disciplining, or dismissing workers and managers who fail to achieve their targets (Sewell and Wilkinson, 1992). Hence, while the lean narrative may encourage movement towards the adoption of certain elements of the normative HRM models, it certainly does not encourage adoption in their entirety.

However, while lean may have been important in shaping HRM practices, it does not explain much about the role of the HR function within corporate life. This too, as discussed above, has changed radically over time. A key driver of more recent change has been the normative model of the HR role developed by US academic Dave Ulrich and his collaborators. Their approach has been to study the evolution of the HR function in large, successful businesses, to analyse why they organize HR in the way that they do, and then to extrapolate from this a normative model of how the HR function should be organized.

The 'Ulrich' model is essentially unitarist in conception, the narrative portraying the HR function as a values-based activity capable of delivering value for all stakeholders: workers, shareholders, and the wider community (Ulrich, Younger, and Brockbank, 2008). It essentially comprises the following. First, an HR shared service centre will perform the great bulk of the HR transactional work for the whole organization in one location. This centralization facilitates standardization of processes and economies of scale, both of which reduce costs. Further costs savings are possible through extensive use of human resource information systems, to facilitate 'employee self-service' where employees use web-based menus and advice to perform tasks that would once have required an HR advisor. Further costs may be saved through outsourcing the shared service centres to specialist companies, perhaps located in low labour cost locations such as India (Ulrich, 1995).

Second, 'embedded' HR business partners or strategic partners, located in business units, factories, shops, and offices, will support general and line management in those workplaces and assist with strategy development and implementation. The assumption is that most of the day-to-day business of people management will be undertaken by line management. The role of the HR business partner is to provide expertise and strategic advice on questions of people management as they relate to the execution of business strategy.

Third, an HR centre of expertise/excellence will act as an internal management consultancy, advising HR business partners and the business units that they work with on issues of organizational design and effectiveness, and providing HR business partners with a menu of options and resources (e.g., training programmes, toolkits, examples of effective practice from elsewhere in the business), in response to problems and issues encountered at a business unit level.

Versions of this model have been widely adopted, not least because of the significant cost savings that can be realized from HR shared service centres and associated outsourcing and re-engineering of HR processes and activities. Many large organizations use management consultants to benchmark their HR functions against industry best practice, which creates considerable isomorphic pressures to adopt this approach. However, while it is clear that the adoption of HR service centres and associated outsourcing activities have had a profound effect on the shape and activities of the HR function, it is less clear that it has led to the liberation of the function from operational and transactional tasks, or provided freedom to focus on strategic value-adding activities. A key argument with regard to this it that HR managers are only able to act in a strategic partner capacity if functional and operational managers are willing to embrace them as genuine strategic partners. There is only limited evidence that this has happened (see, for example, Pritchard, 2010). While this may in part be because functional and operational managers are guilty of failing to give sufficient weight to the advice and guidance that HR professionals are able to offer, it may also be because HR strategic partners are often seen as lacking the skills and insight to really understand businesses needs or offer astute business-focused advice (Ulrich, Younger, and Brockbank, 2012).

In addition, the reality of working as an HR strategic partner is often not about offering strategic advice on how to get the best out of the workforce or build a strong culture, but is about supporting line managers in managing poor performers and in recruiting and retaining talent. Transactional and operational HR responsibilities of this nature need to happen close to the business, so cannot be handled effectively by an HR shared service centre. To try to deal with this, Ulrich developed his original model to incorporate the role of 'operational executors', more junior HR generalists who work alongside strategic partners to relieve them of the burden of this day-to-day transactional and operational work. However, as Pritchard (2010) argues, strategic partners often find themselves re-engaging with transactional activity anyway, in part because of their conviction that only they possess the expertise necessary to play transactional roles effectively, but also because of the struggle they often face in getting operational managers to accept them as genuine partners. This in turn can create significant tension within the HR department, with HR generalists viewing business partners as encroaching on their territory and undermining their role.

Hence, although the Ulrich model is supposed to presage a more strategic and less administrative role for HR, the realities of the model's implementation have often failed to live up to this objective. This in part reflects the historic administrative role that HR has typically played (as discussed above), the result being that HR managers will frequently lack the skills and orientations to be effective strategic partners, while operational and functional managers simply do not see HR as fulfilling a strategic role. It is questionable, therefore, how far the Ulrich narrative has led to the emergence of HR departments that are strategically sufficiently well-placed within their organizations to be able to lobby effectively for the introduction of high commitment models of HRM.

Globalization, Financialization, and HRM

Further isomorphic pressure on the approach organizations take to HRM has resulted from changes in broader market and institutional context. Two factors are particularly important here: globalization and financialization. Globalization refers to the dramatic recent increase in global trade and interaction between nation states; the geographic reorganization of production and international trade, and the integration of financial markets (Sideri, 1997: 38). It has been underpinned by technological changes which have reduced transport and communication costs considerably, making it much cheaper and easier to travel for business purposes, to transport goods, and to plan and control production and service delivery over long distances. These changes, combined with political decisions to open up the previously closed economies of China, India, and the global South have dramatically increased the total pool of workers available to undertake industrial work (Freeman, 2007). This has meant that firms operating in the trading sector have faced increasing competition from lower-wage economies, and have responded to this competitive pressure by replacing labour with capital or by sub-contracting labour to lower wage locations.

Financialization refers to the increasing accountability of corporate managers to global financial markets (Froud et al., 2000). When a company's shares are traded publicly, senior management teams of companies who fail to achieve the returns expected by the financial markets face being deposed through hostile take-overs and mergers, and replaced with management better able to meet the expectations of shareholders (Gospel and Pendleton, 2003; Konzelmann et al., 2006). This is likely to be of particular consequence in 'market outsider' systems (as in the UK and the USA) in which there are large and active equity markets and shareholding is widely dispersed, rather than in 'relational insider' systems (as in Germany, for example) in which the relationship between capital and industry is significantly closer (Gospel and Pendleton, 2003).

Both of these dramatic shifts in the contours of capitalism may have acted to undermine some of the more people-centred features of high commitment HRM theory. Financialization, it is argued, creates pressures on firms to focus on short-term profit maximization and to reduce unit labour costs. Globalization provides the means of making these savings. In such circumstances, firms may be unwilling and unable to make open-ended employment guarantees or take a long-term view of investments in human capital, and may not want to risk offering employees greater autonomy, as to do so might involve managers giving up control of unit labour costs. In addition, pressure to produce quarterly financial performance figures that satisfy capital markets deters managers from involving employees, given that the slower pace of decision-making this implies may be seen as detrimental to meeting short-term financial performance targets (see Thompson, 2003, for a more extended discussion). The isomorphic pressures stemming from financialization and globalization may, therefore, have combined to deter organizations from offering workers long-term employment security, greater autonomy over how they work and a greater say in the running of their firms. This in turn will have militated against the adoption of the high commitment models of HRM.

NATIONAL SYSTEMS OF HRM

A final source of isomorphic pressure on organizations' approaches to HRM concerns the way in which national employment systems shape HR practice. National cultures and the political and economic institutions that are produced by these cultures are important for shaping HRM practice, given that organizations have to comply with national laws and norms that result from them in order to secure social legitimacy.

Although Kerr and colleagues (1960) put forward the hypothesis that technological change would lead to the erosion of national differences in HRM practices, because firms using common production and service delivery technologies would converge on a single best practice approach to managing their employees that was essentially an outcome of that technology, this prediction has not been borne out in practice. There is evidence, for example, that in specific industries such as telecoms (Katz and Darbishire, 1999), chemicals (Pot, 2000), automotive manufacture (Katz and Darbishire, 1999; MacDuffie, 1995; Woywode, 2002), while there has been movement towards 'global best practice' models of HRM, the way in which the models have been adopted has varied substantially between nations. This evidence suggests, therefore, that the need for social legitimacy through compliance with local laws and norms may well supersede best practice theories.

With regard to this, the notion of industrial relations 'systems' (Dunlop, 1958) can help to analyse and understand continuing national differences in approaches to HRM that arise from these differences in rules and norms. Dunlop argued that for analytical purposes, a system of industrial relations comprised of: actors (workers, management, and the state); contexts (labour markets, shaped in part by systems of education and training and welfare provision, and product markets, technologies of productions and service delivery); and a system of rules. Different systems of industrial relations emerged in different countries in response to different contexts (differences in labour markets, product markets, and technology) and the strategic choice of governments in response to pressures from those who elected them.

Dunlop's framework has mainly been used as a tool for analysing differences in trade unionism and collective bargaining between countries, but Begin (1997) has extended the approach to consider the wider HRM implications. Begin makes the point that differences in the system of HRM between countries result from significant differences in a range of contextual variables and social norms. He specifically identifies issues such as differences in: the typical and socially accepted basis of promotion (whether seniority or merit-based for example); approaches to work organization and the distribution of tasks within and between jobs; the distribution of work among the labour force; the span of control between managers and workers; the legal regulation of outflows from employment (redundancy, dismissal, retirement); systems of worker participation and voice; the basis of reward (whether pay is contingent on performance, for example); types of fringe benefit; and salary differentials between higher and lower skilled workers.

A good example of what this means in practice is Pot's (1998, 2000) study of the chemicals industry in the USA and the Netherlands. In this industry, there has been global movement towards a high commitment HRM model. However, its adoption has been only partial, with different elements being adopted in the USA and the Netherlands determined by how well they complement or contradict existing HRM systems. In the USA, moves towards greater worker involvement in decision-making were stymied by a lack of willingness on the part of management to cede power and control, while attempts at job enlargement and functional flexibility through multi-skilling initiatives failed because multi-skilled operators were not rotated between jobs, so did not get the chance to develop and maintain the skills to undertake different tasks. By contrast, in the Netherlands, initial plans to increase flexibility over working hours and introduce performance-related pay were modified to preserve the status of previously negotiated terms and conditions following objections from trade unions.

This variation in approach might be best explained by the dual and interactive effects of culture and institutions. In the USA, there is a strong culture of managerial command and control, and an expectation that workers will remain compliant or risk dismissal. This culture is both an expression of and a contributory factor towards an institutional framework in which worker voice is weak and managerial voice is strong. Key aspects of this institutional framework are that employees have no legal protection from dismissal, and trade unions are weak, with the effectiveness of collective voice through unions having been diminishing since the 1970s (Farber and Western, 2001). By contrast, in the Netherlands, there is a much stronger culture of management through negotiation, consensus, and persuasion. Once again, this culture is both a cause and a consequence of the institutional framework, in which workers expect long-term employment with an organization, are legally protected from dismissal, and where management are legally required to consult and agree changes with worker representatives (Pauwe, 2000: 175).

These differences in contextual factors have therefore resulted in significant variations between the USA and the Netherlands in terms of the manner in which the high commitment models of HRM are interpreted and incorporated into practice. In a similar vein, research into the introduction of team-based work organization to facilitate lean production and total quality management within the automotive industry found that national differences in vocational education and training and in worker representation systems resulted in significant differences in the way in which work teams were organized and managed in France compared to Germany (Woywode, 2002).

The above discussion also highlights the centrality of differences in employment protection regulation in explaining variation between countries, this often being viewed as a codification of cultures and norms within a given society (Deakin and Sarkar, 2008). Studies have shown that stronger regulation encourages firms to use labour more productively (Rubery and Edwards, 2003), promotes a cooperative industrial relations climate (Feldmann, 2008), and encourages firms to train, as employment protection legislation means they are less likely to view their workforce as a disposable resource (Gospel and Pendleton, 2003). The lack of labour market regulation in some national contexts (the UK and the USA as well as most developing nations) may therefore be a key influence on the approach taken to HRM, with there being little regulatory pressure in such contexts to encourage the adoption of a high commitment approach.

HR ANALYTICS AND THE FUTURE OF HR

The chapter thus far has offered a number of explanations for the lack of uptake of the 'high commitment' models of HRM. What, however, are the prospects for the future?

The discussion in this section of the chapter turns to the issue of HR analytics and the role this might play in enhancing the strategic position of the HR function, thereby boosting its ability to lobby successfully for the introduction of a high commitment approach.

With regard to this, Boudreau and Ramstad (2007) argue that the heart of the argument concerning the potential of HR analytics is the current inadequacy of HR metrics. While other functional areas of management are able to use data on business performance to identify critical business issues and calculate how business decisions affect bottom-line financial performance, the HR function is typically unable to answer equivalent questions about how 'key talent' contributes to the business. They go on to argue that the solution lies in the development of HR analytics capability, as this will provide the HR function with the capacity to understand and demonstrate convincingly how people contribute to business performance. The essential idea is that every organization can develop an empirically grounded model of how people and talent contribute to the bottom line, and then adjust its HR policies and practices to optimize performance in the light of this model (Boudreau and Jesuthasan, 2011; Cascio and Boudreau, 2014). This is a beguiling vision, but is it achievable?

The development of HR analytics is facilitated by two related developments. The first is the growth of large data warehouses of HR-related data, which have arisen from the automation of much HR transactional work. Large organizations will typically accumulate data during recruitment and selection processes on the employment history, skills and competencies, formal educational qualifications, and demographic characteristics of both successful and unsuccessful applicants. Once a worker is employed by the firm, data on hours worked and pay will then be collected and stored as a matter of routine. Depending on the job role, there may also be information on employee performance (sales made, hours billed to clients, measures of individual output, etc.). Additionally, 'soft' performance data might be collected from appraisal and performance management systems, along with information on training and development that the worker has undertaken. The organization will also have information on grievances, capability and disciplinary cases and dispute resolution issues, and data from internal communications, participation schemes, and staff attitudes surveys. Often, HR databases constitute part of wider enterprise resource planning (ERP) software suites, allowing HR data to be analysed in concert with data from supply chain management and logistics, customer relationship management, and management accounting fields.

The second development is the growth of the discipline of analytics, which has emerged at the intersection of engineering, computer science, decision-making and quantitative methods to organize, analyse, and make sense of the increasing amounts of data being generated by contemporary societies (Mortensen, Robinson, and Doherty, 2015).

While the promise of HR analytics is clear, its utility will depend on whether the HR profession can rise to the challenge of mastering this way of thinking and acting. A concern is that much of the existing HR function may lack the skills or aptitude to fully grasp the capabilities of analytics. This matters, because developing an HR analytics programme can be an expensive and time consuming business (CAHRS, 2014a, 2014b). It is necessary to mobilize significant resources, and to negotiate access to data held in other functional silos. If the HR function cannot articulate a vision of what it wants to achieve, it is unlikely this process will get underway. Also, if the HR function is unable to take a lead, it is likely that HR analytics will eventually develop as part of wider analytics programmes led by other functional areas (Rasmussen and Ulrich, 2015). This might, however, prove problematic in two ways. First, other areas of management may misunderstand the nature of human inputs into processes of production and service delivery. If models treat labour as a fixed cost to be minimized rather than a flexible input that can deliver significant boosts to performance if handled correctly, it is likely that both job quality and business performance will suffer (Ton, 2009). Second, all hope of a strategic role for HR will evaporate if the HR function essentially becomes the servant of an analytics model that it has had little role in developing (Angrave et al., 2015). In short, the advent of analytics offers the HR function a route to strategic influence within organizational hierarchies, but if the HR function cannot rise to the challenge, then analytics may lock HR into the essentially administrative service role from which it has long been struggling to escape.

Conclusions

This chapter has offered an analysis of why the adoption of the high commitment models of HRM has remained limited, and also why the HR function tends to play the role it does within organizational life in advanced industrial economies. It has argued that despite relatively recent developments in management theory, which have tried to position HR as a strategic discipline that offers tools and approaches (notably a high commitment approach to HRM) which turn people into a source of inimitable competitive advantage, in most organizations most of the time, HR is a primarily administrative activity in the service of production and operational management, with a mandate to ensure compliance with local rules and customs. Although there are organizations which exemplify the theory, they tend to be the exceptions to the rule. This is because HRM is shaped by the contexts in the HR function operates. Historically, HR has tended to be a catch-all department for a range of administrative activities related to staffing. Issues of work design and organization have been settled by functional and production managers and engineers with minimal HR input. Recent organizational responses to the uncertainty and competitive pressures created by technological change, financialization, and globalization have pushed organizations to adopt other best practice ideas which are at best only partially compatible with high commitment HRM theories. Developments in the field of analytics offer new pathways for HRM to become a more strategic function, but only if HR leaders are able to rise to the challenges that this technology presents. If they fail to do so, analytics are likely to lock HR into its traditional unstrategic service role.

References

Angrave, D., Charlwood, A., Kirkpatrick, K., Lawrence, I., and Stuart, M. (2015). 'Why HR Is Set to Fail the Big Data Challenge', Working Paper, Leeds University Business School.

Appelbaum, E., Bailey, T., Berg, P., and Kalleberg, A. (2000). *Manufacturing Advantage: Why High Performance Work Systems Pay Off*. Ithaca, NY: ILR Press.

Appelbaum, E. and Batt, R. (1994). *The New American Workplace: Transforming Work Systems in the United States*. Ithaca, NY: Cornell University Press.

Appleyard, M. and Brown, C. (2001). 'Employment Practices and Semi-conductor Manufacturing Performance'. *Industrial Relations*, 40(3): 26–41.

Arthur, J. (1994). 'Effects of Human Resource Systems on Manufacturing Performance and Turnover'. *Academy of Management Journal*, 37(3): 670–87.

Batt, R. (2007). 'Service Strategies: Marketing, Operations and Human Resource Practices', in P. Boxall, J. Purcell, and P. Wright (eds.), *The Oxford Handbook of Human Resource Management*. Oxford: Oxford University Press, 533–51.

Beer, M., Spector, B., Lawrence, P., Quinn Mills, D., and Walton, R. (1984). *Managing Human Assets*. London: Collier Macmillan.

Begin, J. (1997). *Dynamic Human Resources Systems*. Berlin: Willem de Gruyter.

Bloom N., Eifert, B., Mahajan, A., McKenzie, D., and Roberts, J. (2013). 'Does Management Matter? Evidence from India'. *Quarterly Journal of Economics*, 128(1): 1–51.

Bloom, N., Lemos, R., Sadun, R., Scur, D., and Van Reenen, J. (2014). 'The New Empirical Economics of Management'. Centre for Economic Performance Occasional Paper 41, London: Centre for Economic Performance.

Boudreau, J. and Jesuthasan, R. (2011). *Transformative HR: How Great Companies Use Evidence Based Change for Sustainable Competitive Advantage*. San Francisco, CA: Jossey Bass.

Boudreau, J. and Ramstad, P. (2007). *Beyond HR: The New Science of Human Capital*. Boston, MA: HBR Press.

CAHRS (2014a). 'CAHRS Working Group on HR Analytics Summary Report, Part 1', Cornell University Centre for Advances Human Resources, Ithaca, NY. Available at: <http://cahrs.ilr.cornell.edu/CentersofExcellence/data.aspx?n=HR%20Analytics/Metrics#Research> (accessed 21 October 2014).

CAHRS (2014b). 'CAHRS Working Group on HR Analytics Summary Report, Part 2', Cornell University Centre for Advances Human Resources, Ithaca, NY. Available at: <http://cahrs.ilr.cornell.edu/CentersofExcellence/data.aspx?n=HR%20Analytics/Metrics#Research> (accessed 21 October 2014).

Caldwell, R. (2003). 'The Changing Role of Personnel Managers: Old Ambiguities, New Uncertainties'. *Journal of Management Studies*, 40(4): 983–1004.

Caldwell, R. and Storey, J. (2007). 'The HR Function: Integration or Fragmentation?', in J. Storey (ed.), *Human Resource Management: A Critical Text*. London: Cenage, 21–38.

Cappelli P. and Neumark, D. (2001). 'Do "High Performance" Work Practices Improve Establishment Level Outcomes?' *Industrial and Labor Relations Review*, 54(4): 737–75.

Cascio, W. and Boudreau, J. (2014). *Investing in People: The Financial Impact of Human Resources Initiatives*, 2nd edn. Upper Saddle River, NJ: Pearson Press.

Combs, J., Liu, Y., Hall, A., and Ketchen, D. (2006). 'How Much Do High-Performance Work Practices Matter? A Meta-Analysis of Their Effects on Organizational Performance'. *Personnel Psychology*, 59(3): 501–28.

Deakin, S. and Sarkar, P. (2008). 'Assessing the Long-run Economic Impact of Labour Law Systems: A Theoretical Reappraisal and Analysis of New Time Series Data'. *Industrial Relations Journal*, 39(6): 453—87.

Delbridge, R. (2007). 'HRM in Contemporary Manufacturing', in P. Boxall, J. Purcell, and P. Wright (eds.), *The Oxford Handbook of Human Resource Management*. Oxford: Oxford University Press, 405–27.

Delbridge, R., Lowe, J., and Oliver, N. (2000). 'Shopfloor Responsibilities under Lean'. *Human Relations*, 53(11): 1459–79.

Delery, J. and Doty, D. (1996). 'Modes of Theorizing in Strategic Human Resource Management: Test of Universalistic, Contingency and Configurational Performance Predictions'. *Academy of Management Journal*, 39(4): 802–35.

De Menezes, L. and Wood, S. (2006). 'The Reality of Flexible Work Systems in Britain'. *International Journal of Human Resource Management*, 17(1): 106–38.

DiMaggio, D. and Powell, W. (1983). 'The Iron Cage Revisited: Institutional Isomorphism and Collective Rationality in Organizational Fields'. *American Sociological Review*, 48(1): 147–60.

Dunlop, J. (1958). *Industrial Relations Systems*. Boston, MA: Harvard Business School Press.

Faems, D., Sels, L., De Winnie, S., and Maes, J. (2005). 'The Effects of Individual HR Domains on Financial Performance: Evidence from Belgian Small Businesses'. *International Journal of Human Resource Management*, 16(5): 676–700.

Freeman, R. (2007). 'The Great Doubling: The Challenge of the New Global Labor Market', in J. Edwards, M. Crain, and A. L. Kalleberg (eds.), *Ending Poverty in America: How to Restore the American Dream*. New York: The New Press, chapter 4.

Farber, H. and Western, B. (2001). 'Accounting for the Decline of Unions in the Private Sector, 1973-1998'. *Journal of Labor Research*, 22(3): 459–85.

Feldmann, H. (2008). 'The Quality of Industrial Relations and Unemployment Around the World'. *Economics Letters*, 99(1): 200–3.

Froud, J., Haslam, C., Sukhdev, J., and Williams, K. (2000). 'Shareholder Value and Financialisation: Consultancy Promises and Market Moves'. *Economy and Society*, 29(1): 80–110.

Gospel, H. and Pendleton, A. (2003). 'Finance, Corporate Governance and the Management of Labour: A Conceptual and Comparative Analysis'. *British Journal of Industrial Relations*, 41(3): 557–82.

Grey, C. (2013). *A Very Short, Fairly Interesting and Reasonably Cheap Book about Studying Organizations*. London: SAGE.

Guest, D. (2011). 'Human Resource Management and Performance: Still Searching for Some Answers'. *Human Resource Management Journal*, 21(1): 3–13.

Guest, D. and Conway, N. (1999). 'Peering into the Black Hole: The Downside of the New Employment Relations in the UK'. *British Journal of Industrial Relations*, 3(3): 367–89.

Hope Hailey, V., Farndale, E., and Truss, C. (2005). 'The HR Department's Role in Organisational Performance'. *Human Resource Management Journal*, 15(3): 49–66.

Huselid, M. (1995). 'The Impact of Human Resource Management Practices on Turnover, Productivity and Corporate Performance'. *Academy of Management Journal*, 44(3): 13–28.

Ichniowski, C., Shaw, K. and Prennushi, G. (1997). 'The Effects of Human Resource Management Practices on Productivity: A Study of Steel Finishing Lines'. *American Economic Review*, 87(3): 291–313.

Katz, H. and Darbishire, O. (1999). *Converging Divergences: World Wide Changes in Employment Systems*. Ithaca, NY: Cornell University Press.

Kaufman, B. (2007). 'The Development of HRM in Historical and International Perspective'. in P. Boxall, J. Purcell and P. Wright (eds.), *The Oxford Handbook of Human Resource Management*. Oxford: Oxford University Press, 19–47.

Kerr, C., Dunlop, J., Harbison, F., and Myers, C. (1960). *Industrialism and Industrial Man: The Problems of Labour and Management in Economic Growth*. Cambridge, MA: Harvard University Press.

Kersley, B., Alpin, C., Forth, J., Bryson, A., Bewley, H., Dix, G., and Oxenbridge, S. (2006). *Inside the Workplace: Findings from the 2004 Workplace Employment Relations Survey*. London: Routledge.

Konzelman, S., Conway, N., Trenberth, L., and Wilkinson, F. (2006). 'Corporate Governance and Human Resource Management'. *British Journal of Industrial Relations*, 43(3): 541–67.

Lawler, E. (1986). *High Involvement Management*. San Francisco, CA: Jossey Bass.

Legge, K. (1995). *Human Resource Management: Rhetoric and Realities*. London: Palgrave Macmillan.

McCann, L., Hassard, J., Granter, E., and Hyde, P. (2015). 'Casting the Lean Spell: The Promotion, Dilution and Erosion of Lean Management in the NHS'. *Human Relations*, 68(9): 1557–77.

MacDuffie, J. (1995). 'Human Resource Bundles and Manufacturing Performance: Organizational Logic and Flexible Production Systems in the World Auto Industry'. *Industrial and Labor Relations Review*, 48(2): 197–221.

Messersmith, J. and Guthrie, J. (2010). 'High Performance Work Systems in Emergent Organisations: Implications for Firm Performance'. *Human Resource Management*, 49(2): 241–64.

Mortensen, M., Robinson, S., and Doherty, N. (2015). 'Operational Research from Taylorism to Terrabytes: A Research Agenda for the Analyticis Age'. *European Journal of Operational Research*, 241(3): 583–95.

Parker, M. and Slaughter, S. (1988). *Choosing Sides: Unions and the Team Concept*. Detroit, MI: Labor Notes.

Patel, P. and Conklin, B. (2012). 'Perceived Labor Productivity in Small Firms: The Effects of High-Performance Work Systems and GROUP CULTURE through Employee Retention'. *Entrepreneurship Theory and Practice*, 36(2): 205–35.

Pauwe, J. (2000). *HRM and Performance: Achieving Long Term Viability*. Oxford: Oxford University Press.

Pfeffer, J. (1994). *Competitive Advantage through People: Unleashing the Power of the Workforce*. Boston, MA: Harvard University Press.

Pfeffer, J. (1998). *The Human Equation*. Boston, MA: Harvard University Press.

Pot, F. (2000). *Employment Relations and National Culture*. Cheltenham: Edward Elgar.

Pritchard, K. (2010). 'Becoming an HR Strategic Partner'. *Human Resource Management Journal*, 20(2): 175–88.

Purcell, J. and Kinnie, N. (2007). 'HRM and Business Performance', in P. Boxall, J. Purcell, and P. Wright (eds.), *The Oxford Handbook of Human Resource Management*. Oxford: Oxford University Press, 533–51.

Rasmussen, T. and Ulrich, D. (2015). 'Learning from Practice: How HR Analytics Avoids Becoming a Fad'. *Organizational Dynamics*, first online publication, doi:10.1016/j.orgdyn.2015.05.008.

Rubery, J. and Edwards, P. (2003). 'Low Pay and the National Minimum Wage', in P. Edwards (ed.), *Industrial Relations: Theory and Practice*. Oxford: Blackwell, 447–69.

Schmitt, J. and Mitukiewicz, A. (2012). 'Politics Matter: Changes in Unionization Rates in Rich Countries, 1960–2010', *Industrial Relations Journal*, 43(3): 260–80.

Sels, L., De Winne, S., Maes, J., Delmotte, J., Faems, D., and Forrier, A. (2006). 'Unravelling the HPWS-Performance Link: Value-Creating and Cost-Increasing Effects of Small Business HPWS'. *Journal of Management Studies*, 43(2): 319–45.

Sewell, G. and Wilkinson, B. (1992). '"Someone to Watch Over Me": Surveillance, Discipline and the Just-in-Time Labour Process'. *Sociology*, 26(2): 271–89.

Sideri, S. (1997). 'Globalisation and Regional Integration'. *European Journal of Development Research*, 9(1): 38–82.

Sparrow, P., Hird, M., and Cooper, C. (2015). *Do We Need HR? Repositioning People Management for Success*. Basingstoke: Palgrave Macmillan.

Storey, J. (1992). *Developments in the Management of Human Resources*. Oxford: Blackwell.

Taylor, F. (1911). *Principles of Scientific Management*. New York: Harper.

Thompson, P. (2003). 'Disconnected Capitalism: Or Why Employers Can't Keep Their Side of the Bargain'. *Work, Employment and Society*, 17(2): 359–78.

Ton, Z. (2009). 'The Effect of Labor on Profitability: The Role of Quality'. Harvard Business School Working Paper 09–040, Harvard Business School, Boston, MA.

Ulrich, D. (1995). 'Shared Services: From Vogue to Value'. *Human Resource Planning*, 18(3): 12–23.

Ulrich, D., Younger, J., and Brockbank, W. (2008). 'The Twenty-First Century HR Organization'. *Human Resource Management*, 47(4): 829–50.

Ulrich, D., Younger, J., and Brockbank, W. (2012). *HR from the Outside In: Six Competencies for the Future of Human Resources*. Maidenhead: McGraw-Hill.

Van Wanrooy, B., Bewley, H., Bryson, A., Forth, J., Freeth, S., Stokes, L., and Wood, S. (2013). *Employment Relations in the Shadow of Recession*. London: Palgrave Macmillan.

Walton, R. (1985). 'From Control to Commitment in the Workplace'. *Harvard Business Review*, 63(2): 77–84.

Way, S. (2002). 'High Performance Work Systems and Intermediate Indicators of Firm Performance within the US Small Business Sector'. *Journal of Management*, 28(6): 765–85.

Western, B. (1999). *Between Class and Market: Postwar Unionization in the Capitalist Democracies*. Princeton, NJ: Princeton University Press.

Woywode, M. (2002). 'Global Management Concepts and Local Adaptations: Working Groups in the French and German Car Manufacturing Industry'. *Organization Studies*, 23(4): 497–524.

Youndt, M., Snell, S., Dean, J. W., and Lepak, D. (1996). 'Human Resource Management, Manufacturing Strategy, and Firm Performance'. *Academy of Management Journal*, 39(4): 836–66.

CHAPTER 10

MANAGING OPERATIONS

NICOLA BATEMAN AND ZOE RADNOR

INTRODUCTION

THE purpose of this chapter is to examine how operations are currently managed with a particular focus on managing processes and so it builds on Chapter 4, which laid the foundations of the discipline of Operations and set it in the context of other management disciplines. As such, one of the major movements for operations management (OM) in terms of academic study has been the shift from production to service with a change of emphasis from industrial engineering to more managerial approaches. As a discipline one of the challenges for OM has been to mark its place alongside other management disciplines in terms of theory. In Chapter 4, Martin Spring outlined the concept of OM, its standing in terms of theory and practice. He also discussed the development from a manufacturing to service context. In this chapter we aim to build on that with some reflection on the past and present through further analysis of journal publications from the key OM journals and recognition in practice, before considering in more depth the future of OM with a reflection on the 'fit' of OM for the public sector given its roots in manufacturing and latter application to service. This review will be presented though a reflective analysis of the implementation of 'Lean' in public services. A philosophy and methodology much hailed as a way to manage operations effectively.

In terms of implementation and management of processes, aspects of OM have been very much evident in managerial activity with ideas of quality management, lean, and performance measurement becoming mainstream in terms of 'what managers do'. This is evidenced in the use of quality standards ISO 9000 (International Standards Organisation, 2015) becoming widespread with over a million certificates in 187 countries issued in 2013 according to the International Standards Organisation survey (2013) the manifestation of lean in all its guises (Radnor, 2010b) and use of operational measures to assess activities as widespread as ambulance quality (NHS England, 2014) to fish conservation (Oregon Department of Fish and Wildlife, 2013).

The democratic nature of managing operations—pretty much any manager will recognize operations activities—be it planning, scheduling, design of processes, improvement, managing capacity means that the challenges and complexities will be well known. As Slack et al. (2009) state, 'operations management is accepted as being founded on the idea of managing processes, and because managers in all functions are now accepting that they spend much of their time managing processes it is clear that, to some extent all managers are operations managers'.

Different industrial sectors across the world have also acknowledged the need to improve their operations management expertise and there have been many initiatives launched to achieve this. Examples include Industry Forum launched by Society of Motor Manufacturers and Traders along with the UK's Department of Trade and Industry in 1996 (Industry Forum, 2015) to improve the automotive supply chain, or more broadly the 2014 Reith lectures (Gawande, 2014a, 2014b) identified this as the century of the system and OM has much to offer managers across industries.

So, what has been the focus on OM and managing operations to date within the academic literature? Has this reflected the demands and expectations of industry and organizations, particularly public services, for their understanding in how to manage operations more effectively? The following sections present an overview of the research activity before one approach, lean, is considered in more detail.

RESEARCH PUBLICATION PROFILE

To put into context the focus of OM and managing operations an analysis of research is presented. Building on a database which has been used to investigate the theoretical perspectives in operations management (Walker et al., 2015) this analysis is of the key operations management journals, *International Journal of Operations and Production Management* (IJOPM), *Journal of Operations Management* (JOM), and *Production and Operations Management* (POM) from 1980 to 2014 has a population of 3,607 papers in the OM field. These can be analysed in a range of ways to reveal research activity in the recent past. The rise of service operations as a research subject can be detected in this analysis and of the 128 (3.5%) papers that specifically address a service sector such as healthcare or education and training just over a quarter have been published since 2012. Lean operations—a development Japanese manufacturing addressed in Chapter 4—represents 172 (4.7%) from 1980 to 2014. Lean papers started to appear in the early 1990s reaching a peak in 2004, declining, and then peaking again in 2013. The fact that these major movements only represent quite small percentages of the academic output is acknowledged in the literature (Walker et al., 2015). As well as the work of Walker (2015), Slack, Lewis, and Bates (2004) conducted research comparing the priorities of their MBA students versus the number of papers in OM subjects. They found salient differences including lean being ranked

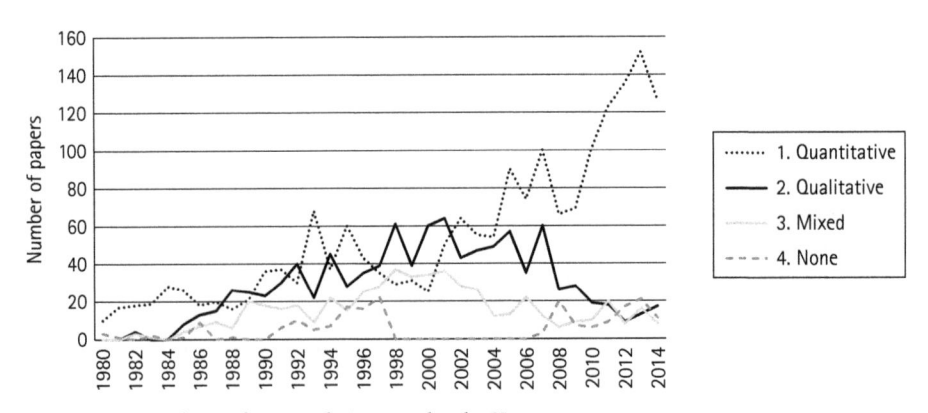

FIGURE 10.1 Analysis of Research Approaches by Year.
Sources: International Journal of Operations Management, Journal of Operations Management, Production and Operations Management issues from 1980 to 2014

more highly by MBA students than in the literature whereas performance management was the other way round.

The type of research approach conducted is also striking overall: quantitative methods are the most popular with 52.23%, qualitative was 27.67%, and mixed methods only account for fewer than one in six papers (14.72%). Over time, the number of quantitative papers has increased steadily, and significantly since the early 2000s; qualitative papers have declined from about the same time (Figure 10.1).

The gap between quantitative papers and other approaches is substantial. Over the last four years the average number of quantitative papers per year was: 127.75, qualitative: 14.75, mixed: 13.5, and other: 13.25. One might explain the rise of quantitative papers as maturity in the field: theories have been laid out and researchers are in a position to test hypotheses. An alternative view is that researchers are responding to an understanding that quantitative papers are easier to publish and so researchers pursue this type of research in order to meet institutional demands for publication.

The dominance of quantitative research is reflected in the research methods used with nearly a quarter of all papers being surveys. Other popular methods were case studies and simulations (Figure 10.2).

Conceptual papers were represented, with fewer than 13% of papers, and one would expect that this might expand the theoretical underpinning of the subject, but instead the vast majority—nearly 75% of papers—do not specify a theoretical foundation. Of those papers that do cite a specific theoretical foundation there is no dominant theoretical approach. The most common with fewer than 8% of the theoretical papers was game theory, followed closely by contingency theory. It seems that OM as a field has not really seriously engaged with management theory nor has it laid its own theoretical foundations (Walker et al., 2015).

Given OM's applied roots, is it appropriate that it should? There is an argument to be made both ways. The argument for engaging with wider management theory is that a broader view could expand and inform OM positively, widening its foundations

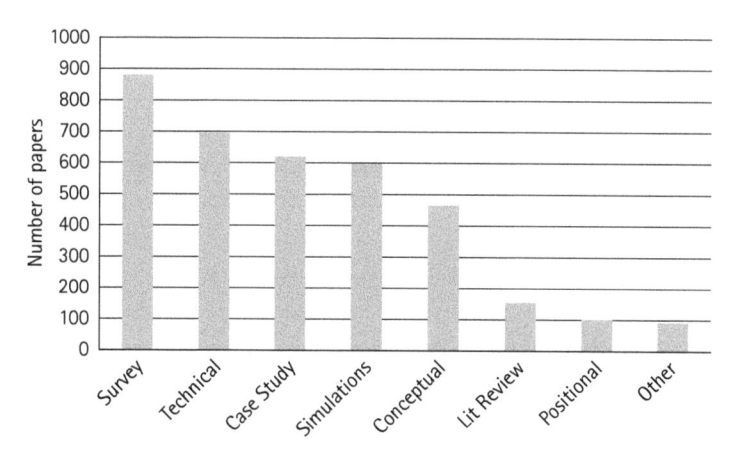

FIGURE 10.2 Comparison of Research Methods, 1980–2014.

Sources: International Journal of Operations Management, Journal of Operations Management, Production and Operations Management issues from 1980 to 2014

providing better insights and fulfilling its remit both in terms of industrial application but also in terms of informing broader management theory. The argument against is that OM does not fit well with management theory and attempts to do so are just vanity projects by OM researchers attempting to assimilate their business school environments rather than fulfilling their main purpose to serve operations practitioners.

Examining publication by country reveals that the United States was the subject of most papers with the UK and Spain second and third respectively. The range of countries examined in papers was very wide with research papers focused in fifty-seven different countries. Regionally the dominance of the USA meant that the Americas represented 20% of the papers published, followed by Europe (10%), followed by Asia, Australasia, Africa, and the Middle East (Figure 10.3).

In this chapter and in Chapter 4 we have abstracted the origins, profile, and recognition of the discipline. Through exploring more deeply 'managing operations' we have unpacked some key areas of focus and development. One of these areas still emerging through the literature is the application of OM for public services. In the journal paper analysis of 3607 papers published, 114 were explicitly focused on the public sector with a further 140 as mixed public and private. The peak of publication for public sector (including mixed) was 2011, whilst during 1980–91 only a handful of papers were published and in some years none at all. In the past decade there has been consistent publication focusing on public service and mixed public and private, however it may be that the 41% of papers (1980–2014) where no sector is stated did have a public sector element that the authors chose not to explicitly state. The predominant types of paper published were surveys and case studies, representing 30% and 31% of the 254 papers. This reveals that most research published is trying to establish the current state of public service OM. Whereas papers that set the agenda, that are positional and conceptual, only represent 1.2% and 3.9% of the public service OM papers. Of the 254 papers in public and mixed categorizing by sector, healthcare was revealed the biggest with 30% of papers. The next

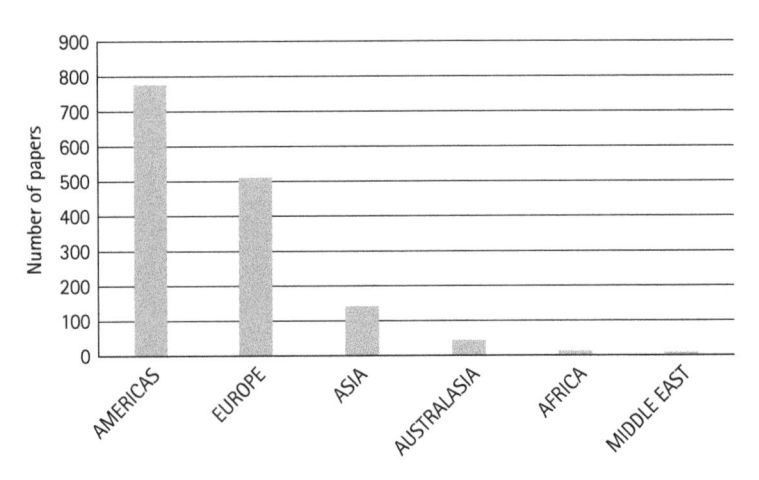

FIGURE 10.3 Number of Publications by Region.
Sources: International Journal of Operations Management, Journal of Operations Management, Production and Operations Management issues from 1980 to 2014

largest single sector was education with 8%, but papers that examined multiple sectors represented 24% of the papers. This may be a lack of research in this area, difficulty publishing this type of papers, or a reflection of the need for greater levels of field data and in-depth analysis to develop new concepts and theory in the area.

In a recent edited book (Radnor et al., 2016) 'Public Service Operations Management' is conceptualized. Focusing on one strand on this, for illustration, the remainder of the chapter will review the application of lean in public services illustrating that to date there has been an over focus on technical tools without an understanding of the principles and assumptions of lean or the context in which it is being implemented. The chapter concludes that to develop further there needs to be greater consideration of the underlying logic and theories of service management for not just lean but OM to have greater influence across the public sector.

Fit for Purpose: Managing Operations in Public Services

Public service reform has been on the political agenda since the late 1970s and has included such approaches as the 3Es (economy, efficiency, and effectiveness) through to Best Value and New Public Management (NPM) (Rashman and Radnor, 2005). 'Lean Thinking' has become a recent prominent and popular approach to public service reform. In the current era of constrained and reduced public spending it has promised to maintain service productivity, improve resource utilization, and maintain service quality. In short, it has been promoted as enabling public service providers to 'do more, with less' (Radnor, Holweg, and Waring, 2012).

In the USA and UK in 2005 the total outlay on public services as a percentage of national gross domestic product (GDP) was 35.9% and 44.5% respectively (Pettigrew, 2005) rising from 12.7% and 24.0% in 2001 (Karwan and Markland, 2006). In 2011 the Index of Economic Freedom reported that government spending as a percentage of national GDP was 38.9% for the USA and 47.3% for the UK (Index of Economic Freedom, 2011). During this same period (2005–11) both countries, as well as other countries such as Greece and Portugal, have experienced a profound recession leading to budgetary and spending cuts across the public sector. In England, for example, the Operational Efficiency Report (HM Treasury, 2009) in April 2009 stipulated that potential savings of around £10 billion a year should be sought over three years across public services.

This growing pressure on public services across the Western world has led to a focus on increased efficiency over and above the outcome measures of effectiveness and equity. Both public services, including health (Fillingham, 2008; Guthrie, 2006) and local government (Krings, Levine, and Wall, 2006; Office of the Deputy Prime Minister, 2005), and central and federal government (Richard, 2008; Radnor and Bucci, 2010) have responded by implementing a range of business process improvement methodologies including Lean Thinking, Six Sigma, Business Process Reengineering (BPR), Kaizen, and Total Quality Management. Tellingly, in the literature review presented in this chapter focusing on the use of these methodologies in the public sector 51% of publications sourced focused on lean, with 35% of these within health services (Radnor, 2010a).

The research on lean has suggested it can offer significant impact related to quality, cost, and time and even to the satisfaction of both staff and service users. The UK Ministry of Defence, for example, reported a fall in the cost of maintaining one aircraft from £711 to £328 together with a reduction in manpower required for this activity by 21%; the Connecticut Department of Labour eliminated 33.5 staff hours in its work by the redesign of its processes, saving $500,000 in staff time over a year; and Solihull Borough Council produced £135,000 saving in the postal costs for its fostering service, through a Lean review (Radnor, 2010b). Other reported benefits have included the reduction of waiting time for public services and a reduction in service costs through a reduction in resource utilization (Silvester et al., 2004) as well as intangibles such as increased employee motivation and satisfaction and increased customer satisfaction (Radnor and Boaden, 2008).

This apparent success story marks a starting point. Although lean appears to have had a successful impact within public services, the actuality has been one of easy successes and a lack of sustainability and resilience in the benefits achieved. It could be argued the majority of studies about Lean thinking in the public sector to date are not comparative or rigorous (Lilford et al., 2003). Carefully selected case studies have been used to promote benefits in public services without a balanced view of the negative aspects or consideration of the influence of other factors. Radnor and Boaden (2008) stated in a recent article Lean may be a panacea—because there is evidence indicating that it can support and help in addressing some of the inefficiencies in public services focused around processes and practices. But it may also be a paradox—because many public service managers appear to be attempting to apply it without fully understanding its underlying principles, seeing it merely as another policy or set of tools. More recently Radnor and Osborne (2013) argued that lean could be a failed theory for public services as there have been easy successes but a lack of sustainability and resilience in the benefits achieved. It argues that Lean does have the potential to have a substantial impact upon public services reform. To achieve this, however, it should not be treated as a theory in its own right. Rather it needs to be situated in within *public-service-dominant business logic* (Osborne, Radnor, and Nasi, 2013) to achieve enduring benefits for public services and their users.

What Is Lean?

Lean (also referred to as the Toyota Production System or TPS) originated within the Toyota Motor Corporation for the manufacture of cars as a then radical alternative to the traditional method of mass production and batching principles for optimal efficiency, quality, speed, and cost (Holweg, 2007). Lean seeks to 'design out' overburden (muri), inconsistency (mura), and waste (muda) in operational processes. The five core principles of lean thinking have been effectively summarized by Womack and Jones (1996). The first is to specify the 'value' created by the operational process. This should not be dominated by provider interests, but instead should reflect what the customer will value. The second involves identifying 'value streams' or those processes that will ultimately add value to the product or service. This can be achieved through forms of problem-solving and change management, often through re-drawing activities that add value, whilst eliminating those that do not. The third involves creating 'flow' throughout these processes. This means breaking down the boundaries and divisions between organizational and occupational groups to ensure work streams are continually attuned to the creation of value. The fourth highlights the importance of demand or 'pull', through responding to the needs of customers, rather than suppliers. Finally, Womack and Jones (1996) talk about the need to embed 'lean thinking' as a continuous activity within the culture of the organization.

Through all the principles it is argued that lean thinking centres around better configuring operational processes, as well as fostering behavioural cultural change by focusing on value creation. Crucially in lean, 'value' is defined by the customer or consumer, not the organization (Womack and Jones, 1996).

Building on this point it is important to reflect the key assumptions which lean is based on. Without these, lean cannot work. These assumptions have been defined as (Radnor, Holweg, and Waring, 2012):

- determining 'value' and 'waste' from a customer's point of view,
- creating value either by reducing waste and thus the cost of a product or service, or by increasing the value-adding activities without increasing the cost of the service or product,

- appreciating that there is a defined and measurable benefit to the organization in reducing non-value adding activities—in the private sector this has been seen as a reduction in cost, or an increase in competiveness against the peers,
- freeing up resources through the above processes to help a business, and
- understanding that at the heart of Lean is the concept of 'customer value'.

This genealogy for lean raises three important challenges for its implementation in public services—in that they are not manufactured goods but services, that the focus of the operating processes and systems of public service organizations (PSOs) are often internal rather than external, and that the indicators of success are different than for private sector businesses. When considering the use of Lean in healthcare, for example, Radnor, Holweg, and Waring (2012) reported that these contextual differences have created significant challenges for the implementation of lean in public services. First, unlike in the private sector, the customer (or service user) and commissioner of public services are not the same, which presents difficulties in determining 'customer value'. Second, public services are currently designed to be capacity-led, and hence there is limited or no ability, or willingness, to influence demand, or to re-use freed-up resources to grow the business. Finally, the private sector raison d'etre of lean is on efficiency and cost reduction—yet public services must also consider effectiveness and equity (Radnor, Holweg, and Waring, 2012).

The implementation of lean is often described as 'a journey'—with the various stages of the implementation being landmarks of the total journey (Bicheno, 2004; Hines, Found, and Harrison, 2008). This journey is described by some authors as about developing a Lean philosophy suggesting that organizations should aim to create *a lean lifestyle* (Hines, Found, and Harrison, 2008). Hines, Found, and Harrison (2008) note that the framework of lean often exists at two levels—at a strategic level focusing on the principles and, an operational level focusing on the tools and techniques. Hines, Found, and Harrison (2008) develop this concept with the aid of an iceberg model illustrating two main elements: below the water the enabling elements of strategy and alignment, leadership and behaviour, and engagement, and above the waterline and visible, technology, tools and techniques, and process management.

This model indicates that strategy should be the foundation, supported by decisive leadership and an engaged workforce to understand the processes and then use a range of tools and techniques to improve the processes. A number of tools are used throughout the model including policy deployment, visual management,[1] standardized work, 5S, and process mapping (Hines, Found, and Harrison, 2008).[2] This model illustrates the technical (above waterline) and culture (underwater) aspects of lean and supports

---

[1] Visual management is a concept of using visible information via performance boards to manage the work.
[2] 5S represents a housekeeping approach through Sorting, Setting in Order, Sweeping and Shining, Standardizing, and Sustaining.

the idea that Lean is a journey which takes time with people needing to engage with and embed ideas (Radnor and Walley, 2008).

Implementing Lean in Public Services

Some significant challenges have been identified in the implementation of lean in public services (Radnor and Bucci, 2010; Radnor, 2010b, 2010a; Radnor and Bucci, 2007). Many of these could be described as 'common' for most change management initiatives and not specific to lean. These include a lack of commitment from senior management, change objectives that are not aligned to customer requirements, a lack of training for staff, and a poor selection of projects for implementation (Antony, 2007; Lucey, Bateman, and Hines, 2005; Oakland and Tanner, 2007; Radnor et al., 2006). However, four challenges were identified in this body of research that are particular to lean. These are:

- A focus and over reliance on lean workshops ('Rapid Improvement Events'),
- A toolkit-based approach to lean implementation, but without an understanding of the key principles or assumptions,
- The impact of public sector culture and structures, and particularly the competing professional and managerial role in relation to lean implementation, and
- A lack of focus on the centrality of the customer (or service user) and understanding of the service process.

A focus and over reliance on lean workshops. There are two main approaches to lean implementation in public services. These are the use of discrete workshops or events taking place over a concentrated set of time, often known as rapid improvement events (RIEs), or a comprehensive implementation or programme approach across the whole PSO. Both of these approaches often used the same tools but are different in the breadth, depth, and regularity of their use—with RIEs being short to medium term in focus and the programmatic approach being committed, at least in principle, to continuous improvement.

RIEs (sometimes called 'Kaizen' events) are workshops involving staff from across the organization, often with multiple functions, getting together to make small and quick changes. RIEs comprise three phases, beginning with a preparation period, followed by a five-day event to identify potential lean changes and a three–four-week follow-up period when these changes are implemented. The approach is often favoured by staff as it provides an apparently fast return for effort, is visible, and does not challenge existing management control styles (Radnor and Walley, 2008). However, in isolation this approach can be problematic. RIEs tend to be more focused on short-term outcomes than longer-term developmental issues (Radnor and Walley, 2008). Spear (2005) has noted that a series of such small-scale successful Lean projects can have a dramatic impact in the longer term. However, he also notes that, in order to achieve this longer-term impact, it is important that these small-scale projects are all focused around a clear long-term improvement strategy. Currently, this appears not to be case in many public service RIE events (Radnor, Holweg, and Waring, 2012).

The full programme approach requires the entire PSO to be engaged in the implementation of Lean. RIEs may be used to change key areas or departments but fundamentally the programme is focused on developing behaviours throughout the organization which continuously improves value, flow, and performance through the use of a range of lean tools—including performance boards/ visual management, daily meetings, workplace audits, problem-solving, and experimentation (Holweg, 2007; Spear and Bowen, 1999). The key issue in such programmes is not so much the application and use of these tools. Rather it is about building a more fundamental understanding of the underlying principles of lean through their application. They are a means to an end rather than the end itself (Shah and Ward, 2007).

A toolkit-based approach to lean implementation. Drawing from the extant literature, typical tools and techniques associated with lean include Kaizen events, process mapping, '5S', value stream mapping, and visual management (Radnor, 2010b).[3] Assessing these tools, Radnor (2010) has argued that they can be used for three purposes within PSOs as part of lean implementation. These purposes are:

- **Assessment:** To assess service delivery processes at organizational level, for example value stream mapping, process mapping,
- **Improvement:** To support and improve the processes of service delivery, for example RIEs, 5S, structured problem-solving, and
- **Monitoring:** To measure and monitor the impact of the processes and their improvement, for example control charts, visual management, benchmarking, work place audits

As an example lean implementation in a large central government department in the UK (HM Revenue and Customs) began in April 2006 across a number of sites (Radnor and Bucci, 2007). It consisted of introducing revised processes in the four key customer-facing operations at each of the sites: performance boards which reflected the teams' performance, resource planning mechanisms, targets, and problem-solving. These operations were supported by daily meetings (ten minutes each morning) to motivate the staff to reflect upon the achievements of the previous day, to plan the coming day's work, and to resolve any outstanding problems or issues with the lean implementation process. Other tools were also introduced to support ongoing problem-solving (Radnor, 2010a).

The HMRC case study demonstrated a pre-occupation in public service Lean programmes with the tools of Lean rather than the over-arching approach itself. These tools may, and often did, lead to short-term success in improving the internal efficiency of the PSOs concerned. However, rarely, if ever, did they consider the issue that is actually

---

[3] Value stream mapping is the identification of all the specific activities occurring along a value stream for a product or product family (or service).

central to true Lean implementation—the centrality of the customer and customer value to organizational effectiveness.

Radnor (2010b) has stressed the importance of organizational readiness factors for the implementation of lean. These factors include an understanding of the processual nature of public services delivery, an appreciation of what 'value' actually comprises within public services, an external orientation for the lean process and the PSO, the active engagement of staff in process redesign, and the centrality of co-production to effective lean (Radnor, 2010b). She has argued further that an absence of focus on these factors in lean implementation in public services has resulted in a lack of sustainability in the longer term for these lean initiatives (Radnor and Bucci, 2007; Radnor, 2010b). Tools have been focused on to the exclusion of strategic intent.

The impact of public sector culture and structure. McNulty (2003) notes that across PSOs as a whole, policy is invariably focused at the senior level and undertaken by managers, whereas practice occurs at the operational level and undertaken by professionals (such as clinicians, teachers, or social workers). He describes further how professional work is broken down into specialities that very rarely cross departmental boundaries and that professionals control the flow of their work. Consequently they can resist managerial attempts to make their work more predictable, transparent, and standardized.

Within healthcare in particular, it has been argued that this challenge can cause conflict. Clinical acceptance of change initiatives proposed by service managers can be difficult because of resistance to being told how to do things, because they are uninterested in process improvements across departments that are apparently aimed at efficiency gain alone and because they perceive these initiatives as in conflict with their professional values (Cauldwell, Brexler, and Gillem, 2005; Wysocki, 2004). This has been especially so in the case of process re-design initiatives, such as lean (Woodard, 2005). Despite this opposition, clinical buy-in is critical to the success of the initiatives, as clinicians invariably have a strong power-base within the health service and have the power and credibility to convince colleagues that these initiatives can improve patient care—or not (Cauldwell, Brexler, and Gillem, 2005; Massey and Williams, 2005; Guthrie, 2006).

Gulledge and Sommer (2002) point out that the mandates and structure of the implementation of these process improvement methodologies are based on the traditional 'command and control' structures that will be found most commonly in private sector firms and that their implementation in PSOs has been predicated upon the existence of this model. Significantly, the research has revealed that many lean initiatives are actually top-down, driven by policy and public spending necessities, rather than bottom-up, based upon expressed need. Lean programmes have been decided upon and designed to the exclusion either of the professional staff who would be responsible for their implementation or of the service users who were purportedly to benefit from these reform programmes. Consequently the lean initiatives became policy, or finance, facing rather than oriented to the benefits of the end-users of services—a core element of true Lean. As a consequence, both Gulledge and Sommer (2002) and Seddon and Caulkin (2007) have suggested that this has meant that lean can never achieve its potential in public services, precisely because it is policy and finance facing, rather than end-user facing.

Frontline staff end up reacting to internal measures and targets rather than to external customers (i.e., their end-users). This is an anathema to the true vision of Lean.

A lack of focus on the centrality of the customer (or service user) and understanding of the service process. Proudlove, Moxham, and Boaden argue that a key problem for lean in healthcare is of 'identifying customers and processes in a healthcare setting and the use of clear and appropriate terminology' (2008: 33). Halachmi (1996) has also contended that it is hard to specify value in public service delivery because some organizational functions and procedures do not contribute directly to value, at least in the eyes of the customer (Halachmi, 1996).

Within a commercial organization, the definition and requirements of the customer are comparatively straightforward and directly impact upon turnover and profit. It therefore becomes easier to identify value and value-added activities. Within public services, though, the concept of a 'customer' is not so straightforward and can be contested. It can include direct end-users, unwilling or coerced users, multiple users of a service, citizens who indirectly benefit from a service and future users of a service (Osborne, Radnor, and Nasi, 2013). Moreover, the terminology of 'customer' or 'consumer' is itself problematic, rooted as it is in the discourse of commercial and business firms. The concept of the end-user is perhaps more appropriate. It does not assume the presence of a market exchange or commercial relationship—though it too suffers from some of the multiple meanings identified above.

Moving on to the issue of the role of 'process' in successful Lean implementation, Denison has described the ideal type of 'process-organisation' as one 'wherein the primary issue of organisational design is creating value and organising is understood not as a series of functional units or business units but as a collection of interrelated processes that create value' (1997: 31). A key problem for lean in PSOs has been, in contrast, that it has focused upon internal departmental efficiency rather than external, service-user driven, value (Radnor, Holweg, and Waring, 2012).

Three brief examples will make this point. First, across HMRC, in response to the question 'who is the customer?' the response was often 'everyone'! When asked whether the requirements of these customers were understood the answer was invariably 'yes—high quality quick information' but with little articulation as to what that meant in terms of standards and requirements. Therefore, there was no clear understanding either of who their end-users were, or of what level of quality and timing of information would result in better service delivery processes and more satisfied end-users (Radnor and Johnston, 2013).

Second, it is a truism within healthcare that the delivery of patient care is largely a human process and consequently that the causes of variability are often difficult to quantify. Walley, Silvester, and Steyn (2006) and Seddon (2005) have both argued that there is a need to better understand how demand varies across healthcare and to remove activities that do not add value to the patient or that create bottlenecks in the system. An example of such an improvement might be transferring patients from emergency departments to theatres more quickly by removing unnecessary paperwork, reducing the number of different staff involved in the process to minimize handover time, and/

or to improve the physical layout of hospitals (Lister, 2006; Walley, Silvester, and Steyn, 2006). This is a classic lean approach—it seeks to reduce queues by managing the variation in process. All too often, though, the public service approach has been to focus on increasing the number of public goods provided, in a situation where demand is, literally, inexhaustible. Like de-marketing, lean approaches seek to control either the level of demand for value and/or the processes used to deliver it.

Finally, Seddon and Brand (2008) outline two different types of demand—value demand ('what we are here to provide', or mission-driven demand) and failure demand ('failure to do something or do something right for the customer'). They report that in local government departments in the UK, the level of failure demand can be as high as 80%, severely limiting the ability of such departments to deal with value, mission-driven, demand. Understanding this key distinction in types of demand is vital to PSOs. Yet the findings of the HMRC evaluation clearly indicate that the reform focus was not on how patterns of work could be changed to better meet the demands of service users but rather on how the demand could be moved around to fit with the existing work patterns of the organization. The organizations were capacity not demand led and this only led to an increase, not decrease, in failure demand (Radnor and Bucci, 2010; Radnor and Bucci, 2007).

Fit for Purpose? Lean in Public Services

The extant literature clearly indicates that there are potential benefits from introducing lean approaches into public services delivery and that these benefits can add real value to the end-users of these public services (see Radnor, 2010: 370, 500 for some examples across public services). First, it is true that PSOs have made some time and cost savings that have benefited the public purse. HMRC, for example, has saved £400m from the implementation of the Pacesetter initiative (National Audit Office, 2011). Arguably though, these savings were primarily a product of addressing the prior poor design of these public services—what could be termed as 'picking the low hanging fruit (and windfalls!) of public management reform'. This may be an important goal in its own right, but it is not the intent of lean. This intent is rather to improve the effective delivery of end-outcomes to the external users of public services and to add value to their lives in doing so.

Second, it is vital to its success to understand that lean is context dependent (Radnor, Holweg, and Waring, 2012). It derives originally from a private sector, manufacturing context (Toyota) and this context has affected, and limited, its early implementation in public services. However, it cannot be simply transferred across to a public service context and assume that it can offer the same benefits. If this is the intent then lean will indeed be a 'failed theory' with little to offer public services beyond the correction of previous design faults (Radnor and Osborne, 2013). If lean, and indeed other OM concepts, is to go beyond this and to offer a genuine route to increased public service effectiveness and increased end-user value then a modified theory of lean needs to be developed which is suited to the public service context. Based on this the remainder of this chapter will sketch out some reflections and ideas for lean, managing operations, and OM for public services.

REFLECTIONS ON MANAGING OPERATIONS IN PUBLIC SERVICES

Due to the GDP percentage spent on public services, the financial situation and, the response by public organizations in using OM concepts and methodologies (given as example lean) there never has been a more important time for OM scholars to both research and publish on OM in the public sector. This has to go beyond merely reporting case study examples, giving survey results, or focusing on healthcare and developed countries but to use the opportunity to develop new OM thinking and theory which can be applied to public sector organizations and public services in general which should be defined as 'Public Service Operations Management'. This new discipline needs to adapt the traditional frameworks and concepts, developed through manufacturing and private service organizations, and develop on new frontiers taking into account the digital and information age (Radnor et al., 2016).

However, the challenge is not just how the OM discipline should adapt to the context/sector but also how the context/sector adapts to the discipline. Public sector organizations have struggled to recognize that they are a service based organization but instead considered themselves in terms of policy and product orientation.

It has been argued that the increasingly fragmented and inter-organizational context of public services delivery (Haveri, 2006) necessitates asking new questions about public services delivery. It is now no longer possible to continue with a focus solely either upon administrative processes or upon intra-organizational management—the central pre-occupations of public administration and (new) public management, respectively. Rather, these foci must be integrated with a broader paradigm that emphasizes both the governance of inter-organizational (and cross-sectorial) relationships and the efficacy of public service delivery systems rather than discrete public service organizations. This broader framework has subsequently been termed 'The New Public Governance' (Osborne, 2010). This framework does not replace the previous foci of course, but rather embeds them in a new context, an argument similarly made by Thomas (2012).

A second argument is that much contemporary public management theory has been derived conceptually from prior 'generic' management research conducted in the manufacturing rather than the services sector. This has generated a 'fatal flaw' (Osborne, Radnor, and Nasi, 2013) in public management theory that has viewed public services as manufacturing rather than as service processes—and that are created by professional design and input and then delivered to the user even though the business of government is, by and large, not about delivering pre-manufactured products but to deliver services.

Nor are most relationships between public service users and public service organizations characterized by a transactional or discrete nature, as they are for such products (Osborne, Chew, and McLaughlin, 2009). On the contrary, the majority of 'public goods' (whether provided by government, the non-profit and third sector or the private sector) are in fact not 'public products' but rather 'public services' that are integrated into people's lives. Social work, healthcare, education, economic and business support services, community development and regeneration, for example, are all services provided but service organizations rather than concrete products, in that they are intangible, process driven, and based upon a promise of what is to be delivered. Public services can of course include concrete elements (healthcare or communications technology, for example). But these are not 'public goods' in their own right—rather they are required to support and enable the delivery of intangible and process driven public services.

This product-dominant flaw has persisted despite the growth of a substantive body of services management and service operations management theory that challenges many of its fundamental tenets for the management of services (Gronroos, 2007; Johnston and Clark, 2008; Normann, 1991). It is this latter body of service management theory, it is argued here and within the book, that should inform our theoretical and conceptual understanding and analysis of the management and delivery of public services.

So should public sector organizations be investing in managing operations? The answer is probably yes as evidence indicates that Lean is potentially a good framework for public services as the principles give managers something to 'hang onto' with simple tools and techniques to use. However, it needs to be fully understood as a philosophy and seen more than just a policy and a set of tools. It needs to be set within a service management context and logic.

We would suggest, as shown in the lean exploration, that uncritically applying manufacturing ideas to public service is flawed, although many of the approaches and ways of thinking that helped evolve these original manufacturing ideas are useful. This approach of adapting operations management to the public service environment, whilst learning from existing thinking, should also recognize themselves as services, with the distinctive service operations management logic and managerial challenges that this implies, and hence reject the potential flaw contained within current, product-dominant public management theory.

In conclusion, we have argued in this chapter. managing operations in the future should be across sectors drawing on a range of disciplines, theory, and concepts. We hope when analysing journal content fifteen years from now the range of type of article, international and sector profile would be far wider than we have found to date.

REFERENCES

Antony, J. (2007). 'Is Six Sigma a Management Fad or Fact?'. *Assembly Automation*, 27: 17–19.
Bicheno, J. (2004). *The New Lean Toolbox*. Buckingham: Picsie books.

Cauldwell, C., Brexler, J., and Gillem, T. (2005). 'Engaging Physicians in Lean Six Sigma'. *Quality Progress*, 38: 42–6.
Denison, D. R. (1997). 'Towards a Process Based Theory of Organizational Design: Can Organizations Be Designed around Value-Chains and Networks?'. *Advances in Strategic Management*, 14: 1–44.
Fillingham, D. (2008). *Lean Healthcare: Improving the Patient's Experience*. Chichester: Kingsham Press.
Gawande, A. (2014a). 'The Century of the System', 2nd BBC Reith Lecture' (available at: <http://downloads.bbc.co.uk/radio4/open-book/2014_reith_lecture2_wellcome.pdf> (accessed 19 January 2015).
Gawande, A. (2014b). 'The Idea of Wellbeing', 4th BBC Reith Lecture <http://downloads.bbc.co.uk/radio4/open-book/2014_reith_lecture_4_delhi.pdf> (accessed 17 December 2014).
Gronroos, C. (2007). *Service Management and Marketing*. Chichester: John Wiley & Sons.
Gulledge Jr, T. R. and Sommer, R. A. (2002). 'Business Process Management: Public Sector Implications'. *Business Process Management Journal*, 8: 364–76.
Guthrie, J. (2006). 'The Joys of a Health Service Driven by Toyota'. *Financial Times*.
Halachmi, A. (1996). 'Business Process Reengineering in the Public Sector: Trying to Get Another Frog to Fly'. *National Productivity Review*, 15: 9–18.
Haveri, A. (2006). 'Complexity in Local Government Change'. *Public Management Review*, 8: 31–46.
Hines, P., Found, P., and Harrison, R. (2008). 'Staying Lean: Thriving, Not Just Surviving', Lean Enterprise Research Centre, Cardiff University, Cardiff.
HM Treasury (2009). 'Operational Efficiency Programme: Final Report', HM Treasury, London.
Holweg, M. (2007). 'The Genealogy of Lean Production'. *Journal of Operations Management*, 25: 420–37.
Index of Economic Freedom (2011). Available at: <*http://www.heritage.org/index/*> *Wall Street Journal*, New York (accessed 22 May 2011).
Industry Forum (2015). Available at: <https://www.industryforum.co.uk/who-we-are/> (accessed 19 January 2015).
International Standard Organisation (2013). 'The ISO Survey of Management System Standard Certifications—2014' (available at: <http://www.iso.org/iso/iso_survey_executive-summary.pdf?v2013> (accessed 9 July 2015).
International Standard Organisation (2015). Available at: <http://www.iso.org/iso/iso_9000> (accessed 12 January 2015).
Johnston, R. and Clark, G. (2008). *Service Operations Management*. Harlow: FT/Prentice Hall.
Karwan, K. R. and Markland, R. E. (2006). 'Integrating Service Design Principles and Information Technology to Improve Delivery and Productivity in Public Sector Operations: The Case of South Carolina DMV'. *Journal of Operations Management*, 24: 347–62.
Kim, J. and Robb, D. (2014). 'New Dimensions: How 3D Printing May Change the Scope of Industry'. *Apics Magazine*, 24: 40–2.
Krings, D., Levine, D., and Wall, T. (2006). 'The Use of "Lean" in Local Government'. *Public Management*, 88: 12–17.

Lilford, R. J., Dobbie, F., Warren, R., Braunholtz, D., and Boaden, R. (2003). 'Top Rate Business Research: Has the Emperor Got Any Clothes?'. *Health Services Management Research*, 16: 147–54.

Lister, S. (2006). 'Bloated NHS Is to Receive the Tesco Treatment'. *The Times*, 6 June 2015.

Lucey, J., Bateman, N., and Hines, P. (2005). 'Why Major Lean Transitions Have Not Been Sustained'. *Management Services*, 49(2): 9–13.

McNulty, T. (2003). 'Redesigning Public Services: Challenges of Practice for Policy'. *British Journal of Management*, 14: 31–45.

Massey, L. and Williams, S. (2005). 'Cando: Implementing Change in an NHS Trust'. *International Journal of Public Sector Management*, 18: 330–49.

National Audit Office (2011). 'Pacesetter: HMRC Programme to Improve Business Operations'. National Audit Office, London.

NHS England 2014 Ambulance Quality Indicators Data 2014–15. Available at: <https://www.england.nhs.uk/statistics/statistical-work-areas/ambulance-quality-indicators/ambulance-quality-indicators-data-2014-15/> (last accessed 28 November 2016)

Normann, R. (1991). *Service Management: Strategy and Leadership in Service Business*. New York: Wiley.

Oakland, J. S. and Tanner, S. J. (2007). 'Lean in Government: Tips and Trips'. Oakland Consulting White Paper.

Office of the Deputy Prime Minister (2005). 'A Systematic Approach to Service Improvement', Office of the Deputy Prime Minister, London.

Oregon Department of Fish and Wildlife (2013). Oregon Native Fish Status Report. Available at: <http://www.dfw.state.or.us/fish/ONFSR/report.asp#coho> (last accessed 28 November 2016).

Osborne, S. P. (2010). *The New Public Governance?* London: Routledge.

Osborne, S. P., Radnor, Z., and Nasi, G. (2013). 'A New Theory for Public Service Management? Toward a (Public) Service-Dominant Approach'. *The American Review of Public Administration*, 43(2): 135–58.

Osborne, S., Chew, C., and McLaughlin, K. (2009). 'Developing the Marketing Function in UK Public Service Organizations: The Contribution of Theory and Practice'. *Public Money and Management*, 29: 35–42.

Pettigrew, A. (2005). 'The Character and Significance of Management Research on the Public Services'. *Academy of Management Journal*, 48: 973–77.

Proudlove, N., Moxham, C., and Boaden, R. (2008). 'Lessons for Lean in Healthcare from Using Six Sigma in the NHS'. *Public Money & Management*, 28: 27–34.

Radnor, Z. J. (2010a). 'Review of Business Process Improvement Methodologies in Public Services', Advanced Institute of Management, London.

Radnor, Z. J. (2010b). 'Transferring Lean into Government'. *Journal of Manufacturing Technology Management*, 21: 411–28.

Radnor, Z. J., Bateman, N., Esain, A., Kumar, M., Williams, S., and Upton, D. (eds.) (2016). *Public Service Operations Management*. Oxon: Routledge.

Radnor, Z. J. and Boaden, R. (2008). 'Lean in Public Services: Panacea or Paradox?'. *Public Money and Management*, 28: 3–7.

Radnor, Z. J. and Bucci, G. (2007). 'Evaluation of Pacesetter: Lean Senior Leadership and Operational Management, within HMRC Processing'. HM Revenue and Customs, London.

Radnor, Z. J. and Bucci, G. (2010). 'Evaluation of the Lean Programme in HMCS: Final Report'. HM Court Services, London.

Radnor, Z. J., Holweg, M., and Waring, J. (2012). 'Lean in Healthcare: The Unfilled Promise?'. *Social Science and Medicine*, 74: 364–71.

Radnor, Z. J. and Johnston, R. (2013). 'Lean in UK Government: Internal Efficiency or Customer Service?'. *Production Planning and Control*, 24: 903–15.

Radnor, Z. J. and Osborne, S. P. (2013). 'Lean: A Failed Theory for Public Services?'. *Public Management Review*, 15: 265–87.

Radnor, Z. and Walley, P. (2008). 'Learning to Walk Before We Try to Run: Adapting Lean for the Public Sector'. *Public Money and Management*, 28: 13–20.

Radnor, Z. J., Walley, P., Stephens, A., and Bucci, G. (2006). 'Evaluation of the Lean Approach to Business Management and Its Use in the Public Sector'. *Government Social Research*.

Rashman, L. and Radnor, Z. (2005). 'Learning to Improve: Approaches to Improving Local Government Services'. *Public Money and Management*, 25: 19–26.

Richard, G. (2008). *Performance Is the Best Politics: How to Create High-Performance Government Using Lean Six Sigma*. Fort Wayne, IN: HPG Press.

Seddon, J. (2005). 'Watch Out for the Toolheads!' Available at: <https://vanguard-method.net/library/articles/non-academic-articles/systems-thinking-and-lean/watch-out-for-the-tool-heads/> (last accessed 28 November 2016).

Seddon, J. and Brand, C. (2008). 'Debate: Systems Thinking and Public Sector Performance'. *Public Money and Management*, 28: 7–10.

Seddon, J. and Caulkin, S. (2007). 'Systems Thinking, Lean Production and Action Learning'. *Action Learning: Research and Practice*, 4(1): 9–24.

Shah, R. and Ward, P. T. (2007). 'Defining and Developing Measures of Lean Production'. *Journal of Operations Management*, 25: 785–805.

Silvester, K., Lendon, R., Bevan, H., Steyne, R., and Walley, P. (2004). 'Reducing Waiting Times in the NHS: Is Lack of Capacity the Problem?'. *Clinician in Management* 12: 105–11.

Slack, N., Chambers, S., Johnston, R., and Betts, A. (2009). *Operations and Process Management: Principles and Practice for Strategic Impact*. Harlow: FT/ Prentice Hall.

Slack, N., Lewis, M., and Bates, H. (2004). 'The Two Worlds of Operations Management Research and Practice: Can They Meet, Should They Meet?'. *International Journal of Operations & Production Management*, 24(4): 372–87.

Spear, S. (2005). 'Fixing Health Care from the Inside'. *Harvard Business Review*, 83: 78–91.

Spear, S. and Bowen, H. K. (1999). 'Decoding the DNA of the Toyota Production System'. *Harvard Business Review*, 77(5): 97–106.

Thomas, J. C. (2012). *Citizen, Customer, Partner: Engaging the Public in Public Management*, Armonk, NY: ME Sharpe.

Walker, H., Chicksand, D., Radnor, Z., and Watson, G. (2015). 'Theoretical Perspectives in Operations Management: An Analysis of the Literature'. *International Journal of Operations and Production Management*, 35: 1182–206.

Walley, P., Silvester, K., and Steyn, R. (2006). 'Managing Variation in Demand: Lessons from the UK National Health Service'. *Journal of Healthcare Management*, 51: 309–20.

Womack, J. P. and Jones, D. T. (1996). *Lean Thinking*. New York: Simon & Schuster.

Woodard, T. D. (2005). 'Addressing Variation in Hospital Quality: Is Six Sigma the Answer?'. *Journal of Healthcare Management*, 50: 226–36.

Wysocki Jr, B. (2004). 'Industrial Strength: To Fix Health Care, Hospitals Take Tips from Factory Floor; Adopting Toyota Techniques Can Cut Costs, Wait Times; Ferreting Out an Infection; What Paul O'Neill's Been Up To'. *Wall Street Journal (Eastern Edition)*, 9 April 2004.

CHAPTER 11

MANAGING PROJECTS

JEFFREY K. PINTO AND PEERASIT PATANAKUL

THE UBIQUITY OF PROJECTS

PROJECTS and project-based work continue to proliferate in both the developed and developing economies around the world. Current estimates suggest that approximately 65% of all work being done in modern organizations today is project-based (Morris, 2013a), while projects themselves, including broad industrial categories of infrastructure, research and development (R&D), information technology (IT), process improvement account for some trillions of dollars per annum. In fact, there is a worldwide demand for nearly $57 trillion in infrastructure projects over the next twenty years and 41% of the world's capital investments is in projects (Morris, 2013a). Not only do projects themselves serve as the chief value generator for firms in multiple industries, but project organizational approaches are routinely used as the means for addressing and solving societal problems (including arable land development and programs for inoculation), emergency response (Haitian earthquake relief or Japanese tsunami recovery), and economic development (creation of alternative fuel vehicles, natural resource exploration, and urban education initiatives). Projects hold the promise of giving organizations, both large and small, the means to positively impact the world around them, while also providing a means to maximize profitability and firm value.

Projects are defined as: temporary endeavours undertaken to create a unique product, service, or result (PMI, 2013). Alternatively, the Association of Project Management offers a similar definition, suggesting that a project is 'a unique, transient endeavour, undertaken to achieve planned objectives, which could be defined in terms of outputs, outcomes or benefits'. Thus, projects are characterized in terms of critical elements (Pinto, 2013), including:

1. *They are complex, one-time processes.* Projects are undertaken to address a specific purpose or to meet a stated goal. They are complex because they often require the coordinated inputs of multiple actors from different parts of the

organization—different departmental units, geographical regions, or even other, cooperating organizations.
2. *They are limited by budget, schedule, and resources.* Projects are not intended to run indefinitely. Project-based work requires the completion of a set of specified outcomes or results, while working within the constraints of specified budget and schedule.
3. *Projects have a clear goal or set of goals.* Project goals, or deliverables, define the nature of the project and its purpose. Projects are undertaken with a specific purpose in mind, either a new product, service, or other outcome. Specific goals that give a measureable result are the driving force behind project-based work. Once the goals are achieved, the project is concluded and project team disbanded.
4. *Projects are customer-focused.* In addition to being bounded by a set of clearly defined constraints, projects have a client or customer for whom they were developed. That is, a project is undertaken for and intended to respond to the needs of either an internal or external customer.
5. *Projects are the building blocks in the design and execution of organizational strategies.* Projects are the principal means whereby companies operationalize corporate-level objectives; they are the vehicles for realizing organizational goals (Loch and Kavadias, 2011). For example, Apple's strategy of competitive advantage through breakthrough technologies is just the realization of multiple technology-based new product development projects.
6. *Projects have a clear life cycle.* Coupled with the notion that projects are ad hoc, one-off endeavours is the important idea that they pass through well-recognized stages of a life cycle. For this chapter, we will identify four stages of a project's life cycle: conceptualization, planning, execution, and termination. There are multiple management responsibilities and challenges that occur within each of these life cycle stages.

With a better sense of the nature of projects, we can elaborate the challenge of project management, itself defined as 'the application of knowledge, skills, tools, and techniques to project activities to meet the project requirements' (PMI, 2013: 5). Thus, the goal of project management is to bring a project to successful fruition (meeting the project requirements). Project management 'success', in this sense, is typically seen as satisfying the 'quadruple constraint'; completing projects on time, on budget, to requirements, and satisfying the customer. While seemingly straightforward, when we actually begin managing projects, we quickly understand that these four success criteria often involve a juggling act on our part: spending money can make the project finish faster, but at the expense of budget overruns and potential compromises in quality. Spending extra time to get the project's functionality (quality) right can jeopardize critical deadlines in the project schedule. In short, although the quadruple constraint is an important target to aim for, successfully satisfying all elements that define a successful project can often be extremely challenging.

We noted above that one critical characteristic of projects is their life cycle. Further exploring the concept of project life cycles, we can observe a simplified representation in Figure 11.1, where the X-axis is the elapsed time for project development and the Y-axis shows the level of effort, often referred to as man-hours, resources committed, or budget spent. At the completion of each stage, some deliverable is created, all of which contribute to the eventual successful conclusion of the project. So, for example, at the conclusion of the conceptualization phase, a business case for the project has been made, feasibility studies have verified its development, and the project charter is created, committing the project organization and critical department heads to support the project about to be undertaken. Following completion of the planning phase, all critical scope documentation is completed, including detailed plans and schedules for critical milestones and project delivery. The execution stage in the project life cycle refers to the actual 'work' of the project, at which point all important tasks are completed. As Figure 11.1 shows, it is during project execution that the majority of organizational resources are committed to the project, with overall expenditures reaching their highest level. Finally, terminating a project involves a number of administrative details, transfer of the project to its intended users, satisfying all legal or contractual obligations, and archiving critical documentation, including lessons learned materials, for future reference. Life cycles are a critical component of the project management experience because they illustrate both

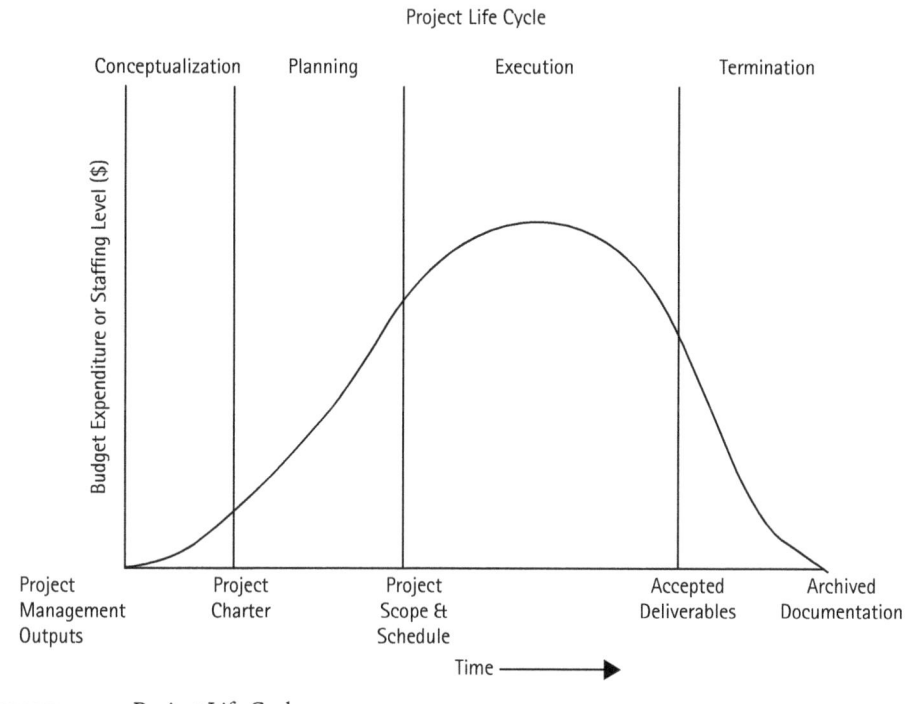

FIGURE 11.1 Project Life Cycle.

Adapted from: PMI (2013)

the uniqueness of each project and one of its chief constraints; that is, the time-bound nature of the project work itself.

The rise of project-based work reflects a response to the profound changes that have occurred in the industrial world over the past twenty years. Among the critical changes that organizations have seen are:

1. *Shortened product life cycles.* Product development at most corporations is a nearly continuous process; that is, as new products are being introduced to the marketplace, modifications or upgrades are already on the drawing board for development. Consider the recent introductions of software packages, smart phones, or other consumer goods. The life cycles of many of these products is now being measured in terms of months or even weeks, rather than years. As the time between upgrades has shortened significantly, it has caused organizations' project teams to be always thinking in terms of the 'next' or 'newest'.
2. *Narrow product launch windows.* With the emergence of global competition, organizations must be conscious of the optimal launch point for new products; that is, for many organizations, product introductions have to be carefully managed to coincide with market opportunities (e.g., the critical 'Black Friday' start to the Christmas shopping season in the USA). Careful planning and the coordination of multiple partners is critical to successfully hitting these launch windows. For example, in the global environment, it is necessary to link with multiple business partners, coordinate efforts, and respond quickly to opportunities as they emerge. The launch window theme emphasizes the criticality of market timing for maximum effect with projects being the best means to realize optimal timing.
3. *Increasingly complex and technical products.* Most of us are familiar with the observation that the average automobile's onboard computers today have more power than the systems that allowed man to land on the moon in 1969. This point illustrates a profound feature of modern commercial economies: products are complicated, technically sophisticated, and often difficult to produce quickly. The public's appetite for 'the next big thing' leads to requirements for products that are faster, lighter, better, and more complex than the old ones. As a result, organizations employ multiple project teams for a variety of purposes: to scan the environment for possible new technologies, identify competitors, and gauge consumer expectations; to investigate the potential for developing products through R&D; and to bring likely candidates to market as rapidly and error-free as possible.

As the above discussion suggests, projects, once traditionally viewed as a specialized organizational operation within some well-understood settings (construction, new product development, oil and gas exploration, and so forth), has evolved to becoming the principle means by which both public and private organizations can make positive changes to their operating environment. Hence, the need for project management skills has never been greater, as more and more organizations seek to adopt project-based work as a proactive method for engaging their customer bases.

Unfortunately, the track record for project performance in many industries remains unsatisfactory. Put another way, the reality of project management practice to date has not kept pace with the need for adopting project methods. Project success rates in some industries like IT are appalling; for example, according to the 2004 PriceWaterhouseCoopers Survey of 10,640 projects valued at $7.2 billion, across a broad range of industries, large and small, only 2.5% of global businesses achieved 100% project success, and more than 50% of global business projects failed. The Chaos Summary survey by The Standish Group (2013) reported similar findings: the majority of all projects were either 'challenged' (due to late delivery, being over budget, or delivering less than required features) or 'failed' and were cancelled prior to completion, or the product developed was never used. Researchers have concluded that the average success rate of business-critical application development projects is 39%. Even more troubling, their statistics have remained remarkably steady since 1994. Nor are construction projects immune: the Special Inspector General for Iraq Reconstruction (SIGIR) reported that more than $8 billion of the $53 billion the US Pentagon spent on thousands of Iraqi reconstruction projects was lost due to 'fraud, waste, and abuse'. Hundreds were eventually cancelled, with 42% of the terminated projects ended because of mismanagement or shoddy construction. As part of their final 2013 report, SIGIR noted: 'We found that incomplete and unstandardized databases left us unable to identify the specific use of billions of dollars spent on projects' (Kelley, 2008; Mulrine, 2013; Francis, 2014). Ultimately, the Project Management Institute notes that for every $1 billion invested in projects, some $280 million is at risk (*PMI Today*, 2013).

There are a number of reasons why the performance of the majority of projects in many industries continues to lag expectations; among them are a failure to appreciate the unique challenges of managing projects. Despite the rise of interest in project management and the numbers of certified professional project managers, research suggests that for many organizations, project managers receive little specialized training in their new jobs and are simply expected to learn as they proceed. The proliferation of these 'accidental project managers' is a common feature across public and private organizations (Pinto and Kharbanda, 1995). Another recurring problem is the lack of understanding of how a project's unique characteristics must alter a manager's approach to their discipline. The project life cycle, cross-functional staffing, and the lack of clear lines of authority are all associated with managing projects and must be considered, as we will do presently. Finally, many project managers approach their challenges with an inadequate or incomplete model of the knowledge base they must master. We will demonstrate the distinction between the traditional 'execution-based' project management model and the more comprehensive 'management of projects' paradigm that offers a far richer and more inclusive synthesis of the professional challenges in managing projects to successful completion.

Lastly, many projects fail because their organizations misjudge the manner in which project managers can most optimally be employed. Project managers work best when they are granted a significant amount of autonomy for decision-making and action.

Chiefly, this is because of the sheer breadth of responsibilities they face in performing their duties. Successful project managers are called upon to develop and manage budgets, recruit and lead human resources, develop work schedules and project activity networks, manage client relationships (both external to the organization and internal departments), negotiate with senior management, perform risk assessment and mitigation, among other myriad duties. In successful project-based firms, nowhere short of the Chief Executive's office is one likely to find organizational personnel with this degree of autonomy and responsibility. Many organizations fail at project management because they first fail to train and equip their project managers to face the sheer breadth and depth of their managerial challenge.

THE PROJECT MANAGEMENT BODY OF KNOWLEDGE

Professional project management organizations, including the Project Management Institute (US), Association of Project Management (UK), International Project Management Association, and Japanese Project Management Association have sought to codify and articulate the critical body of knowledge necessary to successfully manage projects. These bodies of knowledge vary to a degree, with some organizations placing more emphasis on some functions over others, but there is a general agreement regarding the critical knowledge areas that inform our ability to manage projects. In the interest of brevity, we would like to briefly address each of these knowledge areas and then examine the way in which these models of the body of knowledge affect (both positively and negatively) our ability to successfully manage projects. The ten knowledge areas proposed by PMI include:

1. Integration Management—All processes and activities for identifying, unifying, and integrating the various elements of the project, its chief clients, and other stakeholders, as well as all planning, monitoring, and controlling functions.
2. Scope Management—All processes required to ensure that the project includes all the work (and *only* the work) required to successfully complete the project, starting from collecting requirements, defining project scope, and creating Work Breakdown Structures to verifying and controlling scope.
3. Time Management—All processes required to manage the timely completion of the project, including defining activities and their sequence, estimating resources and duration of each activity, and developing and controlling project schedule.
4. Cost Management—All the elements involved in planning, estimating, budgeting, financing, funding, managing, and controlling costs so the project will be completed within the approved budget.

5. Quality Management—The processes and activities of the organization that determine quality policies, objectives, and responsibilities so that the project will satisfy the needs for which it was undertaken.
6. Human Resource Management—The processes that organize, manage, and lead the project team.
7. Communications Management—The processes required to ensure the timely planning, collection, creation, distribution, storage, retrieval, management, control, monitoring, and disposition of project information.
8. Risk Management—Processes for conducting risk management planning, identification, analysis, response planning, and controlling risk on a project.
9. Procurement Management—The processes necessary to purchase and acquire products, services, or results needed from outside the project team and includes contract management.
10. Stakeholder Management—The processes required to identify the people, groups, or organizations that could impact or be impacted by the project, to analyse stakeholder expectations and their impact on the project, and develop appropriate strategies for engaging stakeholders in critical project decisions.

This is necessarily a cursory review of the critical elements in the project management body of knowledge but it should serve to solidify our previous point regarding the breadth of demands that project management can place on prospective managers. The comprehensive nature of mastering cost estimation and budgeting, network analysis and scheduling, group development and leadership behaviours, communications and stakeholder relationship management, as well as contracting and supply chain procurement responsibilities demonstrates the unique challenge that project managers accept when working to lead their teams to successful project completion. Regardless of the industry within which projects are undertaken, the key themes remain constant and constantly challenging.

The Management of Projects Paradigm

Historically, project management was conceptualized in terms of a relatively straightforward, execution-based model. Figure 11.2 shows this simplified 'delivery' model, with its ten critical knowledge areas (time, cost, scope, risk, etc.) laid out against a timeline with life cycle stages embedded. The delivery model implicitly posits the role of project manager as that of an efficient executor of projects for which they were presumed to have had little input during project definition. Their role is relegated to an engaged onlooker who played no role in the critical ('fuzzy') front-end, when strategic issues are raised, technologies to be used are agreed to, supply chains are developed and suppliers vetted, and so forth. Scholars have criticized this traditional model as one that may have

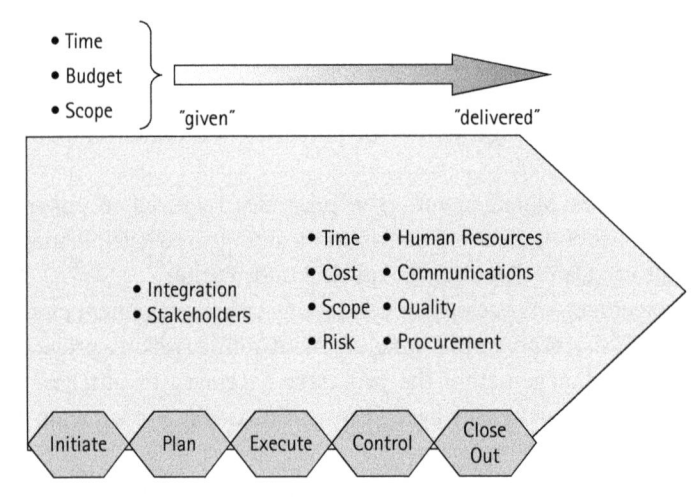

FIGURE 11.2 Traditional Execution-based Approach to Project Delivery.

Source: Morris (2013b: 62).

held true at one time and for specific classes of project, such as construction, but modern project management and the wide variety of demands placed on project managers today demonstrate that it is a myopic and far-too-limiting way of viewing the real role of the project manager (Morris, 1994, 2013b).

In 1994, Professor Peter Morris proposed an alternative model, termed 'Management of Projects' (MoP) to challenge the traditional view with a far more comprehensive perspective on the 'real' duties of modern project managers. In his conceptualization, project management is seen as not simply a delivery system, or technique-laden toolbox, but an equal partner in developing the critical interfaces, both internally and externally, that successful projects require. Figure 11.3 shows the full MoP model. Note how the delivery sub-system from traditional project management is embedded within the larger model, which also distinguishes between those activities that are related to 'definition' and others that comprise project 'delivery.' Further, the MoP paradigm proposes several key interactions with external stakeholders, including interactions with the business and general environment, affecting both definition and delivery stages, as well as interactions with the larger organization, source of strategy development, project financing, technology, commercial, and organizational systems. Morris's argument is cogently expressed in the observation that projects cannot be developed (delivered) without sufficient work being performed to ensure that they are fully defined and linked to critical elements within and without the organization. Finally, the MoP model creates a 'meta' life cycle, suggesting that a true representation of project development must include a reconfigured five-stage process, including concept, feasibility, definition, execution, and close-out.

One of the advantages of the MoP framework is that it more accurately defines the 'real' duties of project managers to be far more comprehensive than the traditional model of simple delivery. In the updated MoP, project managers' roles are much broader, taking into consideration the need to immerse themselves in previously unaddressed

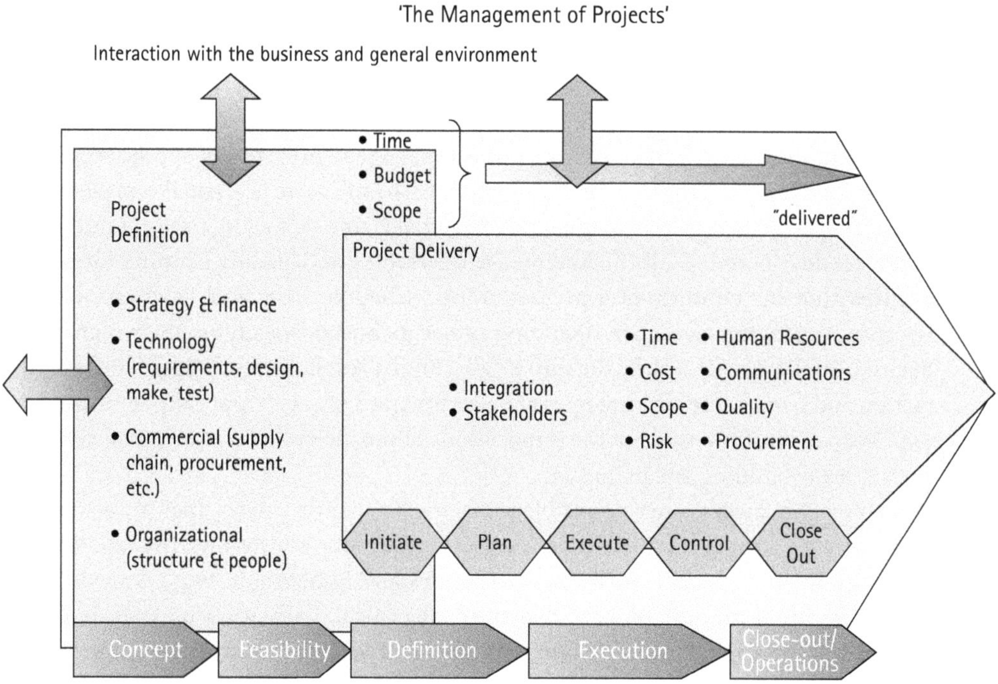

FIGURE 11.3 The Management of Projects.

Source: Morris (2013b: 62).

tasks such as supply chain development, contracting, or requirements management. The modern project manager is required to become more fully qualified, not only in the technical details of the project but as an individual who must interface with top management and critical stakeholders early in the project's development; in fact, far earlier and with far greater responsibilities than the outdated execution model. The MoP offers an expansive perspective of the challenge modern project managers face in a complex and rapidly changing commercial environment, by making clear the far broader nature of the challenges they need to address for successful project management.

CHALLENGES IN MANAGING PROJECTS

The previous sections sought to put project management in context; to highlight its challenges, constraints, and the myriad duties required to successfully shepherd a project to completion. Within this setting, there are several challenges embedded within the fabric of the project management process with which all novice project leaders must acquaint themselves. While by no means a complete list of contemporary challenges in managing projects, the following offer a perspective on the significant problems one is likely to face.

Life Cycle Implications

We noted earlier that projects have a clear life cycle that identifies their critical stages of development. While the life cycle has been used to identify the project's activities to be completed, the life cycle also informs project management in terms of other responsibilities; for example, project team development. The life cycle is a visual representation of a principle challenge in managing projects; that is, the deliberate time-bound nature of project development. All efforts aimed at developing and leading a project team must occur within the confines of a predetermined schedule. The clock is always ticking. Because project managers are operating under a constant deadline, their managerial decision-making methods, leadership styles, conflict resolution techniques, negotiating tactics, and team-building strategies are all a function of this temporally-bounded system. We can illustrate some of the implications of the life cycle on managerial activities such as team-building and planning.

As project managers are responsible for facing key delivery dates, they are also working to create a strong, supportive team under similar time constraints. Because they are operating in a 'temporary organization' (Lundin and Söderholm, 1995), knowledge of leadership and team development dynamics are critical. Early work on team-building, particularly the Tuchman and Jensen (1977) model, came under criticism for its single-sequence phasing and lack of multiple decision paths, disregard of external influences, and so forth. Further, although it reflects the dynamism of the evolving team, it lacks a time pressure element; that is, the notion that these stages cannot be allowed to evolve at their own pace because a time-bound objective exists (Hirokawa and Poole, 1986). Some of the most useful work on team development dynamics from a project (time-sensitive) perspective come from Connie Gersick under the model of punctuated equilibrium (Gersick, 1988, 1989). Punctuated equilibrium refers to the phenomenon whereby teams progress through alternating inertial change and revolution in the behaviours and themes through which they approach work (Gersick, 1991). When challenged to produce results in projects, teams do not progress through a uniform series of developmental stages, nor through linear, additive building block sequences. They instead must find ways to work together, deal with outside expectations, and meet established deadlines.

Project life cycle challenges inform not only our understanding of developing and leading project teams, but also our understanding of the use of project management tools and techniques. There are many project management tools and techniques available for project managers and project team members. The pressing questions include: what are the appropriate tools and techniques to use that will lead to better project performance and when should such tools and techniques be used? Since each phase of the project life cycle has its own required deliverables, the project managers should use the tools and techniques appropriately in order to deliver the outcomes required for each phase. This means that the project managers do not only use the tools and techniques that are commonly known or frequently used by others, but also the ones that contribute to the success of their project.

Research has shown that during the conceptual phase, the main deliverables and activities are to develop a preliminary project scope, which is not yet developed in detail. Among other frequently used tools and techniques, project managers will employ feasibility studies and communication plans to improve the likelihood of subsequent project success (Patanakul, Iewwongcharoen, and Milosevic, 2010). During the planning phase, project managers are required to develop a detailed project scope, which includes cost estimation, time estimation, resource assignment, procurement plans, and so forth. Tools and techniques such as analogous estimation, contingency planning, cost baseline, Critical Path Method, and hierarchical scheduling are also usually necessary. In the execution phase, milestone analysis and earned value methodologies are techniques that help project managers successfully monitor project performance status. As the chief conduit to critical project stakeholders, the project manager should also be constantly assessing the level of customer satisfaction. For project closure at the termination phase, the use of cost baseline, lessons learned, archiving all relevant materials, contract satisfaction and when necessary, remediation and negotiation are all required skills for project managers.

The project life cycle is a continuous and persistent reminder that the project is constantly going through some stage in its development, with each of these stages requiring knowledge of the specific activities necessary for completion, critical stakeholders who have to be kept apprized, and myriad duties that project managers are expected to master and perform. Clearly, the challenge of managing projects from a life cycle perspective should demonstrate the unique and valuable skill set that successful project managers possess and the degree of careful selection and training needed to make a productive project manager in modern organizations.

Responsibility Is Clear; Authority Is Murky

Because project teams are often comprised of members from different functional departments outside of the direct authority of the project manager, there are several unique challenges in managing project teams. Project managers are responsible for successful completion of their projects but their actual authority over their own project teams may be minimal. Within the organization structure literature, we refer to matrix designs as those that share power between project managers and functional department heads. In matrix structures, the expectation is that project managers first assess their resource needs to complete a project ('How many engineers will I need? How many programmers?') and then work with department heads who control these resources to get temporary staffing support for some period of the project's life. However, power differentials are rarely equal between the two sides. In some settings, termed 'strong matrix', the project manager will actually have sufficient power to requisition the needed personnel for the team. On the other hand, a weak matrix suggests that final authority for staffing support remains with the functional manager. The balanced matrix assumes an equal power distribution and staffing occurs as the result of cooperative consultation between the parties to ensure that the best people are assigned to work on the project.

In reality, within most organizations the project managers occupy a shaky position; one that affords them full responsibility for project delivery but often accords them little real power in interacting with other key organizational stakeholders. As a result, successful project managers quickly learn the importance of influence skills to do their jobs effectively. Influence has been defined by organizational researchers in varying ways. At its most basic, we can think of influence as the ability to affect the behaviour of others in a particular way (DuBrin, 2012). While power has a stronger base and is viewed as a capacity to influence, the tactics of influence themselves are predicated on the presumption that the manager does not have sufficient power to unilaterally force compliance. Thus, ingratiation, persuasion, bargaining and exchange, and pressure serve as legitimate methods for influencing different organizational stakeholders. This is particularly relevant because these same project managers frequently lack formal power or positional authority to mandate action. In addition to influence ability, the most important interpersonal skill for project managers to master is negotiation. Project leaders negotiate constantly with clients regarding project specifications, with department heads to secure resources, with top management for additional funding if needed, with team members to develop and enforce specification requirements, and so forth. In a setting where their formal power may be nil and actual authority remains unclear, it is critical that project managers recognize more informal but equally effective methods to affect the behaviour of others.

Planning and Optimism Bias

The Management of Projects (MoP) paradigm as shown in Figure 11.3 raises some critical implications for not only the effective management of a project in development; it also represents a clear picture of the role project managers play in project definition. As we noted previously, the traditional, 'delivery' model of project management puts project managers squarely into the operationalization camp; their role in this paradigm is to plan the project and work the plan as efficiently as possible. However, as the MoP makes clear, this abbreviated model ignores the critical role that project managers play on the critical front-end of the project, working with internal and external stakeholders to get the definition right before moving to delivery.

Managing the front-end successfully is particularly important due to recent research that has shed light on a number of errors in project planning, especially the problems of planning and optimism bias. Projects, as we have noted, are undertaken for a variety of reasons but there is no gainsaying their popularity in multiple industries. For example, the sheer number and costs associated with infrastructure projects undertaken on an annual basis are staggering. As the dismal performance of these projects (in terms of cost overruns, poor quality, and/or significant schedule slippages) becomes widely known, it is imperative to consider some of the reasons why there are recurring and systematic problems with cost estimation, poor project delivery, and spiralling overages, again and again. Why, for example, have Olympic Games routinely overrun their budgets, sometimes by appalling amounts? Why are the construction of giant 'megadams' often a greater hindrance to third world economies than a boon? In short, why are large numbers and sometimes whole classes of projects routinely late and over budget?

It was to begin to address some of these questions that Professor Bent Flyvbjerg (Flyvbjerg, 2005, 2011; Flyvbjerg, Bruzelius, and Rothengatter, 2003; Flyvbjerg, Garbuio, and Lovallo, 2009) and his colleagues have undertaken systematic, longitudinal research into project performance. Their findings suggest that several dynamics are at work when it comes to project definition, many of which relate to the inability of project sponsors to establish a reasonable point of departure for why they support projects in the first place. Further, many projects are initiated with less-than-full information or based on unrealistically optimistic assumptions. The irony is that many of these false assumptions are derived in spite of clear, historical evidence to the contrary. Thus, London's 2012 Olympics were originally budgeted to cost £2.3 billion despite Beijing's 2008 final cost of £9.8 billion and Barcelona's 1992 cost of £8.06 billion. When the costs of developing the Olympics were finally calculated, the price tag sat at well over £11 billion, representing a huge overrun from the original target. Flyvbjerg points to the problems of the *planning fallacy, optimism bias*, and *strategic misrepresentation* as key drivers of poor project performance.

The planning fallacy is derived from prospect theory, developed by Kahneman and Tversky (1979) as a way to explain bias in human decision-making. Their work demonstrates that human beings are prone to emphasize the positive, ignore competing and negative information, overestimate benefits, and underestimate costs as part of the planning process. An important study in understanding the implications of the planning fallacy was undertaken by Buehler, Griffin, and Ross (1994), who studied the manner in which people are prone to making optimistic time predictions regarding projects. In particular, they found three dynamics at work:

1. People tend to underestimate their own, but not others' completion times. They termed this effect 'optimistic prediction bias'.
2. People focus on plan-based scenarios rather than relevant past experience when generating estimates. The implication here is an over-reliance on projected expectations at the expense of practical experience.
3. Peoples' attributions diminish the relevance of past experiences. Poor past performance was routinely attributed to external or unstable causes.

The implications of this research on the problem of optimism bias are starkly apparent. When key stakeholders and other project sponsors develop time and cost estimates for prospective new projects, they have a tendency to routinely ignore past experiences, *no matter how relevant or similar to current projects*. Further, optimism predication bias suggests that estimates are always shaded in a positive light. Finally, strategic misrepresentation is the conscious decision of critical project sponsors and stakeholders to purposely misrepresent the advantages while minimizing disadvantages of project opportunities. As Flyvbjerg and colleagues have pointed out, the roots of strategic misrepresentation (otherwise known as 'lying'!) are political, not psychological, as in the case of optimism bias and the planning fallacy. With strategic misrepresentation, key actors deliberately obscure critical information in order to get a project approved, knowing that the release of honest estimates or actual historical data would condemn many new project opportunities to outright rejection. Political or organizational pressures, the pursuit of favourable opportunities through managing high-profile projects within the firm, and a desire to have their name associated with famous projects, are all reasons why strategic misrepresentation is so prevalent. For a variety of reasons, key stakeholders have routinely 'cooked the books' to exaggerate benefits and minimize drawbacks in order to get projects approved, knowing that for many public and private organizations, getting the project initially funded means the commitment is likely to continue to escalate through multiple budget adjustments and rescheduling to account for the inevitable slippages.

These tendencies have major implications for projects and by extension, conscientious project managers. In fact, one of the critical but underappreciated roles of project managers is to serve as a gate-keeper to work to prevent these errors from becoming embedded within the firm's operating procedures. The more project managers are permitted (and encouraged) to engage in front-end project definition, they become full partners in the project's development and governance process (Pinto, 2014). As resident experts on cost and time estimation, scope development, and so forth, good project managers can become a crucial voice of reason in trying to militate against these errors of planning and optimism bias. On the other hand, if firms maintain the classical, delivery model for projects (with the concomitant expectation that the project manager's role is simply that of an implementer of other people's dreams), there is the very real threat that these systematic errors will continue, guided by stakeholders' faulty misconceptions or presumptions.

Managers of Multiple Projects

As project management is implemented across industries, projects can be found in various sizes and levels of complexity. In some industries or among project types (e.g., IT or residential construction), projects typically have smaller budgets and shorter durations. In these settings, it is becoming very common for project managers to be tasked with leading more than one project at a time. These projects are not necessary mutually dependent in terms of objectives and goals but are assigned to the same project manager in an attempt to improve management efficiency and possibly, knowledge transfer. These project managers are referred to as *multiple-project managers,* and such a management condition has been called the management of a group of multiple projects (MGMP) (Patanakul, 2013).

There are a number of fundamental differences in management tasks between traditional single-project managers and multiple-project managers. The responsibility of single-project managers is to lead one project towards its overall goal. On the other hand, multiple-project managers are tasked to lead multiple projects with different goals. The challenges inherent in leading multiple-project teams include being forced to switch contexts multiple times per day, attending to different projects at various stages in their life cycles, dealing with different stakeholder considerations, and supporting multiple organizational goals (Fricke and Shenhar, 2000; Patanakul, 2013). In these circumstances, multiple-project managers have to coordinate among the interdependencies between projects so that each project can achieve its goal. Research has tended to suggest that the projects led by multiple-project managers are smaller than the ones run by single-project managers; nevertheless, being responsible for a number of diverse types of projects, focusing on different project goals, and leading multiple project teams (multiple combinations of team members) can create a high degree of management complexity (Patanakul and Milosevic, 2008).

To address the aforementioned challenges, researchers have suggested that multiple-project managers should possess a set of competencies that are distinct from, and may not be necessary for, single-project managers (Patanakul and Milosevic, 2008). One of those competencies is *interdependency management*, necessary for managing resources and technology interdependencies to benefit all projects under multiple-project manager's lead. Interdependency management is increasingly challenging when projects have different goals. Further, multiple-project managers should be proficient in *multitasking* so that they can effectively switch contexts from project to project with minimal loss in productivity. In addition, they have to be able to *simultaneously lead* multiple teams; that is, they have to possess a flexible leadership style that can adapt to different teams and be capable of practicing leadership in a discontinuous manner—engage, lead one team, disengage, lead another team, and so forth. The dynamics and intensity of multiple project management are significant and can post a significant challenge. Not every project manager can be successful in managing multiple projects.

Virtual Project Teams

The availability of information and communication technology enables many organizations to implement projects in a virtual environment. That is, instead of traditional co-located settings, many projects have team members in geographically dispersed locations and rely on interactive technology to work together. However, the seamless collaboration can be challenging because of the differences in time, location, and culture.

To successfully manage a virtual project team, project managers must have skills in articulating project goals, assigning responsibilities, and providing continuous feedback (Kayworth and Leidner, 2000). In addition to leading the project team, it is important that the project managers act as a team coordinator as they are usually the stable part of the team. It is important to keep all team members in the communication loop.

Each member must understand how their contribution fits into the overall project success. In addition to clear goals, assignment, and responsibilities, the project managers should facilitate the formation of desired norms and values among team members. This set of norms and values will shape the behaviour of the team. This includes what are acceptable and unacceptable by the team. Research also shows that trust among team members is significant. Trust is often perceived as a necessary condition for collaboration (Jarvenpaa, Knoll, and Leidner, 1998) and can help alleviate conflicts among team members. Additionally, dispersed project teams are likely to involve members from different countries and cultural backgrounds that can be the sources of misunderstanding and conflict. The project manager must to foster a global mindset among team members.

Information and communication technologies are at the heart of managing virtual project team. New technologies have been constantly introduced but many project managers rely heavily on phone calls and emails. When selecting the technology to support virtual work, project managers should focus on the criteria that shape their daily behaviour. Typical criteria include simplicity, reliability, and accessibility. The selected technology should allow team members to focus more on the messages than worrying about the medium itself. In addition to using technology, the project manager should augment virtual communication with face-to-face opportunities. These face-to-face meetings may be done at key points during the project life cycle. One or two initial meetings can be scheduled at the beginning of the project to identify the scope and nature of the project, and to help build a project team and develop trust.

Concluding Thoughts

In this chapter, we have attempted to place the challenges of managing projects within the larger context of management in modern organizations. We have argued that a fundamental appreciation for the sheer number and diversity of projects is necessary, as well as noting that over the past decades, corporate work has moved inexorably in the direction of projects as a critical vehicle for positive change, process improvement, new product development, and so forth. At the same time as projects are proliferating, the availability of cadres of skilled project managers continues to lag behind. In the vacuum created by a need that cannot be satisfied with current supply, organizations have been forced to rely on temporary solutions and on-the-job training, all while still fundamentally misunderstanding the myriad roles that project managers must adopt to do their jobs well.

Successfully managing projects requires a unique set of skills that must be clearly appreciated so that organizations can most effectively establish mechanisms for identifying, recruiting, and training project managers. Equally, stable mentorship programmes would serve as a useful method for imparting important skills and judgement alternatives to new project managers. In many organizations, demographics are leading to the retirement of senior project personnel, many of whom possess invaluable skills and knowledge of organizational operations. Because the concept 'knowledge management' is so critical in the field of project management, it is vital that organizations engaging in project-based work develop a strategic human resource plan that allows for the training and transfer of the most critical project management skills to a new generation of managers (Reich, Gemino, and Sauer, 2014; Pollack, 2012). Challenges of the global economy, increasingly technical products, infrastructure requirements, public demands for improved efficiency and renewal resource usage, all point to the need for organizations to do more with less, the very characteristics and limiting constraints that make project management such a valuable skill set for modern economic and commercial realities.

REFERENCES

Buehler, R., Griffin, D., and Ross, M. (1994). 'Exploring the 'Planning Fallacy': Why People Underestimate Their Take Completion Times'. *Journal of Personality and Social Psychology*, 67: 366–81.

DuBrin, A. J. (2012). *Leadership: Research Findings, Practice, and Skills*, 7th edn. Mason, OH: South-Western.

Flyvbjerg, B. (2005). 'Design by Deception: The Politics of Megaproject Approval'. *Harvard Design Magazine*, 22(Spring): 50–9.

Flyvbjerg, B. (2011). 'Over Budget, Over Time, Over and Over Again', in P. W. G. Morris, J. K. Pinto, and J. Söderlund (eds.), *The Oxford Handbook of Project Management*. Oxford: Oxford University Press, 321–44.

Flyvbjerg, B., Bruzelius, N., and Rothengatter, W. (2003). *Megaprojects and Risk: An Anatomy of Ambition*. Cambridge: Cambridge University Press.

Flyvbjerg, B., Garbuio, M., and Lovallo, D. (2009). 'Delusion and Deception in Large Infrastructure Projects: Two Models for Explaining and Preventing Executive Disaster'. *California Management Review*, 51(2): 170–93.

Francis, D. (2014). 'How Squandered U.S. Money Fuels Iraqi Insurgents'. *Fiscal Times*, 12 June. Available at: <http://www.thefiscaltimes.com/Articles/2014/06/12/How-Squandered-US-Money-Fuels-Iraq-s-Insurgents> (accessed 9 July 2016).

Fricke, S. E. and Shenhar, A. J. (2000). 'Managing Multiple Engineering Projects in a Manufacturing Support Environment'. *IEEE Transactions on Engineering Management*, 47(2): 258–68.

Gersick, C. (1988). 'Time and Transition in Work Teams: Toward a New Model of Group Development'. *Academy of Management Journal*, 31: 9–41.

Gersick, C. (1989). 'Making Time Predictable Transitions in Task Groups'. *Academy of Management Journal*. 32: 274–309.

Gersick, C. (1991). 'Revolutionary Change Theories: A Multilevel Exploration of the Punctuated Equilibrium Paradigm'. *Academy of Management Review*, 16: 10–36.

Hirokawa, R. Y. and Poole, M. S. (1986). *Communication and Group Decision-Making*. London: SAGE.

Jarvenpaa, S. L., Knoll, K., and Leidner, D. E. (1998). 'Is Anybody Out There?' Antecedents of Trust in Global Virtual Teams'. *Journal of Management Information Systems*, 14: 29–64.

Kahneman, D. and Tversky, A. (1979). 'Prospect Theory: An Analysis of Decisions under Risk'. *Econometrica*, 47: 313–27.

Kayworth, T. and Leidner, D. (2000). 'The Global Distributed Manager: A Prescription for Success'. *European Management Journal*, 18(2): 183–94.

Kelley, M. (2008). '$600M Spent on Canceled Contracts'. *USA Today*, 18 November: 1

Loch, C. and Kavadias, S. (2011). 'Implementing Strategy through Projects', in P. W. G. Morris, J. K. Pinto, and J. Söderlund (eds.), *The Oxford Handbook of Project Management*. Oxford: Oxford University Press, 224–51.

Lundin, R. A. and Söderholm, A. (1995). 'A Theory of the Temporary Organization'. *Scandinavian Journal of Management*, 4: 437–55.

Morris, P. W. G. (1994). *The Management of Projects*. London: Thomas Telford.

Morris, P. W. G. (2013a). 'Trends and Strategy', presentation given at 4th International Symposium on Project Management, Monterrey, Mexico, November.

Morris, P. W. G. (2013b). *Reconstructing Project Management*. Chichester: Wiley-Blackwell.

Mulrine, A. (2013). 'Rebuilding Iraq: Final Report Card on US Efforts Highlights Massive Waste'. *Christian Science Monitor*, 12 July. Available at: <http://www.csmonitor.com/USA/Military/2013/0712/Rebuilding-Iraq-Final-report-card-on-US-efforts-highlights-massive-waste> (accessed 9 July 2016).

Patanakul, P. (2013). 'Key Drivers of Effectiveness in Managing a Group of Multiple Projects'. *IEEE Transactions on Engineering Management*, 60(1): 4–17.

Patanakul, P., Iewwongcharoen, B., and Milosevic, D. Z. (2010). 'An Empirical Study on the Use of Project Management Tools and Techniques across Project Life-Cycle and Their Impact on Project Success'. *Journal of General Management*, 35(3): 41–65.

Patanakul, P. and Milosevic, D. Z. (2008). 'A Competency Model for Effectiveness in Managing Multiple Projects'. *Journal of High Technology Management Research*, 13(2): 118–31.

Pinto, J. K. (2013). *Project Management: Achieving Competitive Advantage*, 3rd edn. Upper Saddle River, NJ: Prentice-Hall.

Pinto, J. K. (2014). 'Project Management, Governance, and the Normalization of Deviance'. *International Journal of Project Management*, 32: 376–87.

Pinto, J. K. and Kharbanda, O. P. (1995). 'Lessons for an Accidental Profession'. *Business Horizons*, 38(2): 41–50.

PMI Today (2013). 'State of the Profession'. 8–9 March.

Pollack, J. (2012). 'Transferring Knowledge about Knowledge Management: Implementation of a Complex Organizational Change Program'. *International Journal of Project Management*, 30: 877–86.

PMI (Project Management Institute) (2013). *Project Management Body of Knowledge*, 5th edn. Newtown Square, PA: Project Management Institute.

Reich, B. H., Gemino, A., and Sauer, C. (2014). 'How Knowledge Management Impacts Performance in Projects: An Empirical Study'. *International Journal of Project Management*, 32: 590–602.

Standish Group (2013). 'Chaos Manifesto 2013'. Boston, MA.

Tuchman, B. W. and Jensen, M. A. (1977). 'Stages in Small Group Development Revisited'. *Group and Organizational Studies*, 2: 419–27.

CHAPTER 12

MANAGING DATA, INFORMATION, AND KNOWLEDGE

WENDY L. CURRIE

INTRODUCTION

MANAGEMENT scholarship compartmentalizes data, information, and knowledge as three distinct teaching and research areas. Within the field of management information systems (MIS) these labels can be traced back to three eras or phases of computerization: (1) data-processing from 1964 to 1974; (2) management information systems from 1975 to 1984, and (3) strategic information systems era from 1985 to 1994 (see Hirschheim and Klein, 2011; Moschella, 1997). Since the mid-1990s, the Internet and world wide web (WWW) have spawned a new era of computerization with new topics of digital business, e-commerce, e-business, and the networked society providing teaching and research opportunities spanning a range of management disciplines (Galliers and Currie, 2011).

In this chapter, we consider the topics of data, information, and knowledge as important focal areas in management scholarship. We observe how these terms have been used in chronological order over four decades in the management disciplines of MIS and finance. The MIS discipline emerged in the 1960s, focusing on data processing and data management, moving to the 1970s, shifting the focus from data to information management, and expanding its disciplinary repertoire in the 1980s, focusing on the strategy-technology connection (Kantrow, 1980). Combining ideas from MIS with strategy, many publications looked at how information technology could provide strategic benefits to organizations or industries (Porter and Miller, 1985; Willcocks, Feeny, and Islei, 1997).

These shifting interests may be dismissed simply as *management fashions* reflecting changing priorities and interests in business school curriculums (particularly in MBA and executive management teaching). Yet a deeper analysis of the history of technological change, looking at the chronology of events and evolution in computerization over four decades, points to significant 'disruptive' changes in the workplace (Christensen, 2007). Put simply, the development of mainframe computing in the 1960s (e.g., IBM's 360 model), to application software in the 1970s (e.g., with new companies including Microsoft, Oracle, and SAP), the launch of the personal computer and word processor in the 1980s (e.g., IBM, Apple, and Amstrad) and the commercialization of the Internet in the 1990s, have changed the nature and shape of industries, organizations, and management. MIS, as a management discipline, has examined these changes through the decades. Yet management research has paid little attention to the relationships between each of these stages or eras in technological change, particularly in how each one has presented management with new data and information challenges, and in the growth of so-called, *knowledge work*. This is a missed opportunity for MIS research, as most studies lack an historical dimension and focus instead on the current trends in technology or *IT artefacts*, including hardware and software for the mainframe, PC, or Internet age.

In addition, the unit of analysis is often at the organizational level, rather than seeking to explain the significance of moving from one stage or era to another, such as new management challenges and changes in work practices. So while the MIS field contains many interesting studies which relate to a specific point in time, it is noteworthy that MIS fashions have changed where the concept of *data* in management research became almost forgotten in the 1980s as *information management* became the more popular term, only to be replaced by *knowledge management* a decade later. This has led to criticisms that, despite the vast numbers of studies on knowledge management, only a few make the distinction between information management and knowledge management, and others re-label less fashionable terms, such as organizational learning as knowledge management (Wilson, 2002).

The inter-disciplinary and cross-functional implications of computerization have seen data, information, and knowledge becoming perennial terms in the broader management scholarship. The influence of the general strategy literature is found in seminal studies in MIS where researchers have examined the strategic potential of information technology to increase the competitive advantage of firms (see Benjamin et al., 1984; Earl, 1989; McFarlan, 1984). Whereas the focus in the 1980s looked at how the strategic management of *information* could provide a competitive advantage, later work examined *knowledge* flows and processes within firms (Gupta and Govindarajan, 2000).

In finance, which has a long history of using information technology, the concepts of data, information, and knowledge are used in a variety of ways. A rich literature has emerged on the use of technology in financial trading, differentiated by quantitative studies which build models to simulate trading behaviour and qualitative work on the sociology of finance, which considers the social and behaviour aspects of technological change in financial markets (MacKenzie, 2006; Knorr Cetina and Preda, 2004).

In this chapter, we combine academic scholarship from MIS and finance to the wider concept of *financialization* which refers to 'the increasing role of financial motives, financial markets, financial actors and financial institutions in the operation of the domestic and international economies' (Epstein, 2005: 3). We suggest the plurality of the concept financialization is a good starting position to understand some of the fundamental changes in information technology in financial markets. Financialization also relates to other sectors, such as, the not-for-profit (government, charity) and manufacturing and retailing, among others. For this chapter, we confine our discussion to the financial sector.

Noting that management scholarship has not made any significant inroads in understanding the complex and dynamic events leading up to the financial crisis of 2008, despite the significance of this global catastrophe for business and society more generally (Starkey, 2015), our primary objective is to promote much closer collaboration between the management disciplines of MIS and finance. By so doing, we are not suggesting that other management disciplines, such as strategy and organizational behaviour, are less relevant. Rather, we identify opportunities for MIS and finance based upon our reading of the literature and empirical phenomena (financial trading) under scrutiny.

We identify four broad literature streams within the MIS and finance disciplines which are relevant for understanding the role of technology in financial markets. We provide a brief overview of these themes and suggest that future researchers need to contextualize these debates from both an historical (chronological) and a cross-disciplinary (MIS-finance intersection) perspective. By encouraging a broader dialogue across the management disciplines, we believe future research will benefit from moving away from its current single-disciplinary focus to one which adopts an eclectic approach by engaging with the debates and themes from other management disciplines. This broader theoretical and empirical focus will hopefully provide greater policy direction and guidance for decision-makers. Not simply to isolate examples of *best practice* for managers and employees, but also to *problematize* research topics to gain a better academic and practitioner understanding of the range and complexity of the subject-matter under investigation (Alvesson and Sandberg, 2011). We build our argument by first considering how the terms data, information, and knowledge have been presented in the MIS field.

Data, Information, and Knowledge

Data, information, and knowledge are generic terms which relate to all areas of management theory and practice. Our interest is to observe how the field of Management Information Systems (MIS) has drawn heavily on these terms over several decades (Currie and Galliers, 1999) with each one representing a distinctive time period in the development of business computing. Figure 12.1 represents a common illustration where data, information, and knowledge are segmented, suggesting they are interrelated as part of a trilogy. However, our review of the MIS literature shows that each

```
      /\
     /  \
    /Data\
   /------\
  /Information\
 /------------\
/  Knowledge   \
/----------------\
```

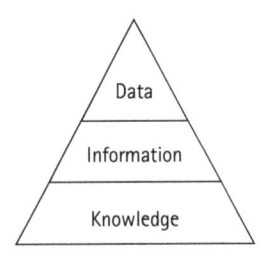

FIGURE 12.1 The Trilogy of Data, Information, and Knowledge.

term represents a particular period in the development of MIS, with relatively few studies which pay close attention to their inter-relationship.

Data Management

During the 1960s and prior to the development of the MIS field, computer and information science fields viewed data as representing unorganized and unprocessed facts. This static representation of data looked at data as a set of discrete facts about events. Data could be either structured or un-structured. Data was a pre-requisite to information. The field of data management emerged in the 1960s, for 'the development, execution and supervision of plans, policies, programs and practices that control, protect, deliver and enhance the value of data and information assets' (DAMA-DMBOK, 2015). Technology moved from sequential processing (first cards, then tape) to random access processing. As technology advanced, applications moved towards real-time, interactive applications, with the growing requirement for data to be well-defined and easy to use across different applications.

The term *data* was not evident in mainstream management education and research for several decades, unlike the current and fashionable term 'big-data' which attracts much more attention today (George, Haas, and Pentland, 2014). Indeed, *data* and *data management* were largely seen as the domain of computer and information science disciplines, rather than of particular interest to senior managers across the business functions. As technology advanced, the need for data processing (DP) became more important in organizations. The period between the 1960s and early 1970s became known as the DP era, with new courses being launched in management schools. Yet despite the promise of new technology, managers continued to take a *hands-off* approach to DP, which remained the domain of the DP department and specialist technical managers and staff. More importantly, DP managers did not occupy a board-room position, as the management functions taking priority were finance, strategy, and marketing. This early lack of interest from senior managers about the potential of information technology has been linked to the numerous *computer failures* which followed in the decades subsequent to the DP era (Sauer, 1993). Delegating data management responsibilities to a single department became increasingly unviable as the proliferation of data stored on computers continued to increase during this period, particularly in the banking sector which was one of the pioneers of business computing.

Information Management

Following the mid-1970s, the DP era gave way to the information management (IM) era, where information was increasingly seen as an aggregation of data (e.g., processed data) to help in the decision-making process. Unlike data, which is static, information management gives meaning and purpose to data. It involves the collection and management of information from one or more sources and its distribution to one or more target audiences. Management involves the organization of, and control over, the planning, structure, processing, manipulating, evaluating, controlling, and reporting of information. Throughout the 1970s, this largely involved managing information in paper-based files, file maintenance, and the life cycle management of files. With the proliferation of information technology continuing with the creation of companies like Microsoft, Oracle, and SAP during this decade, information management expanded to include other activities. Information management would no longer be a routine activity, performed mainly by lower level administrative staff. Instead, it became more automated as the use of information technology expanded in organizations.

Unlike the earlier DP era where data management was siloed within the functional domain of a single department (e.g., data processing), the information management era witnessed the dispersal of data management responsibilities as managers and staff were increasingly required to use computers for various business processes, applications, and tasks. The traditional role of the DP manager morphed into an information manager, with organizations like the British Computer Society calling for people with *hybrid skills* combining technical expertise with business knowledge (Earl and Skyrme, 1992). This requirement was met with mixed views as increasingly complexity of technology hardware and software, coupled with raised expectations for information managers to understand business issues, was difficult to find in one individual. The solution to this problem was often to encourage people with IT skills (e.g., engineers and computer scientists) to pursue a business qualification (e.g., an MBA or specialist masters in management or one of the management functions like finance, marketing, or human resources). Within management education, the IM era saw the development of the subject as distinctive from the mainstream management disciplines. Whilst this offered the advantage of developing MIS as a discipline in its own right, the proliferation of information technology pointed to a closer coupling of management disciplines and functions rather than their segmentation into discrete (siloed) fields with their own associations, journals, conferences and the like. In management education, a separate MIS discipline aimed to secure information management as a core part of the management curriculum. But turf wars developed as other disciplines also became interested in the role and impact of information technology in functional management areas, such as finance, human resources management (HRM), and marketing. MIS scholars, keen to demonstrate the subject matter of their own discipline extended beyond *hardware and software* to include social and cultural factors, looked towards building new theories of technology management (Currie, 1995). Yet MIS struggled in many management schools to secure its position as a *core* discipline on MBA programmes, as other disciplines continued to be dominant. This was a surprising development in management education given the proliferation of new technology throughout the 1970s and 1980s.

Knowledge Management

By the 1990s, a new term *knowledge management* became fashionable with the publication of several books and journal papers linking the pervasive use of information technology with how individuals acquire skills and experience which they apply in the workplace. Knowledge management, defined as the process of capturing, developing, sharing, and effectively using organizational knowledge (Davenport, 1994) reinforced the view that technology is the responsibility of all managers and staff, and should not be confined to a single department or function. Cognitive, social, and organizational learning processes were seen as essential ingredients for the success of a knowledge management strategy. Combined with performance measurement and benchmarking, knowledge management was promoted to accelerate the learning process and to drive cultural change in organizations (Bray, 2013).

Over two decades, knowledge management expanded its repertoire as a descriptive and analytical term to cover a wide range of organizational, managerial and technical issues and activities. With further advances in information technology leading up to the millennium, knowledge management included: Intranet-based systems; electronic document management; groupware, knowledge-based systems; business intelligence; innovation support tools and knowledge portals. The origin of these concepts can be traced to information science, database management, and artificial intelligence, raising the question as to whether knowledge management offers something new and distinctive or instead is simply a more fashionable label to cover perennial MIS topics from the earlier DP and IM eras.

Advocates of *knowledge management* have been keen to promote its multi-disciplinary focus on *organizational learning*, where knowledge can be used to achieve strategic objectives (Sanchez, 1996; Nonaka and Hirotaka, 1995), often conflating the terms (Wilson, 2002). Knowledge is perceived as distinct from data and information. While information is derived from data, knowledge is derived from information. Since the 1990s, the concept of knowledge management has gained popularity across the management disciplines, reflected in numerous journal publications and case studies targeted to academic and practitioner audiences. The conceptual plurality of knowledge management (Nonaka and Peltokorpi, 2006) extends the earlier focus on cross-national comparisons of cultural norms that influence the behaviour of managers and employees towards a more complex and mixed-bag of idealistic concepts without a coherent theoretical base (Alvesson and Kärreman, 2001). Critics suggest knowledge management covers a variety of organizational activities where the concepts of knowledge and information are used interchangeably, with little relevance to either knowledge or information (Wilson, 2002). Even in the wider management scholarship, knowledge management is a key topic with multiple definitions and meanings, and again, often without any reference to data or information.

Financialization and Management Information Systems

In this section, we link the above concepts of data, information, and knowledge to contemporary debates about financialization to provide a more contextual and focused discussion of the link between MIS and finance. Following the global financial crash of 2008, financialization is used by economists, sociologists, and political scientists to describe the 'transformation in which financial activities (rather than services more generally) have become increasingly dominant' in world economies over several decades (Krippner, 2011: 2). Financial markets have become more fragmented and complex where global interconnections pose new demands on regulators to develop and apply new laws, directives, and rules to prevent disruptive market events. Data, information, and knowledge play a large role in debates about financialization as financial innovation in the form of new products and services increasingly use information technology in what has become a global and networked economy. Financial trading is now an international marketplace where investors can buy and sell shares across exchanges located in many countries.

Deregulation of Financial Markets

A central theme of the financialization thesis is the increasing fragmentation and complexity of financial markets (Styhre, 2015). Following deregulation in the 1970s, the revenues generated from the financial services sector and have become increasingly important to domestic and international economies (Epstein, 2005). Global interconnections pose ongoing challenges for financial regulators who aim to apply new laws, directives, and rules to prevent disruptive market events. In the European Union, policy-makers have sought to harmonize the relationship between the twenty-eight member states through banking directives and regulatory mandates. Financial services have been a source of increased profits, influencing the objectives and operating criteria of many banks and governments.

Academic scholarship using the umbrella term financialization is varied with studies on the role of shareholders in corporate governance (Williams, 2000) the rise in the economic power of the rentier class, new types of instruments and indexes that have boosted financial investments (Philips, 1994) activities that create value to improve the efficiency of an economy (Turbeville, 2013) the growth and importance of such activities within national economies (Krippner, 2011) and whether financialization as a process is sustainable in the long term (Palley, 2007).

Financial markets have changed considerably over several decades, particularly as a result of financial intermediation. This is the outcome of two closely coupled areas: retail banking and the financial stock market. Both have existed since the earliest banks were formed in the seventeenth century, and government regulation to control their activities has occurred in a cyclical wave following successive financial crises. In its simplest form, a bank is an organization that receives deposits from investors, collects taxation from state laws, and uses this revenue to invest in loans to a business or an individual, or government sponsored programmes (from building roads or paying for a war). It is the promise of interest income to encourage deposits to be made and based on gearing, where the economy will benefit from increased cash flows. This underpins all investment and is vital for any economy to maintain the *virtuous cycle* of economic growth.

Capital intermediation occurs through the operation of the stock market with investment banks. Here a company offers new securities in return for financial investment that promises growth and income. Rather than depositing their money into a retail bank, an investor will purchase securities because they hold the potential for increased returns and growth. These holdings are usually much more liquid than those that are accumulated following a bank loan (such as the deposit for a house) and offer the potential for short term profit. The opportunities to benefit from new markets where the early speculator will earn attractive rewards for risky bets are tempting to the investor. There are obvious similarities between the South Sea Bubble of 1720 and dot.com bubble of 2000, where extraordinary profits were promised to many people—despite being unrealistic to others. The 1990s dot.com boom saw rocketing valuations as the Nasdaq Composite hit 5,048.62 before collapsing to under 1,300 during the 2008 financial crisis.

Investment banks are involved with creating the primary market and are also an important part of the secondary market, where they ensure liquidity exists. If this declines, then the market in those securities ceases to offer any benefits over rival securities or even more traditional retail bank deposits. Over the past few decades there has been a substantial increase in the instrument products that are offered by these market makers as this represents another stream of profits. Derivative types have grown phenomenally and securitization has created numerous market opportunities for investors to diversify their risk. Additional products such as Exchange Traded Funds (ETF) and new Indexes have fuelled the demand for the ever increasing need for new types of investment opportunity, encouraging investors to take on higher risk for short term returns. By creating more new instruments, risk taking becomes more common and accepted. In sum, two important issues arise from the financialization thesis. First, financial markets have undergone significant deregulation over many decades made possible by financial market technology. Second, an emerging research issue is the role played by information technology in developing new financial products and services, and how financial regulators need to monitor and evaluate these changes in the interests of investors.

Financial Market Technology (FinTech)

Coupled with deregulation in financial markets, the relentless pace of technological change beginning in the 1960s and continuing after the 1980s 'Big Bang' in global stock markets, saw electronic communications networks (automated trading) replacing open outcry trading (human floor traders). This fundamentally changed the dynamics, economics, and processes of financial trading. The term 'financial technology' (FinTech) captures the use of software and applications in financial services. Financial technology, defined as 'innovation in financial services' (NDRC, 2015) includes new solutions which demonstrate incremental or radical/disruptive innovation development of applications, processes, products, or business models in the financial services industry (Puschmann, 2012).

A key development is the growth of high frequency and algorithmic trading, which is computerized trading using proprietary algorithms. This form of trading does not involve the direct intervention of *humans* to carry out trading decisions (MacKenzie, 2015) and is a modern example of radical/disruptive innovation in financial markets. The topic has attracted the interest of international regulatory bodies, such as the Securitis and Exchange Commisison (SEC) in the USA and European Commission (EU) as campaigners have called for more regulation to tackle loopholes in financial (trading) markets. The focus is on preventing market abuse and manipulation by improving transparency and monitoring trading strategies. Financial regulatory interest to moderate the technological arms race among financial firms is controversial, as the desire to create a more level playing field for market participants is at odds with the ideology of free market competition (Currie and Seddon, 2015).

Unpacking Financialization, Finance, and Technology

In the post-financial crisis period, the intersection of MIS and finance is central to the Financialization thesis, as businesses, institutions, governments, and individual investors examine the role of financial technology in the most recent financial meltdown. Information technology has played a large part in the development of financial innovation (e.g., new financial products and services) made possible by mainframe computing, the personal computer, and the Internet. The physical transformation of financial trading from the traditional 'open-outcry' pits became increasing obsolete after 2000, where most stocks and futures contracts now use electronic trading, which is faster, cheaper,

Finance	Models of Financial Trading	Sociology of Finance
Information Technology	IT Artefacts	Social Studies of Technology

FIGURE 12.2 Unpacking Financialization, Finance, and Technology.

and more efficient. But while advances in technology have enabled these vast changes to financial markets and trading, we note from the academic literature that debates around finance, markets, trading, and technology have fragmented into distinct theoretical and empirical contributions within management disciplines. In this section, we identify four literature streams from finance and MIS: (1) models of financial markets, (2) the sociology of finance, (3) IT artefacts, and (4) the social studies of technology. Each of these literature streams produces quantitative and qualitative studies where some overlap exists in the research topics selected, the issues and debates that are raised, the content in the scholarly journals, and conferences and workshops where academics discuss FinTech. In selecting high frequency trading (HFT) as a relevant example of how financial markets have been significantly changed by information technology, we recommend closer collaboration between MIS and finance scholarship, particularly as each discipline has much to learn from the other (Figure 12.2).

Models of Financial Trading

Towards the end of the twentieth century, financial markets underwent their most significant changes due to increased automation and revised financial regulation (Funk and Hirschman, 2014). Electronic trading began in 1971 when NASDAQ opened the world's first electronic stock market. Since then, the financial markets have become fragmented, where new securities and trading volumes have increased exponentially (Dombret, 2013). In 1985 the London Stock Exchange (LSE, and the third largest exchange in the world) matched over 20,000 trades each day. By 2015 this figure was over thirty times larger. Computerization in financial markets has been relentless, changing the shape of trading. One development which has gained some attention in the past decade is the emergence of HFT which is a subset of algorithmic trading and carried out in two ways: (1) a large order implemented via a computerized algorithm using a program designed to secure the best price, where the order may be split into smaller pieces (tranche) and executed at different times; and (2) algorithms that seek small trading opportunities in the market rather than executing a set order (Nasdaq, 2015). HFT is a step change in financial trading which embodies the transition from human traders to algorithmic trading (MacKenzie, 2015).

Developments such as HFT, enabled by the prolific changes in computerization in finance, raise important questions not only about the differences between the material features of the technology, and how the technology is used to make judgements in financial markets, but also about the use of data and information, and knowledge-based processes. Currently, the main body of work on HFT is found in the finance literature. Many studies use quantitative (mathematical) models to simulate HFT activities. Unlike traditional forms of financial trading, where large investment firms hire fund managers to handle investment portfolios on behalf of their clients, the need for human intervention is greatly reduced in HFT, as computerized algorithms execute trading activities. HFT is carried out in fragmented and interconnected markets. Traders may operate in *dark pools* with little transparency of trade execution and where trading systems are co-located to access the exchanges at rapid speed (MacKenzie, 2015).

In the early 2000s HFT accounted for less than 10% of equity orders (Kumar, Goldstein, and Graves, 2011). Following the 2008 financial crisis, the first quarter of 2009 saw total assets under management for hedge funds with HFT strategies around $141 billion, down about 21% from their peak before the worst of the crises (Rogow, 2009). In 2009, HFT was estimated to account for 60–73% of all US equity trading volume, decreasing to approximately 50% in 2015 (Nasdaq, 2015). In the US in 2014, HFT represented almost 49% of equity and 60% of futures volumes. In 2015 it was estimated that of the 7 billion shares traded each day, two-thirds were generated by computer programmes (Mayer-Schönberger and Cukier, 2013).

Despite the wider implications of high frequency and algorithmic trading for management scholarship, most studies are found in the finance discipline and use quantitative techniques to examine how HFT has impacted foreign exchange markets (Chaboud et al., 2014), improved liquidity, and lowered latency (Menkveld and Zoican, 2014). While data moving at high speed is a key attribute of HFT, another relates to the synthesis of information using complex trading algorithms and powerful computers, often co-located near the electronic matching systems within securities exchanges. By co-locating trading systems in close proximity to the exchanges' matching engines, and utilizing microwave technology, firms can speed up their orders to the exchanges by milliseconds and increase their competitive advantage over rival firms and traders with slower connections. Expensive technology enables traders to *compete on speed* (Pagnotta and Philippon, 2012; Menkveld and Zoican, 2014). But significant fixed costs in technology to execute HFT strategies is outside the financial reach of many smaller firms leaving them unable to compete with their larger rivals (Biais, Foucault, and Moinas, 2011).

Models of financial trading make a significant contribution to the body of work on computerization in financial markets. But within the finance discipline and management scholarship more generally, a gap exists 'between the academic research on HFT and its perceived impact on markets in the public, media and regulatory' fields (Gomber et al., 2011). We suggest this presents an opportunity for closer collaboration between quantitative finance research which builds models and frameworks of HFT strategies and qualitative research from financial sociology on the societal and cultural practices of HFT, and FinTech more widely.

Sociology of Finance

The literature on the sociology of financial markets primarily broadens debates about financial technology through the trilogy of *governance, regulation, and compliance* or GRC. As a social and cultural phenomenon, technology is integral to financial markets since it structures and shapes the transactions and the rules that perform the markets. The sociology of finance combines the material and behavioural aspects of financial technology where theoretical perspectives embrace the wider context of international financial markets (Knorr-Cetina and Preda, 2004). Financial markets are viewed both as formal and mechanistic systems where rational (economic-man) models *perform the market*, and as socio-technical systems where economic agents display routines and habits which may contribute to market stability or conversely, engage in behaviour driven by perceived or actual market uncertainty (Calvo and Mendoza, 2000).

Key concepts for analysing financial markets include: *fields, networks, and performativity*. The first views financial markets as institutional fields with specific contributions on the financial services industry (Fligstein, 1990; Fligstein and McAdam, 2012). Financial markets can be theorized as *fields* and *sub-fields* where multiple interrelated institutions and agents negotiate their *positions* or *stakes* (Bourdieu, 1977) in a highly competitive and dynamic environment. The second considers economic action and social structure as a network of relationships (Knorr-Cetina and Preda, 2004). Contrasting economic agents as either under-socialized or over-socialized, we can observe how global micro-structures embrace the sociological aspects of technology that facilitate 'culturally specific social actions performed at a distance' (Granovetter, 1985: 909). The third introduces concept of performativity which asserts that economics does not simply describe economic phenomena since it also produces the phenomena it analyses (Callon, 1998). We observe a tendency in financial sociology to treat technology as a *black-box*, where scholars rarely unpack how specific technologies are designed, applied, and evaluated in specific industry, organizational, and managerial settings. By treating technology as a homogenous entity, it becomes difficult to unpack the relationship between technology and its impact on work practices. An example is in the context of financial regulation and technology (Williams, 2012). A recent article notes that many studies focus on how regulatory regimes impact financial innovation (e.g., products and services) with fewer looking at this relationship in the opposite direction (Funk and Hirschman, 2014).

Our focus on HFT offers an interesting example of how technology plays an increasing part in policy development in financial regulation (Currie and Seddon, 2015). While the literature on the sociology of finance is complementary to research which builds models of financial trading, HFT is a phenomenon with much wider societal, organizational and managerial implications, particularly as government agencies increasingly look towards regulating HFT to mitigate 'unfair' practices where some HFT firms use sophisticated technological infrastructure and applications unavailable to others.

IT Artefacts

The MIS discipline focuses on people, organizations, and technology with many studies looking at *IT artefacts* as socially embedded instruments for work and communication (Orlikowski and Iacono, 2001). Much of this work considers the design, use, and evolution of IT artefacts using both quantitative and qualitative methodologies. In the recent literature, MIS researchers call for more studies which theorize the material and social practices in the context of IT artefacts (Feldman and Orlikowski, 2011).

From our review of computerization in financial markets since the mid-1960s, there are surprisingly few studies in MIS which focus on the IT artefact in the context of financial markets and trading. Studies published prior to the financial crisis of 2008 feature work on asymmetric information and insider trading, information technology and time-based competition in financial markets, financial technology as a decision-making tool (Zopounidis, Doumpos, and Matsatsinis, 1997), and artefacts used in electronic trading and banking (Clemons and Weber, 1996; Weber, 2006; Barrett and Scott, 2004).

Following the financial meltdown, studies have looked at investor competence and trading, experimentation in financial markets, and financial objects in investment banking (Muniesa et al., 2011). Other studies have looked at computerization and regulatory compliance (Bamberger, 2009) with better electronic audit trails, improvements in order and trade transparency, enhanced ability of market participants to develop and apply automated risk controls, and greater monitoring and use of those controls.

As an IT artefact, we observe that HFT is discussed in a number of finance studies which build models on HFT strategy, and from the sociology of finance which look at the displacement of *humans* in algorithmic trading (MacKenzie, 2015). Yet a disconnection exists between the fields of MIS and finance on the debates and issues covered on HFT, even though each field has much to learn from the other. HFT is an IT artefact with social and material properties. Yet an effective and meaningful approach must also consider cross-disciplinary perspective. HFT is a contemporary example of computerization in financial markets. The IT artefact which comprises the social and material properties of HFT needs also to be considered in the wider socio-political and economic context of financial trading, not just at the organizational level, for example the individual HFT firm, but also at the intra- and inter-organizational levels. By so doing, it then becomes important to consider the multi-jurisdictional conditions in which HFT operates, as different international, national and regional government institutions and agencies impose policy decisions which have far-reaching effects on firm and individual behaviour. MIS and finance scholarship may look towards the social studies of technology as a way of complementing work on the models of financial trading, the sociology of finance and IT artefacts.

Social Studies of Technology

The combined work from MIS on the IT artefact and the social studies of technology offers a rich theoretical contribution, but often lacks empirical clarity about how technology is used in a practical setting. While calls are made to extend the concept of the IT artefact to include the material and social properties, the social studies of technology, like financial sociology, shares a tendency to *black-box* technology. Financial technology is viewed as a *socio-technical device* (dispositive socio-technique in French) where the concept of *agencement* describes socio-technical arrangements in their capacity to act and to give meaning to action (Callon and Caliskan, 2005). Unlike the concept of *performativity*, which is used widely in finance and economics, where agents *perform the market*, the term 'agencement' is deployed as a *catch-all* sociological concept. Here, IT artefacts comprise the tools, equipment, technical devices, and algorithms in financial markets. Devices viewed as agencements demonstrate how agency is situated in spatial and temporal fields across networks.

The notion of market device is relevant to the theorization about financial technology, as it embraces 'the material and discursive assemblages that intervene in the construction of markets' (Muniesa, Millo, and Callon, 2007). A material device constitutes an *object of agency*, either at a minimalist, instrumental version or at a maximalist, determinist version. But caution is needed about perceiving a device as a bifurcation of agency, where the human (social) agent is situated on one side and the device (material) agent is on the other. Thus, 'Instead of considering distributed agency as the encounter of (already "agenced") persons or devices, it is always possible to consider it as the very result of these compound agencements' (Muniesa, Millo, and Callon, 2007: 2). In sum, rather than the subject being viewed as external to the device, subjectivity is enacted in a device.

Our example of financial trading, the sociological analysis of a device as an object of agency which exerts different forces on social behaviour, provides an interesting starting position to observe the traditional relationship where the trader sits opposite the trading screen and more contemporary trading environments, exemplified by HFT, where the trader no longer interacts directly with the technology.

Another concept, *sociomateriality*, has gained ground in the social studies of technology, which asserts, 'there is no social that is not material, and no material that is not also social' (Orlikowski, 2007). Combining social materiality with the notion of agencement offers some theoretical building blocks for understanding the social and material properties of HFT. In particular, how HFT strategies combine the physical attributes of the technology with the values and ideologies of financial traders and the wider stakeholder communities including financial regulators, market (industry) participants, private investors, and citizens among others. The importance of this literature, of which we only provide a snapshot in this chapter, is demonstrated in HFT practices that become increasingly entangled with existing and emerging sociomaterialities, where materiality is not therefore an 'incidental or intermittent aspect of organizational life: it is integral to it' (Orlikowski, 2007: 1436).

DISCUSSION AND CONCLUSION

In this chapter, we have looked at the concepts of data, information, and knowledge in relation to the three stages or eras of MIS, starting in the 1960s where data management focused almost exclusively on the hardware and software of information technology, moving in the 1970s to information management, where MIS became more established as a discipline in its own right, through to the 1980s, where information technology began to be viewed as a strategic tool to enhance competitive advantage. These early developments in the MIS field were significant for understanding how technology has become an integral part of work and organization; and also how the *ebb and flow* of different fashions in management education have changed how data, information and knowledge have been used in academic scholarship. In recent years, the growing interest in the concept of *big data* has been embraced across the management disciplines. In MIS, big data is the subject of a growing number of research papers, with many focussing on large data sets which require increased technological capacity to capture, store, manage, and process data. To some extent, the attention on big data has eclipsed the popularity of knowledge management.

But, like knowledge management, big data is in danger of becoming an umbrella term which conflates a wide spectrum of topics relating to data, information, and knowledge. Current fashions in academic scholarship identify the five 'V's of big data: Volume, Variety, Velocity, Variability, and Veracity. Volume refers to the quantity of data generated. In the context of HFT, the size of big data may be measured in terabytes or petabytes. Variety is demonstrated by structured and unstructured data types that need to be stored, processed, and interpreted. These different sources and data types increase the inefficiency of how information is shared across financial markets, because each source will generate data in different formats and sizes. Velocity describes the ever decreasing time it takes for data to be transmitted, stored, processed, or structured into new data feeds. The continuous investment that HFT firms make to eliminate performance bottlenecks has led to a technical arms race, with billions of dollars spent on technology trading infrastructure. Because all activities are generated by computers, it is difficult to comprehend the thousands of orders sent every second throughout the day and the need to send them as quickly as possible. Variability illustrates how insights from the media constantly change as the same data and information is interpreted in a different way, or new feeds from other sources help to shape a different outcome in real time. In financial markets, large data analysis companies like Bloomberg provide important business and market news and information to HFT traders. HFT strategies are influenced by the 24/7 news media where information about world events is now available as *real time* data. Veracity is the quality of the data being captured and how this may vary. Accuracy of analysis depends on the veracity of the source data. Veracity has enabled HFT firms to emerge as a sub set of algorithmic trading, accounting for almost 49% of the USA and 39% of the European equity market (World Federation Exchange, 2013).

As the above HFT example demonstrates, data, information, and knowledge management is a highly complex process, as financial markets channel large volumes of data from multiple sources. These data are linked, connected, and correlated to generate information to be used by traders, which can be described as knowledge generation. As an example of the financialization of global trading, HFT is a small segment in a much wider landscape where computerization has changed the shape of financial markets. While we have only scratched the surface of financialization, FinTech, and HFT in this chapter, our overview of the four literature streams suggests that academic scholarship needs to embrace a cross-disciplinary approach to gain a deeper understanding of the complex issues underpinning these three themes. Financialization is a multi-disciplinary phenomenon which embraces wider debates from economics, sociology, and technology management.

As our FinTech example of HFT shows, financial modelling may help us simulate HFT strategies to understand its mechanics and technical drivers. This work is more meaningful combined with financial sociology which examines the wider regulatory, organizational, and managerial aspects of the financial industry. Work from MIS which seeks to unpack the IT artefact may further be linked with emerging debates in the social studies of technology, such as sociomateriality. In summary, while we may accept that social and material properties are entangled, our focus on HFT shows that technologies are situated across multiple, complex and diverse data networks, potentially making them difficult to observe by traditional methods of empirical enquiry, such as surveys and interviews. This becomes even more problematic as the role of *humans* is further removed from the day-to-day activities and processes in financial trading, making the social and cultural aspects almost impossible to distinguish from the material and infrastructure of the technology.

References

Alvesson, M. and Kärreman, D. (2001). 'Odd Couple: Making Sense of the Curious Concept of Knowledge Management'. *Journal of Management Studies*, 38(7): 995–1018.

Alvesson, M. and Sandberg, J. (2011). 'Generating Research Questions through Problematization'. *Academy of Management Review*, 36(2): 247–71.

Bamberger, K. A. (2009). 'Technologies of Compliance: Risk and Regulation in a Digital Age'. *Texas Law Review*, 669.

Barrett, M. and Scott, S. (2004). 'Electronic Trading and the Process of Globalization in Traditional Futures Exchanges: A Temporal Perspective'. *European Journal of Information Systems*, 13: 65–79.

Benjamin, R. I., Rockhart, J. F., Scott-Morton, M. S., and Wyman, J. (1984). 'Information Technology: A Strategic Opportunity'. *Sloan Management Review*, (Spring): 3–10.

Biais, B., Foucault, T., and Moinas, S. (2011). 'Equilibrium Fast Trading', Working Paper. Available at: <http://idei.fr/doc/wp/2013/wp_idei_769.pdf> (accessed 10 July 2016).

Bourdieu, P. (1977). *Outline of a Theory of Practice*. Cambridge: Cambridge University Press.

Bray, D. (2013). 'Literature Review—Knowledge Management Research at the Organizational Level', Social Science Research Network. Available at SSRN: <http://ssrn.com/abstract=991169> or <http://dx.doi.org/10.2139/ssrn.991169> (accessed 10 July 2016).

Callon, M. (1998). 'Introduction: The Embeddedness of Economic Markets in Economics', in *The Laws of the Market*. Oxford: Blackwell, 1–57.

Callon, M. and Caliskan, K. (2005). 'New and Old Directions in the Anthropology of Markets', Paper presented to Wenner-Gren Foundation for Anthropological Research, New York, 9 April.

Calvo, G. and Mendoza, E. (2000). 'Rational Contagion and the Globalization of Securities Markets'. *Journal of Economic Perspectives*, 10: 123–39.

Chaboud, A. P., Chiquoine, B., Hjalmarsson, E., and Vega, C. (2014). 'Rise of the Machines: Algorithmic Trading in the Foreign Exchange Market'. *The Journal of Finance*, 69(5): 2045–84.

Christensen, C. M. (1997). *The Innovator's Dilemma: When New Technologies Cause Great Firms to Fail*. Boston, MA: Harvard Business School Press.

Clemons, E. K. and Weber, B. W. (1996). 'Alternative Securities Trading Systems: Tests and Regulatory Implications of the Adoption of Technology'. *Information Systems Research*, 7(2): 163–88.

Currie, W. L. (1989). 'The Art of Justifying New Technology to Top Management'. *Omega*, 17(5): 409–18.

Currie, W. L. (1995). *Management Strategy for IT*. London: Pitman Publishing.

Currie, W. L. and Galliers, R. D. (1999). *Rethinking Management Information Systems: An Interdisciplinary Perspective*. Oxford: Oxford University Press.

Currie, W. L. and Seddon, J. J. M. (2015). 'Computerized High Frequency and Algorithmic Trading: Correlation and Causation', Presented at the Conference on High Frequency and Algorithmic Trading, Stuart School of Business, Chicago, USA, 2 November.

DAMA-DMBOK (2015). 'Guide (Data Management Body of Knowledge) Introduction and Project Status'. Available at <https://www.dama.org>.

Davenport, T. H. (1994). 'Saving IT's Soul: Human Centered Information Management'. *Harvard Business Review*, 72(2): 119–31.

Dombret, A. (2013). 'How to Overcome Fragmentation in the European Financial Market. Speech at the 23rd European Banking Congress'. Available at: <http://www.bundesbank.de/Redaktion/EN/Reden/2013/2013_11_22_dombret.html> (accessed 6 March 2015).

Earl, M. J. (1989). *Management Strategies for Information Technology*. New York: Prentice Hall.

Earl, M. J. and Skyrme, D. J. (1992). 'Hybrid Managers—What Do We Know about Them?'. *Information Systems Journal*, 2(3): 169–87.

Epstein, G. (2001). 'Financialization, Rentier Interests, and Central Bank Policy', Manuscript, Department of Economics, University of Massachusetts, Amhert, MA, December.

Epstein, G. (ed.) (2005). *Financialization and the World Economy*. Northampton, MA: Edward Elgar.

Feldman, M. S. and Orlikowski W. J. (2011). 'Theorizing Practice and Practicing Theory'. *Organization Science*, 22: 1240–53.

Fligstein, N. (1990). *The Transformation of Corporate Control*. Cambridge, MA: Harvard University Press.

Fligstein, N. and McAdam, D. (2012). *A Theory of Fields*. Oxford: Oxford University Press.

Funk, R. J. and Hirschman, D. (2014). 'Derivatives and Deregulation: Financial Innovation and the Demise of Glass-Steagall'. *Administrative Science Quarterly*, 59(4): 669–704.

Galliers, R. D. and Currie, W. L. (2011). *The Oxford Handbook of Management Information Systems: Critical Perspectives and New Directions*. Oxford: Oxford University Press.

George, G., Haas, M. R., and Pentland, A. (2014). 'Big Data and Management'. *Academy of Management Journal*, 57(2): 321–26.

Gomber, P., Arndt, B., Lutat, M., and Uhle, T. (2011). 'High Frequency Trading. E-Finance Lab', Goethe University, Germany. Available at: <http://ssm.com/abstract+1858626> (accessed 10 July 2016).

Granovetter, M. (1985). 'Economic Action and Social Structure: The Problem of Embeddedness'. *American Journal of Sociology*, 91(3): 481–510.

Gupta, A. K. and Govindarajan, V. (2000). 'Knowledge Flows within Multinational Corporations'. *Strategic Management Journal*, 21(4): 473–96.

Hirschheim, R. and Klein, H. K. (2011). 'Tracing the History of the Information Systems Field', in R. D. Galliers and W. L. Currie (eds.), *The Oxford Handbook of Management Information Systems*. Oxford: Oxford University Press, 16–61.

Kantrow, A. M. (1980). 'The Strategy-Technology Connection'. *Harvard Business Review*, 58(4) (July–August): 6–21.

Knorr Cetina, K. and Preda, A (ed.) (2004). *The Sociology of Financial Markets*. Oxford: Oxford University Press.

Krippner, G. R. (2011). *Capitalizing on Crisis*. Cambridge, MA: Harvard University Press.

Kumar, P., Goldstein, M., and Graves, F. (2011). 'Trading at the Speed of Light: The Impact of High Frequency Trading on Market Performance, Regulatory Oversight, and Securities Litigation', The Brattle Group (2).

Leonardi, P. M. (2013). 'Theoretical Foundations for the Study of Sociomateriality'. *Information & Organization*, 23: 59–76.

McFarlan, F. W. (1984). 'New Electronics Systems Can Add Value to Your Product and Throw Your Competition Off Balance'. *Harvard Business Review* (May/June): 98–103.

MacKenzie, D. (2006). *An Engine, Not a Camera: How Financial Models Shape Markets*. Cambridge, MA: MIT Press.

MacKenzie, D. (2015). 'Dark Markets'. *London Review of Books*, 37(11): 29–32.

Mayer-Schönberger, V. and Cukier, K. (2013). *Big Data: A Revolution That Will Transform How We Live, Work and Think*. Boston, MA: Houghton Mifflin Harcourt.

Menkveld, A. J. and Zoican, M. A. (2014). 'Need for Speed? Exchange Latency and Liquidity', Discussion Paper TI 14-097/IV/DSF78. Available at: <http://papers.tinbergen.nl/14097.pdf> (accessed 10 July 2016).

Millo, Y. and MacKenzie, D. (2009). 'The Usefulness of Inaccurate Models: Towards an Understanding of the Emergence of Financial Risk Management'. *Accounting, Organizations and Society*, 34(5): 638–53.

Moschella, D. C. (1997). *Waves of Power: The Dynamics of Global Technology Leadership, 1964–2010*. New York: Amacom.

Muniesa, F., Chabert, D., Ducrocq-Grondin, M., and Scott, S. V. (2011). 'Back Office Intricacy: The Description of Financial Objects in an Investment Bank'. *Industrial and Corporate Change*, 20(4): 1189–213.

Muniesa, F., Millo, Y., and Callon, M. (2007). An Introduction to Market Devices. *The Sociological Review*, 55: s", 1–12. Available at: <http://onlinelibrary.wiley.com/doi/10.1111/j.1467-954X.2007.00727.x/abstract>.

Nasdaq (2015). Available at: <http://www.nasdaq.com/investing/glossary/h/high-frequency-trading>.

NDRC. Available at: <http://www.ndrc.ie/about-us/>.

Nonaka, I. and Hirotaka, T. (1995). *The Knowledge Creating Company: How Japanese Companies Create the Dynamics of Innovation*. New York: Oxford University Press.

Nonaka, I. and Peltokorpi, V. (2006). 'Objectivity and Subjectivity in Knowledge Management: A Review of Top Articles'. *Knowledge Process Management*, 13(2): 73–82.

Orlikowski, W. J. (2007). 'Sociomaterial Practices: Exploring Technology at Work'. *Organization Studies*, 28(9): 1435–48.

Orlikowski, W. J. and Iacono, C. S. (2001). 'Desperately Seeking the IT in IT Research: A Call to Theorizing the IT Artefact'. *Information Systems Research*, 12(2): 121–34.

Pagnotta, E. and Philippon, T. (2012). 'Competing on Speed', April Working Paper. Available at: <http://pages.stern.nyu.edu/~tphilipp/papers/Speed.pdf> (accessed 10 July 2016).

Palley, T. I. (2007). 'Financialization: What It Is and Why It Matters'. Working Paper Series, No. 153, University of Massachusetts, Amherst.

Philips, K. (1994). *Arrogant Capital: Washington, Wall Street and the Frustration of American Politics*. New York: Little Brown and Company.

Porter, M. and Miller, V. (1985). 'How Information Gives You a Competitive Advantage'. *Harvard Business Review* (July/August): 149–60.

Puschmann, A. R. (2012). 'The Rise of Customer-Oriented Banking: Electronic Markets Are Paving the Way for Change in the Financial Industry'. *Electronic Markets*, 22(4): 203–15.

Rogow, G. (2009). 'Rise of the (Market) Machines', *Wall Street Journal*, 19.

Sanchez, R. (1996). *Strategic Learning and Knowledge Management*. Chichester: Wiley.

Sauer, C. (1993). *Why Information Systems Fail: A Case Study Approach*. Oxfordshire: Alfred Waller.

Starkey, K. (2015). 'The Strange Absence of Management during the Current Financial Crisis'. *Academy of Management Review*, 40(4): 652–63.

Styhre, A. (2015). *The Financialization of the Firm*. London: Edward Elgar.

Turbeville, W. (2013). 'Financialization and a New Paradigm for Financial Markets'. Available at: <http://www.demos.org/sites/default/files/publications/Tuberville.pdf> (accessed 10 July 2016).

Weber, B. (2006). 'Adoption of Electronic Trading at the International Securities Exchange'. *Decision Support Systems*, 41(4): 728–46.

Willcocks, L. P., Feeny, D., and Islei, G. (1997). *Managing IT as a Strategic Resource*. McGraw-Hill Higher Education.

Williams, J. W. (2012). *Policing the Markets*. New York: Routledge.

Williams, K. (2000). 'From Shareholder Value to Present-day Capitalism'. *Economy and Society*, 29(1): 1–12.

World Federation of Exchanges (2013). Report on High Frequency Trading. Available at: <https://www.world-exchanges.org/home/index.php/news/world-exchange-news/world-federation-of-exchanges-reports-on-high-frequency-trading-hft>.

Wilson, T. D. (2002). '"The Nonsense of "Knowledge Management"'. *Information Research*, 8(1).

Zopounidis, C., Doumpos, M., and Matsatsinis, N. F. (1997). 'On the Use of Knowledge-Based Decision Support Systems in Financial Management: A Survey'. *Decision Support Systems*, 20(3): 259–77.

CHAPTER 13

MANAGING MEANING—CULTURE

VIOLINA P. RINDOVA AND SANTOSH SRINIVAS

Introduction

> The world as we deal with it is always constituted by those in it, so that ... it can always be re-viewed, re-constituted and thus transcended by making use of possibilities for reframing, or for redefining the way in which the world is understood. (Turner, 1990: 3–4)

THE management of meaning as a key management task was established clearly with Pfeffer's (1981) seminal paper 'Management as Symbolic Action.' In this paper Pfeffer (1981: 1) advanced the argument that the 'analysis of management or leadership in organizations must proceed on two levels. On the level of substantive actions and results, decisions are largely the result of external constraint and power-dependence relationships. On the expressive and symbolic level, the use of political language and symbolic action serves to legitimate and rationalize organizational decisions and policies.' He highlighted the differences between substantive and symbolic actions, associated them with different goals and outcomes, and located the management of meaning in the symbolic realm with the purpose of explaining and rationalizing substantive actions. Pfeffer's article not only focused research attention on the management of meaning as a core managerial task, but also defined the research agenda on the topic emphasizing the socio-political dynamics of meaning management as a means for building social cohesion within the organizational boundaries, and managing conflict with external audiences.

In the thirty-five years since the publication of his seminal article, the management of meaning has emerged as a central area of inquiry in organizational science. The concept has attracted wide scholarly attention across research streams ranging from micro research on cognition and decision-making, to meso-level studies on organizational culture, image, and identity, and macro-level research on organizational strategies, competitive and stakeholder interactions, and institutional logics.

This research has shown that organizations, and their environments, are systems of beliefs, shaped and transformed by managers' use of symbolic means—language, narratives, frames, concepts, rituals, and visual images that inform, direct, motivate, and facilitate organized action (Smircich and Morgan, 1982; Gioia and Chittipeddi, 1991; Rindova and Fombrun, 1999; Lounsbury, 2007; Thornton, Ocasio and Lounsbury, 2012). Leaders' and managers' own interpretative processes have been found to be central to the strategic choices and possibilities they envision and pursue (Pettigrew, 1977; Smircich and Stubbart, 1985; Barr, Stimpert, and Huff, 1992; Kaplan, 2008; Martins, Rindova and Greenbaum, 2015). The management of meaning has also been increasingly recognized as an essential part of a firm's strategy for managing relationship with stakeholder audiences by influencing external perceptions about the organizational identity, image, reputation, and celebrity (e.g., Hatch and Schultz, 1997; Gioia, Schultz, and Corley, 2000; Ravasi and Schultz, 2006; Rindova, Pollock, and Hayward, 2006; Rindova, Petkova, and Kotha, 2007). In entrepreneurship research, meaning-making has been related to resource acquisition and wealth generation (e.g., Aldrich and Fiol, 1994; Lounsbury and Glynn, 2001; Garud and Giuliani, 2013; Petkova, Rindova, and Gupta, 2013). Taken together, these theoretical and empirical works highlight the management of meaning as a basis for mobilizing internal and external action, and for generating advantageous positions in exchange relationships with resource holders. The research further shows that the management of meaning in pursuit of internal cohesion and external support involves overlapping and interrelated activities that increasingly blur the boundaries between internal and external processes of meaning exchanges.

We organize our discussion of the findings of this research as follows: the first section highlights some important distinctions and debates that surround the meaning of meaning; the second section reviews studies on the substantive consequences of managing meaning in organizational and strategic management research, emphasizing that strategic activities are 'simultaneously symbolic and substantive, involve reciprocal processes of cognition and action, and entail cycles of understanding and influence' (Gioia and Chittipeddi, 1991: 447). The third section provides some directions for future research.

Understanding Meaning and Meaning-making

The concept of meaning has a long and complex intellectual history spanning psychology, philosophy, semiotics, linguistics, hermeneutics, sociology, anthropology, and, of course, marketing and management (e.g., Ogden and Richards, 1923; Schiffer, 1972; Bruner, 1990; Baumeister, 1991; Shore, 1996; Zilber, 2008; Park, 2010; Brown, Colville, and Pye, 2014; Maitlis and Christianson, 2014; Gee, 2015). Across these different disciplines many different definitions and perspectives on meaning and meaning-related processes have been advanced.

It is therefore not surprising that organizational science lacks agreement both about what constitutes 'meaning' and what processes are involved in meaning-making. As Gray, Bougon, and Donnellon (1985) argued, meaning, as it pertains to organizational life, can be considered from a variety of perspectives—from a cognitive perspective as concepts and schemas, from a relational perspective as maps and networks, and from an institutional perspective as logics and ideologies. Meaning-making therefore is invoked in a variety of ways in the literature, with some definitions emphasizing its cognitive aspects 'focused on appraisal and interpretation, which is described in terms of developing frameworks, schemata, or mental models', others emphasizing its social nature in that it 'occurs between people' and is 'negotiated, contested, and mutually co-constructed' (Maitlis and Christianson, 2014: 62 and 66), while others yet highlighting that it is shaped by the ideational and symbolic aspects of institutions (Thornton, Ocasio, and Lounsbury, 2012). Not only organizational scholars differ in how they view meaning-making, but a proliferation of meaning-related constructs have been observed in the literature. In a recent review of the organizational sensemaking literature, Maitlis and Christianson (2014: 69) document the introduction of terms such as 'sensebreaking', 'sensedemanding', 'sense-exchanging', 'sensehiding', and 'sense-specification', in addition to the now well-established construct of 'sensegiving' (Gioia and Chittipeddi, 1991). While this phenomenon reveals the intensification of scholarly interest in meaning-making, it also highlights the need for finding the common threads in the diversity. We highlight three important issues in this regard.

First, we concur with Baumeister (1991) that meaning is not easy to define, as to define it is to already use meaning. He defines it as 'shared mental representations of possible relationships among things, events, and relationships. Thus, meaning *connects* things' (1991: 15, emphasis in original). In a similar vein, Weick (1995: 111) described sensemaking as *connecting* cues and frames in stating that 'The combination of a past moment + connection + present moment of experience creates a meaningful definition of the present situation (…) Frames tend to be past moments of socialization and cues tend to be present moments of experience. If a person can construct a relation between these two moments, meaning is created.' Thus, to understand meaning and meaning-making, scholars need to investigate connections and connecting—what is being connected and through what processes.

Second, much disagreement surrounds the answers to both questions—what is being connected and how. Researchers working from the perspective of either cognitive or social psychology espouse an information-processing paradigm and study how observed stimuli are given meaning through the application of schemas (Fiske and Taylor, 1991). Schemas are cognitive structures that represent 'knowledge about a concept or type of stimulus, including its attributes and the relations among attributes' (Fiske and Taylor, 1991: 98) and that provide frames for interpreting new information. Research suggests that whereas meaning-making as a type of cognition is not necessarily 'conscious, verbal, deliberate, or rational' (Fiske and Taylor, 2013: 364), individuals are motivated to engage in meaning-making in order to reduce the discrepancy between 'situational meaning'—derived from the experience in a particular environmental encounter—and 'global meaning' based on their broad orienting systems consisting of beliefs, goals, and subjective feelings (Park, 2010). Such meaning-making requires 'relatively stable mental models or schemas by means of which people maintain a sense of fundamental stability in their apprehension of reality' (Shore, 1996: 157).

The notion of schemas is also central to the Carnegie School approach to the study of organizations (Simon, 1955; March and Simon, 1958; Cyert and March, 1963) that highlights the importance of cognitive frames of reference for the regularity in the way people construct meanings (see Cornelissen and Werner, 2014, for review). The neo-Carnegie School (Gavetti, Levinthal, and Ocasio, 2007) has further emphasized how mental representations impose structure 'on an information environment to give it form and meaning' (Walsh, 1995: 281), anchoring organizational action in a schematic, top-down, theory-driven information processing perspective.

In new-institutional theory schemas are viewed as 'the realm of institutionalized culture, of typification, of the habitus, of the cognitive shortcuts that promote efficiency at the expense of synoptic accuracy' (DiMaggio, 1997: 269). Institutionalists have argued that stable meaning structures become further organized in 'logics' defined as socially constructed, coherent, and integrated sets of 'assumptions, values, beliefs, and rules' (Thornton and Ocasio, 1999: 804) that prescribe legitimate ends and means (Friedland and Alford, 1991). Logics direct attention, activate identities, goals, and schemas, and shape the social interaction of actors (Thornton, Ocasio, and Lounsbury, 2012). They further provide building blocks for meaning construction, and meaning construction serves as a mechanism by which logics are brought to bear on organizational practices and identities (Dalpiaz, Rindova, and Ravasi, 2016).

Scholars working from sociological and communication perspectives tend to espouse a symbolic view of meaning-making as mediated by the operation of signs, symbols, and concepts in a given cultural world (Mead, 1934; Blumer, 1969; Goffman, 1974). This view—often summarized by the 'semiotic triangle' that consists of a stimulus (a referent), a symbol, and an interpretation (a reference) (Ogden and Richards, 1923)—emphasizes that multiple interpretations of the same stimulus can be evoked by different symbolic devices. Meaning emerges from 'a three-step interface of action: sending a symbolic cue, responding to the cue, and responding to the response' (Allan, 2006: 22). Thus, in contrast to the socio-cognitive perspective emphasizing how information cues and the organization of knowledge in structures, both subjective and intersubjective, affect meaning-making, the socio-cultural perspective incorporates the role of signification, communication, and contextualized interaction. The symbolic interactionist view stresses that analyzing how meaning-making is influenced through the use of symbolic devices deployed in some form of communication is critical for understanding collective processes of meaning-making, the emergence of shared understandings, as well as the management of meaning as a purposeful act. Research in this tradition conceptualizes meaning-making as a 'bottom-up' process in which language and other symbols are seen not simply as priming 'a separate "internal" cognitive process, but as potentially formative of individual and collective meaning construction' (Cornelissen and Werner, 2014: 196).

Third, acknowledging that meaning is both an individual and a social construct (Flower, 1994), researchers stress that meaning is neither directly transferrable, nor controllable, but is instead constructed (Crotty, 1998) and negotiated (Schultz and Wehmeier, 2010). This means that the symbols employed by the actors, and the influence they have on the actions of others are not only determined by either the stimuli, or the symbols, or the receiver's interpretations alone, but by the interaction among them in a given social interaction context. Further, the socially and collectively generated meanings can have multiple roles in organizations and their environments—as contested outcomes, as well as media through and within which power struggles for change take place (Hardy and Maguire, 2008). On the one hand, organizations are systems of shared meanings developed through socialization and sustained by leadership and power. On the other hand, organizing is precarious as contradictory meanings emerge from multiple sources, including stratification, occupational and group differences, as well as differences in individual goals and cultural experiences. The collective meanings and their representations therefore serve both as resources for action, and as contextual constraints. Co-constructions 'need not reflect widespread agreement in the collective', and 'meaning in an organization is best captured by a multiplicity of stories' (Maitlis and Christianson, 2014: 95).

Managing Meaning Internally and Externally

Pfeffer (1981: 1) conceived of the management of meaning as a key managerial task because organizations are 'systems of shared meanings and beliefs' and 'the construction and maintenance of belief systems' is necessary for 'continued compliance, commitment, and positive affect on the part of participants regardless of how they fare in the contests for resources'. By managing meaning, he argued, managers render the activities of an organization sensible and consensually understood and agreed upon, thereby motivating organizational members and satisfying the demands of external audiences. Through management of meaning, managers accomplish two critical tasks: lower opposition and conflict, thereby mobilizing organizational action, and reduce scrutiny by external audiences. We turn to a discussion of organizational research related to each of these themes next.

Organizational Culture and Identity

In the 1980s research on organizational culture and symbolism emerged as a central perspective for understanding the management and construction of organizational meanings (Dandridge, Mitroff, and Joyce, 1980; Smircich and Morgan, 1982; Schein, 1985; Smircich and Stubbart, 1985; Donnellon, Gray, and Bougon, 1986; Turner, 1986; Martin, 1992). This work showed that effective leadership depends as much upon symbolic modes of action as on instrumental modes of influence. It demonstrates the crucial role of leadership in the structuring and transformation of organizational reality through the use of symbolic resources such as language, rituals, dramas, stories, and myths to 'frame and shape the context of action' (Smircich and Morgan, 1982: 261). Smircich (1983) showed how a system of shared meanings in an organization emerges as a product of its unique history, personal interactions, and circumstances of action, as well as purposeful design by managers using symbolic means. Hatch (1993: 686) proposed that culture is 'constituted by continuous cycles of action and meaning-making shadowed by cycles of image and identity formation'. Identifying the role of meaning in the continuous production and reproduction of culture, she suggested that whereas symbolization involves 'culturally contextualized meaning creation via the prospective use of objects, words, and actions' (1993: 673), interpretation evokes 'a broader cultural frame as a reference point for constructing an acceptable meaning' (1993: 675).

Subsequent work extended the analysis of the interplay between organizational culture and identity. Hatch and Schultz (1997) characterized organizational identity as a 'self-reflexive product' (1997: 361) 'grounded in local meanings and organizational symbols, and thus embedded in organizational culture' (1997: 358). Others have suggested that identity is a 'cultural meaning or sensemaking focused on itself' (Fiol, Hatch and Golden-Biddle, 1998: 58) constituted by tensions between 'substantive reflections and symbolic expressions' (Rindova and Schultz, 1998: 47). Using a longitudinal case study, Ravasi and Schultz (2006) illustrated how organizational culture provides resources for leaders to both make sense of and give sense about organizational identity.

Gioia, Schultz, and Corley (2000) departed from the original Albert and Whetten's (1985) formulation of organizational identity 'as that which is central, enduring, and distinctive about an organization's character' (2000: 63) by attending to the difference of expressed values from which identity is imputed and to the notion that 'the *interpretation* of those values is not necessarily fixed or stable' (2000: 65, emphasis in original). Because of this difference, they argued organizational identity has a degree of fluidity arising from varying member interpretations. In a recent review of multiple perspectives on organizational identity, Gioia et al. (2013) further emphasized the importance of recognizing organizational members as 'meaning creators' (2013: 170).

Organizational and Strategic Change

Gioia and Chittipeddi (1991: 444) drew attention to strategic change as a critical time when the rich implications of meaning-making can be understood. They showed how strategic change instigation involves attempts by the chief executive officer (CEO) and top management team to first 'figure out and ascribe meaning to strategy-relevant events, threats, opportunities, etc. and then to construct and disseminate a vision that stakeholders and constituents could be influenced to comprehend, accept, and act upon to initiate desire [sic] changes'. Researchers have further shown that the imposition of meanings to strategic issues characterized by ambiguity, for example, whether issues are categorized as threats or opportunities, affects strategic actions taken such as changes to product-service offerings (Dutton and Jackson, 1987; Thomas, Clark, and Gioia, 1993).

Because strategic changes frequently involve symbolic struggles over meanings, processes such as framing of actions are seen as critical to secure understanding and negotiate support for the proposed strategic re-orientations (Fiss and Zajac, 2006). Research in this vein shows that the success of strategic change efforts rests not only on the substantive changes in vision, goals, structures, and processes, but also on the use of symbols to trigger a 'cognitive reorientation' and stakeholders' acceptance of the change (Gioia et al., 1994). In a study of conditions that trigger sensegiving, Maitlis and Lawrence (2007) suggested that organizational change creates an imperative for leaders to construct shared accounts, as change increases the ambiguity and unpredictability of a broad set of issues, and the salience of interest divergence for stakeholder audiences. Rindova, Dalpiaz, and Ravasi (2011) similarly showed that ongoing redefinitions of organizational identity accompany fundamental shifts in organizational strategies of action. Finally, Sonenshein and Dholakia (2012) drew attention to how managerial communication influences the requisite psychological resources of employees, and ultimately their belief that they could implement the change, closely linking interpretations of strategic change to the likelihood of change implementation behaviours.

Innovation

The management of meaning has also been related to organizational innovation. For instance, Bartel and Garud (2009) argued that sustaining innovation in organizations requires 'real-time coordination among people with different kinds of knowledge, systems of meaning, and modes of acting' (2009: 109), and that such coordination can be achieved using cultural mechanisms, which they referred to as 'innovation narratives'. They suggested that such narratives facilitate the translation of ideas and ambiguous situations in a way that provides both coherence and flexibility to interactions during the innovation process. Boland and Tenkasi (1995) similarly argued that in the context of knowledge-intensive organizations, creative meaning-making is central for success as work processes are characterized by 'indeterminacy, ambiguity, and uncertainty' and work is 'emergent, exploratory and often moves through multiple pathways with understandings being developed and changed as the work proceeds' (Tenkasi and Boland, 1993: 30). Thus, sensemaking is seen as a central process that supports organizational innovation capabilities and activities. Stigliani and Ravasi (2012: 1253) provided an ethnographic account of the interplay between social practices and cognitive processes that link individual and collective level sensemaking in the innovation activities of a leading design firm. They found that the combination of conversations and use of material and symbolic artefacts (e.g., thumbnails and frameworks) enables collaborative construction of meaning, with members making sense together, rather than, or in addition to 'giving sense to one another'. Taking a different view on the relationship between managing meaning and innovation, Martins, Rindova, and Greenbaum (2015) propose that organizations can use structured meaning management for business model innovation by designing processes that resemble naturally occurring cognitive processes for meaning transfer and recombination—namely, analogical reasoning and conceptual combination.

Environmental Enactment

A new perspective on the management of meaning in organizations emerged from strategic management research conducted from a socio-cognitive perspective. Porac, Thomas, and Baden-Fuller (1989) pioneered the study of industries as socio-cognitive communities. They articulated the core tenets of the interpretative view in strategy research which sees meaning-making as ongoing and continuously constructed through micro-momentary interactions among participants, with interpretations and actions being closely intertwined. From this perspective, organizational activities are an 'ongoing input-output cycle in which subjective interpretations of externally situated information become themselves objectified via behavior' (1989: 398). As a result of this continual exchange interpretations become shared and 'material conditions and mental models become inextricably intertwined' (1989: 412). Reger and Huff (1993) similarly showed that shared interpretations of the past, present, and future of industry groups shape industry evolution and reinforce economic realities.

The recognition of the intertwining of interpretations and actions was associated with the view of environments as 'enacted' rather than objective (Weick, 1979; Smircich and Stubbart, 1985), in which the role of strategists is not to go '"out" to collect facts' for the purposes of environmental scanning, decision-making, implementing a structure, and controlling of events. Instead, Smircich and Stubbart (1985: 730) proposed, the task of strategists is 'an imaginative one, a creative one, an art' that involves the effective use of various 'value/symbol systems' to generate the context for other actors to interpret organizational life. Accordingly, they criticized strategic management for ignoring the social nature of strategy formation, and the systems of shared meanings that facilitate or constrain strategy implementation.

Rindova and Fombrun (1999) build on these ideas and characterize market exchanges as unfolding through cycles of resource exchanges that connect firms' production processes to product and factor markets and cycles of interpretative exchanges that connect organizational belief systems (knowledge, culture, and identity) to field-level belief systems reflected in industry macro-cultures, competitive categorizations, and reputational orderings. Their framework suggests that firms compete not only over material resources, but also over favourable constituents' interpretations about various dimensions of value creation. A firm's competitive advantage depends not only on the resources it possesses and deploys, but also on the processes through which it communicates about the value its resource allocations create, and through which it responds to the definitions of success provided by resource holders. Meaning management therefore needs to be viewed as a strategic process, central to both securing superior competitive positions, and influencing the perception of value in organizational environments.

Rindova, Becerra, and Contardo (2004) similarly re-conceptualized competitive interactions as a combination of competitive actions and 'language games' (Wittgenstein, 1953). They argued that the language that surrounds competitive interactions 'subtly but persuasively shapes the competitive reality both inside and around warring firms' and that 'by attending to the constructive power of language, researchers and managers alike can better cope with the complexities of current market environments, where the pursuit of meaning and competitive advantage are closely intertwined' (2004: 683–4). Nadkarni and Narayanan (2007: 689) built on these ideas in empirical analysis of firms in the aircraft and semiconductor industries, and showed that industry velocity was not necessarily objectively pre-determined but reflected 'collective strategy frames' 'about industry boundaries, competitive rules, and strategy-environment relationships available to a group of related firms in an industry'. Weber and Mayer (2014) address how the cognitive frames of exchange parties affect transaction costs and exchange relationships, arguing that frame misalignment gives rise to 'interpretative uncertainty'.

Taken together the contributions of the interpretative research in strategy have led to a new perspective on the management of meaning as a key strategic activity. From this perspective, by managing meaning, managers not only mobilize internal action and appease powerful external actors, but instead tightly couple symbolic and substantive actions to increase strategic fit with audience perceptions of value. Meaning-making, in this view, is a key boundary-spanning process through which firms manage interactions with stakeholders (Rindova and Fombrun, 1999), competitors (Porac, Thomas, and Baden-Fuller, 1989; Porac and Thomas, 1990; Reger and Huff, 1993), and exchange partners (Weber and Mayer, 2014).

Communicating with External Stakeholder Audiences

Whether a firm uses communications purposefully to influence perceptions of itself or not, external audiences ascribe meanings to its actions and develop images of it. Put differently, the meaning-making processes of audiences about organizations do not rely on organizational communication alone because 'associations [in a broader sense, including perceptions of quality, loyalty and awareness] are created by anything linked to the brand' (Aaker, 1992: 164), and the firm as a whole.

Organizational communication provides firms with opportunities to draw attention to actions and accomplishments they deem important, to reduce information asymmetry about managerial intentions and investments, and to supply 'ready made' interpretative frameworks for stakeholders to apply to interpreting their behaviours (Rindova and Fombrun, 1999). Indeed, several strands of organizational and strategy research have focused on how firms use communication to influence the meaning-making process of stakeholder audiences. Working from an organizational culture and identity perspective, Hatch and Schultz (1997: 361) argued that the externally and internally directed management of meaning connects culture, identity, and image in a mutually interdependent circular process, so that 'who we are is reflected in what we are doing and how others interpret who we are and what we are doing'. They suggest the need for managers to simultaneously attend to, and bridge, the internal and external symbolic contexts of organizations. Suchman (1995) highlighted the debate between the institutional and strategic approaches to legitimation, with the latter research stream studying how 'organizations instrumentally manipulate and deploy evocative symbols in order to garner societal support' (1995: 572), and the former stream arguing that organizations that try to actively manage their legitimacy may be perceived as manipulative (Ashforth and Gibbs, 1990).

The strategic approach to legitimation has been particularly productive in the analysis of how new firms gain legitimacy and improve access to resources. Following a social constructivist view, Aldrich and Fiol (1994) argued that for entrepreneurs, social contexts 'represent not only patterns of established meaning, but also sites within which renegotiations of meaning take place' (1994: 649). They proposed that through strategic use of symbolic resources, new ventures could gain cognitive legitimacy more quickly and develop new meanings that alter established expectations and norms. Lounsbury and Glynn (2001) extended these ideas in articulating a cultural view of entrepreneurship emphasizing the use of symbolic resources, such as stories to evocatively represent the venture's potential, making it more attractive to funders and other resource holders. Holt and Macpherson (2010) contrasted the cultural view of entrepreneurship to the myth of entrepreneurs as lone 'heroic' actors noting that by using stories entrepreneurs 'cast their actions within a wider institutional frame' to enlist stakeholder support.

Current research on managing meaning with stakeholder audiences shows that organizations may be usefully viewed as skilled cultural operatives that draw on cultural resources such as categories to furnish a set of meanings—emotional, behavioural, social, and economic—that renders themselves more understandable to relevant stakeholders, and thereby enables success (e.g., Wry, Lounsbury and Glynn, 2011; Glynn and Navis, 2013). Hatch and Schultz (2009), however, warn against the mistaken belief that organizations own the meanings of their expressions and that stakeholder perceptions are congruent with their intentions. In fact, research suggests that stakeholder interpretations of firms' actions and identities become a reality—an enacted environment—that further commits the firm to a given course of action (Rindova, Becerra, and Contardo, 2004; Rindova, Pollock, and Hayward, 2006; see also Rindova, Reger, and Dalpiaz, 2012). This poses a challenge to organizations to re-orient from being the sole producers of meaning to facilitators for its co-creation with multiple stakeholders.

Future Research Directions

In the preceding section we reviewed some of the core developments in organizational research on the management of meaning as shaped by Pfeffer's (1981) seminal article. In this article he argued that symbolic and substantial aspects of organizational activity are most likely only loosely coupled because 'management action operates largely with and on symbolic outcomes, and that external constraints affect primarily substantive actions and outcomes in formal organizations' (1981: 6). He suggested the need for further research on the relationship between symbolic actions and substantive outcomes.

As we have shown, in the thirty-five years since the publication of his article, a great deal of progress has been made in understanding how meaning-making affects the mobilization of action inside and outside organizations, with the growing consensus that substantive and symbolic have mutually reinforcing effects that enhance the outcomes of both. Put differently, researchers have shown that not only symbolic actions have substantive outcomes, but that substantive actions themselves are born from meaning-making processes embedded in symbolic systems. This perspective is most evident in interpretative strategy research (Porac, Thomas, and Baden-Fuller, 1989; see also Kaplan, 2011, for a review).

Further, the focus of analysis on the effects of the management of meaning on stakeholder audiences has shifted away from avoiding potentially negative effects by reducing scrutiny and conflict, and towards generating additional value by enacting and shaping the environment—the notion of 'endogenous environments' (Kaplan, 2011: 686)—and developing social approval assets, such as legitimacy, status, and reputation (see Rindova, Reger, and Dalpiaz, 2012). As a result, the topic of the management of meaning has gained prominence in the research agendas of scholars who study entrepreneurship (e.g., Hill and Levenhagen, 1995; Lounsbury and Glynn, 2001; Dodd, 2002; Nicholson and Anderson, 2005; Santos and Eisenhardt, 2009; Petkova, Rindova, and Gupta, 2013; Garud, Schildt, and Lant, 2014), strategic and institutional change (e.g., Schultz and Wehmeier, 2010; Zilber, 2011; see Greenwood et al., 2008; Cornelissen et al., 2015) and the social construction of value in markets (Westphal and Zajac, 1998; Rindova, Pollock, and Hayward, 2006; Rindova and Petkova, 2007; Rindova, Dalpiaz, and Ravasi, 2011; Eisenman, 2013).

Overall, the research on the management of meaning increasingly emphasizes the substantive consequences of symbols, the need for developing skills for using symbols substantively, and the coupling of substantive instrumental action and symbolic expression to ensure stakeholder understanding, positive evaluation, and support. Further, with the expanding scope and diversity of research in entrepreneurship, organizational studies, and strategy that incorporate meaning-making in the analysis, some exciting new areas of research have emerged. Below we highlight two such areas ripe with opportunities for significantly advancing the analysis of meaning-making in organizations and their environments.

Meaning Management as a Managerial versus Organizational Capability

With the growing recognition of the substantive consequences of the use of symbols to manage meaning-making within and across organizational boundaries, the question of whether some managers and organizations are more skilful in doing so, and why, has gained central importance. The traditional research on organizational culture and identity we discussed was largely embedded in a view of culture as a relatively unified system of values or norms that unequivocally guides and constrains cognition and action (Giorgi, Lockwood, and Glynn, 2015). This traditional research portrayed organizations as different in the content of the meanings they manage but similar in the processes through which they do so. It therefore did not consider the variation in processes through which organizations develop and change their cultures and identities (managing meaning internally), and their images and reputation (managing meaning externally).

In contrast, some of the recent work in cultural sociology and organizational research suggests that individuals and organizations vary in how much culture they hold or use, and how diverse their cultural resources are (Swidler, 2001; for reviews, see Weber and Dacin, 2011; Giorgi, Lockwood, and Glynn, 2015). For example, in a study of French gastronomy setting Rao, Monin, and Durand (2005) demonstrate how actors engage in a 'cultural bricolage' by borrowing and recombining cultural materials from across categorical boundaries to effectively address market problems and opportunities. Rindova, Dalpiaz, and Ravasi (2011) show how Italian manufacturer Alessi gradually expanded the set of cultural resources it used to guide its strategy making. They develop the construct of 'cultural repertoire enrichment' to highlight the possibility for organizations to expand their ability to use cultural resources through effortful investment in wide-ranging changes in their practices. Zott and Huy (2007: 74) show that entrepreneurs vary in both what symbolic actions they perform and how they perform them. Their findings suggest that those entrepreneurs who are 'skilled cultural managers'—that is, those who deploy a wide variety of symbols and do so more frequently—attract more resources than others. Organizations can use even unconventional cultural resources, such as conceptions of time, to enable interpretive shifts and address conflictual issues in pluralistic environments (Reinecke and Ansari, 2015).

Scholars have further argued that we lack adequate theory about the specific resources and capabilities organizations need in order to manage meanings strategically. They have suggested that the economic value of strategy is culturally constructed, and that an organization's ability to engage in cultural works—that is, purposive actions of creating, maintaining, and disrupting the cultural elements in its institutional context—influences its competitive advantage (Maurer, Bansal, and Crossan, 2011). Dalpiaz, Rindova, and Ravasi (2010) further argue that the management of meaning involves the development of a set of intangible assets that resemble knowledge and reputation, but are distinct from them. They build on Bourdieu's (1984) ideas about cultural and symbolic capital as resources that determine how individuals manage their positions in the competition for status in the socio-cultural world to argue that organizations also can develop cultural and symbolic capital to claim desirable positons in markets.

Taken together, these studies suggest that organizational abilities to manage the deeper meaning systems have implications for organizational performance, effectiveness, and competitive advantage. Further, they suggest that there are multiple processes through which individuals and organizations use cultural resources, and that these processes occur at different levels of analysis (individual versus organizational) and vary in effectiveness in selection and deployment of cultural resources in specific individual and collective activities. They point to the importance of investigating what processes constitute capabilities related to the management of meaning and whether these capabilities differ from other type of organizational capabilities studied in management research such as technological (Helfat and Raubitschek, 2000) and knowledge integration capabilities (Grant, 1996; Verona and Ravasi, 2003).

Interplay between Organizational Culture as Systems of Beliefs (Shared and Fragmented) and Societal Culture as a Toolkit

Related to the set of questions above is the question about how organizational cultures and other cultural processes such as identity and image management relate to the broader societal culture and the variety of meanings generated in organizational environments. Whereas organizational researchers have moved away from the analysis of organizational environments as objective and given, they continue to assign actors in organizational environments to relatively passive roles as evaluators with fixed expectations (Hsu, 2006; Hsu, Hannan, and Koçak, 2009). However, as Wry, Lounsbury, and Glynn (2011) show, actors have considerable cultural agency in constructing and managing the symbolic boundaries—that is, conceptual distinctions used to categorize—and thereby in actively and strategically shaping their environment. Further, in a study of the emergence of modern Indian art as a category, Khaire and Wadhwani (2010) show that the meaning construction is a collaborative enterprise, and therefore, organizations keen on participating in it should attend to distributed agency and interpretive shifts in their fields, and skilfully engage in the collective discourse through which meanings are constructed. Similarly, Weber, Heinze, and DeSoucey (2008), in their study of the emergence of the grass-fed meat and dairy products market in the United States as social movement, show how the movement participants mobilized broad cultural codes to create the new market segment. Their analysis showed that the activists opposed the dominant industrial logic of agricultural production by elaborating a shared meaning system based on semiotic codes with oppositional structures, and that this emergent meaning system stimulated producer activities, as well the development of a collective producer identity. In sum, these studies (see also Glynn and Navis, 2013) advance a socio-cultural perspective in which organizations and other social actors are seen as actively engaging in an interactive co-construction of meanings.

Scholars seeking to advance research in this direction can draw on current research in media and communications that has increasingly focused on the active production and co-production of meaning by audiences, and organizations that serve as platforms for display and aggregation of user-generated content (Bruns, 2008; Jenkins, Ford, and Green, 2013). Given how active audiences have become in the explicit production of meaning, and how the costs of distributing such symbols and content have decreased, we suggest that the next important frontier in the analysis of the management of meaning is in the exploration of the ongoing and fluid exchanges of meanings between and within the various communities in which organizations are increasingly embedded. Such analyses can respond to recent calls from institutional scholars for developing a truly interactive understanding of meaning co-construction (see Cornelissen et al., 2015).

References

Aaker, D. (1992). *Managing Brand Equity: Capitalizing on the Value of a Brand Name*. New York: Free Press.

Albert, S. and Whetten, D. (1985). 'Organizational Identity', in L. L. Cummings and B. M. Staw (eds.), *Research in Organizational Behavior*, 7: 263–95. Greenwich, CT: JAI Press.

Aldrich, H. E. and Fiol, C. M. (1994). 'Fools Rush In? The Institutional Context of Industry Creation'. *Academy of Management Review*, 19(4): 645–70.

Allan, K. (2006). *Contemporary Social and Sociological Theory: Visualizing Social Worlds*. London: SAGE.

Ashforth, B. E. and Gibbs, B. W. (1990). 'The Double-Edge of Organizational Legitimation'. *Organization Science*, 1(2): 177–94.

Barr, P. S., Stimpert, J. L., and Huff, A. S. (1992). 'Cognitive Change, Strategic Action, and Organizational Renewal'. *Strategic Management Journal*, 13(S1): 15–36.

Bartel, C. A. and Garud, R. (2009). 'The Role of Narratives in Sustaining Organizational Innovation'. *Organization Science*, 20(1): 107–17.

Baumeister, R. F. (1991). *Meanings of Life*. New York: Guilford Press.

Blumer, H. (1969). *Symbolic Interactionism: Perspective and Method*. Berkeley, CA: University of California Press.
Boland Jr, R. J. and Tenkasi, R. V. (1995). 'Perspective Making and Perspective Taking in Communities of Knowing'. *Organization Science*, 6(4): 350–72.
Bourdieu, P. (1984). *Distinction: A Social Critique of the Judgement of Taste*. London: Routledge & Kegan Paul.
Brown, A. D., Colville, I., and Pye, A. (2014). 'Making Sense of Sensemaking in Organization Studies'. *Organization Studies*, 36(2): 265–77.
Bruner, J. S. (1990). *Acts of Meaning*. Cambridge, MA: Harvard University Press.
Bruns, A. (2008). *Blogs, Wikipedia, Second Life, and Beyond: From Production to Produsage*, vol. 45. New York: Peter Lang.
Cornelissen, J. P., Durand, R., Fiss, P. C., Lammers, J. C., and Vaara, E. (2015). 'Putting Communication Front and Center in Institutional Theory and Analysis'. *Academy of Management Review*, 40(1): 10–27.
Cornelissen, J. P. and Werner, M. D. (2014). 'Putting Framing in Perspective: A Review of Framing and Frame Analysis across the Management and Organizational Literature'. *The Academy of Management Annals*, 8(1): 181–235.
Crotty, M. (1998). *The Foundations of Social Research: Meaning and Perspective in the Research Process*. London: SAGE.
Cyert, R. M. and March, J. G. (1963). *A Behavioral Theory of the Firm*. Englewood Cliffs, NJ: Prentice-Hall.
Dalpiaz, E., Rindova, V., and Ravasi, D. (2010). 'Where Strategy Meets Culture: The Neglected Role of Cultural and Symbolic Resources in Strategy Research', in J. A. C. Baum and J. Lampel (eds.), *Advances in Strategic Management*. Volume 27. Emerald Group Publishing Limited, 175–208.
Dalpiaz, E., Rindova, V., and Ravasi, D., (2016), 'Combining Logics to Transform Organizational Agency: Blending Industry and Art at Alessi', *Administrative Science Quarterly*, 61(3): 347–92.
Dandridge, T. C., Mitroff, I., and Joyce, W. F. (1980). 'Organizational Symbolism: A Topic to Expand Organizational Analysis'. *Academy of Management Review*, 5(1): 77–82.
DiMaggio, P. (1997). 'Culture and Cognition'. *Annual Review of Sociology*, 23: 263–87.
Dodd, S. D. (2002). 'Metaphors and Meaning: A Grounded Cultural Model of US Entrepreneurship'. *Journal of Business Venturing*, 17(5): 519–35.
Donnellon, A., Gray, B., and Bougon, M. G. (1986). 'Communication, Meaning, and Organized Action'. *Administrative Science Quarterly*, 31(1): 43–55.
Dutton, J. E. and Jackson, S. E. (1987). 'Categorizing Strategic Issues: Links to Organizational Action'. *Academy of Management Review*, 12(1): 76–90.
Eisenman, M. (2013). 'Understanding Aesthetic Innovation in the Context of Technological Evolution'. *Academy of Management Review*, 38(3): 332–51.
Fiol, C. M., Hatch, M. J., and Golden-Biddle, K. (1998). 'Organizational Culture and Identity: What's the Difference Anyway', in D. A. Whetten and P. C. Godfrey (eds.), *Identity in Organizations: Building Theory through Conversations*. London: SAGE, 56–9.
Fiske, S. T. and Taylor, S. E. (1991). *Social Cognition*. New York: McGraw-Hill.
Fiske, S. T. and Taylor, S. E. (2013). *Social Cognition: From Brains to Culture*. London: SAGE.
Fiss, P. C. and Zajac, E. J. (2006). 'The Symbolic Management of Strategic Change: Sensegiving via Framing and Decoupling'. *Academy of Management Journal*, 49(6): 1173–93.
Flower, L. (1994). *The Construction of Negotiated Meaning: A Social Cognitive Theory of Writing*. Carbondale, IL: Southern Illinois University Press.

Friedland, R. and Alford, R. (1991). 'Bringing Society Back In: Symbols, Practices and Institutional Contradictions', in W. Powell and P. DiMaggio (eds.), *The New Institutionalism in Organizational Analysis*. Chicago, IL: University of Chicago Press, 232–63.

Garud, R. and Giuliani, A. P. (2013). 'A Narrative Perspective on Entrepreneurial Opportunities'. *Academy of Management Review*, 38(1): 157–60.

Garud, R., Schildt, H. A. ,and Lant, T. K. (2014). 'Entrepreneurial Storytelling, Future Expectations, and the Paradox of Legitimacy'. *Organization Science*, 25(5): 1479–92.

Gavetti, G., Levinthal, D., and Ocasio, W. (2007). 'Perspective-Neo-Carnegie: The Carnegie School's Past, Present, and Reconstructing for the Future'. *Organization Science*, 18(3): 523–36.

Gee, J. (2015). *Social Linguistics and Literacies: Ideology in Discourses*. New York: Routledge.

Gioia, D. A. and Chittipeddi, K. (1991). 'Sensemaking and Sensegiving in Strategic Change Initiation'. *Strategic Management Journal*, 12(6): 433–48.

Gioia, D. A., Patvardhan, S. D., Hamilton, A. L., and Corley, K. G. (2013). 'Organizational Identity Formation and Change'. *The Academy of Management Annals*, 7(1): 123–93.

Gioia, D. A., Schultz, M., and Corley, K. G. (2000). 'Organizational Identity, Image, and Adaptive Instability'. *Academy of Management Review*, 25(1): 63–81.

Gioia, D. A., Thomas, J. B., Clark, S. M., and Chittipeddi, K. (1994). 'Symbolism and Strategic Change in Academia: The Dynamics of Sensemaking and Influence'. *Organization Science*, 5(3): 363–83.

Giorgi, S., Lockwood, C., and Glynn, M. A. (2015). 'The Many Faces of Culture: Making Sense of 30 Years of Research on Culture in Organization Studies'. *The Academy of Management Annals*, 9(1): 1–54.

Glynn, M. A. and Navis, C. (2013). 'Categories, Identities, and Cultural Classification: Moving beyond a Model of Categorical Constraint'. *Journal of Management Studies*, 50(6): 1124–37.

Goffman, E. (1974). *Frame Analysis: An Essay on the Organization of Experience*. Boston, MA: North Eastern University Press.

Grant, R. M. (1996). 'Prospering in Dynamically-Competitive Environments: Organizational Capability as Knowledge Integration'. *Organization Science*, 7(4): 375–87.

Gray, B., Bougon, M. G., and Donnellon, A. (1985). 'Organizations as Constructions and Destructions of Meaning'. *Journal of Management*, 11(2): 83–98.

Greenwood, R., Oliver, C., Sahlin, K., and Suddaby, R. (eds.) (2008). 'Introduction', in R. Greenwood, C. Oliver, K. Sahlin, and R. Suddaby (eds.), *The SAGE Handbook of Organizational Institutionalism*. Thousand Oaks, CA: SAGE, 1–46.

Hardy, C. and Maguire, S. (2008). 'Institutional Entrepreneurship', in R. Greenwood, C. Oliver, K. Sahlin, and R. Suddaby (eds.), *The SAGE Handbook of Organizational Institutionalism*. Thousand Oaks, CA: SAGE, 198–217.

Hatch, M. J. (1993). 'The Dynamics of Organizational Culture'. *Academy of Management Review*, 18(4): 657–93.

Hatch, M. J. and Schultz, M. (1997). 'Relations between Organizational Culture, Identity and Image'. *European Journal of Marketing*, 31(5/6): 356–65.

Hatch, M. J. and Schultz, M. (2009). 'Of Bricks and Brands: From Corporate to Enterprise Branding'. *Organizational Dynamics*, 38(2): 117–30.

Helfat, C. E. and Raubitschek, R. S. (2000). 'Product Sequencing: Co-evolution of Knowledge, Capabilities and Products'. *Strategic Management Journal*, 21(10–11): 961–79.

Hill, R. C. and Levenhagen, M. (1995). 'Metaphors and Mental Models: Sensemaking and Sensegiving in Innovative and Entrepreneurial Activities'. *Journal of Management*, 21(6): 1057–74.

Holt, R. and Macpherson, A. (2010). 'Sensemaking, Rhetoric and the Socially Competent Entrepreneur'. *International Small Business Journal*, 28(1): 20–42.

Hsu, G. (2006). 'Jacks of all Trades and Masters of None: Audiences' Reactions to Spanning Genres in Feature Film Production'. *Administrative Science Quarterly*, 51(3): 420–50.

Hsu, G., Hannan, M. T., and Koçak, Ö. (2009). 'Multiple Category Memberships in Markets: An Integrative Theory and Two Empirical Tests'. *American Sociological Review*, 74(1): 150–69.

Jenkins, H., Ford, S., and Green, J. (2013). *Spreadable Media: Creating Value and Meaning in a Networked Culture*. New York: New York University Press.

Kaplan, S. (2008). 'Framing Contests: Strategy Making under Uncertainty'. *Organization Science*, 19(5): 729–52.

Kaplan, S. (2011). 'Research in Cognition and Strategy: Reflections on Two Decades of Progress and a Look to the Future. *Journal of Management Studies*, 48(3): 665–95.

Khaire, M. and Wadhwani, R.D. (2010). 'Changing Landscapes: The Construction of Meaning and Value In a New Market Category—Modern Indian Art'. *Academy of Management Journal*, 53(6): 1281–304.

Lounsbury, M. (2007). 'A Tale of Two Cities: Competing Logics and Practice Variation in the Professionalizing of Mutual Funds'. *Academy of Management Journal*, 50(2): 289–307.

Lounsbury, M. and Glynn, M. A. (2001). 'Cultural Entrepreneurship: Stories, Legitimacy, and the Acquisition of Resources'. *Strategic Management Journal*, 22(6/7): 545–64.

Maitlis, S. and Christianson, M. (2014). 'Sensemaking in Organizations: Taking Stock and Moving Forward'. *The Academy of Management Annals*, 8(1): 57–125.

Maitlis, S. and Lawrence, T. B. (2007). 'Triggers and Enablers of Sensegiving in Organizations'. *Academy of Management Journal*, 50(1): 57–84.

March, J. G. and Simon, H. A. (1958). *Organizations*. New York: Wiley.

Martin, J. (1992). *Cultures in Organizations: Three Perspectives*. New York: Oxford University Press.

Martins, L. L., Rindova, V. P., and Greenbaum, B. E. (2015). 'Unlocking the Hidden Value of Concepts: A Cognitive Approach to Business Model Innovation'. *Strategic Entrepreneurship Journal*, 9(1): 99–117.

Maurer, C. C., Bansal, P., and Crossan, M. M. (2011). 'Creating Economic Value through Social Values: Introducing a Culturally Informed Resource-Based View'. *Organization Science*, 22(2): 432–48.

Mead, G. H. (1934). *Mind, Self and Society: From the Standpoint of a Social Behaviorist*. Chicago, IL: University of Chicago Press.

Nadkarni, S. and Narayanan, V. K. (2007). 'The Evolution of Collective Strategy Frames in High- and Low-Velocity Industries'. *Organization Science*, 18(4): 688–710.

Nicholson, L. and Anderson, A. R. (2005). 'News and Nuances of the Entrepreneurial Myth and Metaphor: Linguistic Games in Entrepreneurial Sense-Making and Sense-Giving'. *Entrepreneurship Theory and Practice*, 29(2): 153–72.

Ogden, C. and Richards, I. (1923). *The Meaning of Meaning*. New York: Harcourt, Brace & World.

Park, C. L. (2010). 'Making Sense of the Meaning Literature: An Integrative Review of Meaning-making and Its Effects on Adjustment to Stressful Life Events'. *Psychological Bulletin*, 136(2): 257.

Petkova, A. P., Rindova, V. P., and Gupta, A. K. (2013). 'No News Is Bad News: Sensegiving Activities, Media Attention, and Venture Capital Funding of New Technology Organizations'. *Organization Science*, 24(3): 865–88.

Pettigrew, A. M. (1977). 'Strategy Formulation as a Political Process'. *International Studies of Management & Organization*, 7(2): 78–87.

Pfeffer, J. (1981). 'Management as Symbolic Action: The Creation and Maintenance of Organizational Paradigms'. *Research in Organizational Behavior*, 3: 1–52.

Porac, J. F. and Thomas, H. (1990). 'Taxonomic Mental Models in Competitor Definition'. *Academy of Management Review*, 15(2): 224–40.

Porac, J. F., Thomas, H., and Baden-Fuller, C. (1989). 'Competitive Groups as Cognitive Communities: The Case of Scottish Knitwear Manufacturers'. *Journal of Management Studies*, 26(4): 397–416.

Rao, H., Monin, P. and Durand, R. (2005). 'Border Crossing: Bricolage and the Erosion of Categorical Boundaries in French Gastronomy'. *American Sociological Review*, 70(6): 968–91.

Ravasi, D. and Schultz, M. (2006). 'Responding to Organizational Identity Threats: Exploring the Role of Organizational Culture'. *Academy of Management Journal*, 49(3): 433–58.

Reger, R. K., and Huff, A. S. (1993). 'Strategic Groups: A Cognitive Perspective'. *Strategic Management Journal*, 14(2): 103–23.

Reinecke, J. and Ansari, S. (2015). 'When Times Collide: Temporal Brokerage at the Intersection of Markets and Developments'. *Academy of Management Journal*, 58(2): 618–48.

Reordon, K. K. (1981). *Persuasion: Theory and Context*. Beverly Hills, CA: SAGE.

Rindova, V. P., Becerra, M., and Contardo, I. (2004). 'Enacting Competitive Wars: Competitive Activity, Language Games, and Market Consequences'. *Academy of Management Review*, 29(4): 670–86.

Rindova, V., Dalpiaz, E., and Ravasi, D. (2011). 'A Cultural Quest: A Study of Organizational Use of New Cultural Resources in Strategy Formation'. *Organization Science*, 22(2): 413–31.

Rindova, V. P. and Fombrun, C. J. (1999). 'Constructing Competitive Advantage: The Role of Firm-Constituent Interactions'. *Strategic Management Journal*, 20(8): 691–710.

Rindova, V. P. and Petkova, A. P. (2007). 'When Is a New Thing a Good Thing? Technological Change, Product Form Design, and Perceptions of Value for Product Innovations'. *Organization Science*, 18(2): 217–32.

Rindova, V. P., Petkova, A. P., and Kotha, S. (2007). 'Standing Out: How New Firms in Emerging Markets Build Reputation'. *Strategic Organization*, 5(1): 31–70.

Rindova, V. P., Pollock, T. G., and Hayward, M. L. (2006). 'Celebrity Firms: The Social Construction of Market Popularity'. *Academy of Management Review*, 31(1): 50–71.

Rindova, V. P., Reger, R. K., and Dalpiaz, E. (2012). 'The Mind of the Strategist and the Eye of the Beholder: The Socio-Cognitive Perspective in Strategy Research', in G. B. Dagnino (ed.), *Handbook of Research on Competitive Strategy*. Northampton, MA: Edward Elgar Publishing, 147–64.

Rindova, V. P. and Schultz, M. (1998). 'Identity within and Identity Without: Lessons from Corporate and Organizational Identity', in D. A. Whetten and P. C. Godfrey (eds.), *Identity in Organizations: Building Theory through Conversations*. New York: SAGE, 46–51.

Santos, F. M. and Eisenhardt, K. M. (2009). 'Constructing Markets and Shaping Boundaries: Entrepreneurial Power in Nascent Fields'. *Academy of Management Journal*, 52(4): 643–71.

Schein, E. H. (1985). *Organizational Culture and Leadership*. San Francisco, CA: Jossey-Bass.

Schiffer, S. (1972). *Meaning*. Oxford: Clarendon Press.

Schultz, F. and Wehmeier, S. (2010). 'Institutionalization of Corporate Social Responsibility within Corporate Communications: Combining Institutional, Sensemaking and Communication Perspectives'. *Corporate Communications: An International Journal*, 15(1): 9–29.

Shore, B. (1996). *Culture in Mind: Cognition, Culture, and the Problem of Meaning*. New York: Oxford University Press.

Simon, H. A. (1955). 'A Behavioral Model of Rational Choice'. *The Quarterly Journal of Economics*, 69: 99–118.

Smircich, L. (1983). 'Organizations as Shared Meanings', in L. R. Pondy, P. J. Frost, G. Morgan, and T. C. Dandridge (eds.), *Organizational Symbolism*. Greenwich, CT: JAI Press, 55–65.

Smircich, L. and Morgan, G. (1982). 'Leadership: The Management of Meaning'. *Journal of Applied Behavioral Science*, 18(3): 257–73.

Smircich, L. and Stubbart, C. (1985). 'Strategic Management in an Enacted World'. *Academy of Management Review*, 10(4): 724–36.

Sonenshein, S. and Dholakia, U. (2012). 'Explaining Employee Engagement with Strategic Change Implementation: A Meaning-Making Approach'. *Organization Science*, 23(1): 1–23.

Stigliani, I. and Ravasi, D. (2012). 'Organizing Thoughts and Connecting Brains: Material Practices and the Transition from Individual to Group-Level Prospective Sensemaking'. *Academy of Management Journal*, 55(5): 1232–59.

Suchman, M. C. (1995). 'Managing Legitimacy: Strategic and Institutional Approaches'. *Academy of Management Review*, 20(3): 571–610.

Swidler, A. (2001). *Talk of Love: How Culture Matters*. Chicago, IL: University of Chicago Press.

Tenkasi, R. V. and Boland, R. J. (1993). 'Locating Meaning-making in Organizational Learning: The Narrative Basis of Cognition'. *Research in Organizational Change and Development*, 7: 77–103.

Thomas, J. B., Clark, S. M., and Gioia, D. A. (1993). 'Strategic Sensemaking and Organizational Performance: Linkages among Scanning, Interpretation, Action, and Outcomes'. *Academy of Management Journal*, 36(2): 239–70.

Thornton, P. H. (2002). 'The Rise of the Corporation in a Craft Industry: Conflict and Conformity in Institutional Logics'. *Academy of Management Journal*, 45(1): 81–101.

Thornton, P. H. and Ocasio, W. (1999). 'Institutional Logics and the Historical Contingency of Power in Organizations: Executive Succession in the Higher Education Publishing Industry, 1958–1990'. *American Journal of Sociology*, 105(3): 801–43.

Thornton, P. H., Ocasio, W., and Lounsbury, M. (2012). *The Institutional Logics Perspective: A New Approach to Culture, Structure, and Process*. Oxford: Oxford University Press.

Turner, B. A. (1986). 'Sociological Aspects of Organizational Symbolism'. *Organization Studies*, 7(2): 101–15.

Turner, B. (ed.) (1990). *Organizational Symbolism*. Berlin: de Gruyter.

Verona, G. and Ravasi, D. (2003). 'Unbundling Dynamic Capabilities: An Exploratory Study of Continuous Product Innovation'. *Industrial and Corporate Change*, 12(3): 577–606.

Walsh, J. P. (1995). 'Managerial and Organizational Cognition: Notes from a Trip Down Memory Lane'. *Organization Science*, 6(3): 280–321.

Weber, K. and Dacin, M. T. (2011). 'The Cultural Construction of Organizational Life: Introduction to the Special Issue'. *Organization Science*, 22(2): 287–98.

Weber, K., Heinze, K. L., and DeSoucey, M. (2008). 'Forage for Thought: Mobilizing Codes in the Movement for Grass-Fed Meat and Dairy Products'. *Administrative Science Quarterly*, 53(3): 529–67.

Weber, L. and Mayer, K. (2014). 'Transaction Cost Economics and the Cognitive Perspective: Investigating the Sources and Governance of Interpretive Uncertainty'. *Academy of Management Review*, 39(3): 344–63.

Weick, K. E. (1979). *The Social Psychology of Organizing*, Topics in Social Psychology Series. Reading, MA: Addison-Wesley.

Weick, K. E. (1995). *Sensemaking in Organizations*, vol. 3. Thousand Oaks, CA: SAGE.

Westphal, J. D. and Zajac, E. J. (1998). 'The Symbolic Management of Stockholders: Corporate Governance Reforms and Shareholder Reactions'. *Administrative Science Quarterly*, 43(1): 127–53.

Wittgenstein, L. (1953). *Philosophical Investigations*. New York: Macmillan.

Wry, T., Lounsbury, M., and Glynn, M. A. (2011). 'Legitimating Nascent Collective Identities: Coordinating Cultural Entrepreneurship'. *Organization Science*, 22(2): 449–63.

Zilber, T. B. (2008). 'The Work of Meanings in Institutional Processes', in R. Greenwood, C. Oliver, K. Sahlin and R. Suddaby (eds.), *The Sage Handbook of Organizational Institutionalism*. Thousand Oaks, CA: SAGE, 151–69.

Zilber, T. B. (2011). 'Institutional Multiplicity in Practice: A Tale of Two High-Tech Conferences in Israel'. *Organization Science*, 22(6): 1539–59.

Zott, C. and Huy, Q. N. (2007). 'How Entrepreneurs Use Symbolic Management to Acquire Resources'. *Administrative Science Quarterly*, 52(1): 70–105.

CHAPTER 14

MANAGEMENT AND LEADERSHIP

RONALD E. RIGGIO

Management vs Leadership: Definitions, Distinctions, and Early Theories

'Managers do things right, leaders do the right thing.'

THIS is one of the most commonly cited quotes on management and leadership. It has been attributed to Peter Drucker, the 'Father of Modern Management', and to leadership guru, Warren Bennis. Neither of them admitted to coining the phrase, but it points out the heart of the distinction between management and leadership. Management is seen as handling the more mundane and routine tasks of the manager's job—assigning duties, measuring performance, monitoring work behaviour—while leaders focus on the big picture of setting direction, articulating a vision, keeping the collective on the 'right' path, and inspiring and motivating followers. The reality, however, is that management and leadership are intertwined.

For purposes of understanding what researchers mean by 'leaders', most typically leaders are identified as those holding management or supervisory positions, or outside of work organizations, are identified as people with appointed or elected positions of power and authority. It was assumed through much of the research on management and leadership that 'leaders lead' and 'followers follow'. Today, however, we realize that the roles and relationships of leaders and followers are interrelated and much more complex.

Since ancient times, both leadership and management have been about power relationships. Persons with status, authority, or valuable resources were able, through force, or through social exchange, to get others to do their bidding. Sociologist Max

Weber (1947) outlined different types of authority: *traditional authority* (e.g., monarchies, patriarchies), *bureaucratic authority* (e.g., legal or position-oriented authority), and *charismatic authority* (i.e., willingly following because of a belief in the leader). All involve one individual having power over others, although the forms of power differ.

Management in the early days of the industrial revolution was based on bureaucratic authority and a system of rewards/incentives for positive behaviour (i.e., productivity) and punishments for undesirable behaviour or an inability to produce. For example, Adam Smith (1776) in the *Wealth of Nations* suggests that the goal of management in industry is to maximize productivity. Frederick Taylor (1911) and Scientific Management sought to increase efficiency in labor with a goal of improving productivity, offering workers additional monetary compensation in exchange for following the 'best methods' for performing their jobs. This, at the time, was the dominant philosophy of management.

It was the pioneering, and often overlooked, writings of Mary Parker Follett (1949) that brought followers into the manager–worker interaction. Follett advocated managers sharing power with followers, soliciting their input, and focusing on a shared purpose that would unleash their motivation and initiative. Later, psychologist Elton Mayo (1933) and the Human Relations movement, focused on effective management as fostering good interpersonal relationships with and among workers as a key to motivation and improving workplace productivity. Perhaps the biggest impact on understanding the complexity of successful management, and the role of manager and subordinate/follower comes from Peter Drucker (1954) who viewed management in such broad terms that he felt the term 'leadership' was not necessary. According to Drucker, a good manager leads and leads well.

While the study of management focused on the technical skills and the effective use of power to manage work groups, the concept of leadership extended beyond the work setting, and involved a focus on those individuals who were at the top levels of nations, organizations, or social movements. Emerging from sociology, political science, and especially psychology, leadership looked beyond the everyday management of people to creating a vision for the collective, developing strategy, inspiring and motivating, and making key decisions.

In early research on leadership, psychology's influence led to a focus on leadership qualities—particularly the traits of effective leaders. Intelligence, extraversion-sociability, self-confidence, dominance, and dozens of other traits were investigated as correlates of leadership (see Lord, deVader, and Alliger, 1986, and Mann, 1959, for reviews). One aspect of this research looked at traits as predictors of attainment, or emergence, into positions of leadership, while another line examined whether possession of these traits predicted the effectiveness of the leader (either measured through group output or through evaluations/ratings of the leader's effectiveness). The trait approach was criticized because of seemingly small relationships between traits and leadership outcomes (e.g., Stogdill, 1948), so research on leadership traits was practically abandoned for decades.

The post-Second World War era in psychology saw the rise of the behaviourists, so the focus shifted from leadership traits to leader behaviours. Two research programmes, one at Ohio State University, and the other at the University of Michigan, examined the behaviours enacted by effective leaders (Kahn and Katz, 1960; Stogdill and Coons, 1957). Through factor analyses of leader behaviours, two general categories were derived: one category was focused on the task and on group productivity, while the other category consisted of behaviours aimed at enhancing the leader–follower relationship. The resulting categories were labelled *Initiating Structure* (by the Ohio State researchers), or *Task-Oriented* behaviours (by the Michigan scholars); *Showing Consideration* (Ohio State), or *Relationship-Oriented* behaviours (Michigan). The obvious conundrum was that these very different categories of leadership behaviours—nearly diametrically opposed—were both associated with effective leadership. This led scholars to search for situations under which each category of leader behaviour would be most effective.

The 1960s and 1970s saw the introduction of a number of what might be called 'situational' or 'interactional' theories of leadership. These theories looked at the interaction of leader behaviour and situational variables, with a goal of determining the best possible combination that would result in positive outcomes (i.e., leader effectiveness, group performance, etc.). In nearly all cases, these theories built off of the earlier work on leader behaviours—task-oriented or relationship-oriented behaviours or styles.

An example of one such theory emanating from the management literature was originally known as the Life-Cycle Theory, which postulated that a leader needed to adjust his or her behaviour in order to best accommodate the level of supervision needed by a subordinate (Hersey and Blanchard, 1969). According to this theory, the 'situation' consisted of the level of maturity possessed by a subordinate. A highly mature subordinate possesses high levels of job-related skills and knowledge and is highly self-motivated. The manager's task is to adjust his or her behaviour (task-focused or relationship-oriented) to the maturity level of the subordinate. According to the theory, a manager/leader should be extremely directive and task-focused with a low maturity subordinate, and more supportive and relationship-focused with moderately mature subordinates. This relatively simple theory became quite popular and was later renamed Situational Leadership Theory (SLT), and became the cornerstone of one of the largest management/leadership training and development programs (Hersey and Blanchard, 1993).

Another situational leadership theory of the 1970s focused on leaders as decision makers, and postulated that the primary task of leaders is to make important, work-related decisions. However, the decision-making strategy that a leader should use is dependent on critical elements of the situation. This theory, known as the Decision-Making Model, suggests that leaders can make decisions using different strategies, ranging from autocratic decision-making, to consultative decision-making (a process that involves subordinates by consulting with them to gain their input), to purely democratic decision-making (majority-rule strategies whereby the leader allows the group or team to vote and decide; see Vroom and Yetton, 1973).

In the Decision-Making Model, the leader conducts a careful analysis of the situation before making a decision by asking a series of questions. For example, the first question is: 'Is a high quality decision required?' An affirmative answer begins to suggest that the leader might want to get his or her subordinates' input. Additional questions focus on whether or not subordinates will accept and implement the decision once it is made, and whether the leader possesses enough information to make a good decision. The result is a rather complex 'decision-tree' framework that directs the leader towards autocratic decision-making (where the leader makes the decision alone), consultative decision-making, or a pure democratic decision-making process. Based on research, the Decision-Making Model directs leaders towards more effective decision-making.

Another popular situational model was proposed by psychologist Fred Fiedler, and is known as the Contingency Model of Leadership (Fiedler, 1967). According to Fiedler, a leader's behavioural style is more fixed than malleable. In other words, Fiedler believes that leaders are either more oriented towards the task, or the relationship, and this orientation is a behavioural and motivational style. As a result, leaders need to be matched with situations that allow them to be the most effective.

Fiedler distinguishes between what he terms 'task-motivated' and 'relationship-motivated' leaders, and uses a psychological measure to assess which style a leader possesses. A detailed analysis of the situation is then performed, focusing on how liked and respected leaders are in a particular situation (termed 'leader-member relations'), how structured or unstructured the group's task is, and the power that the leader is given by the organization (termed 'position power'). Based on extensive empirical research, Fiedler determined that task-motivated leaders perform better in situations that are either highly favourable (good leader–member relations, structured, strong position power) or highly unfavourable (poor leader–member relations, unstructured, weak position power) from the leader's perspective. On the other hand, relationship-motivated leaders do better in the 'middle ground' situations. However, because leadership style is relatively fixed, Fiedler does not believe that leaders can adjust their behaviour to fit the situation, as suggested by the other situational theories of leadership. Instead, Fiedler and his colleague advocate matching leaders to particular situations in which they will be more effective (Fiedler and Chemers, 1984).

All of the situational leadership theories have one thing in common: they all attempt to 'engineer' effective leadership by matching leader behaviour to variables associated with the leadership situation (Fiedler, 1965; Riggio, 2011a). This is a very limited and unidirectional view of management/leadership—conceptualizing it as a process whereby leaders behave in particular ways that lead to group and organizational outcomes. We shall see that more contemporary theories of leadership focus more on the interaction of leaders and followers, working together to get things done.

Contemporary Theories of Leadership

Currently, the two most popular theories of leadership focus on the relationship between leaders and followers as the key to leadership effectiveness. The first of these two theories is termed 'Leader-Member Exchange (LMX) Theory', and suggests that effective leadership is determined by the quality of the interaction between the leader and a particular work group member (Dansereau, Graen, and Haga, 1975; Graen and Uhl-Bien, 1995). This theory begins with the observation that the dyadic relationships that develop between leaders and particular followers tend to differ in quality. According to LMX Theory, leaders develop stronger relationships with particular followers, termed the 'in-group', and give less time and consideration to those in the 'out-group'. High-quality leader–member relationships are characterized by frequent communication and positive and supportive interactions. In low-quality LMX relationships, communication is less frequent and less positive in tone. As one might expect, high-quality LMX relationships lead to higher levels of performance and greater follower satisfaction and loyalty (Gerstner and Day, 1997; Graen, Novak, and Sommerkamp, 1982).

There are two important advancements contributed by LMX Theory to the understanding of leadership. First, LMX stands in direct contrast to most other theories of leadership that focus on leaders behaving in a uniform way with all followers. Instead, LMX Theory highlights the common-sense notion that leaders will value and treat certain followers differently—leading to more accurate prediction of workplace outcomes (Graen, 1976). Second, the role of the follower is highlighted in more recent work on LMX Theory which emphasizes that LMX is a two-way street, influenced by the effort and motivation put into the relationship by both leaders and followers (Maslyn and Uhl-Bien, 2001).

Although the concept of charismatic leaders can be traced back to Weber's (1947) notion of charismatic authority, the study of charismatic leadership in the management/leadership literature is relatively new. A number of leadership scholars have focused on the qualities associated with charismatic leadership, charismatic behaviours, and the effects of leader charisma on followers. For example, House and colleagues (House, 1977; Klein and House, 1995) suggest that charismatic leaders are particularly effective in communicating confidence and shared goals to followers. In addition to ability to communicate, scholars have focused on the ability of charismatic leaders to communicate emotions and inspire followers (Hogan, Raskin, and Fazzini, 1990; Riggio, 1987). Conger and Kanungo (1987, 1988) suggest that the key characteristics of charismatic leaders include a sensitivity to the followers and to the environment, a desire to change the status quo, and ability to inspire followers. Charismatic leadership is also viewed as situational to some extent, as charismatic leaders may be more effective in situations that are highly uncertain or unstable, or when change or transformation is needed (House and Singh, 1987). Finally, it is clear in most formulations of charismatic leadership theory that the followers play an important role. To be effective, a charismatic leader must gain the respect and admiration of followers and align the leader's goals with those of the follower.

The most prominent of contemporary theories of leadership builds on the notion of leader charisma, and is known as Transformational Leadership Theory (Bass, 1985; Bass and Riggio, 2006). In terms of published research, transformational leadership is easily the most popular contemporary leadership theory, with thousands of publications utilizing the construct. This theory emanates from the work of political historian James MacGregor Burns (1978), who distinguished between the more traditional 'transactional' leadership (involving a social exchange, such as work effort for pay) and transformational leadership, in which leaders and followers work together to achieve higher levels of motivation and performance. Psychologist Bernard Bass and colleagues (Bass, 1985; Bass and Avolio, 1994) developed the theory, outlining its various elements, and created a measurement instrument, the Multifactor Leadership Questionnaire (MLQ; Bass and Avolio, 1990), to measure transformational leadership. The various components of transformational leadership are presented in Table 14.1.

The 'charisma' associated with transformational leaders comes from two sources: the idealized influence component, whereby the leader is a positive, and moral, role model for the followers, and the inspirational motivation component that allows leaders to influence followers at the emotional level—moving them to greater levels of performance. The intellectual stimulation component helps to stimulate followers to engage in problem-solving behaviour, and to be creative, also helping to achieve group or team success. Finally, through individualized consideration, the transformational leader builds a strong relationship with each follower, assesses his or her strengths, abilities, needs, and desires, using that knowledge to motivate, as well as develop followers' leadership capacity.

Transformational leadership, as its name suggests, involves the leader working with followers to raise the collective motivation and effort in order to deal with change, or to reach extraordinary levels of performance. The transformational leader is charismatic, but the theory goes beyond simply the leader's charisma. Transformational leadership theory also focuses on the leader's ability to motivate and stimulate follower creativity,

Table 14.1 The Components of Transformational Leadership Theory

Idealized Influence—The leader serves as a positive (and moral) role model for followers. The leader focuses on the purpose and mission of group or organization and behaves consistently. In other words, the leader 'walks the talk'. This component builds follower admiration and trust in the leader. Idealized influence is reflected both in the behaviours that the leader performs, and in the attributions of 'charisma' that followers give to the leader.

Inspirational Motivation—This element involves the leader's ability to motivate and inspire followers by providing meaning and challenge, and 'moving' followers with inspiring words and affect. Combined with idealized influence, this is the source of the transformational leader's 'charisma'.

Intellectual Stimulation—Through encouraging followers to question assumptions, reframe problems, and try new approaches, the transformational leader stimulates follower innovation and creativity. As the saying goes, the leader stimulates followers to 'think outside the box'.

Individualized Consideration—The leader works to establish a good interpersonal relationship with each follower, paying special attention to each follower's needs and concerns. Through mentoring, coaching, and empowering/delegating, the transformational leader helps build each follower's individual leadership capacity.

and to engage followers in such a way that they become empowered, individually motivated, and focused on developing their own leadership capacity.

Meta-analyses of studies on transformational leadership suggest that followers of transformational leaders are more satisfied (Dumdum, Lowe, and Avolio, 2002), and have higher levels of performance than followers of non-transformational leaders (Lowe, Kroek, and Sivasubramaniam, 1996). Moreover, individuals led by transformational leaders report less stress and burnout, suggesting that the strong relationship between transformational leaders and followers somehow buffers followers from the experience of stress (Seltzer, Numerof, and Bass, 1989).

The many ethical debacles in business and government that came to light in the new millennium led to a greater focus on leadership ethics. As a result, a number of contemporary and emerging theories of leadership emphasize the ethical and moral dimensions of leadership. Although Authentic Leadership Theory (ALT) is the most prominent amongst them, there are a number of newer theories that focus on leadership ethics. Authentic Leadership Theory suggests that authentic leaders promote positive psychological capacities in followers, and foster a positive ethical climate (Walumbwa et al., 2008). There are four components to ALT: (1) *self-awareness* on the part of the leader, who knows his/her strengths and weaknesses as a leader; (2) an *internalized moral perspective*; (3) *balanced processing* of information, which allows the leader to explore other's opinions and approach decision-making in an objective, unbiased manner; and (4) *relational transparency*, which refers to being open and honest in dealings with others—not having any 'hidden agendas'.

In addition to ALT, there are a number of other theoretical approaches that focus on leader ethics/morality, including Ethical Leadership which focuses more explicitly on ethical leader behaviours (Brown and Trevino, 2006), Spiritual Leadership, which emphasizes the role of a spiritual 'calling' to lead followers through value alignment (Fry, 2003), and Virtuous Leadership, which focuses on the role of the leader's character and possession of cardinal virtues to keep the leader from behaving unethically (Riggio et al., 2010). A very different approach to leadership is offered by the notion of Servant Leadership. Emanating from the writings of Robert Greenleaf (1972, 1977), the notion of servant leadership puts followers first. The servant leader nurtures and empowers followers and works towards their benefit, and the benefit to larger society. Although resurfacing an older construct, research on servant leadership has been spurred recently by the development of measures designed to assess it (Barbuto and Wheeler, 2006; Liden et al., 2008).

One problem with nearly all leadership theories is that they are 'leader-centric', viewing leaders as the force that operates on followers and situations to achieve certain outcomes. Meindl and his colleagues (Meindl, 1990; Meindl, Ehrlich, and Dukerich, 1985) referred to this as the 'romance of leadership'. In recent years, there has been greater research attention paid to the role of followers and followership. Akin to the trait and behavioural approaches to leadership, one line of research has examined the characteristics and behaviours of exemplary followers (Kelley, 1988; Chaleff, 2003). This approach to studying followers in the leadership equation amounts to a 'reversing the lens' approach—examining the role that followers play in helping to construct leadership (Uhl-Bien et al., 2014). Indeed, the idea that followers help to 'construct' leaders and leadership is central to the Social Identity Theory, which postulates that group members choose to follow an individual who best represents the ideals and goals of the collective (Hogg, 2001; Hogg, van Knippenberg, and Rast, 2012). This approach is quite consistent with the notion discussed earlier of a leader's charisma partly residing in the followers' perception of the leader.

Another approach to understanding the role of the follower in the leadership equation is known as the 'constructionist' perspective. This view suggests that leaders and followers work together to co-create both leadership and followership. For example, DeRue and Ashford (2010) propose that leaders and followers engage in a sort of social negotiation of claiming identities, and granting, or recognizing, the other's role. Leaders claim a leader identity, and followers must then grant them that identity and claim the role of follower. In other words, followers accept the leader's authority and position and choose to follow the leader. If the claiming and granting process works out, then leadership is co-created by leaders and followers fulfilling their roles. However, if either party does not cooperate (the follower refuses to recognize the leader, or accept the follower role; the leader chooses not to play the leadership role), then no leadership is constructed. DeRue and Ashford (2010) thus see leadership occurring through a mutual influence process whereby leader influence followers and vice versa.

Lastly, the context of the leader–follower interaction is also quite important (Collinson, 2006). Followers may only follow a leader if the time or setting is right, withdrawing their support for the leader when circumstances change. As Uhl-Bien et al. state, the study of followership 'is *not* the study of leadership from the follower perspective. It is the study of how followers view and enact following behaviors in relation to leaders' (2014: 96).

Assessing, Selecting, and Developing Leaders

A great deal of effort and resources are invested in trying to assess and select managers with good leadership potential, measuring leadership in managers, and developing their leadership capabilities in order for them to grow into better and more effective leaders of teams, departments, and organizations. In this section, we review research on the assessment, selection, and development of managers and leaders.

Two general approaches are used in identifying and selecting individuals for leadership positions. The first is to focus on internal candidates—lower-level members who have potential to be promoted to higher-level leadership positions (so-called 'high potentials'). The second strategy is to recruit external candidates with some proven leadership experience or potential to lead. Lower-level leadership positions are more often filled with internal candidates, while higher-level positions, such as department head or CEO, are more likely to focus on external candidates, or explore both internal and external candidates (Howard, 2007; see also Thornton, Hollenbeck, and Johnson, 2011).

Ideally, a model is used to guide assessment and selection of leaders. In selection, most often a competency model is used that focuses on what are believed to be the core knowledge, skills, abilities, and other characteristics (KSAOs) that leaders will need for success in the particular leadership position and in the organization. A variety of techniques can be used to attempt to assess leadership competencies, ranging from inferences made from interviews, to various forms of tests for specific competencies, to leadership simulations. We will briefly discuss the strengths and weaknesses of these various methods of assessing leadership potential.

The use of interviews, reference checks, and review of resumes and other biographical information is quite common. Indeed, it is unlikely to be selected for any leadership position without first submitting a resume, undergoing one or more interviews, and having some sort of background or reference check. There are many weaknesses associated with these methods, including biased responding (i.e., giving desirable responses, presenting only positive information), assessing only perceptions/descriptions of leader behaviour rather than the behaviours themselves, and concerns over the reliability and validity of selection interviews (see Dipboye and Johnson, 2013, for an overview of the selection interview and its use). On the positive side, interviews and reference checks can often identify critical liabilities or limitations, and are relatively easy to implement.

The use of standardized tests for assessing leadership potential has some benefits and drawbacks as well. Most commonly used tests include tests of cognitive ability, various personality tests that assess traits associated with leadership potential, and situational judgement tests that try to determine how a leader might perform in a specific situation. While tests typically have known levels of reliability and validity, they measure competencies associated with leadership—making inferences about leadership behaviours, rather than assessing the behaviours themselves (Howard, 2007).

Leadership simulations, such as the situational exercises that are part of a managerial assessment centre (see Thornton and Rupp, 2006, for an overview), allow observation and evaluation of actual leadership behaviours. Some of these exercises are used to assess administrative, decision-making, and written communication skills simulations. A typical example is the managerial 'in-box', with correspondence (i.e., memos, emails, etc.) that requires the participant to make decisions, communicate responses, and plan and schedule meetings. Other simulations exercises, such as simulated team meetings, employee 'coaching' sessions, and formal presentations, are used to assess leadership and team skills, decision-making, mentoring/coaching, performance management skills, and oral communication. Because assessment centres focus on demonstration of managerial/leadership behaviours, they are considered a 'best practice' in assessing leadership potential (Howard, 2007). Regardless of the methods used for leader selection, a key to success is the ability to ascertain the competencies, behaviours, and other qualities that will lead to effective leadership in the actual position.

Another important concern is the ongoing assessment of effective leadership in individuals currently holding leadership positions in organizations. Two general strategies are used in determining leadership effectiveness. The first involves ratings of leader effectiveness from supervisors, subordinates, or others who have the opportunity to see the leader in action. The second method for assessing leader performance uses more objective outcomes, such as team or departmental performance, as expressed in terms of measures of productivity, financial measures such as profit, or other concrete outcomes.

The most common means of assessing managerial/leadership performance involves the ratings made by direct supervisors. For those in higher-level leadership positions, subordinate ratings are also common. These methods involve raters' perceptions of leader effectiveness, and are subjective and prone to biases. Liking for the leader, fear or retribution for providing critical evaluations, or an inability to connect the leader's behaviour to performance outcomes, can all bias leader ratings. Moreover, any particular rater—be they superior, subordinate, or peer—reflect only that person's perspective on the rated leader's performance.

A comprehensive rating method that has gained increasing popularity, is the use of 360-degree feedback. This involves collecting leadership performance ratings from all persons who have contact with the target leader, including supervisors, subordinates, peers, and external customers/clients. The advantage of 360-degree feedback is that it offers a wide range of different perspectives on the target leader, and allows determination of the agreement among the different raters (i.e., reliability). The obvious drawbacks to 360-degree feedback include the costs of such a comprehensive process, confusion if the different raters are in disagreement, and the fact that it still represents perceptions of a leader's performance rather than actual performance (see Smither, London, and Reilly, 2005, for a review of 360-degree feedback).

An important function of assessment of leader performance is to guide performance management of leaders. To that end, many of the leadership assessment techniques, including 360-degree feedback, are used to monitor and improve leader performance, and to identify candidates for promotion. Many of the assessment methods play an important role in the development of leaders.

A major enterprise in organizations, and by various consulting organizations, is the development and honing of leadership skills in managers. Kellerman (2012) describes it as the 'leadership industry', whereby billions of dollars are spent each year trying to develop managerial and leadership skills. These leadership development programmes range from workshops lasting a few hours to several days, to multifaceted, integrated leader development programmes that can last over a period of years. Day (2000) makes an important distinction between 'leader development' and 'leadership development'. Leader development focuses on individual leaders and trying to develop their competencies and strategies to be more effective leaders. Leadership development focuses more on the collective—the group, department, or organization—in an effort to improve the shared leadership capacity of both leaders and followers.

Historically, leader development efforts received a boost with the situational leadership theories. For example, the Situational Leadership Theory led to a programme designed to apply the behavioural theories of leadership with the premise that the best leaders are high on both task- and relationship-orientation. This programme was initially known as the Managerial Grid, but was later renamed the Leadership Grid (Blake and McCanse, 1991; Blake and Mouton, 1985). Grid training has been used to train hundreds of thousands of managers, despite criticisms about the soundness of the underlying theory (Vecchio, 2007). Likewise, Fiedler's Leader Match programme was also quite popular, although it took the opposite strategy of making sure that different types of leaders (task-motivated vs relationship-motivated) were in situations that were best suited to their leadership style (Leister, Borden, and Fiedler, 1977).

Currently, a number of the more popular leadership theories (e.g., Transformational Leadership Theory, LMX Theory) have been used as a framework for leader development programmes. There are also a variety of techniques to improve leadership. These range from the standard seminars or workshops to ongoing leader development efforts. For example, 360-degree evaluations have moved from use as a leader performance assessment method to an ongoing effort to recognize a particular leader's strengths and areas that should be targeted for improvement (Atwater, Brett, and Waldman, 2003). A longitudinal study of managers who received ongoing 360-degree feedback found improved managerial competence over time (Bailey and Fletcher, 2002). Another ongoing programme to develop leaders is the use of leadership coaches. Usually utilized for higher-level, executive positions, a coach provides frank, ongoing feedback to the leader to help him or her develop and improve leadership performance (Kilburg, 2000; McKenna and Davis, 2009).

Leadership simulations are also a common method for improving leader capacity. These include various sorts of management 'games' (e.g., Devine et al., 2004) to developmental assessment centres that simulate a typical managerial workday(s) (Siegfried, 2006). A very different sort of leadership development program—one that builds both individual and shared leadership capacity—is action learning. Action learning is a programme where teams of employees are assembled in order to work on an actual assignment, such as developing a new product or solving an organizational problem (Conger and Xin, 2000). The idea is that managers learn and develop their leadership by doing.

How effective are leader development efforts? One meta-analysis of all sorts of leadership development efforts, found a significant impact—one that was small, but statistically significant (Avolio et al., 2009). Of course, the amount of time invested, the type of leadership development programme, and the participants' motivation to develop all matter. One important suggestion is for leadership development practitioners to assess the return on investment of development programs by looking at the programme's costs and the resulting increase in group performance (Avolio, Avey, and Quisenberry, 2010).

The Future of Management and Leadership Studies

Leadership is a 'hot' topic among managers, and an important concern for organizations across all sectors. In business, politics, education, healthcare, and nonprofits there is great concern about having high-quality leadership, and a great deal of energy and resources are invested in trying to attract and retain top-level leaders. While the educational market for MBAs has seemed to plateau, the number of graduate programmes (Masters and PhD) that involve leadership (e.g., organizational leadership, educational leadership, leadership studies, etc.) are growing at a rapid rate (Riggio, 2011b). Moreover, organizations are putting more resources into leadership development efforts. All in all, the future 'market' for leadership seems bright.

What are some of the most important trends in leadership research and practice, and what are the implications for the management of organizations?

Clearly, the complexity of the leadership scenario is of foremost importance. We know that the leader-centric bias has led us to ignore or diminish the importance of the follower in co-constructing leadership (Carsten and Uhl-Bien, 2012). In other words, it is leaders and followers working together that create leadership. Moreover, the situation matters, as does the level at which leadership takes place in an organization (e.g., whether leadership is coming from the top, or bubbling up from the bottom levels of the organization). One promising avenue is the development of complexity theory, which takes into account a large number of variables, to the understanding of leadership (Uhl-Bien, Marion, and McKelvey, 2007).

Studying the complex nature of organizational leadership requires sophisticated methodology and solid research designs. In organizations, leadership occurs at multiple levels, with a hierarchy of leaders and followers. Moreover, followers constitute both individuals, with a dyadic relationship with the leader/supervisor, and a member of a collective (team or department). State-of-the-art research, therefore, requires multi-level models and analyses (e.g., Yammarino et al., 2005). An overview of key research issues in the study of leadership is presented in Day and Antonakis (2013).

While we know quite a bit about the characteristics of leaders, the correlates of leadership, and leadership outcomes, we understand relatively little about the leadership process. For example, we know little about the mechanisms of how leaders motivate followers, and we know even less about the process by which followers influence leaders. Indeed, a greater focus on the follower, and the follower's role in leadership, is clearly an area that has received more attention in recent years, and will continue into the future (Uhl-Bien et al., 2014).

Another area that has received some research attention, but represents fertile ground for increasing our understanding of leadership, is the process by which leadership develops, both in terms of the earliest precursors of leadership (e.g., Murphy and Johnson, 2011; Riggio and Mumford, 2011), but also across the adult years (Day, Harrison, and Halpin, 2009). A better understanding of how leadership competencies develop will help both with the selection of leaders, but particularly in understanding how to better develop leaders.

Finally, we know relatively little about leadership in diverse cultures and among diverse people. Given the scarcity of women in top-level leadership positions, it makes sense that there has been a flurry of research on gender in leadership over the past dozen years (e.g., Chin, 2014; Eagly and Carli, 2007). The multi-nation, multi-culture GLOBE study (Chhokar, Brodbeck, and House, 2007; House et al., 2004) has spurred the study of leadership internationally, and the increasing number of leadership scholars from non-Western nations, suggests that the future will see a much better understanding of leadership and diversity.

REFERENCES

Atwater, L. E., Brett, J. F., and Waldman, D. (2003). 'Understanding the Benefits and Risks of Multi-Source Feedback', in S. E. Murphy and R. E. Riggio (eds), *The Future of Leadership Development*. Mahwah, NJ: Lawrence Erlbaum, 89–106.
Avolio, B. J., Avey, J. B., and Quisenberry, D. (2010). 'Estimating Return on Leadership Development Investment'. *The Leadership Quarterly*, 21(4): 633–44.
Avolio, B. J., Reichard, R. J., Hannah, S. T., Walumbwa, F. O., and Chan, A. (2009). 'A Meta-Analytic Review of Leadership Impact Research: Experimental and Quasi-Experimental Studies'. *The Leadership Quarterly*, 20(5): 764–84.
Bailey, C. and Fletcher, C. (2002). 'The Impact of Multiple Source Feedback on Management Development: Findings from a Longitudinal Study'. *Journal of Organizational Behavior*, 23: 853–67.
Barbuto Jr, J. E. and Wheeler, D. W. (2006). 'Scale Development and Construct Clarification of Servant Leadership'. *Group and Organization Management*, 31: 300–26.
Bass, B. M. (1985). *Leadership and Performance beyond Expectations*. New York: Free Press.
Bass, B. M. and Avolio, B. J. (1990). *Multifactor Leadership Questionnaire*. Palo Alto, CA: Consulting Psychologists Press.
Bass, B. M. and Avolio, B. J. (1994). *Improving Organizational Effectiveness through Transformational Leadership*. Thousand Oaks, CA: SAGE.
Bass, B. M. and Riggio, R. E. (2006). *Transformational Leadership*, 2nd edn. New York: Lawrence Erlbaum/Taylor & Francis.
Blake, R. R. and McCanse, A. A. (1991). *Leadership Dilemmas—Grid Solutions*. Houston, TX: Gulf.
Blake, R. R. and Mouton, J. S. (1985). *The Managerial Grid*. Houston, TX: Gulf.
Brown, M. E. and Trevino, L. K. (2006). 'Ethical Leadership: A Review and Future Directions'. *The Leadership Quarterly*, 17: 595–616.
Burns, J. M. (1978). *Leadership*. New York: Harper & Row.
Carsten, M. K. and Uhl-Bien, M. (2012). 'Follower Beliefs in the Co-Production of Leadership: Examining Upward Communication and the Moderating Role of Context'. *Zeitschrift fur Psychologie*, 220(4): 210–20. doi:10.1027/2151-2604/a000115.
Chaleff, I. (2003). *The Courageous Follower: Standing Up to and for Our Leaders*, 2nd edn. San Francisco, CA: Berret-Koehler.
Chhokar, J. S., Brodbeck, F. C., and House, R. J. (eds) (2007). *Culture and Leadership across the World: The GLOBE Book of In-Depth Studies of 25 Societies*. Mahwah, NJ: Lawrence Erlbaum.
Chin, J. L. (2014). 'Women and Leadership', in D. V. Day (ed.), *The Oxford Handbook of Leadership and Organizations*. New York: Oxford University Press, 733–53.
Collinson, D. (2006). 'Rethinking Followership: A Post-Structuralist Analysis of Follower Identities'. *The Leadership Quarterly*, 17: 179–89.
Conger, J. A. and Kanungo, R. N. (1987). 'Toward a Behavioral Theory of Charismatic Leadership in Organizational Settings'. *Academy of Management Review*, 12: 637–47.

Conger, J. A. and Kanungo, R. N. (1988). 'The Empowerment Process: Integrating Theory and Practice'. *Academy of Management Review*, 13: 471–82.

Conger, J. A. and Xin, K. (2000). 'Voices from the Field: Executive Education among Global Corporations'. *Journal of Management Education*, 24: 73–101.

Dansereau, F., Graen, G., and Haga, B. (1975). 'A Vertical Dyad Linkage Approach to Leadership within Formal Organizations: A Longitudinal Investigation of the Role Making Process'. *Organizational Behavior and Human Performance*, 13: 46–78.

Day, D. V. (2000). 'Leadership Development: A Review in Context'. *The Leadership Quarterly*, 11: 581–613.

Day, D. V. and Antonakis, J. (2013). 'The Future of Leadership', in H. S. Leonard, R. Lewis, A. M. Freedman and J. Passmore (eds), *The Wiley-Blackwell Handbook of the Psychology of Leadership, Change and Organizational Development*. Oxford: John Wiley & Sons, 221–35.

Day, D. V., Harrison, M. M., and Halpin, S. M. (2009). *An Integrative Approach to Leader Development: Connecting Adult Development, Identity, and Expertise*. New York: Routledge.

DeRue, S. and Ashford, S. (2010). 'Who Will Lead and Who Will Follow? A Social Process of Leadership Identity Construction in Organizations'. *Academy of Management Review*, 35: 627–47.

Devine, D. J., Habig, J. K., Martin, K. E., Bott, J. P., and Grayson, A. L. (2004). 'TINSEL TOWN: A Top Management Simulation Involving Distributed Expertise'. *Simulation & Gaming*, 35: 94–134.

Dipboye, R. L. and Johnson, S. K. (2013). 'Understanding and Improving Employee Selection Interviews', in K. F. Geisinger, B. A. Bracken, J. F. Carlson, J. C. Hansen, N. R. Kuncel, S. P. Reise, and M. C. Rodriquez (eds), *APA Handbook of Testing and Assessment in Psychology*, vol. 1. Washington, D.C.: American Psychological Association, 479–99.

Drucker, P. F. (1954). *The Practice of Management*. New York: Harper & Row.

Dumdum, U. R., Lowe, K. B., and Avolio, B. J. (2002). 'A Meta-Analysis of Transformational and Transactional Leadership Correlates of Effectiveness and Satisfaction: An Update and Extension', in B. J. Avolio and F. J. Yammarino (eds), *Transformational and Charismatic Leadership: The Road Ahead*. Oxford: JAI/Elsevier, 35–66.

Eagly, A. H. and Carli, L. L. (2007). *Through the Labyrinth: The Truth about How Women Become Leaders*. Boston, MA: Harvard Business School Press.

Fiedler, F. E. (1965). 'Engineer the Job to Fit the Manager'. *Harvard Business Review*, 43: 115.

Fiedler, F. E. (1967). *A Theory of Leadership Effectiveness*. New York: McGraw-Hill.

Fiedler, F. E. and Chemers, M. M. (1984). *Improving Leadership Effectiveness: The Leader Match Concept*, rev. edn. New York: Wiley.

Follett, M. P. (1949). *Freedom and Co-ordination: Lectures in Business Organization*. London: Management Publications Trust.

Fry, L. W. (2003). 'Toward a Theory of Spiritual Leadership'. *The Leadership Quarterly*, 14: 693–727.

Gerstner, C. R. and Day, D. V. (1997). 'Meta-Analytic Review of Leader-Member Exchange Theory: Correlates and Construct Issues'. *Journal of Applied Psychology*, 82: 827–44.

Graen, G. B. (1976). 'Role-Making Processes within Complex Organizations', in M. D. Dunnette (ed.), *Handbook of Industrial and Organizational Psychology*. Chicago, IL: Rand McNally, 1201–45).

Graen, G. B., Novak, M., and Sommerkamp, P. (1982). 'The Effects of Leader-Member Exchange and Job Design on Productivity and Satisfaction: Testing a Dual Attachment Model'. *Organizational Behavior and Human Performance*, 30: 109–31.

Graen, G. B. and Uhl-Bien, M. (1995). 'Relationship-Based Approach to Leadership: Development of Leader-Member Exchange (LMX) Theory of Leadership over 25 Years: Applying a Multi-Level, Multi-Domain Perspective'. *The Leadership Quarterly*, 6: 219–47.

Greenleaf, R. K. (1972). *The Servant as Leader*. Westfield, IN: The Greenleaf Center for Servant Leadership.

Greenleaf, R. K. (1977). *Servant Leadership: A Journey into the Nature of Legitimate Power and Greatness*. New York: Paulist Press.

Hersey, P. and Blanchard, K. H. (1969). 'Life-Cycle Theory of Leadership'. *Training and Development Journal*, 23: 285–91.

Hersey, P. and Blanchard, K. H. (1993). *Management of Organizational Behavior: Utilizing Human Resources*, 6th edn. Englewood Cliffs, NJ: Prentice Hall.

Hogan, R., Raskin, R., and Fazzini, D. (1990). 'The Dark Side of Charisma'. In K. E. Clarek and M. B. Clark (eds), *Measures of Leadership*. West Orange, NJ: Leadership Library of America, 171–84.

Hogg, M. A. (2001). 'A Social Identity Theory of Leadership'. *Personality and Social Psychology Review*, 5: 184–200.

Hogg, M. A., van Knippenberg, D., and Rast, D. E. (2012). 'The Social Identity Theory of Leadership: Theoretical Origins, Research Findings, and Conceptual Developments'. *European Review of Social Psychology*, 23: 258–304.

House, R. J. (1977). 'A 1976 Theory of Charismatic Leadership', in J. G. Hunt and L. L. Larsen (eds), *Leadership: The Cutting Edge*. Carbondale, IL: Southern Illinois University Press, 189–207.

House, R. J., Hanges, P. J., Javidan, M., Dorfman, P. W., and Gupta, V. (eds), (2004). *Culture, Leadership, and Organizations: The GLOBE Study of 62 Societies*. Thousand Oaks, CA: SAGE.

House, R. J. and Singh, J. V. (1987). 'Organizational Behavior: Some New Directions for I/O Psychology'. *Annual Review of Psychology*, 38: 669–718.

Howard, A. (2007). 'Best Practices in Leader Selection', in J. A. Conger and R. E. Riggio (eds), *The Practice of Leadership: Developing the Next Generation of Leaders*. San Francisco, CA: Jossey-Bass, 11–40.

Kahn, R. L. and Katz, D. (1960). 'Leadership Practices in Relation to Production and Morale', in D. Cartwright and A. Zander (eds), *Group Dynamics: Research and Theory*, 2nd edn. Elmsford, NY: Row, Peterson, 554–71.

Kellerman, B. (2012). *The End of Leadership*. New York: Harper Business.

Kelley, R. E. (1988). 'In Praise of Followers', *Harvard Business Review*, 66: 141–8.

Kilburg, R. R. (2000). *Executive Coaching: Developing Managerial Wisdom in a World of Chaos*. Washington, D.C.: American Psychological Association.

Klein, K. J. and House, R. J. (1995). 'On Fire: Charismatic Leadership and Levels of Analysis'. *The Leadership Quarterly*, 6: 183–98.

Leister, A., Borden, D., and Fiedler, F. E. (1977). 'Validation of Contingency Model Leadership Training: Leader Match'. *Academy of Management Journal*, 20: 464–70.

Liden, R. C., Wayne, S. J., Zhao, H., and Henderson, D. (2008). 'Servant Leadership: Development of a Multidimensional Measure and Multi-Level Assessment'. *The Leadership Quarterly*, 19: 161–77.

Lord, R. G., de Vader, C. L., and Alliger, G. M. (1986). 'A Meta-Analysis of the Relation between Personality Traits and Leadership Perceptions: An Application of Validity Generalization Procedures'. *Journal of Applied Psychology*, 71: 402–10.

Lowe, K. B., Kroeck, K. G., and Sivasubramaniam, N. (1996). 'Effectiveness Correlates of Transformational and Transactional Leadership: A Meta-Analytic Review of the MLQ Literature'. *The Leadership Quarterly*, 7: 385–425.

McKenna, D. D. and Davis, S. L. (2009). 'Hidden in Plain Sight: The Active Ingredients of Executive Coaching'. *Industrial and Organizational Psychology*, 2(3): 244–60.

Mann, R. D. (1959). 'A Review of the Relationships between Personality and Performance in Small Groups'. *Psychological Bulletin*, 56: 241–70.

Maslyn, J. M. and Uhl-Bien, M. (2001). 'Leader-Member Exchange and Its Dimensions: Effects of Self-Effort and Other's Effort on Relationship Quality'. *Journal of Applied Psychology*, 86: 697–708.

Mayo, E. (1933). *The Human Problems of an Industrial Civilization*. Cambridge, MA: Harvard University Press.

Meindl, J. R. (1990). 'On Leadership: An Alternative to the Conventional Wisdom'. *Research in Organizational Behavior*, 12: 159–203.

Meindl, J. R., Ehrlich, S. B., and Dukerich, J. M. (1985). 'The Romance of Leadership'. *Administrative Science Quarterly*, 30: 78–102.

Murphy, S. E. and Johnson, S. K. (2011). 'The Benefits of a Long-Lens Approach to Leader Development: Understanding the Seeds of Leadership'. *The Leadership Quarterly*, 22(3): 459–70.

Riggio, R. E. (1987). *The Charisma Quotient*. New York: Dodd Mead.

Riggio, R. E. (2011a). 'The Management Perspective: Engineering Effective Leadership in Organizations', in M. Harvey and R. E. Riggio (eds), *The Dialogue of Disciplines: Research Companion to Leadership Studies*. Cheltenham: Edward Elgar, 119–28.

Riggio, R. E. (2011b). 'Is Leadership Studies a Discipline?', in M. Harvey and R. E. Riggio (eds), *The Dialogue of Disciplines: Research Companion to Leadership Studies*. Cheltenham: Edward Elgar, 9–19.

Riggio, R. E. and Mumford, M. D. (2011). 'Introduction to the Special Issue: Longitudinal Studies of Leadership Development'. *The Leadership Quarterly*, 22(3): 453–56.

Riggio, R. E., Zhu, W., Reina, C., and Maroosis, J. (2010). 'Virtue-Based Measurement of Ethical Leadership: The Leadership Virtues Questionnaire'. *Consulting Psychology Journal*, 62(4): 235–50.

Seltzer, J., Numerof, R. E., and Bass, B. M. (1989). 'Transformational Leadership: Is it a Source of More or Less Burnout or Stress?' *Journal of Health and Human Resources Administration*, 12: 174–85.

Siegfried Jr, W. D. (2006). 'Introduction to Special Issue: Developmental Assessment Centers'. *The Psychologist-Manager Journal*, 9(2): 71–4.

Smith, A. (1776). *The Wealth of Nations*. London: W. Strahan and T. Cadell.

Smither, J. W., London, M., and Reilly, R. R. (2005). 'Does Performance Improve Following Multisource Feedback? A Theoretical Model, Meta-Analysis, and Review of Empirical Findings'. *Personnel Psychology*, 58(1): 33–66.

Stogdill, R. M. (1948). 'Personal Factors Association with Leadership: A Survey of the Literature'. *Journal of Psychology*, 25: 35–71.

Stogdill, R. M. and Coons, A. E. (eds) (1957). *Leader Behavior: Its Description and Measurement*. Columbus, OH: Ohio State University, Bureau of Business Research.

Taylor, F. W. (1911). *The Principles of Scientific Management*. New York: Harper.

Thornton, G. C., Hollenbeck, G. P., and Johnson, S. K. (2011). 'Selecting Leaders: Executives and High Potentials', in J. L. Farr and N. T. Tippins (eds), *Handbook of Employee Selection*. New York: Routledge, 823–41.

Thornton, G. C. and Rupp, D. E. (2006). *Assessment Centers in Human Resource Management: Strategies for Prediction, Diagnosis, and Development.* Mahwah, NJ: Erlbaum.

Uhl-Bien, M., Marion, R., and McKelvey, B. (2007). 'Complexity Leadership Theory: Shifting Leadership from the Industrial Age to the Knowledge Area'. *The Leadership Quarterly,* 18(4): 298–318.

Uhl-Bien, M., Riggio, R. E., Lowe, K. B., and Carsten, M. K. (2014). 'Followership Theory: A Review and Research Agenda'. *The Leadership Quarterly,* 25: 83–104.

Vecchio, R. P. (2007). 'Situational Leadership Theory: An Examination of a Prescriptive Theory', in R. P. Vecchio (ed.), *Leadership: Understanding the Dynamics of Power and Influence in Organizations,* 2nd edn. Notre Dame, IN: University of Notre Dame Press, 318–34.

Vroom, V. H. and Yetton, P. W. (1973). *Leadership and Decision-Making.* Pittsburgh, PA: University of Pittsburgh Press.

Walumbwa, F. O., Avolio, B. J., Gardner, W. L., Wernsing, T. S., and Peterson, S. J. (2008). 'Authentic Leadership: Development and Validation of a Theory-Based Measure'. *Journal of Management,* 34(1): 89–126.

Weber, M. (1947). *The Theory of Social and Economic Organizations,* trans. A. M. Henderson and T. Parsons. New York: Free Press.

Yammarino, F. J., Dionne, S. D., Uk Chun, J., and Dansereau, F. (2005). 'Leadership and Levels of Analysis: A State-of-the-Science Review'. *The Leadership Quarterly,* 16: 879–919.

CHAPTER 15

FRAGMENTATION IN STRATEGIC MANAGEMENT

Process and Agency Issues

MARK SHANLEY

Introduction

STRATEGY is one of the oldest areas of teaching in business schools and today remains one of the most widely taught subjects in business school curricula. It is also arguably among the youngest and least understood research areas within business scholarship, with its professional origin in the 1970s (Khurana, 2007). Currently best known as 'Strategic Management', the area comprises a wide range of topics of continuing interest to practitioners but is often seen as lacking a compelling identity as a distinct field (Jarzabkowski, 2005). Its core topics overlap in its subject matter with a number of core social science disciplines, such as economics, sociology, and psychology (Nag, Hambrick, and Chen, 2007). Perhaps because of these factors, the field also suffers from a sense of intellectual fragmentation that has been recognized at various times throughout its history and that continues to the present (Ronda-Pupo and Guerras-Martin, 2012).

While a number of factors contribute to this fragmentation, the complexity of strategy's object of study is certainly one of them, since most definitions of the field involve its efforts to understand how large organizations make decisions on a consistent basis across multiple decision units and across diverse geographic markets through the actions of thousands of employees. This complexity has led scholars to develop dozens of definitions of the field that differ on general assumptions regarding: 1) the actors involved; 2) the decisions and actions taken by actors that have been identified as 'strategic' as opposed to 'operational' or 'tactical'; 3) the presumed organizational context in which strategic decisions are made and implemented; and 4) the broader business environment of strategic action, whether at the level of industry or some larger social aggregation (Herrmann, 2005). This list is not inclusive.

Academic perspectives on strategy are complicated further by the felt need of many scholars to address the perspectives of practitioners, whether consultants, top managers, or planners, who are primarily interested in how strategic choices influence firm performance. Indeed, it is arguable that the strategy field has been so focused for so long on how strategy influences performance that research on a large number of alternative dependent variables has been neglected. Given the broad range of topics in the field, the overlapping disciplinary bases for addressing these topics, and the limited range of dependent variables that have attracted interest, it is not surprising that research results have failed to accumulate in an integrated fashion in strategy as they have in other academic areas. This fragmentation has been a longstanding source of concern among strategy scholars since the area's beginnings (Schendel and Hofer, 1979; Rumelt, Schendel, and Teece, 1994).

This chapter reviews these issues in more detail, inspired by the results of some recent bibliographic review studies. The major issues contributing to the fragmentation of strategy are seen as of two sorts. The first concerns undertheorized aspects of decision and implementation processes. The second area of problematic issues concerns undertheorized assumptions of action behind strategy theories, especially concerning how top managers make decisions in multiple temporal frames, complex organizational settings, and based on prior experiences and the expectations of conflicting environmental demands. Suggestions are offered to improve conceptualization of process issues concerning interconnected linkages, intertemporal linkages, and inter-relational linkages. Suggestions regarding action assumptions of the field are considered in terms of a craft approach to organizational agency (Sennett, 2008).

Recent Studies of Strategic Management Fragmentation

Some recent studies have attempted to develop a clarified definition of strategic management by studying how published studies in the field have been presented to members of the scholarly community and their students. This is akin to a scholarly 'crowdsourcing' of field definitions and is premised on an assumption that the field's dimensions can be gleaned from an analysis of how previous scholars have developed their efforts. This research is described in more detail below.

Nag, Hambrick, and Chen (2007) see the fragmentation of the strategic management field as a problem and attempt to address it by articulating a definition of the field based upon the modes of expression and assumptions that are explicitly or tacitly held by its members. To do this, they survey 585 authors of papers presented at national meetings to obtain their characterization of a pool of 447 published articles (at least 18 articles per respondent) that were seen as part of the field. In addition, respondents also evaluated a set of articles that were not generally thought to be part of the field. Based on their analysis of these ratings, a definition of the strategy field was generated and validated. The resultant definition can be summarized as:

> The field of strategic management deals with the major intended and emergent initiatives taken by general managers on behalf of owners, involving utilization of resources, to enhance the performance of firms in their external environments. (Nag, Hambrick, and Chen, 2007: 242)

Nag, Hambrick, and Chen (2007) also examine the explicit definitions of strategy provided by other scholars to determine the nature of conceptual overlaps between strategic management and core disciplines like economics, sociology, management, and marketing. They conclude that there is substantial implicit consensus among scholars regarding the basic elements of the field, but also considerable intellectual diversity and fragmentation regarding non-core aspects of the field and variety in how aspects of the field are combined for particular studies. While Nag, Hambrick, and Chen (2007) is informative regarding the fragmentation of the field and the various ways in which it might be addressed, it is less helpful in other ways. The results of this study support claims about conceptual fragmentation in the field, but the authors end up downplaying the importance of that fragmentation. Core members of the strategy field have an implicit and shared understanding regarding the definition of the field and this permits their research programs to prosper and allows them to work productively on research with members of other research communities. In effect, they conclude that the same factors which contribute to perceived fragmentation also contribute to shared understandings among core researchers.

This is a puzzling conclusion, in that a thorough empirical investigation of the field comes to conclusions that do not seem highly tied to the data. In effect, the field is studied and found to be fragmented but that result is not seen as important to core researchers. Nag, Hambrick, and Chen (2007) provide less guidance regarding how the conceptual fragmentation can be mitigated and conceptual integration furthered. They suggest that their results will enable scholars to better frame debates about the nature of the field, although how such new debates might develop is left unstated. The perspective taken here is that better developing the implied theoretical implications of current strategy perspectives will help the field to achieve more conceptual integration and also permit current researchers to develop their studies more effectively.

Ronda-Pupo and Guerras-Martin (2012) build on this idea of clarifying the basis of the strategic management field by examining the evolution of the field's core concept, strategy. They do this through a bibliometric analysis of how definitions of strategy have developed in the course of three consecutive time periods. They start with 91 different definitions in these periods and examine the key words and cluster relationships among key words for each period. By examining how their analytical results change over time, they develop a composite set of critical terms that underlie the most important theoretical approaches to strategy. In summarizing their results, they conclude that strategy involves:

> the dynamics of the firm's relationship with its environment for which the necessary actions are taken to achieve its goals and/or its performance by means of the rational use of resources. (Ronda-Pupo and Guerras-Martin, 2012: 182)

Ronda-Pupo and Guerras-Martin (2012) find that definitions of strategy were characterized in the initial time period by low levels of consensus. Over the subsequent periods, the level of consensus increased steadily, but only to levels of 'slight' or 'fair' levels. They suggest that consensus over the concept of strategy is likely to increase further, although it is unclear by how much. The authors conclude that despite the lack of consensus over its core constructs, strategy developed steadily during the time periods of the study, a conclusion that is consistent with that reached by Nag, Hambrick, and Chen (2007).

Ronda-Pupo and Guerras-Martin's (2012) conclusions regarding consensus around the strategy construct are not very strong and the authors position their study more in terms of a methodological contribution, based on their use of novel bibliometric techniques. Most interestingly, they conclude their paper with questions about whether consensus over key terms is important to the growth of a discipline and what the causes of the lack of consensus over strategy might be. In effect, the fragmentation of the strategy field is reaffirmed by these results, although little is added to debates about why this fragmentation has occurred or what should be done about it.

In considering the results of Nag, Hambrick, and Chen (2007) and Ronda-Pupo and Guerras-Martin (2012), neither presents a theoretical basis for the fragmentation of the strategy field or any hypotheses regarding impediments to greater integration of the field, so it is not surprising that the results of these studies are inconclusive. The rich findings of these studies do suggest some ways to understand the causes of strategy's fragmentation. Strategy in its many variants concerns (or can concern): 1) actions taken by a firm after an intentionally rational decision process; 2) actions taken by a firm to skillfully deploy its resources and capabilities; 3) actions taken by a firm in order to achieve goals and improve performance on varied dimensions; or 4) actions taken to manage the dynamic interactions between a firm and its environment. Fundamental questions arise for each of these sets of actions and a wide range of possibilities are readily apparent in the literature. Several points are apparent from considering the fundamental aspects of strategy shown by these studies.

A first point concerns the theoretical complexity of Strategic Management. Each of the core areas identified by these studies has a distinct set of perspectives on strategy and is the focus of considerable research. In the general areas, and often in more specific subareas, entire scholarly careers are generated. The disciplinary focus of researchers also varies by area in predictable ways due to the theoretical interests of their core disciplines (economics versus sociology versus psychology) as well as the different approaches to research design and data analysis associated with different disciplines. This is understandable and reasonable in terms of an academic division of labour, in which researchers are rewarded for systematic research programs and large numbers of high quality publications. It is doubtful, however, that the managers of firms making strategic decisions have similar incentives or focus their attention on the same set of strategic drivers as those pursued by academics. This suggests that how scholars define their research problems relative to practitioners will strongly influence the extent to which researchers shed light on how strategic decisions are made and implemented within firms and how the resulting performance of these firms is assessed.

A second point suggested by these study results is that researchers in different core strategy areas do not interact well. While numerous strategy studies make some reference to related areas, it is unusual for a study to attempt a meaningful integration between different core areas. Consider research on mergers, acquisitions, and strategic alliances. These transactions are important for practitioners and have a persistent presence in developed economies. They are also among the most popular targets for strategy research (see Gomes-Casseres, 2015 for a review.). Even with the popularity of mergers and acquisitions (M&A) research in strategy, consistent results have not accumulated in these areas and merger research displays the same fragmentation identified by Nag, Hambrick, and Chen (2007) and Ronda-Pupo and Guerras-Martin (2012)for the broader strategy field. Studies of merger determinants focus on industry and financial market factors, while studies of merger integration and alliance management are much more likely to adopt managerial perspectives and focus on psychological or organizational factors. While large sample data analysis is common for industry and financial approaches, case studies are more common for integration studies. In attempting to present general rules for these transactions, Gomes-Casseres shows that these rules represent the findings of very different research areas that are tied together by the fact of a transaction rather than by a unifying logic for how merger planning fits with merger integration or how valuation research fits with ideas of creating bundles of resources and capabilities. What is missing is a logic for M&A and alliances that permits a unified approach to research design and data collection. How the various aspects of the M&A process fit together is arguably a critical factor for developing knowledge about these transactions and their outcomes. Management and consulting practice has increasingly focused on the entire process, including post-merger integration. Academic work has not matched this level of focus and integration (Calipha, Tarba, and Brock, 2010).

A third point suggested from these studies is that while strategy perspectives espouse a dynamic and interactive view of strategic management, empirical studies that actually incorporate such a view are unusual. A fundamental premise of the field is that managers plan their strategic decisions, take action based on those decisions, and reap higher performance results by doing so. This presumes a temporal sequence that is critical to strategic theories but is seldom followed up on adequately in studies. There are a large number of studies that utilize longitudinal data sets, but relatively few that build the theoretical assumptions behind a longitudinal analysis into theory and research design. As Mosakowski and Earley (2000) suggest, while strategy papers often employ a diverse set of temporal assumptions, few do so explicitly. The theoretical and practical problems in operationalizing a dynamic and interactive view of strategy are well known. In a dynamic view, performance variables become not only outcomes of a period's activities but also informational inputs for subsequent actions and decisions. For a strategy perspective to make sense, managers must learn from their past results and adjust their activities in light of new expectations.

To make sense of the findings of Nag, Hambrick, and Chen (2007) and Ronda-Pupo and Guerras-Martin (2012), it is necessary to consider whether the issues identified by these studies are fundamental or transitional and a function of the 'youth' of the field. The argument in this chapter is that the fragmentation reported by Nag, Hambrick, and Chen (2007) and Ronda-Pupo and Guerras-Martin (2012) (and others) has fundamental bases within strategic management theory and is unlikely to change until some theoretical issues have been clarified. Four issues areas suggested by the studies discussed above have implications for the theoretical fragmentation of the strategy field: complexity, process, time, and performance.

Complexity

The domain of interest to strategic management is highly complex. This complexity contributes to the three other issue areas mentioned below. While demographic studies show that most business organizations are small, those that receive attention for their strategies are large—and often very large—employing tens of thousands and sometimes millions of workers. These firms compete in multiple and diverse product and geographic markets and span multiple institutional and regulatory systems. The reality of how these firms make and implement strategic decisions involves the activities of tens of thousands of actors, spans multiple organizational levels with complex and often overlapping authority systems, and depends on a technological context characterized by change that is rapid and difficult to predict.

Addressing the complexity of firms in their environment and market settings will of necessity influence future research by reducing the comparability of firms in research designs. The complexity of even moderately sized firms will make the overall set of strategic choices of firms into an increasingly custom bundle, such that even supposedly close competitors of a firm will appear on a closer examination to be quite different. Recognizing the complexity of firms does obviate the need for sampling designs but places a burden on researchers to justify data driven designs that neglect the specificity of firm strategies in their industry and geographic settings. Integrating areas within the field, however, will also reduce the likelihood of obtaining a sufficiently large sample to pursue a design that is publishable in many major journals. Better reflecting the complexity of strategic actors may thus bring researchers into conflict with current norms in the field regarding the size and composition of samples for studies that are publishable in major journals. Sampling has long been a problem in strategy research, whether one is concerned with reflecting the complexity of the actors or attempting to obtain a randomized sample for studies of firm strategies (Short, Ketchen, and Palmer, 2002).

Activity/Process Linkages

A second issue that is implicit by the work of Nag, Hambrick, and Chen (2007) and Ronda-Pupo and Guerras-Martin (2012) is that for sub-areas within strategic management to become better integrated, the processes by which different activities of firms are linked need to be better specified. At the most general level, firms deploy their resources and capabilities to meet perceived environmental demands and then revise and readjust those deployments based on performance results. Penrose (1959) articulates this general logic well and it is common in the strategy research literature. How such a generic process actually occurs within complex firms, however, is anything but obvious for firms possessing even modest levels of complexity. This is not solely a problem of description, but rather one of understanding how the activities and functions highlighted by Penrose for generic situations are linked in large complex bureaucracies. How do corporate planning processes differ in their ability to perceive the demands of the environment? How do firms translate their strategic decisions into implementation activities in subsidiaries? How does one assess the degree of continuity between how top managers make various types of decisions and how those decisions are carried out by their subunits? A firm's strategic decisions can be embedded in multiple processes that overlap and whose demands on the firm are inconsistent, such as when the processes by which products are brought to market are different in their timing from the firm's accounting and financial processes.

Better process specification does not require a resort to thick description. It does involve viewing process linkages as central rather than peripheral for strategy theories and viewing firm processes as more than just occurring within a 'black box' (Dobbin and Baum, 2000). For example, Parmigiani and Holloway (2011) study the antecedents of parent firm implementation capabilities and their performance implications by examining relationships between headquarters and business units in food service franchising chains. These are the questions discussed above and the authors note the methodological problems of studying such processes. To obtain a large sample for the study, however, the authors must restrict their attention to the characteristics and capabilities of these units and assess performance in terms of associations with subsequent results. The actual processes are not studied. Implementation and coordination are inferred rather than directly identified. The actual processes remain a black box.

Time

A third issue implied by Nag, Hambrick, and Chen (2007) and Ronda-Pupo and Guerras-Martin (2012) concerns the failure of strategic management theories and research to clarify their assumptions regarding time. This was referenced above, but is considered in more detail here.

Nobody denies that time is a fundamental dimension of the world that underlies all physical and social action. The basic presumptions of strategy theories, however, often go beyond commonsense ideas of linear time and involve more specialized assumptions. Theories of strategy assume intertemporal linkages between actors, resources, events, and results. Some of these claims are explicit, and central to a theoretical view such as in Helfat and Peteraf (2003) or evolutionary theories of strategy and economics (Nelson and Winter, 1982). However, Mosakowski and Earley (2000) note that while there are numerous implicit temporal aspects in strategy studies, there is little explicit recognition of specialized notions of time. Souder and Bromiley (2012), for example, report on a similar lack of explicit temporal orientation in their study of capital investments by firms. More generally, the prevalence of correlation-based designs in strategy research suggests that researchers are accustomed to thinking in cross-sectional terms. In such settings, recognizing temporal constraints is a matter of lagged correlation designs, such as that conditions at a given time correlate with performance measures at a subsequent time, while more nuanced views of time receive scant attention.

There are other examples of distinct temporal aspects of strategic decisions. Productive assets have different productive lifetimes. Differences in the time orientation of the firm's assets imply differences in capabilities as well as differences in how adaptable the firm is to environmental changes. There may also be a discontinuity between the firm's productive operations and its administrative systems. Yearly operating results may be concentrated in a particular time period while the firm needs to secure regular financing throughout a year, a situation common in industries like fashion. Discontinuities among the temporal dimensions of a firm's activities may be behind some significant strategic problems. For instance, the disconnect between the long-term nature of mortgage loans and the short term nature of firm borrowing to finance their mortgage operations was critical to the problems many mortgage firms faced during the financial crash of 2008.

Theories of strategy often imply multiple coexisting temporal frames and clarifying the interrelationships among these frames is theoretically important. Regular operations may be understood in a linear sequence, while planning and control processes operate on clear cycles of defined lengths. If the firm's strategy involves longer term investments or initiatives, such as to build market share in new areas, additional time frames may be relevant. Many of a firm's most important assets, including capability levels and reputation, may accumulate over time on the basis on persistent good performance. Firms that invest to obtain the benefits of these cumulative intangible assets stand to benefit greatly from them once they mature. Competitors who have not made such long-term investments may be impaired in competing due to their temporal disadvantage. This will be the case if competitors need to go through the same learning process that incumbents did and thus are unable to jump ahead in capabilities without putting in the required effort over time. If this is the case, then not only will competitors need to spend the requisite time in imitation, but trying to hurry the process will lead to increased costs and reduced performance due to what

Cool and his colleagues call 'diseconomies of time compression' (Cool, Dierickx, and Costa, 2012).

Temporal framing is also linked to strategies through the interrelationships assumed among firm activities, results, and subsequent adjustments. These relationships, and the activities through which they are maintained, take up time. The temporal orientation of the firm as a decision-maker is not reducible to the time frame implied by the activities of individual managers. The organization is more than the sum of its individual parts and the time frame in which the organization acts is longer than that for individual actors. Performance needs to be assessed in terms of the minimum time needed for the firm to make and implement decisions, including the time taken up by the firm's decision-making and operational processes.

Firm-level time frames also need to be matched with different and potentially conflicting temporal expectations from stakeholders. Different groups of firm stakeholders may have conflicting time requirements for information with which to evaluate firm decisions and results. Regulators will have one set of temporal needs for their decisions while investors may have different ones. For example, mergers, acquisitions, and other corporate control transactions are often evaluated by investors on the basis of share price changes immediately following the announcement of a transaction, even though regulatory filings and decisions associated with a transaction may occur over a more extended period and even though the actual performance of the transaction in question may not be known to investors for several years, if at all.

Performance

The central role of corporate performance in all areas of strategy suggests that clarifying issues around performance will be critical to improving the integration of the field. Two issue areas are especially relevant. The first is that strategic actors have multiple stakeholders, for whom different performance demands are relevant. The second concerns the endogeneity of performance variables. For any overall performance metric, the measure obtained is both an outcome that reflects on the results of firm activities from prior decisions and an input to subsequent strategic decisions that allows decision-makers to change their activities based on results and adapt to expected environmental changes.

The implication of multiple stakeholders with differing performance expectations is that performance becomes more complex and harder to understand than it is for any single summative measure, such as stock price. Bondholders will be interested in the ability of the firm to repay its debts. Equity investors will be interested in the potential for firm growth to make investments profitable. Employees will be concerned with the stability of the firm and the maintenance of employment prospects. Suppliers will be concerned with the firm's ongoing viability. Government regulators could be concerned with firm compliance in a variety of different performance domains. Local communities, industry associations, and other private actors may well have different performance expectations. It is frequently claimed that single performance measures, such as stock price, capture all of the demands placed on managers but that claim is far from clear theoretically or empirically. Different stakeholders may have their own residual risks from associating with a firm, while the residual risks of investors may be more diversifiable than often claimed. In addition, whether a multiple dimension view of performance is more helpful in explaining how firms behave than is a unidimensional view is an empirical question (Mueller, 2013).

While the idea of multiple stakeholders has a long history in strategic thinking, it has not made much headway in influencing performance ideas in current research. The complexity of performance expectations has often been papered over by reference to overall profitability or capital market measures, but the reality is more complex. For example, the product market success of a firm, in terms of market share or pricing power, will influence its ability to raise money in capital markets. The linkage of capital market performance and product market performance will in turn affect the labour market performance of the firm, such as when firm management incentives are heavily oriented towards stock options. While the stock price is growing, managers with stock incentives will be highly incented to perform. That situation changes once share price growth slows and the firm's markets mature. Some studies have addressed conflicting goals in more limited contexts. Barnett and Salomon (2012) studied the relationship between profitability and ethical performance over a large sample found a complex and inconsistent relationship, in which neither was clearly more important for firms in all circumstances.

Strategic management theories often presume that managers intend to make choices so as to maximize performance—or at least satisfice on performance goals (March and Simon, 1958). They hypothesize about how their firms arrive at the best fits with their environments and make their choices accordingly. This means that managers do not make their strategic choices randomly but instead choose on the basis of their expectations regarding how their firms will perform under different choices. This is what is meant by the *endogeneity* of strategic performance. That top managers appear to act this way is not indicative of a bad state of affairs for managers or their firms—indeed it has long been a major normative emphasis of strategic management as a field (Hamilton and Nickerson, 2003).

Even though most strategy researchers hold assumptions consistent with endogeneity, few strategy theories have been developed to work out the details of endogenous choices. Little is known about how strategic managers set performance expectations or articulate various options for comparison. The feedback mechanisms by which managers obtain data on the results of their choices and then readjust their choices based on data are not well understood. If one considers a broader array of strategic outcomes it is even less clear how managers balance data that concern more complex performance situations. So while a firm's performance in a given period may be part of a dynamic system of actions and adjustments as managers try to forge an environmental fit, research has not progressed to capture the workings of these relationships and managerial efforts to bring the firm's activities into alignment with its environment. A simpler more linear form of the system is typically provided instead.

If strategic choices are endogenous, however, statistical adjustments must be made in research designs, irrespective of whether the study's motivation fully articulates the relevant processes. Failing to account for endogeneity can lead to serious distortions in results that can be substantial enough to change the signs of statistical findings. Bascle (2008) compares endogeneity to the problem of assessing the efficacy of random trials when the trials are not random but instead driven by the researcher's expectation for one treatment option versus another. Hamilton and Nickerson (2003) discuss endogeneity problems for strategy research, given the widespread presumption of endogenous choices, and document the large number of studies in major journals that fail to make any adjustments for it.

What to Do? Process Theories and Craft Perspectives

The issues raised above suggest that some alternative approaches to thinking about strategy may be helpful in addressing the fragmentation in the field. These are not concerned with revamping current theory and empirical research in detail. Addressing the issues raised above involves more the overall view of the tasks and domain of the strategy area that motivates more specific research projects. The argument here is that strategy researchers, in pursuit of publishable papers, underemphasize and treat as peripheral or of secondary importance some aspects of the phenomena they are studying that may be much more important for understanding the strategic behaviours of large firms. These include issues of complex time frames, multiple goals, firm-level decision processes, and endogenous decisions. Neglecting these issues, which concern the overall identity and processes of the firm as a strategic actor, makes it difficult to integrate research results in a manner consistent with the overarching stories of how firms behave that motivate current research, whether based on economic or industry perspectives, the 'resource-based' view of the firm, or a view of firms as embedded institutional actors.

Refocusing on the firm as a strategic actor is not just a problem of describing the firm's activities and processes in more detail. Doing this will make the picture of strategy that emerges from a study more consistent with the details of how strategy takes place in firms. This is part of the approach of scholars studying 'strategy as practice' (Jarzabkowski, 2005). Researchers using such approaches examine the 'messy realities' of how strategic change takes place in firms and the 'lived experience' of those who take part in such processes. The issues raised by these researchers are consistent with those motivating this chapter and support claims about the fragmentation of the strategy area (Johnson et al., 2007).

While such inductive approaches are valuable, they are not germane to the issues of interest in this chapter, which concern modifying theory and research practice to mitigate fragmentation and improve coherence within the field. At a basic level, effective explanation is premised on reducing detail through abstraction and then making sense of the reduced picture reality that results, and which the researcher chooses to focus upon. Greater detail may render a study more consistent with practice, but will not of its own accord ensure more effective explanation. Inductive research approaches that fail to address theoretical issues run the risk of being both less informative and more costly. They will also have trouble contributing to a general understanding of strategy relative to that provided by more abstract approaches.

Providing greater detail without facilitating better explanation will turn strategic management research into a process for producing case studies. Even though the number of cases in use in business schools has proliferated and cases are widely available, they have been the subject of little research themselves. It is clear, however, that these studies have not contributed to the integration of the field in research journals. Gibbert, Ruigrok, and Wicki (2008) analysed 159 case studies published in journals that published strategic management research and found that while cases were strong on external validity, this came at the expense of internal and construct validity. While there appears to be a market for case based strategy research, this work has not provided an antidote to the fragmentation of the field.

The issue then is not a more realistic account of firms, but a change in which assumptions are made regarding strategy. Following the recommendations of Friedman (1953), simplified theoretical assumptions are often presumed in strategic studies, out of a concern for predictive results. Tsang (2006) notes the complexity of the phenomena in strategy studies and argues for distinguishing between assumptions that can facilitate prediction even if unrealistic from assumptions that need to be sufficiently realistic to ensure the viability of the theoretical mechanisms that researchers use in generating their predictions. More realistic assumptions can help improve predictions and allow for the integration of research results.

An important feature of strategic management is that decision and planning processes are not just concerns of researchers but are also central to top managers in large firms who make and implement strategies—and who are thus the objects of study for strategy researchers. This has been the case from the beginnings of the strategy research in studies of strategic planning and control systems (Lorange and Vancil, 1976; Lorange, 1984). The modelling of firm-level processes was also central to 'Carnegie School' researchers, such as March, Simon, and Cyert (March and Simon, 1958; Cyert and March, 1963), as well as to the influential studies of decision processes based on the work of Allison and Quinn (Allison, 1971; Quinn, 1980). There has been continuing interest in planning and decision processes among researchers, but this work has generally not been published in top journals but in practitioner journals or trade volumes (Mintzberg, 1994; Hamel and Prahalad, 1994).

Wiltbank et al. (2006) make use of the earlier planning and decision literature to consider the merits of strategy approaches focusing on prediction versus control. They present a decision process for firms to adapt to their environmental demands, pursue multiple goals, and control the implementation of choices. They conclude by arguing for an approach to strategy that is non-predictive but rather enables top managers to make choices that effectively adapt to changing environments and control the implementation of their choices. They highlight the suggestion above that the predictive orientation of strategic research is not well aligned with the interests of top managers and practitioners in making predictions and strategizing for their firms. This lack of alignment may be a correlate of the factors contributing to the intellectual fragmentation of the strategy field.

A related view on these issues concerns the practices and policies of editors at the top strategy journals and how scholars respond to them. Richard Bettis, a coeditor of *Strategic Management Journal*, writes about the 'search for asterisks' (Bettis, 2012). By this he means the focusing of researcher effort on studies most likely to product statistically significant results (noted in articles by asterisks). His argument links three practices that are common to strategy researchers. First, exceptional statistical results are sought and written up for submission to journals. Second, exceptional results if published are seldom followed up on for confirmation through replication studies. Third, the normal expectations regarding firms and their strategies, which form the 'null hypothesis' in tests, are seldom if ever tested. Null results do not get published. Bettis argues that these practices, however understandable, are at odds with the norms of scientific investigation that are claimed to be underlying the research and publication process. Harrison et al. (2016) present empirical results consistent with these observations.

Scientific enquiry, once faced with reported exceptions, should pursue such exceptions to determine if they are ultimately replicable. Bettis also decries that common habit of requiring nearly all empirical work to include a significant portion on theory development covering the test of interest in a paper. The overall implication of Bettis' concerns is to avoid a process that systematically publishes exceptional findings, seldom if ever works to validate those findings, seldom if ever validates or updates baseline theoretical expectations or allots insufficient journal space for theory development that is distinct from empirical testing. The impact of all of these issues is probably consistent with the intellectual fragmentation that is the subject of this chapter, with growing numbers of separate exceptional results that are insufficiently validated by follow-up research and inadequately integrated by overall theoretical perspectives into which research in the field can be best understood. While the journal reviewing and publication policies are much too involved to consider in detail here, the concerns raised by Bettis are consistent in their implications with the arguments presented here.

It does imply that without some more thought about general theoretical approaches, the fragmentation of the field noted in the studies reviewed above is unlikely to change significantly. In the remainder of this chapter, two general approaches are developed to address integration issues. One is an idea of process research that is oriented towards better integrating aspects of the strategy field. The second is a suggestion for reframing strategic management in terms of craftsmanship, a view that will permit the integration of process theories, dynamic performance processes, and complex sets of performance objectives that potentially span multiple audiences.

A Pragmatic Approach to Strategic Processes

Process approaches to strategy have a mixed history within the field. Process is a frequently invoked concept in management (Pettigrew, 1992). In spite of this, what constitutes process research has been difficult to define and what is called a 'process' has had multiple meanings. Examples range from the literature on strategic planning and control (Lorange and Vancil, 1976; Lorange, 1984) to decision theories of the 'Carnegie School' (Cyert and March, 1963) to economic studies of innovation and industry evolution (Nelson and Winter, 1982), to sociological studies of institutionalization (Oliver, 1991; Kostova, Roth, and Dacin, 2008).

For all of its multiple uses in strategy, process is not well developed theoretically. What is meant by a process perspective? Van de Ven (1992) identifies the three basic ways in which strategic process is considered. Process is invoked to identify a causal logic leading to some outcome. Process can also detail the sequence of activities by individuals in pursuit of some goal or outcome. At this general level, however, process is sufficiently broad that these same characterizations may lay behind varied strategic perspectives as well. It is difficult to see how such a diffuse and general view of process helps to improve theoretical integration in strategy. Van de Ven suggests that for process views to better develop, they need to be better linked to theories of strategic content and organization.

Shanley and Peteraf (2006) suggest an approach for building up process views of strategy not in terms of a comprehensive theory but in terms of the theoretical contributions that process ideas bring to a given research question. They start with the general notion of process as helping to understand complexity in strategic actors. They suggest three traits of process views that can help reduce complexity in particular situations. These are: 1) interconnectedness; 2) intertemporal linkages; and 3) inter-relational linkages.

Interconnectedness

Strategy frameworks often focus on how and why firms deploy their resources and capabilities across dispersed geographic and product markets. Industry approaches to strategy that view firms in the context of sets of suppliers, buyers, competitors, potential entrants, and even providers of substitute and complementary providers, presume processes by which industry transactions occur and industry structure evolves (Porter, 1998; McGahan, 2004). Not only market structure, but market subgroupings such as strategic groups and industry networks do not emerge instantaneously but develop in particular ways such that the processes involved matter (Peteraf and Shanley, 1997). How strategy is influenced by its geographic context remains an open question generating considerable interest, especially in such areas as mergers and acquisitions (Yurov et al., 2013).

This connectedness is not just a matter of linkages across geographic and product markets. A distinctive characteristic of large firms is that their action is inherently connected across levels of analysis. Top managers report to their boards of directors regarding their goals and performance expectations for a coming year. Corporate plans, in turn, depend on the activities of divisions and other subunits, whose managers are better connected with and knowledgeable regarding the subunits and their served markets. This does not begin to address the ways in which firms are able to coordinate their activities going forward with those of suppliers, buyers, and complementary actors. While progress in information systems has helped flatten these structures in recent decades, the processes by which goals are set, funds are provided, performance reviewed, and future activities revised must of necessity cross organizational levels, often multiple times in a given cycle.

It is tempting to assume that cross-level linkages occur, and this is indeed the approach taken in studies that seek to obtain a larger sample of organizations. It is risky to make such an assumption for a number of reasons. There could be a failure of coordination across levels caused by poor training or communication. The activities of interest may have occurred through different sets of linkages or through multiple lines of action that harmed coordination with later activities or with other units. The failure of linkage may not be consequential by itself but may correlate with some deeper problems with a firm's strategy.

Spanning of levels of analysis has been of theoretical interest in strategy since the field's inception. The problems that prompted the growth of the field were those related to the growth of large firms in modern economies (Barnard, 1938; Chandler, 1962, 1977). Strategy research developed as a problem-focused area oriented towards the problems faced by managers as their firms grew larger than most other firms, often by a wide margin. To accomplish this growth, managers had to solve organizational problems that greatly complicated the ways in which their firms were managed and their performance was assessed. For example, as shown by Chandler (1977), if growth was to be profitable, it had to be accompanied by an internal division of labour, task specialization, and a managerial hierarchy, that along with size allowed economies of scale and scope to be realized. These newly grown firms also collaborated at an industry level to consolidate competitive markets into oligopolies and permit survivors from industry shakeouts to establish sustainable strategies through collective action.[1]

The industries in which firms developed these capabilities often possessed underlying technical and scientific systems that forced firms to make substantial investments in research and development to support existing products and keep managers abreast of technical changes that affected their firms. Given the increased reach of these firms, it is understandable that they developed skills that enabled them to successfully relate to other actors in the environment affected by the firm's actions, whether these included lobbying, negotiating, or complying with government regulations.

Firms changed management processes in response to these changes in organization and activities. To succeed on a longer-term basis, firms had to institutionalize these

---

[1] See Besanko et al., 2016, chapter 13 for recent studies of corporate structures.

innovations in their management and control systems. A key to these changes was the ability to bridge levels to allow these complex firms to succeed. Some firms, such as General Electric, have engaged in such management innovation from their founding. GE, for instance, came into existence linking three distinct business areas—electric power generation, power distribution, and consumer products that helped grow the overall demand for electricity. For most firms, organizational and management processes evolved as firms faced new challenges. These management processes were central to the founding of the strategic management field (Schendel and Hofer, 1979).

Intertemporal Linkages

Strategy perspectives that presume a specialized time frame also require an enhanced basis for a process perspective. This is needed when specific activities must occur in an appropriate sequence for a theoretical perspective to be validated. Sometimes these time frames are explicit, but they are often not explicitly developed. Not all temporal claims are the same, however, and surprisingly few strategy perspectives incorporate them as features of competition, learning, or research and development.

Consider the place of contingency perspectives on strategy. The idea that firms search to achieve some degree of 'fit' between the demands of their business environment and the particular capabilities and resources available for competition has been a common theme in strategy theories from the beginning of the field. Indeed, it is arguably one of the central constructs of strategy. It is present in the classical management writings of Barnard and Penrose and clearly articulated in structural contingency theory (Child, 1972). Subsequent incarnations of fit approaches can be found in a wide range of strategy perspectives, including competitive strategy, generic strategies, the resource based view of the firm, resource dependence theory, and institutional theories of industries and markets. All of these approaches share the perspective that firms act to establish a beneficial relationship with actors in their environment who can aid its survival, growth, legitimacy, profitability, or some other desirable outcome that can be linked to environmental positioning.

The earliest and most influential antecedents of contingency approaches clearly articulated the importance the temporal processes that firms followed in growing, responding to challenges, developing capabilities, and improving their performance on multiple dimensions in their business environments. The work of Chandler (1962, 1977; Chandler and Hikino, 1990) is most noteworthy in establishing the idea of strategy and showing how strategy, structure, and industry evolution interact for corporate actors. Other early theorists also incorporated iterative adaptation processes as central features of their work. Penrose (1959) made an interactive process of how top managers bring their firms into alignment with their environment a central part of her theory. Penrose (1960) supported these ideas with a detailed historical case study of the Hercules Powder Company to illustrate her principles. Fligstein (1993) provides an influential sociological critique of Chandler and others while assuming similar temporal processes.

As ideas of fit and contingency moved into the mainstream of strategy research, how the research was conducted changed, consistent with increased biases towards large sample designs. As this happened, attention on explicitly testing firm evolutionary processes waned and study designs became more focused upon showing associations between firm and environmental characteristics across a wide sample. Without attention to the processes by which firms move into and out of alignment with their environments, it is not surprising that the meaning of 'fit' becomes progressively unwieldy and results fail to accumulate. Child (1972) raised these issues early on noting the problems caused by the failure to recognize the endogenous role of managerial choice in theories of firm-environment fit. In a broader review, Venkatraman (1989) identifies multiple meanings of the relationships between an organization and its environment that could be relevant to fit, noting the different statistical tests that are needed for different meanings. While numerous studies have looked at fit, the processes by which fit develops or unravels at a given time or in given environmental conditions received less attention and remain undertheorized (Drazin and Van de Ven, 1985). While fit approaches remain common in strategy research, they are increasingly employed more as metatheories than as explicit theoretical motivations for studies.

An exception to these issues is research on *dynamic managerial capabilities* (Helfat and Martin, 2014), which considers how firms align with their environments but addresses the issues with traditional fit studies by emphasizing the role of managerial capabilities, in particular cognitive skills, human capital, and social capital. The intuition is that firms whose managers possess greater dynamic capabilities can better address the demands of the environments, defined in terms of a variety of goals. It is unclear that this research sheds light on the processes by which firms change and move into or out of environmental alignment—or even how the capabilities of particular managers contribute to firms' change processes. These studies link capabilities to outcomes with intervening processes being imputed. That does not necessarily pose a problem, unless the nature of the underlying process is unclear, which is often the case. There are many ways in which firms can adapt to environmental demands, just as there are many ways for firms to compete. How a process leads to a given result is important but seldom clarified. If a firm manages to respond to an environmental demand, is that an example of successful adaptation? Has that firm developed a new skill or capability? When is it defensible to impute a process from a result and when does doing so constitute the assuming away of process?

Intertemporal linkages are also critical for understanding more limited strategic domains where the issues raised above for strategy management field appear in a microcosm. Consider M&A. These transactions continue to generate huge volumes of research, despite the complexities associated with the combination of large freestanding firms and the lack of much consensus about how these transactions work (Gomes-Casseres, 2015; Calipha, Tarba, and Brock, 2010). The continuing interest in these transactions is understandable, due to their monetary value and the large number of people they affect. The lack of consensus about M&A is harder to understand but is likely due to the temporal structuring of how M&A transactions occur and the lack of explicit temporal linkages for researchers regarding the steps in the merger process. There is a clear legal event called a merger or acquisition, which takes place at a specific time and must follow an elaborate set of institutional rules. This event sets out separate action domains that are studied separately with different theoretical perspectives. Pre-merger issues, including planning, valuation, due diligence, and negotiations, are the focus of some researchers. Post-merger issues, including communications and public relations, integration, and even divestiture, typically concern different actors and are studied by different researchers, often using reduced samples and more qualitative research methodologies.

Analysing strategic M&A performance has proven difficult, due to problems of specifying performance expectations—or even when the merger event itself is sufficiently complete. Post-merger performance in the acquired firm is often highly problematic, given the turnover of decision-makers and the lack of continuity between pre-and post-acquisition processes and management regimes. These problems make it more understandable why the principal performance measures for M&A research remain those based on stock price changes upon a deal's announcement, even though such measures are at best expectations of events yet to occur (Sirower, 1997). Studies of large samples of mergers and their performance or studies of how particular transactions fit into broader programs of corporate development, have been unusual (Ravenscraft and Scherer, 1987; Porter, 1987). Detailed studies of individual merger cases have been unusual as well, and a recent review of the literature called for efforts at consolidating research on post-merger integration (Calipha, Tarba, and Brock, 2010).

Inter-relational Linkages

The people at the top of large firms, the decisions they make, and the actions they take have long had a central role in strategy research. Barnard (1938) focused on top managers, and studies of CEOs, the top management team (TMT), and middle managers have been consistent focal points of researchers ever since. Despite its central role in strategy perspectives, it is not surprising that the study of managers (especially 'top managers') is a distinct and complex area of study in its own right (Finkelstein, Hambrick, and Cannella, 2009). What managers actually do on the job, however, is far from obvious and attempts to identify the key tasks of top managers or integrate what we know about them have not provided clear results. What is particularly important for top managers is that much of their work is inter-relational, especially areas such a coordination and control. This makes it highly problematic to view managers as repositories of capabilities that can be summed up across a management team. How managers interact with other managers and with the rest of the firm is also important.

More importantly, the choices of top managers determine their firms' strategic postures, the ways in which they change direction and respond to the environment, and the commitments that make their positions hard to change. In effect, top managers provide the content that is carried out through the firm's administrative structures and processes (Hambrick and Mason, 1984). Understanding managers is critical for understanding how their firms make decisions, deploy resources in pursuit of those decisions, and adjust activities going forward on the basis of new information and feedback on past choices. Whether the construct is 'manager' or 'decision-maker', it is tempting to analogize from what we know about individuals to the situation faced by large and complex firms. Such analogies may not be warranted. Not only are individual managers likely to be highly limited decision-makers, but the actual decision-maker for large firms is more likely to be a collective rather than an individual.

The firm's top management team (TMT)—or C-Suite—is composed of individuals of different experiences and skills who are organized in a complex senior management division of labour. The TMT comprises traditional senior executive ranks, along with the leaders of the firm's major subunits. In addition to these executives, there are also more specialized senior staff positions, such as the General Counsel and the chief financial officer (CFO).and a variety of senior staff positions with responsibility for legal, financial, regulatory, and other specialized parts of the firm. In recent years, there has been a proliferation of newer 'chief' functional positions, such as the chief information officer (CIO) and the chief marketing officer (CMO). The size of these teams has increased substantially since the 1980s (Guadalupe, Li, and Wulf, 2013).

How TMTs operate as collective decision-makers is complex. At one level, the TMT is a group of individuals, led by the chief executive officer (CEO). These individuals vary in their areas of expertise and responsibility and thus in what they bring to the team's deliberations. They also vary in their level and basis of compensation. Within the team there are subgroups, some formal, such as an executive committee or specialized subcommittee. There can also be informal subgroups, as well as a general climate based on how the TMT has operated in the past in responding to environmental pressures. Finally, many members of the TMT represent subunits or other groups within the firm. While there may well be regularities in TMT behaviours over a given period, due to such factors as CEO tenure, it is hard to justify a simplistic view of such a team as analogous to a unitary rational decision-maker. Studies that fail to recognize the complexity of relationships in the decision-making function of large firms will likely generate confusing and inconclusive results. This situation can be improved by developing theory about how the firm comes to operate as a consistent decision-maker—at least for its strategic decisions. Related to this is a need to clarify how the TMT is embedded in the organizational context of the broader firm—the context in which strategic decisions are implemented.

Agency, Strategy, and Craft

The argument to this point has noted the perceived fragmentation of strategic management as an area of inquiry that has been noted at various points since the area's inception and that persists today, as shown by Nag, Hambrick, and Chen (2007) and Ronda-Pupo and Guerras-Martin (2012). The results of these studies suggest some broad issue areas that may have contributed to the field's fragmentation. These concern the complexity of the topical domain, the lack of compelling ideas about activities and processes are linked in complex firms, the lack of articulated assumptions regarding the multiple time frames in which strategic action is embedded, and a failure to accommodate endogenous managerial choice into theories of strategic action. Suggestions were offered for enhancing the process issues with strategy by enhancing theories along dimensions where process issues have been most pronounced, especially in areas of inter-relational, intertemporal, and interconnected action. Addressing only the process issues raised above would likely not lead to improved integration. Along with better theory on process, better theory is needed on how strategic actors make decisions, act to carry them out through large organizations in complex contexts, and reevaluate and revise their decisions on the basis of performance and environmental interactions. This forms what social theorists sometimes refer to as an agency construct (Emirbayer and Mische, 1998).[2] There are presumptions regarding human action in most theories, although they often remain implicit. How the theorized idea of agency in a situation accords with the behaviours and choices of real actors provides the empirical side to agency theorizing.

Emirbayer and Mische (1998) note the difficulties of social theorists in accounting for purposeful action in complex settings. These difficulties lead to explanations that either overemphasize rational choice freed from contextual constraints or else presume a highly contextualized setting that overly limits the potential for understanding how individuals can influence their settings and act effectively. This is a longstanding problem of social theory that goes back to classical debates about free will versus determinism. Emirbayer and Mische present an enhanced idea of agency that seeks to understand action as embedded in ongoing relationships, informed by the past, and oriented towards the future. Their idea of human agency has three elements: iteration, projectivity, and practical evaluation. *Iteration* refers to the selective reactivation by actors of past patterns of thought and action. This aspect of agency promotes the consistency of actions and decisions with past experiences and enables the maintenance of the actor's identity over time. *Projectivity* involves the generation by actors of possible future courses of action. This aspect of agency concerns how actors are able to make use of the past to generate options for the future. *Practical Evaluation* refers to the capacity of actors to make practical and normative judgements among alternative courses of action, based on dilemmas of experience, emerging demands, and situational ambiguities. These elements involve processes of problem identification, judgement, choice, and follow through on choices.

---

[2] This is not to be confused with *Agency Theory* (Eisenhardt, 1989), an economics-based theory of incentives and information frequently used in strategy research.

Strategy and the Agency Construct

While there may be other candidates, the set of agency assumptions behind strategic management can best be summarized in terms of the idea of endogenous top management strategic choices discussed above. The top manager is the strategic actor who makes decisions that match the skills, capabilities, and resources of his firm with his perceptions of the demands placed on the firm by the business environment. Those decisions are then implemented, performance is assessed, and changes are made in subsequent activities to improve on prior performance or new information and move the firm into better alignment with the environment. Penrose (1959, chapter 3) is an early example of this, but similar sets of assumptions are noted by others, such as Hamilton and Nickerson (2003), who raise the issue in the context of endogeneity issues in strategy research.

The Emirbayer and Mische agency framework is informative for understanding the fragmentation of the strategy field. Many of these points match up well with those already made above and suggest the need for greater clarity. At a basic level, the identification of the strategic decision-maker is unclear. Is it the top manager? Is it the manager of a division or some other subunit? Among managers, are some strategic and some not? Is there collective decision-making involved in a choice, and if so, how does the collective decision-maker operate?

In terms of the embeddedness of decisions and actions, the assumptions regarding strategic decisions tend to focus on rational decision models, often financial in nature. The embedded nature of strategic management is seldom emphasized, although it receives more attention in case studies. There is if anything more popular attention on research approaches that eschew the embedded nature of decisions in favour of more 'disruptive' approaches (Christensen, 1997). This detachment can also be extended to more complex decision processes. The common distinction between decision-making and implementation is a common form of this. As mentioned above with mergers and acquisitions, the individuals who negotiate and value mergers may be different from the corporate decision-makers who approve them, who in turn are different from the business unit managers who are most involved in integrating new acquisitions into the acquiring firm, or the acquired firm managers who turn over in large numbers following mergers.

Linking current action and anticipated 'projective' action with past actions and decisions is also undertheorized in strategy research. Apart from some prominent firms with established well known histories, there is little indication of strong organizational memories, especially given the tendencies of CEO and their teams to turn over frequently. The resistance of firms to the maintenance of corporate records for any time longer than required by law also contributes to the lack of linkage with or knowledge of past events. Ideas of 'corporate memory' have little basis in current strategic research. While there has been theoretical interest in path dependence, evolution, and related ideas (Nelson and Winter, 1982; Pettigrew, 1985; North, 2005), these are more exceptional in strategy than in economic history or technology studies (the work of Chandler notwithstanding).

Paradoxically with strategy research, while there has been much attention on the choice of particular strategies, this has not been matched by attention to how particular strategic choices solve the problems faced by the firms adopting them and how these choices are or are not consistent with the historical actions of these firms. For example, while the resource-based view of the firm emphasizes the matching of firm capabilities and resources with environmental opportunities, there is little theory on how these matching processes occur. More often the logic is invoked to explain a strategic configuration already in place.

At a basic level, the linking of past actions, current situations, and future actions implied by the Emirbayer and Mische framework is not just a matter of information systems and data, but a matter of collectively held beliefs about the firm's past, its current situation, and future prospects. Even with adequate data, the absence of some minimal consensus regarding the firm in time would render firm decision-making problematic. The nature of such consensus could differ by problem area and by the managers involved in a decision. It could be threatened by significant turnover in the TMT, whether intentional or not. Such contingencies make better understanding of the TMTs of large firms an even more important research priority.

Kaplan and Orlikowski (2013) apply these ideas of Emirbayer and Mische in their field study of strategy-making in a communications firm facing an industry crisis following the end oif the Internet bubble. Using a detailed ethnographic research design and focusing on strategy practice, they look at five product teams involved concurrently in determining how the firm would respond to its crisis through changes in the management of particular products. As they observed the teams, they noticed that the progress of the teams in making product strategy decisions depended on the degree to which team members were able to mesh their conflicting individual interpretations of what had happened in the past, what the current problems were, and what was a reasonable expectation of future developments. When the teams were able to maintain a basic level of agreement regarding these temporal issues, the project moved ahead towards resolution. When events or changes in people brought these agreements into question, progress on a project stalled. When this occurred, the teams had to engage in what Kaplan and Orlikowski (2013) refer to as 'temporal work' to recast a consensus on temporal understandings as a basis for getting projects back on track. They provide detailed characterizations of team processes as they engaged in this time work and argue that this process work around securing team agreement on temporal issues is as crucial for understanding how teams work in times of crisis as any formal descriptions or plans of the project teams.

Kaplan and Orlikowski (2013) are persuasive for how temporal issues are negotiated and managed by active teams. Their results raise issues for how such temporal understandings are arrived at elsewhere in the firm, such as by the TMT that mandated project reviews or in other divisions of the firm with different histories and technical mandates. Their work makes it clear that a firm's temporal orientation is more complex in practice than the straightforward scheme of Emirbayer and Mische (1998) would suggest and can vary both across levels within the firm as well as across major subunits, raising the question of just which temporal orientation is relevant for a given situation.

In the next section, an alternative set of assumptions regarding agency is proposed, one based on the work of Sennett (2008) and employing ideas of 'craft', 'craftwork', and 'craftsmanship'. This is presented below, along with some material on related approaches.

Craftsmanship as an Agency Assumption

Sennett (2008) presents a set of micro level assumptions about action in private domains that, despite some similarities, appears at odds with the basic agency assumptions of strategic management discussed earlier. He defines craftsmanship as 'an enduring, basic human impulse, the desire to do a job well for its own sake'. While talking about 'craft' and 'craftsmanship' brings up images of musicians, chefs, carpenters, writers, painters, and sculptors, Sennett develops an abstract set of assumptions that is meant to cover much if not all 'knowledge work.' This includes such modern occupations as programmers and physicians. That craft work has a quality requirement means that there are quality standards than can be written down to some degree and also communicated to an individual in training so that the craft can be learned.

Sennett suggests a potentially broad applicability for his view of craft by extending the idea to such activities as parenting and citizenship. Indeed, any work that is not amenable to automation and routinization could be organized around craft principles. As a basic assumption, craft refers to the organization of work rather than to the capabilities of workers. Most people possess the capabilities to work towards quality standards and become intelligent craftsmen. This includes tasks whose principal activities involve coordinating and cooperating with others. Cooperation is part of craft. Managers can be craftsmen.

How do craftsmen act? How does the craftsman gain skill? Sennett presumes the linkage of thought and action and by implication attacks the distinction between skilled and deskilled work traditionally common in the organization of industry. He assumes a linkage of thought and action and in particular that all skills, even highly abstract ones, have their origins in a person reflecting on their physical efforts. In a work situation, an individual attempts to accomplish some tasks with a given set of tools, in an environment characterized by ambiguity and resistance. Ambiguity and resistance are not only characteristics of the natural environment but also of the social environment in which the craftsman is embedded. As the craftsman repeats his efforts and considers his successes and failures, he uses his imagination to identify the most effective ways to proceed and thus develops technological knowledge and skills. Over time, he learns to develop routines that free up his attention and enable him to identify and resolve other more advanced or more salient problems. Through this iterative interaction of goals, actions, and imaginative reflection on results, the craftsman develops and prospers. This is not a deskilled and boring iteration, but a process in which the craftsman is engaged and anticipatory. It is not a linear process but an irregular one, due to the ambiguities of environmental resistance and the unpredictability of imagination and individual learning.

The craftsman is embedded in a social order and is not an isolated worker. His social order provides the craftsman with his tasks, his problems to solve, his quality standards, and his feedback. Craftsmanship is thus 'joined skill in community.' Workshops provide a communal atmosphere and social structure that guides skill development through personal contact rather than written instruction. The value of disciplined skill versus other success criteria such as inspiration, genius, personal favouritism, or family connections is enforced through the authority of the workshop and its denomination of masters and apprentices. Guilds and other forms of collective organization also enforce work standards collectively and enable cooperation.

To illustrate these dynamics, Sennett discusses the case of how Renaissance artists broke away from the constraints of the commune and guild system to gain more autonomy in relation to their wealthy court patrons and more independence in the design and execution of their artistic work. The key to this attempt at change from medieval order was to project a new image for themselves and their work to their new publics. Rather than being under the astrological sign of Mercury, as had other skilled craftsmen, the new artists projected themselves as being under Saturn, with its associated brooding and mysterious nature. This attempted shift was only partially successful, but this case provides an example of the potential for social movement, and even a client focused strategy, in the context of the Renaissance. Wittkower and Wittkower (1963) provide a detailed history of this case.

Craftsmanship assumptions, while framed in terms of individuals and small groups, are also intended to be applicable to more complex organizations. Sennett clearly notes the importance of coordination and cooperation in how craft enterprises work. This suggests that classes of positions that tend to be found in larger organizations, such as managers and boundary spanners, fall into the domain of craft management. The applicability of these arguments to larger scale settings is also evident in Sennett's examples, which span a wide range of different workshop settings, some quite large. Since Sennett's approach is largely historical, many of his examples will be from medieval or early modern sources. In addition to these examples, however, major examples are also drawn from large modern undertakings such as the Manhattan Project (to develop the first atomic bomb during the Second World War) or the software development team at the Linux Corporation, in its cooperative development of open source code.

Regarding assumed goals, it was mentioned above that craftsman assumptions presume endogenous performance expectations. Craftsmen have objectives regarding what they wish to achieve. Sennett's arguments also lead to a multiple goals situation with potential conflicts among goals. The key here is the idea of quality driven work and the presumption that craftsmen will pursue that work 'for its own sake', out of a commitment to doing a high quality job. This commitment to quality provides a potential motivational benefit. By being involved in their work and its definition and by being committed to its quality, craftsmen will be more highly motivated to succeed. This increased motivation—Sennett refers to it as an 'obsession'—will make the craftsman more effective overall than the non-craftsman for similar work.[3] Pursuing craft work for its own sake also opens up the potential for goal conflicts, since projects will be commissioned for reasons potentially in conflict with craft-driven perfection. For example, a client may want a particular outcome under time pressures. The particular circumstances of a project may restrict the raw materials that can be brought to bear on it. If a craftsman is part of a larger workshop, the multiple projects of the workshop may also conflict in their demands on the craftsman. There may also be conflicts over competing time frames. This suggests that the active balancing of multiple objectives and their related performance demands is central to the craftsman's work and that there is no overall goal, including the quality of the work itself, to which other goals can be subordinated. Balancing conflicting demands is central to the work.

Craftsmanship and Strategy

What are the implications of Sennett's craftsman perspective for the issues raised earlier concerning the fragmentation of strategy as an area of inquiry? The intent here is twofold: 1) to consider what the craftsman assumptions suggest that is at variance with the current orientation of the field; and 2) to consider what the craftsman assumptions suggest that are currently latent in the strategy field.

To begin with, Sennett's work suggests much greater clarity is needed regarding who in the firm is part of the strategic decision-making team. At the level of assumptions, Sennett's craftsman learns by thinking, doing, and reflecting about his or her core tasks with commitment to quality work. If large firms are run by a top management teams (TMTs), then research on how the TMT goes about its business as a collective decision-maker is an important place to start. TMT research has not been prominent in the strategy field in recent years, despite the development of new approaches to organizing the TMT in practice, as well as new thinking on the role of the board in the firm's strategic decisions (Guadalupe, Li, and Wulf, 2013).

Sennett's claim that nearly everyone is capable of taking part in quality-driven work suggests that continuity within strategic processes of the firm is both worthwhile and possible. Sennett's work also suggests that the links between the actors involved in strategic decisions and those involved in the implementation of those decisions needs more theorizing. The implication is that the number of individuals who potentially influence the strategic decisions of a firm is much larger than strategy research typically presumes. Recall that the TMT research noted above was noteworthy because of its expansion of the decision-making function in the firm beyond the traditional focus on managers at the very top of the firm's hierarchy. If strategy and implementation are strongly linked, and if strong links are important for performance, then some reconceptualization of theories about the decision processes of large firms may be in order. These points were already alluded to above in discussing of M&A decisions where the

---

[3] See Sennett, 2008, part 3 for a discussion of quality 'obsession'.

failure to 'get everyone on the same page' could lead to significant implementation risks. Poor implementation could even be accompanied by resistance from those who were not involved in or committed to decisions but who are threatened by their consequences (Vallas, 2006).

Sennett's work also suggests the need for research on how firms identify strategies from past performance and how new strategic options are generated linking the firm's past experiences with it projected challenges. As suggested above, it is likely that firms generally do not base their strategic decisions on their past experiences, except to the extent that they are committed by the past decisions or constrained by environmental factors. This may be less of a problem for smaller firms who may possess a recoverable memory and some continuity in leadership, but that is less likely for larger firms. The role of key advisory firms in strategic decision processes is also of interest, especially to the extent that these advisors help or hinder the efforts of firms to ground their decisions on their experience, their profile of capabilities, and the projections of top managers regarding environmental demands. If these advisory firms prove to be substitutes for the development of a management capacity to learn from experience rather than complements, then their employment may prove more harmful than helpful to performance.

Some rethinking is also needed on matters of corporate goals if Sennett's assumptions about the need for balancing of potentially conflicting goals is taken seriously. While large firms know this very well, there is some confusion in theory and sometime rhetoric among researchers about the degree to which the performance demands of potentially competing stakeholders must be understood. It is not theoretically clear that the demands of one set of stakeholders (shareholders) dominate those of other stakeholders. It is also unclear that if a firm maximizes on some overarching goal (profitability; share price) then the satisfaction of other stakeholder performance expectations will follow. At a minimum, this suggests that some alternative models of studying how firms relate to multiple stakeholders could be considered and tested.

Mintzberg, Strategy, and Craft

Mintzberg (1987) applied the idea of craft to strategy before Sennett. He provides an analogy between the activity of a stereotypical craftsman artist and the tasks facing strategic managers. His point is that what a single craftsman does can be informative regarding what managers should do in strategizing for large firms—'face other way as a potter must manage her craft, so too managers must craft their strategy.' Mintzberg raises a number of issues that are related to those covered in this chapter, for example that strategy is a mixture of intention, action, and reflection that is often difficult to disentangle. He also notes the difficulty in analogizing about how an organization must of necessity make decisions on the basis of how individual craftsmen go about their work. Craftsmen are not linear and 'rational' in their work and neither should corporate decision-makers be strictly linear in their work. Craftsmen both decide and implement and managers would make better decisions if they linked decision-making and implementation.

Mintzberg's analogical reasoning gets in the way, however, and it is far from clear what the point of his article is, apart from the need to eschew overly rational stereotypes of managerial decision-making and reflect the messy but richer approach of craftsmen. His intuition of the nature of managerial work is insightful and appealing for a practitioner audience. The analogy linking craft and strategy is well taken and his points are consistent with many of Sennett's observations. Mintzberg's essay is not analytically developed, however, and that was not his intention. This makes it unclear what the implications of his perspective are for those seeking to craft better strategy research by making use of his portrait of the craftsman.

Conclusion

There have long been concerns regarding the theoretical integration of strategy as an area of academic enquiry. These were evident since the earliest key texts in the field, and have continued to arise, more or less, at regular intervals until today. Fragmentation is not necessarily a problem for an area. After all, a major development in the field has been its receiving increasing interest from social science disciplines like economics, sociology, and psychology, and there is a growing acceptance of strategy topics in core discipline journals. To the extent that strategic management maintains its interest in being an interdisciplinary area with strong roots in practice, however, the issue of fragmentation becomes a larger concern.

Recent studies have considered fragmentation issues and sought to validate them using innovative bibliometric methods. These studies found fragmentation in the field and low levels of consensus on such matters as the definition of strategy—the core construct of the field. Despite these results, the researchers associated with these studies reached few conclusions regarding the causes of fragmentation, its importance for the field, or steps that may help mitigate it. These conclusions in the face of results confirming fragmentation are puzzling.

Addressing the theoretical integration of strategic management does not necessarily require that core researchers change their activities or limit their productive research programs. A field more integrated and less fragmented by *fiat* is not a substitute for the field as it currently stands. What is needed are efforts to improve and extend current theoretical approaches to address issues that are conducive to fragmentation. This is not necessarily a matter of developing new theory, although that could certainly be part of the effort.

At some level, a degree of fragmentation is to be expected and even welcomed. As economic conditions change, technology progresses, and globalization continues, it is reasonable to expect strategies to change and for researchers to experience a disconnect of sorts between what they are currently studying and the state of practice among the elite firms that researchers hope to understand through their studies. Even among cutting edge firms, however, the development of practice is likely to be uneven, as nimble start-ups develop into large bureaucracies and find that the practices that work well in some industries fail to work in others or that the innovative practices of small ventures cannot easily be transplanted into large firms due to conflicts with bureaucratic routines and incentives towards volume and growth. These developments in the broader world may actually serve to invigorate researchers and permit them to update entire research agendas that may have grown stale or out of touch with practice.

Having said this, the fragmentation in the strategy field appears to be real and grounded in how strategy researchers go about their work of developing theory and crafting study designs. The results of Nag, Hambrick, and Chen (2007) and Ronda-Pupo and Guerras-Martin (2012) are compelling, even if their interpretations are less so. These results are consistent with critiques of the field that have been raised occasionally since the field's inception. This chapter has discussed issues associated with this fragmentation, as well as some issues where the incentives of scholars for publishing and the biases at some journals regarding what is chosen for publication may contribute to fragmentation. In concluding the chapter, it is reasonable to discuss some general directions for addressing fragmentation.

As already suggested, a first step towards reducing fragmentation is to make explicit the background assumptions regarding levels of analysis, temporality, or multiple stakeholders, so that process issues behind a decision a can be identified, understood, and assessed. For example, a study of a firm's use of internal competition for innovation among subunits will benefit from clarifying the organizational conditions underlying such a strategy, the market and technological conditions making such a strategy plausible, and the evolving experience of the firm in managing such innovation. As Jarzabkowski and her colleagues have recently argued (2016), practices are embedded in organizational contexts and studying them in isolation is risky. While such designs will lead to richer results, they will also reduce the potential for comparing across firms and require more focus on the firm's evolving performance.

Rethinking research designs will prove valuable for making decisions about how concrete studies should be. At one extreme, a broad large sample study that covers whole groups of firms, such as entire industries, will purchase its generalizability at the expense of its usefulness to particular managers. The idea that broad studies will contribute to accumulated knowledge about strategy or even tell practising managers something that they do not already know is often a chimera. The other extreme of an N = 1 study of strategy-making in a large firm runs the risk of being a consulting effort whose results are privileged by management or of little or no generalizability if not privileged. If the aim of researchers is to find a middle position between these extremes, then addressing fragmentation becomes similar to the practice development problem faced by consulting firms decades ago and which brought the strategy field some of its most enduring conceptual frameworks (Kiechel, 2010). To avoid mimicking the consultants, strategy researchers should give much thought to how they proceed.

An alternative approach to addressing fragmentation would be to employ a *configuration* approach, which involves articulating a set of organizational types comprising patterned sets of organizational, strategic, and environmental variables that provide a framework within which a larger set of firms can be productively studied. Such a typology would embed a firm's strategic efforts within its broader organizational and environmental context and thus mitigate many of the issues associated with fragmentation. Configuration approaches became widespread in research motivated by contingency approaches, so that profiles of firms that had a greater degree of 'fit' with their environments could be compared with those that enjoyed less fit.

Configuration approaches became more widespread in the early decades of the strategy field, with the work of Danny Miller and his colleagues being perhaps the most visible. Miller (1981) explicitly motivates a search for configurations—what he calls 'organizational gestalts' in terms of the need to address issues similar to those raised above concerning theoretical fragmentation. He argues that employing such configurations will lead to a richer, more complex, and multifaceted characterization of the process by which organizations adapt and change. Configuration studies remain popular but their popularity has given rise to concerns about their theoretical bases, whether inductive or deductive approaches are most useful, the types of data that are most appropriate for grouping algorithms, and the applicability of configurations to different organizational and industry contexts. Ketchen, Thomas, and Snow (1993) and Short, Payne, and Ketchen (2008) provide detailed reviews of this research. More recently, organizational configurations have received attention from economists, who are interested in how complementarities and substitution effects among organization design variables influence the number of configurations obtained as well as their characteristics (Roberts, 2004).

This chapter has suggested theoretical issues around process theory and agency assumptions that may be helpful for rethinking strategy research. There are obvious issues involved in motivating researchers to pursue more complex and more highly situated studies with limited study budgets or in motivating journal editors and reviewers to appreciate the value of such studies. Changes in longstanding practices take time. These issues deserve a more involved discussion than can be attempted here. However, suggesting how to improve theory to foster integration and reduce fragmentation is a good place to start.

References

Allison, G. (1971). *Essence of Decision: Explaining the Cuban Missile Crisis*. Boston, MA: Little, Brown & Co.
Barnard, C. (1938). *The Functions of the Executive*. Cambridge, MA: Harvard University Press.
Barnett, M. L. and Salomon, R. M. (2012). 'Does it Pay to be Really Good? Addressing the Shape of the Relationship between Social and Financial Performance'. *Strategic Management Journal*, 33(11): 1304–20.
Bascle, G. (2008). 'Controlling for Endogeneity with Instrumental Variables in Strategic Management Research'. *Strategic Organization*, 6(3): 285–327.

Besanko, D., Dranove, D., Shanley, M., and Schaefer, S. (2016). *Economics of Strategy*, 7th edn. Hoboken, NJ: Wiley.
Bettis, R. A. (2012). 'The Search for Asterisks: Compromised Statistical Tests and Flawed Theories'. *Strategic Management Journal*, 33(1): 108–13.
Calipha, R., Tarba, S., and Brock, D. (2010). 'Mergers and Acquisitions: A Review of Phases, Motives, and Success Factors', in S. Finkelstein and C. L. Cooper, (eds.), *Advances in Mergers and Acquisitions*, vol. 9, Bingley: Emerald Group, 1–24.
Chandler, A. (1962). *Strategy and Structure*. Cambridge, MA: MIT Press.
Chandler, A. (1977). *The Visible Hand*. Cambridge, MA: Belknap.
Chandler, A. and Hikino, T. (1990). *The Dynamics of Industrial Capitalism*. Cambridge, MA: Belknap.
Child, J. (1972). 'Organization Structure, Environment, and Performance: The Role of Strategic Choice'. *Sociology*, 6: 1–22.
Christensen, C. M. (1997), *The Innovator's Dilemma: When New Technologies Cause Great Firms to Fail*. Boston, MA: Harvard Business School Press.
Cool, K., Dierickx, I., and Costa, L. A. (2012). 'Diseconomies of Time Compression', INSEAD Working Paper 2012/78/ST.
Cyert, R. and March, J. (1963). *The Behavioral Theory of the Firm*. Englewood Cliffs, NJ: Prentice-Hall.
Dobbin, F. and Baum, J. A. C. (2000). 'Introduction: Economics Meets Sociology in Strategic Management'. *Advances in Strategic Management*, 17: 1–26.
Drazin, R. and Van de Ven, A (1985). 'Alternative Forms of Fit in Contingency Theory'. *Administrative Science Quarterly*, 30: 514–39.
Eisenhardt, K. M. (1989). 'Agency Theory: An Assessment and Review'. *Academy of Management Review*, 14(1): 57–74.
Emirbayer, M. and Mische, A. (1998). 'What is Agency?' *American Journal of Sociology*, 103(4): 962–1023.
Finkelstein, S., Hambrick, D. C., and Cannella, A. A. (2009). *Strategic Leadership: Theory and Research on Executives, Top Management Teams, and Boards*. New York: Oxford University Press.
Fligstein, N. (1993). *The Transformation of Corporate Control*. Cambridge, MA: Harvard University Press.
Friedman, M. (1953). *Essays in Positive Economics*. Chicago, IL: University of Chicago Press.
Gibbert, M., Ruigrok, W., and Wicki, B. (2008). 'What Passes as a Rigorous Case Study?' *Strategic Management Review*, 29(13): 1465–74.
Gomes-Casseres, B. (2015). *Remix Strategy: The Three Laws of Business Combinations*. Boston, MA: Harvard Business School Press.
Guadalupe, M., Li, H., and Wulf, J. (2013). 'Who Lives in the C-suite? Organizational Structure and the Division of Labor in Top Managements'. *Management Science*, 60(4): 824–44.
Hambrick, D. C. and Mason, P. A. (1984). 'Upper Echelons: The Organization as a Reflection of its Top Managers'. *Academy of Management Review*, 9(2): 193–206.
Hamel, G. and Prahalad, C. K. (1994). *Competing for the Future*. Boston, MA: Harvard Business Review Press
Hamilton, B. H. and Nickerson, J. A. (2003). 'Correcting for Endogeneity in Strategic Management Research'. *Strategic Organization*, 1(1): 51–78.
Harrison, J. S., Banks, G. C., Pollack, J. M., O'Boyle, E. H., and Short, J. C. (2016). 'Publication Bias in Strategic Management Research'. *Journal of Management*, 42: 5–20.
Helfat, C. E. and Martin, J. A. (2014), 'Dynamic Managerial Capabilities: Review and Assessment of Managerial Impact on Strategic Change'. *Journal of Management*, 41(5): 1281–312.

Helfat, C. E. and Peteraf, M. A. (2003). 'The Dynamic Resource-based View: Capability Lifecycles'. *Strategic Management Journal*, 24(10): 997–1010.
Herrmann, P. (2005). 'Evolution of Strategic Management: The Need for New Dominant Designs'. *International Journal of Management Reviews*, 7(2); 111–30.
Jarzabkowski, P. (2005). *Strategy as Practice: An Activity based Approach*. London: SAGE.
Jarzabkowski, P., Kaplan, S., Seidl, D., and Whittington, R. (2016). 'On the Risk of Studying Practices in Isolation: Linking What, Who, Aad How in Strategy Research'. *Strategic Organization*, 14(3): 248–59.
Johnson, G., Langley, A., Melin, L., and Whittington, R. (2007). *Strategy as Practice: Research Directions and Resources*. Cambridge: Cambridge University Press.
Kaplan, S. and Orlikowski, W. J. (2013). 'Temporal Work in Strategy Making'. *Organization Science*, 24(4): 965–95.
Ketchen, D. J., Thomas, J. B., and Snow, C. C. (1993). 'Organizational Configurations and Performance: A Comparison'. *Academy of Management Journal*, 36(6): 1278–313.
Khurana, R. (2007). *From Higher Aims to Hired Hands*. Princeton, NJ: Princeton University Press.
Kiechel, W. (2010). *The Lords of Strategy*. Boston, MA: Harvard Business School Press.
Kostova, T., Roth, K., and Dacin, M. T. (2008), 'Institutional Theory in the Study of Multinational Corporations: A Critique and New Directions'. *Academy of Management Review*, 33(4): 994–1006.
Lorange, P. (1984). 'Strategic Control', in R. Lamb (ed.), *Competitive Strategic Management*. Englewood Cliffs, NJ: Prentice-Hall, 247–71.
Lorange, P. and Vancil, R. (1976). 'How to Design a Strategic Planning System'. *Harvard Business Review*, 54(5): 75–81.
McGahan, A. M. (2004). *How Industries Evolve: Principles for Achieving and Austaining Superior Performance*. Boston, MA: Harvard Business School Press.
March, J. G. and Simon, H. A. (1958). *Organizations*. Oxford: Wiley.
Miller, D. (1981). 'Toward a New Contingency Approach: The Search for Organizational Gestalts'. *Journal of Management Studies*, 18(1): 1–26.
Mintzberg, H. (1987), 'Crafting Strategy'. *Harvard Business Review*, 65(3): 66–75.
Mintzberg, H. (1994). *Rise and Fall of Strategic Planning*. New York: Free Press.
Mosakowski, E. and Earley, P. C. (2000). 'A Selective Review of Time Assumptions in Strategy Research'. *Academy of Management Review*, 25(4): 796–812.
Mueller, D. C. (2013). *The Corporation: Growth, Diversification, and Mergers*. New York: Routledge.
Nag, R., Hambrick, D., and Chen, M. (2007). 'What is Strategic Management, Really? Inductive Derivation of a Consensus Definition of the Field'. *Strategic Management Journal*, 28: 935–55.
Nelson, R. and Winter, S. (1982). *An Evolutionary Theory of Economic Change*. Cambridge, MA: Belknap.
North, D. C. (2005). *Understanding the Process of Economic Change*. Princeton, NJ: Princeton University Press.
Oliver, C. (1991). 'Strategic Responses to Institutional Processes'. *Academy of Management Review*, 16(1): 145–79.
Parmigiani, A. and Holloway, S. S. (2011). 'Actions Speak Louder than Modes: Antecedents and Implications of Parent Implementation Capabilities on Business Unit Performance'. *Strategic Management Journal*, 32(5): 457–85.
Penrose, E. (1959). *The Theory of the Growth of the Firm*. Oxford: Oxford University Press.
Penrose, E. (1960). 'The Growth of the Firm: A Case Study, the Hercules Powder Company'. *Business History Review*, 34: 1–23.

Peteraf, M. and Shanley, M. (1997). 'Getting to Know You: A Theory of Strategic Group Identity'. *Strategic Management Journal*, 18 (Summer Special Issue): 165–86.

Pettigrew, A. (1992). 'The Character and Significance of Strategy Process Research'. *Strategic Management Journal*, 13: 5–16.

Pettigrew, A. (1985), *The Awakening Giant: Continuity and Change at ICI*. Oxford: Basil Blackwell.

Porter, M. E. (1987). 'From Competitive Advantage to Corporate Strategy'. *Harvard Business Review*, 63(3): 43–59.

Porter, M. E. (1998). *Competitive Advantage*. New York: Free Press.

Quinn, J. (1980). *Strategies for Change: Logical Incrementalism*. Homewood, IL: Irwin.

Ravenscraft, D. and Scherer, F. (1987). *Mergers, Sell-offs, and Economic Efficiency*. Washington, D.C.: Brookings.

Roberts, J. (2004). *The Modern Firm: Organizational Design for Performance and Growth*. Oxford: Oxford University Press.

Ronda-Pupo, G. A. and Guerras-Martin, L. A. (2012). 'Dynamics of the Evolution of the Strategy Concept: 1962–2008: A Co-word Analysis'. *Strategic Management Journal*, 33(2): 162–88.

Rumelt, R. P., Schendel, D. E., and Teece, D. J. (eds.) (1994). *Fundamental Issues in Strategy: A Research Agenda*. Boston, MA: Harvard Business School Press.

Schendel, D. and Hofer, C. (1979). *Strategic Management: A New View of Business Policy and Planning*. Boston, MA: Little, Brown.

Sennett, R. (2008). *The Craftsman*. New Haven, CT: Yale University Press.

Shanley, M. and Peteraf, M. (2006). 'The Centrality of Process'. *International Journal of Strategic Change Management*, 1(1): 4–19.

Short, J. C., Ketchen, D. J., and Palmer, T. B. (2002). 'The Role of Sampling in Strategic Management Research on Performance: A Two-Study Analysis'. *Journal of Management*, 28(3): 363–85.

Short, J. C., Payne, G. T., and Ketchen, D. J. (2008). 'Research on Organizational Configurations: Past Accomplishments and Future Challenges'. *Journal of Management*, 34(6): 1053–79.

Sirower, M. (1997). *The Synergy Trap*. New York: Free Press.

Souder, D. and Bromiley, P. (2012). 'Explaining Temporal Orientation: Evidence from the Durability of Firms' Capital Investments'. *Strategic Management Journal*, 33(5): 550–69.

Tsang, E. W. K. (2006). 'Behavioral Assumptions and Theory Development: The Case of Transaction Cost Economics'. *Strategic Management Journal*, 27(11): 999–1011.

Van de Ven, A. (1992). 'Suggestions for Studying Strategy Process: A Research Note'. *Strategic Management Journal*, 13: 169–88.

Vallas, S. P. (2006), 'Empowerment Redux: Structure, Agency, and the Remaking of Managerial Authority'. *American Journal of Sociology*, 111(6): 1677–717.

Venkatraman, N. (1989). 'The Concept of Fit in Strategy research: Toward Verbal and Statistical correspondence'. *Academy of Management Review*, 14(3): 423–44.

Wiltbank, R., Dew, N., Read, S., and Sarasvathy, S. D. (2006), 'What to Do Next? The Case for Non-Predictive Strategy'. *Strategic Management Journal*, 27(10): 981–98.

Wittkower, M. and Wittkower, R. (1963). *Born under Saturn*. New York: NYRB.

Yurov, K., Greenstein, S. M., Shanley, M. T., and Potter, R. E. (2013). 'The Role of Geographic Location of High-Technology Firms: Evidence from the Computer Networking Industry'. *Thunderbird International Business Review*, 55(4): 371–85.

CHAPTER 16

MANAGEMENT PRACTICE— AND THE DOING OF MANAGEMENT

STEFAN TENGBLAD

Introduction

This chapter describes management from a practice perspective. The focus is the routine work of managers in everyday settings. In its review of the main conceptualizations of everyday management, the chapter examines the differences and similarities in how textbooks, scientific articles, and management education programmes present managerial work behaviour. The chapter also addresses the relatively modest effect that valid, reliable, and sustained research findings have had on management research and education.

Management refers to the handling of people, equipment, and other assets (not least, financial assets), often in the organizational or economic context. The word management derives from the Latin noun *manus* (hand) and from the Vulgar Latin verb *manidiare* (to handle). In Italian, the verb derivation is *maneggiare* (to control a horse). In English, management is used in everyday language in the sense that 'to handle a situation (in a good way)' means 'to manage' (Tengblad, 2015).

There are various ways to conceptualize management. In management theory, management is typically thought of as the way in which people handle goal-oriented, related activities. The acronym POSDCORB (Planning, Organizing, Staffing, Directing, Co-Ordinating, Reporting, and Budgeting), for example, is often used to conceptualize an administrative management perspective that is based in large part on the work the French industrialist Henri Fayol (1841–1925). This view of management has an inherent normative dimension. For instance, managers may be criticized if they fail to plan activities or if they engage in activities outside approved managerial scope (e.g., gossiping, politicking, bonding, acting emotionally or ceremonially, or simply reacting to stimuli).

A second way to conceptualize management is to see it primarily as the work practices of professionals, or semi-professionals as some managers are described. In this conceptualization of management, other aspects emerge as important, and the formalized way of understanding management is challenged by the nature of management work which is a messier, more hectic, informal, and verbal than the textbook version of management.

In short, in comparing these two conceptualizations of management we are looking at the gap between theory and practice. Differences between theoretical and practical insights arise because scientists (i.e., researchers/theorists) and practitioners (i.e., managers/executives) have different agendas, goals, and experiences. This chapter gives an overview of the most important studies within the management practice perspective on the work of managers.

The Research on Management Practice

The research on management practice since the 1940s falls mainly into two streams. The first stream is the functionalist stream that emphasizes the classic conceptualizations and analyses of managerial work behaviour. The second stream is the ethnographic stream that emphasizes the study of managerial culture and knowledge. In this section we describe these two streams. For a fuller discussion, see Tengblad (2013) and Tengblad and Vie (2012).

Management Practice Research: The Functionalist Stream

Some of the management practice researchers, especially in earlier times, have been rather critical to their study objects fragmented and reactive way of working. They have seen functional management theory as a guide when they have discussed how managerial work practices should be improved.

The Pioneering Study

Sune Carlson, a Swedish Professor of Business Administration, is generally considered to be the founder of the managerial work research tradition (Mintzberg, 1973). In his book *Executive Behaviour* Carlson (1951/1991) published findings from his extensive investigation of the work behaviour of ten corporate managing directors. He reported the difficulties the directors had in working as efficiently and productively as they (and Carlson) thought most beneficial to their companies (Tengblad, 2003). Carlson coined the term 'administrative pathologies' to describe the conditions that cause a managing director to act inefficiently and unproductively. An example is the diary complex. In this pathology, directors focus on the day's scheduled tasks rather than on the day's most important (and often impromptu) tasks.

Carlson made a number of other original observations on work behaviour. He reported on the high degree of fragmentation in the directors' workdays that, combined with high work pressure, left little time for planning and reflecting. He observed that the directors, who saw their work situation as atypical and exceptionally challenging, relied somewhat on wishful thinking in their decision-making rather than on clear assessments of evidence and reality. The directors hoped and believed that future conditions would somehow turn current chaos into stable and controllable order.

Carlson's *Executive Behaviour* describes managerial work as hectic, fragmented, complex, and often disorganized. Habits and the logic-of-events model control work more than reflective and deliberate planning. Carlson concluded that executive behaviour should be studied in context, taking both the social and physical environments into consideration. He later wrote that when he began his research, he imagined directors as orchestra conductors; at the end of his research, he saw them more as marionette puppets.

Early Studies on Supervisory Work

In the 1950s research in industrial sociology resulted in a number of studies of individual foremen and supervisors. One notable example is *The Foreman on the Assembly Line* in which Walker, Guest, and Turner (1956) reported on interviews with fifty-five foremen. These interviews revealed the foremen's reflections on their work with particular reference to staffing, personal work relationships, product quality issues, and emergency/accident measures. One key finding was that the foreman has the role of the 'shock absorber' that absorbs, but does not transmit, work pressure. In an article on time and the foreman, Guest (1956) reported on a parallel study of full-day, minute-by-minute, observations of fifty-six foremen, He described the foremen's work as a hectic round of activities, each lasting on average only forty-eight seconds. In particular, Guest highlighted the foremen's lack of idle time, the constant interruptions in their work, the great variety of their contacts, and the many and varied problems that arose simultaneously.

Variation in Managerial Work

In her book *Managers and Their Jobs* (1967, revised in 1988), Rosemary Stewart reported on the work activities in a four-week period of 160 managers employed in a broad range of management positions. With this large sample, Stewart was able to compare a number of manager positions and the variations in work practices among managers in similar positions. She concluded that it is misleading to talk about managerial positions in general terms without acknowledging these variations. For example, she noted that general managers spend only 7% of their time on paper work whereas chief accountants are involved with paper work 84% of their time.

Using computer factor analysis, Stewart identified the following five categories of managers:

- *Emissaries*: Managers who travel widely and spend much of their time away from the organization.
- *Writers*: Managers who read, analyze, and write.
- *Discussers*: Managers who work mainly through staff meetings.
- *Troubleshooters*: Managers who work mainly with disturbances, including operational problems.
- *Committee Members*: Managers who work with committees that consist of members from various organizational areas.
- *The Committee Men*: Managers with a high level of intra-organizational horizontal contacts.

In a study on managerial choices, Stewart (1982) found that despite the existence of work practice variations, most of the study's participants did not choose their behaviour proactively.

Like Sune Carlson, Stewart commented on the problems caused by the fragmentation in managerial work. She saw the fragmentation as extremely disruptive to the well-functioning of the organizations. In her vivid analogy, managers are like grasshoppers; they hop from one problem to another as 'a perpetual excuse for postponing considerations of the long-term ones' (Stewart 1967/1988: 111).

The Nature of Managerial Work

In his book *The Nature of Managerial Work* Henry Mintzberg (1973) presented what is now the most renowned model of managerial roles. The model, which consists of ten roles, is summarized in what follows. The term 'organization' is used here in a general sense to mean the entity, the unit, the department.

Interpersonal Roles

- *Figurehead*: A manager who represents the organization. Work tasks typically have a ceremonial character.
- *Leader*: A manager who creates a positive atmosphere and motivates subordinates. Work tasks include employee hiring and compensation.
- *Liaison*: A manager who is the contact link between peers and outsiders. In modern management literature, this work task is often described as networking.

Informational Roles

- *Monitor*: A manager who is knowledgeable about various conditions related to the organization—for instance, environmental issues, technological developments, and other trends.

- *Disseminator:* A manager who circulates information (both factual data and value-based opinions) in the organization.
- *Spokesman:* A manager who publicizes information externally that is in the best interests of the organization—for example, information intended to persuade consumers or to establish/re-establish external legitimacy.

Decisional Roles

- *Entrepreneur:* A manager who initiates change that exploits opportunities and improves operations—for example, change that increases productivity with new technology.
- *Disturbance handler:* A manager who deals with negative events in the organization such as product quality problems, workplace conflicts and accidents, and poor employee job performance.
- *Resource allocator:* A manager who makes decisions or approves/disapproves decisions related to the allocation of financial and personnel resources and to the authorization and scheduling of various activities.
- *Negotiator:* A manager who mediates between the organization and union representatives, customers, and business partners.

Mintzberg's book also includes an authoritative summary of earlier research, a synthesis of the nature of managerial work in thirteen propositions, and an observational study of five chief executives. His synthesis of the nature of managerial work in the following four characteristics is perfectly consistent with the contemporary work environment:

1) Much work at an unrelenting pace
2) Activities characterized by brevity, variety, and fragmentation
3) Preference for live action
4) Attraction to the verbal media.

Mintzberg's book, like those of Carlson and Stewart, is in the tradition that concludes managerial work practices are largely dysfunctional and should be replaced with work practices developed by management scientists. Mintzberg attributed this dysfunctionality to managers' constant preoccupation with immediate, ad hoc problems and their constant round of meetings. Managers, under such pressure, find it difficult to get real work done. In general, Mintzberg concluded, scheduling managerial work is a very complex and challenging task.

The Rationality of Work Fragmentation

In 1982, before he became a 'management guru', John P. Kotter published *The General Managers* in which he described fifteen general managers at nine major US companies. He used multiple research methods in his study (e.g., observations, shadowing, and interviews with managers and co-workers). In addition, Kotter listed financial indicators, together with appraisals from peers, subordinates, and superiors, to rate general managers' performance.

Kotter's major findings relate to the concepts of 'agenda' and 'network'. Using these concepts, Kotter emphasized general managers' choices and their opportunities to influence their work by setting agendas and by building and utilizing personal networks to implement those agendas. The concept of agenda is similar to the concept of strategy implementation while the concept of network refers to interaction, preferably informal contact, with numerous people inside and outside the corporation. Kotter also argued that differences in managerial performance result from differences in how the general managers establish and use their networks when implementing their agendas.

Kotter (1982: 89) concluded that chaotic conversations might be highly effective: 'the agendas and network allowed all the GMs to engage in short and disjointed conversations that were often extremely efficient'. Because of the inevitable ambiguity and uncertainty in the general manager's job, managerial decisions emerge from social processes rather than from rational and calculative analysis of data. Kotter also noted that joking, kidding, and talking about non-work matters are integral parts of managerial conversations. Such small talk, Kotter argued, is important for creating and maintaining networks.

Perhaps Kotter's most important finding, however, is that fragmented interactions in problem-solving situations may be effective in implementing long-term agendas (Tengblad and Vie, 2012). Kotter's contribution is its departure from the management science paradigm with its rigid emphasis on working systematically (i.e., deductively, deliberatively, logically, and sequentially).

A New Synthesis of Management as Work Practice

In his book *Managing* (2009) Henry Mintzberg updated his previous research on managerial work with new, empirical material. For this book, he observed twenty-nine managers from numerous sectors. Basing his conclusions on these observations, Mintzberg criticized organizational research that highlights the role of leadership and downplays other aspects of managerial work. He concluded that the image of the manager/leader as a visionary and a goal-setter is a flawed representation that results from the popular and rather well-accepted separation of management and leadership.

Mintzberg acknowledged the highly complex, fragmented, hectic, and often chaotic nature of management. Thus, he presents a multifaceted and integrated model of management that, in a rather complex way, avoids the either/or reasoning that is typical of popular management textbooks. According to Mintzberg, a manager requires both the generalist's ability to think, communicate, lead, and execute, and the specialist's ability to think about fine-grained organizational operations.

Management, according to Mintzberg, at best is insightful, engaging, and mindful; at worst, it is disconnected from reality, de-spiriting, and disorganized. He concluded that while no manager can master all aspects of management, it is crucial that the manager avoids one-dimensionality, narcissism, and self-aggrandizement.

Management Practice Research: The Ethnographic Stream

The ethnographic research stream, which is willing to examine managerial work from a more general social science perspective, includes activities such as gossiping, identity-making, politicking, and revealing emotions as integral factors in management work practices. This research stream also examines ethical issues related to subordination, inequality, and domination.

First Studies of Middle Management Behaviour

Tom Burns (1954, 1957) made two diary studies in the UK in the mid-1950s. In these studies, he examined how 76 senior and middle managers at eight companies worked in timeframes of three, four, or five weeks. Burns observed that the differences in how managers communicated depended on whether their companies experienced high or low degrees of change. He concluded: 'Generally speaking, the faster the rate of change, the more time is spent by managers in talking with each other' (1957: 51). Burns and Stalker (1961) developed this idea as the contingency perspective on the management of innovation.

Burns (1954, 1957) also noted several discrepancies in the managers' records of their activities. For instance, the managers overestimated the amount of time they spent on production and underestimated the amount of time they spent on personnel. Burns concluded the managers were unaware of the extent of their involvement in 'human relationships'.

Burns, who was the first researcher to take a significant interest in the social aspects of managerial work, proposed a view of the organization as a system of personal relationships rather than a hierarchy of authority. In an article on small groups, Burns (1955) elaborated on this idea in his observation that an individual's political behaviour leads to the formation of coalitions, cliques, and cabals. This research inspired his influential work on the micro-politics of organizations. In a subsequent article, Burns (1961) observed the presence of intense rivalry for position and rewards when people work in situations where cooperation is required around common organizational goals.

Unofficial aspects of managerial work

In his book *Men Who Manage*, Melville Dalton (1959) presented perhaps the most extensive account of the unofficial and informal aspects of managerial work. By taking formal staff positions, Dalton applied a covert, if unorthodox, research approach to data collection at four companies in the same city in the United States. He conducted formal and informal interviews, kept a work diary, made participant observations, and attended company social events.

Among the many informal aspects of managerial work he observed, Dalton emphasized the power struggles between management cliques that compete for resources and trade information and favours. He also described the strained collaboration between line and staff, the informal rewards system, and the active re-interpretation of company policies at the local level. He detailed the unofficial influences on promotions and careers such as managers' ethnicity, religion, club memberships (e.g., the yacht club and the Masons), and political affiliations. Thus, managers' private lives merge with their professional lives in this highly complex 'web of commitments' and 'workable arrangements' at work. The picture Dalton paints is of managers caught up in a whirl of ambiguity, complexity, and conflict; to make sense of this confusion, they engage in unofficial and informal activities outside the boundaries set by their formal positions.

Pioneer study on gender in management

Men and Women of the Corporation by Rosabeth Moss Kanter (1977) is a classic study in the field of gender and management. Her book made a major contribution to the managerial work tradition in its study of how structural factors influence management practice.

Kanter worked as researcher and consultant in a Quality of Work Life program at a Fortune 500 company she called Indsco. Most managers at the company, which was very conformist, felt very insecure in their positions. The pressure to conform was a self-perpetuating process that she labelled 'homosexual reproduction' (1977: 48). Because actual work performance was so difficult to measure, social acceptance was the decisive factor in promotions. Thus, Indsco managers frequently resorted to the use of organizational politics for advancement: creating networks, building relationships, manoeuvring for position and power, and monitoring behind-the-scenes action.

Kanter described Indsco managers' work as very demanding and complex. The unwritten rule was that working to the utmost of human capacity signalled loyalty to the company and to the managerial hierarchy. Kanter concluded, however, that no matter how much managers worked, there were always unfinished tasks. Such was the intention when managerial positions were designed.

Kanter also analysed the ideology of managerialism and the bureaucratic corporation in the context of the enormous work inequities such an ideology produces. She argued that the managers, in order to legitimize the importance of their organizational roles, claimed they acted rationally in their quest for logical and efficient solutions to problems. Successful managers, they implied, are therefore people in control of their emotions. Because women are often stereotyped as too emotional, they are not qualified to be managers. Women are said to lack masculine rationality.

Networking for advancing personal interests

In the book *Real Managers*, Fred Luthans (1988) and his team at the University of Nebraska identified more selfish reasons for networking than Kotter had. The team's goal was to examine the differences, if any, between the work activities of managers with successful careers and the work activities of managers perceived as most effective. Using a four-activity model with twelve descriptive work categories and trained observers who recorded the activities of 248 managers over a two-week period, the team made more than 20,000 observations. A breakdown of the observed activities was as follows:

- *Traditional management* (32%—Planning, Decision-making, Controlling)
- *Routine communications* (29%—Exchanging information, Handling paperwork)
- *Human Resource Management* (20%—Motivating, Disciplining, Managing conflict, Staffing, Training/Development)
- *Networking* (19%—Interacting with outsiders, Socializing/Politicking)

Luthans et al. found very small overlap of the two manager categories: managers were either successful and effective, or unsuccessful and ineffective. Moreover, they found that successful managers spent far less time on traditional management activities than less successful managers. Their major (and non-traditional) activity was networking, especially socializing and politicking. The effective managers also spent very little time on traditional management activities, and worked more with routine communications and human resource management. Furthermore, of the twelve descriptive work categories, decision-making had the weakest relationship with effectiveness.

The morality of management

Robert Jackall's *Moral Mazes* (1988), consistent with Dalton's (1959) theme that managers adapt to their social environment, offered numerous examples of the moral and political dimensions of managerial work. Jackall presented evidence from 143 intensive, semi-structured interviews with managers and evidence from extensive participant and non-participant observations of managers at various levels. The data were collected at four US companies.

Jackall's book highlighted the ethical ambiguity inherent in the management position. According to Alvesson (2004), ambiguity (contrasted with uncertainty when additional facts do not clarify a situation) results when several plausible interpretations of the same event or data exist. Jackall described how managers in ambiguous situations experience unusually strong pressure to comply with 'what the guy above you wants from you' (Jackall, 1988: 6). Compliance means acquiescence with superiors as well as with corporate rules and procedures. Since the corporation is an intricate matrix of individual and group rivalries, each seeking advantages and advancements, survival depends on the ability to live with the ambiguity of this moral maze.

Jackall observed that managers continually express excitement about their work even as they hide their anxieties. Although they constantly worry about making mistakes and being blamed for others' mistakes, they feel the pressure to appear cheerful and in total control, whatever the situation. Combined with the vague criteria used in their performance evaluations, this nervous anxiety increases managers' insecurity.

Jackall found an interesting connection between managers' long work hours and their social bonding in management teams. Managerial work in general (working late at night, in particular) appears to have a rather large social and ritualistic element. Managers often chat informally among themselves and pop in and out of offices with cartoons and jokes. According to Jackall, managers who do not work such long hours and who do not engage in this endless round of informal encounters risk being 'sidelined'.

Managerial identity in times of change and transformation

One of the most cited studies of managerial work in recent decades is *In Search of Management* by Tony J. Watson (1994/2001). Watson was a participant observer for a year at a British company recognized for its ambitious effort to create a new organizational culture that included elements of total quality management, performance-related compensation, teamwork, and personal development. His study, which is an ethnographic account of the everyday thinking and attitudes of the company's middle managers, quotes extensively from his in-depth interviews with these managers.

The major contribution of Watson's book is its depiction of the chaos, uncertainties, ambiguity, and contradictions that the managers described as they struggled with coming to terms with their role as managers. In particular, the book reveals the managers' disillusion and cynicism when the top management claimed that their traditional and hierarchical management approach had been replaced with an empowerment oriented management style. The managers experienced anguish, insecurity, and doubt as they struggled with the company's change programmes, mission statements, and policies that conflicted with their own values. In his analysis, 'Dr. Watson' concludes that top management increased the complexity and ambiguity of the work of the middle managers.

Recent Research about Managerial Work/Management Practices

In recent years the research on managerial work/management practices has investigated new areas and themes. For example, Hales (2002), Matthaei (2010), and Tengblad (2002, 2006) examined the changes in managers' work. Florén (2006) investigated management at small firms, in particular owner-managers of small firms. Arman et al. (2009) studied healthcare managers. Vie (2010) studied R&D managers. These and other studies are described in this section.

Stability and Change in Management Practices

Many management issues are timeless and always worthy of analysis. The time and context of such issues are often relatively unimportant. However, with the appearance of new work developments and trends (increased competition, globalization, advanced technologies, and fresh organizational theories) the research on management practices has expanded.

A turning point in management practice occurred in the early 1980s. In these years, new economic policies appeared that were less concerned with full employment and regulation. In addition, as free trade policies began to open protected national markets, companies expanded internationally. Advances in information technology simplified/improved certain organizational activities. Companies responded to these changes, among other things, with staff reductions and general restructuring. As such changes became more the rule than the exception, managers' job security diminished, even vanished. The umbrella term 'post-bureaucracy' was used to describe this new era in managerial practices.

Post-bureaucratic organizations are characterized by flexible and non-hierarchical structures and practices built on shared values, dialogue, and trust rather than by inflexible and adherence to authority and rules (Grey and Garsten, 2001; Tengblad, 2006). Many authors (e.g., Drucker, 1988; Handy, 1989; Kanter, 1989; Morgan, 1993; Peters, 1989; Zuboff, 1988) claim that the emergence of the post-bureaucracy era has had, or will have, a profound effect on how managers perform their work. Kanter (1989: 85 ff.), for instance, argued that managerial work is undergoing 'an enormous and rapid change' spurred by new technology, increasing customer demands, and competitive pressures that weed out traditional forms of organizing.

Colin Hales (1999, 2002, 2005; see also Hales and Tamangani, 1996) has investigated the effects of decentralization and other ideas related to post-bureaucracy in the United Kingdom, Malaysia, and Zimbabwe. He has looked for evidence of the breakdown in traditional management authority and of changes in middle managers' roles that might result from the post-bureaucratic relaxation of rigid rules, power sharing achieved by dialogue and trust, more self-organized units, and more decentralized decision-making. His research reveals little progress in these settings towards the post-bureaucratic ideal. The traditional, authoritarian managerial roles and behaviours, in which managers are held personally responsible for subordinates, persist. He has found little evidence that employees are, or will be, treated as partners or that the close monitoring of their work has been, or will be, abandoned. Hales concludes (2002: 64) the new way of organizing is not post-bureaucratic but rather 'bureaucracy-lite: all the strength of bureaucracy control with only half the hierarchical calories'.

Tengblad (2006) investigated how and if post-bureaucratic thinking and advances in information technology have influenced management practices. In a research project, designed to replicate Mintzberg's study from 1973, Tengblad observed a similar number of Swedish executives for a week each. He found some important differences. Compared to the executives in the Mintzberg study, the executives in the Tengblad study worked longer hours, generally experienced less work fragmentation, travelled more, and worked out of the office more. Moreover, whereas the executives in the Mintzberg study were closely involved in operational decisions, the executives in the Tengblad study focused more on financial reports and strategic priorities. Tengblad's executives also showed greater interest in spreading company cultural values, promoting company goals, and communicating expectations to subordinates.

Tengblad (2006: 1453) concluded: 'The difference between the two studies—using Selznick's (1957) terminology—can be interpreted as indicating a relative shift in behaviour from *administrative management* to *institutional leadership*' (emphasis in the original).

Despite these differences with Mintzberg's study, Tengblad found many similarities in his test of twelve of Mintzberg's propositions. Tengblad's test (2006: 1451–2) supported the following eight propositions (numbers correlate with Mintzberg's propositions):

1. Managerial work consists of great quantities of work conducted at an unrelenting pace.
4. The manager gravitates towards live action.
5. The manager prefers verbal media.
6. The manager gives mail cursory treatment.
7. Telephone and unscheduled meetings are mainly used for brief contacts between persons that know each other.
8. The scheduled meetings consume more of the manager's time than any other medium.
9. Tours can give valuable information, but the manager spends little time on them.
12. The manager spends relatively little time with superiors (Boards of Directors).

Two propositions were partially supported:

10. External contacts generally consume one-third to one-half of the manager's contact time.
11. Subordinates generally consume one-third to one-half of the manager's contact time.

Two propositions were not supported:

2. Managerial work is fragmented and interruptions are commonplace.
3. Managers prefer brevity and interruptions.

In his examination of the work behaviour of twelve top executives at German companies, Matthaei (2010) found a pattern of executive work that was quite similar to Tengblad's (2006) findings. The executives in the Matthaei study conducted most of their work in lengthy conference meetings with others rather than in brief, unplanned meetings. They worked an average of 65.6 hours a week: 64% of the time was in meetings,

17% in travel/tours, 9% in telephone conversations, and 10% in miscellaneous activities. Although the executives valued meetings as the best place for discussing complex issues and for establishing work relationships, they still worked in many other locations. With the introduction of email and other technologies, they could easily work from home, hotels, trains, and other venues.

Vie (2010) studied post-bureaucratic work changes including comparisons with the Mintzberg (1973) and Tengblad (2006) studies. His research focused on front-line and middle managers in R&D departments. His study shows that such managers in the post-bureaucratic environment, who still carry a large administrative burden, do not act as institutional leaders although they have a dialogue-oriented leadership style. Compared to the top executives in the Mintzberg study, Vie's managers spent more time in unscheduled meetings than in scheduled meetings. Vie's managers also spent more time talking with subordinates and superiors than with people external to their companies. One of Vie's findings is especially interesting: 16% of the managers' verbal contacts at work consisted of social chitchat, humorous exchanges, social greetings, and expressions of concern for others.

The research on continuity and change in management practices in recent years, summarized in this section, reveals there may be more continuity than change. Management practices, backed by tradition and authority, are slow to change even when new technologies, company policies, and leadership ideas are introduced and promoted. Work supervision especially is resistant to change. Managers at the operational level are fire-fighters who are forced to deal with immediate and serious problems in a way that leaves them little time for reflection and consultation. However, some change in management practices is visible in managers' use of technological communication devices and in their increase in travel, planned meetings, and interaction with subordinates. Managerial work at the executive level has changed more than the work of middle and front-line managers in these regards.

Management Practices in Small Companies and in Public Healthcare

Florén (2006) and Florén and Tell (2012) studied management practices in small and entrepreneurial companies. In their five studies, they found the work of the owner-managers is relatively informal and characterized by intensity, brevity, and fragmentation. The number of managerial activities per day varied in these studies from thirty-five to eighty, with an average of fifty-six activities per day. The great majority of these activities took fewer than nine minutes; only a few activities took more than one hour.

O'Gorman, Bourke, and Murray (2005) compared the communication patterns of small firm managers to those of managers at larger organizations. They found that small firm managers use less structured and less ceremonial communications. This informality is also evident in the willingness of small firm managers to work on the operations floor, both at work peaks and at other times.

Many studies of public healthcare management have been conducted. For example, in their various studies on first-line and second-line managers Arman et al. (2009), Dellve and Wikström (2009), and Wikström and Dellve (2009) found that most of the managerial work in public healthcare is conducted in brief activities. First-line managers have many unscheduled meetings whereas second-line managers have more scheduled meetings. The researchers also found that nurse-managers, sometimes faced with conflicting goals, have to reconcile their dual identity as both manager and nurse. These managers must negotiate their identity daily in a network of competing financial, organizational, professional, societal, and personal structures and demands.

Ten Theses of Managerial Work

Tengblad (2012: 339–47), in a review of the last sixty years of studies on management work practices, summarizes the research findings in ten theses. An abbreviated version of these ten theses is presented next. Each thesis derives from the results from several studies conducted at various times, in various countries, at various hierarchical levels, and in various sectors.

Theses on the context of managerial work

1) *Managerial work is subject to various expectations and high-performance pressures*

Managers typically face pressure and expectations that may often seem overwhelming. Moreover, managers' work demands are often contradictory, even mutually exclusive. For example, shareholders and superiors in the management hierarchy may expect greater financial returns, customers want better service and terms, employees want higher salaries, more personal development, and better work environments, and union representatives want more influence.

2) *Managerial work exists in complex and often ambiguous environments*

Managers are partially responsible for a social system. By their very nature, social systems are complex because they consist of different value sets, economic exchange patterns and dependencies, cultural and institutional frameworks, and power relationships. Managers must both give and follow instructions as they try to meet organizational objectives and satisfy assorted (internal and external) demands—even as they try to exert their work autonomy by adopting proactive, enterprising, and resourceful work styles and methods.

3) *Managerial work involves much uncertainty and many unforeseen events*

Managers experience a great deal of uncertainty at work. It is impossible for managers to predict all external events or always foresee the consequences of their own and others' actions. Chance and randomness are factors that inevitably disrupt careful planning.

Theses on the characteristics of managerial work

4) Managerial work involves a hectic work pace and long working hours

Managers work long hours, often in chaotic and stressful conditions. For many managers, the outcome is a poor work–life balance and symptoms of physiological and psychological stress. Mintzberg (1973) summarizes this often-observed research finding in his Proposition 1 about managerial work: 'Managerial work consists of great quantities of work conducted at an unrelenting pace'.

5) Managerial work is usually fragmented

Managers' workdays are usually fragmented because of frequent interruptions and because of the huge variation in their tasks. Such unavoidable work fragmentation is a source of frustration for many managers. Managers at the operational level, with significant administrative responsibility, including frequent meetings, normally have more work fragmentation than managers at the executive level.

6) Managerial work is conducted in a processual and adaptive manner

Most managers prefer following detailed schedules and well laid-out plans. However, they often have to spend much of their time dealing with surprise events and disruptions to administrative routines. Ambitious plans are rarely of use when such situations arise. The ability to manage fuzzy work situations is often more important for success than planning skills and strategic thinking.

7) Managerial work is a collective accomplishment

Managers, who are responsible for groups of people, are involved in many intra-group interactions. This means managers are followers as well as leaders. Their work requires managing people in a collective effort. The people they manage are not simply passive recipients of top-down visions, ideas, decisions, and instructions—they are actively influencing the administrative processes.

8) Managerial work is emotionally intense

Managers' work is often of a highly emotional character. The rather widespread preference for non-emotionality in management is inconsistent with the reality of managerial work. Managers, like everyone else, sometimes make choices influenced by complex and often irrational emotions.

9) Managerial work requires symbolic actions

Managers have a greater responsibility than producing positive financial and operational results. Managers must also achieve and maintain internal and external legitimacy. Organization results are affected by many more factors than managerial work competence and effort. The more difficult it is to measure performance in output terms; the more important it is for managers to display their performance in input terms (e.g., workplace presence, physical appearance, and compliance with value systems, rules, and requests).

10) *Managerial work involves substantial participation in informal activities*

Managers who engage in informal activities often strengthen their positions in the organization, advance their careers, and are rewarded with larger salaries/bonuses and other perquisites. Real decision-making often takes place in informal settings, apart from external scrutiny. Formal activities, such as meetings with their rituals and pretence of objectivity and perhaps also democratic decision-making, frequently are mere covers for the informal activities.

Conclusions

Managers' work, which is enormously varied, is conducted at hectic speeds and in chaotic situations that are seldom described in management textbooks. The thoughtful and precise goal setting and planning that students study in management programmes are rarely the norms in actual practice. Managers' work consists of fragmented, rushed activities that are often reactive and ad hoc. Numerous research studies confirm the reality of this observation. Goals and plans are often revised, even rejected. Managers lack the luxury of time to act as they might like or as others might like them to act. Hill (1992: 192) quotes a manager on the stress this pressure produces:

> A lot of days, I'm here early and out late. Still I accomplish nothing that I was supposed to accomplish. I have so many interruptions and have to keep shifting my priorities. By the end of the day I feel drained, with nothing to show for all my work.

Nevertheless, managers have to make choices and decisions. Then they have to explain and legitimize their actions to the people who set expectations and exert pressure. Thus, management can be compared to a theatrical performance: a manager is an actor before an audience when all that the manager says may not exactly match the reality. A host of emotional factors, which managers may or may not be consciously aware of, influence their decision-making, but behind the scene. Anger, fear, suspicion, and egoism in its various forms, for example, are not the rational and systematic decision-making factors that the functionalist research stream identifies and promotes. Management theorists, authors, and educators serve students better when they admit not only the uses but also the limitations of systematic, rational management practices in the real world of managerial complexity, chaos, and doubt.

References

Alvesson, M. (2004). *Knowledge Work and Knowledge-Intensive Firms*. Oxford: Oxford University Press.

Arman, R., Dellve, L., Wikström, E., and Törnström, L. (2009). 'What Health Care Managers Do: Applying Mintzberg's Structured Observation Method'. *Journal of Nursing Management*, 17(6): 718–29.

Burns, T. (1954). 'The Directions of Activity and Communication in a Departmental Executive Group: A Quantitative Study in a British Engineering Factory with a Self-Recording Technique'. *Human Relations*, 7(1): 73–97.

Burns, T. (1957). 'Management in Action'. *Operational Research Quarterly*, 8(2): 45–60.

Burns, T. (1955). 'The Reference of Conduct in Small Groups: Cliques and Cabals in Occupational Milieux'. *Human Relations*, 8(4): 467–86.

Burns, T. (1961). 'Micropolitics: Mechanisms of Institutional Change'. *Administrative Science Quarterly*, 6(3): 257–81.

Burns, T. and Stalker, G. M. (1961). *The Management of Innovation*. London: Tavistock Publications.

Carlson, S. (1951/1991). *Executive Behaviour*. Reprinted with contributions by Henry Mintzberg and Rosemary Stewart. Uppsala: Studia Oeconomiae Negotiorum.

Dalton, M. (1959). *Men who Manage: Fusions of Feeling and Theory in Administration*. New York: John Wiley.

Dellve, L. and Wikström, E. (2009). 'Managing Complex Workplace Stress in Health Care Organizations: Leaders' Perceived Legitimacy Conflicts'. *Journal of Nursing Management*, 17(8): 931–41.

Drucker, P. (1988). 'The Coming of the New Organization'. *Harvard Business Review*, 66, January/February: 45–53.

Florén, H. (2006). 'Managerial Work in Small Firms: Summarising what we Know and Sketching a Research Agenda'. *International Journal of Entrepreneurial Behavior & Research*, 12(5): 272–88.

Florén, H. and Tell, J. (2012). 'Managerial Behaviour in Small Firms: Does it Matter what Managers Do?', in S. Tengblad (ed.), *The Work of Managers: Towards a Practice Theory of Management*. Oxford: Oxford University Press, 245–63.

Grey, C. and Garsten, C. (2001). 'Trust, Control and Post-bureaucracy'. *Organization Studies*, 22(2): 229–50.

Guest, R. H. (1956). 'Of Time and the Foreman'. *Personnel*, 32(6): 478–86.

Hales, C. (1999). 'Leading Horses to Water? The Impact of Decentralization of Managerial Behaviour'. *Journal of Management Studies*, 36(6): 831–51.

Hales, C. (2002). '"Bureaucracy-lite" and Continuities in Managerial Work'. *British Journal of Management*, 13(1): 51–66.

Hales, C. (2005). 'Rooted in Supervision, Branching into Management: Continuity and Change in the Role of First-line Manager'. *Journal of Management Studies*, 42(3): 471–506.

Hales, C. and Tamangani, Z. (1996). 'An Investigation of the Relationship between Organizational Structure, Managerial Role Expectations and Managers' Work Activities'. *Journal of Management Studies*, 33(6): 731–56.

Handy, C. (1989). *The Age of Unreason*. London: Business Books.

Hill, L. A. (1992). *Becoming a Manager: Mastery of a New Identity*. Boston, MA: Harvard Business School Press.

Jackall, R. (1988). *Moral Mazes: The World of Corporate Managers*. New York: Oxford University Press.

Kanter, R. M. (1977). *Men and Women of the Corporation*. New York: Basic Books.

Kanter, R. M. (1989). 'The New Managerial Work'. *Harvard Business Review*, 67, November/December: 85–92.

Kotter, J. P. (1982). *The General Managers*. New York: The Free Press.

Luthans, F., Hodgetts, R. M., and Rosenkrantz, S. A. (1988). *Real Managers*. Cambridge, MA: Ballinger.

Matthaei, E. (2010). *The Nature of Executive Work*. Wiesbaden: Gabler.

Mintzberg, H. (1973). *The Nature of Managerial Work*. New York: Harper & Row.
Mintzberg, H. (2009). *Managing*. San Francisco, CA: Berrett-Koehler Publishers.
Morgan, G. (1993). *Imaginization*. London: SAGE.
O'Gorman, C., Bourke, S., and Murray, J. A. (2005). 'The Nature of Managerial Work in Small Growth-Oriented Small Businesses'. *Small Business Economics*, 25(1): 1–16.
Peters, T. (1989). *Thriving on Chaos*. London: Pan.
Selznick, P. (1957). *Leadership in Administration: A Sociological Interpretation*. New York: Harper & Row.
Stewart, R. (1967/1988). *Managers and Their Jobs: A Study of the Similarities and Differences in the Ways Managers Spend Their Time*, 2nd edn. Basingstoke: Macmillan.
Stewart, R. (1982). *Choices for the Manager*. Englewood Cliffs, NJ: Prentice-Hall.
Tengblad, S. (2002). 'Time and Space in Managerial Work'. *Scandinavian Journal of Management*, 18(4): 543–66.
Tengblad, S. (2003). 'Classic, but not Seminal: Revisiting the Pioneering Study of Managerial Work'. *Scandinavian Journal of Management*, 19(1): 87–103.
Tengblad, S. (2006). 'Is there a "New Managerial Work"? A Comparison with Henry Mintzberg's Classic Study 30 Years Later'. *Journal of Management Studies*, 43(7): 1437–61.
Tengblad, S. (2012). 'Conclusions and the Way Forward', in S. Tengblad (ed.), *The Work of Managers: Towards a Practice Theory of Management*. Oxford: Oxford University Press, 337–56.
Tengblad, S. (2013). 'Management Roles', in E. H. Kessler (ed.), *Encyclopedia of Management Theory*. Thousand Oaks, CA: SAGE, 462–70.
Tengblad, S. (2015). 'Management and Leadership', in S. M. Dahlgaard-Park (ed.), *Encyclopedia of Quality and the Service Economy*. Thousand Oaks, CA: SAGE, 385–9.
Tengblad, S. and Vie, O. E. (2012). 'Management in Practice: Overview of Classic Studies on Managerial Work', in S. Tengblad (ed.), *The Work of Managers: Towards a Practice Theory of Management*. Oxford: Oxford University Press, 18–44.
Walker, C. R., Guest, R. H., and Turner, A. N. (1956). *The Foreman on the Assembly Line*. Cambridge, MA: Harvard University Press.
Watson, T. J. (1994/2001). *In Search of Management: Culture, Chaos and Control in Managerial Work*, rev. edn. London: Thomson Learning.
Vie, O. E. (2010). 'Have Post-bureaucratic Changes Occurred in Managerial Work?'. *European Management Journal*, 28(3), 182–94.
Wikström, E. and Dellve, L. (2009). 'Contemporary Leadership in Health Care Organizations: Fragmented or Concurrent Leadership'. *Journal of Health Organization & Management*, 23(4): 411–28.
Zuboff, S. (1988). *In the Age of the Smart Machine*. New York: Basic Books.

CHAPTER 17

MANAGING CHANGE

DAVID A. BUCHANAN

What's the Problem?

That this is an age of change is an expression heard frequently today. Never before in the history of mankind have so many and so frequent changes occurred. These changes that we see taking place all about us are in that great cultural accumulation which is man's [sic] social heritage. It has already been shown that these cultural changes were in earlier times rather infrequent, but that in modern times they have been occurring faster and faster until today mankind is almost bewildered in his effort to keep adjusted to these ever increasing social changes. This rapidity of social change may be due to the increase in inventions which in turn is made possible by the accumulative nature of material culture. (Ogburn, 1922: 199)

FROM a management perspective, organizational change is seen as problematic. How do we persuade people to accept new technologies that will make their skills, knowledge, and working practices obsolete? How quickly can people who find themselves with new roles, and new relationships, learn how to operate effectively after a major reorganization? How about this new system for capturing and processing customer information? We prefer the old system because it works well. Change can be difficult. Change that is not well managed, however, can generate frustration and anger.

Most estimates put the failure rate of planned changes at around 60%–70% (Rafferty et al., 2013). There are three main problems. First, there is a widespread belief that change is resisted, as a feature of 'human nature'. Second, there is a perception that organizations struggle to change as rapidly as the trigger conditions—competitive, economic, social, legislative, technological. Third, there is concern about the growing scale of change. There is, therefore, no shortage of advice on how to handle resistance, on how to accelerate the pace, and on managing 'transformational' change.

Kotter and Schlesinger (1979/2008) identify strategies for dealing with resistance, including education, participation, facilitation and support, negotiation, manipulation, and coercion. The first four take time to implement, but can improve relationships among those involved. The other two strategies can be implemented quickly, but can generate lasting distrust and resentment. It is often assumed that resistance is inevitable, but Rafferty, Jimmieson, and Armenakis (2013) argue that individual readiness for change can be strengthened through socialization and communication processes. Resistance is also presented as undesirable, from a management standpoint, but that is not necessarily the case. Resistance can open up debate, and stop inappropriate ideas from going ahead. Research into middle managers—those stereotyped change blockers—more often shows them subverting top team plans due to a perceived likelihood of failure (for which middle managers would get the blame) in favour of more effective and profitable initiatives (Boyett and Currie, 2004; Rouleau and Balogun, 2011).

The pace of change has also come to be regarded as particularly challenging. We seem to think of our own time as distinct in this regard. Witness, for example, the speed of geo-political events, the rapid spread of financial crises, and the constant stream of new technologies, in medicine, entertainment, communications, manufacturing, defence; smart phones, phablets, wristputers, 3-D printing, social media. The consultancy firm Deloitte (2013) advises clients with an approach called 'organization acceleration'. Mintzberg (2000), however, observes that each succeeding generation tends to perceive its own situation as more turbulent than that of its predecessors', as William Fielding Ogburn did, in 1922. So perhaps we should not over-react. Change is always accompanied by continuity, and is indeed defined by and with reference to what has not changed, but organizations announcing change rarely articulate what is going to stay the same, thus heightening anxieties unnecessarily.

The scale of change, small and localized versus large and systemic, is also problematic. Management consultants specializing in strategy often use a 'three whiteboards' exercise with the top management teams of their client organizations. The whiteboard on the left is headed, 'Where are we now?'. The board on the right is headed, 'Where do we want to be in two to five years' time?' (choose an appropriate period). The board in the middle is of course headed, 'How will we get there?'. With most organizations, the board on the right indicates large-scale, strategic, transformational change.

Depth is one metaphor that can be used as a basis for categorizing different types of change, as illustrated in Figure 17.1. At the bottom of this figure sits the 'small stuff' that may not even be regarded as 'change'. Mid-scale includes 'sustaining innovation' that involves improving on current practices. At the top of the scale is 'disruptive innovation' which involves radically new business models and working methods (Christensen, 2000). Managing small changes may be easier than implementing frame-breaking initiatives. The former are likely to involve few departures from the familiar. Deep or 'off the scale' change is often abrupt, painful, and can stimulate greater resistance.

The consultants' exercise implies that 'deep' change is more prevalent and necessary. This may be appropriate in some organizational contexts. However, research also suggests that small scale changes should not be overlooked. Moore and Buchanan (2013),

↑	Off the scale	disruptive innovation frame-breaking, mould-breaking redraw dramatically organization and sector boundaries
	Deeper	paradigm shift, strategic change new ways of thinking and solving problems, whole system change new ways of doing business
	Deep change	change the mission, vision, values, the organization's philosophy, in order to symbolize a radical shift in thinking and behaviour
		change the organization's definition of success create new goals, objectives, targets
	Sustaining innovation	improve business planning to symbolize a shift in thinking tighten up on documentation, reporting, controls
		reallocate resources grow some departments, cut others, create new units
	Shallow change	fine tuning: cut costs, improve efficiencies constantly 'nibble away' making minor improvements
↓	Not on the scale	'sweat the small stuff' - quickly solve the minor annoying problems that nobody has bothered to fix; 'grease the wheels'

FIGURE 17.1 Assessing Depth of Change.

for example, demonstrate how an initiative designed to fix small problems rapidly in an acute hospital generated a number of major performance improvements for almost no cost. In this case, 'sweating the small stuff' enabled deeper changes to happen, by getting people involved (the small problems were identified by staff), establishing a reputation for getting things done, and thus creating the platform for subsequent larger-scale initiatives. Shallower changes can facilitate, enable, and complement the deeper initiatives, and evidence suggests that these should not be underestimated. Although most commentary focuses on deep change, in most organizations, at any given time, changes are likely to be taking place across the scale. Recognizing this, many organizations have thus set up corporate project or programme management offices (PMOs) to support and coordinate their initiatives (Ward and Daniel, 2013).

The label 'managing change' thus offers the promise that this is a process that should and can be planned, coordinated, and controlled in a proactive, predictable, and effective manner. The volume of commentary on the subject, theoretical and practical, is now vast and fragmented, reflecting a number of contrasting perspectives and approaches. The manager in search of guidance is thus faced with a wealth of choice. A Google search (November 2013) produced the results shown in Table 17.1. Some of these 'hits' lead to academic sources, some to government agencies and professional bodies, and many to management consulting organizations selling change management perspectives, techniques, and tools. Within the range of perspectives, however, guides to practice tend to offer similar recommendations. With so much advice, and consistent advice available, why do so many changes fail?

Table 17.1 Managing Change on Google

Search term	Number of 'hits'
Managing organizational change	10.7 million
Organizational change management	59.5 million
Managing change	278 million
Change management	1,090 million

Given the breadth of this diverse field, this chapter focuses selectively on five key issues. First, *practical guidelines* or change management 'recipes' are assessed. Second, *process theory* perspectives on change are explored. Third, the issues raised by the *pace of change* are considered. Fourth, *change leadership skills* are examined. Finally, suggestions for *future research* in this area are outlined.

Change Management Recipes

The hand of the American social psychologist Kurt Lewin, whose work dates from the mid-twentieth century, still hovers over the field of change management today. Contemporary interest in the subject—theoretical and practical—dates from his contribution. Lewin argued that it was necessary first to 'unfreeze' current attitudes, to create an understanding of the need for change. Following implementation, he observed that it was necessary to 'refreeze' attitudes and behaviours, before those involved could revert to previous ways of working. This simple 'unfreeze–move–refreeze' model has face validity, and is still cited in change management commentary. However, with regard to the third phase in the model, and given the ongoing stream of change initiatives that many organizations seem to experience, 'permanent thaw' has become a more accurate metaphor.

Most contemporary change models have followed Lewin's approach, offering more detail, and using different terms. Kotter's (1995) eight-phase approach to transformational change, for example, opens with 'create a sense of urgency' (unfreeze), passes through 'empower people to act' (move), and ends with 'institutionalize new approaches' (refreeze). The US Institute for Healthcare Improvement (IHI) advocates a five-step change implementation framework (Figure 17.2) which begins with 'make the status quo uncomfortable', reaches a fifth, 'execute change', which closes with 'sustain improved levels of performance' (Reinertsen, Bisognano, and Pugh, 2008: 4). Recognize the language?

These 'n-step recipes' ('n' can be any number higher than two) dominate the landscape of practical guidance on change management. These approaches codify what is usually

```
                    ┌──────────────────────────────────────────────┐
                    │  1. Set Direction: Mission, Vision, and Strategy │
       ➡            │                                              │            ➡
      PUSH          │  Make the status quo uncomfortable   Make the future attractive  │          PULL
                    └──────────────────────────────────────────────┘
```

3. Build will	5. Generate Ideas	5. Execute Change
• Plan for Improvement • Set Aims/Allocate Resources • Measure System Performance • Provide Encouragement • Make Financial Linkages • Learn Subject Matter • Work on the Larger System	• Read and Scan Widely, Learn from Other Industries and Disciplines • Benchmark to Find Ideas • Listen to Customers • Invest in Research and Development • Manage Knowledge • Understand Organization as a System	• Use Model for Improvement for Design and Redesign • Review and Guide Key Initiatives • Spread Ideas • Communicate Results • Sustain Improved Levels of Performance

2. Establish the Foundations

- Reframe Operating Values
- Build Improvement Capability
- Prepare Personally
- Choose and Align the Senior Team
- Build Relationships
- Develop Future Leaders

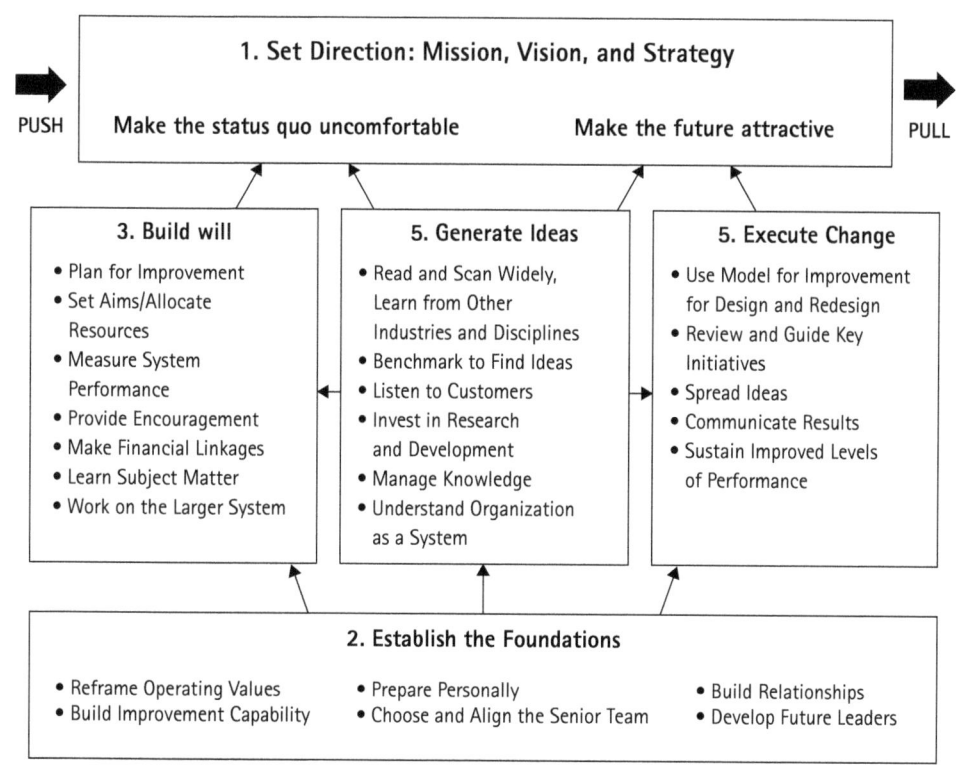

FIGURE 17.2 The Institute for Healthcare Improvement Large-scale Change Framework.

a messy, iterative process, and offer the busy change leader straightforward advice on what do to in order to improve the chances of success. It is also probably accurate to observe that, in most cases, if your organization does not broadly follow the advice of Kotter and the IHI, then your change programme could be in trouble.

Another illustration of the genre is provided by Keller, Meaney, and Pung (2010), who identify the methods that make 'transformational change' successful. They define transformational change as 'any large-scale change, such as going from good to great performance, cutting costs, or turning around a crisis' (Keller, Meaney, and Pung, 2010: 1). Their model is based on a global survey of 2,500 executives carried out by McKinsey & Co, a management consulting firm. Those executives identified four sets of tactics which had contributed to the success of their changes. The tactics concerned goals, structures, involvement, and leadership, and are summarized in Table 17.2.

Goals, structures, engagement, leadership—these are common themes in change management advice. However, Keller and colleagues also found that these tactics were more effective when they were combined. Of the organizations which used all of these tactics, 80% met their aims, compared with only 10% of those organizations which had used none of these approaches. Even with defensive transformations, the chance of success using all of these tactics was 64%.

Table 17.2 The McKinsey & Co. Recipe for Successful Transformational Change

Tactic	Explanation
Goals	go for growth and progressive, developmental change, with 'stretch' targets avoid defensive transformations which are reactive and focus on cost cutting focus on strengths and achievements, not just problems set unambiguous measures of success and monitor progress
Structures	logical programme design break processes down into clearly defined initiatives allow those involved to co-create the programme clear roles, responsibilities, and accountabilities
Involvement	high levels of engagement and collaboration front line ownership of events initiative to drive change also comes from the front line high levels of communication and involvement at all stages
Leadership	personal commitment and visible involvement of the chief executive leaders 'role model' the desired changes and 'mindset' develop capacity and capability for continuous improvement culture becomes more receptive to further innovation

One problem with these recipes is that the change process *is* messy and iterative. There is a danger of oversimplification in reducing the process to three, four, or eight steps. Things do not always go according to plan or happen on time, external events interfere, and it may often be necessary to jump ahead, and to backtrack. In addition, change is politicized, as those who feel disadvantaged seek to undermine the process when they discover that their arguments against what is about to happen are being ignored. A second problem relates to a lack of detail behind the principles. It may be appropriate to 'make the status quo uncomfortable' and to 'avoid defensive transformations', but these frameworks do not explain how to accomplish those steps. Exploring practice in other organizations can be a source of ideas, but what has worked in one setting rarely works in another, without modification. A third problem concerns the lack of attention to context. Not all change is 'transformational' (management consultants can charge higher fees for advice on transformations than with more mundane initiatives). In some contexts, a relaxed pace may be desirable, but time may be of the essence elsewhere. Does the same advice apply in different contexts?

These complexities have been addressed by Stace and Dunphy (2001) who from their research in the finance sector in Australia develop a contingency model. They first define the scale of change, from fine-tuning to corporate transformation, and then identify four styles of change: collaborative (widespread participation), consultative (limited involvement), directive (authoritative decisions), and coercive (imposed change). Stace and Dunphy argue that participative strategies are time-consuming as they expose

	Incremental change strategies	Transformative change strategies
	Participative evolution	*Charismatic transformation*
Collaborative–consultative modes	use when the organization needs minor adjustment to meet environmental conditions, where time is available, and where key interest groups favour change	use when the organization needs major adjustments to meet environmental conditions, where there is little time for participation, and where there is support for radical change
	Forced evolution	*Dictatorial transformation*
Directive–coercive modes	use when minor adjustments are required, where time is available, but where key interest groups oppose change	use when major adjustments are necessary, where there is no time for participation, where there is no support for strategic change, but where this is necessary for survival

FIGURE 17.3 The Stace-Dunphy Contingency Model of Change Implementation.

conflicting views that are difficult to reconcile. Where organizational survival depends on rapid and strategic change, dictatorial transformation is appropriate. Their model of change is summarized in Figure 17.3, advocating different approaches to fit different contexts.

Hope Hailey and Balogun (2002) and Balogun (2006) also advocate context sensitive approaches to the design and implementation of change. Their framework identifies a number of contextual features in what they call 'the change kaleidoscope', including: the necessary speed of change; the scope of the change agenda; the need to maintain continuity on some dimensions; diversity of attitudes and values among those affected; individual change capabilities and organizational capacity for change; readiness for change; and the power of the change agent. These context features, they argue, should influence decisions concerning the starting point and path of change, the chosen implementation style, specific change levers and mechanisms, and the nature of change roles (top down, bottom up, dispersed).

These recipes and contingency models are 'high level' guides and not detailed roadmaps. They seem to be useful in practice as long as they are used in that way, although academic critics complain of their a-theoretical nature. Change leaders resorting to these models thus have to 'fill in the blanks' themselves, with an appropriate blend of local knowledge, informed judgement, and creative flair.

Returning to the question posed earlier, why is the failure rate of planned change attempts so high? Most recipes offer the same straightforward guidance: clear goals, powerful change leaders, good communications, high levels of participation, invest in training, celebrate success, embed. None of this advice is difficult to implement. So, what is the problem? The answer may lie, in part, in an analogy with the circus performer. The change leader has to keep numerous plates spinning, usually for a prolonged period, while colleagues (the resistance) try to knock some of the plates off their sticks, and to divert the change leader's attention from the others, so that they also fall.

Processual Perspectives

It is a truism to observe that change is a process, and not an event. Nevertheless, processual perspectives have been influential in demonstrating the nature and implications of the untidy, non-linear characteristics of change. This influence has been more significant with regard to theory, and process accounts have been criticized, perhaps unfairly, for their relative lack of practical change management advice. However, processual accounts advise change leaders to prepare for the messy and unpredictable nature of change, in contrast to the more orderly sequences of events that are implied by the change recipes and contingency models discussed earlier.

Process accounts explain how phenomena such as organizational change unfold over time through the combination and interaction of factors at different levels of analysis (Pettigrew, Woodman, and Cameron, 2001). Process theories are also examples of 'conjunctural causality' (Goldstone, 2003), also known as configurational or combinatorial explanations. Time, and event sequence are central to understanding (Langley et al., 2013). Dawson and Andriopoulos (2014) argue that change processes are influenced by the interaction of three sets of factors: context, substance, and politics (Figure 17.4).

The past, present, and future external and internal context of the organization are thus important influences. Previous events can of course shape current and future

The context of change (past, present, and future)

External context: Market, legislation, political events

Internal context: Human resources, job design and work structures, technology, product/service, history and culture

The change process

The politics of change

External activity: Political lobbying, strategic alliances, stakeholder discussions

Internal activity: Negotiation, conflicts and resistance

The substance of change

Scale and scope
defining characteristics
timeframe
perceived centrality

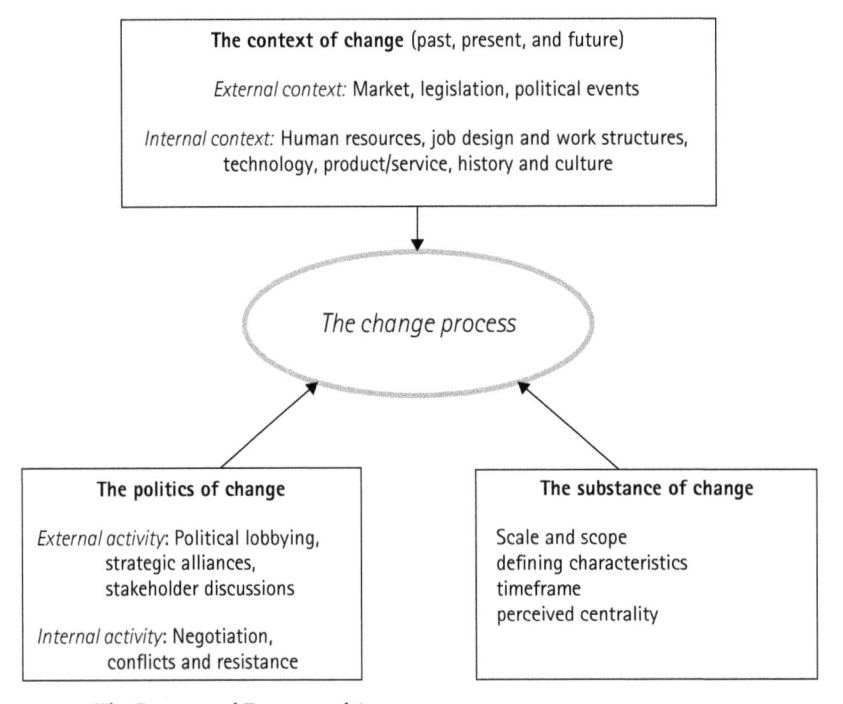

FIGURE 17.4 The Processual Framework*.

* based on Dawson and Andriopoulos, 2014

perceptions and responses. The substance of change is significant, with regard to scale, timeframe, and 'perceived centrality', or how important the change is to the survival of the organization. Processual accounts emphasize the role of political tactics, both external (lobbying, alliances, stakeholder management) and internal (conflict and resistance). Change agents must therefore be willing and able to intervene in the politics of the organization if they are to succeed (Buchanan and Badham, 2008). A key part of this aspect of the role involves symbolic actions which seek to legitimize proposals in the face of competing ideas, to establish the credibility of particular definitions of problems and solutions, and to gain consent and compliance from other organizational members. Part of the change leader's task, therefore, concerns 'the management of meaning' (Pettigrew, 1985: 442). This involves 'the way you tell it', or more accurately with 'the way you *sell* it' to others.

The discussion so far has concerned changes that are deliberately *planned*. However, some changes are *emergent*. In the absence of management direction, most organizations are constantly changing anyway. People find better ways of doing things. Problems arise for which novel and more-or-less permanent solutions are found. Most management and professional job descriptions incorporate, explicitly or implicitly, responsibilities for cutting costs, increasing revenue, improving quality, business development, and so on—in other words, identifying and implementing change initiatives.

Plowman et al. (2007) give a fascinating account of emergent change, described as 'radical change accidentally'. They document the turnaround of 'Mission Church', a failing organization with declining membership, which was able to grow that membership, to include a much wider cross section of the community, with benefit to the surrounding area. This was not the result of a deliberate plan, but was triggered by a breakfast meeting at which the introduction of a new 'breakfast for the homeless' service was suggested. This relatively insignificant event took place in the context of a declining organization, experiencing changes in leadership, combined with internal conflict, and lack of clarity over the organization's purpose. Small actions were amplified in this unstable context, making radical change possible, although this was emergent and slow. This is a good example of a processual account of successful change unfolding over time, illustrating the phenomenon of conjunctural causality, as factors at different levels of analysis combined to produce the outcomes.

From their processual account, Dawson and Andriopoulos (2014) identify eight 'general lessons' concerning change management practice. First, there are no universal prescriptions or simple recipes for how best to manage change. Second, change is a political process, and change leaders need be politically sensitive and astute. Third, time, planning and flexibility are essential, in changing attitudes and behaviours, and in gaining commitment for change.

Fourth, they advocate 'critical reflection', challenging taken-for-granted assumptions, for example with regard to resistance, which may be desirable if it subverts a weak initiative. Fifth, it is important to learn from both positive and negative experiences, rather than concentrating on successes. Sixth, education, training, and development should be aligned with the needs of new operating procedures. Seventh, communication is a fundamentally important vehicle in steering processes in desired directions. Finally, 'contradictions provide health food for critical reflection': change requires constant adaptation to contextual circumstances.

Has process theory been unable to offer practical advice for change leaders? Plowman et al. (2007) encourage sensitivity to context and small actions, but do not set out further guidelines. Most of the advice from Dawson and Andriopoulos (2014) also relates to how the change process should be understood, rather than to implementation. In sum, where recipe accounts recommend 'do this', processual accounts advise, 'be aware of this'. In the context of understanding and managing organizational change, both sets of advice appear to have value, particularly in combination.

THE QUESTION OF PACE

Previous research suggested that organizations typically experience periods of relative stability, interrupted from time to time by larger-scale changes. This was known as the theory of 'punctuated equilibrium' (Tushman and Romanelli, 1985; Tushman, Newman, and Romanelli, 1986), which required the organization to balance a 'workable equilibrium' with sharp 'frame-breaking' systemic changes when required. In other words, the pace of change was determined by the frequency of those frame-breaking intervals.

Kotter and Schlesinger (1979/2008) offered a more nuanced perspective, advocating a contingency approach to determining the 'optimal speed' of change, depending on the situation. Not surprisingly, they suggested moving quickly if performance was declining rapidly, and the survival of the organization was in jeopardy. They advocated a more modest pace where resistance was expected to be intense, where the commitment of others was required to help design and implement the changes, and where the change leaders had less organizational power than the resistance. Time pressure is also a decision criterion in the Stace–Dunphy contingency model discussed earlier.

Most managers today, however, feel that they are denied the luxury of choice with regard to whether and when to launch the next round of organizational changes. Punctuated equilibrium is an unfamiliar pattern. As noted earlier, 'permanent thaw' is a more appropriate metaphor than 'refreezing'. With regard to internal systems, structures, and working practices, most organizations need to match the pace of developments in financial markets, new technology and materials, and competition, accompanied by constant shifts in domestic and international government priorities, policies, and regulatory requirements. There seems to be little or no stable equilibrium to be found in this pattern.

Kotter (2012a: 52) thus offers advice on how to speed up change, with eight 'change accelerators':

1. Create a sense of urgency with regard to a single, big opportunity;
2. Build and maintain a guiding coalition;

3. Form a strategic vision, and develop initiatives to capitalize on major opportunities;
4. Communicate the strategy and vision to create a 'volunteer army';
5. Ensure that your network removes barriers in the way of achieving the vision;
6. Celebrate significant short-term wins;
7. Be persistent and keep learning from experience, but do not declare victory prematurely;
8. Make sure that changes become part of the organization culture.

These 'accelerators' are based on Kotter's (1995) change model, but with three differences. First, Kotter argues that these accelerators must operate concurrently, rather than in sequence. Second, change must not rely on a small powerful core group, but on many change agents from across the organization. Third, traditional hierarchy must be complemented by flexible and agile networks.

Accelerating the pace of change may be damaging in some circumstances. Abrahamson (2000, 2004) claims that constant rapid change is destabilizing and causes burnout, and argues instead for 'painless change'. Echoing the research of Tushman and Romanelli (1985), Abrahamson argues that organizations should aspire to 'dynamic stability', which means interspersing major initiatives among carefully timed periods of smaller 'organic' changes, identifying two organic processes:

- *Tinkering*   fiddling with the nuts and bolts to create inspired solutions to contemporary problems, rather than trying to create something new from scratch.
- *Kludging*   tinkering on a larger scale, using internal and external resources (skills, technologies, models), maybe creating a new division or business.

Effective change thus involves careful pacing, implementing patterns of large and smaller scale changes at appropriate intervals. Organizations that have avoided change may need to transform rapidly, while those which have changed rapidly may have to start tinkering and kludging. Abrahamson's advice again implies that organizations can choose which changes to implement when, on what scale, and at what pace. Environmental pressures often shape, if not make, those decisions.

Bruch and Menges (2010) also argue that rapid change can lead to corporate burnout, observing that, in many organizations, intense market pressures encourage management to increase the number and speed of activities, raise performance goals, shorten innovation cycles, and introduce new systems and technologies. When the chief executive makes this furious pace 'the new normal', the achievements turn into chronic overloading. Working constantly under time pressure, with priorities frequently changing, focus is scattered, staff become tired and demotivated, and customers get confused.

Bruch and Menges call this 'the acceleration trap'. They found that in companies that were 'fully trapped', 60% of employees felt that they lacked the resources to get their work done, compared with only 2% in companies that were not 'trapped'. They also identified three typical patterns.

- *Overloading* staff have too much work to do, but not enough time or resources
- *Multiloading* staff have too many different kinds of tasks, thus reducing focus
- *Perpetual loading* the organization operates close to capacity all the time, giving employees no chance to rest or retreat, but only to ask, 'When is the economizing going to come to an end?'. (Bruch and Menges, 2010: 83)

An organization probably has an 'acceleration culture' if staff answer 'yes' to five or more of the following nine statements (Bruch and Menges, 2010: 85):

- Is it hard to get important things done because too many other activities diffuse focus?
- Is there a tendency to drive the organization to the limits of its capacity?
- Does the company value hard effort over tangible results?
- Are employees made to feel guilty if they leave work early?
- Do employees talk a lot about how big their workload is?
- Are managers expected to act as role models by being involved in multiple projects?
- Is 'no' a taboo word, even for people who have already taken on too many projects?
- Is there an expectation that people must respond to emails within minutes?
- After work, do staff keep their mobile phones on because they feel they need to be reachable?

An organization can break free from the acceleration trap with a combination of strategies. First, clarity with regard to strategy and goals is important. Second, less important work should be brought to a halt. Third, a system for prioritizing initiatives should be developed. Finally, senior management should 'declare an end to the current high-energy phase' (Bruch and Menges, 2010: 83). At one company studied by Bruch and Menges, the chief executive insisted that managers identify only three 'must-win battles', to concentrate attention and energy, instead of the 'ten top priority goals' with which they used to work.

The question of pace is of pressing practical concern, given the perceived need for speed to survive, on the one hand, and the potential dangers of individual and corporate burnout, on the other. This is an oversimplification; moderately-paced change may be effective in some settings, and it is surely possible to change at pace without the drawbacks, given careful anticipation and management of the issues. However, most of the commentary in this section draws on practitioner sources. Processual accounts have had little to say about the pace of change, despite emphasizing the importance of temporal factors. Better understanding of the nature, benefits, and drawbacks of different rates of change in different contexts requires longitudinal research methods. Sadly, trends in research funding, and in the performance management of researchers, encourage short term outputs, thus discouraging longitudinal studies that could take years to produce convincing results.

The Change Leader

- *Researcher* 'We would like to speak to the change agents who implemented your whole-hospital redesign programme.'
- *Human resources director* 'What, all four and a half thousand of them?'

Terminology has become a problem: change agents, change managers, change leaders. Are these terms interchangeable? For most of the second half of the twentieth century, the term 'change agent' referred to an external facilitator or consultant hired to design the interventions that would produce the changes that management desired. The term now tends to be used more loosely, to include anyone who is involved in helping to design and implement change, either inside or from outside the organization, whether or not they have a formal change role or job title.

Kotter (2012b) maintains a distinction between change managers and change leaders. The role of managers is to keep small change initiatives under control and running smoothly. Change leaders supply the vision and the driving force for major transformations. Kotter thus argues that change leadership capabilities are at a premium in an unpredictable and fast-moving business environment. (Cynics might note that consultants can sell leadership advice at a higher premium than management advice.) This discussion echoes the wider debate about the difference between management and leadership, where similar contrasts between maintaining order and providing vision appear.

Mintzberg (2009) adopts a different view, observing that while it may be possible to separate management and leadership roles conceptually, it is not possible to do so in behavioural terms. He asks if we would like to be managed by someone who could not lead, or to be led by someone who could not manage, concluding that 'We should be seeing managers *as* leaders, and leadership as management practiced well' (Mintzberg, 2009: 9). In this chapter, we will stick with Mintzberg. However, following fashion, the term 'change leader' will be used here in preference to other terms.

Change leadership, as with leadership in general, has thus become a widely distributed function (Gronn, 2009; Denis, Langley, and Sergi, 2012). Buchanan et al. (2007) describe the implementation of a complex change agenda which dramatically improved the treatment given to men with prostate cancer in an acute hospital. While the contributions of four individuals (one of whom was employed by an external agency) were key, there was no project leader, and implementation involved a further 23 individuals, and 26 managerial, administrative, and clinical groups, patients, representatives, and other organizations. Responsibility for the changes shifted between individuals and groups as the work progressed, apparently without the need for any supervisory or coordinating roles or structures. Many of those implicated in this process had little or no change leadership background or training.

Does this mean that everyone is now a change leader? No, but the possibility of being involved in a change initiative is ever present, and the need for basic skills in this area is thus increased. It may be appropriate in many organizations to offer change leadership development opportunities to staff other than those in formal change management roles. As indicated previously, Kotter (2012a) advocates the dispersal of change leadership responsibilities as a tactic for accelerating the pace of change.

Considering the capabilities that change leaders require, it is difficult to escape from competency frameworks. Table 17.3 summarizes the framework developed by the global Change Management Institute (Leys, 2012). Competency frameworks have been

Table 17.3 Change Management Institute Competency Model

Skill area	Demonstrates understanding of/capabilities in
Facilitating change	principles of change; the environment business focus; change readiness; culture awareness
Strategic thinking	vision; assess readiness strategic view; sustainable outcomes
Thinking and judgement	analytical thinking; holistic perspective; decision-making
Influencing others	customer/stakeholder focus; professional presence networking; interpersonal skills (selling ideas; use of power)
Coaching for change	adult learning principles; change management needs analysis; organizational capability to manage change role model; champion new skills
Project management	plan development; monitor and manage progress cost management; risk and opportunity management review project outcomes
Communication	relationships building; empathy; oral and written communication measures effectiveness of communication
Self-management	personal responsibility; prioritization and time management resilience; flexibility; emotional intelligence
Facilitation—meetings and workshops	design; participatory environment structure (agenda, physical environment) process (facilitation tools, inclusion, timing)
Professional development	updates knowledge and develops skills promotion of change management
Specialist expertise (1) Learning and development	needs identification; training plan solution delivery; evaluation
Specialist expertise (2) Communication	needs identification; plan; solution design and development; solution delivery; evaluation

criticized for the fragmented and over-simplified manner in which expertise is represented (Hollenbeck, McCall, and Silzer, 2006). Political skill can be central to change leader effectiveness (Ferris, Davidson, and Perrewé, 2005; Buchanan and Badham, 2008) but is rarely recognized. Beeson (2009), however, in identifying what he calls 'core selection factors' in executive career advancement, emphasizes the importance of 'soft skills' such as 'Getting things done across internal boundaries (lateral management); demonstrating organizational savvy; influencing and persuading colleagues; dealing with conflict'. Nevertheless, these frameworks are commonly used in practice as assessment and development tools. Do the twelve skill areas in Table 17.3 present an unrealistic picture of the 'hypercompetent' change leader? Not necessarily. Most if not all of those skills, including the 'specialist expertise', apply to most if not all general management roles.

Another criticism of competency frameworks is that they do not capture the nature of the work, and therefore the attitudinal and personality characteristics that contribute to change leadership effectiveness. Being involved in leading a large-scale change project can be a challenging task, with regard to the commitment of time and energy. Someone looking for a conventional nine-to-five commitment will probably be uncomfortable in a change leadership role. Here is an account of an exchange between the author of this chapter and a Finnish woman who had joined a team working on a particularly demanding change project with an organization in Adelaide, South Australia:

> 'You have described this job as making very heavy demands on your time and energy. It sounds exhausting. Why did you decide to accept this job?'
>
> 'I wanted a job to look forward to in the morning, and not want to leave in the evening. I saw it as a great opportunity to learn. I get charged up with more learning. I need that. I needed to get my hands dirty. It gave me a chance to show my capabilities. It is a very tiring and frustrating job. On the other hand, it gives you a great opportunity to excel. I am a risk taker. I need some excitement and powerplay while at work. I believe that the only way to meet the challenges of the external business environment is to offer the customer what they really want. It gave me an opportunity to work with some highly motivated and committed individuals. Together we were able to make it happen. I have thick skin. I realized that I was going to make some enemies during the change process—as well as some very influential and powerful friends. I was able to accept the challenge due to the stage of my personal lifestyle (boyfriend overseas, dog at home). I sacrificed my spare time for the company—and for the financial and non-financial rewards. Even though I was an inexperienced change agent, I was confident that I had skills, knowledge and attributes to make it happen. Or that I could find an expert (internal or external) to assist me to make it happen. If I would fail, I could still work with [this organization]—or elsewhere, because I am tolerant of ambiguity.'

This person was motivated by the challenge, the excitement, and the personal development opportunities, and was not concerned about the long hours, due to lifestyle factors and the stage that she had reached in her career. She also displays several significant personality traits: need to learn and develop, need for risk and power, desire to make things happen, tolerant of ambiguity, thick skin.

The rewards for working in such an intense and pressured role include personal development and wider future career opportunities. Change leaders are typically exposed to corporate issues and to stakeholders that they would not meet in a conventional professional or operational role. As a result, they enhance their employability and often have 're-entry' problems with regard to returning to their previous roles, and pursue promotion opportunities instead (Buchanan, 2003).

Issues that appear to be assuming greater significance thus include the implications of distributed change leadership, the role of political expertise in shaping the nature, direction, and pace of change, and the motives of change leaders. There is, however, a lack of research evidence in these areas.

The Research Agenda

Change is one area of organization and management studies where theory and practice do not appear to inform or to complement each other. There is no 'core' research tradition, and no set of shared concepts or frameworks. The recipes people find processual accounts obscure; the process people regard the recipes as atheoretical. This gap arises from transatlantic differences in epistemology. American researchers remain wedded to positivist, variance-based perspectives which seek to isolate and operationalize variables and to establish covariation. British and European researchers are more comfortable with constructivist epistemology, processual perspectives, and theoretical narratives. This distinction is captured by Mohr (1982) who argues that, in the field of organizational behaviour, variance perspectives are of limited value, and that process theory is a more appropriate vehicle for developing understanding. That argument has been received with more favour on one side of the Atlantic than the other. This observation does not apply to Canadian researchers, who have consistently advocated processual perspectives (e.g., Langley et al., 2013).

The fragmentation of the field means that we do not fully understand why, with broadly consistent and non-contentious practical guidelines, a high proportion of change efforts fail to achieve their aims. Diversity of perspectives can be a strength, enlivening debate, as well as a weakness, sowing confusion. However, given the perceived need for constant, often rapid, and predominantly large-scale organizational changes, and the damage caused by the apparent mis-management of change, better understanding of the critical success and failure factors, in different context, would have a range of individual, organizational, social, and economic benefits.

At least five sets of research questions merit closer attention.

First, there is little research exploring the nature and prospects for organizational change in different economic conditions, such as growth versus recession. Most case study accounts of change appear to involve progressive, developmental change agendas. Detailed case accounts of defensive, reactive, cost cutting agendas are rare, although Keller, Meaney, and Pung (2010) argue that these are less likely to succeed. Does organizational change become easier to manage in a recession, where the sense of urgency is likely to be widespread, along with an understanding of the rationale (Meaney and Wilson, 2009)?

Second, the notion of 'transformational' change appears to be clear and taken-for-granted, sitting at the top of the scale, or 'off the scale', in Table 17.1. This may be unhelpful in two regards. First, this conceptualization overlooks the facilitative and potentially cumulative effects of shallower, smaller-scale change initiatives. For many organizations, 'the small stuff' may be an appropriate starting point, while launching into deep change could be a miscalculation. Second, this approach to transformation focuses attention on the *substance* of change; the new organization structure, the new IT system, the new service delivery model. Many organizations, however, are experimenting with novel *approaches* to developing that substance in the first place, through staff engagement. For example, the director of transformation at an acute hospital in England explained:

> If anything, I think the most radical things that we have done are the genuine engagement and asking people as to what do you think would be better, and allowing them to do it. So it's the approach and the culture and the leadership and the mindset change. And the bravery that has to go alongside that from a senior leadership perspective, to put the umbrella up and shield people from any external criticism or demands if it weren't to go right immediately.

Transformational change may thus be more appropriately conceptualized as a multidimensional phenomenon which takes different guises, depending on substance, scale, relationship to other ongoing initiatives, timing, sequencing, pace, and intended outcomes.

Third, a new style of 'recipe' has emerged, relating not to change implementation, but to establishing and maintaining the *capability* to implement change continuously. Mohrman and Lawler (2012: 42) argue that organizations must focus on 'next practice' as well as 'best practice', because:

> The major challenge for organizations today is navigating high levels of turbulence. They operate in dynamic environments, in societies where the aspirations and purposes of various stakeholders change over time. They have access to ever-increasing technological capabilities and information. A key organizational capability is the ability to adapt as context, opportunities, and challenges change.

Describing the 'Building Capacity to Change' (BCC) project at Capital One, a financial services company, Worley and Lawler (2009) and Lawler and Worley (2006) identify four 'built to change' features. First, a strong focus on future trends, possibilities, and implications. Second, a 'test and learn' strategy that is constantly seeking 'momentary advantages' and opportunities for new revenue streams. Third, flexible organization design, with flat structures, frequent reorganizations, and empowered employees. Finally, having the capability to change as a matter of routine. There has been little research into this construct. One key issue concerns the problems potentially generated by the constant flux and uncertainty implicit in the model. Another concerns the applicability of this approach in public sector organizations, where constant change is also an imperative, but where bureaucratic, legislative, and regulatory barriers may block the approach.

Fourth, the concept of path dependence has been used by political scientists to study national revolutions, involving (transformational) government and regime change, between for example democracy and dictatorship (Mahoney and Rueschemeyer, 2003; Goldstone, 2003). Path dependence explains how a society, or an organization, can become predisposed, committed, or 'locked in' to a future course of action through the influence of past decisions and events. This perspective has not been widely used to understand the nature of organizational changes. Sydow, Schreyogg, and Koch (2009) develop a model of organizational path dependence, which is a 'tapering social process' with three phases: preformation, where the scope for action is broad, but still conditioned by the past; formation, when a dominant pattern emerges, narrowing the options, and making the process increasingly irreversible; and lock in, when the dominant pattern becomes fixed and gains a deterministic character. Resonating with a processual perspective, tracing events over time in context, research conducted through this lens could generate fresh insights into why some changes succeed, and others do not.

Finally, there is a paradox in this field that has attracted little interest, concerning post-crisis change. Accidents, failures, serious incidents, and other extreme events provide the organizations involved with a 'brutal audit' of their structures, systems, procedures, and management styles (Lagadec, 1993). Such events are normally followed by investigations, with the remit to identify what went wrong, and to develop recommendations to prevent a recurrence. Those recommendations, however, are often not implemented (Elliott, 2009). Why not? Research has focused on event causality and crisis management, and on the role of public inquiries. Post-crisis change management has been overlooked (Buchanan and Denyer, 2013). Understanding why change does not happen under conditions where readiness and receptiveness should be high could shed fresh light on the nature and success of change in 'normal' organizational settings, as well as contributing to a reduction in those extreme events.

Underpinning these suggestions is the assumption that the methodologies that would generate the evidence are available to researchers. The study of change in different economic conditions, studying different modes of transformational change, investigating the development of continuous change capability, exploring path-dependent explanations of change processes, tracing the fate of post-crisis recommendations—these issues require longitudinal methods. It is unfortunate that research funding and performance management systems now discourage such methodological approaches. Changing those systems would appear to be difficult.

REFERENCES

Abrahamson, E. (2000). 'Change without Pain'. *Harvard Business Review*, 78(4): 75–9.

Abrahamson, E. (2004). *Change Without Pain: How Managers Can Overcome Initiative Overload, Organizational Chaos, and Employee Burnout*. Boston, MA: Harvard Business School Press.

Balogun, J. (2006). 'Managing Change: Steering a Course between Intended Strategies and Unanticipated Outcomes'. *Long Range Planning*, 39(1): 29–49.

Beeson, J. (2009) 'Why You Didn't Get that Promotion: Decoding the Unwritten Rules of Corporate Advancement'. *Harvard Business Review*, 87(6): 101–5.

Boyett I. and Currie, G. (2004). 'Middle Managers Moulding International Strategy: An Irish Start-Up in Jamaican Telecoms'. *Long Range Planning*, 37(1): 51–66.

Bruch, H. and Menges, J. I. (2010). 'The Acceleration Trap'. *Harvard Business Review*, 88(4): 80–6.

Buchanan, D. A. (2003). 'Demands, Instabilities, Manipulations, Careers: The Lived Experience of Driving Change'. *Human Relations*, 56(6): 663–84.

Buchanan, D. A. and Badham, R. (2008). *Power, Politics, and Organizational Change: Winning the Turf Game*, 2nd edn. London: SAGE.

Buchanan, D. A. and Dawson, P. (2007). 'Discourse and Audience: Organizational Change as Multi-Story Process'. *Journal of Management Studies*, 44(5): 669–86.

Buchanan, D. A. and Denyer, D. (2013). 'Researching Tomorrow's Crisis: Methodological Innovations and Wider Implications'. *International Journal of Management Reviews*, 15(2): 205–24.

Buchanan, D. A., Addicott, R., Fitzgerald, L., Ferlie, E., and Baeza, J. (2007). 'Nobody in Charge: Distributed Change Agency in Healthcare'. *Human Relations*, 60(7): 1065–90.

Christensen, C. M. (2000). *The Innovator's Dilemma: When New Technologies Cause Great Firms to Fail*. New York: Harper Collins.

Dawson, P. M. B. and Andriopoulos, C. (2014). *Managing Change, Creativity and Innovation*, 2nd edn. London: SAGE.

Deloitte (2013). *Organization Acceleration: The New Science of Moving Organizations Forward*. London: Deloitte Touch Tohmatsu Limited.

Denis, J.-L., Langley, A., and Sergi, V. (2012). 'Leadership in the Plural'. *Academy of Management Annals*, 6(1): 1–73.

Elliott, D. (2009). 'The Failure of Organizational Learning from Crisis: A Matter of Life and Death?'. *Journal of Contingencies and Crisis Management*, 17(3): 157–68.

Ferris, G. R., Davidson, S. L. and Perrewé, P. L. (2005). *Political Skill at Work: Impact on Work Effectiveness*. Mountain View, CA: Davies-Black Publishing.

Goldstone, J. A. (2003). 'Comparative Historical Analysis and Knowledge Accumulation in the Study Of Revolutions', in James Mahoney and Dietrich Rueschemeyer (eds.), *Comparative Historical Analysis in the Social Sciences*. Cambridge: Cambridge University Press, 41–90.

Gronn, P. (2009). 'Leadership Configurations'. *Leadership*, 5(3): 381–94.

Hollenbeck, G. P., McCall, M. W., and Silzer, R. F. (2006). 'Leadership Competency Models'. *The Leadership Quarterly*, 17(4): 398–413.

Hope Hailey, V. and Balogun, J. (2002). 'Devising Context Sensitive Approaches to Change: The Example of Glaxo Wellcome'. *Long Range Planning*, 35(2): 153–78.

Keller, S., Meaney, M., and Pung, C. (2010). *What Successful Transformations Share*. Chicago and London: McKinsey & Company.

Kotter, J. P. (1995). 'Leading Change: Why Transformation Efforts Fail'. *Harvard Business Review*, 73(2): 59–67.

Kotter, J. P. (2012a). 'Accelerate!', *Harvard Business Review*, 90(11): 44–52.

Kotter, J. P. (2012). *Leading Change*, 2nd edn. Boston, MA: Harvard University Press.

Kotter, J. P. and Schlesinger, L. A. (1979, republished 2008). 'Choosing Strategies for Change'. *Harvard Business Review*, 86(7/8): 130–9.

Lagadec, P. (1993). *Preventing Chaos in a Crisis*. Maidenhead: McGraw-Hill.

Langley, A., Smallman, C., Tsoukas, H., and Van de Ven, A.H. (2013). 'Process Studies of Change in Organization and Management: Unveiling Temporality, Activity, and Flow'. *Academy of Management Journal*, 56(1): 1–13.

Lawler, E. E. and Worley, C. G. (2006). *Built to Change: How to Achieve Organizational Effectiveness*. San Francisco, CA: Jossey Bass.

Lewin, K. (ed.) (1951). *Field Theory in Social Science: Selected Theoretical Papers by Kurt Lewin*. London: Tavistock Publications (UK edition published 1952).

Leys, F. (2012). *Change Management Practitioner Competencies*. Sydney: Change Management Institute.

Mahoney, J. and Rueschemeyer, D. (2003). 'Comparative Historical Analysis: Achievements and Agendas', in James Mahoney and Dietrich Rueschemeyer (eds.), *Comparative Historical Analysis in the Social Sciences*. Cambridge: Cambridge University Press, 3–38.

Meaney, M. and Wilson, S. (2009). 'Change in Recession'. *People Management*, 15(10): 62.

Mintzberg, H. (2000). *The Rise and Fall of Strategic Planning*. Harlow: FT Prentice Hall.

Mintzberg, H. (2009). *Managing*. Harlow, Essex: Financial Times Prentice Hall.

Mohr, L. B. (1982). *Explaining Organizational Behaviour: The Limits and Possibilities of Theory and Research*. San Francisco, CA: Jossey-Bass Publishers.

Mohrman, S. A. and Lawler, E. E. (2012). 'Generating Knowledge that Drives Change'. *Academy of Management Perspectives*, 26(1): 41–51.

Moore, C. and Buchanan, D. A. (2013). 'Sweat the Small Stuff: Minor Problems, Rapid Fixes, Major Gains'. *Health Services Management Research*, 26(1): 9–17.

Ogburn, W. F. (1922). *Social Change: With Respect to Culture and Original Nature*. New York: B. W. Huebsch.

Pettigrew, A. M. (1985). *The Awakening Giant: Continuity and Change in ICI*. Oxford: Basil Blackwell.

Pettigrew, A. M., Woodman, R. W., and Cameron, K.S. (2001). 'Studying Organizational Change and Development: Challenges for Future Research'. *Academy of Management Journal*, 44(4): 697–713.

Plowman, D. A., Baker, L. T., Beck, T. E., Kulkarni, M., Solansky, S. T., and Travis, D. V. T. (2007). 'Radical Change Accidentally: The Emergence and Amplification of Small Change'. *Academy of Management Journal*, 50(3): 515–43.

Rafferty, A. E., Jimmieson, N. L., and Armenakis, A. A. (2013). 'Change Readiness: A Multilevel Review'. *Journal of Management*, 39(1): 110–35.

Reinersten, J. L., Bisognano, M., and Pugh, M. D. (2008). *Seven Leadership Points for Organization-Level Improvement in Health Care*, 2nd edn. Cambridge, MA: Institute for Healthcare Improvement.

Rouleau, L. and Balogun, J. (2011). 'Middle Managers, Strategic Sensemaking, and Discursive Competence'. *Journal of Management Studies*, 48(5): 953–83.

Stace, D. and Dunphy, D. (2001). *Beyond the Boundaries: Leading and Re-creating the Successful Enterprise*. Sydney: McGraw Hill.

Sydow, J., Schreyogg, G., and Koch, J. (2009). 'Organizational Path Dependence: Opening the Black Box'. *Academy of Management Review*, 34(4): 689–709.

Tushman, M. L. and Romanelli, E. (1985). 'Organizational Revolution: A Metamorphosis Model of Convergence And Reorientation'. *Research in Organizational Behaviour*, 7: 171–222.

Tushman, M. L., Newman, W. H., and Romanelli, E. (1986). 'Convergence and Upheaval: Managing the Unsteady Pace of Organizational Evolution'. *California Management Review*, 29(1): 29–44.

Ward, J. and Daniel, E. (2013). 'The Role of Project Management Offices in IS Project Success and Management Satisfaction'. *Journal of Enterprise Information Management*, 26(3): 316–36.

Worley, C. G. and Lawler, E. E. (2009). 'Building a Change Capability at Capital One Financial'. *Organizational Dynamics*, 38(4): 245–51.

PART III
THEMES

CHAPTER 18

MANAGEMENT AS A PRACTICE OF POWER

DAVID COURPASSON

MANAGEMENT can be defined as a practice of power; in that sense it involves the capacity to frame the conduct of others, as well as oneself (Clegg, 2009: 310). Management as power is a form of government that involves an active practice of shaping the relevant contexts and structures within which people are likely to 'be managed', that is, to obey prevalent order and principles. Management as power is the process through which a non-equivocal relationship between mandates and obedience can be established. Weber (1978) defined power as 'the probability that one actor within a social relationship will be in a position to carry out his will despite resistance' (53). As such, many have come to define management as the bundle of tactics and strategies that actors devise to articulate this power, to resist power, to act in conflicting situations, or to cope with uncertainty (Crozier, 1964). Management could also have been equated with 'organizational politics' and all the negative behavioural associations, such as backroom deals, nasty influence over others etc (Clegg, Courpasson, and Phillips, 2006). Equating management of power with organizational politics runs the risk of seeing it as a rather individualistic process (French and Raven, 1959) depending on what resources actors would *possess*. Relational perspectives have rather emphasized the structural nature of power relationships, suggesting that power is enshrined in networks of dependencies (Pfeffer and Salancik, 1974). More recently, post-structuralist versions drawing from Foucault have argued that power resides *between* individuals, actors and organizations (Sewell, 1998; Fleming and Spicer, 2014). In a nutshell, seeing management as a practice of power entails to study how people 'work out' their power relationships, that is the concrete situations they face within organizations (Courpasson, Golsorkhi, Sallaz, 2012: 15).

For the purposes of this chapter, we will broadly observe that managing power consists of activities that create arrangements between people through relations and structures that permit the distribution of work and responsibilities. Power is mobilized as a capacity to influence other actors because of the fundamental frictional and conflicting nature of organizational life; it cannot be reduced to abstract interpretations of conformity, obedience or resistance. Moreover, it is also a capacity to construct specific organizational forms that we call here *infrastructures of power*, within which people will be able to accomplish tasks because they will share certain goals and meanings over what they do and what they have to do. Contestation and acceptation are simultaneously generated by the practice of power, which is therefore also considered in this chapter as a practice of debate and deliberation around the means, ends, and meanings of the workplace.

Therefore, constructing management as a practice of power supposes to define the nature of the subordination that permits this relationship to endure. For instance, Lukes (2005) contends that power is expressed in three faces, ranging from the most observable dimensions (when power is what people actually do) to the most invisible or implicit expressions like manipulation and subjectification (Fleming and Spicer, 2014). Fleming and Spicer (2014) offer a complementary vision by identifying four faces of power: coercion, manipulation, domination, and subjectification, all being either episodic or systemic expressions of power (Clegg, 1989). Coercion and manipulation are episodic modes of influence relying upon 'identifiable acts that shape the behaviour of others' (Fleming and Spicer, 2014: 240). Domination and subjectification are more systemic forms because 'they mobilize institutional, ideological and discursive resources to influence organizational activity' (Fleming and Spicer, 2014: 240). Beyond the faces of power, this chapter will strive to highlight and illustrate the interrelations between management as power and the 'infrastructures' of power that organizations have been inventing since the inception of bureaucratic regimes, to generate obedience and overcome recalcitrance from the part of workers and employees. In particular, we will shed light on the everlasting issue of the relationship between the *centre* of organizations, and its *peripheral* actors, to suggest that management power is a practice aiming to regulate the tensions existing between these spaces. Power is the mirror of a social order that is also produced from interactions and negotiations among actors around the proper rule to be applied in a certain space, at a certain moment (Crozier, 1964).

What is distinctive about a worker is that it is presumed to be an obedient subject in exchange for an income; traditional organization meant that there was a continuity between task and the structures organizing scales of status and hierarchical prerogatives: one moved up the status hierarchy by 'displaying mastery of task' (Clegg, 2009: 311) and obedient behaviour. But recent organizational forms like polyarchies (Dahl, 1971; Courpasson and Clegg, 2012) or post-bureaucracies (Heckscher and Donnellon, 1994) have dismantled this secular statutory dynamic to produce more uncertain and more unbalanced and temporal workplaces.

The chapter begins with rapid overviews of both theories of power that we acknowledge as shaping the field today, and of a genealogy of the infrastructures of power that give to management its essential political nature. Then we highlight the pressing issue of the centre-periphery debate before suggesting some avenues for further research.

A Rapid Overview of Theories of Power: the 'Faces' Approach

In this chapter we retain the four dimensions of power as highlighted by Fleming and Spicer (2014). Among the manifold of frameworks dealing with power issues, this dimensional perspective is interesting because it emphasizes the diversity of power relationships and the number of ways through which power relations regulate the interaction between individual agencies and institutional-organizational apparatuses.

Power as Coercion

The focus of power can be the direct exercise of power by certain individuals or groups to achieve their own political ends. This tradition builds on Dahl's one dimensional view of power (Dahl, 1957; Lukes, 2005). The issue is what is the process through which individuals will end up doing something that they do not want or plan to do? Possession of certain resources (Pfeffer and Salancik, 1974), control over uncertainty (Crozier, 1964), official power endowed by the 'bureau" (Weber, 1978; Merton, 1957) are the most travelled notions explaining this first dimension. In that instance, management as power implies seeking to use resources and bases of power which they have at their disposal to get people to do what they would not otherwise do (to paraphrase Dahl's canonical definition, 1957).

Power as Manipulation

Here there is an 'implicit shaping of issues considered important or relevant' (Fleming and Spicer, 2007: 17). Studies in this perspective investigate the processes through which agendas are shaped. For instance, Selznick (1949) demonstrated how certain topics are prevented from arising because of apparently objective criteria. Also Gouldner (1970) showed how workers' perceptions of themselves are shaped by ideas of powerlessness thus letting the room to more influential groups to set agendas through the mobilization of bias (Bachrach and Baratz, 1970). In that instance, management as power implies agenda setting, a less direct form of influence aiming to carefully assess what is to be put in the debate and who participates to this debate.

Power as Domination

Many theories of organizational power view it as a process of domination. According to Fleming and Spicer (2007: 19), 'this dimension of power shapes our very preferences, attitudes and political outlook'. This perspective draws from Lukes' radical vision, where he explains how people come to become obedient through a specifically constructed understanding of their situation. Lukes (2005) highlights that individuals are prevented from 'having grievances by shaping their perceptions, cognitions and preferences in such a way that they accept her role in the existing order of things …'.

Domination rests upon the capacity of management to articulate hierarchical relationships that appear unchangeable and unquestioned to the employees. This perception is shaped by a range of techniques largely investigated like corporate cultures (Kunda, 1992), and societal assumptions (Alvesson, 1987). The way through which certain assumptions are made legitimate and eventually standardized also corresponds to a lively research terrain in institutional analysis (Lawrence and Suddaby, 2006). In that instance, management as power implies that managerial actors seek to ideologically determine the terrain of action and inaction, thus curbing and confronting others' interests and claims.

Power as Subjectification

Subjectification defines and determines an actor's sense of self, including emotions and identity. To quote Fleming and Spicer (2014: 244), 'the focus is not on decision-making or non-decision making (…) but the constitution of the very person who makes decisions. (…) Power therefore, produces the kind of people we feel we naturally are' (Fleming and Spicer, 2007: 23).

Research has largely investigated the means and systems through which subjectification can be produced in contemporary organizations. Teams (Barker, 1993), Human Resource Management discourses (Townley, 1993), organizational indoctrination (Phillips and Oswick, 2012) or disciplinary mechanisms of identification (Thornborrow and Brown, 2009) are examples that show the subtlety of political practices that are likely to organize and orient the everyday conduct of actors and how they see and evaluate what is and is not a proper conduct. In that instance, management as power implies that forms of control are inextricably linked to one's sense of self.

These four faces of power can interestingly be related to a genealogy of how power has been developing over time in organizations through the creation of specific infrastructures. We define infrastructures of power as the regimes through which management establishes legitimate and understandable connections between concrete organizational forms and settings within which people work and live at work, and ideological foundations of its action and meanings. Put differently, infrastructures encompass organizational forms and practices and deeper structures and reasons to act through power.

A Rapid Genealogy of Managing Power and the Infrastructures of Power: from Taylor to Google

The Taylorist Disciplinary Infrastructure

Taylorism is the first technology of power that is sustained by a specific infrastructure aimed to produce a 'political economy of the body' (Clegg, 2009: 312). Strict obedience to the plan is the central operating goal of management as a basic utilitarian ideology aiming to construct a principle of 'national efficiency' (Taylor, 1911). Aiming to the fusion of the function of utility and efficiency with a social function of individual differentiation of outputs and merits through metrics, the management of power consists of creating disciplinary programs to shape people, work, and the organizational infrastructure in order to minimize the always possible imperfections of the system-like resistance. Thus the Taylorist infrastructure is the constant production of managerial knowledge aiming to rearrange the everyday practices of power that permits the workshop to function, based on a pragmatic science of calculation. As reminded by Clegg (2009), managing in the Taylorist infrastructure means 'constituting central aspects of identity through relations of power; thus when one is managing this implies that one is exercising power-over both people and things' (313). Managing means power, also because some are born to manage and others to execute and be directed. The power/knowledge relation is therefore reshaped and placed exclusively in the hands of management, for the sake of the reproduction of the one best way to do things. Power is therefore not only embedded in the everyday practice of management, it becomes management, the normalcy and the very condition of the organizational infrastructure. It links efficiency to power through the optimal use of the human body. Power is oriented towards producing new mechanisms to manage bodies at work, what Clegg (2009) calls a 'political economy of the body' aiming to subject worker's bodies to the superior intelligence of the manager and to the physical strength of the factory machinery (Canguilhem, 1992: 63), all that legitimized by productive economic purposes.

This 'anatomical politics' (Foucault, 1977) is congruent with a hierarchical infrastructure that helps rendering the body docile and cooperative. Subjecting the body goes hand in hand with an impersonal system of relationships clearly delineating boundaries of accountability and authority.

The Fordist Moral Infrastructure

In 1913 Henry Ford introduces the assembly line as a new way of producing automobiles. The relations of power in these settings were shaped by a growing catalogue of routines, but also by a subtler moral machinery of power.

The moral side of Fordism comes mostly from the fact that routinized assembly lines generated high levels of turnover that forced Ford to hire thousands of workers in 1912 and 1913 to maintain the workforce (see Clegg, 2009: 317). Ford announced the five-dollar day so that workers could share the company profits and become active consumers, ownership being something that they could come to realize. But the five-dollar day was also implying the existence of rules governing eligibility: demonstrating that one was a clean and sober man, and industrious and worthy worker was *key* to get eventually a recommendation from one's supervisor. Investigators of the Ford Sociological Department visited workers' houses and suggested ways to achieve the company standards for 'better morals'. All forms of excesses in which individual energies could be wasted (such as jazz music, see Porter, 2002) were considered trouble-making practices. Ensuring the moral probity of employees was the moral investment necessary to ensure an efficient and disciplined workforce, devoid of irrational behaviours and activities involving passion and wasteful actions, because 'manners of the body share the potential for becoming a stage on which the struggle for social legitimacy and control is dramatized' (Appelrouth, 2005: 1497), pushing people to an inability to follow rules; 'a general lack of moral qualities were not what Mr. Ford required in his employees' (Clegg, 2009: 320). From this moral concern grew a practice of severe control and terrorization of workers so as to prevent unionization. Ford's Service Department would grow to be the largest private police force in the world at that time.

The moral infrastructure of Fordist factories suggests that power in the organization is a reflection of power in the wider society: running an efficient factory means that management has to have control over what kind of persons it employs, thus leading management to exercise control and power over private lives and generate a specific culture within which people are subjected to the imperatives of management.

The Human Relations Infrastructure

Fordist infrastructures strongly suggested that managing power in the workplace required disciplining not only the body but also the lives of employees, where cultures and identities could transcend the working space itself.

The Hawthorne studies somehow extended this reflection by highlighting how sources of productive power could come from a kind of *group morale*:

'The improvement in production (…) reflects rather a freer and more pleasant working environment, supervisor who is not regarded as a "boss", a "higher morale". (…) Their opinion is of course mistaken: in a sense they are getting closer supervision than ever before, the change is in the quality of the supervision' (Mayo, 1975: 75).

From this insight, management of power shifts toward the mental states, the consciousness and unconsciousness, the 'soul' of the employees (Clegg, 2009: 321). The locus of power does not reside mostly in complex engineering of job design, selection and training, as well as correct reward policies; it is reflected in the figure of the manager, invested with the capacity to shape the social milieu constituting the workplace, a space of motivation and astute communication founded on a vision of informality as enmeshed with formal rules and procedures. Managing power means working through positive power, so as to attain the soul, to shape what employees have to see in sorts of therapeutic confessional sessions with managers, now that the body has been properly disciplined. The underlying idea framing power relations is that management has to convince the worker that s/he wants to be an obedient subject and that no external machinery will coerce her to think that way. Patterns of spontaneous obedience are elaborated, like standard operating procedures. Managing power means managing subjectivity seen as a group phenomenon, and a central resource for the efficient organization.

Google's Politics: the Return of Corporate Culturalism?

Organizational power is not always the enactment of direct [and brutal] force by a dominating actor over another less powerful. Power is also often infused in specific circuitries where ideas and identities can be strongly oriented and weigh upon peoples' view of their interests; it can also curb the willingness to resist or to exercise critical dissent in organizational settings where the multidimensionality and multiple forms taken by power pushes people to share, genuinely or not, the neo-normative imperatives of efficiency. *Google's politics* is an expression that helps us to see how recent forms of management of power are likely to produce an employee who ends up thinking that s/he likes and is proud of what s/he does and where s/he works. In that perspective, power is located in non-visible aspects of political life; it works through fluid and fragmented relationships where actors may have a significant degree of autonomy but are nevertheless subordinated to the ever more oppressive cultural configuration of post-industrial or post-capitalist forms of organizations.

Attempts to 'emotionalize' the work ethos (Weber, 1978) in neo-human relations models are well known. Corporations became interested in 'soft' modes of management (Courpasson, 2000); Bendix (1956/1999) also contends that management has always included ideological imperatives to persuade workers to accept their fate of obedient subjects. Google politics seeks to foster an all-encompassing environment 'in which our very personhood becomes a loyal reflection of the company' (Fleming, 2013: 4). Company such as Google are 'greedy institutions' (Coser, 1974) systematizing control and shaping the practical 'consciousness' of individuals (Willmott, 1993: 523) through cultural and material devices. What Edwards termed the 'IBM approach' may enable to construct workers' allegiance so that they see little difference between their 'wellness' and that of the company (Barley and Kunda, 1992). Ray (1986) goes as far as to predict that corporate culture programs, as long as they are functioning, might help corporations to conquer 'the last frontier of control'—the unconscious political loyalties of workers (Fleming, 2013: 5). This type of management of power is about generating synergies between the emotional needs of workers and the economic rationality of the company, thus 'mixing up' the worker and the management. Marcuse (1964) explained how emotion and rationality, once tied together, can become perverse modalities of power in authoritarian regimes. Is Google an authoritarian regime of power and control? At least what can be noticed at this stage is that, in the bureaucratic regime, the power mediated by impersonal rules let little leeway for action but the 'good employee' could think freely; in neo-managerial enterprises à la Google, even people's thoughts seem to be policed, in the very name of autonomy, creativity, and emancipation (Willmott, 1993; Fleming, 2013).

The interesting conundrum regarding power in Google type corporations is that despite the widespread disenchantment that includes workers, managers, and even CEOs alike, people still continue to work longer and harder than ever (Fleming, 2013). The expression 'my work is my life' (Michel, 2012: 344) epitomizes the curious admixture between private spheres and corporations, in a society where overworking seems not being equated with being alienated. This means that the scope of managerial power has augmented in today's neo-capitalist enterprises. A kind of 'neo-normative' control has emerged in large corporations where workers are encouraged to 'just be themselves' (Fleming and Sturdy, 2011). Making a difference in a highly competitive workplace is a necessity in an otherwise 'liberative' context of management that largely defines the post-industrial workplace. Even certain transgressions and subversive attitudes can be celebrated by some 'funky CEOs' wearing Che-Guevara tee shirts …' (Cremin, 2011, in Fleming, 2013: 14).

This post-industrial infrastructure of power displaces the old boundaries that separated work from non-work in the Taylorist world; working and being productive is likely to become a life project. The closed social system defined by Taylorist boundaries is progressively dismantled and replaced by the Google model of production whereby the extra-anti economic qualities, even a form of critical distance from the capitalist imperatives, are exploited for economic purposes. Thus workers do not know any longer when work begins and when it ends: all time becomes work time (Fleming, 2013: 15). And the worker is advised to forget some old distinctions that were the central signifiers of his personal and occupational identity.

Quickly put, it seems that infrastructures of management power would have evolved from the construction of closed and controlled organizations, relatively impervious to outside lives and projects, to all-encompassing machineries devising much more open worlds of strong cultures to which workers are in great part subjected despite the persistence of certain forms of resistance. In these infrastructures, management power aims to valorize a culture of 'free labor' as a form of extension of the corporate gaze to the non-work sphere. The objective of management power is here to be highly inclusive, so that extra economic life skills can be mobilized for economic purposes.

This transformation is not entirely founded on managerial discourses, far from it. It is also fabricated and concretely processed by structural dynamics entailing the modification of organizational forms of work and cooperation. For the purposes of this chapter, we shall concentrate on one of these main dynamics: the relationship between centres and peripheries in organizations. Indeed, if in strong infrastructures of power workers were forced to align their efforts to unquestioned forms of centralized authority—centrally incarnated authorities—new forms of management power impose to address the consequences on the distribution of power that new organizational regimes may entail.

NEW FORMS OF ORGANIZATIONS: CENTRAL VS PERIPHERAL POWERS

The question of power is reshaped in new organizations. More particularly, new power asymmetries and new power channels arise in new bureaucracies. Managing power is mostly about regulating the balance between the autonomy of local actors and the necessities of respecting central rules of operation. Although that sounds like an old story, the changing context of contemporary organizations raises different important questions for sociologists and organizations theorists: how are people reworking their forms of collaboration in supposedly less stable and less hierarchical settings? How are the boundaries between central and peripheral actors evolving in terms of reciprocal control and responsibility? How, in particular, are central and peripheral actors reshaping their respective domains of power in settings where authority is supposed to be more distributed and norms of behaviours more diverse? Is managerial power more or less obtrusive in decentralized forms of work? These questions raise, in a slightly different manner, one of the core issues of organizational sociology: the relationships between centre(s) and periphery(ies) in the political dynamics of change. In a nutshell, one of the original contributions of Shils (1961) is to contend that membership in society [in organizations] is mostly constituted by the relationship and the distance to the central zones of society [of organizations]. The centre is defined as a phenomenon of culture (values and beliefs) and as a 'phenomenon of the realm of action', that is to say, a 'structure of activities, of roles and persons.' (Shils, 1961). In this perspective, it is possible to understand the political dynamics of neo-bureaucracies and the transformation of power relationships through the analysis of the interaction between central authorities and peripheral actors. That is where new organizations are interesting to study. More particularly, talking about 'new centres' in new organizations as new structures of reciprocal roles and attributions between central and peripheral actors invites to study the transformation of organizations through the redistribution of responsibilities between the two.

Scholars contend that traditional bureaucratic structures function because of very entrenched repertoires of action. On the contrary, neo-bureaucracies are supposed to be more volatile and virtual (Child and McGrath, 2001; Heckscher and Donnellon, 1994), and internal boundaries more ambiguous. The organization, described as a process of 'continuous morphing' (Rindova and Kotha 2001), is seen as more open and adaptive. Beyond this well-known catechism of new firms, depicted as 'heterarchies' (Girard and Stark, 2002), or 'post-bureaucracies' (Kellogg, Orlikowski, and Yates, 2006), political changes do affect the actual power of peripheral actors to influence change in their working environments and the subsequent degree of responsibility that they might receive in this very change. We define peripheral actors here as all organizational members who do not belong to the 'inner circles' of power in organizations, nor to central departments at the headquarters of companies: they are not part of technocratic work teams (Daday and Burris, 2008). Those actors evolve today in shifting centres of expertise and accountability where the question of responsibility is posed in different terms, because the relationships of those actors to the centres of expertise of organizations are fundamentally relations of control. Being held responsible and constantly under control is one of the major difficulties of peripheral managerial work today. What is more, peripheral actors are working to build temporary settlements within more collaborative and diffuse systems of work, they are working through short-term assignments, in heterogeneous project teams: responsibility is therefore not only distributed but fragmented according to different time frames and places, thus blurring the boundaries of who is accountable for what and who is entitled to do what and when. At the same time, hierarchs are also more volatile while their work is to bring together groups of people who do not know each other and who need to work interdependently under growing constraints (Bechky, 2006). The idea here is that new bureaucracies are ambivalent systems with respect to the relationship between centres and peripheries and, therefore, with respect to the question of power and responsibility—they are both extremely polarized and centralized, provoking a cultural marginalization of peripheral actors, and more politically distributed. This ambivalence has already been evoked by theorists (Courpasson and Reed, 2004) but how actors deal with it is still very unclear. Contrary to what theorists of post-capitalist resistance contend (Fleming, 2013), we suggest that peripheral actors exercise power by creating new forms of resistance so as to cope with this ambivalence, and that this resistance reshapes the organizational workplace and, in particular, how the relationship between the centre and the periphery is changing. This resistance is important because new forms of work in neo-bureaucracies tend to obscure managerial power and the sources of control and responsibility, which is more unobtrusive and volatile, operating through the fluid channels of changing hierarchies.

Changes in Peripheric Actors' Power

In neo-bureaucratic contexts, the question of peripheral actors' power is different than in traditional bureaucratic settings for several reasons: (1) uncertainty is becoming more a growing constraint instead of being the core of actors' political resources to influence the workplace and to negotiate arrangements (Crozier and Friedberg, 1980); (2) responsibility is seen more and more as short-term and accountability is more individualized, while people are confronted to situations of growing interdependence, in other words, the issue of responsibility is more and more political because it is mostly seen by actors as how to escape the judgement of central powers as well as the constant lateral control of colleagues; (3) solidarity between workers is rapidly evolving toward short-term cohesion oriented towards accomplishing tasks rather than defending community practices and rules; and (4) actors' resistance is less channelled than in Weberian classical 'channels of appeal' (Weber, 1978), because it is also expressed through diverse, temporary, and more subjective everyday corridors of action (Mumby, 2005).

The rapid transformations of the contemporary workplace partly accounts for these political shifts (Vallas, 2008). For instance, Kuhlmann and Schumann (2008) show that the new division of labour in the industry opens up new possibilities for criticism and debate for actors, because workers gain more capacity to reason and exchange with their peers and with their employers in more lateral structures. Thus, a new type of peripheral actor may be emerging, more prone to escaping the coercive working relationships, thus redefining the meaning of work (see Hernandez, 2008). Less optimistic accounts see a greater diversity in how workers cope with new ambivalent forms of organizations. For instance, Vallas (2006) sees the emergence or the entrenchment of traditional defiant cultures of work, as well as the potentialities of more creative new cultures where the negotiation on the 'rules of the game' is allowed by the very quality of workers' claims. Still, the emergence of new cultures of work does not imply that peripheral actors would be more powerful. New cultures of work can be a direct consequence of the strengthening of central technocratic zones of expertise, forcing workers at the periphery to create locally embedded modalities of action 'against' the centre, so as to cope with increasing degrees of descending and lateral control and simultaneous increasing degrees of peripheral responsibility.

Consent and Resistance in New Bureaucracies

Classical studies of bureaucratic dynamics have demonstrated for a while that bureaucracy emerged out of struggles around the legitimacy of internal resistance against specific forms of authority (Gouldner, 1954). Studies have also highlighted the ways in which bureaucracy was designed as a control solution to problems of resistance always likely to emerge out of working communities (Langton, 1984). Consequently, the legitimacy of internal resistance in the workplace is a key issue when trying to understand the transformation of bureaucratic power, that is to say, how internal resistance affects bureaucratic efficiency and its repertoire of routines. In the political volatility of neo-bureaucratic contexts, resistance is developing in situations of ambiguity, fluidity, and emergence of unexpected strategies, tactics, and behaviours. The repertoires of resistance are expanding as much as central powers are gaining ground because of the technocratic expertise required to control more and more complex and interconnected settings.

New bureaucracies could therefore offer more numerous occasions of confrontation, if only because they are founded on a principle of actors' empowerment. The logic of empowerment entailed in new organizations is likely to be overtly used and endorsed by certain key employees to resist specific decisions and/or to take unplanned and sometimes unorthodox initiatives (Courpasson and Thoenig, 2008). These initiatives are likely to reinstall a certain balance of power between the centre and the periphery, because challenges from below can gain an entrepreneurial legitimacy, as long as they are not stigmatized as 'trouble-making' activities (Ford, Ford, and D'Amelio, 2008): more often than not, resistance is still seen implicitly as an irrational reaction against central authorities, instead of being considered as a resourceful and positive 'peripheral' behaviour. Responsibility is therefore here requested by central powers to emphasize the 'irresponsibility' of resisters who would not share or understand organizational policies and who, because of this discrepancy in meanings, would hinder change processes and diminish organizational development.

Despite this persistent stigmatization which derives from bureaucratic habits, resistance in new bureaucratic contexts is a process of *self-empowerment*, because rebels gain and retain an autonomous power to act without being hierarchically empowered to do so (Courpasson, Golsorkhi, and Sallaz, 2012). This lack of authorization to contest is significant in terms of responsibility because it means that peripheral actors decide to bypass usual 'chains of command' to act and that judgements of responsibility can be made outside of those official channels in polyarchic infrastructures of power (Dahl, 1971; Courpasson and Clegg, 2012). Acts of resistance in neo-bureaucratic contexts therefore deliberately question the very notion of power in the workplace: resisting a decision entails the redistribution of roles within work teams because all members do not necessarily share resisting claims. At the same time, resisting tactics and strategies involve often a high degree of commitment and expertise, as well as risk taking. All in all, that means that resisting acts dovetail nicely with current definitions of the 'good employee' who is supposed to be 'entrepreneurial' (Du Gay, 2000) although resisting implies to transgress usual zones of prerogatives and runs counter to the efforts of technocratic experts to impose standardized forms of work and cooperation. Power is therefore partly located in peripheral resistance but it supposes to divert the places and actors who judge whether peripheral resistance is legitimate or not.

This dilemma between peripheral resistance as a legitimate and responsible action and the necessities of centres to keep control over actors obliges us to reconsider the classical vision of centre and periphery.

Revisiting the Question of Centre and Periphery

If relationships of power and responsibility in new bureaucracies are reshaped by the capacity of peripheral actors to resist the directives of the centre, then the very nature of the relationship between centres and peripheries has to be rethought.

Shils (1961) suggests that there are two kinds of centrality. First, the centre is constituted by the sacred nature of authority; it is the locus of the sacred—this is particularly true for bureaucracies, in which the affirmative attitude of members towards established authority is partly based on the sentiments of sacredness aroused by the constant and ethical application of central rules (Du Gay, 2000). Second, the centre is constituted by elite members—the latter, by their very possession of authority, 'attribute to themselves an essential affinity with the sacred elements of their society of which they regard themselves as the custodians' (Shils, 1961: 118). Put differently, the centre is made of circles of power conferring legitimacy and responsibility to their very members, hence the oligarchical tendencies of organizations that Michels noted a long time ago (Michels, 1915; Zald and Lounsbury, 2010).

The idea that we present here is that new organizations modify the sacred dimension of the centre because they modify the attachment and dedication of members to its unquestioned authoritative dimension, as well as the actual distribution of 'judgemental' attributions between actors. New organizations are of course not authority-free systems; they retain the sacred dimensions of the centre but the everyday conditions of work increase the extent of active dissent or even rejection of central rules and values. This is particularly true within the managerial body. Volatile and more distributed organizations amplify the distance between *central* managers, who feel a growing sense of *affinity* with the centre, and *peripheral* managers (in particular managers in charge of production, manufacturing, sales and R&D) who feel a growing sense of *disconnection* to the centre, also because of the financialization of the workplace (Thompson, 2013). Managerial elites and sub-elites are more fragmentary, and local fragments of the managerial body (such as Business Unit managers, or factory managers) are more and more dispossessed of their attachment to the actual central value system of the organization. Likewise, their willing participation to this system is vanishing, which creates an unprecedented tension between centre and periphery in organizations.

The feeling of remoteness from the centre of peripheral managers is experienced by individuals as a growing ambivalence and incoherence—peripheral actors are more distant from the centre and feel at the same time a greater concern with the centre, because the latter exercises more authority through the non-coercive and non-authoritative new forms of work and control that we have rapidly depicted. Thus, peripheral managers have an acute sense of being 'outsiders', sometimes even of being excluded or put at the margins of 'what counts' in the organization, of what Shils calls the *vital zones* surrounding the centre, while being extremely pressurized by central technocrats who check their performance on a daily basis and who are thus more present although more remote than ever.

In that context, the feeling of moral responsibility for observing the rules of the organization and for sharing its authority tends to get lost—peripheral actors sense the necessity of acting on their own, as egoistical entrepreneurs looking for 'safety valves' (Fleming, 2013) or personal initiatives, or as local 'strategizers' inventing the relevant peripheral rules and willingly bypassing a central system that they do not respect any more. When peripheral actors despise central rules while feeling increasingly constrained to act through those rules, organizations cannot develop or maintain the sacredness of their centre—they resemble more and more distributed and temporary systems of action where responsibility is a volatile and secondary criterion for action. Of course, alternative political modalities do exist, like polyarchic systems (Dahl, 1971; Courpasson and Clegg, 2012) where resisting activities can be seen as loyal and responsible behaviours as long as they do not damage the legitimacy of central authorities. But new organizations are far from taking this route. In a sense, addressing management as a practice of power obliges to consider the growing divergence and dysfunctionality between organizational objectives and workers' commitment to the corporate cause—individuals are asked to invest more of themselves (up to mixing up life and work as we noted above), yet employers seem to retreat from true investment in human capital—declining security, career ladders, pensions and the like (Thompson, 2013: 473). This growing divergence is crucial to understand the practice of power in today's workplaces.

Future Developments

No theoretical approach to power offers a generally satisfying and informative definition, but all say something true and relevant—power as control of behaviour (Dahl, 1957), power as the capacity to realize a will, an intention (Weber, 1978; Russell, 1938); power as a system resource (Parsons, 1937). In all cases the research question oscillates between locating power ('Who rules whom?'), the focus being on the command–obedience relationship (Lukes, 1986), or on politics as praxis, as a process generating outcome, be it based on coercion or consensus (or both). Lukes insists that 'the very search for such a definition is a mistake (…) what unites the various views of power is too thin and formal to provide a generally satisfying definition, applicable to all cases' (Lukes, 1986: 4–5).

The most exciting concerns emerging from the transformations of organizational power are not mostly theoretical; we may agree with Lukes to see power as a capacity 'to make a difference to the world' (Lukes, 1986: 5). More importantly, novel areas of empirical research can provide fertile grounds for developing novel theories, simply because current theories do not adequately explain certain new phenomena. We suggest two main areas of empirical development that are crucial for the theory of power as management and management as power.

The Impact of New Technologies on Hierarchies

For quite a long time, it is legitimate to ask why there is so little resistance in the workplace and why do 'subordinate' groups often consent to their subjugation to managerial rules that are not devised for their wellness. The prevalence of passivity remains a puzzling ingredient of social life in organizations. Despite attempts to show instances of oppositional powerful and consequential resistance (Courpasson, Golsorkhi, and Sallaz, 2012), the manufacturing of consent seems to remain the core feature of managerial 'ideological hegemony' (see Clegg, 1989), where a 'structure of power relations is fully legitimized by an integrated system of cultural and normative assumptions' (Hyman and Brough, 1975: 199). At the level of organizations, it means that the sacrosanct principle of hierarchy remains the hallmark of most organizations. Then a question arises: What will be the consequence of the rapid spread of the web inside the organizational hierarchy? In a sense, the web is a direct 'attack' against the most widespread and enduring model of power. As Hamel (2007) would put it, 'thoughtocracy' exists on the web, but not in organizations. In other words, how can organizations continue to function according to bureaucratic and vertical univocal channels of power while people watch and participate in the deployment of alternative forms of power where knowledge and the generation of ideas is *de facto* distributed?

The question behind the scene is to get back to the conceptualization of organizations as power regimes—systems of concentration/distribution of power, depending on specific visions of what is legitimate or not to exercise power and influence. Here the question is more about the impact of new technologies in the shaping of new political subjects within organizations (like in research on recent social movements, see Milkman, Luce, and Lewis, 2013) than in devising alternative post-bureaucratic models that largely follow the fundamentals of the targeted initial model (Hecksher and Donnellon, 1994). Future power is likely to be dependent on the emergence of a 'post-managerial organization', where management could be a collective task, the central collective action for organizations to survive and develop.

Violence in Organizations

The relationship between management power and violence or threat of violence has received scant attention from organizational scholars. However it is a central characteristic of workplace relations. Not only direct and physical violence are commonplace in certain settings (bodily injuries, consequences of work on health and safety like stress and psychological sufferings); extreme acts of aggression in work settings have been reported as well as incivility 'spirals' (Anderson and Pearson, 1999). More symbolic violence is also widespread. Symbolic violence refers to the 'imposition of any symbolic representation (languages, conceptualization, and portrayals) on recipients who have little choice about whether to accept or reject them' (Bourdieu, 1986: 812). In that sense, power relations come to be perceived not for what they are in a structure, but in a form which renders them obligatorily legitimate in the eyes of those subject to power. This study is crucial in contemporary workplace settings that have developed a soft infrastructure of power, as we have suggested above. The threat to use power is even more intimidating than the actual exercise of power. This type of issue is not only valid in military organizations (Fleming and Spicer, 2014); the use of ritualistic activities to generate feelings of kinship and solidarity are also important to study in institutions such as the police, or elite schools, where violence becomes part of the 'toolkit' to generate a culture of honour and solidarity among 'friends'.

Conclusion

Organization and management theory have not always been addressing power and related issues like resistance conceptually. But the development of organizational theory is somehow ridden by power. Indeed, if we define power as the relations through which organizational structures can facilitate or hinder practices of cooperation with others, power should be the centre of attraction of organizational scholars. The power/knowledge nexus is fundamentally what defines the orientation of contemporary organizations, largely based on practices of generation and use of knowledge. Management as a practice of power, as we have suggested in this chapter, is the set of attitudes that managers can adopt to encourage people to act in concert to do things that they would not have done otherwise. In that sense, power over and power to should become indistinguishable and be the active forces through which management not only gains legitimacy, but permits people to freely contribute to the pursuit of acceptable goals. As research has shown numerous times, if the foundations of organization are therefore the relations of power (Clegg, 2009), it is also the innumerable opportunities for power as resistance that derive from the willingness of management to secure organizations as relatively closed social and cultural entities. The practice of power lies also in the creative cracks and interstices that will always be beyond the control of managerial instruments and prerogatives (Hjorth, 2005). That is what can also render structures of domination more transparent and open to change (Clegg, Flyvbjerg, and Haugaard, 2014). The systems of meanings and subjectivation that have been created by management for decades have been largely taken for granted by organization scholars as 'the truth'. But they are in fact largely conventional, which means that they could have been otherwise if the makings of managerial power were more transparent and less inspired by elitist aspirations. In that perspective, power can be seen as the set of means used by people to falsify the supposedly truthful management principles of bureaucracy, Taylorism, and the more recent approximations of emancipatory utopian projects of 'free labour'.

REFERENCES

Alvesson, M. (1987). *Organization Theory and Technocratic Consciousness: Rationality, Ideology and Quality of Work*. New York: De Gruyter.

Anderson, L. M. and Pearson, C. M. (1999). 'Tit for Tat? The Spiraling Effect of Incivility in the Workplace'. *Academy of Management Review*, 24(3): 452–71.

Appelrouth, S. (2005). 'Body and Soul: Jazz in the 1920s'. *American Behavioral Scientist*, 48(11): 1496–1509.

Bachrach, P. and Baratz, M. S. (1970). *Power and Poverty: Theory and Practice*. New York: Oxford University Press.

Barker, J. R. (1993). 'Tightening the Iron Cage: Concertive Control in Self-managing Teams'. *Administrative Science Quarterly*, 38: 408–37.

Barley, S. R. and Kunda, G. (1992). 'Design and Devotion: Surge of Rational and Normative Ideologies of Control in Managerial Discourse'. *Administrative Science Quarterly*, 37: 363–99.

Bechky, B. A. (2006). 'Gaffers, Gofers, and Grips: Role-based Coordination in Temporary Organizations'. *Organization Science*, 17(1): 3–21.

Bendix, R. (1956/1999). *Work and Authority in Industry; Managerial Ideologies in the Course of Industrialization*. New Brunswick: Transaction Publishers.

Bourdieu, P. (1986). 'The Force of Law: Toward a Sociology of the Juridical Field' (Intro. by R. Terdiman). *The Hastings Law Journal*, 38: 805–53.

Canguilhem, G. (1992). 'Machine and Organism', in J. Crasy and S. Kwinter (eds.), *Incorporations*. New York: Zone Press, 45–69.
Child, J. and McGrath, R. G. (2001). 'Organizations Unfettered: Organizational Form in an Information-intensive Economy'. *Academy of Management Journal*, 44(6): 1135–48.
Clegg, S. R. (1989). *Frameworks of Power*. London: SAGE.
Clegg, S. R. (2009). 'The Foundations of Organization Power'. *The Journal of Power*, 2(1): 35–64.
Clegg, S. R., Courpasson, D. and Phillips, N. (2006). *Power and Organizations*. London: SAGE.
Clegg, S. R., Flyvbjerg, B., and Haugaard, M. (2014). 'Reflections on Phronetic Social Science: A Dialogue'. *Journal of Political Power*, 7(2): 275–306.
Coser, L. (1974). *Greedy Institutions: Patterns in Undivided Commitment*. New York: Free Press.
Courpasson, D. (2000). 'Managerial Strategies of Domination: Power in Soft Bureaucracies'. *Organization Studies*, 21(1): 141–61.
Courpasson, D. (2006). *Soft Constraint; Liberal Organizations and Domination*. Copenhagen: CBS Press and Liber.
Courpasson, D. and Clegg, S. (2012). 'The Polyarchic Bureaucracy: Cooperative Resistance in the Workplace and the Construction of a New Political Structure of Organizations'. *Research in the Sociology of Organizations*, 34: 55–81.
Courpasson, D., Golsorkhi, D., and Sallaz, J. (2012). 'Rethinking Power in Organizations, Institutions and Markets: Classical Perspectives, Current Research, and the Future Agenda'. *Research in the Sociology of Organizations*, 34: 1–21.
Courpasson, D. and Reed, M. (2004). 'Introduction: Bureaucracy in the Age of Enterprise'. *Organization*, 11(1): 5–12.
Courpasson, D. and Thoenig, J. C. (2008). *When Managers Rebel*. London: Palgrave.
Cremin, C. (2011). *Capitalism's New Clothes*. London: Polity.
Crozier, M. (1964). *The Bureaucratic Phenomenon*. Chicago, IL: Chicago University Press.
Crozier, M. and Friedberg, E. (1980). *Actors and Systems*. Chicago, IL: Chicago University Press.
Daday, G. and Burris, B. (2008). 'Technocratic Teamwork: Mitigating Polarization and Cultural Marginalisation in an Engineering Firm'. *Research in the Sociology of Work*, 10: 241–62.
Dahl, R. (1957). 'The Concept of Power'. *Behavioral Science*, 20: 201–15.
Dahl, R. (1971). *Polyarchy: Participation and Opposition*. New Haven, CT: Yale University Press.
Du Gay, P. (2000). *In Praise of Bureaucracy: Weber, Organization, Ethics*. London: SAGE.
Fleming, P. (2013). 'Down with Big Brother! The End of Corporate Culturalism?'. *Journal of Management Studies*, 50(3): 474–95.
Fleming, P. and Spicer, A. (2007). *Contesting the Corporation: Struggle, Power and Resistance*. Cambridge: Cambridge University Press.
Fleming, P. and Spicer, A. (2014). 'Power in Management and Organization Science'. *The Academy of Management Annals*, 8(1): 237–98.
Fleming, P. and Sturdy, A. (2011). 'Being Yourself in the Electronic Sweatshop: New Forms of Normative Control'. *Human Relations*, 64: 177–200.
Ford, J. D., Ford, L. W., and D'Amelio, A. (2008). 'Resistance to Change: The Rest of the Story'. *Academy of Management Review*, 33(2): 362–77.
Foucault, M. (1977). *Discipline and Punish: The Birth of the Prison*. London: Allen and Lane.
French, J. R. P. and Raven, B. (1959). 'The Bases of Social Power', in D. Cartwright and A. Zander (eds.) *Group Dynamics*. New York: Harper & Row.
Girard, M. and Stark, D. (2002). 'Distributing Intelligence and Organizing Diversity in New Media Projects'. *Environment and Planning A*, 34: 1927–49.
Gouldner, A. (1954). *Patterns of Industrial Bureaucracy*. New York: The Free Press.

Gouldner, A. (1970). *The Coming Crisis of Western Sociology*. New York: Basic Books.

Hamel, G. (2007). *The Future of Management*. Boston, MA: Harvard Business School Press.

Heckscher, C. and Donnellon, A. (eds.) (1994). *The Post-Bureaucratic Organization: New Perspectives on Organizational Change*. London: SAGE.

Hernandez, S. (2008). 'Workers Rule: Relations in Production at a Cooperative Workplace in Mexico'. *Research in the Sociology of Work*, 10: 215–40.

Hjorth, D. (2005). 'Organizational Entrepreneurship: With de Certeau on Creating Heterotopias (or Spaces for Play)'. *Journal of Management Inquiry*, 14(4): 386–98.

Hyman, R. and Brough, I. (1975). *Social Values and Industrial Relations: A Study of Fairness and Equality*. Warwick Studies in Industrial Relations. London: Blackwell.

Kellogg, K. C., Orlikowski, W. J., and Yates, J. (2006). 'Life in the Trading Zone: Structuring Coordination across Boundaries in Postbureaucratic Organizations'. *Organization Science*, 17(1): 22–44.

Kuhlmann, M. and Schumann, M. (2008). 'What's Left of Workers' solidarity? Workplace Innovation and Worker's Attitudes Toward the Firm'. *Research in the Sociology of Work*, 10: 189–215.

Kunda, G. (1992). *Engineering Culture: Control and Commitment in a High-Tech Corporation*. Philadelphia, PA: Temple University Press.

Langton, J. (1984). 'The Ecological Theory of Bureaucracy: The Case of Josiah Wedgwood and the British Pottery Industry'. *Administrative Science Quarterly*, 29(3): 330–54.

Lawrence, T. B. and Suddaby, R. (2006). 'Institutions and Institutional Work', in R. Clegg, C. Hardy, T. B. Lawrence, and W. R. Nord (eds.), *Handbook of Organization Studies*, 2nd edn. London: SAGE, 215–54.

Lukes, S. (ed.) (1986). *Power*. New York: New York University Press.

Lukes, S. (2005). *Power: A Radical View*, 2nd edn. London: Palgrave.

Marcuse, H. (1964). *One-Dimensional Man: Studies in the Ideology of Advanced Industrial Society*. New York: Beacon Press.

Mayo, E. (1975). *The Social Problems of Aan Industrial Civilization*. New York: Viking.

Merton, R. K. (1957). *Social Theory and Social Structure*. New York: Free Press.

Michel, A. (2012). 'Transcending Socialization: A Nine-year Ethnography of the Body's Role in Organizational Control and Knowledge Workers' Transformation'. *Administrative Science Quarterly*, 56(3): 325–68.

Michels, R. (1915). *Political Parties: A Sociological Study of the Oligarchical Tendencies of Modern Democracy*. New York: Free Press.

Milkman, R., Luce, S., and Lewis, P. (2013). *Changing the Subject: A Bottom-Up Account of Occupy Wall Street in New York City*. New York: The Murphy Institute, CUNY.

Mumby, D. K. (2005). 'Theorizing Resistance in Organization Studies: A Dialectical Approach'. *Management Communication Quarterly*, 19(1): 19–44.

Parsons, T. (1937). *The Structure of Social Action: A Study in Social Theory with Special Reference to a Group of Recent European Writers*. New York: Free Press.

Pfeffer, J. and Salancik, G. R. (1974). 'Organizational Decision Making as a Political Process: The Case of a University Budget'. *Administrative Science Quarterly*, 25 (4): 637–53.

Phillips, N. and Oswick, C. (2012). 'Organizational Discourse: Domains, Debates, and Directions'. *The Academy of Management Annals*, 6(1): 435–81.

Porter, E. (2002). *What is this Thing Called Jazz? African American Musicians as Artists, Critics and Activists*. Berkeley, CA: University of California Press.

Ray, C. A. (1986). 'Corporate Culture: The Last Frontier of Control?'. *Journal of Management Studies*, 23: 287–97.

Rindova, V. P. and Kotha, S. (2001). 'Continuous "Morphing": Competing through Dynamic Capabilities, Form, and Function'. *Academy of Management Journal*, 44(6): 1263–80.

Russell, B. (1938). *Power: A New Social Analysis*. London: George Allen & Unwin.

Selznick, P. (1949). *TVA and the Grass Roots: A Study in the Sociology of Formal Organization*. Berkeley, CA: University of California Press.

Sewell, G. (1998). 'The Discipline of Teams: The Control of Team-based Industrial Work through Electronic and Peer Surveillance'. *Administrative Science Quarterly*, 43: 397–428.

Shils, E. (1961). *The Logic of Personal Knowledge: Essays Presented to Michael Polanyi*. Glencoe, IL: Free Press.

Taylor, F. W. (1911). *Principles of Scientific Management*. New York: Harper.

Thompson, P. (2013). 'Financialization and the Workplace: Extending and Applying the Disconnected Capitalism Thesis'. *Work, Employment and Society*, 27(3): 472–88.

Thornborrow, T. and Brown, A. D. (2009). 'Being Regimented: Aspiration, Discipline, and Identity Work in the British Parachute Regiment'. *Organization Studies*, 30(4): 355–76.

Townley, B. (1993). 'Foucault, Power/Knowledge, and its Relevance for Human Resource Management'. *Academy of Management Review*, 18(3): 518–45.

Vallas, S. P. (2006). 'Empowerment Redux: Structure, Agency, and the Remaking of Managerial Authority'. *American Journal of Sociology*, 111(6): 1677–1717.

Vallas, S. (ed.) (2008). *The Transformation of Work*. Research in the Sociology of Work, vol. 10. Bradford: Emerald Publishers.

Weber, M. (1978). *Economy and Society*. Berkeley, CA: University of California Press.

Willmott, H. (1993). Strength is Ignorance, Slavery is Freedom: Managing Culture in Modern Organizations'. *Journal of Management Studies*, 30: 515–52.

Zald, M. N. and Lounsbury, M. (2010). 'The Wizards of Oz: Towards an Institutional Approach to Elites, Expertise and Command Posts'. *Organization Studies*, 31(7): 963–96.

CHAPTER 19

MANAGEMENT AND MORALITY/ETHICS— THE ELUSIVE CORPORATE MORALS

MICHEL ANTEBY AND CAITLIN ANDERSON

MORALS are shared understandings in which humans' highest aspirations and dreams come to fulfilment, and the underpinnings of many, if not all, collective human pursuits. Whether in everyday settings or at critical life junctures, morals allow us to distinguish right from wrong and good from bad. They guide and justify thought and action in all arenas of social life. But are there any such things as corporate morals? Put otherwise, do members of corporations (particularly those leading them) have a shared understanding of their world, and the world more broadly? And if so, what might this shared understanding look like? What are corporate morals?

Before corporations gained the prominence they have today, Émile Durkheim dismissed the notion of corporate morals. He viewed what he called, at the time, business morals, like any other kind of morals—family morals, say, or civic morals—as shared meanings that emanate from a given social structure and the communal life of its members (Durkheim, 1973). As he explained, 'If there is one fact that history has irrefutably demonstrated, it is that the morality of each people is directly related to the social structure of the people practicing it (…) The connection is so intimate that, given the general character of the morality observed in a given society (…) one can infer the nature of that society, the elements of its structure and the way it is organized' (Durkheim, 1961: 87). By this definition, Durkheim allowed that some occupational groups, such as government functionaries or physicians, did have professional moral codes: those groups congregated regularly in the course of their daily work or in a professional association from which morals could arise. But in his view, this condition did not hold for the business professions. Financiers, industrialists, and heads of mercantile houses came together in competition or to do deals, but these were 'chance meetings and concern[ed] only the individuals.' This 'lack of organization in the business professions', Durkheim went on, 'has one consequence of the greatest moment: that is, that in this whole sphere of social life, no professional ethics exist' (Durkheim, 1958: 9). Put otherwise, business morals prove non-existent.

Whether or not Durkheim's claim held true when he made it in the late 1890s, subsequent social shifts have made it increasingly difficult to defend. Since the managerial revolution of the first half of the twentieth century, business, far from being characterized by a 'lack of organization', is often thought to be plagued by an overabundance of it. The suggestion that business only coalesces 'by chance' is equally problematic: business has become 'management' (Chandler, 1977; Dalton, 1959; Gouldner, 1955; Mintzberg, 1973) and the vast majority of professionals employed in the pursuit of profit find themselves engaged in an intensely social experience—one not only grounded in corporate life, but also increasingly engineered via business school education (Abend, 2014; Anteby, 2013; Jennifer Louise and Gianpiero, 2010; Joel, Linda, and Raghu, 2013; Khurana, 2007; Starkey and Tiratsoo, 2007). If, as sociologists maintain, morality emanates from collective organization (Hitlin and Vaisey, 2010; Lamont, 2000; Vaisey, 2009; Wuthnow, 1987; Zelizer, 1979), then business may be the most 'moral' sphere of all.

This chapter reviews the evolving state of knowledge regarding corporate morals, from the middle of the twentieth century with the consolidation of management as a profession to recent developments in the making of corporate cultures. We advance three main contentions about this body of research. First, that the empirical work conducted to date yields ample evidence that the complex organizations in which most businesspeople now live out their working lives are indeed profoundly moral structures. We take a sociological rather than a normative perspective on morals, defining the term as what a given community deems appropriate.[1] As an example, if a typical policeman on a given force believes 'laying low' and making no waves is the best way to behave on the job, then such behaviour would be labelled moral within that community of police officers (Van Maanen, 1973). Though outsiders sometimes object to the content of corporate morals, they nonetheless are rich and internally coherent codes of conduct. It does not follow, however, that the volume and density of corporate morals makes them easy to discern.

Our second contention is that one of the defining features of corporate morals is their elusive and often unspoken quality, compounded by problems of field access. Large private organizations tend to be fairly closed worlds. Corporate leaders typically regard nosy outsiders hoping to study their morals with suspicion and are reluctant to grant these researchers access: a 1997 review of Calvin Morrill's study of high-level American executives still described his research sites, without irony, as 'exotic' (Smith, 1997: 223). 'Studying-up' or trying to document the culture of the powerful (like high-level executives) proves always challenging for researchers (Nader, 1972). As an illustration, almost no published fieldwork has been conducted in boardrooms. Because of these problems of access, and because corporate morals so often go unstated, researchers have focused their efforts on documenting the behavioural manifestations of morals: the

---

[1] For a similar use of morality, see Marcel Mauss, 'Morality is the art of living communally as evidenced by the presence of the notion of right' (authors' translation) (1967: 279).

moral 'rules-in-use' that govern conduct in organizations (Jackall, 1988: 5); the 'rules of the game' (Morrill, 1995: 190–7); or the 'cues' that guide organizational members to the proper course of action (Anteby, 2013: 13, 83). Recent scholarship has succeeded at documenting many such unspoken cues, for instance, the ways in which managers look up to their hierarchy for moral guidance (Jackall, 1988); their avoidance of overt conflict (Morrill, 1995); and how they rely in part on their own experience of frequent job changes as a justification for 'liquidating' others (Ho, 2009). Thus, despite the difficulty of specifying corporate morals, scholars have been able in some settings to infer managers' moral worldviews from observation of their moral rules-in-use and normative cues. Yet progress in that regard still appears slow. Our third contention sheds a different light on this elusiveness.

Finally, our third contention is that scholars' difficulty in pinpointing the contents of corporate morals via empirical observation might tell us more about those morals themselves than previously realized. Specifically, their very elusiveness may confirm recent research suggesting that the most meaningful dimension of business morals is not their first-order normative views but their background, or *metaethical*, content (Abend, 2014). In contrast to normative ethics, which consists of specific views regarding what kinds of actions are virtuous or what kinds of institutional arrangements are just, metaethics comprises the nature of morality and moral language. We argue that managers' apparent underspecification of morals suggests a underlying metaethical commitment to pluralism or relativism in moral affairs. That is, that there is a consensus in corporate contexts that there is value in accommodating multiple moral viewpoints at once. The moral 'silence' that researchers have observed both in corporations and in business schools (Anteby, 2013; Jackall, 1988: 5; Morrill, 1995: 17) is therefore a mechanism that supports this deeper metaethical rejection of fixed or objective morals. Thus the elusiveness of corporate morals might be an artifact of the morals themselves (Anteby, 2013: 142), rather than merely a sign of limited field access. This desired moral silence might be a form of morality after all—whether we agree with it or not.

BUSINESS MORALS AND THE MANAGERIAL REVOLUTION

One of the key insights of the first-generation investigations into corporate culture was the insight that new trends in managerial morals could be traced back to systemic shifts in the structure of business. The distinctive traits of *corporate* morals come into clearer view in comparison to the system of *business* morals that preceded them. Durkheim, in the late 1890s, described a form of small-proprietor capitalism that had more in common with the world of Adam Smith than of General Motors. The morals that emanated from it were the morals of the marketplace—emphasizing primarily transparency in transactions—rather than the morals of managerial capitalism, which (as C. Wright

Mills observed in his classic study, *The Power Elite*) shared many essential features with those of other large institutions in neo-liberal society (Mills, 1956). As the large, multi-divisional manufacturing corporation came to dominate developed economies (Perrow, 2002), observers catalogued their distinctive structural elements and the moral implications that flowed from them. As a classic study of US business education noted in 1959, 'No one would argue that there is a clear and precise code of conduct applicable to business (...), but the norms within which employees operate are nonetheless real' (Pierson, 1959: 92).

The sheer size of corporations is an obvious but morally freighted feature of managerial life. By 1933, the 500 largest non-financial firms in the United States accounted for nearly 60% of all non-financial firm assets, a figure that changed little through the 1990s (Mizruchi, 2013: 10). At its peak in 1972, the General Motors Corporation, the largest American employer, had more than three quarters of a million employees (*Fortune Magazine*, 1973). As organizations ballooned in size, the work lives of their managerial ranks became increasingly social. Coordinating the scaled-up manufacturing, marketing, sales, and distribution activities of large corporations meant the emergence of a large cadre of employees whose work lives revolved less and less around technical expertise or productivity, and more and more around getting along with others. As C. Wright Mills noted, 'business success' no longer meant the patient and diligent shepherding of an enterprise. Rather, it became a function of 'conformity with the criteria of those who have already succeeded' (Mills, 1951: 141). Survival of the fittest gave way to the survival of those who socially and morally fit in. For observers who grew up with the nineteenth-century gospel of success, emphasizing thrift, industry, and persistence, the ascendancy of social adroitness over technical expertise meant a troubling divorce of hard work from reward (Jackall, 1988: 7–10; Mills, 1951, 1956; Riesman, 1950; Whyte, 1956). At both its higher and middle managerial levels, Mills concluded, success came to be conceived as little more than 'a network of smart rackets' (1956: 347).

The emergence of corporate morals is also related to members' length of tenure in and identification with organizations. In 1870 just three in ten top executives began their careers within the organization they led (or had been with it since its inception); by 1950 nearly seven in ten had spent their entire work lives within one organization. Fewer than one in ten entered from a different professional or government background (Mills, 1956: 139). A key moral implication of long corporate careers was the ascendancy of procedural or organizational goals over the operational ones: in other words, organizational maintenance became its own rationale. Also, the notion that employees increasingly identified with the organizational identity (usually engineered and promoted by managers) gained popularity in scholarly inquiries into workplace dynamics (Albert and Whetten, 1985; Alvesson, Ashcraft, and Thomas, 2008; Bartel, Blader, and Wrzesniewski, 2007; Pratt, 2000). Thus, employees' assumed identification with the preferred managerial collective identity set the grounds for an intense socialization process into corporate institutional norms (Glynn, 2008).

One morally significant feature of managerial structure was the hierarchical nature of corporate authority. As Robert Jackall observed, managers identify and locate themselves in a network of fealty relationships with their nearest superiors and subordinates. '[A]uthority is embodied in their personal relationships with their immediate bosses and in their perceptions of similar links between other managers up and down the hierarchy' (Jackall, 1988: 17). The structure of career advancement reinforces the organizational chart as a guide to morality. Because the (mostly subjective) judgements of superiors are the criteria by which promotions, bonuses, and other rewards are meted out, long-time inhabitants of organizations come to realize that they must look to their superiors for guidance on issues of right and wrong. In the words of a former vice-president of a large firm, 'What's right in the corporation is what the guy above you wants from you. That's what morality is in the corporation' (Jackall, 1988: 6).

Particularly in the post-war decades, a chorus of business leaders and scholars articulated a body of arguments regarding the unique ability of corporations to pursue the public interest. The separation of capital (shareholders) from management created a cadre of disinterested leaders capable of pursuing growth in large organizations 'without destroying human values in the process', in the 1957 words of Theodore Houser, then-CEO of Sears, Roebuck (quoted in Ho, 2009: 196). Economist Carl Kaysen told the American Economic Association that 'the modern corporation was a soulful corporation' led by a 'management [that] sees itself as responsible to stockholders, employees, customers, the general public and, perhaps most important, the firm itself as an institution' (quoted in Ho, 2009: 195). A range of professional business organizations, from the comparatively conservative corporate public relations body the National Association of Manufacturers (NAM) to the more progressive Committee on Economic Development (CED) argued business leaders' claim to speak in the public interest (Jackall, 1988: 162– 90; Mills, 1956: 122; Mizruchi, 2013: 37–44, 55–62).

Observers offered diverging analyses of the public discourse of corporate morals. In the eyes of many contemporaries, business leaders' claims to represent the public interest was mere hypocrisy. 'Every such naked interest, every new unsanctioned power of corporation, farm bloc, labour union, and governmental agency that has risen in the past two generations has been clothed with morally loaded slogans. For what has *not* been done in the name of public interest?' (Mills, 1956: 344). It was, Robert Jackall concurred, merely a 'magic lantern' of corporate public relations (Jackall, 1988: 162–90). Loud protestations of corporate social responsibility simply cloaked a deeper moral vacuum. In hindsight, however, others have suggested that the statements and associations that articulated the corporate public interest in the post-war decades may have had a salutary effect on corporate behaviour. Mark Mizruchi (2013) suggests that by participating in public-spirited associations, or by giving an address arguing that corporations are pillars of the community, corporate leaders tied their hands somewhat by thus committing themselves publicly to a vision of corporate social responsibility. It was, in a sense, a case of 'fake it till you make it': a corporate moral culture that included such statements operated as a check on some of the worst excesses and enabled some public-spirited gestures, such as the CED's 1966 open letter in support of President Johnson's efforts to rehabilitate urban slums, signed by twenty-two of the most visible and respected corporate leaders. Other initiatives in the same decade included campaigns for tax increases to support both innovative social programs and the Vietnam War (Mizruchi, 2013: 67–72). Overall, the managerial revolution begged for a deeper scholarly dive into the contents of corporate morals.

The Many Flavours of Corporate Morals

In contrast to the first-generation investigations of managerial professions, which presumed that managers and their morals were comparatively invariant across the corporations and sectors that employed them—that 'organization man' was a uniform type and 'white collar' a singular culture (Mills, 1951; Whyte, 1956)—second-generation studies convey instead a clear sense that corporate morals come in multiple flavours. The key insight of Mills, Whyte, Riesman, Dalton, and others was that the rise of the large, multi-divisional corporation signaled a paradigm shift for business morals, from a transactional morality of the marketplace to an organizational morality of managerialism; the lesson of their successors in the 1980s–2000s is that far subtler tweaks in organizational context and other situational factors could be shown to be associated with significant differences in corporate normative orders.

Robert Jackall's research on three corporations in the 1980s reveals the effects that an uncertain business climate can have on corporate morals. In contrast to the monolithic corporate Leviathans portrayed in Whyte or Mills, the large organizations of the 1980s and later are 'houses of cards' (Jackall, 2010: 204). Acquisitions were constant threats, and even in their absence corporations engaged in frequent restructuring and redundancies on their own initiative in the hope of pre-empting hostile takeovers. Accordingly, there emerged great pressures—and rewards—for managers to show high profits on a relatively short time-line. At the chemical company that Jackall studied, these pressures were evident in the widespread practice of 'milking' the corporation's plants: plant managers deferred capital expenditures such as maintenance or innovative investments so as to inflate profits in the short term, then changed jobs or engineered a transfer within the firm before the plant's deterioration became impossible to ignore. Costly expenditures thus affected the 'numbers' of the manager's successor (Jackall, 1988: 90–100). Though Jackall provides ample evidence of managers' private misgivings about this practice, in public they unanimously censured a vice president who rebuked a subordinate for milking plants. 'The code is this', explained one respondent. 'You milk the plants (…) and exercise authoritative prerogatives at will with subordinates and other lesser mortals (…) *But you also don't play holier than thou*' (Jackall, 1988: 97, emphasis in the original). Thus, in this corporate context, being 'holy' equated to adopting almost any behaviour that enhanced short-term profitability.

The uncertainty of late twentieth-century corporate life also amplified the commitment to keeping options open that Mills identified earlier, with the consequence that 'flexibility' became the primary corporate virtue (Jackall, 1988). Managers know from experience that business is unpredictable, and that 'a tremendous amount of plain luck is involved in advancement' (Jackall, 1988: 70). Accordingly, they strive to maintain the freedom of manoeuvre to distance themselves from poor results and affiliate themselves with successful ones. In C. Wright Mills' memorable phrase, corporations are 'systems of organized irresponsibility' (1951: 111, 149, 160, 349) in which 'details and decisions are pushed down, and credit is pulled up' (Jackall, 1988: 95). Accordingly, passing the buck, dragging one's feet until important decisions 'make themselves', spreading responsibility as widely as possible, and being careful not to over-commit one's boss come to be seen as moral practices. 'Speak like the quiet competent man of affairs and never personally say No', Mills advised aspiring members of the power elite. 'Hire the No-man as well as the Yes-man. Be the tolerant Maybe-man and they will cluster around you, filled with hopefulness' (1956: 141). Taking care to commit to as little as possible comes to be seen as a morally right course of action.

Changes in organizational structure as well as business climate can yield vastly different flavours of corporate morals. Calvin Morrill's study of conflict management among executives reveals the significant impact that comparatively subtle shifts in organizational form might entail. The thirteen firms he studied were all publicly held, for-profit organizations with an executive corps of between ten and seventy-six members (median seventeen). There were a number of themes common to executive life across all of his research sites, including perks unavailable to lower echelons of the firm (limos, private planes; special office furniture and other accoutrements; special staff such as security personnel or concierges); long hours at work; comparatively little intimacy with colleagues; and comparatively low representation of women and other minorities (Morrill, 1995: 28–45). Despite their many similarities, executives in these thirteen firms acted according to widely different normative orders when it came to conflict management. Broadly speaking, Morrill found no fewer than three normative orders that varied according to type of managerial structure.

Morrill's first two types of corporate structure upheld the 'pervasive societal myth' that corporations are consensus-driven organizations where conflict is avoided when possible, and hidden when not (Dalton, 1959: 263; Morrill, 1995: 45). The first and best-known corporate structure Morrill calls the 'mechanistic bureaucracy'. In a mechanistic bureaucracy, authority flows through hierarchical chains of command and members exhibit a tendency towards rule-orientation—concern with obeying proper bureaucratic procedures. Conflict management, too, proceeds through these hierarchical chains of command and proper bureaucratic procedures. Executives pursue grievances against subordinates in a unilateral, penal mode; that is, by diktat—though these orders are typically given in private. For example, an executive concerned that a junior executive was too hard on his staff would request regular meetings at his private club to discuss his progress in 'making over' his management style (Morrill, 1995: 109). Executives of similar rank refer their differences to the appropriate higher power. Subordinates also frame their grievances with superiors in penal terms, but seldom pursue them. When they do, it tends to take the form of sabotage: three VPs at a financial firm, for example, colluded to introduce errors and omissions into their SVP's presentations, resulting in his demotion (Morrill, 1995: 2–4). Negotiation or formal grievance procedures that reach outside the operational chain of command are rare: following the mere threat of formal action by a subordinate, a manager 'spent several months attempting to repair his reputation (…) as an executive who could not contain management problems within his own span of control' (Morrill, 1995: 132).

In 'atomistic' organizations, such as professional service firms like accounting or management consulting, conflict is even further sublimated. Because executives in such contexts are highly autonomous, operating with their own support staff on individual client accounts, they can—and do—simply avoid those with whom they have friction (Morrill, 1995: 141–76). This is not to say that conflict was less common in atomistic organizations. Executives nursed numerous grievances, particularly over claims to clients: when a partner resigned, for example, and his or her accounts were distributed among his colleagues; or when an executive exploited a personal connection to gain an account that might have gone to a colleague with more expertise in the content area. Both in mechanistic and atomistic organizations, resort to open conflict, formal grievance procedures, or third-party adjudication is regarded as a loss of face to be strenuously avoided; as symptomatic of a manager's fundamental inability to manage. Remaining silent on points of disagreement is accordingly a primary corporate virtue.

In organizations that deploy the more innovative 'matrix' system, by contrast, conflict is expressed in a radically different manner. In a matrix organization, project teams are overlaid on top of existing functional units. Because there are two competing lines of formal authority, each one is correspondingly weakened, which lends itself to disputes over issues of administrative jurisdiction and organizational strategy. Such ambiguity promotes both lone-wolf behaviour and informal coalition-forming. Morrill shows how executives in matrix organizations interpreted such jurisdictional ambiguity through a lens of personal honour. Executives who felt their turf infringed and their honour slighted engaged in a 'moralistic tit for tat' with their foes, sometimes escalating into vengeance games that drew in supporters and occasionally even culminated in physical violence. In a matrix organization, corporate morality involved the aggressive—and overt—defence of one's turf, and by extension one's honour. In that sense, organizational structures seem to condition in part corporate morals.

The Wall Street world explored in Karen Ho's *Liquidated: An Ethnography of Wall Street* (2009) reveals yet another flavour of corporate morality. One signal example is the culture of smartness in the world of high finance. In contrast to the more traditional corporations that Mills or even Jackall describe, where 'brilliance' is seen as a liability (Jackall, 1988) and ambitious managers were advised to 'never let your brains show' (Mills, 1956: 141), 'smartness' is a central virtue in the financial world. For one thing, 'smartness'—defined and represented by educational pedigree, impeccable dress and grooming, mental quickness, and aggressiveness—is an essential credential for employment as an investment banker.[2] But it also serves as a justification for forcibly

---

[2] Research has suggested that recruiters for investment banks and consulting firms often screen applicants on extra-curricular activities (typically the types of sports practised) to identify a good cultural match between candidates and firms (Rivera, 2012).

restructuring American business. 'The 'culture of smartness' is central to understanding Wall Street's financial agency, how investment bankers are personally and institutionally empowered to enact their worldviews, export their practices, and serve as models for far-reaching socioeconomic change' (Ho, 2009: 41). In the world of high finance, smart makes right.

Wall Street, and the influence it exerts on the business world at large, also offers a distinct contrast to the stability and longevity once associated with large corporations—and once blamed for some of their moral failings. As Karen Ho documents, the culture of employment insecurity in investment banks offers their members a rationale for cutting jobs in the firms they restructure: frequent job-changing comes to seem like a universally-shared feature of employment. Whether they jump ship for a better position, or get caught in one of the regular 'self-downsizings' that take place on Wall Street (investment banks conduct an average of two rounds of layoffs per year), Ho's respondents told the same story of frequent job changes. Moreover, they suggested, the instability and disruption made them better employees, and their employers better, more efficient, and nimbler enterprises (Ho, 2009: 231–43). Still further, Wall Streeters habitually employed job-hopping as a means of maximizing their compensation, often leaving right after bonus season for a new position (Ho, 2009: 268–71). Wall Street's is a corporate morality in which value resides in timing and agility.

Moral Silence and Relativism

The effort to view corporate morals as a whole, thus, seems to end in an impasse. On the one hand, prescriptive statements of business values tend to be characterized by a high degree of surface uniformity: play by the rules; don't lie, cheat, or steal; and treat your employees well. These exhortations vary little by context, and have changed little for centuries (Abend, 2014). On the other hand, the empirical work by Jackall, Morrill, Ho, and others suggests that managers' moral rules-in-use and other manifestations of normative orders in practice appear to be highly variable and context-dependent. Such conclusions—simultaneously contradictory and wide-ranging—would seem to nullify the effort to draw any overarching conclusions regarding corporate morals. Accordingly, we draw attention to a different manifestation of corporate morals—moral silence—that is, we contend, a common thread running through existing research on corporate morals and one that may yield more insight into the nature of those corporate morals than previously acknowledged.

Though they do not analyse it at length, several empirical researchers have remarked on a certain degree of obfuscation, indirection, or silence as a common manifestation of corporate morality. Morrill notes that the moral worldviews of managers and executives consist of 'tacit knowledge (…) acquire[d] on the fly' (1995: 17); Jackall notes along similar lines that '[m]anagers typically do not discuss ethics [or] morals (…) in a direct way with each other (…). Actual organizational moralities are thus contextual, situational, highly specific, and, most often, unarticulated' (1988: 5).

Some of their readings of this phenomenon are less generous than others. For Robert Jackall, silence is a strategy to which managers resort to manage the tension between the moralities of their organizations, and those moralities proper to other groups or structures: professional codes, for example, or those of the broader community. The story of one whistleblower, an accountant who uncovered evidence of systematic falsification of financial information in his organization, illustrates this divergence well. After struggling with his conscience, the accountant concluded that his loyalty to his professional code of conduct required that he blow the whistle on the malfeasance. His colleagues, however, condemned his actions as destructive of the very fabric of managerial functioning. His actions 'called others' organizational morality, their acceptance of the moral ethos of bureaucracy, into question, made them uncomfortable, and eroded the fundamental trust and understanding that makes cooperative managerial work possible' (Jackall, 2010: 116). Rather, his colleagues told Jackall, the accountant should have remained silent in moral matters. As Jackall's interviews make clear, his respondents are aware of the contrast between their organizational morality and the broader or 'abstract' morality of the accountancy profession. Silence is their prescribed strategy for managing that tension.

A similar code of silence is mandated by the bankers' worldview in Karen Ho's ethnography of high finance. Her Wall Street interview subjects typically take the position that it is a moral imperative for business leaders to stay silent in matters of morals. This position originates in the neoclassical logic of shareholder value, which holds that it is the sole duty of the firm to maximize the profits that flow to its stock owners. Recognizing the claims of other stakeholders (such as employees, customers, or the broader public) is both pernicious and 'immoral'. It is pernicious because firms best maximize social welfare by maximizing total firm value in the economy; it is immoral because it is theft committed against the stock owners (Ho, 2009: 207–12; for another statement of these arguments, see Margolis and Walsh, 2003). Mark Mizruchi confirms that the rise of the theory of shareholder value in the 1980s and after coincided with the decline of the CED and other forums in which business leaders once articulated the values of business as a whole and a constituent part of societies more broadly. Today, he writes, business groups devoted to political relations do not seek to speak for their industry, or for industry as a whole, but simply work to reduce the role of government and the power of labour (Mizruchi, 2013: 176–9). When it comes to moral vision beyond the imperative to maximize shareholder value, business leaders and industry associations alike tend to remain silent.

Given the ubiquity of silence and covert dynamics in accounts of corporate morals, it is worth considering the possibility that the phenomenon might be more than anecdotal; instead, silence might be an artifact of the *contents* of corporate morals (Anteby, 2013: 142). Could silence itself be a moral position? Here it is useful to draw on the theoretical infrastructure of moral philosophy. For moral philosophers, ethics come in three varieties: applied ethics (the moral dilemmas of particular cases, such as the well-known trolley dilemma); normative ethics (general statements about the good life, or just social arrangements); and metaethics (the study of the nature of ethics and moral language). Recent work by Gabriel Abend has suggested that, when it comes to business ethics, applied and normative ethics are comparatively uneventful. Things get interesting, by contrast, at the level of metaethics, where Abend—perhaps confirming others' assertions that the empirical study of business ethics may always face 'metatheoretical' problems (Treviño and Weaver, 2003: 1–64)—shows older statements of 'moral realism' (the view that ethics are fixed and objective) being eclipsed by contrary statements of 'moral relativism' particularly associated with institutions like large corporations and business schools (Abend, 2014: 290–305).

Recent ethnographic work has more closely addressed the role of silence as a mechanism supporting such a metaethic. A study of faculty socialization at the Harvard Business School (HBS) suggests that the School's MBA curriculum's apparent restraint from endorsing any given set of morals might be 'a form of morals after all' (Anteby, 2013: 142). Senior HBS faculty members' recent description of the School's first-year required ethics course as one that does not endorse any particular point of view seems to supports such an interpretation (Datar, Garvin, and Cullen, 2010: 162). They note that 'students must feel that the classroom is a safe, protected environment in which they can openly explore and question one another's deeply held beliefs without the need to parrot back a prescribed philosophy or point of view.' Thus the difficulty of specifying corporate morals may not be the result of a lack of morals, but an artifact of the content of corporate morals, namely a desire to keep in play multiple viewpoints.

Such an aspiration to accommodate multiple viewpoints (within limits) has been apparent throughout the School's history. For example, Charles Gragg, a faculty member who authored the 1940 teaching note 'Because Wisdom Can't Be Told', explained that 'the principal object of professional education is to accelerate a student's ability to act in a mature fashion under conditions of responsibility' (Gragg, 1940: 3–5). What constituted a mature fashion was purposely left unspecified. Gragg added that 'each student is free to present and hold to his own views.' With respect to moral decision-making, faculty members involved in the School's current formal ethics course offerings seem to agree with Gragg: they note that managers' actions need to 'be guided and consistent with relevant ethical standards' or to meet 'relevant' ethical 'requirements', but steer clear of specifying what those standards or requirements are (Paine, 2006; Sucher and Hsieh, 2011; Sucher, 2011). Another School teaching note posits that managers' actions build on 'personal, family, and cultural values, tenets of our religious beliefs and personal philosophies, past experiences, prior knowledge, and general understanding of what morality means', but refrains from of articulating what such morals might entail. Put otherwise, moral thinking is essentially viewed as a process that can accommodate (within limits) multiple moral viewpoints. For all corporate managers to coalesce under a tent, its size needs to be sufficiently large. To paraphrase and qualify Durkheim's statement opening this chapter, those involved in commerce and industry might obey multiple morals rather than no morals at all. Thus, in the corporate world, being relatively silent about endorsing any unique moral perspective might indeed be a form of morals.

Conclusion

Between abstract morals and concrete individuals lie intermediary groups entrusted with ensuring proper socialization into those shared understandings. The families, schools, and faith communities we grow up in are obvious examples of such intermediaries. Sidewalks, street corners, and neighbourhood restaurants can also act as intermediaries (Duneier, 1999; Whyte, 1943). But many other entities, including professional groups and work organizations, also participate in the socializing enterprise (Biggart, 1989; Chan, 2009; Hitlin and Vaisey, 2010; Jackall, 2010; Zelizer, 1979). These entities offer their members an affiliation intimate enough to pervade the core of their everyday lives, yet distinct enough from any given individual for members to envision themselves part of broader pursuits. While such entities do not always succeed at their respective goals, they often foster shared views among members (Vallas, 1991; Vaughan, 1996). Corporations are no exceptions: they train their members in developing a shared, normative understanding of the world and in some cases, such as the definition of job discrimination and equal opportunity, develop moral codes within their walls that are later exported to society at large (Dobbin, 2009: 221–34). Because of their preeminence in contemporary life, we need to better grasp what corporate morals entail. We hope this chapter offers a starting point for readers to better understand these corporate morals.

References

Abend, G. (2014). *The Moral Background: An Inquiry into the History of Business Ethics*. Princeton, NJ: Princeton University Press.

Albert, S., and Whetten, D. A. (1985). 'Organizational Identity'. *Research in Organizational Behavior*, 7: 263–95.

Alvesson, M., Ashcraft, K. L., and Thomas, R. (2008). 'Identity Matters: Reflections on the Construction of Identity Scholarship in Organization Studies'. *Organization*, 15(1): 5–28.

Anteby, M. (2013). *Manufacturing Morals: The Values of Silence in Business School Education*. Chicago and London: University of Chicago Press.

Bartel, C., Blader, S. L., and Wrzesniewski, A. (eds.) (2007). *Identity and the Modern Organization*. Mahwah, NJ: Lawrence Erlbaum Associates.

Biggart, N. W. (1989). *Charismatic Capitalism: Direct Selling Organizations in America*. Chicago, IL: University of Chicago Press.

Chan, C. S. (2009). 'Invigorating the Content in Social Embeddedness: An Ethnography of Life Insurance Transactions in China'. *American Journal of Sociology*, 115(3): 712–54.

Chandler, A. D. (1977). *The Visible Hand: The Managerial Revolution in American Business*. Cambridge, MA: Belknap Press.

Dalton, M. (1959). *Men Who Manage: Fusions of Feeling and Theory in Administration*. New York: Wiley.
Datar, S. M., Garvin, D. A., and Cullen, P. G. (2010). *Rethinking the MBA: Business Education at a Crossroads*. Boston, MA: Harvard Business Press.
Dobbin, F. (2009). *Inventing Equal Opportunity*. Princeton, NJ: Princeton University Press.
Duneier, M. (1999). *Sidewalks*. New York: Farrar, Straus and Giroux.
Durkheim, É. (1958). *Professional Ethics and Civic Morals*. Glencoe, IL: Free Press.
Durkheim, É. (1961). *Moral Education: A Study in the Theory and Application of the Sociology of Education*. New York: Free Press.
Durkheim, É. (1973). *Émile Durkheim on Morality and Society* (ed. R. N. Bellah). Chicago, IL: University of Chicago Press.
Fortune Magazine. (1973). *Fortune 500 Historical Database*. Available at: <http://money.cnn.com/magazines/fortune/fortune500_archive/snapshots/1972/563.html> (accessed 22 May 2014).
Glynn, M. A. (2008). 'Beyond Constraint: How Institutions Enable Identities', in R. Greenwood (ed.), *The SAGE Handbook of Organizational Institutionalism*. Los Angeles and London: SAGE, 413–30.
Gouldner, A. W. (1955). *Patterns of Industrial Bureaucracy*. London: Routledge and Kegan Paul.
Gragg, C. I. (1940). *Because Wisdom Can't Be Told (HBSP Case 9- 451- 005)*. Cambridge, MA: President and Fellows of Harvard College.
Hitlin, S., and Vaisey, S. (2010). 'Back to the Future', in S. Hitlin and S. Vaisey (eds.), *Handbook of the Sociology of Morality*. New York: Springer, 3–14.
Ho, K. Z. (2009). *Liquidated: An Ethnography of Wall Street*. Durham, NC: Duke University Press.
Jackall, R. (1988). *Moral Mazes: The World of Corporate Managers*. New York: Oxford University Press.
Jackall, R. (2010). 'Morality in Organizations', in S. Hitlin and S. Vaisey (eds.), *Handbook of the Sociology of Morality*. New York: Springer, 203–10.
Jennifer Louise, P. and Gianpiero, P. (2010). 'Identity Workspaces: The Case of Business Schools'. *Academy of Management Learning and Education*, 9(1): 44–60.
Joel, G., Linda K., T., and Raghu, G. (2013). 'Values Work: A Process Study of the Emergence and Performance of Organizational Values Practices'. *Academy of Management Journal*, 56(1): 84–112.
Khurana, R. (2007). *From Higher Aims to Hired Hands: The Social Transformation of American Business Schools and the Unfulfilled Promise of Management as a Profession*. Princeton, NJ: Princeton University Press.
Lamont, M. (2000). *The Dignity of Working Men: Morality and the Boundaries of Race, Class, and Immigration*. New York and Cambridge, MA: Russell Sage Foundation and Harvard University Press.
Margolis, J. D. and Walsh, J. P. (2003). 'Misery Loves Companies: Rethinking Social Initiatives by Business'. *Administrative Science Quarterly*, 48(2): 268–305.
Mauss, M. (1967). *Manuel d'Éthnographie*. Paris: Éditions Payot.
Mills, C. W. (1951). *White Collar: The American Middle Classes*. New York: Oxford University Press.
Mills, C. W. (1956). *The Power Elite*. New York: Oxford University Press.
Mintzberg, H. (1973). *The Nature of Managerial Work*. New York: Harper and Row.

Mizruchi, M. S. (2013). *The Fracturing of the American Corporate Elite*. Cambridge, MA: Harvard University Press.
Morrill, C. (1995). *The Executive Way: Conflict Management in Corporations*. Chicago, IL: University of Chicago Press.
Nader, L. (1972). 'Up the Anthropologist: Perspectives Gained from Studying Up', in D. H. Hymes (ed.), *Reinventing Anthropology*, 1st edn. New York: Pantheon Books, 284–311.
Paine, L. S. (2006). *Instructor's Guide to Leadership and Corporate Accountability (LCA) (HBSP Note 5- 307- 032*. Boston, MA: President and Fellows of Harvard College.
Perrow, C. (2002). *Organizing America: Wealth, Power, and the Origins of Corporate Capitalism*. Princeton, NJ: Princeton University Press.
Pierson, F. C. (1959). *The Education of American Businessmen; A Study of University-College Programs in Business Administration*. New York: McGraw-Hill.
Pratt, M. G. (2000). 'The Good, the Bad, and the Ambivalent: Managing Identification among Amway Distributors'. *Administrative Science Quarterly*, 45(3): 456–93.
Riesman, D. (1950). *The Lonely Crowd: A Study of the Changing American Character*. New Haven, CT: Yale University Press.
Rivera, L. A. (2012). 'Hiring as Cultural Matching: The Case of Elite Professional Service Firms'. *American Sociological Review*, 77(6): 999–1022.
Smith, V. (1997). 'Review of *White-Collar Blues: Management Loyalties in an Age of Corporate Restructuring* by Charles Heckscher; *The Executive Way: Conflict Management in Corporations* by Calvin Morrill'. *Contemporary Sociology*, 26(2): 220–3.
Starkey, K. and Tiratsoo, N. (2007). *The Business School and the Bottom Line*. Cambridge and New York: Cambridge University Press.
Sucher, S. J. (2011). *Action Planning: An LCA Perspective. Harvard Business School Module Note 605- 079*. Boston, MA: President and Fellows of Harvard College.
Sucher, S. J. and Hsieh, N. (2011). *A Framework for Ethical Reasoning. Harvard Business School Background Note 610-050*. Boston, MA: President and Fellows of Harvard College.
Treviño, L. K. and Weaver, G. R. (2003). *Managing Ethics in Business Organizations: Social Scientific Perspectives*. Stanford, CA: Stanford Business Books.
Vaisey, S. (2009). 'Motivation and Justification: A Dual-process Model of Culture in Action'. *American Journal of Sociology*, 114(6): 1675–715.
Vallas, S. P. (1991). 'Workers, Firms, and the Dominant Ideology: Hegemony and Consciousness in the Monopoly Core'. *The Sociological Quarterly*, 32(1): 61–83.
Van Maanen, J. (1973). 'Observations on the Making of Policemen'. *Human Organization*, 32(4): 407–18.
Vaughan, D. (1996). *The Challenger Launch Decision: Risky Technology, Culture, and Deviance at NASA*. Chicago, IL: University of Chicago Press.
Whyte, W. F. (1943). *Street Corner Society: The Social Structure of an Italian Slum*. Chicago, IL: University of Chicago Press.
Whyte, W. H. (1956). *The Organization Man*. New York: Simon and Schuster.
Wuthnow, R. (1987). *Meaning and Moral Order: Explorations in Cultural Analysis*. Berkeley, CA: University of California Press.
Zelizer, V. A. R. (1979). *Morals and Markets: The Development of Life Insurance in the United States*. New York: Columbia University Press.

CHAPTER 20

MANAGEMENT AND MODERNITY

GRAHAM SEWELL

What is Modernity and Why Does it Matter to Management? Autonomy, Mastery, and Modernity

TRYING to identify the very essence of Modernity and when and where this essence originated will always be confounded by some kind of 'First Cause' problem. How could we definitively pin down the one event, idea, or momentous work that heralded the instant in time when we became modern, or the time when we stop being unmodern for that matter? In this sense, my definition is no more or less arbitrary than anyone else's but it also carries with it the implicit understanding that some kind of definition is nevertheless required in order that we might proceed. It starts with Wagner's (2012) observation that two themes continue to dominate our self-understanding of what it means to be a human being living in the modern era: that we are self-determining subjects and that we can exercise this autonomy to choose reason as the basis for the pursuit of domination over nature. But this self-understanding also involves an ambivalence that tempers our reflexive historical consciousness by recognizing that there is a problem at the heart of the pursuit of mastery. This stems from the tension between the fatalistic recognition that our present circumstances must change and our understandable desire for stability and, with it, certainty and security. Localized variations of this tension pull us in different directions to such an extent that Modernity is now best thought of in terms of pluralities and transformation rather than convergence and stability (Clegg, 1990; Wagner, 2012); a concept that must accommodate many and diverse oppositions. Of course, the observation that we are ambivalent about Modernity has a long pedigree in social theory. For example, Lash (1999) locates it in something as early as the inter-textual dialogue Kant conducts in his three critiques of reason. I shall return to Lash's work later on but, for my immediate purposes, Zygmunt Bauman's concept of ambivalence is as good a place as any to start this discussion of Modernity and its relation to management (see Bauman, 1991). He sees Modernity as a cultural and social project of the Enlightenment that is characterized by a drive towards order, design, naming, and segregating. Most importantly for us, however, is Bauman's attempt to put something resembling an everyday understanding of the concept of management at the heart of this project in that to manage is a common feature of all these characteristics; a means to the end of creating order and stability through rational design, classification, and the promotion of a spatial and temporal division of labour. For Bauman what is central to such differentiation is the maintenance of symmetry around the pairing of inside and outside, with the classification of others as friends or enemies being the example par excellence of setting apart things like truth and falsity, good and evil, beauty and ugliness, etc. Ambivalence rears into view in the form of the stranger who sits outside such categorical dyads, giving rise to the 'horror of indetermination' which must be overcome by minimizing the destabilizing hermeneutical problem of being faced by the presence of such an undecidable third category (cf. Latour, 1993—especially his comment on our fear of 'hybrid' objects). Here Bauman's sociological inclinations leads him to concentrate on the way in which we use territorial and functional separation to avoid the necessity of confronting such horrors. Thus, carving up the social world into things like administrative regions or domains of professional expertise reduces the potential for strangers to disrupt matters by restricting our social interactions to 'sectors of assumed common understanding and mutual interest' (Barth, 1969, quoted in Bauman, 1990). In short, we can conceive of management as a reflexive act that involves the exercise of mastery over ourselves and others so that we can erect, police, and ultimately deploy rational principles to dismantle the spatial and functional boundaries associated with a complex and dynamic division of labour. Thus, determining who has the legitimate authority to exercise mastery others in large part forms the basis for debates around managerial control. It used to be that there was an invisible but nevertheless recognized fault line between managers who managed and workers who did as they were told but now it seems that everyone everywhere is expected to be a self-managing entrepreneur. Likewise, working through who claims the right, on the basis of their privileged access to a body of technical knowledge, to determine which course of action is preferable over another in large part forms the basis for debates about management expertise. For example, it used to be taken for granted that something like strategy was the responsibility of a priestly caste of senior professional managers but what organization today would risk a major change in strategy without calling in external consultants?

Having arrived at a working definition of Modernity as a condition of ambivalence borne of the opposition between change and stability, management can thus be seen as a conscious act that tries to reconcile this contradiction at the heart of modern culture by constantly trying to shore up a division of labour that is inherently unstable. This puts us in mind of the broad sweep of Weber's critique of Modernity where bureaucracy is but a contingent feature of domination through rationalization (Clegg and Lounsbury, 2009) and where the obligations of the bureaucratic office holder frequently run counter to our basic human instincts (Turner, 1991). The most common take on this tension stems from Parsons' tendentious translation of *Stahlhartes Gehäuse* (Cohen, Hazelrigg, and Pope, 1975; Clegg and Lounsbury, 2009) as the 'Iron Cage'. This is now universally recognizable and has taken on a life of its own but its fails to capture the subtlety of Weber's German term (Baehr, 2001; Clegg and Lounsbury, 2009). This has led us to underplay Weber's metaphorical use of bureaucracy as a characteristic configuration of power relations to convey the moral dimension of a rationalizing technology whose main locus of action is the human body (Turner, 1992). I make this point early on to signal that in the last section of this chapter I shall reexamine the role of management under bureaucracy as a mode of rationalization via an alternative reading of *Stahlhartes Gehäuse*. This will allow us to reconsider management as a set of practices that are part of a wider 'science of Man' (Hennis, 1988) that orders human bodies through forms of classification (such as 'friend' or 'enemy', 'good' or 'bad', 'productive' or 'unproductive', etc.) in an attempt to avoid Bauman's 'horror of indetermination'. I will start off in a more predictable manner, however, by looking at prominent representatives of what Clegg (1990) called 'formal theories of administration'. I then consider authors whose critiques of Modernity draw on European traditions of social theory before contrasting this with 'new' institutional theory and the way it deals with the relationship between management and Modernity. Finally, I turn to Lash's notion of 'another modernity' to develop an alternative take on Weber's concept of *Stahlhartes Gehäuse* as a personal disposition rather than an all-enveloping iron cage that stifles human thriving through what he described elsewhere as the rational organization of formally free labour (Weber, 1961).

Management in Pursuit of Progress

This mention of formally free labour is important, for much of Weber's understanding of the administration of modern organizations turns on the way in which contractual arrangements between employers and employees had superseded feudal arrangements (Münch, 1983). Under feudalism serfs could not easily be evicted from the land they tended and this limited its productive efficiency. Contrast this rigidity with the notional flexibility inherent in a contract between a principal and an agent in a modern organization—the principal can choose who they contract with based on some assessment of the agent's suitability for the task at hand and the cost of hiring them. Likewise, an agent can ostensibly choose whether or not to serve a principal based on the nature of the task and the compensation on offer. Moreover, if either party fails to fulfil their obligations under the contract then redress can be sought. For Weber (1968) this transition to such a new social institution meant that modern organizational administrators were now expected to select employees on the basis of a technical assessment of skills in the context of a competitive labour market; something that effectively established the need for a new profession who possessed expertise in techniques of rational calculation (Münch, 1983). It is this notion of expertise and its possession that underpins the concept of mastery found across many of the formal theories of administration that we have come to associate with late nineteenth and early twentieth century management thinkers—that is, disinterested managers' rights to exercise legitimate authority over others derives from their privileged access to a body of specialized technical knowledge. Most assessments of early management thinkers usually place Henri Fayol second only to Frederick Taylor but, on closer inspection, it is Fayol who arguably took a more integrated approach to the management of organizations as a coherent group made up of individuals who subordinate themselves to some notion of the general interest, à la Weber's (1961) notion of a 'corporate body'. Moreover, anyone coming across Fayol's (1916) fourteen general principles of management for the first time would also see much that still resonates with the exhortations of management consultants today (Peaucelle and Guthrie, 2013; Wren, Bedeian, and Breeze, 2002). In light of this, I shall briefly consider how Fayol's more nuanced conception of management as a vocation goes beyond Taylor's rather narrow horizons to unexpectedly echo some of Weber's better known concerns about the ethically ambiguous nature of Modernity.

Although Fayol was an admirer of Scientific Management, the Frenchman recognized that *administration industrielle et générale* required an appreciation of ambiguity that many critics (e.g., Kanigel, 1996) suggest was largely absent in the work of Taylor. Consider the following comment:

> The soundness and good working order of the body corporate depend on certain conditions termed indiscriminately principles, laws, rules. For preference I shall adopt the term principles whilst dissociating it from any suggestion of rigidity, for there is nothing rigid or absolute in management affairs, it is all a question of proportion. Seldom do we have to apply the same principle twice in identical conditions; allowance must be made for different changing circumstances, for men are just as different and changing as many other variable elements. (Fayol, 1949: 181)

Nevertheless, Fayol was just as adamant as Taylor that a privileged access to a body of specialist knowledge was the source of managers' authority to instruct subordinates and a division of labour along these lines was part of the 'natural' order of things based on the distribution of intelligence throughout the population (Fayol, 1916). This led Fayol to write extensively on how his five functions of management—*Prévoyance, Organisation, Commandement, Coordination,* and *Contrôle* (hence his acronym, POCCC)—could form the institutional basis for the systematic education of managerial elites. Although there is no evidence to suggest Fayol was familiar with Weber, he shared the German's ambivalence about the march of rational calculation, its embodiment in bureaucracy, and their relationship to the project of Modernity—that is, they are all human creations yet the pursuit of rationality via bureaucracy as a technically superior form of organization (Weber, 1968) also creates seemingly inevitable conditions that fatefully compromise human thriving (Clegg, 1990). In this way, Fayol's appreciation of the ambiguities involved in management and his fear of the stultifying effects of rules and universal standardized procedures can still be seen as a corrective to an emerging technocratic consciousness where highly trained managers could somehow identify and implement the 'one best way' of human organization (cf. Aitken, 1960). In this respect Fayol's awareness that enforcing the division of labour between 'thinkers' and 'doers' was a practical impossibility in most organizational situations where there would always be exceptions to managerial rules and where employees would inevitably know more than their superiors about what they were doing.

This realization that employees had access to knowledge that was unavailable to their managers is also evident in the work of Mary Parker Follett. If the work of Fayol provides us with a more nuanced take on the danger of taking scientific management at face value then Follett serves a similar function when it comes to the Human Relations School. Bruce and Nyland (2012) point to the tendency to beatify Elton Mayo for his alleged role in humanizing scientific management but he yearned for a return to a mythical age where the relationship between 'masters' and 'men' was built on a natural order of superiority and subordination (see Mayo, 1919). In this respect, Mayo was criticizing Modernity from a pre-modern position (see my comments on Burrell below). In contrast, Follett looked forward to an age of cooperation that would come about as an inevitable part of an evolutionary process, thus substituting Mayo's misplaced nostalgia for a Golden Age with a modernist belief in social progress. Nevertheless, Follett's and Mayo's prescriptions for reaching their shared ideal of organizational harmony were very similar in that they both focused on how social groups inevitably formed even in the most rationalized organizations and that they should thus be the focus of formal organizational design (Miller and Form, 1964). Follett's response was to advocate for the devolvement of management responsibility throughout the organization, noting that even the 'lowliest delivery driver' would be best left to determine the order in which he should make his rounds (Follett, 1941). She also noted that different people possessed varied but complementary leadership qualities that were rarely found in one person. Furthermore, she considered the highest quality of leadership to be the ability to take on board and reflect back the collective will of a group. Thus, management is a social achievement of collaboration and cooperation that arises through interpersonal relationships; a form of mutual normative control if you will. The continuing persuasiveness of this approach rests on Follett's recognition of the important distinction between power and authority or, as she put it, 'power over' and 'power with'. Again, although there is no evidence to suggest she was well acquainted with the work of Weber this nevertheless chimes with his warning that we should not subordinate value-based rationality to the technocratic consciousness of instrumental rationality where things like efficient command and control become ends in themselves.

Reassessing Management in a Postmodern World

It may seem almost inconceivable now but there was a time not so long ago when many people were exercised about whether we left Modernity behind and found ourselves in a postmodern condition. In this section I wish to focus on three authors—Gibson Burrell, Stewart Clegg, and Paul du Gay—who made important contributions to this debate by drawing on Continental theorists to build on the insights of the key thinkers of the modernist project such as Marx, Durkheim, and Weber.

When considering Gibson Burrell's individual contribution to the matters at hand in this chapter, it is useful to start with an article he produced in the late 1980s with Robert Cooper. They situate their critique of Modernity in the collective failure of nerve that beset the social sciences from the late 1960s onwards (Cooper and Burrell, 1988). One consolation of this decline of confidence in grand narratives of progress was that it freed organization and management studies from the compulsion to be relevant in an instrumental sense, thereby giving us license to reconnect with Weber's project of understanding the role of organizations in the variegated rationalization of social life that accompanies the disenchantment of the world (Cooper and Burrell, 1988). From focusing on *the* organization as a discrete and autonomous rational object we can thus turn our attention to organizing as the expression of the desire to establish mastery over the natural and social worlds (cf. Weick, 1974—especially his comments on organization as a noun and organizing as a verb). This stance is representative of a broader revival of interest in the work of a 'de-Parsonized' Weber (Cohen, Hazelrigg, and Pope, 1975) for, as the Marxist project (and even its diluted social democratic version) faltered, why not turn to a figure whose contribution had seemed destined to be overshadowed by Marx (Blau, 1963)? In reconnecting with Weber, the extended contribution of Burrell has been crucial in developing a critical appreciation of now familiar continental thinkers such as Michel Foucault (Burrell, 1988) and Jürgen Habermas (Burrell, 1994). Intellectually, this embrace of such diverse thinkers initiated by Burrell has been very liberating as it has been part of an opening up of a terrain that seems almost boundless; a place where discussions of the organizational aspects of the New Orleans Mardi Gras (Islam, Zyphur, and Boje, 2008) can aspire to the same degree of scholarly legitimacy as discussions of the design and implementation of business strategies in transnational corporations. Importantly, it means that under the rubric of Modernity, management is not simply something that people called 'managers' do but a name we give to the desire to order social relations according to a particular model of functional rationality; a place where corporations, in their position as 'as the dominant social subsystem, become the paradigmatic organizations of systemic modernism' (Cooper and Burrell, 1988: 96). By systemic modernism, Cooper and Burrell mean a continuation of the instrumental reason originally associated with Auguste Comte and his successors. This is contrasted with the critical modernism of the late Frankfurt School approach of Jurgen Habermas which opposes the creeping rationalization of all aspects of life via an appeal to a Kantian notion of emancipation through reason (Cooper and Burrell, 1988). It is as if everything would be fine if we could only get back in touch with the authentic experience of everyday life; a desirable mode of living that is distorted by the instrumental and calculative language of systemic modernism which ultimately legitimates coercion in the name of efficiency. Guess (1981) characterises this historically as a gradual (indeed, almost imperceptible) shifting of the normative basis of Modernity so that the social institutions that were once supposed to guarantee freedom from the irrational restrictions of tradition and superstition themselves become repressive and thwart us in the pursuit of many desires yet are still widely tolerated because their operation is seen as being formally or procedurally correct. This gives rise to the ironic situation that managers may sincerely believe they are acting in the interests of all through enacting rational principles of organization such as measurement, calculation, and control when, to all intents and purposes, they are actually cementing the interest of a few (Sewell and Barker, 2006a).

Burrell's eclectic intellectual stance on the problems of management and Modernity is at its most ambitious in his book, *Pandemonium*; a text that ominously announces its intentions as something intended 'to be disruptive, randomizing, and reliant on the reader's creativity' (Burrell, 1997: 2). Central to Burrell's claims about a life today largely lived in, around, and through organizations is that our confidence in the Enlightenment had effectively put the Middle Ages behind us is wishful thinking. This recognition does not, however, provoke an appeal for a return to superstition and a belief in divine providence at the expense of rationality and objectivity. Rather, it is an impassioned plea for us to avoid the privileging of the knowledge of technocrats in and around organizations by recognizing the contribution of 'folk' knowledge—that is, how groups other than managers (and, for that matter, management scholars) have important things to say about organizational life. Importantly, this also gives us license to consider the continued role of things like myth (Blumenberg, 1985, 2010) and superstition (Gell, 1988; Stivers, 2001) as we try to reconcile the modernist expectation that we can order social relations according to a universal model of functional rationality with the refractory nature of localized human experience.

The tension between the desire to find one best way to organize and the geographically distinct and pragmatic responses to the challenge of organizing is the central theme of Stewart Clegg's major contribution to our understanding of Modernity and management (Clegg, 1990). Here he examines the emergence of 'different modes of rationality' that arise from the 'the interplay of local cultures with processes of institutional framing and regulation which derive from both from the state and from other agencies of rationalization' (Clegg, 1990: 176). In this way Clegg can be seen as a forerunner of what has become known as the 'Varieties of Capitalism' approach (Hall and Soskice, 2001) to this potentially bewildering mix of anthropology, sociology, and political economy. Drawing on the work of Blunt (1990), Clegg shows how Modern organizations have typically responded to the challenges of mastery over society and nature through what he calls the 'imperatives of organization'. Although we might have hoped that these responses would be timeless and universal, it turns out they were associated with a moment in time and space that has already passed. Emblematic of this ephemeral nature of modern organizations is the rise of Asian economic powers that manage to thrive in the global market by combining apparently contradictory social institutions. Although Clegg took the now troubled Japan as his exemplar, even as this country's economy has stagnated, new telling examples have emerged such as South Korea's *Chaebol* conglomerates (effectively family-run fiefdoms) or, more recently, Chinese state-owned enterprises whose managers are Communist Party members with MBAs from major international business schools.

This leaves us with Paul du Gay who, like Burrell and Clegg, develops his take on Modernity via a de-Parsonized reading of Weber. In many ways du Gay has been more active than the other two in maintaining an interest in the personal and ethical aspects of Weber's project through his sustained interest in the moral imperatives of bureaucracy. Thus, while it is fair to say that Burrell and, to a lesser extent, Clegg use social theory to understand organizations, du Gay thinks about organizing as a way of developing social theory. Nowhere is this more evident than in his powerful critique of Zygmunt Bauman and this takes on a double significance for this chapter—not only is du Gay's treatment of Bauman important in its own right but also we must give it serious consideration given that I wish to return to Bauman's definition of Modernity later on.

Du Gay's principal objection to Bauman's claims about the nature of Modernity is that he singled out science and rational-legal bureaucracy as the primary cause of the decline of individual moral action and responsibility in organizational settings. This is because these two defining features of the modern world combine to put a (physical and psychological) distance between us as social actors that undermines 'responsibility for the Other born of proximity to the Other' (du Gay, 2000: 36). This is exacerbated by a fine-grained functional division of labour where, by concentrating on their localized and narrow duties, bureaucrats lose sight of the overall purposes they are serving. In other words, managers can pursue their duties unencumbered by doubt or moral culpability if they don't know (or, perhaps, don't wish to know) the harm it is doing to others. The logical (and shocking) conclusion Bauman draws from this is that, by removing the obligation to act with individual moral responsibility in this way, the potential for a Holocaust to occur lurks in all modern societies. In support of this he invokes Weber's comment that organizations now operate 'according to calculable rules and without regard to persons' (Bauman, 1989: 193). Du Gay argues that this position is unfounded on sociological and historical grounds, both of which stem from Bauman's tendentious misreading of Weber. Sociologically speaking, and contra Bauman, Weber did not predict that rationalization inevitably creates a homogenized social singularity (du Gay, 2000); indeed, bureaucratic conduct is compatible with a variety of political and social ends, including those associated with liberal pluralism *and* Bolshevism (see Gouldner, 1955; cf. Clegg, 1990). This suggests that we should look to the historical and cultural conditions which give rise to particular configurations of bureaucracy that serve as the means to divergent political and social ends (Sewell and Barker, 2006a). In light of this, we can partially account for the rise of Nazism by considering the continued influence of romantic myths that were invented to stoke nationalism leading up to German political unification in 1871 (see my comments on Burrell above). Importantly, the Nazis exploited the humiliations of defeat in the Great War by skilfully appropriating such myths to promote the pre-modern notion of the mechanical solidarity of a single *Volksgemeinschaft* bound by common values and beliefs, rather than a modern notion of organic solidarity achieved through a diverse but interdependent division of labour (Durkheim, 1984). This found its most obvious expression in the way Hitler was depicted as literally embodying the manifest destiny of a unified German nation in the same way that, say, Henry IV had previously done. Thus, Nazi functionaries did not pledge allegiance to an abstract ideal of a disinterested vocation or office but to the personal service of Hitler himself (du Gay, 2000). In short, they were not cogs in faceless bureaucratic machines but myrmidons of the Führer who were, despite later denials, fully aware of the ends to which Nazism was being directed (Eatwell, 2003).

In summary, if Burrell has given us license to consider management as part of a broader modern project of mastery of nature and society then Clegg has showed how this mastery still plays out in organizations that do not fit the one-size-fits-all models of early management thinkers. This leaves du Gay to remind us that Weber's depiction of the bureaucratic office as a vocation can inspire us to re-evaluate the moral status of recently maligned modern institutions such as the agencies of the social democratic state.

Modern Institutions, Modern Managers

In parallel with this mainly European interest in the broader scope of social theory as it pertains to organizing, in North America there developed a more focused exploration of the way in which relatively stable rules, conventions, and norms of conduct (or, alternatively, habits, customs, and codes, depending on your preferences) shape the social relations of organizations. This is the stuff of organizational institutional theory; a mainly North American intellectual tradition that is to postmodernism what yacht rock it to punk (i.e., like punk never happened). It is, however, an undoubtedly venerable tradition that is at least as old as Durkheim's injunction to study 'social facts as things' (DiMaggio and Powell, 1991), although the term 'institution' may well date back as far as the early seventeenth century (Hodgson, 2006). Most mainstream social science disciplines have their own take on institutions (e.g., Douglas, 1986; Lipset, 1959; North, 1991) but when we speak of their organizational implications today we tend to use terms developed by the 'new' institutional theory over the last thirty years or so (Scott, 2008). Nevertheless, at the most abstract level this distinctive approach still shares with other disciplines the common assumption that rules, conventions, and norms of conduct are man-made (as opposed to naturally occurring) phenomena and, as such, they could somehow be otherwise if the circumstances or the personnel were different. With this in mind any institutional approach has to include an adequate account of how human agency brings institutions into being as well as an adequate account of how human agency is constrained by those very institutions. Stated in this way, we can begin to see the potential logical contradiction at the heart of institutionalism: if our theories of institutional effects are too deterministic then there would never be any social change, for institutions would always preserve the status quo; but, then again, if our theories of institutional creation are too voluntaristic then no institution could ever take hold, and we would constantly live in a state of disorder (see Holm, 1995). Seo and Creed (2002) called this the paradox of embedded agency and, thought of in this way, at the conceptual heart of institutionalism lies the same ambiguous status that we earlier attributed to Modernity—that is, there is a tension between the tendency towards social change and the desirability for stability and certainty. Most organizational approaches to institutions have looked to the likes of Giddens (1984), Bourdieu (1977), and Sewell (1992) to deal with this tension through some recursive relationship between structure and agency, in the process popularizing Eisenstadt's (1980) concept of the 'institutional entrepreneur' to take account of 'the activities of actors who have an interest in particular institutional arrangements and who leverage resources to create new institutions or to transform existing ones' (Maguire, Hardy, and Lawrence, 2004: 657). Of course, under this definition of institutional entrepreneurship such actors do not necessarily have to be managers in a nominal sense, for any person could conceivably transform existing institutions or invent new ones, so long as they had the inclination and enough of the right resources (DiMaggio, 1988). Other things being equal, however, you might reasonably expect that if anyone had the inclination and resources to shape institutions—that is, do institutional 'work' (see Lawrence and Suddaby, 2006)—at the organizational level it would be managers, as traditionally they have been the very people who, under formal theories of administration, are expected to use their specialist technical skills to balance stability and change through some sort of risk assessment. In other words, there is an institutional aspect to the taken-for-granted expectation that managers can initiate changes in rules, conventions, and norms in organizations which is, of course, one of the main assumptions of the culture change literature with its constant talk of 'change agents' (e.g., Cameron and Quinn, 2011).

This last observation is a good example of Bloor's (2000) point that an institution is, like one of Durkheim's social facts, both an object and also its own subject. For example, thinking of change management from an institutional perspective involves identifying recognizable human practices through the use of language supplied by the institutions that impinge on change management itself—that is, 'the thing talked about, and the talk itself, are one and the same' (Bloor, 2000: 161). This raises an obvious and important methodological question: Is it impossible get 'outside' an institution to obtain an objective grasp of which aspects of managers' activities involve the conscious application of expertise and which merely involve unconsciously following rules, conventions, and norms? In addition to this, we can add another level of methodological complexity in that if managers, like anyone else, 'live across' several institutions (Friedland and Alford, 1991) then how do we filter out the institutions that do not matter to change management?

The most common response of new institutional theory to these types of challenge has been to revert to methodological individualism via what has come to be known as the 'cognitive turn' (DiMaggio, 1997). This locates the micro-foundation of institutionalization somewhere in the minds of presumed-to-be rational actors who are working through the practical implications of routines, scripts, and cognitive schemas supplied by the relevant institutions that they encounter in and around organizations (DiMaggio, 1997, 2002; Hirsch and Lounsbury, 1997). A prominent example of this cognitive turn in the organizational literature is the 'institutional logics approach' (see Thornton, Ocasio, and Lounsbury, 2012). This draws heavily on Coleman's (1990) celebrated causal model of how the rational, self-conscious, and purposive actions of individuals combine to cause institutional logics—that is, 'either a set of rule-like structures that constrain organization or a set of cultural toolkits that provide opportunities for change in existing cultures and practices' (Thornton, Ocasio, and Lounsbury, 2012: 81)—that direct the attention of organizational agents towards a limited range of legitimate courses of action (Thornton and Ocasio, 1999; Thornton, 2004). In such circumstances, and acting under conditions of bounded rationality, managers (as a certain type of rational organizational actor) would make specific decisions related to their organizations and, in doing so, are engaged in the reproduction or transformation of institutional logics. While this is a necessarily brief description of a comprehensive and sophisticated way of thinking about the relationship between structure and agency, it does capture the way in which the cognitive turn leads us to consider an institution as a discrete social object only insofar as it is an aggregated representation of individuals acting in recognizably similar ways under similar circumstances (Swedberg, 1998). This general position has been subjected to extended critique (Udehn, 2002; Jepperson and Meyer, 2011) but, for the purposes of this chapter, I wish to dwell on its distinctly modernist tendency to place the presumed-to-be rational agent at the heart of its analysis. Here our two methodological challenges can be brought together under one question: How do we isolate the discrete macro-social phenomena (be they ideologies, cultures, or institutional logics) that impinge on a manager's decision-making when the manager as a rational actor is itself an institution (Hacking, 2004; Bloor, 2000; Willmott, 2011)? In other words, managers as the embodiment of the autonomy and mastery of Modernity have been taken-for-granted in institutional theory's cognitive turn. If, however, we adopt Douglas's (1986) line that institutions 'do the thinking for us' by providing socially embedded and coherent systems of knowledge that supply characteristic classifications, logical operations, and taken-for-granted forms of ratiocination then we can see in a new light Meyer's (2008) observation that much organizational research is fixated on understanding conscious and rational decision-making when few decisions are ever made in this way. So, while it should thus come as no surprise that we will be inclined to privilege analytically the purposeful activities of intentional agents like managers or institutional entrepreneurs when we concentrate on micro-foundations as part of the cognitive turn, we can also look to the way in which Modernity's dual foci of autonomy and mastery (Wagner, 2012) play out through institutional theory's own taken for granted assumptions. This opens up the enticing prospect that we can indeed be true to the original intentions of Berger and Luckmann (1966) and attempt to unite the two main streams of classical sociology—that is, Weberian methodological individualism and Durkheim's more methodologically holistic approach (Dobbin, 2009)—in a reflexive accommodation that locates institutional theory within the intellectual, political, and cultural project of Modernity itself. After all, institutional theory and the object it presupposes—the rational, autonomous, and atomized actor—is just as much a creature of Modernity as management.

MANAGEMENT AND A REFLEXIVE MODERNITY

This last observation provides us with an opportunity to reconsider some of the recurrent themes in this chapter. The first of these is the enduring power of the image of the modern manager as an autonomous actor who practises impartial mastery over the natural and social realms in the pursuit of rational objectives that are beneficial to all. This sits squarely with the notion of progressive change that we associate with Modernity—things are (or, at least, could be) getting better and all we need to improve is to get a little bit more rational, with managers at the forefront of this progress. Yet, as Bauman and others have noted, much of the energy of managers is actually expended in shoring up existing social and technical arrangements that advantage some and disadvantage others. This tension between change and stability gives rise to the ambivalence we have towards management—are managers simply disinterested technocrats or servants of established interests? Thus, the institution of modern management is reflexive in that it is part of a wider ambivalent consciousness we associate with Modernity while modern managers themselves have to make sense of their roles as participants in organizations who find themselves balancing the ideal of impartial rationality with the compromises they have to make on a day-to-day basis just to hold things together. Lash (1999) styles this as a tension between 'determinate' judgement (which can be undertaken by anyone, so long as they are competent at following universal rules of cognition) and 'aesthetic' judgement (a form of casuistry performed in the face of risk, ambivalence, and contingency). This latter form of reasoning is at the heart of 'reflexive modernity' where 'individuals must find the rules [of cognition] to use to encounter specific situations. They must innovate rules in a bricolage of their own identities, a process that is as dependent on analogic reason as on the rules of logic' (Lash, 1999: 3). In light of this, living with risk, ambivalence, and contingency in organizations is all the more difficult if the basis of our analogic reasoning is the dominant institutionalized metaphor of the rigid 'iron cage' (Tiryakian, 1981). Regardless of whether this iron cage creates the space for us to act within the rules or protects from the actions of others who do not live up to the expectations of those same rules (Adler and Borys, 1996; Sewell and Barker, 2006b), it is still as if it is something that is external to our experience and leaves our will (if not our ability) to act in certain ways unaffected (Baehr, 2001). In contrast, Baehr (see also Chalcraft, 1994) provides us with an alternative translation of Weber's original *Stahlhartes Gehäuse* metaphor that is simultaneously more amenable to Lash's notion of reflexive modernity and is also consistent with du Gay's appeal for us to consider the ethical status of the activities of bureaucratic office holders under the particular configurations of bureaucracy associated with different historical and cultural conditions of morality.

Although *Stahlhartes Gehäuse* can be variously rendered as a steel box, case, or jacket (Tiryakian, 1981), Baehr (2001) adopts the translation of a hardened steel shell. On its own it conveys the image of constraint that is much more intimate than an external cage—something we carry around with us, shaping our very physical make-up—but, when we consider what Weber set this hard shell against, then Parsons' translation seems even more clumsy (or, more likely, tendentious, considering he was a fluent German speaker who had spent several years studying in Heidelberg). Indeed, Weber's mention of the *Stahlhartes Gehäuse* is not in the narrow context of what we have come to think of as a description of reified bureaucratic social structures, but the much broader context of a modern economic order where our experiences of being part of the machine-like division of labour associated with the production and consumption of goods and services on an industrial scale take on an ascetic quality where our rational conduct is like a religious obligation or calling. On this Weber makes reference to the British Puritan theologian Richard Baxter who thought that, for the Godly, any concern for material goods and other worldly things should sit on our shoulders 'like a light cloak, which can be thrown aside at any moment'. In a modern secular world, however, any such concerns cannot easily be thrown aside because the cloak, which moulds itself to our form, has now become a steel-hard shell that we always carry with us and shapes us to its form. In other words, for Puritans of the Reformation the pursuit of rational goal-oriented conduct was part and parcel of the moral decision to follow a spiritual calling and the material and social trappings of temporal life paled into insignificance but, for modern citizens in a secular age, rational goal-oriented conduct has become an economic compulsion. It is as if the pursuit of material and social trappings of the temporal life is all we have as modern humans. On this, it is Baehr's (2001) contention that, in choosing the steel-hard shell as his metaphor, Weber was signalling that we should consider that modern capitalism has created a new way of being. He continues,

> The habitation of a steel shell implies not only a new dwelling for modern human beings, but a transformed nature: homo sapiens has become a very *different* being, a degraded being. A cage deprives one of liberty, but leaves one otherwise unaltered, one's powers still intact even if incapable of full realization. A shell, on the other hand, hints at organic reconstitution of the being concerned: a shell is part of an organism that cannot be dispensed with. (Baehr, 2001: 164—emphasis in original)

This is, to use another of Weber's most powerful metaphors, a good example of how coherent ideas—be it the Reformation's focus on an individual's personal relationship with God or Modernity's focus on the moral responsibly of individual agents in organized social relationships—act as a 'switchman' that pushes ends-oriented action in certain directions by informing characteristic 'strategies of action' (Swidler, 1986). Thus, the strategies of action associated with Lash's (1999) deliberate judgement translate to an organizational context where managers pursue ends-oriented behaviour based on a symbolic reality of standardized practices of measurement, control, and classification (cf. Bauman, 1991). According to Swidler (1986), such strategies of action are most suited to periods of cultural stability but, as we struggle to accommodate the many and diverse oppositions like the ones I identified at the start of this chapter under the progressive rubric of a single universal Modernity, we can look to an alternative and reflexive modernity where managers are skilled at developing rules of right conduct and ethical behaviour in localized settings based on a new symbolic reality that accommodates identities outside traditional modern categories and simple one-size-fits-all models of human motivations and organizational behaviour (Beck, Bonss, and Lau, 2003). In short, managers should slough off the hardened steel shell of determinate judgement and wrap themselves in the cloak of aesthetic judgement.

References

Adler, P. S. and Borys, B. (1996). 'Two Types of Bureaucracy: Enabling and Coercive'. *Administrative Science Quarterly*, 41: 61–89.

Aitken, H. (1960). *Taylorism at Watertown Arsenal*. Cambridge, MA: Harvard University Press.

Baehr, P. (2001). 'The "Iron Cage" and the "Shell as Hard as Steel": Parsons, Weber, and the Stahlhartes Gehäuse Metaphor in the Protestant Ethic and the Spirit of Capitalism'. *History & Theory*, 40: 153–69.

Barth, F. (1969). *Ethnic Groups and Boundaries: The Social Organization of Culture Difference*. New York: Little, Brown.

Bauman, Z. (1989). *Modernity and the Holocaust*. Oxford: Polity Press.

Bauman, Z. (1990). 'Modernity and Ambivalence'. *Theory Culture & Society*, 7: 143–69.

Bauman, Z. (1991). *Modernity and Ambivalence*. Ithaca, NY: Cornell University Press.

Beck, U., Bonss, W., and Lau, C (2003). 'The Theory of Reflexive Modernization: Problematic, Hypotheses and Research Programme'. *Theory Culture & Society*, 20: 1–33.

Berger, P. and Luckmann, T. (1966). *The Social Construction of Reality: A Treatise in the Sociology of Knowledge*. Garden City, NY: Doubleday.

Blau, P. (1963). 'Critical Remarks on Weber's Theory of Authority'. *American Political Science Review*, 52: 305–16.

Bloor, D. (2000). 'Collective Representations as Social Institutions', in W. S. F. Pickering (ed.), *Durkheim and Representations*. London: Routledge, 157–66.

Blumenberg, H. (1985). *Work on Myth*. Cambridge, MA: MIT Press.

Blumenberg, H. (2010). *Paradigms for a Metaphorology*. Ithaca, NY: Cornell University Press.

Blunt, P. (1990). 'Strategies for Human Resource Development in the Third World'. *Public Administration & Development*, 10: 299–313.

Bourdieu, P. (1977). *Outline of a Theory of Practice*. Cambridge: Cambridge University Press.

Bruce, K. and Nyland, C. (2012). 'The Demonization of Scientific Management and the Deification of Human Relations', in N. Lichtenstein (ed.), *The American Right and U.S. Labor Politics, Ideology, and Imagination*. Philadelphia, PA: University of Pennsylvania Press, 42–76.

Burrell, G. (1988). 'Modernism, Postmodernism and Organizational Analysis 2: The Contribution of Michel Foucault'. *Organization Studies*, 9: 221–35.

Burrell, G. (1994). 'Modernism, Postmodernism and Organizational Analysis 4: The Contribution of Jürgen Habermas'. *Organization Studies*, 15: 1–19.

Burrell, G. (1997). *Pandemonium: Towards a Retro-Organization Theory*. London: SAGE.

Cameron, K. S. and Quinn, R. E. (2011). *Changing Organizational Culture*. New York: John Wiley.

Chalcraft, D. (1994). 'Bringing the Text Back in: On Ways of Reading The Iron Cage Metaphor in the Two Editions of the Protestant Ethic', in L. J. Ray and M. Reed (eds.), *Organizing Modernity: New Weberian Perspectives on Work, Organization and Society*. London: Routledge, 16–45.

Clegg, S. R. (1990). *Modern Organizations: Organization Studies in the Postmodern World*. London: SAGE.

Clegg, S. R. and Lounsbury, M. (2009). 'Weber: Sintering the Iron Cage – Translation, Domination, and Rationality', in P. Adler (ed.), *Oxford Handbook of Sociology and Organization Studies: Classical Foundations*. Oxford: Oxford University Press, 118–45.

Cohen, J., Hazelrigg, L. E., and Pope, W. (1975). 'De-Parsonizing Weber: A Critique of Parsons' Interpretation of Weber's Sociology'. *American Sociological Review*, 40: 229–41.

Coleman, J. S. (1990). *Foundations of Social Theory*. Cambridge, MA: Harvard University Press.

Cooper, R. and Burrell, G. (1988). 'Modernism, Postmodernism and Organizational Analysis: An Introduction'. *Organization Studies*, 9: 91–112.

DiMaggio, P. (1988). 'Interest and Agency in Institutional Theory', in L. Zucker (ed.), *Institutional Patterns and Culture*. Cambridge, MA: Ballinger Publishing Company, 3–22.

DiMaggio, P. (1997). 'Culture and Cognition'. *Annual Review of Sociology*, 23: 263–87.

DiMaggio, P. (2002). 'Why Cognitive (and Cultural) Sociology Needs Cognitive Psychology', in K. A. Cerulo (ed.), *Culture in Mind: Toward a Sociology of Culture and Cognition*. London: Routledge, 274–82.

DiMaggio, P. J. and Powell, W. W. (1991). 'Introduction', in P. J. DiMaggio and W. W. Powell (eds.), *The New Institutionalism in Organizational Analysis*. Chicago, IL: University of Chicago Press, 1–38.

Dobbin, F. (2009). 'How Durkheim's Theory of Meaning-Making Influenced Organizational Sociology', in P. S. Adler (ed.), *The Oxford Handbook of Sociology and Organization Studies: Classical Foundations*. Oxford: Oxford University Press, 200–22.

Douglas, M. (1986). *How Institutions Think*. Syracuse, NY: Syracuse University Press.

du Gay, P. (2000). *In Praise of Bureaucracy: Weber – Organization – Ethics*. London: SAGE.

Durkheim, E. (1984). *The Division of Labor in Society*. New York: Free Press.

Eatwell, R. (2003). *Fascism: A History*. London: Random House.

Eisenstadt, S. N. (1980). 'Cultural Orientations, Institutional Entrepreneurs and Social Change: Comparative Analyses of Traditional Civilizations'. *American Journal of Sociology*, 85: 840–69.

Fayol, H. (1916). *Administration Industrielle et Générale*. Paris: Dunod.

Fayol, H. (1949). *General and Industrial Management*. London: Pitman.

Follett, M. P. (1941). *Dynamic Administration: The Collected Papers of Mary Parker Follett*. New York: Harper.

Friedland, R. and Alford, R. R. (1991). 'Bringing Society Back in: Symbols, Practices, and Institutional Contradictions', in P. J. DiMaggio and W. W. Powell (eds.), *The New Institutionalism in Organizational Analysis*. Chicago, IL: University of Chicago Press, 232–63.

Gell, A. (1988). 'Technology and Magic'. *Anthropology Today*, 4(2): 6–9.

Giddens, A. (1984). *The Constitution of Society*. Cambridge: Polity Press.

Gouldner, A. W. (1955). 'Metaphysical Pathos and the Theory of Bureaucracy'. *American Political Science Review*, 49: 496–507.
Guess, R. (1981). *The Idea of a Critical Theory*. Cambridge: Cambridge University Press.
Hacking, I. (2004). 'Between Michel Foucault and Erving Goffman: Between Discourse in the Abstract and Face-to-Face Interaction'. *Economy & Society*, 33: 277–302.
Hall, P. and Soskice, G. (2001). *Varieties of Capitalism: The Institutional Foundations of Comparative Advantage*. Oxford: Oxford University Press.
Hennis, W. (1988). *Max Weber: Essays in Reconstruction* (trans. K. Tribe). London: Allen and Unwin.
Hirsch, P. M. and Lounsbury, M. (1997). 'Ending the Family Quarrel: Toward a Reconciliation of "Old" and "New" Institutionalisms'. *American Behavioral Scientist*, 40: 406–18.
Hodgson, G. M. (2006). 'What are Institutions'. *Journal of Economic Issues*, 40: 1–25.
Holm, P. (1995). 'The Dynamics of Institutionalization: Transformation Processes in Norwegian Fisheries'. *Administrative Science Quarterly*, 40: 398–422.
Islam, G., Zyphur, M. J., and Boje, D. (2008). 'Carnival and Spectacle in Krewe de Vieux and the Mystic Krewe of Spermes: The Mingling of Organization and Celebration'. *Organization Studies*, 29: 1565–89.
Jepperson, R. and Meyer, J. W. (2011). 'Multiple Levels of Analysis and the Limitations of Methodological Individualism'. *Sociological Theory*, 29: 55–73.
Kanigel, R. (1996). *The One Best Way: Frederick Winslow Taylor and the Enigma of Efficiency*. Cambridge, MA: MIT Press.
Lash, S. (1999). *Another Modernity: A Different Rationality*. London: Wiley-Blackwell.
Latour, B. (1991). 'Technology is Society Made Durable', in J. Law (ed.), *A Sociology of Monsters: Essays on Power, Technology and Domination*. London: Wiley, 103–32.
Latour, B. (1993). *We Have Never Been Modern*. Cambridge, MA: Harvard University Press.
Lawrence, T. and Suddaby, R. (2006). 'Institutional Work', in S. Clegg, C. Hardy, amd T. Lawrence (eds.), *Handbook of Organization Studies*, 2nd edn. London: SAGE, 215–54.
Lipset, S. M. (1959). 'Some Social Requisites of Democracy: Economic Development and Political Legitimacy'. *American Political Science Review*, 53: 69–105
Maguire, S., Hardy, C., and Lawrence, T. B. (2004). 'Institutional Entrepreneurship in Emerging Fields: HIV/AIDS Treatment Advocacy in Canada'. *Academy of Management Journal*, 47: 657–79.
Mayo, E. (1919). *Democracy and Freedom: An Essay in Social Logic*. Melbourne: Macmillan.
Meyer, J. W. (2008). 'Reflections on Institutional Theories of Organization', in R. Greenwood, C. Oliver, K. Sahlin, and R. Suddaby (eds.), *The SAGE Handbook of Organizational Institutionalism*. Thousand Oaks, CA: SAGE, 790–812.
Miller, D. C. and Form, W. H. (1964). *Industrial Sociology: The Sociology of Work Organizations*. New York: Harper & Row.
Münch, R. (1983). 'From Pure Methodological Individualism to Poor Sociological Utilitarianism' (trans. R. Kalberg). *Canadian Journal of Sociology*, 8: 45–76.
North, D. (1991). 'Institutions'. *Journal of Economic Perspectives*, 5: 97–112.
Nyland, C., Bruce, K., and Burns, P. (2014). 'Taylorism, the International Labour Organization, and the Genesis and Diffusion of Codetermination'. *Organization Studies*, 35: 1149–69.
Peaucelle, J.-L. and Guthrie, G. (2013). 'Henri Fayol', in M. Witzel and M. Warner (eds.), *Oxford Handbook of Management Theorists*. Oxford: Oxford University Press, 49–73.
Scott, W. R. (2008). 'Approaching Adulthood: The Maturing of Institutional Theory'. *Theory & Society*, 37: 427–42.

Seo, M.-G. and Creed, W. E. D. (2002). 'Institutional Contradictions, Praxis, and Institutional Change: A Dialectical Perspective'. *Academy of Management Review*, 27: 222–47.

Sewell Jr., W. H. (1992). 'A Theory of Structure: Duality, Agency, and Transformation'. *American Journal of Sociology*, 98: 1–29.

Sewell, G. and Barker, J. R. (2006a). 'Coercion Versus Care: Using Irony to Make Sense of Organizational Surveillance'. *Academy of Management Review*, 31: 934–61.

Sewell, G. and Barker, J. R. (2006b). 'Max Weber and the Irony of Bureaucracy', in M. Korczynski, R. Hodson, and P. K. Edwards (eds.), *Social Theory at Work*. Oxford: Oxford University Press, 56–87.

Stivers, R. (2001). *Technology as Magic: The Triumph of the Irrational*. New York: Continuum.

Swedberg, R. (1998). *Max Weber and the Idea of Economic Sociology*. Princeton, NJ: Princeton University Press.

Swidler, A. (1986). 'Culture in Action: Symbols and Strategies'. *American Sociological Review*, 51: 273–86.

Thornton, P. M. (2004). *Markets from Culture: Institutional Logics and Organizational Decisions in Higher Education Publishing*. Stanford, CA: Stanford University Press.

Thornton, P. M. and Ocasio, W. (1999). 'Institutional Logics and the Historical Contingency of Power in Organizations: Executive Succession in the Higher Education Publishing Industry, 1958–1990'. *American Journal of Sociology*, 1(5): 801–43.

Thornton, P. H., Ocasio, W., and Lounsbury, M. (2012). *The Institutional Logics Perspective: A New Approach to Culture, Structure, and Process*. Oxford: Oxford University Press.

Tiryakian, E. A. (1981). 'The Sociological Import of a Metaphor: Tracking the Source of Max Weber's Iron Cage'. *Sociological Inquiry*, 51: 27–33.

Turner, B. S. (1991). 'Preface', in H. H. Gerth and C. Wright Mills (eds.), *From Max Weber: Essays in Sociology*. London: Routledge, xii–xxx.

Turner, B. S. (1992). *Max Weber: From History to Modernity*. London: Routledge.

Udehn, L. (2002). 'The Changing Face of Methodological Individualism'. *Annual Review of Sociology*, 28: 479–507.

Wagner, P. (2012). *Modernity: Understanding the Present*. Oxford: Polity Press.

Weber, M. (1961). *Basic Concepts in Sociology*. Secaucus, NJ: Carol Publishing Group. 1983.

Weber, M. (1968). *Economy and Society: An Outline of Interpretive Sociology*. New York: Bedminster Press.

Weick, C. (1974). 'Middle Range Theories of Social Systems'. *Behavioral Science*, 19: 357–67.

Willmott, H. (2011). 'Institutional Work for What? Problems and Prospects of Institutional Theory'. *Journal of Management Inquiry*, 20: 67–72.

Wren, D. A., Bedeian, A. G., and Breeze, J. D. (2002). 'The Foundations of Henri Fayol's Administrative Theory'. *Management Decision*, 40: 906–18.

PART IV

MANAGEMENT IN SOCIETY AND MANAGEMENT ORGANIZATIONS/ INSTITUTIONS

CHAPTER 21

EVIDENCE-BASED MANAGEMENT

KEVIN MORRELL AND MARK LEARMONTH

Introduction

THE 'evidence-based' approach has been advocated widely across several social science disciplines (Cartwright and Hardie, 2012; Nutley, Walter, and Davies, 2007). It has its origins in a model of clinical research and practice: evidence-based medicine. This seeks to ensure clinical judgements about the care of individual patients are made through the application of 'the conscientious, explicit, and judicious use of current best evidence' (Sackett et al., 1996: 71). Evidence-based medicine places central, heavy emphasis on situated expertise, 'the proficiency and judgment that individual clinicians acquire through clinical experience and clinical practice' and ethics, 'compassionate use of individual patients' predicaments, rights, and preferences in making clinical decisions' (Sackett et al., 1996: 71).

Since the evidence-based approach began in healthcare, early contributions discussed the appropriateness or inappropriateness of taking this model of clinical practice, and applying it to healthcare management. Walshe and Rundall (2001: 432-3) describe a 'paradigm shift' to evidence-based healthcare in terms of moves 'from' and 'to' across a number of dimensions. In terms of *research direction*, the paradigm shift meant moving from being '[r]esearcher-led; tied to academic agendas; little coordination'—to 'needs led; tied to health service priorities; focused on major service areas/needs; well co-ordinated'. There are similar moves across *research methods*—from 'frequent mismatches between research questions and methods'—to 'appropriate use of research methods'; *research outputs*—from 'peer-reviewed academic journals seen as researchers' primary goal' to 'changes in clinical practice seen as primary aim (…) with publication as one step towards that goal'; *practitioner understanding*—from 'focused on reports of individual research studies' to 'focused on meta-analyses and systematic reviews of relevant, appraised research'.

This account comes comparatively early in terms of writing on the evidence-based approach, and refers to healthcare management. Even so, it is a useful start point from which to consider subsequent arguments and the general claims contemporary advocates make for evidence-based management (EBMgt). These later claims typically rely on a similar 'from ... to' movement. For instance, a special issue editorial of the *Academy of Management Learning and Education*, also proposed a paradigm shift, encouraging people to 'change the world' (Rynes, Rousseau, and Barends, 2014). As others have, this set out advantages wholesale adoption of EBMgt would bring—improvements and standardization in research methods and research practices, in research quality, dissemination and practitioner engagement, and influence. They contrast this (2014: 319) with the current state of affairs:

> By ignoring evidence, billions of dollars are spent on ineffective management practices, to the detriment of employees and their families, communities, and the society at large (...) As teachers of the next generation of managers, we have a moral obligation to change this situation. We can do this by helping future managers acquire content knowledge based upon a solid and extensive body of research, teaching them how to find the best available evidence and then critically appraise its trustworthiness, and encouraging critical thinking and dialogue about academic (and other) texts and their underlying assumptions. So, let's go into the classroom and make a change in the world by teaching EBP [evidence-based practice].

To evaluate these claims and connect EBMgt to the central concerns in this Handbook of Management we begin by examining this paradigm shift in more detail, then review the history of this approach. This sets the context for considering two aspects of EBMgt's use of the management-as-medicine-motif (MAMM): (1) as science, and (2) as profession. We conclude with a case illustrating how problems can arise in medicalizing a phenomenon that resists simplification—employee turnover.

The Paradigm Shift

The clarity and simplicity of Walshe and Rundall's (2001) 'from ... to' paradigm shift is useful. It helps us to see continuing comparison in terms of the *content* of claims and arguments made by advocates of EBMgt (superior research, superior engagement with practice and so on). It also helps us to see a continuation in terms of how the content of those claims and arguments is *organized*. In other words, the appeal to a paradigm shift is an important rhetorical device in the case for EBMgt. This 'from ... to' contrast Legge (1995) identifies in relation to the argument for a shift from 'Personnel Management' (PM) to human resource management (HRM). Models of PM tended to describe or caricature, models of HRM were idealized. (Legge argued there was little or no difference between the normative ambitions of PM and HRM.)

This from-to move is often used in political campaigns, when an opposition is challenging an incumbent government. Any opposition can always identify flaws in the existing government's programme of action (and it would not spend time praising any strengths of course). This is because government is messy, there are always decisions that can be criticized, and there are always some events that happen while governments are in power that are negative, and that they can be tarnished with. The opposition meanwhile, who have been denied power but at least have the luxury of not being responsible for the past, can always promise a rosy future. This is why so many political campaigns are framed in terms of a need for change. It is important to remember that what propels appeals for wholesale change with respect to EBMgt is a rhetorical device: of contrast. Moreover, this contrast is not symmetrical. It relies on a move from selective, pejorative criticism of the past to a similarly selective and aspirational account of the future (which is therefore impossible to disprove).

The Paradigm behind the Shift

In policy terms, and in terms of engaging with practice, evidence-based rhetoric has been popular because it has allowed those responsible for making decisions to present their interventions as guided purely by pragmatism rather than ideology. This is signalled in the appeal to an interest in 'what works'. However, several evaluations of supposedly evidence-based approaches call into question whether these actually do 'work' (see Archibald, 2015; Hope, 2004; House, 2006; Lather, 2004 below). An alternative perspective would be that evidence-based language is simply used to furnish credibility to decisions that would have been taken anyway.

In management studies, what remains in our view the fullest and most considered account of advocates for evidence-based management (EBMgt) came in a paper in the *British Journal of Management* (Tranfield, Denyer, and Smart, 2003). This set out an extremely well argued and persuasive case for the adoption of the systematic review in organization studies. The contribution was timely in that it was in keeping with the contemporary political emphasis on pragmatism and 'what works', a wider political zeitgeist associated with the New Labour government in the UK, and its desire to appear post-ideological. The New Labour government was an enthusiastic adopter of evidence-based discourse, and channelled funding towards bodies and institutions promoting this approach. However, evaluations of particular initiatives associated with the evidence-based approach suggested they were not post-ideological, but simply replaced one ideology for another. The account by Hope (2004) of a government programme of evidence-based practice in the justice system (trying to reduce burglaries) found it was not a case of seeing 'what works', but of 'pretend it works' (the title of his paper). Latterly, House (2006) and Lather (2004) outline negative effects on US educational research, where there has come to be a dogmatic insistence on narrow forms of 'evidence' to solve any and all research questions. Archibald (2015: 146) in comparative, country-level case analysis of programs in non-formal education (in the USA and Kenya) concludes, 'the dominant approach to making non-formal education more evidence-based (…) is seriously flawed'.

Academic ideas do not win through solely because they are intrinsically the best in the marketplace for ideas. Throughout the history of science and social science, the role of influential promoters is key. We have discussed the influence of the New Labour government and the appeal of EBMgt as post-ideological and pragmatic. Arguably though, the landmark event increasing the profile of EBMgt in academia was Denise Rousseau's (Rousseau, 2006) Presidential Address to the 2005 Academy of Management Conference. Some ten years after this, we now have a dedicated handbook on EBMgt, some very well cited academic articles, and several forums promoting EBMgt to management scholars, and to managers (see Morrell and Learmonth, 2015 for a recent review).

Over this time, there has been a great deal of consistency in what EBMgt involves. A recent account of EBMgt defined it as:

> making decisions through the conscientious, explicit and judicious use of the best available evidence from multiple sources (…) to increase the likelihood of a favorable outcome. (Barends, Rousseau, and Briner, 2014: n.p.)

We have abridged this quote slightly but not changed the sentiment. It is the same language as the account of evidence-based medicine by Sackett et al. (1996) that we cited earlier, though minus consideration of ethics or situated expertise. Underpinning this account of making decisions, and of evidence, is a common approach to understanding problems. This aspires to the same protocols used in evidence-based medicine. Indeed, EBMgt has been supported most strongly by scholars who favour modes of knowledge production that are closer to the natural sciences and positivism. Superior forms of evidence in *medicine* are those that are the result of randomized controlled trials, and from systematic reviews of the results of such trials. These offer the promise of the greatest body of research evidence and the appeal of being able to weight research differentially—not just in terms of quantity, but quality too. Approaches to understanding management that challenge the principles of aggregation and commensuration—such as critical ethnographies, or forms of critique that question whether we should start with the interests of 'management'—cannot be incorporated into this approach. Critics of EBMgt are not against evidence, therefore, they are against the particular construction of evidence in EBMgt (Morrell and Learmonth, 2015).

The evidence-based movement continues to grow in social science. It has ardent advocates. It is interesting though, that even in medicine, where there is more consensus about methods than in management, the evidence-based approach has been criticized for the narrowness of its horizons (Holmes et al., 2006). Similar concerns have been voiced about the evidence-based movement in management. Building on existing critique (Learmonth and Harding, 2006; Morrell, 2008; Morrell and Learmonth, 2015), we set out some problems, and dangers, attendant to evidence-based management, focusing on the mobilization of the central aspirational motif by advocates—the medicine as management motif (MAMM). At its core is the belief that management research and practice are comparable to medical research and medical practice. To sustain this motif the evidence-based approach relies on simplistic and one-sided comparisons between management and medicine—striving to find similarities rather than being awake to differences. We organize and criticise these comparisons in terms of two themes: EBMgt as science and EBMgt as profession.

EVIDENCE-BASED MANAGEMENT AS SCIENCE

Underlying the assertion that the 'evidence' promoted in EBMgt is a superior form of knowledge are a set of assumptions: about the status of social science, about the nature of the social world, and about management research. We will explain these briefly and then illustrate how they are interconnected in an account of EBMgt. In relation to the status of social science, EBMgt is a contemporary expression of the idea that there is a hierarchy of sciences (Cole, 1983), and that the kinds of knowledge claim different disciplines make can be ranked depending on where they lie on the hierarchy. In terms of the nature of the social world, EBMgt depends on realism and a correspondence theory of truth (the better the evidence, and the more of it, the more likely it is we will find the right answer—the 'what works'). In terms of management research, EBMgt devalues work that does not pursue realism, and the methods associated with the superior science of medicine. We can use two connected ideas to expand on these: a hierarchy of the sciences (Cole, 1983), and the concept of positivism (Gartrell and Gartrell, 2002).

Figure 21.1 shows a hierarchy of the sciences, where science can be understood as an attempt to explain empirical phenomena and to build theories that are open to being falsified. Those disciplines at the bottom of the hierarchy are presumed to command greater certainty in terms of the phenomena they investigate, to be able to predict with increasing certainty, and to enjoy greater consensus. Cole (1983) contests this last presumption in particular.

This is a simplification of course. For instance, some disciplines are difficult to place (economics, law, philosophy), and sub-disciplines or schools within one discipline can diverge radically from the mainstream of their parent discipline in terms of their aspirations to be scientific—some scholars have approached literary criticism as science. Management studies itself is broad in this way, indeed it is more diverse than longer established disciplines. The travelling salesman problem (a challenge in operations management; see e.g., Laporte, 1992) is mathematics, whilst a great deal of work in other sub-disciplines draws on the humanities (see Morrell and Learmonth, 2015 for a recent review). Even so, the hierarchy is helpful to connect the three assumptions in EBMgt: about the status of social science, about the nature of the social world, about management research. Using this heuristic, EBMgt is an attempt to try to change the field, so that we move from the top two rungs, to approach the same status and (presumed) confidence and consensus as medicine. The way to do so is by adopting humanities (not 'science' because theories are unfalsifiable)

v

sociology (& management studies)

v

psychology

v

medicine

v

biology

v

chemistry

v

physics

v

mathematics (not 'science' as it is not empirical and - partly - deals in proof)

FIGURE 21.1 A Simple Hierarchy of the Sciences.

the assumptions disciplines lower down have about the world (realism, positivism), and using techniques that psychology has in common with medicine (statistics, meta-analysis).

To take the second idea connecting these three assumptions in EBMgt (the status of social science, the nature of the social world, the nature of management research), it is helpful to set out the links between EBMgt and positivism. Gartrell and Gartrell (2002: 640) identify positivism as:

> General law-like statements relating abstract concepts, nominal and operational definitions of terms; formal language such as logic or mathematics used to express laws; derivation of hypotheses; relations among variables; and statistical analysis.

EBMgt advocates often set forward broad and expansive definitions of evidence which do not suggest an attachment to positivism. Yet these expansive definitions also shrink quite quickly. For instance, Barends et al., (2014: n.p.) set out what might be called a generous account of evidence:

> When we say 'evidence', we basically mean *information*. It may be based on numbers or it may be qualitative or descriptive (…) from scientific research suggesting generally applicable facts (…) from local organizational or business indicators, such as company metrics or observations of practice conditions. Even professional

experience can be an important source of evidence, for example an entrepreneur's past experience of setting up a variety of businesses should indicate the approach that is likely to be the most successful (…) Regardless of its source, all evidence may be included if it is judged to be trustworthy and relevant.

This generous definition later shrinks and positivism finds expression in the ways quantitative methods, statistical analysis and general statements are favoured. This quote is again from Barends, Rousseau, and Briner (2014: n.p.):

> Forecasts or risk assessments based on the aggregated (averaged) professional experience of many people are more accurate than forecasts based on one person's personal experience (…)
> Professional judgments based on hard data or statistical models are more accurate than judgments based on individual experience (…)
> Knowledge derived from scientific evidence is more accurate than the opinions of experts (…)
> A decision based on the combination of critically appraised experiential, organizational and scientific evidence yields better outcomes than a decision based on a single source of evidence.

There is an additional aspect to the tag of 'positivist' we give to EBMgt. This is interesting, in terms of the connections between a search for status, and moving up the hierarchy of sciences. Even though positivism very quickly becomes the norm as one moves up the hierarchy of sciences, it is a label social scientists shun, because it is associated with an overly simplistic view of the world (Gartrell and Gartrell, 2002). The quotes above and our critical reviews elsewhere (e.g. Morrell and Learmonth, 2015) say to us that this tag fits.

Another aspect to the hierarchy model that is helpful is that it shows how EBMgt can be understood as reductionist. Reductionism has several senses but at the core is the idea that it is a mode of explanation that involves taking one thing and explaining it in terms of something that is taken as having superior and overriding explanatory power (in the hierarchy above sciences ranked lower down the page have priority in this regard):

> to reduce Xs to Ys is to show that Xs are *nothing but* Ys. The aim is to give an account of Xs in terms of Ys, which are given a privileged status (…) Genes are nothing but DNA molecules. A flash of lightning is nothing but an electric discharge. Heat is mean kinetic energy of molecule movements. (Mautner, 2000: 474)

EBMgt is reductionist because it seeks to aggregate and make things the same in terms of one criterion of 'quality' evidence. For instance, though evidence-based medicine emphasized ethics and situated expertise, those advocating an evidence-based approach to management have focused almost exclusively on the techniques of review and synthesis, and on promoting a central epistemological assumption: that the best evidence in management studies is analogous to evidence in medicine (Morrell, 2008). Only comparatively recently has ethics been professed to be an important concern. Ethics is now 'one of the four fundamental activities' of EBMgt (Rousseau, 2012: 4), while it was absent in both Tranfield, Denyer, and Smart (2003) and Rousseau (2006). But advocates write quite clumsily about ethics (Morrell, Learmonth, and Heracleous, 2015 has more on this). One explanation (for omission and then clumsy introduction of ethics) is it is impossible to write coherently about ethics and to pursue reductionism.

Connecting back to our hierarchy of sciences heuristic, reductionism in EBMgt comes because of the aspirational attachment to the techniques and values of science in medicine. EBMgt takes problems, phenomena, and complexities that could be addressed from several perspectives—from humanities or neighbouring social sciences, and claims they can be explained using the techniques and approaches of psychology. This is reductionist because EBMgt depends on the claim (per the extract above) that all problems in management studies can be addressed in this way. Simply referring to 'making decisions' gives broadest possible scope, offering no room to acknowledge the limitations of this approach, nor to consider problems where EBMgt might be unsuitable.

Evidence-based Management as Profession

Underpinning the medicine as management motif (MAMM) are a number of themes and narrative devices. Key to EBMgt's appeal to legitimacy is management's intellectual similarities with medicine; arguably this is just one of the latest manifestations of 'physics envy'—the longing that social scientists have for the same certainties and prestige that are associated with knowledge in the natural sciences. Advocates often recognize the possibility that management and medicine may be different. But rather than acknowledging that such difference would severely curtail their aspirations, they seem irritated that difference remains as much of a threat now as it was in the earliest inceptions of EBMgt. Indeed, commenting even before the main works in EBMgt had been written, Young et al. complained about 'the increasingly tired debate about the extent to which medical and social knowledge differ' (Young et al., 2002: 219). What this comment overlooked is that the reason debate was tired was because none of the problems raised by critics had been satisfactorily answered. It still remains the case that medical and social knowledge are different. This is a continuing problem for supporters of EBMgt. Whilst the debate may be no less tired, criticisms that question the legitimacy of this comparison are still unanswered.

Some are bullish about the problem; Kepes, Bennett, and McDaniel (2014: 450) argue any apparent difference is not down to two disciplines looking at different questions, but that 'scientific evidence in management may be untrustworthy because of several problems within the scientific process in our field.' This is a reductionist's explanation. To infer that consensus in one field implies fields with less consensus are deficient is only valid if the problems of one can be reduced to the other. The reading across of such deficiency does not just seem an example of the physics envy social scientists are sometimes accused of, it appears to be a severe dose of 'physician envy' (Morrell, 2008: 621).

Advocates who are less bullish often acknowledge but then ignore the differences between medicine and management; or pay lip-service to differences; or occasionally tie themselves in a knot. In the recent AMLE SI, we see all three variations in one sentence:

> Although medicine is not the same as management, what can evidence-based management educators learn from their more experienced colleagues in medicine? (Barends and Briner, 2014: 476–7)

This is the premise of the paper, '[t]o find out, we spoke to two pioneers of evidence-based medicine' (Barends and Briner, 2014: 477). But it is an ungainly argument. It begins: 'medicine and management are not the same'; and ends: 'let us follow best practice in medicine'. If medicine is not the same as management, how could colleagues in medicine be 'more' experienced? If the two are different, they would not be more experienced, they would be experienced in something different.

Rather than believing MAMM, different stories about the relationship of management and medicine can be at least equally as plausible, depending on the context. Indeed, one simple alternative—that we prefer—is that management is *not* like medicine. If the force of this disarmingly simple sentiment is acknowledged, the wind goes out of the sails of EBMgt. (See Grey, 2004 for a more detailed account of why management might be fundamentally dissimilar to medicine.) The more general point though is that there is diversity and variety in any context—multiple stories can always be told about any social phenomenon—and it is this diversity and variety which the EBMgt approach overlooks or ignores. In the sense that it denies difference and variety, the EBMgt approach seems not just reductionist, but inimical to generating new knowledge. In certain situations it might be sensible or useful to tell stories about the links between management and medicine; in many other contexts, however, very different stories would probably be far more appropriate.

A further example of MAMM at work in the SI comes in an exchange during the course of Steven Charlier's interview with Gary Latham (Charlier, 2014: 472):

> [Charlier:] Some critics of EBMgt have stated that unlike medical research, 'evidence' from management research (…) features 'paradigmatic disagreement' over what should be considered as 'evidence' (Learmonth and Harding, 2006). How would you respond to these criticisms?
>
> [Latham:] I have close friends who are medical doctors. They can't agree on whether a pregnant woman should take aspirin! This issue is not at all unique to our field.

This analogy would be useful if the paper Charlier refers to had said, 'management scholars typically disagree about what course of action is best, whereas doctors typically agree what course of action is best.' What the paper says is different. It concerns (as Charlier correctly summarizes) paradigmatic disagreement: disagreement about ways of seeing. Moreover, the argument in that paper actually *depends* on identifying disagreement between doctors. Learmonth and Harding (2006: 248), argue that for doctors, 'disagreement [is] within certain parameters and limits.' They then contrast this with the kind of disagreement we have in management studies:

> lack of an agreed paradigm means that disputes and divergences over foundations (for example, about what counts as evidence and quite possibly about what counts as a problem) are likely to arise with such regularity that appeals to evidence as a means to resolve these disputes would become worthless. (Learmonth and Harding, 2006: 249)

Let us take Latham's analogy and interrogate it. In an important sense, doctors agree on, and 'know' rather a lot when it comes to aspirin. They would agree aspirin is the same thing as acetylsalicylic acid, that it is an analgesic, an anti-inflammatory, that it is non-steroidal, an anti-pyretic, an anti-platelet, it has a number of interaction effects with other drugs, it should not be taken by people with certain allergies, it should only be taken in certain doses, etc. All this agreement comes a long way before we even start asking 'evidence-based' questions about aspirin—e.g., does it typically reduce or increase risks of cancers? Moreover, underpinning this knowledge would be a shared way of seeing from fields such as physics, chemistry, biology, pharmacy, and physiology. For instance, and without even necessarily knowing the values, doctors would agree that under constant pressure, in its purest form, it will always melt at a certain temperature, that it has a chemical formula ($C_9H_8O_4$), that it will have a molecular weight, and so on. Underneath this there would be agreed and law-like givens about how our bodies work: a theory of blood circulation for instance. And there is an even more primitive fact about any drug: a drug is not conscious and it does not have a mental state. Notwithstanding any talk of a placebo effect, administering a drug is fundamentally unlike any management intervention. In management there is a recursive and complex relationship between the managed and manager: a double hermeneutic—because a management theory does not just describe or explain, it makes the world (see Ghoshal, 2005). This is even before considering additional layers of complexity caused by group interactions and effects, and things we struggle to make sense of but give names to—like 'culture' or 'leadership.' None of this is to say that research is not possible, or not valuable, or that we cannot know anything; it is a reason, however, to be cautious about what kinds of claims we make and to be careful in drawing analogies.

In management studies we can agree conventions, and we can quote what people have said, or attribute positions to a more or less successful school or tradition. Some fields associated with management have formulae, axioms, or even proofs, but these are never about the direct business of management—people trying to do things with, for, and to people. Nowhere is there a level of agreement about any intervention as basic and important as aspirin in medicine. We do not even agree, for example, on what an organization is. We do not have a universally accepted definition of work. We do not agree what managers do, or on what you have to do to be a manager, or whether any action counts particularly as management. We do not agree on how to define and measure performance, or innovation, learning, satisfaction, commitment, entrepreneurship, etc. There are many different ways of seeing all of these things, because social phenomena are interpreted and constructed according to values and ideologies that precede empirical inquiry, and that depend on particular framings and contexts.

Medicalizing Management

We conclude by discussing a systematic review in the *Cochrane Database of Systematic Reviews* (CDSR). CDSR normally contains medical reviews, but occasionally other phenomena following the same logic. The review we discuss has, at the time of writing, been published five times (a protocol, a review, and three updates). But it has never reviewed any evidence. We explain this paradox starting with the design, then the review.

The Design

Systematic reviews start with a protocol—a plan for how the review will be carried out. This protocol by Flint and Webster [FW] (2007: 1) had these objectives: 'To determine the effectiveness of various exit interview strategies in decreasing turnover rates amongst health care professionals working in healthcare organisations'. To address these objectives it planned this comparison: 'Exit interviews compared to no exit interview' (1). The protocol also says the review will only search for two study types, 'Randomized controlled trials (RCT's) or well designed quasi-experimental studies (QES)' (3).

RCTs and QESs are near the apex of a hierarchy of medical evidence, but do not always capture social complexity. They are often simplistic and reductionist. Employee turnover is challenging to understand and model (Morrell, Loan-Clarke, and Wilkinson, 2001, 2004a, 2004b). It is relationally complex, often unfolding unpredictably (Lee and Mitchell, 1994; Lee et al., 1999). Both RCTs and QES use a logic of control and treatment groups, but there is a basic problem with the FW design. Not every organization does exit interviews of course, but of those who do carry out exit interviews we are not aware of any organizations that randomly allocate people who say they are leaving to either 'exit interview' (treatment) or 'no exit interview' (control) groups.

The reason is that employers have a duty of care which does not stop when someone hands in their notice. If someone quits, they have a duty to try to find out why, and may only find out during an exit interview. A treatment and control design creates an exposure. An organization could be accountable for not investigating claims an employee might only feel able to raise in an exit interview (Morrell and Arnold, 2007), e.g., sexual or racial discrimination, bullying or harassment, malpractice, or corruption. If someone leaving on those grounds had been allocated not to have an exit interview, an organization could be culpable for not having done what it should to make sure discrimination, harassment, and malpractice were properly examined. Healthcare organizations are often unionized, so variations in practice about such a fundamental aspect of the employment relationship would be unlikely to be tolerated, if ever suggested by management. One can say, in other words, that an exit interview is not just exit, it is potential for voice (Budd, Golan, and Wilkinson, 2010). For these reasons we suggest FW is unlikely ever to find the evidence it is set up to 'systematically review'.

Even so, the protocol gives an impressive series of undertakings as to what the authors would do if they found evidence. They undertake to:

> base primary analyses on consideration of dichotomous outcome measures [or] extract the primary measure (as defined by the authors of the study) or the median measure (…) For comparisons of RCT and QES designs we will report (separately for each design): Median effect across included study; Inter-quartile ranges of effect size across included studies; Range effect sizes across included studies (…) We will report individual tables comparing effect sizes of interventions grouped according to EPOC taxonomy (…) use the standard statistical methods of the Cochrane Collaboration for pooling of data from randomized and quasi-randomized control trials. For categorical and continuous data, we will calculate the risk ratios (RR) and weighted mean difference (WMD) respectively with 95% confidence intervals. We will use a random-effects model to take into account the heterogeneity of the various studies.

And for secondary analysis to:

> explore consistency of primary analyses with other types of end points (…) calculate standardized effect sizes for continuous measures by dividing the difference in mean scores between the intervention and comparison group in each study by an estimate of the (pooled) standard deviation.

And for re-analysis and presentation to:

> re-analyse RCT and QES designs with potential unit of analysis errors where possible by recalculating results using the appropriate unit of analysis [or] contact the authors of each study for clarification (…) use summary of findings tables (…) to interpret the results and draw conclusions about the effects (benefits, potential harm and costs) of different interventions including the size of effects and quality of the evidence for outcomes (…) We will prepare tables and bubble plots comparing effect sizes of studies grouped according to potential effect modifiers (timing of the interview, person carrying out the interview and location of the interview).

We have suggested the design will not find any evidence, let us consider how the review itself progressed in the four versions published since the protocol.

The Review

Here are the steps taken in the review, described in the latest, 2014 version:

> The original search identified 1560 citations, of which we considered 19 potentially relevant. The two authors independently reviewed the abstracts of these studies and retrieved the full texts of eight studies. We excluded all eight following independent assessment; they were either interviews, commentaries on how to do an exit interview or descriptive studies about reasons for leaving. We found no studies that matched our inclusion criteria. For this first update, we screened 2220 citations and identified no new studies. (1)

The eight studies mentioned above do not give a systematic picture of relevant literature, forming an extremely unlikely distribution. As in social science generally, there is more work published nowadays, and recent work is more available to review. But of these eight studies, two are in the 1950s, two in the 1980s, one in the 1990s then three in 2003, 2007, 2009. The protocol also undertook that 'Studies published in all languages will be included' yet these are all in English. In what is again unlikely, the authors say that since their 2007 protocol they only found one potentially relevant study. This was one they carried out themselves: interviewees with thirteen nurses (though they do not state the sample size in their description of their own study). Yet employee turnover is, empirically, one of the richest topics in management and healthcare management (Morrell, 2005).

There have been several large scale studies of nursing turnover (to take just one category of healthcare professional) since 2007. For instance, work on the European Nurses' Early Exit (NEXT) surveys 623 healthcare organizations (hospitals, care homes, etc.) and includes comparative data on 14,016 stayers and 866 leavers (Estryn-Behar et al., 2010). In the USA, work using the National Sample Survey of Registered Nurses examines turnover among 1,653 newly qualified registered nurses working in hospitals. Of these, 30% left their employers, and an additional 13% changed positions staying with the same employer (Brewer et al., 2012). Work in Canada examines turnover among an initial sample frame of 41 hospitals and 4,481 respondents (O'Brien-Pallas et al., 2010). In the UK, panel data from five waves of the labour force survey has been used in earlier work to track employment and turnover among 5,413 nurses (Frijters, Shields, and Price, 2007). Individually and collectively, these studies allow either national-level, organizational-level, or institutional-level comparative analysis of the effect of different approaches to exit interviews. They collect data at multiple sites, multiple time periods and at different levels of analysis. What they do not discuss is RCTs or QESs, where leavers in one organization are allocated to either having an exit interview or some other intervention. But, as argued, this does not happen. Even so the datasets above offer potential for re-analysis that approximates randomization.

One dimension to the systematic review, often held out as a unique benefit in preference to other modes of reviewing, is it is not just meant to identify published work, but relevant datasets and grey (unpublished) literature. This is where a rhetorical danger of the claim to 'systematic review' surfaces. In conventional reviews, authors never suggest that all work has been considered. But by using the label 'systematic review' and by undertaking to have carried out a scrupulous and conscientious search this can imply or claim that all work relevant to the question, and all relevant datasets, have been considered.

For instance, FW (2013: 6) does not simply state no relevant work was included, it states excluded work was not of sufficient quality, 'we have been unable to identify any trials *or other high quality studies* that have assessed the value of exit interviews to reduce turnover amongst healthcare professionals' (emphasis added). This confuses study design and study quality—which is reductionism. The studies above have been extremely well executed, by teams of researchers led by international authorities in different fields. Other designs could well be 'high quality'. FW imply this of their own (2009) study—they describe it as 'In depth interviews'. (Yet, as mentioned, they do not say how many interviewees: thirteen.)

Systematic reviews are set up to include 'grey literature'—unpublished work and datasets. This is consistent with conscientiously seeking out available evidence. Here is what FW (2007: 4) says in relation to this:

> (f) Authors of relevant papers will be contacted regarding any further published or unpublished work.
> (g) Authors of other reviews in the field of effective professional practice will be contacted regarding relevant studies that they may be aware of.

FW (2013: 4) reads:

> We contacted authors of relevant papers regarding any further published or unpublished work.

The lead author of this chapter doubted this, as his work was one of the eight studies and he had not been contacted. He asked the corresponding author in November 2013 to explain this, and when they did not reply asked again. They asked if he could wait until February 2014 for a reply. He then contacted CDSR raising concerns with the review. During this correspondence CDSR published two updates in March and in August of 2014. Updating is 'a process aiming to identify new evidence to incorporate into a previously completed systematic review' (Moher et al., 2008: 2, writing in CDSR).

Both 2014 'updates' re-describe how the review was carried out, setting out a version that is inconsistent with that in the 2013 review. The inclusion criteria change, the criteria for excluding work change, the claim to have contacted authors is withdrawn, and instead there is a specific justification for why authors were not contacted. Contrary to the above, the two updates read:

> We planned to contact authors of papers meeting our inclusion criteria regarding any further published or unpublished work. (both 2014)

The justification for not contacting authors is the same for two studies that were published 60 years ago as for studies in the 2000s: 'Inclusion criteria not met so the author was not contacted.' We cannot access either 1950s article online, but estimate their authors would be over ninety. The review is thirteen pages in 2011, eleven pages in 2013, twenty-seven pages in March 2014 and thirty pages in August 2014. Author order also changes. But across all these versions FW has not reviewed any evidence.

Conclusion

To borrow MAMM ourselves, these are symptoms of reductionism and medicalization that EBMgt ushers in. This shows that focusing on the protocols derived from reviewing in medicine can lead to an unhelpful and illogical framing of organizational phenomena. It also shows how the protocols and rhetoric of the systematic review do not necessarily lead to superior evidence. Instead they can, inadvertently or not, disguise inaccuracies and inconsistencies in both method and evidence. Of most concern: a systematic review can tell us there is no evidence, when there is.

Our hope in offering critique and this example is to make a positive contribution. Debate has been so one-sidedly for EBMgt that dialectically opposed argument can be helpful. We are not against evidence; we are against a narrow construction of evidence. To borrow MAMM ourselves again, we think the field requires a dose of scepticism—to be taken liberally. This might even help advocates of EBMgt to rethink their position—to discover, tolerate, or even celebrate radically different ways of seeing the world—especially from those scholars who work outside the strictures of the systematic review and positivism more generally. Early on in the development of EBMgt, other social science perspectives, including, for example, the difficulties posed for EBMgt by comparisons with medicine, were acknowledged and debated. We would advocate looking back, for example, at Tranfield, Denyer, and Smart (2003) or Walshe and Rundall (2001). Since Rousseau's (2006) presidential speech to the Academy of Management, however, such acknowledgements of diversity and disagreement have all but disappeared from the EBMgt literature. That particular address ended: 'Please join with me in working to make evidence-based management a reality' (Rousseau, 2006: 268). We would ask the opposite: 'please join with us in working to make evidence-based management a fiction.'

Those hearing about EBMgt for the first time are likely to see the problems inherent in MAMM, and of trying to apply this narrow version of evidence to their particular situation. Managers themselves, certainly those who are thoughtful and critical enough to engage with the ideas in this handbook, are often very keen to learn about the latest and most insightful research evidence. At the same time, many of them will resist the idea that some of the most important questions they face can ever be answered simply by looking at 'a body of evidence.' They will be likely to be as tired as we are of empty appeals to an evidence-base when that is selectively constructed, or assembled post-hoc to justify a decision taken on other grounds.

References

Archibald, T. (2015). "'They Just Know': The Epistemological Politics of 'Evidence-based' Non-formal Education". *Evaluation and Program Planning*, 48: 137–48.

Barends, E. G. and Briner, R. B. (2014). 'Teaching Evidence-based Practice: Lessons from the Pioneers; An Interview with Amanda Burls and Gordon Guyatt'. *Academy of Management Learning & Education*, 13(3): 476–83.

Barends, E., Rousseau, D. M., and Briner, R. B. (2014). *Evidence-Based Management: The Basic Principles*. Amsterdam: Center for Evidence-based Management.

Brewer, C. S., Kovner, C. T., Greene, W., Tukov-Shuser, M., and Djukic, M. (2012). 'Predictors of Actual Turnover in a National Sample of Newly Licensed Registered Nurses Employed in Hospitals'. *Journal of Advanced Nursing*, 68(3): 521–38.

Budd, J., Golan, P., and Wilkinson, A. (2010). 'New Approaches to Employee Voice and Participation in Organisations'. *Human Relations*, 63(3): 303–10.

Cartwright, N. and Hardie, J. (2012). *Evidence-Based Policy: A Practical Guide to Doing it Better*. Oxford: Oxford University Press.

Charlier, S. D. (2014). 'Incorporating Evidence-based Management into Management Curricula: A Conversation with Gary Latham'. *Academy of Management Learning and Education*, 13: 467–75.

Cole, S. (1983). 'The Hierarchy of the Sciences?'. *American Journal of Sociology*, 89: 111–39.

Estryn-Behar, M., Van der Heijden, B. I., Fry, C., and Hasselhorn, H. M. (2010). 'Longitudinal Analysis of Personal and Work-related Factors Associated with Turnover among Nurses'. *Nursing Research*, 59(3): 166–77.

Flint, A. and Webster, J. (no date). 'Exit Interviews to Reduce Turnover amongst Healthcare Professionals'. Available at: <http://onlinelibrary.wiley.com/doi/10.1002/14651858.CD006620.pub3/otherversions>, (this link gives access to five documents—the 2007 protocol, the 2011 review, the 2013 review, and two subsequent versions in 2014—where the title and author order change) (accessed 16 June 2016).

Frijters, P., Shields, M. A., and Price, S. W. (2007). 'Investigating the Quitting Decision of Nurses: Panel Data Evidence from the British National Health Service'. *Health Economics*, 16(1): 57–73.

Gartrell, C. D. and Gartrell, A. W. (2002). 'Positivism in Sociological Research: USA and UK (1966–1990)'. *British Journal of Sociology*, 53: 639–57.

Ghoshal, S. (2005). 'Bad Management Theories are Destroying Good Management Practices'. *Academy of Management Learning and Education*, 4: 75–91.

Grey, C. (2004). 'Reinventing Business Schools: The Contribution of Critical Management Education'. *Academy of Management Learning and Education*, 3: 178–86.

Holmes, D., Murray, S., Perron, G., and Rail, G. (2006). 'Deconstructing the Evidence-based Discourses in Health Sciences: Truth, Power and Fascism'. *International Journal of Evidence-based Healthcare*, 4: 180–6.

Hope, T. (2004). 'Pretend it Works: Evidence and Governance in the Evaluation of the Reducing Burglary Initiative'. *Criminology and Criminal Justice*, 4: 287–308.

House, E. R. (2006). 'Methodological Fundamentalism and the Quest for Control', in N. K. Denzin and M. Giardina (eds.), *Qualitative Inquiry and the Conservative Challenge*. Walnut Creek, CA: Left Coast Press, 93–108.

Kepes, F., Bennett, A. A., and McDaniel, M. A. (2014). 'Evidence-based Management and the Trustworthiness of our Cumulative Management Knowledge: Implications for Teaching, Research and Practice'. *Academy of Management Learning and Education*, 13: 446–66.

Laporte, G. (1992). 'The Traveling Salesman Problem: An Overview of Exact and Approximate Algorithms'. *European Journal of Operational Research*, 59(2): 231–47.

Lather, P. (2004). 'This *is* Your Father's Paradigm: Government Intrusion and the Case of Qualitative Research in Education'. *Qualitative Inquiry*, 10: 15–34.

Learmonth, M. and Harding, N. (2006). 'Evidence-based Management: The Very Idea'. *Public Administration*, 84: 245–66.

Lee, T. W. and Mitchell, T. R. (1994). 'An Alternative Approach: The Unfolding Model of Voluntary Employee Turnover'. *Academy of Management Review*, 19: 51–89.

Lee, T. W., Mitchell, T. R., Holtom, B. C., McDaniel, L. S., and Hill, J. W. (1999). 'The Unfolding Model of Voluntary Turnover: A Replication and Extension'. *Academy of Management Journal*, 42: 450–62.

Legge, K. (1995). *Human Resource Management: Rhetorics and Realities*. London: Palgrave.

Mautner, T. (ed.) 2000. *A Dictionary of Philosophy*. London: Penguin.

Moher, D., Tsertsvadze, A., Tricco, A. M., Grimshaw, J., Sampson, M., and Barrowman, N. (2008). 'When and How to Update Systematic Reviews'. *Cochrane Database of Systematic Reviews*. Issue 1.

Morrell, K. (2005). 'Towards a Typology of Nursing Turnover'. *Journal of Advanced Nursing*, 49(3): 315–22.

Morrell, K. (2008). 'The Narrative of 'Evidence-based' Management: A Polemic'. *Journal of Management Studies*, 45: 613–45.

Morrell, K. and Arnold, J. (2007). 'Look After They Leap'. *International Journal of Human Resource Management*, 18(9): 1683–99.

Morrell, K. and Learmonth, M. (2015). 'Against Evidence-based Management, for Management Learning'. *Academy of Management Learning & Education*, 14(4): 520–33.

Morrell, K., Learmonth, M., and Heracleous, L. (2015). 'An Archaeological Critique of 'Evidence-based Management': One Digression After Another'. *British Journal of Management*, 26(3): 529–43.

Morrell, K., Loan-Clarke, J., and Wilkinson, A. (2001). 'Unweaving Leaving: The Use of Models in the Management of Employee Turnover'. *International Journal of Management Reviews*, 3: 219–44.

Morrell, K., Loan-Clarke, J., and Wilkinson, A. (2004a). 'The Role of Shocks in Employee Turnover'. *British Journal of Management*, 15: 335–49.

Morrell, K., Loan-Clarke, J., and Wilkinson, A. (2004b). 'Organisational Change and Employee Turnover'. *Personnel Review*, 33: 161–73.

Nutley, S. M., Walter, I. C., and Davies, H. T. O. (2007). *Using Evidence: How Research Can Inform Public Services*. London: Policy Press.

O'Brien-Pallas, L., Murphy, G. T., Shamian, J., Li, X., and Hayes, L. J. (2010). 'Impact and Determinants of Nurse Turnover: A Pan-Canadian Study'. *Journal of Nursing Management*, 18(8): 1073–86.

Rousseau, D. M. (2006). 'Is There Such a Thing as Evidence-based Management?'. *Academy of Management Review*, 31: 256–69.

Rousseau, D. M. (ed.) 2012. *The Oxford Handbook of Evidence-Based Management*. Oxford: Oxford University Press.

Rynes, S. L., Rousseau, D. M., and Barends, E. (2014). From the Guest Editors: Change the World: Teach Evidence-based Practice!'. *Academy of Management Learning and Education*, 13: 305–21.

Sackett, D. L., Rosenberg, W. M., Gray, J. A. M., Haynes, R. B., and Richardson, W. S. (1996). 'Evidence Based Medicine: What It Is and What It Isn't'. *British Medical Journal*, 312: 71–2.

Tranfield, D., Denyer, D., and Smart, P. (2003). 'Towards a Methodology for Developing Evidence-informed Management Knowledge by Means of Systematic Review'. *British Journal of Management*, 14: 207–22.

Walshe, K. and Rundall, T. G. (2001). 'Evidence Based Management: From Theory to Practice in Health Care'. *The Milbank Quarterly*, 79: 429–57.

Young, K., Ashby, D., Boaz, A., and Grayson, L. (2002). 'Social Science and the Evidence-based Policy Movement'. *Social Policy and Society*, 1: 215–24.

CHAPTER 22

MANAGEMENT EDUCATION IN BUSINESS SCHOOLS

KENNETH G. BROWN AND ROBERT S. RUBIN

How business schools operate, and in particular educate future managers, is at once a longstanding concern and a topic of intense contemporary focus. For many, business schools are at least in part to blame for the malfeasance of corporate executives at Enron, Worldcom, and Tyco and even for the global financial crisis that began in 2008 (Giacolone and Wargo, 2009; Holstein, 2013; O'Connor, 2013; Plumer, 2009; Polodny, 2009). Concerns about the role of business schools may help explain why the volume and pace of management education research has increased. Seminal reports on business school faculty and curricula by the Carnegie Corporation and Ford Foundation in 1959, and the Porter and McKibbin follow-up in 1988, have been cited more in recent years than when they were first published. For example, of 1,673 total cites on Google Scholar for Porter and McKibbin, 392 (23%) have been since 2011 as compared with 249 (15%) in the first five years of publication.[1] Concerns raised in these reports about how we educate managers resonate even more today than when they were first published.

There has been more than one follow-up to Porter and McKibbin (e.g., Datar, Garvin, and Cullen, 2010; Holtom and Dierdorff, 2013) as well as an overall expansion in the breadth and depth of scholarly work about business schools and the education they provide (Rubin and Dierdorff, 2013). Although much of the follow-up research focuses explicitly on the signature business school degree, the Master's in Business Administration (MBA), the conclusions speak to many dimensions and programs in business schools, including undergraduate programs and the characteristics of faculty and their research. The theme of these follow-up studies, described in more detail in this chapter, continues a theme noted in the original critiques—that business schools could do more for society if they innovated and balanced their emphasis on theoretical,

---

[1] As of 27 July 2016. We acknowledge that the increase in citations is at least in part attributable to the introduction of new journals, but the introduction of these journals also supports the idea that interest in management education scholarship has grown.

disciplinary research and technically oriented training with practical research and blended soft- and hard-skills training.

Given the substantial growth in research since the influential Porter and McKibbin (1988) report, the purpose of this chapter is to provide a snapshot of this emergent literature, identifying key themes and suggesting future research directions. Because the focus of this chapter is scholarly, we do not directly answer the questions, 'how should we run business schools today?' or 'how should we change to better educate future managers?' Instead, we review research related to these and other questions in the hope of encouraging further scholarly work. Further, the review contained within is not a comprehensive one, but rather focuses on foundational research that has either created new research domains, fundamentally changing the direction of previous work, or provided a basis for future work.

Towards this end, first, we review the concept of management education to clarify our focus and explain how the contested nature of its definition may contribute to an overly narrow perspective. Second, we discuss the forces pushing for changes in management education. Third, we provide an overview of scholarly management education literature, noting changes in journals and pinpointing highly cited studies. Fourth, we review research in two popular areas of study—online learning and MBA curricula—and provide suggestions for future research.

Management Education Defined

Management education (much like the term management itself) has contested meanings. In the scholarly community, the term management education is often used to describe the work done by those who teach general management and related behavioural disciplines. This way of thinking about management education is driven by those who teach in departments of management and are supported by organizational entities such as the Academy of Management and OBTS, the Teaching Society for Management Educators. The *Journal of Management Education*, for example, publishes research primarily on the teaching of organizational behaviour, human resource management, and strategy.

Within the general public (and even some scholars outside of the management discipline), the term management education is used to describe general business education as defined by business school accrediting bodies. The major business school accrediting bodies use the term 'management education' in their main descriptions of business school curriculum. The Association of MBAs in the United Kingdom, for example, notes that today their organization's research 'explore[s] global trends and thought leadership in *management education*' (emphasis added, <http://www.mbaworld.com/en/About-us.aspx>, accessed 17 June 2015). EQUIS, coordinated by the Brussels-based European Foundation for Management Development (EFMD), accredits institutions that are 'primarily devoted to *management education*' (emphasis added, <https://www.efmd.org/index.php/accreditation-main/equis>, accessed 17 June 2015). EFMD describes itself as a 'catalyst to enhance excellence in management education and development globally.' Finally, the Association to Advance Collegiate Schools of Business (AACSB) states its mission as follows: 'advance quality *management education* worldwide through education, thought leadership, and value-added services' (emphasis added, <http://www.aacsb.edu>, accessed 17 June 2015). In all cases, these organizations accredit, support, and publish about graduate (and in some cases undergraduate) programs that include a wide range of coursework including accounting, economics, entrepreneurship, finance, management, marketing, operations, and business analytics.

Different definitions are not just a matter of semantics; how management education is defined determines whether those in management departments, and those who publish in journals labelled 'management education,' align perspectives to the generalist needs of managers, organizations, and society, or the interest of our scholarly boundaries rooted in organizational behaviour and similar behavioural disciplines. That is, when viewed narrowly, management education would not include teaching the broad functions of business such as marketing, accounting, finance, and economics. One major concern about management education described by Datar, Garvin, and Cullen (2010) in their study of highly ranked MBA curriculum is the lack of integration across business disciplines, a problem that would be exacerbated by drawing sharp boundaries about what is and is not part of management education. At the same time, Gentile (2010) has argued that divorcing rigorous quantitative analysis from richer, values-driven perspectives contributes to short-term thinking that can harm society. Because of these and similar concerns, we invoke the more inclusive definition of management education that encourages developing the whole range of knowledge and skill that would prepare students for management work. This definition is better aligned with the popular and generalist definition as well as scholars outside of the management discipline.

Forces for Change

A number of major forces have emerged that place pressure on management education to continue to evolve, including financial pressures, student characteristics, course demand, and technology (Holtom and Porter, 2013).

Financial Pressures

Financial pressures are not unique to management education but instead permeate higher education in the United States and the United Kingdom. In these countries, where government support for universities has declined in recent years, tuition has risen at a pace dramatically higher than inflation and student debt has grown (Sheehy, 2013). As compared with countries such as Argentina, Iceland, Norway, and Sweden, where government-supported school tuition is free, US and UK students are paying an increasingly larger share of their educational expenses, much to their dismay (Ratcliffe, 2015). Politicians are responding to public discord by criticizing universities and, at times, constraining tuition increases. Some universities now offer tuition guarantees that limit increases in tuition for the four or five years that a student is enrolled. These constraints put even further financial strain on universities, which must increasingly rely on private fundraising to increase revenue and leaner staff to decrease costs. Universities must also compete with each other to attract not only the brightest students but also the students who yield the highest net tuition. In the case of government-sponsored institutions with differential in- and out-of-state tuition, out-of-state and international students are attractive because they bring additional revenue. In the USA in particular, there has been a dramatic rise in the number of students enrolling from China. In 2013–14 there were over a quarter million students from China studying in the USA, a figure that represents nearly one-third of all international students studying in the country and an increase in 17% from the previous year (Svoboda, 2015).

Student Characteristics

Increases in international students are only one of the changes in student characteristics that business schools are facing. Applicants for graduate management education are also increasingly diverse by age. Drawing on Graduate Management Admissions Test (GMAT) data, Holtom and Porter (2013) note increases in both younger (younger than 25) and older (40 or older) test takers. Given the increased average age of populations in the USA and UK, increased demand for various forms of graduate education by older adults seems likely. The trend for women is less positive and somewhat concerning. Although women are more likely than men to complete college and attend graduate school in general, at least in the USA (Bidwell, 2014), women's applications to online MBA, full-time one-year MBA, and Executive MBA courses declined from 2012 to 2014. To recruit more women, business schools are introducing new programs, some that reach out to students even before they begin college (Gellman, 2015).

Course Demand

One particularly powerful and well-documented trend in the broader business environment has been the move towards the commodification of knowledge (Trank and Rynes, 2003). That is, in the interest of satisfying short-term goals, organizations have looked to schools of business to produce students who are well-versed in narrow tools and techniques rather than broad knowledge (Trank and Rynes, 2003). In order to meet immediate needs in technology and specific job-focused arenas, organizations exert pressure on business schools to provide job candidates who can hit the ground running.

This environmental shift is contributing to changes in course demand. For example, GMAT test takers for full-time MBA courses have declined since 2009 (see Figure 22.1). The AACSB reports that their member schools are continuing to add specialized

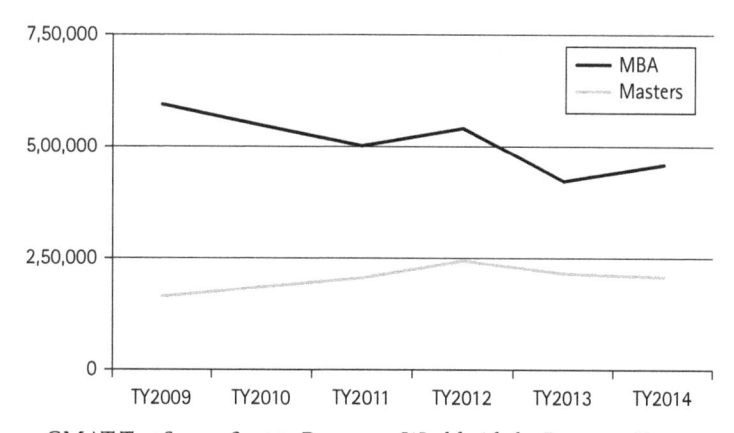

FIGURE 22.1 GMAT Test Scores Sent to Programs Worldwide by Program Type.

Sources: GMAT Trends Tracker 2014: Testing Data

master's courses (AACSB Business School Data Guide, 2015), presumably to continue the efforts to diversify their revenue streams but also address market demands for new employees with a specific, narrow skillset. As such, specialty one-year master's courses in areas such as Finance, Marketing, and Information Systems have gained in popularity (Damast, 2012) and are a key growth strategy for many business schools. But, viewed from our definition, these courses typically do not fall within the domain of management education; they are, instead, vocational courses that prepare students with narrow knowledge and skills specific to a technical role.

Technology

Technology changes are also influencing management education, again in a trend that extends beyond the walls of business schools. Online degree seeking students have risen steadily over the last twenty years and are estimated to include over 5 million learners in the US alone by 2020. While there was much fanfare about for-profit online providers from 2000 to 2010, undergraduate enrolment growth at these providers has actually declined since 2010. In addition, one of the largest private providers in the USA, Corinthian, declared bankupcy in 2015 and liquidated its assets later that same year. Nevertheless, for-profits remain a significant player in the higher education market and 58% of students who enroll in for-profit providers take all of their classes online (IES, 2015). Undergraduate and graduate business degrees are among the most often sought from these providers. For example, 31% of the over 200,000 University of Phoenix students in 2014–15 were studying business administration (US News & World Reports, 2015).

Public institutions have also launched online degree courses. In the area of undergraduate business and MBA courses, publics are gaining attention. Recent *US News & World Report* rankings of online MBA courses had Indiana University, Temple University, University of North Carolina Chapel Hill, Arizona State University, and University of Florida in the top five positions. For other graduate business courses, the top slots were

Indiana University, University of Texas-Dallas, Arizona State University, University of Connecticut, and Pennsylvania State University World Campus. In contrast, the 'Best Business Schools' for traditional MBA courses in the same year were Stanford, Harvard, University of Pennsylvania, University of Chicago, and Massachusetts Institute of Technology (MIT), all private schools.

These lists should not be interpreted to suggest that private schools have ignored online offerings. MIT and Harvard were founding partners in edX, a non-profit consortium that seeks to expand access to education. Many courses offered through edX and a similar consortium called Coursera are offered for free to any interested student who wanted to enrol. Some business schools, including Wharton, offer classes for free but require a fee for a verified certificate of completion.

The term used to describe many of these new online offerings is MOOC, an acronym for massive, open, online course. These courses are not all free, though, and most recently, Arizona State University partnered with edX to offer a Global Freshman Academy that anyone in the world can take for a fee. However, the fee is a fraction of what students would pay for attending Arizona State, and they can take these courses from the convenience of their homes and workplaces. So while some classes maintain the notion of openness, the organizations operating in this space have innovated to create a range of non-traditional, revenue generating post-secondary learning opportunities.

Although enrolments in some MOOC offerings are very high, completion rates have been estimated at only 6.5% (Jordan, 2015). It is difficult to see how non-profit or for-profit companies could survive offering free classes that few people complete. One company who started in this space, Udacity, stopped providing free college education classes and instead has concentrated on paid vocational certification (Byrnes, 2015) under the label of 'nanodegrees.' An interesting innovation specifically in the management education space is HBX, Harvard Business School's entry into online credentialing. In 2014, HBX began enrolling students in HBX CORe (short for Credential of Readiness), a set of three courses intended to provide core knowledge via three Harvard Business School courses. In contrast to a MOOC, the HBX CORe is selective in admissions and fee-based. Many business schools also run fee-based mini-MBA courses that are condensed (e.g., one week) versions of a full MBA including both online and face-to-face options (Damast, 2009).

Central to the work of Udacity, HBX, and schools running online mini-MBA courses is the development of new credentials. It remains to be seen how these credentials will be viewed in the labour market. Research is needed to explore whether and in what ways perceptions of these credentials are changing.

Summary

The overall trends in management education suggest greater diversity in students and courses with pressure to increase tuition revenue and simultaneously reduce costs. It is not surprising in this context to see administrative and technological innovations such as HBX, Arizona State University Global Freshman Academy, and new credentials such as mini-MBA's and nanodegrees. It remains to be seen how much these courses and their associated credentials will displace traditional management education and management degrees. Given how technology has influenced other industries (e.g., music and news, for example Zentner, 2008), traditional business schools stand to lose significant numbers of students to non-traditional courses, further increasing financial strain.

FORMATIVE STUDIES ON MANAGEMENT EDUCATION

Management education as a scholarly discipline has been bolstered by a handful of seminal studies that raised critical concerns about the purpose, practice, perils, and promise of education within schools of business. This era of scholars applying their disciplinary research methods to their own intuitions largely began with Porter and McKibbin (1988); a project commissioned by what was then the American Association of Collegiate Schools of Business (AACSB).[2] Over the course of a few years, the authors visited 60 business schools, interviewed 200 corporate executives, and surveyed nearly 9,000 faculty, students, and alumni. The report was an exhaustive, data-driven examination of the state of business schools.

The major findings of the report included some positive features of business schools such as high levels of faculty qualifications and strong technical skills of graduates. The negatives included a sense of complacency by Deans and faculty, a lack of curricular innovation, and an over-emphasis on quantity rather than quality of faculty research. Their work further highlighted a growing disconnect between what schools were teaching and what practising executives said they desire in business school graduates. Recommendations from their research included greater flexibility in programme delivery, increased attention to the impact of business school research, and increased emphasis on interdisciplinary, cross-functional, and soft-skills teaching.

Two recent scholarly volumes are positioned as follow-ups to Porter and McKibbon: Datar, Garvin, and Cullen (2010) and Holtom and Dierdorff (2013).

Datar and Colleagues

Datar, Garvin, and Cullen (2010) provide both a general argument for what business school should teach and in-depth examinations at how University of Chicago, INSEAD,

---

[2] Now the Association to Advance Collegiate Schools of Business.

Harvard, Yale, Stanford, and The Center for Creative Leadership address these topics. Their review, although focused on a small sample of schools, is rooted in what they describe as the fundamental struggle between two cultures in business schools—rigour (advocated by 'priests of research purity') and relevance (promoted by 'soldiers of organizational performance') (76, terms from March and Sutton, 1997). The dominance of the rigour culture led to MBA graduates having great analytical tools but little practical knowledge. Datar and colleagues argue that hiring from business schools was driven more by their ability to screen high qualified applicants than by the value-added of their education (82).

Datar, Garvin, and Cullen (2010) also suggest that there is agreement on solutions but implementation is difficult (see also Mintzberg, 2004 and Rubin and Dierdorff, 2011). Datar and colleagues identify three curricular needs around which there is considerable agreement: (1) global perspective, (2) leadership development, and (3) integration across disciplines and perspectives. They review in detail the curriculum of elite schools, noting how these needs are being met.

Holtom and Dierdorff

Holtom and Dierdorff (2013) is an edited volume and is less a single study than a collection of essays and specific studies on topics such as graduate management education curriculum, doctoral programmes, teaching, student engagement, and course rankings. One particularly innovative chapter (Rubin and Morgeson) reports on a Graduate Management Admissions Council funded study to measure the quality of management education courses.

Rubin and Morgeson (2013) note limitations in both accreditation and media rankings as measures of course quality and suggest instead a direct measure. Their research process included: (1) multi-method research to develop a quality model, (2) a Q-sort content analysis of quality dimensions, and (3) a survey of subject matters experts to provide validity evidence and reactions to the model. Based on these efforts, they proposed an open systems model of course quality that distinguishes inputs and outputs, over which schools have less control, and throughputs, which are under the school's control and are considered by stakeholders to be key dimensions of quality. Figure 22.2 presents this model with minor modifications. The model places an emphasis on throughputs, which include the quality of the curriculum, faculty, student learning outcomes, and placement at graduation.

The proposal offered by Morgeson and Rubin (2013) is for schools to enhance transparency and report on these dimensions so quality profiles can be communicated to prospective students and other stakeholders. The challenge that remains is the additional work of developing a data collection protocol with buy-in from schools, stakeholders, and accrediting bodies like AACSB, EMBA, and EQUIS.

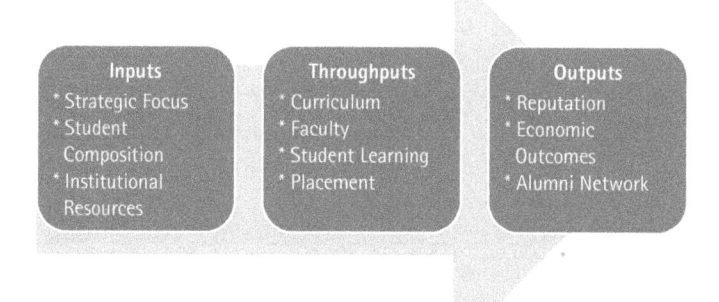

FIGURE 22.2 An Open Systems Model of Program Quality.

Adapted from Rubin and Morgeson, 2013.

THE STATE OF THE ACADEMIC LITERATURE

Porter and McKibbon's work spawned a new enlightenment so to speak with respect to scholarly work focused on management education (Leigh and Beatty, 2008) which had consisted largely of descriptions of classroom teaching practices. Indeed, the literature has ballooned thanks to dedicated new journals including *Academy of Management Learning and Education* (2001), *Statistical Education Research Journal* (2002), *Decision Sciences Journal of Innovative Education* (2003), *International Journal of Management Education* (2002), *International Review of Economics Education* (2003), *Journal of Economics and Finance Education* (2002), *Journal of Emerging Technologies in Accounting Teaching Notes* (2003), and *Management Teaching Review* (2016). Similarly, in the disciplinary field of management, a number of research series have been published (e.g., Wankel and DeFillipi, 2006) as well as a research handbook (Armstrong and Fukami, 2009). Similar volumes have appeared in other business fields, including Accounting (Wilson, 2014) and ethics (Wankel and Stachowicz-Stanusch, 2011) to name but a few.

A review of four journals in the disciplinary management space revealed interesting progress towards management education scholarship, at least the scholarship in traditional management departments, becoming mainstream. Rynes and Brown (2011) compared *Academy of Management Learning and Education, Decisions Sciences Journal of Innovative Education, Management Learning,* and *Journal of Management Education* according to their journal characteristics (who publishes and who reviews) and characteristics of published empirical articles from 2002 to 2007. The results suggest differences across journals but notably, that the *Academy of Management Learning and Education* (*AMLE*) bears some similarity to the most respected empirical journal in management, the *Academy of Management Journal*. Both journals are sponsored by major academic societies, indexed and abstracted by large companies, and have productive scholars as editorial board members. And, increasingly, *AMLE* is listed on journal lists as a world-leading journal (ABS Academic Journal Guide, 2015). In this way, we can say that while management education is not always considered a mainstream sub-discipline of management, it is becoming more mature as an area of study (see also Beatty and Leigh, 2009).

A study of the most cited articles in management education from 1970 to 2013 noted a set of key themes in previous research. Arbaugh, Fornaciari, and Hwang (2014) searched for articles using Google Scholar (via Harzing's Publish or Perish software). As with this chapter, Arbaugh, Fornaciari, and Hwang used an inclusive definition of management education and searched many terms in 'all disciplinary areas housed in business schools and educational research journals that published articles on education delivered by business schools' (9). They organized the top one hundred most highly cited pieces into twenty-one research categories. The two categories with by far the most articles were entrepreneurship education (twenty-three articles) and online teaching and learning (twenty-two articles). The next area, business student ethics, had only twelve articles on the list. Critiques of business schools was the fourth most prevalent theme, with nine articles, but as can be seen in Table 22.1 that shows the Top Twenty-Five cited articles, the top three articles are in this category.

In the next sections we will review key research in two of the most cited domains, online education and critiques of business schools. The topic of entrepreneurial education is an important one, but it has been reviewed in a number of other places (e.g., Mwasalwiba, 2010; Pittaway and Cope, 2007) and is disciplinary in nature rather than broadly applicable across all fields that intersect to examine management education.

Online Teaching and Learning

One of the most obvious trends in higher education, and workplace training as well, has been the increased use of technology to support and even deliver coursework. Technology delivery is not new considering that educational radio began in the United States in the 1920s, and the University of Iowa was the first US university to broadcast television learning opportunities in 1933 (Novak, 2012). While the hopes for widespread educational access via television faded quickly, traditions of distance and eventually computer-aided instruction continue. As noted earlier, there has been tremendous growth in online education in recent years, and the trend is expected to continue.

'Recent developments in computer hardware, software, and communication technologies create exciting new opportunities for the educational use of these technologies' (Alavi, 1994: 159). This quote could have been written in 2015, but it is over twenty years old. Alavi (1994) studied 127 MBA students using a group decision support system. Students who used the system had higher final test grades than those who did not use the system. Leidner and Jarvenpaa (1995) noted a concern that technology was being used to automate delivery, which only serves to speed up ineffective teaching methods. They summarized five learning models to provide an alternative way of thinking about

Table 22.1 Most-cited Articles in Business and Management Education, 1970–2013

Author(s)	Topic	Journal	Citations
1. Ghoshal (2005)	Critiques of Business Schools	Academy of Management Learning and Education	1878
2. Bennis and O'Toole (2005)	Critiques of Business Schools	Harvard Business Review	1219
3. Pfeffer and Fong (2002)	Critiques of Business Schools	Academy of Management Learning and Education	1090
4. Alavi (1994)	Online Teaching and Learning	MIS Quarterly	1048
5. Kolb and Kolb (2005)	Experiential Learning	Academy of Management Learning and Education	1041
6. Leidner and Jarvenpaa (1995)	Online Teaching and Learning	MIS Quarterly	889
7. Piccoli, Ahmad, and Ives (2001)	Online Teaching and Learning	MIS Quarterly	842
8. Webster and Hackley (1997)	Online Teaching and Learning	Academy of Management Journal	580
9. Katz (2003)	Entrepreneurship Education	Journal of Business Venturing	574
10. Kuratko (2005)	Entrepreneurship Education	Entrepreneurship Theory and Practice	566
11. Zhao, Seibert, and Hills (2005)	Entrepreneurship Education	Journal of Applied Psychology	544
12. Gorman, Hanlon, and King (1997)	Entrepreneurship Education	International Small Business Journal	516
13. Alavi and Leidner (2001)	Online Teaching and Learning	Information Systems Research	503
14. Alavi, Wheeler, and Valacich (1995)	Online Teaching and Learning	MIS Quarterly	452
15. Gibb (1993)	Entrepreneurship Education	International Small Business Journal	438
16. Rindova, Williamson, Petkova, and Sever (2005)	Critiques of Business Schools	Academy of Management Journal	419
17. Vesper and Gartner (1997)	Entrepreneurship Education	Journal of Business Venturing	371
18. Arbaugh (2000)	Online Teaching and Learning	Journal of Management Education	366

(Continued)

Table 22.1 Continued

Author(s)	Topic	Journal	Citations
19. Baldwin, Bedell, and Johnson (1997)	Student Teams	*Academy of Management Journal*	360
20. Keys and Wolfe (1990)	Use of Simulations	*Journal of Management*	337
21. Alavi, Yoo, and Vogel (1997)	Online Teaching and Learning	*Academy of Management Journal*	334
22. Fiet (2001b)	Entrepreneurship Education	*Journal of Business Venturing*	316
23. Fiet (2001a)	Entrepreneurship Education	*Journal of Business Venturing*	311
24. Kayes (2002)	Experiential Learning	*Academy of Management Learning and Education*	305
25. Solomon, Duffy, and Tarabishy (2002)	Entrepreneurship Education	*International Journal of Entrepreneurship Education*	302

Source: Arbaugh, Fornaciari, and Hwang, 2014.

information technology in the classroom. They review a number of possible technologies that could be used to provide instructors better access to information about students, including key response pads and email.

It is worth noting how prescient Leidner and Jarvenpaa were in their 1995 article. Key response pads are now generically referred to as audience response technology (Kay and LeSage, 2009) and include stand-alone radio frequency clickers or, more recently, smartphone applications. This technology has been central to the development of *peer instruction*, a pedagogical approach to providing challenging problems to students which they work through in class and provide answers. Students then work in small groups to review the answers. This approach to teaching has been developed and used heavily in physics with great success (Crouch and Mazur, 2001). The current model of flipping classes, where information is provided to students in advance of class and students use class time to work through cases and problems (Bishop and Verleger, 2013), also owes a great deal to the technologies that Leidner and Jarvenpaa examined.

Research that began on using technology *in* the classroom has been supplemented by research on technology *as* the classroom. Arbaugh (2000) examined student satisfaction of online MBA courses. Of note is that, as compared with MOOCs that have high attrition rates, the attrition rate by degree-seeking students in this study was small, less than 3% across four courses. Arbaugh found that students' overall satisfaction was determined by the perceived usefulness of the online delivery technology, the flexibility provided by the class, the ease of interacting with the instructor and other students, and the instructor's emphasis on interaction. Although it sounds dated now, Arbaugh concluded that students see value in an online delivery format. More pertinent today is his conclusion about the importance of participant interaction for satisfaction, a finding that has been confirmed meta-analytically (Sitzmann et al., 2008).

Piccoli, Ahmad, and Ives (2001) report a longitudinal experimental design comparing student IT skills in traditional classroom versus virtual learning environments. They found no learning differences but a trade-off between self-efficacy and satisfaction. Students in the virtual learning environment had higher computer self-efficacy but lower satisfaction with the learning process. This study suggests the importance of not substituting satisfaction, self-efficacy, and learning as outcomes when examining the effectiveness of various teaching technologies. Research confirms that these are distinct constructs with different patterns of relationships with other constructs and thus should not be assumed to be equivalent (Sitzmann et al., 2008, 2010).

Future Research

Research would be useful on how to prepare and support students as they work in virtual environments. Research on learning suggests the importance of guidance and support (Kirschner, Sweller, and Clark, 2006), so research could identify ways to use technology to provide better support to different types of students. The value of technology-mediated learning environment is the capacity to use algorithms to customize the student experience. More theoretically-driven development and empirical testing is needed in this area. Relevant theories include those on technology use (such as the revised Technology Acceptance Model, an earlier version of which was studied by Arbaugh, 2000) and motivation to learn (such as with the Transtheoretical Model of Change as argued by Brown and Charlier, 2013).

Research should also explore potential trade-offs among satisfaction, self-efficacy, learning, and long-term career-related outcomes from management education experiences. When designing classes and courses, instructors should be aware of the ways in which certain events create satisfaction but might interfere with learning (see, for example, the seductive detail effect, Park et al., 2011).

An area that is not useful for future research is a simple comparison of two different technologies. There is a tradition of this research in education, where new innovations led to the question, 'does X + 1 work better than X.' For example, does the use of live video produce better learning than the use of audio only? The answer to this question, when it is limited to differences in technology, is often 'a little' if the new technology is applied thoughtfully. When many factors are controlled, the answer is often 'no significant difference' (Clark, 1984). When judged across a common criterion like learning, it is difficult for a new technology to provide a dramatic improvement unless the comparison is against a straw-man that does not provide sufficient opportunity for the student to interact with the material to be learned.

One example of this point is in research on peer response systems. Does the introduction of peer response systems, or clickers, improve learning in classrooms? When used as a simple way to increase interactivity, it is likely that their effect is small and constrained to increases in satisfaction but not learning. But when used as part of an integrated peer instruction strategy, it has been shown to be effective at increasing both course satisfaction and learning (Crouch and Mazur, 2001; Yun and Lojo, 2010). Key to these improvements is not the technology per se but the use of technology in an instructionally purposeful way to encourage students to solve problems, receive feedback, and discuss with their peers. Future research that examines different technologies should either control for differences in the instructional and learning activities involved with technologies being compared, or articulate the instructional change being studied alongside the new technology and deploy a meaningful control group.

Critiques of Business Schools

In a recent review of MBA-related research published in the *Academy of Management Learning and Education*, Rubin and Dierdorff (2013) found that close to two-thirds of all MBA-related research was dedicated to critiquing curriculum. This focus is evident in the most highly cited critique written by Ghoshal (2005) who noted that theories taught in management classrooms reinforced negative assumptions about managers in ways that led to those assumptions becoming reality. Ghoshal (2005) rebuked business schools for curricula that emphasize the concerns of shareholders over those of stakeholders. He argued that this emphasis on shareholder 'value' that permeates management curricula fostered abdication of managers' and companies' moral responsibilities.

The depth of focus on curriculum is likely justified given the importance of curriculum to a variety of business school stakeholders. For instance, surveys from the Graduate Management Admission Council routinely depict curriculum to be among the most important factors driving student perception of value of their MBA courses (GMAC, 2011, 2015a). Yet, to fully understand why scholars have focused so heavily on curriculum, one must understand a few basic assumptions that underlie graduate management education.

First, historically the purpose of an MBA degree was to build individual capacities for management people and enterprises. The earliest MBA courses were established with the expressed intent of producing a professional class of managers much in the way law schools, medical schools, or engineering schools train groups of professionals, complete with full inculcation of a common body of knowledge and code of professional conduct (for a complete history see Khurana, 2007). However, as MBA courses began to proliferate well into the 1980s, this focus on a professional class of management was being supplanted by a focus on producing technical specialists. Khurana (2007) noted that this shift was largely due to the changes in faculty training moving away from practicing executives towards highly specialized or disciplined PhDs in mathematics, sociology, and psychology as business schools sought to gain increased credibility as academic institutions. Thus, the basic assumptions regarding the educational mission of MBA courses has fluctuated considerably over time and has given rise to myriad questions regarding the appropriate focus of management education curriculum. Second, since the dawn of business schools, there has been substantial debate over the appropriate balance between academic rigour versus practical 'hands-on' training. These debates regarding curriculum content endure with numerous scholars suggesting that today's MBA curriculum lacks relevance to the real-world (Ghoshal, 2005; Pfeffer and Fong, 2002) while others argue that a primary focus on academic rigour is key to producing competent professionals (Rousseau and McCarthy, 2007).

The Ghoshal (2005) article spawned numerous articles that placed the blame for the movement towards shareholders squarely on the ubiquity of economics education as a cornerstone of management education (Ferraro, Pfeffer, and Sutton, 2005; Khurana, 2007; Wang, Malhotra, and Murnighan, 2011). Similarly, scholars who like the general public were horrified by the ongoing corporate ethics calamities have been highly focused on the lack of presence and depth in the area of ethics education. For example, Giacalone (2007) argued that the MBA curriculum rarely engages in deep ethical learning largely because business schools are failing to teach higher order ideals. Instead, the curriculum typically conforms to students' assumptions about values rather than challenging them. Other researchers have focused their attention on improving the way in which the curriculum promotes more critical thinking (Atwater, Kannan, and Stephens, 2008), diversity orientation (Bell, Connerley, and Cocchiara, 2009) and interpersonal skill development (Ferraro, Pfeffer, and Sutton, 2005). Finally, calls for integrating curricula remain constant as business schools grapple with how to best aid students' awareness of the interrelated or systemic aspects of business.

Concomitant with critiques regarding content is an underlying discomfort with the way in which curricula are delivered. Here, researchers frequently focused their work by making distinctions in typical teaching modalities such as experiential and reflective learning. Mintzberg (2004) among others has been particularly vocal in arguing that management is a profession that requires disciplined practice that can only be learned through experiences. He argues for management education courses that support or provide guided practice within real organizational contexts. Tushman and colleagues (2007) found support for Mintzberg's primary arguments showing that direct experience via action-learning provides increased relevance in student learning outcomes.

Although the decades of curriculum research have produced a trove of findings bolstering different perspectives on the development and necessary modification of the curriculum, only a handful of studies have been conducted on a large enough scale that allow for prescriptive conclusions. For example, many thought-provoking studies have chosen to focus on a select number of business schools that appear in media-ranking publications (Datar, Garvin, and Cullen, 2010; Ferraro, Pfeffer, and Sutton, 2005; Segev, Raveh, and Farjoun, 1999) and range in sample sizes from eleven to fifty reducing the overall generalizability of their findings.

One major exception has been Rubin and Dierdorff (2009) who conducted a comprehensive study of required curricula across MBA courses. Specifically, their study encompassed the required coursework from 373 AACSB-accredited schools of business. Guided by the assumption that MBA courses exist to train future managers, Rubin and Dierdorff drew upon a competency model derived from the US Department of Labor's Occupational Information Network (O*NET) which contained 52 managerial occupations from its US nationally representative sample of 8,633 incumbent managers

(Dierdorff, Rubin, and Morgeson, 2009). This competency model depicts six major behavioural competencies as underlying all managerial work; however, two competency domains (managing human capital and managing decision-making processes) were shown by O*NET ratings as significantly more important than the other four (managing administration and control, managing strategy and innovation, managing logistics and technology, and managing the task environment).

Rubin and Dierdorff then cross-referenced these six behavioural competencies to MBA curricula designed to inculcate these competencies, and they found substantial misalignment. This misalignment predominately emerged from MBA courses that overemphasized competencies practising managers rated as less important for performing managerial work (e.g., managing administration and control), while underemphasizing those rated as most important (i.e., managing human capital and decision-making processes). Rubin and Dierdorff (2011) examined perceptions about this curricular misalignment and found that across diverse MBA stakeholders there is significant agreement regarding the need to improve student competencies related to managing human capital.

Incorporating large-scale survey data of business school stakeholders into their comprehensive review of curricula, Rynes and Bartunek (2013) recently concluded that five critical competencies should be taught across all MBA courses: 1) functional and quantitative skills; 2) human capital management including leadership and interpersonal skills; 3) decision-making and problem-solving; 4) ethics and corporate social responsibility; and 5) globalization. Rynes and Bartunek (2013: 211) summarized by remarking:

> There is fairly strong research consensus that, from the employers' point of view, the two areas most in need of curricular enhancement are leadership and management of human capital and decision-making or problem solving. Non-US employers also expect greater emphasis on global and cross-cultural competencies. From a broader societal perspective, there is also a need to enhance ethical, multi-stakeholder and CSR-related decision making capabilities.

Together these large-scale studies suggest that MBA courses currently dedicate the least amount of curricular focus to the areas that matter least to practising managers and that this misalignment with managerial work role requirements are in fact well known by every major stakeholder group associated with business schools. Given the amount of data available to appropriately guide curriculum reform, management scholars ought to apply their tools towards understanding and solving the complex political and institutional barriers that are impinging upon efforts to align the curriculum with the demands of managerial work.

Finally, despite the lengthy criticisms, it's worth observing that extensive research focused on students and external stakeholders shows general satisfaction with the MBA and management education in general. Prospective students see management education as a pathway to increased job opportunities, salary increases, and business knowledge and skills (GMAC, 2015b). Analyses of individual financial return on the

MBA as an educational investment shows strong results (Holtom and Inderrieden, 2007). Employers report that MBA graduates are generally well prepared to succeed in organizations. In a 2012 GMAC survey of over 1,000 companies, 79% of respondents report planning to hire MBA graduates (GMAC, 2012). As Dierdorff et al. (2013) point out, even society appears to benefit from MBA courses programmes, noting that 'to be prosperous, societies require well-functioning organizations' and as such benefits from increased knowledge and skills of MBA graduates.

Future Research

Future research should examine long-term value of various approaches to MBA, specialty master's, and BBA curricula, including the nano and micro credentials that are coming to market. Value here would be defined in terms of benefits for individuals (including satisfaction, self-efficacy, learning, subjective well-being, and career progression) and for the companies that hire them (including job and team performance). In future research, it is important to acknowledge and examine potential trade-offs between satisfaction, self-efficacy, and learning. More broadly, it would be useful to measure social as well as intellectual capital development. Social capital refers to the value contained in the relationships of an individual, team, or organization. Because peer-to-peer interaction may be limited in online environments, social capital may be more difficult to develop online than face-to-face (Brown and Van Buren, 2007). Similarly, changing students' values, beliefs, and world views may be more difficult in some learning settings than in others.

Changes in values and beliefs associated with different teaching approaches are currently understudied. Rynes and Brown (2011) noted that few studies in management education examine changes over time in these constructs, though it is clear that instructors see changing students' beliefs as part of their role (Moosmayer, 2012). One notable exception is Wang, Malhotra, and Murnighan (2011). In a series of three studies, they found that students taking an economics class kept more money in a money allocation task (as compared with those not taking an economics class), students majoring in economics (and those taking three or more economics classes) reported more positively feelings towards greed, and that students who read positive statements about greed led to more positive ratings of the morality of greed. They conclude that economics education is associated with positive attitudes towards greed.

THE FUTURE OF MANAGEMENT EDUCATION RESEARCH

The two topics covered above, online education and MBA curricula, are but a sample of the ongoing scholarship in management education, which is now thriving. New areas are forming and show promise for furthering understanding of management education.

By way of example, we highlight two areas that, in contrast to the domains reviewed above, are nascent.

Engagement and the Informal Curriculum

One new but exciting area deals with the extent to which management education can successfully occur across multiple contexts including the informal, out of classroom experience. Interest in student engagement has begun to grow as business schools attempt to understand more fully the connections between engagement and learning. Feldman (2012) defined student engagement as 'the amount of time, energy, enthusiasm students devote to acquiring new skills and knowledge, participating in professional self-development and extracurricular activities, and self-directing their job search' (263). One interesting conclusion emerging from this body of work suggest that counterintuitively, providing too many development choices for students may in fact decrease students' likelihood of further engagement.

Extending these ideas, recent work has borrowed from economics, notably the concept of the 'informal economy' to suggest that there exist an 'informal curriculum' that operates without prescription, policy, or recognition. Unlike classroom learning, engagement experiences are focused squarely on the student in terms of accountability. Stated more formally, 'the informal curriculum consists of activities provided by the school that lack one or both of the qualities that define the formal curriculum: They are not linked to formally stated goals, or they have no formal assessment' (Caza and Brower, 2015: 98). At times, the informal curriculum may in fact promote institutionally aligned activities such as the case when students promote ideas that support the values or mission of the school. For example, at Harvard Business School, a group of students, taking their cues from medical students, developed the 'MBA Oath' which consisted of a list of statements affirming collective values surrounding professionalism and ethical conduct. The faculty subsequently approved the oath and attempted to institutionalize it within the MBA formal curriculum. It is also possible for the informal or hidden curriculum to undermine institutions attempts to influence students' common experiences because lack of formality is associated with less information sharing and attention (Coff, Coff, and Eastvold, 2006).

Teaching with Problems

Problem-based learning has been around for many years, and has been shown to facilitate skill development (Dochy et al., 2003). The idea is that students should be challenged with authentic problems to encourage them to learn the knowledge necessary to solve the problems and simultaneously develop problem-solving and related skills, such as teamwork in the case of collaborative projects. This teaching approach has been offered, and extended, as a solution to the commodification and miniaturization of management education.

As noted by Waddock and Lozano (2013), holistic development of students requires creative approaches to teaching. They offer examples of classes that use problems to challenge students to use system thinking, reflect, and work in an interdependent and globalized world. Specifically, they examine a course at ESADE and another at Boston College. The ESADE course, entitled Vicens Vives after a famous Catalan historian, blends afternoon sessions, week-end long sessions, and diary reflection. The Boston College course, entitled Leadership for Change, blends all-day sessions, learning team meetings, and diary reflection. Both courses emphasize ongoing reflection, multiple bottom line orientations, and holistic conceptions of managing and leading. They differ in the types of projects that students pursue, as Vicens Vivens emphasizes personal projects and Leadership for Change encouarges work-based projects.

More research is needed on how to prepare students for these types of experiences, and whether these experiences add value for long-term student and organizational outcomes. In addition, as noted by Waddock and Lazano (2013), these courses are time-intensive for faculty and difficult for specialized, research-oriented faculty to teach. Research would be helpful on how to develop faculty interest in and skills for this type of teaching.

As research explores how to blend learning via classroom and technology-mediated environment, research should also explore how to blend learning via classroom and work-related activities. This type of embedding occurs in classes that have been labelled action learning, and offer ways for students to encounter real problems but also have the time to discuss and reflect on what they are learning.

Conclusion

One way to describe the changes in business schools has been as the swing of a pendulum between rigour and relevance. Business schools began as schools of commerce with faculties and curricula that reflected the needs of employers. Beginning with the Ford and Carnegie report of 1959, the pendulum began to swing away from relevance to rigour. Porter and McKibbon found business schools heavily dedicated to rigorous research and quantitative skill development in the classroom. Despite the report's calls for greater relevance with interdisciplinary research and teaching, movement by business schools has been slow. Today, however, the fruits of the labour are apparent. In fact, it might be worth asking whether the pendulum is in fact moving so fast that it will push too far away from rigour. The presence of nanodegrees and just-in-time learning, providing the innovation and curricular flexibility called for by Porter and McKibbon, are mixed blessings. The positives are the increased access and efficiency but the negatives are potential side-effects of emphasizing smaller and more concrete pieces of knowledge and skill. If we push management education into short, online experiences, do we contribute to increasing students' inability to think deeply, sustain their attention over time, and work collaboratively?

To escape the trap of the pendulum, an analogy laden with mechanistic and two-dimensional thinking, it would be helpful to consider how we can engage students more fully in management engagement and involve them in addressing real-world problems. There is not one best way to provide management education but taking these ideas into account will require integration of analytical and values-based, technical, and humanistic perspectives. And it will require even further investigation into the many possible ways to educate students about how to better manage other people and the organizations in which they work.

REFERENCES

AACSB International (2015). AACSB Business School Data Guide. Available at: <http://www.aacsb.edu/publications/datareports/data-guide> (accessed 29 July 2016).

ABS Academic Journal Guide (2015). Available at: <https://charteredabs.org/academic-journal-guide-2015/> (accessed 30 August 2016).

Alavi, M. (1994). 'Computer-mediated Collaborative Learning: An Empirical Evaluation'. *MIS Quarterly*, 18(2): 159–74.

Arbaugh, J. B. (2000). 'Virtual Classroom Characteristics and Student Satisfaction with Internet-based MBA Courses'. *Journal of Management Education*, 24: 32–54.

Arbaugh, J. B., Fornaciari, C. J., and Hwang, A. (2014). 'Development Patterns in Business and Management Education Research: Knowledge-based or Knower-based?'. *Academy of Management Proceedings*, 12321.

Armstrong, S. J. and Fukami, C. V. (2009). *The SAGE Handbook of Management, Learning, Education, and Development*. Thousand Oaks, CA: SAGE.

Atwater, J. B., Kannan, V. R., and Stephens, A. A. (2008). 'Cultivating Systemic Thinking in the Next Generation of Business Leaders'. *Academy of Management Learning & Education*, 7(1): 9–25.

Beatty, J. and Leigh, J. S. A. (2009). 'Taking Stock of Management Education: A Comparison of Three Management Education Journals'. *Journal of Management Education*, 34: 367–92.

Bell, M., Connerley, M., and Cocchiara, F. (2009). 'The Case for Mandatory Diversity Education'. *Academy of Management Learning & Education*, 8(4): 597–609.

Bidwell, A. (2014). 'Women More Likely to Graduate College, but Still Earn Less than Men'. U.S. News and World Report. 31 October. Available at: <http://www.usnews.com/news/blogs/data-mine/2014/10/31/women-more-likely-to-graduate-college-but-still-earn-less-than-men> (accessed 27 July 2016).

Bishop, J. L. and Verleger, M. A. (2013). 'The Flipped Classroom: A Survey of Research'. ASEE Annual Conference & Exposition, Atlanta, GA. Available at: <https://www.asee.org/public/conferences/20/papers/6219/view>.

Brown, K. G. and Charlier, S. D. (2013). 'An Integrative Model of e-learning Use: Leveraging Theory to Understand and Increase Usage'. *Human Resource Management Review*, 23: 37–49.

Brown, K. G. and Van Buren, M. (2007). 'Applying a Social Capital Perspective to Evaluation of Distance Training', in S. M. Fiore and E. Salas (eds.), *Toward a Science of Distributed Learning*. Washington, DC: American Psychological Association, 41–63.

Byrnes, K. (2015). 'Initial Trends in Enrollment and Completion of Massive Open Online Courses'. *The International Review of Research in Open and Distance Learning*, 15(1): 133–59.

Caza, A. and Brower, H. H. (2015). 'Mentioning the Unmentioned: An Interactive Interview about the Informal Management Curriculum'. *Academy of Management Learning & Education*, 14(1): 96–110.

Clark, R. E. (1984). 'Media Will Never Influence Learning'. *Educational Technology Research and Development*, 42: 21–9.

Coff, R. W., Coff, D., and Eastvold, R. (2006). 'The Knowledge Leveraging Paradox: How to Scale Up Without Making Knowledge Imitable'. *Academy of Management Review*, 31: 452–65.

Crouch, C. H. and Mazur, E. (2001). 'Peer Instruction: Ten Years of Experience and Results'. *American Journal of Physics*, 69: 970–7.

Damast, A. (2009). 'The Mini MBA's Big Appeal'. *Bloomberg Business*. Available at: <http://www.bloomberg.com/bschools/content/aug2009/bs20090817_409187.htm> (accessed 27 July 2016).

Damast, A. (2012). 'The Booming Market for Specialized Master's Degrees'. *Businessweek*. Available at: <http://www.businessweek.com/articles/2012-11-21/the-booming-market-for-specialized-masters-degrees> (accessed 27 July 2016).

Datar, S. M., Garvin, D. A., and Cullen, P. G. (2010). *Rethinking the MBA: Business Education at a Crossroads*. Boston, MA: Harvard Business Press.

Dierdorff, E. C., Nayden, D. J., Jain, D. C., and Jain, S. C. (2013). 'Ensuring and Enhancing Future Value'. In B. Holtom and E. Dierdorff (eds.), *Disrupt or be Disrupted: A Blueprint for Change in Management Education*. San Francisco, CA: Jossey-Bass, 21–56.

Dierdorff, E. C., Rubin, R. S., and Morgeson, F. P. (2009). 'The Milieu of Managerial Work: An Integrative Framework Linking Work Context to Role Requirements'. *Journal of Applied Psychology*, 94: 972–88.

Dochy, F., Segers, M., Van den Bossche, P., and Gijbels, D. (2003). 'Effects of Problem-based Learning: A Meta-analysis'. *Learning and Instruction*, 13: 533–68.

Feldman, D. C. (2012). 'Student Engagement: Selection, Management, and Outcomes', in B. Holtom and E. Dierdorff (eds.), *Disrupt or Be Disrupted: A Blueprint for Change in Management Education*. San Francisco, CA: Jossey-Bass: 259–96.

Ferraro, F., Pfeffer, J., and Sutton, R. I. (2005). 'Economics Language and Assumptions: How Theories Can Become Self-fulfilling.' *Academy of Management Review*, 30(1): 8-24.

Gellman, L. (2015). 'Business Schools are Fighting to Recruit Top Women'. *Wall Street Journal*, 6 May. Available at: <http://www.wsj.com/articles/why-business-schools-are-fighting-over-top-women-1430957422> (accessed 8 October, 2016).

Gentile, M. C. (2010). *Giving Voice to Values: How to Speak Your Mind When You Know What's Right*. New Haven, CT: Yale University Press.

Giacalone, R. A. (2007). 'Taking a Red Pill to Disempower Unethical Students: Creating Ethical Sentinels in Business Schools'. *Academy of Management Learning & Education*, 6: 534–42.

Giacolone, R. A. and Wargo, D. T. (2009). 'The Roots of the Global Financial Crisis are in our Business Schools'. *Journal of Business Ethics Education*, 6: 147–68.

Ghoshal, S. (2005). 'Bad Management Theories are Destroying Good Management Practices'. *Academy of Management Learning & Education*, 4: 75–91.

GMAC (2011). *Global Management Education Graduate Survey*. Available at: <http://www.gmac.com/~/media/Files/gmac/Research/curriculum-insight/2011GMAC_GMEGS_SR.pdf> (accessed 29 July 2016).

GMAC (2012). *Corporate Recruiters Survey*. Available at: <http://www.gmac.com/market-intelligence-and-research/research-library/employment-outlook/2012-corporate-recruiters-survey-survey-report.aspx> (accessed 29 July 2016).

GMAC (2015a). *Global Management Education Graduate Survey*. Available at: <http://www.gmac.com/~/media/Files/gmac/Research/curriculum-insight/2015-gmegs-survey-report-final-for-web.pdf> (accessed 29 July 2016).

GMAC (2015b). *mba.com Prospective Students Survey Report*. Available at: <http://www.gmac.com/market-intelligence-and-research/research-library/admissions-and-application-trends/2015-mbacom-prospective-students-survey-report.aspx> (accessed 29 July 2016).

GMAT Trends Tracker (2014). Available at: <http://www.gmac.com/market-intelligence-and-research/research-library/gmat-test-taker-data/gmat-trends-tracker-2014.aspx> (accessed 28 July 2016).

Holstein, W. J. (2013). 'The Multipolar MBA'. *Strategy+Business*. 21 January. Available at: <http://www.strategy-business.com/article/00164?gko=093cf> (accessed 27 July 2016).

Holtom, B. and Dierdorff, E. (eds.) (2013). *Disrupt or Be Disrupted: A Blueprint for Change in Management Education*. San Francisco, CA: Jossey-Bass.

Holtom, B. and Inderrieden, E. (2007). 'Investment Advice: Go for the MBA'. *BizEd*, 6(1): 36–40.

Holtom, B. and Porter, L. W. (2013). 'Introduction: The Change Imperative', in B. Holtom and E. Dierdorff (eds.), *Disrupt or Be Disrupted: A Blueprint for Change in Management Education*. San Francisco, CA: Jossey-Bass, 1–20.

IES (Institute for Education Sciences) (2015). Undergraduate Enrollment. Washington, DC: National Center for Education Statistics. Available at: <http://nces.ed.gov/programs/coe/indicator_cha.asp> (accessed 19 September 2015).

Jordan, K. (2015). 'Initial Trends in Enrolment and Completion of Massive Open Online Courses'. *The International Review of Research in Open and Distance Learning*, 15(1): 134–60.

Kay, R. H. and LeSage, A. (2009). 'Examining the Benefits and Challenges of Using Audience Response Systems: A Review of the Literature'. *Computers & Education*, 53: 819–27.

Khurana, R. (2007). *From Higher Aims to Hired Hands: The Social Transformation of American Business Schools and the Unfulfilled Promise of Management as a Profession*. Princeton, NJ: Princeton University Press.

Kirschner, P. A., Sweller, J., and Clark, R. E. (2006). 'Why Minimal Guidance During Instruction Does Not Work: An Analysis of the Failure of Constructivist, Discovery, Problem-based, Experiential, and Inquiry-based Teaching'. *Educational Psychologist*, 41: 75–86.

Leidner, D. E. and Jarvenpaa, S. L. (1995). 'The Use of Information Technology to Enhance Management School Education: A Theoretical View'. *MIS Quarterly*, 9(1): 265–91.

Leigh, J. and Beatty, J. E. (2008). 'But Where Can I Publish That? Understanding the Management Education Scholarship of Teaching and Learning Domain'. Paper presented at the *Annual Meeting of the Academy of Management*, Anaheim, CA, August.

March, J. G. and Sutton, R. I. (1997). 'Organizational Performance as a Dependent Variable'. *Organizational Science*, 8(6): 698–706.

Mintzberg, H. (2004). *Managers, not MBAs: A Hard Look at the Soft Practice of Managing and Management Development*. San Francisco, CA: Berrett-Koehler Publishers.

Moosmayer, D. (2012). 'A Model of Management Academics' Intentions to Influence Values'. *Academy of Management Learning & Education*, 12(2): 155–73.

Mwasalwiba, E. S. (2010). 'Entrepreneurship Education: A Review of its Objectives, Teaching Methods, and Impact Indicators'. *Education + Training*, 52: 20–47.

Navarro, P. (2008). 'The MBA Core Curricula of Top-ranked U.S. Business Schools: A Study in Failure?'. *Academy of Management Learning & Education*, 7(1): 108–23.

Novak, M. (2012). Predictions for Educational TV in the 1930s. *Smithsonian.com*. Available at: <http://www.smithsonianmag.com/history/predictions-for-educational-tv-in-the-1930s-107574983/?no-ist> (accessed 19 September 2015).

O'Connor, S. (2013). 'The Responsibility of Business Schools in Training Ethical Leaders'. *Forbes*, 15 May. Available at: <http://www.forbes.com/sites/shawnoconnor/2013/05/15/the-responsibility-of-business-schools-in-training-ethical-leaders-2 (accessed 27 July 2016).

Park, B., Moreno, R., Seufert, T., and Brunken, R. (2011). 'Does Cognitive Load Moderate the Seductive Details Effect? A Multimedia Study'. *Computers in Human Behavior*, 27: 5–10.

Pfeffer, J. and Fong, C. T. (2002). 'The End of Business Schools? Less Success than Meets the Eye'. *Academy of Management Learning & Education*, 1: 78–94.

Piccoli, G., Ahmad, R., and Ives, B. (2001). 'Web-based Virtual Learning Environments: A Research Framework and a Preliminary Assessment of Effectiveness in Basic IT Skills Training'. *MIS Quarterly*, 25(4): 401–26.

Pittaway, L. and Cope, J. (2007). 'Entrepreneurship Education: A Systematic Review of the Evidence'. *International Small Business Journal*, 25: 479–510.

Plumer, B. (2009). 'First, Aill all the MBAs'. *UTNE Reader*, July–August. Available at: <http://www.utne.com/politics/reform-mbas-business-schools-economic-crisis.aspx#axzz3C40BIvWf> (accessed 27 July 2016).

Polodny, J. M. (2009). 'Are Business Schools to Blame?' *HBR Blog Network*, 30 March. Available at: <http://blogs.hbr.org/2009/03/are-business-schools-to-blame> (accessed 27 July 2016).

Porter, L. W. and McKibbin, L. E. (1988). *Management education and development: Drift or Thrust into the 21st Century*. New York: McGraw-Hill.

Ratcliffe, R. (2015). 'University Protests Around the World: The Fights Against Commercialization'. *The Guardian*, 25 March. Available at: <http://www.theguardian.com/higher-education-network/2015/mar/25/university-protests-around-the-world-a-fight-against-commercialisation> (accessed 27 July 2016).

Rousseau, D. M. and McCarthy, S. (2007). 'Educating Managers from an Evidence-based Perspective'. *Academy of Management Learning & Education*, 6: 84–101.

Rubin, R. S. and Dierdorff, E. C. (2009). 'How Relevant is the MBA? Assessing the Alignment of Required Curricula and Required Management Competencies'. *Academy of Management Learning & Education*, 8: 208–24.

Rubin, R. S. and Dierdorff, E. C. (2011). 'On the Road to Abilene: Time to Manage Agreement about MBA Curricular Relevance'. *Academy of Management Learning & Education*, 10: 148–61.

Rubin, R. S. and Dierdorff, E. C. (2013). 'Building a Better MBA: From a Decade of Critique Toward a Decennium of Creation'. *Academy of Management Learning & Education* 12: 125–41.

Rubin, R. S. and Morgeson, F. P. (2013). 'Reclaiming Quality in Graduate Management Education', in B. Holtom and E. Dierdorff (eds.), *Disrupt or Be Disrupted: A Blueprint for Change in Management Education*. San Francisco, CA: Jossey-Bass: 297-345.

Rynes, S. L. and Bartunek, J. M. (2013). 'Curriculum Matters: Toward a More Holistic Graduate Management Education', in B. Holtom and E. Dierdorff (eds.), *Disrupt or Be Disrupted: A Blueprint for Change in Management Education*. San Francisco, CA: Jossey-Bass: 179–218.

Rynes, S. L. and Brown, K. G. (2011). 'Where Are We in the 'Long March to Legitimacy?' Assessing the Legitimacy of Scholarship in Management Learning and Education'. *Academy of Management Learning & Education*, 10: 561–82.

Segev, E., Raveh, A., and Farjoun, M. (1999). 'Conceptual Maps of the Leading MBA Programs in the United States: Core Courses, Concentration Areas, and the Rankings of the School'. *Strategic Management Journal*, 20(6): 549–65.

Sheehy, K. (2013). 'Undergrads Around the World Face Student Loan Debt'. *US News & World Report*, 13 November. Available at: <http://www.usnews.com/education/best-global-universities/articles/2013/11/13/undergrads-around-the-world-face-student-loan-debt> (accessed 27 July 2016).

Sitzmann, T., Brown, K. G., Casper, W. J., Zimmerman, R., and Polliard, C. (2008). 'A Meta-analysis of the Nomological Network of Trainee Reactions'. *Journal of Applied Psychology*, 93: 280–95.

Sitzmann, T., Ely, K., Brown, K. G., and Bauer, K. N. (2010). 'Self-assessment of Knowledge: a Cognitive Learning or Affective Measure?'. *Academy of Management Learning & Education*, 9: 169–91.

Svoboda, S. (2015). 'Why Do So Many Chinese Students Choose US Universities?' BBC News, 2 June. Available at: <http://www.bbc.com/news/business-32969291> (accessed 19 September 2015).

Tushman, M. L., O'Reilly, C., Fenollosa, A., Kleinbaum, A. M., and McGrath, D. (2007). 'Relevance and Rigor: Executive Education as a Lever for Shaping Practice and Research'. *Academy of Management Learning & Education*, 6(3): 345-62.

Trank, C. Q. and Rynes, S. L. (2003). 'Who Moved Our Cheese? Reclaiming Professionalism in Business Education'. *Academy of Management Learning & Education*, 2(2): 189–205.

US News & World Reports (2015). 'University of Phoenix'. Available at: <http://www.usnews.com/education/online-education/university-of-phoenix-online-campus-209885/bachelors> (accessed 19 September 2015).

Waddock, S. and Lozano, J. M. (2013). 'Developing More Holistic Management Education: Lessons Learned from Two Programs'. *Academy of Management Learning & Education*, 12(2): 265–84.

Wang, L., Malhotra, D., and Murnighan, J. K. (2011). 'Economics Education and Greed'. *Academy of Management Learning & Education*, 10: 643–60.

Wankel, C. and DeFillipi, R. (eds.) (2006). *New Visions of Graduate Management Education*. Greenwich, CT: Information Age Publishers.

Wankel, C. and Stachowicz-Stanusch, A. (eds.) (2011). *Management Education for Integrity: Ethically Educating Tomorrow's Business Leaders*. Bradford: Emerald Group Publishing.

Wilson, R. M. S. (ed.) (2014). *Accounting Education Research: Prize-Winning Contributions*. New York: Routledge.

Yun, K. A. and Lojo, M. (2010). 'The Effects of Clickers on Student Learning'. *Academic Exchange Quarterly*, 14(1). Available at: <http://rapidintellect.com/AEQweb/cho4563lo.htm> (accessed 28 July 2016).

Zenter, A. (2008). 'Online Sales, Internet Use, File Sharing, and the Decline of Retail Music Specialty Stores'. *Information Economics and Policy*, 20(3): 288–300.

CHAPTER 23

MANAGEMENT AS AN ACADEMIC DISCIPLINE?

DAMIAN O'DOHERTY AND CHRISTIAN DE COCK

INTERRUPTED BEGINNINGS

WHAT remains to be said about 'management as an academic discipline'? And where are we to begin? We could begin with Whitley's (1984) oft-cited summary of the state of management research published in the 20th anniversary issue of the *Journal of Management Studies*. Looking back to the establishment in the USA of *The Institute of Management Sciences* and its major journal *Management Science*, Whitley concluded that the goal of an integrated, coherent, and relevant 'science of management' seemed, if anything, further away than it did in those halcyon 1950s, whilst duly noting an exponential growth of journals, publications, and management academics over those three decades. He also commented on the sense of disillusionment with what had been achieved whilst questioning the intellectual respectability of dominant modes of reasoning in business and management studies. In short, he saw a field 'characterized by fragmentation, proliferation of diffuse and unconnected intellectual standards, goals, techniques and multiple interpretations of research results' (Whitley, 1984: 342).

The next thirty years offer an exemplary case study of *plus ça change*—an irony given the simultaneous desire to give management theory and research an effective presence as a discipline (De Cock and Jeanes, 2006). Riven by endless debates on the respective merits of integration and solidification (e.g. Pfeffer, 1993; Van de Ven, 1999) versus preserving distinctive research 'paradigms' (e.g. Van Maanen, 1995; Westwood and Clegg, 2003), and perennial anxieties about overcoming the conflicting demands of academic rigour and practical relevance to contemporary management practices (e.g. Hambrick, 1994; Hodgkinson and Rousseau, 2009), management studies appears to be very much still in search of discipline. A recent editorial in the *Academy of Management Review* offered yet one more 'summing up' of management theory development and reiterated the by now well-rehearsed theme that 'current management theories have failed to keep pace with changes in the size, complexity, and influence of modern organizations' (Suddaby, Hardy, and Huy, 2011: 237). The authors went on to suggest that 'as a discipline, we have failed to develop our own theories', as 'most of the theories used by contemporary management researchers were formulated several decades ago, largely in the 1960s and 1970s' (236). Suddaby and his colleagues concluded with a rallying call effectively exhorting management scholars to develop what they call 'indigenous theories'. Holt and den Hond (2013: 1590), in their first editorial of the European based *Organization Studies*, interpreted this as a call for the study of management 'to be a discipline, to become a discipline, or to finally accept the consequences of aspiring to be one'.

All this suggests that it is impossible to begin with a grandstand view of 'the discipline' as would be typical of a concluding chapter in a volume such as this. Inexorably, such a beginning would treat disciplinary debates as a progressive standing upon the shoulders of giants or the passing on of the intellectual baton. And yet, as in some never-ending athletics relay race, the finishing line of a proudly established 'management discipline' remains forever out of reach. If this is something we want to question we will therefore need to attempt something different in our chapter, guided by Walter Benjamin's injunction to practice a form of reading and writing that 'brushes history against the grain' (Benjamin, 1999: 257—Thesis VII). Practically this means we aim to render 'strange' that which has become too familiar and to produce effects by showing things that management scholars may realize they have ignored in the rather peculiar body of literature and practices that makes up 'management studies'. This 'producing of effects' means that we adopt a different style or tone of writing from the one with which most readers will be familiar as our chapter grapples with the reading of, and writing about, management *as a discipline haunted by aporia and incoherence*. How to grasp and work with this aporia forms the burden of this chapter. At times irreverent and ill-disciplined, we write on the understanding that discipline is the problem that management leaves as its legacy, but we also want to retain the importance of this legacy so that we can hold open the possibility of its invention, re-invention, displacement, or discarding. Of course this question and the performative tensions the question introduces (i.e. from *where* and *how* does one write about the question of discipline?) into writing is forgotten by most management studies, but the implications of this forgetting define precisely the nihilistic predicaments in which contemporary management finds itself. The chapter invites the reader to participate in a movement of enquiry that helps avoid an unwitting managerialization of academic labour, a movement which takes us back into the necessity of a genealogical attention to our disciplinary origins—discipline thought at the intersection of memory and history, the public and the private. This studied form of enquiry and writing works to create a space from which we might extricate our implication in dominant systems of power/knowledge and better to prepare for the much heralded end(s) of man (Derrida, 1969) for which the coming ecological disaster often summarized as 'the time of the Anthropocene' (Crutzen and Stoermer, 2000) can serve as a marker. In proceeding thus we risk contradiction of course, and so we attempt to write in a way that will compel reading (as opposed to absorption)—perhaps even a 'violent reading' in Blum's

(1973) terms—and will appeal to readers who want to advance towards new questions, as opposed to those who demand simplistic conclusions that reassure and placate.

We have structured this chapter into four parts. Bookending the two central sections on 'histories' and 'critical history and 'post-disciplinarity'' we have composed two sections—'beginnings' and 'endings', where we play rather irreverently with the very notion of 'discipline': they are a deliberate attempt to stay clear of the traditional 'introduction' and 'conclusion' which tend to offer respectively a false impression of solid ground from where to start or arrive. In this spirit 'New beginnings' attempts to re-introduce the paper. In the second section we turn to the standard histories of 'management' and address their claims to provide tangible foundations and delimitations of the subject. Yet, through a close reading, we find a predominantly historicist method (reading the past through the categories of the present) deployed in these histories, which means the research tends to reduce to tautology, marked by an absence of coherence and discipline. In the third section we turn to the genealogical mode of investigation of Foucault who offers an exemplary way out of these dilemmas whilst also showing the importance of a vigilant and permanent questioning of discipline. He teaches us that only an inventive transgression will generate the kind of post-disciplinary method of study that permits us to take the measure of 'management as a discipline'.

(New Beginnings)

So if beginnings and endings are always somewhat arbitrary, why not begin with a single sentence found on the very first page of the inaugural issue of the *Journal of Management Studies*, which itself points to a foundational human beginning: 'Ever since Adam first appraised Eve human beings have been appraising one another' (Rowe, 1964: 1)? It is a sentence that embodies an odd mixture of grandiosity and ambition—if not hubris—but also a restricted and narrow self-regarding reflexivity. Rowe's paper offers an attempt to appraise appraisals, or more strictly, narrates a report on an attempt to appraise appraisals, in a manner that might also resemble the formal experimentation or ludic-play associated with those most dangerous scholars of discipline: the French literary movement known as *Oulip* (*Ouvroir de littérature potentielle*, roughly translated as 'workshop of potential literature'—Becker, 2012). That the formal academic study of management could begin with such a complex tension between self-generating amplification and self-defeating paradox has not attracted the attention it deserves, no doubt—and here we risk ill-founded speculation and a lack of discipline—because the attempt to look straight into the eyes of a founding *aporia* risks blindness. To *begin* with appraisals might also attract those persuaded by dynamics of displacement and psycho-analytical projection to affirm a certain playing out of anxiety and insecurity. Not unsurprisingly then, by the time of the launch of the *British Journal of Management* in 1990 it seemed as if the community had given up any pretence at discipline, the opening editorial declaring the intentions of the journal to provide 'an outlet for *all types of research* and scholarship on *managerially oriented* themes, [that] will especially welcome contributions of a multi-disciplinary or inter-disciplinary nature' (Otley, 1990: 1—emphasis added). What is *not* managerially oriented is left undefined and the possibility of a supra-disciplinary position of appraisal and judgement seems implied even though the exact contours and content of this additional position are left in abeyance. Beginning in confusion and incoherence may not appear to bode well for the subject of management studies and its disciplinary ambition.

Such beginnings may help explain the paradox evident in the treatment of 'discipline' in popular management texts, particularly in those written to introduce and prepare students for employment. On the one hand a survey of recent texts would suggest that discipline is *not* popular at the moment: long gone are the days of thrift, self-discipline, and abstinence essential to the protestant work ethic and the spirit of capitalism as identified by Weber. The writing of Urwick, Fayol, and Taylor—with its militarized language of bureaucracy, spans of control, staff and line, reporting protocols, and office procedures—has been replaced with a fascination for 'thriving on chaos', informality and post-bureaucratic forms of organization, where management should learn how to 'first, break all the rules' (Buckingham and Coffman, 1999). Discipline seems to have been replaced by intoxication with all things creative, thinking outside the box, knowledge leadership, emotional intelligence, and—doing the rounds in the press at the moment—the so-called 'talent pipeline'. It is remarkable how the most popular student textbooks in management shy clear of discipline with an almost embarrassed silence. In Mullins (2013) for example, there is no chapter dealing specifically with discipline, only sporadic and arbitrary references to its use in management theory and practice. Huczynski and Buchanan (2013) provide even less space for the subject. And yet, on the other hand, discipline appears as an omniscient and ever-present term of reference in both Mullins and Huczynski and Buchanan. References to discipline multiply and proliferate as it appears in a diverse and motley range of subjects including pre-modern forms of management practices, more modern human resource policies and procedures, industrial relations disciplinary and grievance procedures, labour discipline, industrial discipline, work discipline, self-discipline, and the academic disciplines from which the hybrid subject of organizational behaviour is forged. Discipline would appear to be nothing if it is not a multiplicity of conceptual promiscuity and ill-discipline!

In what follows we are also attentive to the fact that despite these difficulties, discipline may be on the verge of a return, certainly when one broadens the scope to include business and management outside the boundaries of the US–UK axis of influence. If the rise of Japan stimulated the broadening of the business and management studies curriculum in the USA during the 1980s to include culture, anthropology, and an attention to religion and spirituality in business (Clegg, 2014), then the reassertion of a post-isolationist US expansionism might explain the reappearance of discipline as a more self-conscious subject of attention in Covey's (2013) hugely popular text. Written with a commitment to apostolic forms of Christianity, Covey asserts that 'Management is discipline', and he repeats this formula throughout his text, coupled with a constant reference to the importance of character and self-discipline. It is unfortunately a narrow and restrictive reading. For Covey discipline essentially 'derives from *disciple*—disciple to a philosophy, disciple to a set of principles, disciple to a set of values, disciple to an overriding purpose, to a superordinate goal or a person who represents that goal' (157, emphasis added). If recent textbooks in management are unable to provide much clarity, telling us that discipline is both everywhere and nowhere, perhaps a turn to the historians is required.

Histories: Towards the Inter-zone?

In search of the origins of management we might expect historians to help define the practice and discipline of management; however, this is rarely the case. Pollard's (1965) *The Genesis of Modern Management* is widely regarded as a seminal publication that shows how management is a recent invention emerging only after the industrial revolution in the UK. One of his guiding preoccupations is that better management could have avoided some of the worst social and psychological consequences that accompanied rapid industrialization over the period 1780–1830. In many ways it is a thesis written as an apologia for greater management expertise, but it becomes evident that, for Pollard, management is understood in the most general of terms, covering a range of particularities and differences whilst also extending into public policy and government regulation. In so doing, Pollard extends the scope of 'management' beyond any neatly defined contours and content. Management is identified, inter alia, as an output or outcome of particular political institutions (policy), a stratum of organizational administration, a form of workplace supervision in craft and manufacturing industries, a diffuse but immanent force that manages the economy, and a form of what we might call 'governmentality', namely those practices through which day-to-day party politics is conducted. As a consequence of this prolixity, it becomes difficult to identify something recognizably 'disciplined' in management. In contrast to Pollard, Chandler (1977) is more focused on what he calls the 'visible hand' of management and administration in large organizations which he charts through the so-called second industrial revolution of large capital intensive industries that helped develop the large M-form structure of organization. Yet, once again, distributed across this complex and sprawling form of organization, management designates the work of coordination and control conducted at the corporate level and more mundane operational and supervisory practices exercised in workshops and on 'shopfloors'. Historiological and ideological differences in the practice of historical scholarship further complicate the issue of definition, with management being understood by some as mere agents of capital, whereas for others management designates a novel and relatively autonomous domain of activity forced to mediate and reconcile the contradictory or antagonistic relation between capital and labour (Marglin, 1974; Littler, 1982).

The prodigious scholarship of John Child (1969) identified the emergence of a distinctively twentieth century British 'management movement', in what has now become a standard reference for studies of British Management: *British Management Thought—A Critical Analysis*. Child finds the strong influence of Quaker inspired businesses in the formation of something recognizably 'disciplined' in management thinking and practice. Sir William Mather, Joseph and Seebohm Rowntree, Charles Renold, and Edward Cadbury are considered the pioneers and early intellectuals that forged a set of management principles based on a mixture of paternalism, welfare provision, human relations, liberal-pluralist industrial democracy, and an ethic of 'public service'. However, throughout his study Child is unable to really acknowledge the internal contradictions of this Quaker 'inspired movement'. The commitment to duty and public service, for example, alongside the championing of private profit and the freedom of the entrepreneur means that 'the foundations' are far from coherent or secure. Nor is there great emphasis placed on the disjunction between what was written and said in public, through trade journals and other commercial publications, and what might have been going on in practice in British factories and industries in the early twentieth-century. It has been left to other historians of Victorian and early twentieth-century industry, for example, to chart the violence and degradation, the persistence of slavery and 'child-labour' associated with the management of workers in many industries (Branson and Heinemann, 1971). From the brutal gang master on the dock (Morrison, 1984) to the scourge of miner's lung (Bloor, 2000), working conditions were often violent and dangerous and management an arbitrary physical force of authority and intimidation.

A similar incoherence is evident in Wilson and Thomson's (2006) more recent history of the making of modern management that mixes elements from Williamson's transaction cost economics, Chandler's history of American management, Fligstein and 'environmental control', and schematic 'force-field diagrams' depicting driving forces that promote management and restraining forces that retard the advance of management as a professional expertise. It is perhaps no surprise that with such an eclectic range of influences Wilson and Thomson produce something that resembles the very subject matter of their study: the lack of anything resembling a coherent body of knowledge or practice. Indeed, they rapidly descend into circularity and tautology. A careful reading of their force-field diagrams reveals that the very same factors that are identified as 'driving forces' are also 'restraining forces'. At various points in their thesis they resort to the view that management is located *within* organization, or within a wider context that shapes and influences activities and behaviours, and thereby setting up the familiar sociological dualism that pits structural constraints as something that inhibits the formation of modern management and advanced 'managerial capitalism'. At the same time, however, management as a movement is described as a context-shaping activity itself. In explaining the relative success of American business between 1890 and 1918, for example, Wilson and Thomson conclude that 'the vast and relatively affluent domestic market provided the stimuli for these changes, as well as the reform of competition law in 1890' (88). Where did this affluent market come from if not by management design? Is not a large proportion of this growing domestic market made up of managers who are of course simultaneously consumers? Other driving forces they identify include: educational institutions, financial institutions, physical infrastructure, industrial structure, market structure, product market competition, organizational strategy and theory, orientation to change, and managerial techniques. This miscellany offers a veritable rival for Borges' famous entry on animals in his imaginary encyclopaedia![1] The circularity and tautology could not be clearer. In an effort to explain the rise of management as a modern practice that embraces sophisticated methodologies and practices, Wilson and Thomson tell us that managerial techniques explain ... well, managerial techniques! Essentially it is the large, scale vertically integrated form of business that is prioritized as the master explanation for the rise of management, but the form of business—whether S-form, U-form, or M-form—is precisely the outcome, partly, of managerial activity. This suggests, of course that we have to go beyond and outside the very historicized terms of 'business and management' in order to explain the rise (or not) of management. Yet Wilson and Thomson, like Chandler and other mainstream historians of the discipline, are unwilling to consider the role of wider political economy, empire, slavery, genocide, and so on.

Remarkably there is little attention devoted to the practices of management in either Child or Wilson and Thomson. At the very heart of their project is the study of management, but even after a careful reading of these texts the student keen to learn something more about *the practices* of management will be none the wiser. What is it then that managers do? Pollard (1965) shows that management was practised and the title of 'manager' deployed and used prior to the efforts to codify or systematize practices into a set of principles or rigorous body of knowledge that might form the basis for a self-conscious managerial 'discipline'. But it is Dalton's (1959) *Men Who Manage* and Mintzberg's (1973) *The Nature of Managerial Work* that are often credited as the pioneering studies of day-to-day practices and activities of managers. In the memorable summary of Mintzberg, managers 'were seldom able or willing to spend much time on any one issue in any one session' (33). Instead, their activities were fragmented and often incoherent, characterized by randomness and trivia and treated with episodic attention span, marked by constant interruption and the sense of incompletion and waste. Managers were also constantly assessing what it was that needed their attention, what was significant or insignificant, and what the likely ramifications and implications were of actions and decisions taken on the hoof or improvised for the purposes of moving onto the next interruption. At one time, management might have worked in an office, with the constant to-and-fro of people seeking entrance, telephones ringing, memos arriving, the humming of air-conditioning systems, the irritating flickering of the fluorescent lights, and the unpredictable wobble of a loose wheel never fixed on the executive desk chair.

---

[1] In the essay *The Analytical Language of John Wilkins* Borges refers to a 'certain Chinese encyclopaedia entitled *Celestial Emporium of Benevolent Knowledge*': 'In its remote pages it is written that the animals are divided into (a) belonging to the Emperor, (b) embalmed, (c) trained, (d) suckling pigs, (e) sirens, (f) fabulous, (g) stray dogs, (h) included in this classification, (i) trembling as if they were mad, (j) innumerable, (k) drawn with a very camelhair brush, (l) others, (m) which have just broken the pitcher, (n) which resemble flies from a distance' (Borges, 1952/1973: 103). Borges' excerpt from this fictive Chinese encyclopaedia is a parody that puts into question the very intellectual system it is meant to exemplify (cf. De Cock, 2000: 602).

Today, in the office-less paper-less organization, we might expect that 'managers' still fail to observe timetables and schedules, but added to the fragmentation observed by Mintzberg, the manager today is increasingly mobile and in transit, responding to email on the go, feeding twitter accounts and browsing various other social media sites whilst existing in a dimension of being defined by disorientation and jet-lag in a veritable form of 'non-place' (Augé, 1995) or 'the interzone' (Burrell, 1997).

Critical History and Post-Disciplinarity

> There is no way of telling what may yet become part of history. Perhaps the past is still essentially undiscovered! So many retroactive forces are still needed! (Nietzsche, 1887/1974: 104/#34)

One of the most significant bodies of research to have taken management as a discipline seriously is the work of those allied to industrial relations and labour process study. Where attention is focused on the policies and practices of management, management is seen as a bit part player of more extended systems and institutional ordering—as was enshrined in the UK through collective bargaining and the so-called liberal-pluralist consensus (Clegg, 1979). Here, discipline forms an explicit part of management practice, as in the management of grievance and disciplinary procedures: periodically, labour needs to be *disciplined*. Such a focus, however, has a tendency to restrict its analysis to a limited and circumscribed understanding of discipline, and can result in little more than a detailed chronicle of disciplinary procedures designed to regulate the employment relation. In more radical terms, discrete practices of management are understood to form part of a logic of 'managerialization' that has been forged out of an increasing expropriation of areas of the employment relation previously 'regulated' or managed through trade unions or local craft based labour practices. A more generous treatment of discipline is also evident in variants of Marxist theses where 'discipline' is understood to form part of a dialectic of struggle between capital and labour (see Hyman, 1989), but one tempered by contradiction and unpredictability because of the countervailing pressures in the dynamics of employment relations that compel management to seek forms of commitment beyond disciplinary compliance (Edwards and Whitston, 1989; Edwards, 2005). Labour process study has perhaps done most to advance the claims that management represents a dangerous ideological force in work organizations that works on behalf of capital to control, subordinate, and degrade labour. If Braverman's (1974) *Labour and Monopoly Capital* helped promote a strawman of management, the industry of papers and edited collections that followed in its wake certainly rectified any lack of theoretical and empirical sensitivity (see Knights and Willmott, 1990; Thompson and Smith, 2010).

Beyond Marxism and critical theory, the introduction of the work of Michel Foucault to the study of management and the labour process has been of momentous import in opening up new ways of thinking about the discipline of management. Early advocates of Foucault tended to focus on his major study of the rise of the modern prison in *Discipline and Punish* which offered a fundamentally different and more expansive understanding of discipline than typical in industrial sociology (Foucault, 1979). Many took the 'fruits' of this study, however, in ways that did little more than apply a different set of metaphors and concepts to what remained a very traditional understanding of management and the labour process (Sewell and Wilkinson, 1992). Here management was understood to be driven by the overwhelming preoccupation with control, seeking forms of work and organizational design that 'deskilled' labour, and breaking jobs down into more standardized and repetitive tasks that were then also made more amenable to inspection and 'surveillance'—a key motif in emerging Foucauldian studies of the workplace (see also Knights, 1990; McKinlay and Starkey, 1998). Many of course wondered what this added to the work of people like Goffman (1959), berating the Foucault-turn for its failure to acknowledge the importance of objective material conditions and the political economy of 'structural' features of work organization that constrained what action might be possible at the micro- or meso-level of management and organization (Edwards, 1990; Thompson, 1990). This is a gross mis-understanding of Foucault and the implications that follow from a careful study of his work (Knights and Vurdubakis, 1994; Knights, 2002).

A first reading of *Discipline and Punish* certainly gives the impression that what Foucault was interested in was a detailed genealogy of emerging modern disciplinary practices as they became evident in the form of the prison. Considerable analysis was made of the 'panopticon', the all-seeing but occluded central tower with lines of sight down the main spokes of the aisles of prison cells. More sophisticated versions of labour process study saw that something more was going on in the book and picked up on the link between modern disciplinary practices and what Foucault had studied from Nietzsche, namely the birth of the modern human subject (Knights and Vurdubakis, 1994). Foucault was not interested per se in an empirical study or documentation of prison life or the practices of managing a prison population. In many ways the prison operates as a metaphor for Foucault's thesis, a theatrical *mise-en-scène*, and a concept that opens up a field of forces that converge and diverge around its central motif to make more tangible the complex history that explains the emergence of modern subjectivity. In Bentham's studies of the prison Foucault discovers something like the logic of modernity made manifest in an architectural 'blueprint' and it is obvious to him that this was never realized in its idealized form. Instead of any simple empirical claim, he deploys the prison partly as *dramatis personae* to distil and illustrate what were wider changes to the way in which societies operated. Indeed, it is the birth of the modern nation-state, allied to the emergence of the modern social sciences, which is the dominant target of Foucault's historical research into discipline. His preoccupations are not with whatever might be made empirically of any particular prison or workplace.

Foucault is preoccupied with the task of writing *a history of the present*; in other words, he reconstructs a history of that which is present but largely 'unknown', or in some ways mundane or taken for granted—sexuality, schizophrenia, the classroom, for example—and in writing this history encourages his readership to see the contingency of the categories and arrangements in which we find ourselves, and the possibility that things could be different.[2] This is the critical, 'deconstructive' history that Foucault learns to practise after his reading of Nietzsche. To see a 'transversal' relation across these domains, to uncover an underlying 'episteme' of knowledge that organizes our thinking but which lies 'between' that which we can identify in the terms of an epistemology or ontology, or in his later work, to trace the 'genealogy' of an idea, is to show that what we cherish as our most noble truths or morals finds its 'origin' dispersed in a more contested and uncertain dimension of subjectification, not easily appropriated by knowledge or experience. Hence, the practice of history is a practice of freedom that compels one to excavate the disciplinary practices that have made us who we are and thereby 'enables one to get free of oneself' and 'to know how and to what extent it might be possible to think differently' (Foucault, 1992: 8–9). In doing so Foucault invites us to think how the arbitrary so quickly and easily becomes the rule. This means that all knowledge is dangerous, and if all knowledge is perpetuated through practices—what he calls knowledge-practices—then we are all co-implicated in the unfolding of arbitrary 'logics' for which we have very little understanding of the likely 'systemic' outcomes. For example, we can never be certain that we might not become implicated in practices which may later be condemned as abusive, sexist, or misogynist. In this way he warned us to be wary of the seemingly innocuous and, thereby, helped invent new *objects* of political critique by making political that which had hitherto not been understood as a matter of political controversy.

To be able to do this meant that Foucault had to step outside the disciplinary boundaries of his own intellectual training. His inter- or post-disciplinary status is often the cause of considerable controversy as scholars try to establish whether he was, for example, a historian or a philosopher (Megill, 1987; O'Farrell, 1989). The methods of Foucault's texts were also not explicit, except when institutional and collegiate pressures forced him to publish clarification (Foucault, 1972). What he was up to in *Discipline and Punish* was the exercise of a new form of history, a method he had devised through a careful reading of Nietzsche on genealogy. As Deleuze (1988: 24) wrote, Foucault never worried or had time to explain his methods; he just got on with things and did his historical studies where 'analysis and illustration go hand in hand'. This form of study and writing allowed Foucault to invent effectively a new topology of organization, one where power can be studied in the form of strategies and practices

---

[2] Foucault (1970) starts the preface to his *Les Mots et Les Choses* (*The Order of Things*) with a direct reference to the passage from Borges' fictive Chinese encyclopaedia we quoted earlier in order to emphasize the contingency of any categorization and arrangement: 'This book first arose out of a passage in Borges, out of the laughter that shattered, as I read the passage, all the familiar landmarks of my thought—our thought, the thought that bears the stamp of our age and our geography—breaking up all the ordered surfaces and all the planes with which we are accustomed to tame the wild profusion of existing things…'

not yet organized or consolidated into established forms of property or state power, and prior to the separation of subject and object. This opened up a whole new terrain for historical research and encouraged scholarship to study practices that are simultaneously subject and object-making. In the images of prisoners in cells, bowing down in apparent supplication to the omniscient system of surveillance and control, Foucault also has in mind the hive of workers who man the modern bureaucratization of knowledge, as embodied, for example, in the university. Hence, it is *we* who are disciplined and punished, co-implicated in the formation of the modern nation-state, a form of social organization which is itself soon to be erased under pressure from its internal contradictions and upon which these knowledge practices have been built (Foucault, 1970). Following some of Foucault's work, Readings (1996: 169) already sees the university as a ruined institution, one that has lost its historical *raison d'être* and where gains in critical freedom are being achieved in direct proportion to the reduction in their general social significance. He thus exhorts us to think 'what it means to dwell in those ruins without recourse to romantic nostalgia'.

The scope and scale of this kind of thinking and research practice go beyond any of the customary ambitions of business and management history, industrial relations, or labour process study. For Foucault, we are 'disciplined' by that which is apparently the most innocent and mundane, by that which is in front of our very own eyes, but which nonetheless forms part of an extended chain of practices with far-reaching consequences. And here resides a clue to how, as knowledge workers, we are ensnared in power relations, participating in the production and reproduction of power and inequality, perhaps unbeknownst to ourselves. Power cannot be adequately studied as something which resides in the remote heights of sovereignty, 'the macro', objective laws of political economy, or the machinations of a military-industrial complex supported by the rationales of bourgeois legal practice, all decipherable according to a kind of 'critical realist' analysis. It is not convincing to understand power as something under which we labour, forming an immense structure of oppression and domination. Instead, we might better treat power as something operating more immanently which circulates in complex relays through lateral networks that support a disparate set of 'microphysical' practices—even those most minute and perhaps obvious or apparently trivial elements of the everyday. This means that Foucault might invite us to think about the genealogy of our own citational practices as academics, and how academic authority is achieved through certain rituals and rites of passage (Czarniawska, 1998). He would ask how and why we even come to contemplate writing about management as an academic discipline. We have noted that in the histories of business and management studies, the object of study is very often confused with those resources that make possible the study—the method, in other words—hence producing circularity and tautology. These methods are akin to management techniques and we have already attempted to draw out how these 'management techniques' become both cause and effect of historical analysis through a close reading of Wilson and Thomson (2006). Wilson and Thomson are not untypical. Most studies that have sought to address the emergence of something 'disciplinary' about management thought and practice have tended to produce only very narrow and circumscribed accounts and remain essentially intradisciplinary or self-referential in nature. How to escape this tautology poses one of the most serious challenges for the study of something like discipline in management, or for the quest to identify what is disciplinary about management, which is also our task here.

In tracing the genealogy of something we call 'management', Foucault would examine the historical conditions of possibility that enabled 'management' to become a delimited self-evident object of study or practice. He would also show how 'subjects' were simultaneously created out of the very same conditions that created this object. It is interesting in this respect to consider what we might recognize to be 'managerial techniques' at work in historical scholarship. There are more casual analogies with management in the sense that research and writing necessarily involve a certain management of boundaries, a certain desire for control of material, a certain aspiration for promotion and career, in which the academic journal replicates in many ways the management report. The very collection and harnessing of 'raw materials', the keeping of records, the analysis and then synthesis of these materials into a coherent and digestible form that will 'sell'; all of this can rapidly lead to classic bureaucratization in which the equivalent of managers emerge as experts who enrol and control access to the academic field (O'Doherty, 2009). Beyond this, the contemporary institutional organization of research in universities and the funding arrangements that support the development of major research in the social sciences and humanities all implicate and construct the applicant and fund holder as a manager. One of the most 'managerial' consequences of these arrangements is the increasing demand to tell the funders what it is that one is going to find out. This philistine desire to know in advance is an equivalent of killing curiosity, controlling and inhibiting the creativity necessary to the genuine advance of knowledge. To encourage such progress one must have a far greater tolerance for uncertainty and 'unknowing' and to acknowledge that we are not entirely sure where the research might take us, nor what the 'results' might be. We could go further and suggest that managerial discipline is simultaneously constructed and extended by historical research that does not question its object ('management')—or at least that this expansion and consolidation of discipline proceeds insofar as scholarship avoids treating the more originary questions we are sketching here. Here, of course, is where the Marxist labour process theorists find common ground with celebrants of the vitality and power of management.

To make some advance on our insights we need to trace how something like a 'discipline' is forged. Such a quest will take us into practices that *precede* the existing discourse of management and the categories through which it is understood, and into a space that is interstitial, somewhere in-between the knowledge disciplines and the contemporary social and political institutions with which we are familiar. Such transgression allows us to cut through the circular logic and mutual co-implication of subject and object, in which the answer is already contained in the disciplinary imposed question through which, so to speak, management asks itself about its own history. Hence, it is useless to explain the origins of the business school by studying the internal history of one institution (Wilson, 1992). The rise of the business school in the

UK emerges out of a vast array of forces and interests, much of these international in nature, dating back to the post-Second World War US-led reconstruction of Europe and the UK under the auspices of the Marshall Plan and the later Anglo-American Council for Productivity. Such reconstruction served the 'interests' of the United States in helping to create markets and consumers for American industrial exports and to resist the perceived threat of communism (Cooke, 2004). Much of this can in turn be understood as an extension of a more basic and underlying logic (some might say ideology) that saw the competitive pursuit of ever more material wealth as providing the best answers to more basic and perennial philosophical questions concerned with how we might 'live well'. This is all wrapped up in a complex assemblage of ancillary and supplementary forces that include dominant assumptions about 'the individual', community, and society.

It is not just ideas in the abstract that inform the early development of management studies, but a whole series of practices, objects, artefacts, and materials. If management arises because of coordination and supervisory problems associated with large scale factory production, in which people were taken out of the smaller domestic-based 'putting out' system of primitive manufacture, then it is important to note that factories could not have been built without cheap industrialized construction materials such as iron and brick that allowed large covered open spaces to be built. In this vein, there is also an important history of the stopwatch, the basic tool that facilitated the measurements and 'scientification' of management in the work of Taylor and his followers, to be written here (cf. Thompson, 1967). To explain the emergence of management involves the collection of all these heterogeneous materials and elements. It is vital here that we do not overlook any item, however seemingly minor, innocuous, or even irrelevant, but lay out the elements in a space of formal equivalence so that we might explore possible relations and lines of influence free of the historicist tendencies that read back into history from contemporary categories and classifications with its allied presuppositions about causality and the scale and priority of significance amongst the various possible explanatory elements. In such a display we simultaneously should give chance to the extraction of our own values and prejudices as they are made manifest in the reflexivity which attends such a process of discovery. How these values and prejudices stimulate the selection and interpretation of 'evidence' and lead to the exclusion of other possible explanations provides the possibility for raising the choice of values; and perhaps the possibility of the discovery or invention of new values. Indeed, it was perhaps *the* lesson of structuralism that, 'when faced with a disciplinary project, a crucial way of situating that project is by considering what it is not, what it excludes' (Readings, 1996: 173).

In this short review we have travelled a long way in the quest to understand the discipline of management, and only in entering such a space of enquiry can we begin to discover possible answers to the question of origins and delimitations. But does the study or practice of management amount to 'discipline'? Is it possible to offer a definition of discipline? Historically, the establishment of the modern university was the institutional means by which the established and emerging professions made claims to a monopoly of competence and accreditation—in law and medicine, geography, history, and economics, but also in the sciences and sub-disciplines associated with biology, physics, and chemistry. In the process each discipline sought jurisdictional boundaries for their claims to expertise (Weber, 2001). Each subject then inculcates its students into a venerable tradition and body of knowledge that is formative of certain intellectual skills. To be a disciplined scientist, for example, is to exercise a certain intellectual style which differs from that of the student disciplined into law or history. More than the shaping of minds, however, the experience of disciplinary inculcation is also one of being shaped in heart and mind, in body and soul. In this respect it is useful to recall that management might share affinities with the discipline of archery or even—as a recent study makes clear—the arts of pencil sharpening (Rees, 2013)! Such an understanding of discipline more readily acknowledges the role of the body and its senses, and how these are often overlooked objects of the disciplinary process. This casts new light on that old maxim in which management is defined as 'paper pushers' and when asked what they do the old jokers reply 'sharpening pencils'! There are also of course the more widely recognized bodily techniques of business management and leadership: the handshake, the trained discipline of eye contact, the uniforms and pin-stripe suits, the particular tone with which one 'speaks' management, one's bodily comportment as one 'does' management, the collective arrangement of bodies and distance protocols observed in regular management meetings, etc. Only by virtue of their being commonplace have we forgotten their 'fantastical' qualities, arbitrary but ritualistic, culturally specific, and the distilled historical product of a long process of education and socialization with its roots in manners and taste (O'Doherty, 2016).

Endings (in the Anthropocene)

Management provides no resource for how we might think and write about management as an academic discipline, and tucked away in the end chapters of an edited collection we seem to have been left in an impossible situation. Coming at the end, arriving always too late like Hegel's owl of Minerva, we are tasked to summarize and embrace the field of management studies in order to evaluate its disciplinary boundaries, to conclude with a definitive sign-off. But at the same time being part of this collection of essays, we appear to be implicated *in the field* in ways that make it impossible to delineate its outer boundaries. We are then simultaneously inside and outside, at the end—but announcing the necessity of beginning the enquiry again. We therefore oscillate on the edge of transgression. In many ways our predicament replicates (or mimics) that deconstructive logic we have found in management where it is compelled to assert or search for its own origins in a quest for disciplinary nobility. Yet such an exercise at the same time undoes any claims to discipline, which as we have seen is performatively exemplified in the manner and style in which these studies are conducted. Within the corridors of the business school there certainly exists all manner of playful and creative transgressions that push the boundaries of management practice in ways that a mainstream eager to establish its credentials will find difficult and perhaps embarrassing. From human-dog telepathy (Reason, 1988: 189) to the latest methods and findings reported in the eminent *Academy of Management Journal*, including 'selective coupling as a response to competing institutional logics' (Pache and Santos, 2013), 'compliant sinners' and 'obstinate saints' (Pitesa and Thau, 2013) and 'endo- and exoisomorphism in corporate venture capital programs' (Souitaris, Zerbinati, and Liu, 2012), the ways and methods of management studies remain messy and heterodox.

In this chapter we have been able to question the status of management as a legitimate object of intellectual enquiry and have even raised questions about the very possibility of a rigorous or disciplined study of management. In this way we followed Butler's (2009: 787) notion of critique as 'not merely or only a sort of nay-saying, an effort to take apart and demolish an existing structure (...) [but] the operation that seeks to understand how delimited conditions form the basis for the legitimate use of reason in order to determine what can be known, what must be done, and what may be hoped'. Given that management's 'disciplinary' status, composed of derivative and often awkwardly hybridized social sciences, remains contested in the business school, management might even be considered equivalent to Benjamin's (1999) concept of the *whore of capitalism*, she who accepts all petitions and enquiries. Discipline itself is far from disciplined in management studies and covers what could be described as a promiscuous range of subjects. Moreover, the historians struggle to convince that a self-conscious cadre of professional managers agrees on a core of disciplinary knowledge or expertise that has been accepted and put into practice by practitioners. Child's (1969) notion of a 'management *movement*' therefore lacks credibility, unless we conclude that such movement would have to be equivalent to that of the St Vitus dance.

In the light of what ethnographic studies reveal about the actual everyday practices of managers it seems a wishful fantasy to define management with the venerable and noble title of profession, let alone to grant it the status of discipline. However, as a reputational work of organization, 'management studies' has greatly assisted the development of a distinct labour market for business school professors who thus can claim the possession of academically certified skills and scholarly repute as key criteria for access to increasingly well paid jobs (Whitley, 1984). Furthermore, there can be no mistaking the data on applications to business and management studies degrees which have enjoyed a spectacular growth in recent years. It would seem that everyone wants to be a manager. Now the most popular subject at university, business and management is becoming ubiquitous and indeed synonymous with the university (O'Doherty and Jones, 2005). Not only are there daily launches of new undergraduate programs and an expansion and proliferation of university business schools; everything in education is being constructed in the mirror image of business and management so that some speak of a 'managerialization of everyday life' (Hancock and Tyler, 2009). Even courses in theology and arts, for example, must be written in ways that can answer to the question of employability, as course tutors find themselves confronted by a vast impersonal technologically invested bureaucracy in which the encroachment of rules and regulations on things like course design means that 'content' is increasingly defined by management rather than on scholarly criteria or principles of academic merit. The 'infotainment' lecture or the reduction of knowledge to power-point presentations, the competitive individualistic culture of examination and accountability, and the requirement that lectures be motivational for students, are all examples of a greater managerialization of higher education (Brown and Carasso, 2013; Collini, 2012). You may be studying Latin in an Ivy League or Russell Group university but you are effectively being socialized into the ways and mores of management.

There seems to be something taking place that deserves the title 'disciplinary' though. When we hear students talk about the need to sex-up their CVs or downsize their facebook friendship list, leverage their grade point average or maximize their 'cost/income ratios', there is certainly evidence of disciplinary inculcation into a shared 'managerial' discourse. Students who have become expert in the understanding and practice of progression rules—with its volumes of governance structures made up of compensation, appeals, and mitigating circumstances—will all have become proficient in the logic of administration and litigation. Typically identified as 'game playing', this nonetheless probably offers a better grounding in how to succeed in contemporary business and management (see Lewis, 2014) than the ostensible subject matter of their degree, particularly if they have elected to formally study business and management. Managed and *on-the-road-to-management*, simultaneously subject and object, students today are being enrolled in a silent disciplinary apparatus that forges an ever-greater penetration of managerial logic.

To trace this disciplining we need to step outside the narrow confines in which most management academics ply their trade and explore practices that take place in-between and outside the established institutions of research and methodological discipline promoting management as a profession: in its end-papers, for example; its miscellanea and marginalia. Hence, we need to go beyond the relations that connect up powerful multinational global organizations, consultancies, business schools, and degree curricula (Thrift, 2002). We might take courage from the fact that periodically editorials in major journals issue calls for greater daring and innovation (Holt and den Hond, 2013; Suddaby, Hardy, and Huy, 2011), and even Feyerabend (1975) still receives the occasional name check. However, to cultivate a form of post-disciplinary practice that permits one to take a sideways glance at the historic forces shaping us as social actors and then to further delimit those disciplinary features which ensnare us in a restrictive form of management, demands a more transgressive practice as embodied perhaps in the work of Foucault. The implications that follow from Foucault (and allied advances in continental philosophy—e.g. Derrida, Deleuze and Guattari, Irigaray, Kristeva, Lacan, etc.) compel experimentation with new ways of writing with all the attendant challenges this poses to the mutually constitutive interplay of societal power relations, inequalities, identity and insecurity. However, we might then begin to re-map and re-situate management in an *extended ecology of objects and matter more relevant to the era of the Anthropocene*. Assuming we survive, this will become the dominant problem for management in the future. Reader, you are likely to be baffled by this—but as innovative work, once on the edges of the social sciences, slowly makes its way into management we might anticipate that this re-situating of management will take the form of greater 'strategic partnerships' with a post-human ecology of plants, animals, stones, water, and even weather systems. Hoping to eclipse the all-too-human mindset, the challenge is formidable and will require a certain dedication to the ludic and—dare we suggest—a certain degree of discipline.

REFERENCES

Augé, M. (1995). *Non-Places: Introduction to an Anthropology of Supermodernity*. London: Verso.

Becker, D. L. (2012). *Many Subtle Channels: In Praise of Potential Literature*. Boston, MA: Harvard University Press.

Benjamin, W. (1999). *Illuminations* (trans. H. Zom). London: Pimlico.

Bloor, M. (2000). 'The South Wales Miners Federation, Miners' Lung and the Instrumental Use of Expertise, 1900–1950'. *Social Studies of Science*, 30(1): 125–40.

Blum, A. F. (1973). Reading Marx. *Sociological Inquiry*, 43(1): 23–34.

Borges, J. L. (1952/1973). 'The Analytical Language of John Wilkins', in J. L. Borges (ed.), *Other Inquisitions*. London: Condor, 101–5.

Branson, N. and Heinemann, M. (1971). *Britain in the Nineteen Thirties*. London: Weidenfeld & Nicolson.

Braverman, H. (1974). *Labour and Monopoly Capital*. New York: Monthly Review Press.

Brown, R. and Carasso, H. (2013). *Everything for Sale? The Marketisation of UK Higher Education*. London: Routledge.

Buckingham, M. and Coffman, C. (1999). *Break All the Rules*. New York. Simon and Schuster.

Burrell, G. (1997). *Pandemonium: Towards a Retro Organization Theory*. London: SAGE.

Butler, J. (2009). 'Critique, Dissent, Disciplinarity'. *Critical Inquiry*, 35 (summer): 773–95.

Chandler, A. (1977). *The Visible Hand*. Cambridge, MA: Harvard University Press.

Child, J. (1969). *British Management Thought*. London: George Allen and Unwin.

Clegg, H. A. (1979). *The Changing System of Industrial Relations in Great Britain*. Oxford: Blackwell.

Clegg, S. (2014). 'Managerialism: Born in the USA'. *Academy of Management Review*, 39(4): 566–76.

Dalton, M. (1959). *Men Who Manage*. New York: Wiley.

De Cock, C. (2000). 'Reflections on Fiction, Representation and Organization Studies: An Essay with Special Reference to the Work of Jorge Luis Borges'. *Organization Studies*, 21(3): 589–609.

De Cock, C. and Jeanes, E. L. (2006). 'Questioning Consensus, Cultivating Conflict'. *Journal of Management Inquiry*, 15(1): 18–30.

Collini, S. (2012). *What Are Universities For?* London: Penguin.

Cooke, B. (2004). 'The Managing of the (Third) World'. *Organization*, 11(5): 603–29.

Covey, S. (2013). *The 7 Habits of Highly Effective People*, 25th anniversary edn. New York: Simon and Schuster.

Crutzen, P. J. and Stoermer, E. F. (2000). 'The Anthropocene'. *IGBP Newsletter*, 41: 17–18. Royal Swedish Academy of Sciences, Stockholm.

Czarniawska, B. (1998). *A Narrative Approach to Organization Studies*. London: SAGE.

Deleuze, G. (1988). *Foucault*. Minneapolis, MN: Minnesota University Press.

Derrida, J. (1969). 'The Ends of Man'. *Philosophy and Phenomenological Research*, 30(1): 31–57.
Edwards, P. (1989). 'The Three Faces of Discipline', in K. Sisson (ed.), *Personnel Management in Britain*. Oxford: Blackwell, 296–325.
Edwards, P. K. (1990). 'Understanding Conflict in the Labour Process: The Logic and Autonomy of Struggle', in D. Knights and H. Willmott (eds.), *Labour Process Theory*. Basingstoke: Macmillan, 125–52.
Edwards, P. (2005). 'Discipline and Attendance: A Murky Aspect of People Management', in S. Bach (ed.), *Managing Human Resources: Personnel Management in Transition*. Oxford: Blackwell, 375–97.
Edwards, P. K. and Whitston, C. (1989). 'Industrial Discipline, the Control of Attendance, and the Subordination of Labour: Towards an Integrated Analysis'. *Work, Employment & Society*, 3(1): 1–28.
Feyerabend, P. (1975). *Against Method: Towards an Anarchistic Theory of Knowledge*. Atlantic Highlands, NJ: Humanities Press.
Foucault, M. (1970). *The Order of Things: An Archaeology of the Human Sciences*. London: Tavistock.
Foucault, M. (1972). *The Archaeology of Knowledge*. London: Pantheon Books.
Foucault, M. (1979). *Discipline and Punish*. New York: Vintage.
Foucault, M. (1992). *The Use of Pleasure: The History of Sexuality Volume 2* (trans. Robert Hurley). Harmondsworth: Penguin.
Goffman, E. (1959). *The Presentation Of Self In Everyday Life*. Garden City, NY: Anchor.
Hambrick, D. (1994). What if the Academy Actually Mattered? *Academy of Management Review*, 19(1): 11–17.
Hancock, P. and Tyler, M. (eds.) (2009). *The Management of Everyday Life*. London: Macmillan.
Hodgkinson, G. P. and Rousseau, D. M. (2009). 'Bridging the Rigour–relevance Gap in Management Research: It's Already Happening!'. *Journal of Management Studies*, 46(3): 534–46.
Holt, R. and den Hond, F. (2013). 'Sapere Aude'. *Organization Studies*, 34(11): 1587–600.
Huczynski, A. and Buchanan, D. (2013). *Organizational Behaviour*, 8th edn. Harlow: Pearson Education.
Hyman, R. (1989). *The Political Economy of Industrial Relations*. London: Macmillan.
Knights, D. (1990). 'Subjectivity, Power and the Labour Process', in D. Knights and H. Willmott (eds.), *Labour Process Theory*. Basingstoke: Macmillan, 297–335.
Knights, D. (2002). 'Writing Organizational Analysis Into Foucault'. *Organization*, 9(4): 575–93.
Knights, D. and Vurdubakis, T. (1994). 'Foucault, Power, Resistance and All that', in J. M. Jermier, D. Knights, and W. Nord (eds.), *Resistance and Power in Organizations*. London: Routledge, 167–98.
Knights, D. and Willmott, H. (eds,) (1990). *Labour Process Theory*. Basingstoke: Macmillan.
Lewis, M. (2014). *Flash Boys: A Wall Street Revolt*. New York: W. W. Norton & Company.
Littler, C. R. (1982). *The Development of the Labour Process in Capitalist Societies*. London: Heinemann.
McKinlay, A. and Starkey, K. (eds). (1998). *Foucault, Management and Organization Theory: From Panopticon to Technologies of Self*. London: SAGE.
Marglin, S. (1974). What Do Bosses Do?'. *Review of Radical Political Economy*, 6: 33–60.
Megill, A. (1987). *Prophets of Extremity: Nietzsche, Heidegger, Foucault, Derrida*. University of California Press.
Mintzberg, H. (1973). *The Nature of Managerial Work*. New York: Harper and Row.

Morrison, J. (1984). *Stories of the Waterfront*. Ringwood, Victoria: Penguin.
Mullins, L. (2013). *Management and Organizational Behaviour*. Harlow: Pearson Education.
Nietzsche, F. (1887/1974). *The Gay Science* (trans. W. Kaufman). New York: Vintage.
O'Doherty, D. P. (2009). 'Revitalising Labour Process Theory: A Prolegomenon to Fatal Writing'. *Culture and Organization*, 15(1): 1–19.
O'Doherty, D. P. (2016). 'Manners, Taste, and Etiquette: New Practices of 'Politesse' in Business and Management', in T. Beyes, M. Parker, and C. Steyaert (eds.), *The Routledge Companion to the Humanities and Social Sciences in Management Education*. Abingdon: Routledge, 523–37.
O'Doherty, D. and Jones, C. (eds.) (2005). *Organize! Manifestos for the Business School of Tomorrow*. Stockholm: Dvalin Press.
O'Farrell, C. (1989). *Foucault: Philosopher or Historian?* London: Macmillan.
Otley, D. (1990). 'Editorial'. *British Journal of Management*, 1(1): 1–2
Pache, A. C. and Santos, F. (2013). 'Inside the Hybrid Organization: Selective Coupling as a Response to Competing Institutional Logics'. *Academy of Management Journal*, 56(4): 972–1001.
Pfeffer, J. (1993). 'Barriers to the Advance of Organizational Science: Paradigm Development as a Dependent Variable'. *Academy of Management Review*, 18(4): 599–620.
Pitesa, M. and Thau, S. (2013). 'Compliant Sinners, Obstinate Saints: How Power and Self-focus Determine the Effectiveness of Social Influences in Ethical Decision Making'. *Academy of Management Journal*, 56(3): 635–58.
Pollard, S. (1965). *The Genesis of Modern Management: A Study of the Industrial Revolution in Great Britain*. Harmondsworth: Penguin Books.
Readings, B. (1996). *The University in Ruins*. Cambridge, MA: Harvard University Press.
Reason, P. (ed.) (1988). *Human Inquiry in Action: Developments in New Paradigm Research*. London: SAGE.
Rees, D. (2013). *How to Sharpen Pencils*. New York: Melville House.
Rowe, K. H. (1964). 'An Appraisal of Appraisals'. *Journal of Management Studies*, 1(1): 1–25.
Sewell, G. and Wilkinson, B. (1992). "Someone to Watch Over Me': Surveillance, Discipline and the Just-in-time Labour Process'. *Sociology*, 26(2): 271–89.
Souitaris, V., Zerbinati, S., and Liu, G. (2012). 'Which Iron Cage? Endo-and Exoisomorphism in Corporate Venture Capital Programs'. *Academy of Management Journal*, 55(2): 477–505.
Suddaby, R., Hardy, C., and Huy, Q. N. (2011). 'Introduction to Special Topic Forum: Where Are the New Theories of Organization?'. *Academy of Management Review*, 36(2): 236–46.
Thompson, E. P. (1967). 'Time, Work-discipline, and Industrial Capitalism'. *Past and Present*, 38 (December): 56–97.
Thompson, P. (1990). 'Crawling from the Wreckage: The Labour Process and the Politics of Production', in D. Knights and H. Willmott (eds.), *Labour Process Theory*. Basingstoke: Macmillan, 95–124.
Thompson, P. and Smith, C. (eds.) (2010). *Working Life: Renewing Labour Process Analysis*. London: Palgrave.
Thrift, N. (2002). '"Think and Act like Revolutionaries": Episodes from the Global Triumph of Management Discourse'. *Critical Quarterly*, 44(3): 19–26.
Van de Ven, A. H. (1999). 'The Buzzing, Blooming, Confusing World of Organization and Management Theory: A View from Lake Wobegon University'. *Journal of Management Inquiry*, 8: 118–25.
Van Maanen, J. (1995). 'Style as Theory'. *Organization Science*, 6(1): 133–43.
Weber, S. (2001). *Institution and Interpretation*, expanded edn. Stanford, CA: Stanford University Press.

Westwood, R. and Clegg, S. (2003). 'The Discourse of Organization Studies: Dissensus, Politics, and Paradigms', in R. Westwood and S. Clegg (eds.), *Debating Organization: Point-Counterpoint in Organization Studies*. Oxford: Blackwell, 1–42.

Whitley, R. (1984). 'The Fragmented State of Management Studies: Reasons and Consequences'. *Journal of Management Studies*, 21(3): 331–48.

Wilson, J. F. (1992). *The Manchester Experiment: A History of Manchester Business School, 1965–1990*. London: Paul Chapman Publishing.

Wilson, J. F. and Thomson, A. W. J. (2006). *The Making of Modern Management*. Oxford: Oxford University Press.

CHAPTER 24

CULTURE, CONTEXT, AND MANAGERIAL BEHAVIOUR

LUCIARA NARDON

Introduction

In this chapter, we discuss both theory and research relating to managing across cultures, and argue that the cross-cultural management literature has underemphasized the role of multiple layers of context, or the circumstances that surround a cross-cultural situation, in shaping behaviour. We begin with a brief review of the literature, and then draw on a perspective of situated cognition to examine how various layers of context can influence cognitions and behaviours of various actors. We then discuss the implications of a focus on context for the theory and practice of cross-cultural management.

Culture and Managerial Behaviour

Research and managerial experience have long supported the proposition that culture represents a major influence on individual and group behaviour. Following Hofstede's (1980) path-breaking work on cultural values, as well as later developments by Trompenaars (1993), Schwartz (1992), House et al. (2004), and others, extensive research has focused on developing correlational models of culture in which cultural dimensions representing values or beliefs predict management outcomes. Cultural values were found to be associated with change management, conflict management, decision-making, human resource management, leadership, organization citizenship behaviour, work-related attitudes, negotiation behaviour, reward allocation, and individual behaviour relating to group processes and personality, among others (Kirkman, Lowe, and Gibson, 2006). Clearly, differences in cultural values represent an important variable in research into managerial behaviour across cultures.

While not denying the importance of culture in influencing attitudes and behaviours, there is an increasing recognition among cross-cultural management scholars that an exclusive focus on cultural values and assumptions obscures the relevance of other variables such as individual, organizational, and situational characteristics in influencing behaviour (Cray and Mallory, 1998; Leung et al., 2005; Shenkar, Luo, and Yeheskel, 2008; Taras, Steel, and Kirkman, 2011), leads to hollow models of human behaviour (Peterson and Smith, 2008), and under-represents the messiness and complexity associated with cross-cultural interactions (Shenkar, Luo, and Yeheskel, 2008). In this chapter we focus on the importance of context, or the circumstances surrounding a situation, in shaping the attitudes and behaviours of people across cultures, as well as the role of managers in shaping such contexts.

CULTURE, CONTEXT, AND BEHAVIOUR

While most people recognize the importance of context, or the circumstances surrounding a situation, in defining what is appropriate or inappropriate behaviour in everyday life, cross-cultural management research has underplayed its role in shaping the attitudes and behaviours of people across cultures (Adler, Graham, and Gehrke, 1987; Cray and Mallory, 1998; Leung et al., 2005; Shenkar, Luo, and Yeheskel, 2008; Taras, Steel, and Kirkman, 2011). Instead, cross-cultural management research implicitly assumes culture to be a relatively stable force that shapes individual behaviour across contexts (e.g. Hofstede, 1980; Hampden-Turner and Trompenaars, 1998; House et al., 2004).

Cross-cultural management scholars have begun to recognize that the impact of culture on behaviour does not happen in a vacuum; it occurs within a context made up of an organizational reality, with specific actors involved, who have different levels of power, resources, and interests (Shenkar, Luo, and Yeheskel, 2008). For example, Adler and colleagues (Adler, Graham, and Gehrke, 1987) demonstrated that Japanese, American, and Canadian businesspeople behave differently in cross-cultural negotiations and intra-cultural negotiations, suggesting that how individuals behave within their culture offers limited guidance as to how they may behave in a different cultural context. Similarly, Weisinger and Salipante (2000) found wide variation in the nature of cross-cultural conflicts faced by members of different Japanese-American joint ventures suggesting that the organizational context plays an important role in shaping how national cultures influence behaviour. Moreover, research suggests that some cultures have different norms guiding behaviour towards insiders or outsiders. For example, research on women expatriates suggest that even though local women in Asia may not have as many opportunities as their male counterparts, this difference did not apply to foreign women. They are first and foremost *gaijin* (foreigner in Japanese) and as such receive different treatment than local women (Adler, 1987).

However, despite growing recognition that contextual variables mediate the influence of culture on behaviour, context is seldom articulated, making it an abstract, nebulous, and invisible force (Sommers, 2011). As Swidler suggested, 'The debate over whether or how much culture influences action obscures a crucial insight: that culture's influences vary by context ... [yet] there is remarkably little analysis of the contexts in which culture is brought to bear on action' (Swidler, 2001: 169).

In the next section, we draw on a perspective of *situated cognition*, which proposes that behaviours result from the interaction of cognitive schemas and context (Lant, 2002) and elaborate on the role of context in shaping cognition and behaviour, as well as the role of managers in shaping such contexts.

The Context of Global Work

One could argue that the most important differentiator of international management as a field of study (compared to traditional management research typically focused on one country) is its acknowledgement of and preoccupation with the multiple contexts in which managers must operate. It is widely accepted that what works in New York may not work in Beijing or Berlin, and international management research has been concerned with understanding what makes these contexts different and what attributes managers need to possess in order to deal successfully with numerous cultural contexts simultaneously. However, as illustrated in Figure 24.1, we argue here

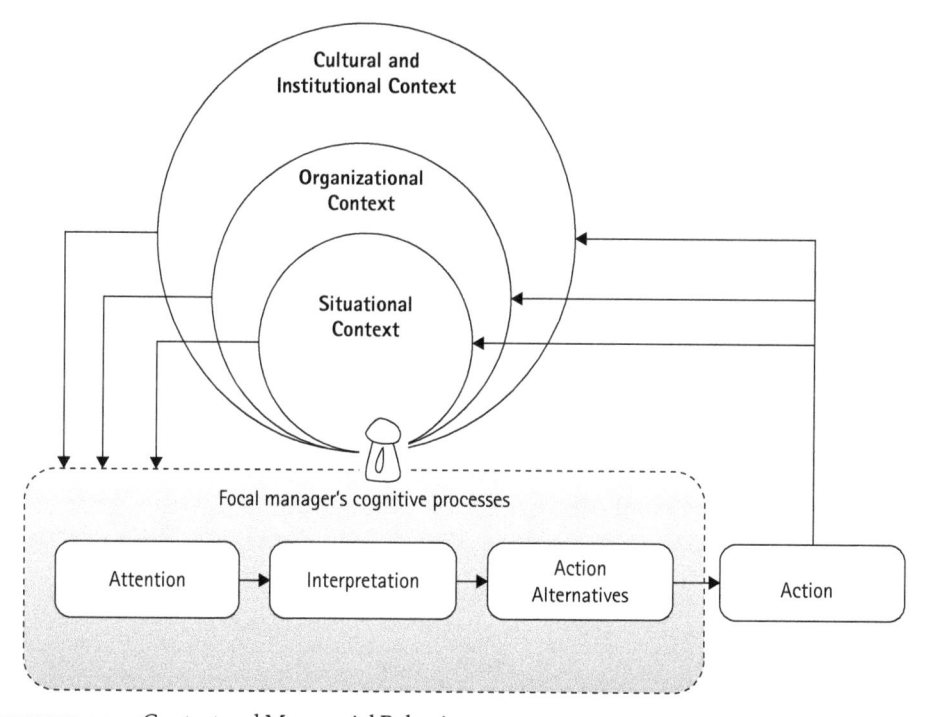

FIGURE 24.1 Context and Managerial Behaviour.

that the field has failed to pay sufficient attention to three important characteristics of context. First, the context in which the manager is located is not just a background for action that needs to be cognitively processed and interpreted, but also a major influence on managers' cognition and action. Second, the context in which the manager is operating consists of multiple layers, each with its own characteristics and influences on cognition and action. Third, contexts are not static, but change constantly based on managers' actions and the actions of others. In Figure 24.1, the weight of the line symbolizes the strength of the relationship between the context and the individual's action and vice-versa. In other words, the situational context exerts more pressures on one individual's action than the cultural and institutional context. At the same time, an individual has more power to modify the immediate situational context than the macro-cultural context, as will be discussed in more detail below. Furthermore, the model recognizes that the three levels of context are not independent. The situational context is embedded in an organizational context, which in turn is embedded in an institutional context.

We build upon a perspective of 'situated cognition' (Lant, 2002; Elsbach, Barr, and Hargadon, 2005; Clancey, 2009), which emphasizes the contextual and dynamic aspects of cognition, and propose that a manager's cognitive process and action result from the interaction between an individual's cognitive schemas and three layers of context: institutional, organizational, and situational (see Figure 24.2). Individual cognitive schemas are 'knowledge structures that represent objects or events and provide default assumptions about their characteristics, relationships, and entailments under conditions of incomplete information' (DiMaggio, 1997: 269) and include cultural knowledge as well as idiosyncratic individual experiences. Further, we propose that actions taken may influence or modify contextual characteristics as well as reinforce or modify existing schemas. We discuss this model in detail below.

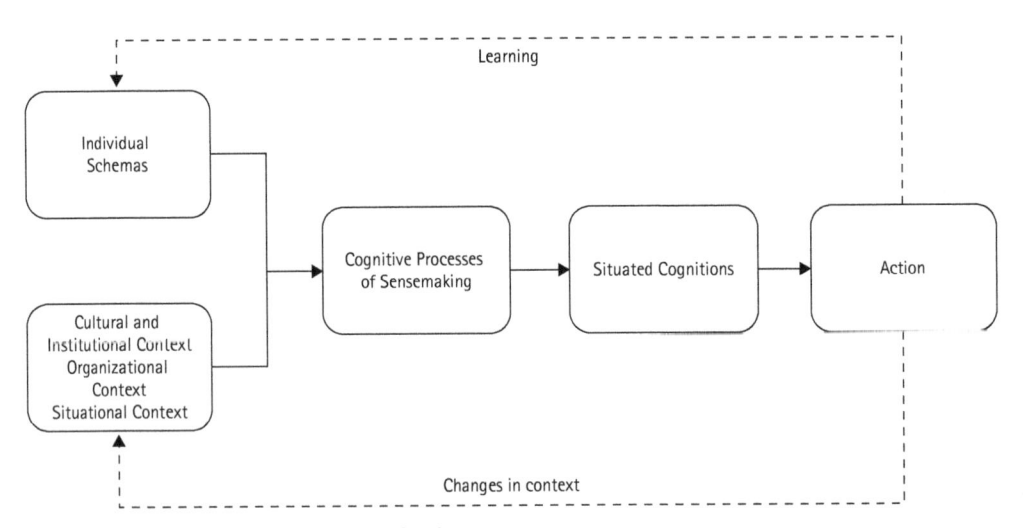

FIGURE 24.2 Context, Cognition, and Behaviour.

Context, Cognition, and Action

While recognizing the importance of an individual's background and biases in information processing (Starbuck and Milliken, 1988; Abrahamson and Hambrick, 1997; Finkelstein, Hambrick, and Cannella, 2008), situated cognition researchers have questioned 'the *primacy* of inside-the-head schemas in cognitive understanding and action' (Elsbach, Barr, and Hargadon, 2005: 423) and suggested that the context in which the manager is located is equally strong in shaping attention and interpretation (Ocasio, 1997; Lant, 2002; Elsbach, Barr, and Hargadon, 2005). The context in which the global manager is operating is not just a background for action that needs to be cognitively processed and interpreted but a major influence on what and how managers notice and interpret as well as the actions they take. Researchers argue that the focus of attention of individuals is triggered by characteristics of the situation, and may be even more important than individual characteristics in influencing action (DiMaggio, 1997; Ocasio, 1997; Lant, 2002; Elsbach, Barr, and Hargadon, 2005). For example, research suggests that individual decisions to litter in public spaces depends more on characteristics of the context, such as amount of visible litter, than on individual littering preferences (Cialdini, Reno, and Kallgreen, 1990). In addition, research suggests that individuals tend to unconsciously conform to the behaviours of others (Sommers, 2011). For example, a study conducted at New York University paired individuals with a partner who constantly shook his foot or rubbed his head. Without realizing it, participants started to mirror this behaviour (Chartrand and Bargh, 1999).

Together this research suggests that action results from the interaction of cognitive schemas and context (DiMaggio, 1997; Lant, 2002) and that 'cognitive activities should be understood primarily as interactions between agents and physical systems and with other people' (Greeno and Moore, 1993: 49). Situated cognition is thus understood as 'temporarily bounded interactions of individuals or collectives engaged in specific cognitive processes, and specific organizational contexts at particular points in time'. As such, situated cognitions are 'transitory perceptual frames that arise from the interactions of cognition and context, and in turn, direct individuals' attention, interpretations and actions' (Elsbach, Barr, and Hargadon, 2005: 424). As Michael Cannon-Brookes, Vice President for Business Development at IBM suggests 'You get very different thinking if you sit in Shanghai or São Paulo or Dubai than if you sit in New York' (*The Economist*, 2008).

Different layers of context situate managers' cognition by influencing attention, interpretation, and action. Contextual characteristics such as symbols, artefacts, and narratives influence managerial attention by structuring the availability and salience of issues and possible responses (Ocasio, 1997). Context also provides individuals with a system of meaning with which to interpret information and behaviours (when in Rome, do as the Romans do). Context also influences individuals' identification and selection of alternatives of action. For example, contextual characteristics such as the degree of embeddedness (Hung, 2005), managerial discretion (Finkelstein and Hambrick, 1990), and cultural tightness (Triandis, 2004) influence the availability and attractiveness of behavioural options.

Each layer of context described below impinges upon managers' cognitive processes and influences attention, interpretation, and action. At the same time, the actions resulting from those situated cognitions alter the managerial context. The dynamic nature of context is discussed in the following section.

Cultural and Institutional Context

The cultural and institutional context of work incorporates much of the macro environment(s) in which the organization operates, which exerts coercive, normative, and mimetic pressures on the global manager and other players with whom the manager must relate (Elsbach, Barr, and Hargadon, 2005). The cultural and institutional environment includes national, regional, industrial, and professional regulations, standards, and norms.

Organizational Context

The organizational context provides managers with a set of rules, procedures, and norms of behaviour to guide action in the form of standard operational procedures and organizational cultural norms that guide attention, interpretation, and action. The organizational context is influenced by the institutional context in which the organization is embedded but independent of it. Organizational culture may either replicate or reject national culture values and norms, creating a microenvironment in which national norms are reinforced or do not apply (Nelson and Gopalan, 2003). Through the development and reinforcement of norms of behaviour, organizations shape the cognitions of its managers by calling attention to some issues and behaviours at the expense of others, by providing input and mechanisms for interpretation, and attempting to regulate action.

Situational Context

The situational context is embedded in and influenced by the organizational and institutional contexts, but exerts influences on the manager that are independent of them. For example, an American manager working for IBM in France, will be embedded to varying degrees into the American and French institutional and cultural environment, and the IBM organizational environment with its rules, norms, and procedures. At the same time, the situation in which the manager finds him or herself is influenced by the very micro circumstances in which a specific interaction is taking place. This can be thought of as the 'point of contact' (Shenkar, Luo, and Yeheskel, 2008). Building on extant literature on organizational influences on attention (Ocasio, 1997) and cognition (Elsbach, Barr, and Hargadon, 2005) we identify three main categories of the situational environment that may influence actors' information processing: structural position, physical settings, and social dynamics.

Structural position

Organization structure and processes are key determinants of the situational context in which actors find themselves, and as such key determinants in their attention and interpretation processes. Within an organization, attention is distributed throughout the multiple functions, procedures, communications, and activities. At each phase of the process, managers' definition of the situation and foci of attention will vary. In other words, through the way the organization is structured, managers become engaged in specific activities, procedures, and communications within the firm, which shape which aspects of a particular situation become important to them (Simon, 1947; Ocasio, 1997), what are the normative expectations of their behaviour (Lieberman, 1956; Yaconi, 2001), and which actions are possible.

Physical setting

The physical setting, including the geographic location, the set-up of equipment and furniture, and nature of available cultural artifacts (Elsbach, Barr, and Hargadon, 2005) where the interaction takes place is a key variable in guiding actors' attention, interpretation, and action.

Whether a meeting takes place at the home or host country; face-to-face or virtually; in an administrative office, plant or off-site; how the equipment is arranged; what furniture or tools are available; and which artifacts are salient all work to guide the attention of actors towards some aspects of the situation and away from others (Ocasio, 1997; Elsbach, Barr, and Hargadon, 2005) triggering behavioural expectations and interpretation schemas. For example, the behaviour of promptly cleaning the lunch table performed by a member of the serving staff has an entirely different meaning than if the same behaviour is performed by the company's president.

Socio-dynamics

Socio-dynamics refer to the nature of interaction between players including individual characteristics and specific processes of interaction (Ocasio, 1997; Elsbach, Barr, and Hargadon, 2005). By players we mean individuals that are directly or indirectly involved in an interaction, including individuals that are participants in a given interaction (people at a meeting) but also people to whom the individuals involved are accountable to (e.g. superior or peers). These individuals may influence what others attend to, how information is presented and interpreted, and which behaviours are accepted.

THE DYNAMIC NATURE OF CONTEXT

Most of the international management literature assumes foreign contexts to be an objective, material, and separate entity, independent of the global manager or organization, and accessible to be discovered and understood. To that end, several models and frameworks have been proposed to understand the nature of the foreign environment in general (e.g., Ghemawat, 2001), and its culture in particular (e.g., Hofstede, 1980; Hampden-Turner and Trompenaars, 1998; House et al., 2004). However, several organizational scholars have questioned the objectivity of the external environment and suggest that organizations and environments are created—or enacted—through the interactions of key actors (Weick, 1979; Smircich and Stubbart, 1985). This perspective sees the context of global work not as objective and static, but rather as a dynamic, changing, and ambiguous field of experience simultaneously shaping and being shaped by the actions of the global manager and other key players.

In other words, as the global manager enters a foreign context, the 'context' is no longer the same, as his or her relationship with individuals and organizations in the foreign context shape and reconstruct that 'context'. The global manager may play an active role in shaping the context around him or her, through interactions with other actors, influencing interpretation and meaning creation (Lant, 2002).

Thus, we conceptualize the global manager as a 'meaning maker', someone actively engaged in assigning meaning to actions and events otherwise ambiguous. The global

Table 24.1 Managers' Influence on Context

Cognitive activity	Managers' influence on objective context	Managers' influence on perceived context
Attention	Manipulate the salience of symbols or aspects of the situation to call attention to issues or solutions. Example: Have a meeting at the factory floor to highlight operational versus strategic issues.	Draw attention of other actors to aspects of the overall experience. Example: Highlighting in communication certain aspects of a situation at the expense of others (e.g. calling attention to the multicultural nature of a team).
Interpretation	Manipulate the environment to provide a system of meaning. Example: Use symbolism to evoke desired interpretations (e.g. public recognition of exceptional customer service).	Provide interpretations or re-interpretations of symbols and experiences. Example: Explicitly proving an interpretation of ambiguous stimuli (e.g. suggesting that the absence of titles is a symbol of a performance based organization).
Selection of action alternatives	Establish rules and procedures that restrict alternatives of action. Example: Have a clear procedure on how to deal customer complaints.	Explicitly suggesting a preferred action alternative. Example: Requesting to be called by the first name.

manager is at the centre of a web of meaning creation in which multiple players are attending, interpreting, and reacting to the actions of the global manager who must attend and respond to multiple players. It is our position that a key to a global manager's success is his or her ability to manage the information processing of multiple actors through increased awareness of how actions are attended and interpreted and of actors' power to shape context. The challenge for global managers is that actors' context is not uniform as some actors may be located in different contexts. The same action may be attended or ignored, and receive varying interpretations by different actors depending on the characteristics of the context that are most salient to them. For example, for the global manager's superiors sitting at headquarters, strategic considerations are likely to be more salient than the local cultural reality. On the other hand, host country employees are more likely to be attending to local cultural norms at the expense of corporate strategy. As these constituencies react to the manager's action, they create a specific situational context for the manager.

We propose that managers have the potential to influence others' cognitions and actions in two ways: by altering the objective context of the interaction or by influencing others' perceptions of the context as it is illustrated in Table 24.1.

Theoretical Implications and Future Research Agenda

We have argued that despite widespread concern with the complexities associated with the multiple cultural contexts surrounding the global manager, for the most part, the context of global management has been reduced to the recognition of different national cultures and their influence on attitudes and behaviours. Addressing calls for further recognition of the role of context in mediating the influence of culture on behaviour, we propose that actions result from the interaction between cognitive schemas and three layers of context—macro-cultural and institutional, organizational, and situational. Further, we propose that the context of global management is not static and independent of the manager, but rather it is shaped by the manager and his or her interactions with other actors. A focus on the context of global management, in addition to cultural and cognitive schemas, has important implications for theory, research, and practice of cross-cultural management. Below we discuss some key theoretical implications of this approach.

Rethink the Prescription that Global Managers Should Adapt to the Host Environment

Conventional wisdom within the international management community is that the key to a successful international assignment is the ability of the manager to adapt to the foreign culture (e.g., Tung, 1982; Black, Mendenhall, and Oddou, 1991; Hendry, 1994; Storey, 1996; Earley and Ang, 2003; Thomas and Inkson, 2004; Earley, Murnieks, and Mosakowski, 2007; Javidan, Teagarden, and Bowen, 2010). A focus on the multiple layers of context in shaping the reality of the assignment suggests that the maxim 'when in Rome, do as the Romans do' obscures significant complexity and ambiguity.

Consider the example of one Anglo-American expatriate working for an American company with Korean business ties (adapted from Steers and Nardon, 2006). The expatriate had a degree in East Asian studies, was fluent in Korean, and was passionate about Korean culture. When his employer needed an executive assistant to be located in Seoul to help manage the day-to-day administration of its joint venture, he seemed like the perfect choice. He was easily able to mix with the local population and quickly embraced many of the characteristics of a typical Korean executive, including listening to subordinate's personal problems and keeping close ties with many of the men in the organization. He even married a Korean woman and moved into a local neighborhood. However, his American superior did not appreciate his adaptation and assimilation into the local culture and soon started perceiving him as an adversary. The expat's assignment was deemed a failure and he was invited to return to headquarters. Instead, he decided to take a position in a local Korean company.

This expat's behaviour is in line with typical advice provided to international managers—he learned the local language, immersed himself in the local environment, and adapted his behaviour to fit local expectations. He clearly had high levels of cultural adaptability. Yet his assignment failed. An analysis of the multiple contexts of the assignment, including the organizations involved, the structural position he occupied, the key players, the socio-dynamic context of their interactions, and the goals and tasks of the assignment would reveal significant more complexity and demonstrate that 'adaptability' is not sufficient to succeed abroad.

The example above highlights the role of the specific context of the assignment in influencing which behaviours are more likely to succeed and reveals the challenges posed by multiple demands and interpretations of multiple players. Future research needs to further investigate the processes involved in managing the dynamic nature of these relationships, including understanding how managers make sense of foreign environments and the mechanisms that help them enact their situational and organizational contexts.

Rethink the Role of Cultural Differences in Global Management

Researchers have recognized that some foreign contexts may present special challenges and barriers to global managers (Johnson, Lenartowicz, and Apud, 2006). A popular notion is that the degree of distance, especially cultural distance, between the home and host country is an important determinant of the difficulties of the assignment. The main assumption is that the more culturally distant or different a host culture is from the individual's home culture, the more difficult it is for him or her to adjust to the new environment (Church, 1982; Mendenhall and Oddou, 1985). A broader conceptualization of context, including its multiple layers and its effect on information processing, opens the possibility to different understandings of the role of cultural differences.

For instance, consider the different circumstances of a Chinese expatriate in England and of an Englishman in China (adapted from *The Economist*, 2010). The Englishman may be pleased with his lifestyle in China, where Western comfort is available and affordable with his expatriate pay, and with his career prospects given the business opportunities in China. On the other hand, the Chinese executive may see his assignment more negatively. Chinese expatriates typically do not enjoy the same pay and perks and need to give up some home comforts such as housemaids. In addition, considering the importance of relationships for career advancements in China, a few years away may hamper one's career.

As the example above illustrates, while cultural and country differences between home and host culture are important, these differences are not inherently good or bad, but will be interpreted differently depending on the specific context of the assignment. Institutional, organizational, and situational variables influence how the expatriate interprets the experience. Rather than focusing on 'cultural distance' or the degree of differences between countries, a more fruitful concept may be that of 'cultural friction' (Shenkar, Luo, and Yeheskel, 2008) which focuses on the encounter of cultural systems and acknowledges the relevance of power differentials and possible conflicts between multinational firms and local actors. A focus on 'friction' suggests 'shifting emphasis from abstract differences towards contact between specific entities, onto to their partisan concerns' (911).

What follows is that cultural adaptability alone is insufficient to predict a manager's success abroad, since several other factors besides cultural differences come into play, including the relationship of the organization with the institutional environment, the players involved and their relationships, and the structural position of the manager, which in turn will influence which differences between the home and host environment are most salient and how these differences are interpreted. Future research needs to further investigate how contextual factors interact with individual expatriates to better understand drivers of success abroad.

Rethink the Relationship between Culture and Behaviour

The observation that context is an important force in shaping action in addition to cultural schemas highlights the possibility of fragmentation in cultural manifestations and challenges the predictive validity of current value-based models. Recent research suggests that while cultural values are strongly related to attitudes, they are not as strong in predicting behaviours, which are more highly influenced by contextual factors (Taras, Steel, and Kirkman, 2011). Placing context in the centre of action suggests that culture influences behaviour through the interaction between cultural schemas and cues embedded in the physical and social environment (Swidler, 1986; DiMaggio, 1997; Nardon, 2011). When facing a context 'People run through different parts of their cultural repertoires, selecting those parts that correspond to the situation or exemplary problem that currently holds their attention' (Swidler, 2001: 25). In other words, 'situations are not merely a neutral field of activity for intentions, which were conceived outside of that situation, but appear to call forth, to provoke certain actions' (Joas, 1996: 160). As such, consistent with recent criticisms of the 'values cause behaviour' paradigm (Swidler, 1986; Earley, 2006; Peterson and Smith, 2008; Nardon, 2011), understanding the link between culture and behaviour must account for the context of the situation in which the behaviour takes place. For example, researchers have noted that most people naturally and unconsciously adapt their behaviour to adjust to new external environments, even though this adaptation may not necessarily improve the fit between individuals and their new context (Berry, 2005). This realization suggests a need to further explore the links between culture, context, and behaviour, moving away from predictive models based solely on cultural values.

Rethink the Role of Global Managers and the Skills Required to Succeed

Positioning the global manager at the centre of a web of sense making in which multiple players are attending, interpreting, and acting, and through this process shaping the context of their actions, suggests a different role for global managers and, as a consequence, requires different sets of skills from managers. When we recognize that context is an important force in shaping behaviour and that individuals have some influence in shaping contexts, we may be able to recognize the potential role of global managers in shaping the interpretive context of their actions. Rather than thinking of a global manager as a 'super-interpreter', someone endowed with cognitive superpowers to absorb, interpret, and integrate multiple sources of information, the global manager becomes a 'meaning maker', entrusted with the role of managing and influencing the information processing of multiple constituencies. Becoming a 'meaning maker' requires a rethinking of management skills required to succeed in a global, multicultural, dynamic environment. Rather than focusing on knowledge acquisition of the other culture, or cultural adaptability, it may be more fruitful to investigate how managers may gain increased awareness of how actions are attended and interpreted by all actors, not just actors in the host culture, as well as identify some more practical skills such as framing communications, identifying and influencing aspects of context, and quickly learning about individual players and their cognitive processes that may aid managers in a dynamic global context.

Conclusion

Several writers in the field of international management have recognized the challenges posed by foreign contexts. Yet, the way in which different aspects of context influence action in general and global management in particular has not been fully examined. In this chapter, we drew on a situated cognition perspective and proposed that action results from the interaction of cognitive schemas, including cultural values and assumptions, and contextual variables. We conceptualized context as a multilayered construct including institutional, organizational, and situational layers which influences what individuals notice, and how they interpret information. Further, we have argued that the context of global management is malleable and changes as a product of the intended or unintended actions of multiple players. Focusing on the role of context in global management challenges some important taken-for-granted assumptions of the field and suggests alternative strategies for working across borders.

From a theoretical point of view, a contextual perspective of cross-cultural management challenges the notion that adaptation to the host culture is a key determinant of success and suggests that managing multiple demands and expectations of players in various contexts is more important. It also challenges the notion that higher levels of cultural difference equal more challenges, and suggests that such differences receive diverse interpretations based on the specific context of the manager. A context-sensitive perspective challenges the validity of value-based predictive models of culture and highlights the need to further explore the relationship between culture and context. Finally, this perspective raises interesting questions about the role of global managers and the skills required to succeed. Rather than focusing on training managers to acquire more knowledge about more cultures, we may do better by focusing instead on increasing awareness of how actions are attended and interpreted and how managers may influence such interpretations.

Acknowledgement

I am grateful to Richard M. Steers for the support, comments, and helpful suggestions provided during the development of this work.

References

Abrahamson, E. and Hambrick, D. C. (1997). 'Attentional Homogeneity in Industries: The Effect of Discretion'. *Journal of Organizational Behaviour*, 18(S1): 513–32.

Adler, N. J. (1987). 'Pacific Basin Managers: A Gaijin, not a Woman'. *Human Resource Management*, 26(2): 169–91.

Adler, N. J., Graham, J. L., and Gehrke, T. S. (1987). 'Business Negotiations in Canada, Mexico, and the United States'. *Journal of Business Research*, 15(5): 411–29.

Berry, J. W. (2005). 'Acculturation: Living Successfully in Two Cultures'. *International Journal of Intercultural Relations*, 29(6): 697–712.

Black, J. S., Mendenhall, M., and Oddou, G. (1991). 'Toward a Comprehensive Model of International Adjustment: An Integration of Multiple Theoretical Perspectives'. *Academy of Management Review*, 16(2): 291–317.

Church, A. T. (1982). 'Sojourner Adjustment'. *Psychological Bulletin*, 91(3): 540.

Chartrand, T. L. and Bargh, J. A. (1999). 'The Chameleon Effect: The Perception–Behaviour Link and Social Interaction'. *Journal of Personality and Social Psychology*, 76: 893–910.

Cialdini, R. B., Reno, R. R., and Kallgreen, C. A. (1990). 'A Focus Theory of Normative Conduct: Recycling the Concept of Norms to Reduce Littering in Public Places'. *Journal of Personality & Social Psychology*, 58(6): 1015–26.

Clancey, W. J. (2009). 'Scientific Antecedents of Situated Cognition', in Philip Robbins and Murat Aydede (eds.), *The Cambridge Handbook of Situated Cognition*. New York: Cambridge University Press, 11–34.

Cray, D. and Mallory, G. (1998). *Making Sense of Managing Culture*. London: International Thomson Business Press.

DiMaggio, P. (1997). 'Culture and Cognition'. *Annual Review of Sociology*, 23(1): 263–87.

Earley, P. C. (2006). 'Leading Cultural Research in the Future: A Matter of Paradigms and Taste'. *Journal of International Business Studies*, 37(6): 922–31.

Earley, P. C. and Ang, S. (2003). *Cultural Intelligence: Individual Interactions across Cultures*. Stanford, CA: Stanford Business Books.

Earley, P. C., Murnieks, C., and Mosakowski, E. (2007). 'Cultural Intelligence and the Global Mindset', in M. Javidan, R. M. Steers, and M. A. Hitt (eds.), *Advances in International Management: The Global Mindset*. Oxford: JAI Press, 75–103.

Elsbach, K. D., Barr, P. S., and Hargadon, A. B. (2005). 'Identifying Situated Cognition in Organizations'. *Organization Science*, 16(4): 422–33.

Finkelstein, S. and Hambrick, D. C. (1990). 'Top-management-team Tenure and Organizational Outcomes: The Moderating Role of Managerial Discretion'. *Administrative Science Quarterly*, 35: 484–503.

Finkelstein, S., Hambrick, D. C., and Cannella, A. A. (2008). *Strategic Leadership: Theory and Research on Executives, Top Management Teams, and Boards*. New York: Oxford University Press.

Ghemawat, P. (2001). 'Distance Still Matters'. *Harvard Business Review*, 79(8): 137–47.

Greeno, J. G. and Moore, J. L. (1993). 'Situativity and Symbols: Response to Vera and Simon'. *Cognitive Science*, 17(1): 49–59.

Hampden-Turner, C. and Trompenaars, F. (1998). *Riding the Waves of Culture: Understanding Diversity in Global Business*. New York: McGraw-Hill.

Hendry, C. (1994). *Human Resources Strategies for International Growth*. London: Routledge.

Hofstede, G. (1980). *Culture's Consequences: International Differences in Work-Related Values*. Beverly Hills, CA: SAGE.

House, R. J., Hanges, P. J., Javidan, M., Dorfman, P. W., and Gupta, V. (2004). *Culture, Leadership and Organizations: The GLOBE Study of 62 Societies*. Thousand Oaks, CA: SAGE.

Hung, S. C. (2005). 'The Plurality of Institutional Embeddedness as a Source of Organizational Attention Differences'. *Journal of Business Research*, 58(11): 1543–51.

Javidan, M., Teagarden, M., and Bowen, D. (2010). 'Managing Yourself: Making it Overseas'. *Harvard Business Review*, April: 109–13.

Joas, H. (1996). *The Creativy of Action* (trans. J. Gaines and P. Keast). Chicago, IL: University of Chicago Press.

Johnson, J. P., Lenartowicz, T., and Apud, S. (2006). 'Cross-cultural Competence in International Business: Toward a Definition and a Model'. *Journal of International Business Studies*, 37(4): 525–43.

Kirkman, B. L., Lowe, K. B., and Gibson, C. B. (2006). 'A Quarter Century of Culture's Consequences: A Review of Empirical Research Incorporating Hofstede's Cultural Values Framework'. *Journal of International Business Studies*, 37: 285–320.

Lant, T. K. (2002). 'Organizational Cognition and Interpretation', in J. Baum (ed.), *The Blackwell Companion to Organizations*. Oxford: Blackwell, 344–62.

Leung, K., Bhagat, R., Buchan, N. R., Erez, M., and Gibson, C. B. (2005). 'Culture and International Business: Recent Advanced and Future Directions'. *Journal of International Business Studies*, 36(4): 357–78.

Lieberman, S. (1956). 'The Effects of Changes in Roles on the Attitudes of Role Occupants'. *Human Relations*, 9(4): 385–402.

Mendenhall, M. and Oddou, G. (1985). 'The Dimensions of Expatriate Acculturation: A Review'. *Academy of Management Review*, 10(1): 39–47.

Nardon, L. (2011). 'Culture, Attention, and Managerial Action: An Application Of Quantitative Content Analysis to Textual Data in Brazil and the U.S.'. *Multidisciplinary Business Review*, 4(1): 35–47.

Nelson, R. E. and Gopalan, S. (2003). 'Do Organizational Cultures Replicate National Cultures? Isomorphism, Rejection and Reciprocal Opposition in the Corporate Values of Three Countries'. *Organization Studies*, 24(7): 1115–51.

Ocasio, W. (1997). 'Towards and Attention-based View of the Firm'. *Strategic Management Journal*, 18: 187–206.

Peterson, M. and Smith, P. (2008). 'Social Structures and Processes in Cross-Cultural Management', in P. Smith, M. Peterson, and D. Thomas (eds.), *Handbook of Cross-Cultural Management Research*. Los Angeles, CA: SAGE, 15–33.

Schwartz, S. (1992). 'Universals in the Content and Structure of Values: Theoretical Advances and Empirical Tests in 20 Countries', in Mark Zanna (ed.), *Advances in Experimental Social Psychology*. New York: Academic Press, 25: 1–65.

Shenkar, O., Luo, Y., and Yeheskel, O. (2008). 'From "Distance" to "Friction": Substituting Metaphors and Redirecting Intercultural Research'. *Academy of Management Review*, 33(4): 905–23.

Simon, H. A. (1947). *Administrative Behaviour: A Study of Decision-Making Processes in Administrative Organizations*. Chicago, IL: Macmillan.

Smircich, L. and Stubbart, C. (1985). 'Strategic Management in an Enacted World'. *Academy of Management Review*, 10(4): 724–36.

Sommers, S. (2011). *Situations Matter: Understanding How Context Transforms your World*. New York: Riverhead Books.

Starbuck, W. H. and Milliken, F. J. (1988). 'Executive's Perceptual Filters: What They Notice and How They Make Sense', in D. C. Hambrick (ed.), *The Executive Effect: Concepts and Methods for Studying Top Managers*. Greenwich, CT: JAI Press, 35–65.

Steers, R. M. and Nardon, L. (2006). *Managing in the Global Economy*. New York: M. E. Sharpe Inc.

Storey, J. (1996). *Human Resource Management: A Critical Text*. London: International Thomson Business Press.

Swidler, A. (1986). Culture in Action: Symbols and Strategies. *American Sociological Review*, 51(2): 273–86.

Swidler, A. (2001). *Talk of Love: How Americans Use Their Culture*. Chicago, IL: University of Chicago Press.

Taras, V., Steel, P., and Kirkman, B. L. (2011). 'Three Decades of Research on National Culture in the Workplace: Do the Differences Still Make a Difference?' *Organizational Dynamics*, 40: 189–98.

The Economist (2008). 'The Empire Strikes Back'. 20 September, p. 12.

The Economist (2010). 'A Tale of Two Expats'. 29 December. Available at: <http://www.economist.com/node/17797134> (accessed 16 August 2016).

Thomas, D. C. and Inkson, K. (2004). *Cultural Intelligence: People Skills for Global Business*. San Francisco, CA: Berrett-Koehler.

Triandis, H. C. (2004). 'The Many Dimensions of Culture'. *Academy of Management Executive*, 18(1): 88–93.

Trompenaars, F. (1993). *Riding the Waves of Culture: Understanding Cultural Diversity in Business*. London: Economist Books.

Tung, R. L. (1982). 'Selection and Training Procedures of US, European, and Japanese Multinationals'. *California Management Review*, 25(1): 57–71.

Weick, K. E. (1979). *The Social Psychology of Organizing*. New York: Random House.

Weisinger, J. Y. and Salipante, P. F. (2000). 'Cultural Knowing as Practicing'. *Journal of Management Inquiry*, 9(4): 376–90.

Yaconi, L. L. (2001). 'Cross-cultural Role Expectations in Nine European Country-Units of a Multinational Enterprise'. *Journal of Management Studies*, 38(8): 1187–1215.

CHAPTER 25

INTERNATIONAL MANAGEMENT

MIKE GEPPERT AND GRAHAM HOLLINSHEAD

Introduction

The subject of international management (IM) is now widely taught across business schools, and is frequently approached as an adjunct or extension to the well-rehearsed disciplines of Business Strategy and Economics. Perusing a selection of popular 'International Management' textbooks, generally published for the consumption of Western audiences by Anglo-American writers, the following headings would appear to be indicative reference points for the parameters of the emergent yet somewhat experimental domain of IM: 'The Political and Legal Environment, Managing Across Cultures, Strategy Formulation and Implementation, Motivation and Leadership Across Cultures, Managing International Assignments'. Yet, arguably, the construction of the subject matter in such fundamentally managerial terms raises as many questions as are potentially resolved. The more critical observer may be disposed to consider, in particular, whether 'best practice' strategic formulations that may be conceived in a 'clean' and pragmatic fashion by both practitioners and theorists, typically residing in 'Western' settings, can readily be transposed from site to site in the modern international enterprise straddling diverse institutional and cultural territories. More generally one senses that the multinational corporation (MNC) is frequently taken for granted as an all pervasive presence in modern economy and society, the alluring image or brand it projects tending to obscure the geographically scattered and diverse managerial groupings that constitute its internal organization, or the workers, frequently located in far flung developing regions, whose labour creates its product or service. In this chapter we seek to bring to the fore the 'reality' of multinational organization by suggesting that the transcendence of MNCs is a manifestation of a particular era in global economic history and that the subsidiary units comprising the MNC totality are 'embedded' in distinctive and diverse socio-economic contexts and are prone to manifest organizational disparity as well as unity. We also argue that the human relations constituting the social fabric of the MNC are scarcely 'clean' or ordered, but rather that they may be characterized by contestation and 'power playing'. In proceeding we will draw upon emerging critical discursive contributions relating to international organization, which are more grounded in the disciplines of sociology, organizational behaviour, and socio-political analysis than derived from strategic management or mainstream economics.

At its core, International Management concerns the study of multinational corporations (MNCs), which evidently constitute an all pervasive force in an era of modernization and globalization, but which have arguably been subject to under-developed theorization in extant literature. Since the inception of the discipline of IM in the early 1950s early rationalistic and unitary views of international enterprise, derived largely from the standpoint of transaction-cost economics or political economy, have tended to give way to more finely grained sociologically informed accounts, which have envisaged the cultures and structures of MNCs as being fundamentally conditioned by the diverse regional institutional arrangements impacting international organization. Recent departures in the study of MNCs have also moved away from early rationalistic paradigms in recognizing the unpredictability and potency of primary social agents in determining the affairs of the MNC. Indeed there is growing recognition of the 'tortuous' relationship between headquarters and subsidiary, which may be characterized through the interplays of power and politics as well as possibilities for harmonious engagement. In this chapter we approach the topic of IM by addressing the following thematic issues: first, why are MNCs dominant actors on the world economic stage and what are the forces which compel companies to internationalize? Second, why are particular elements of production or service delivery processes within MNCs distributed across particular global regions? Third, in the context of such globalization of production, what are the critical dynamics of the relationship between 'parent' and 'subsidiary' elements within the MNC? Fourth, in the light of growing realization that the institutional context for MNC organization 'matters', how do societal and regional effects impinging on dispersed MNC organization contribute to and understanding of MNCs as conflicting 'social spaces' or sites for micro-political interplays.

THE GLOBAL CONTEXT

The growth of the MNC, and corresponding scholarly and popular awareness of international organizational issues, has occurred in an increasingly liberalized global economic environment over the past couple of decades. While the debate continues between those who remain sceptical about the actual extent of globalization (see, for example, Edwards and Rees, 2006; Rugman, 2001), and those 'hyper-globalists' who enthuse about the onset of a new 'global village' (for example Ohmae, 1994; Friedman, 2007), it is undoubtedly the case that significant political and regulative shifts at international and regional levels have facilitated the rise of the MNC to seemingly unprecedented global status. Of particular note are: first, successive GATT (General Agreement on Tariffs and Trade) treaties since the early 1990s which have served to dismantle protective tariffs and quotas; second, the concurrent seismic political shifts in Russia and the former communist bloc, China, India, and Brazil which have engendered market liberalism in these countries and lifted barriers to international trade and investment; and third, the removal of restrictions to the free movement of capital and labour *within* trade blocs such as the North American region (the North American Free Trade Agreement—NAFTA) and the European Union (EU). More recently, the three 'megaregional' groupings of the TPP (The Trans-pacific Partnership), TTIP (Transatlantic Trade and Investment Partnership) and RCEP (Regional Comprehensive Common Partnership—including India, China, and Japan) (UNCTAD, 2014) have gained prominence as international trading entities.

Furthermore, in seeking to understand the anatomy of numerous modern MNCs, which are increasingly characterized by their 'footloose' regional investment strategies, it should be noted that powerful international institutions, specifically the World Bank, International Monetary Fund (IMF), and World Trade Organization (WTO), have paved the way for the incursions of predominantly Western-based corporations into the 'Global South'. As a condition attached to loans extended to developing economies through the auspices of the World Bank and IMF to catalyse growth and alleviate poverty in these regions *structural adjustment programmes* have been implemented which typically require debtor countries to privatize state owned utilities and, more generally, to engage in economic deregulation. In consequence, the physical and social infrastructures of economies in the developing world have been opened up for foreign investment, and corporate expansion or relocation from the advanced economies, exposing relatively inexpensive reserves of labour or other forms of capital. In reflecting, therefore, on the nature of globalization, a major element of which has been the rise of MNCs as dominant actors on the global socio-economic stage, it is instructive to note that the 'new world order' has, to a considerable extent, been constructed by governmental and trans-governmental actions, as well as by the autonomous strategies of MNCs themselves. In comprehending, therefore, the geo-political background for the playing out of 'international management', the application of free market principles to a new global economic order has to be acknowledged, and concomitant economic and political asymmetries between the advanced and underdeveloped world. Such increasing asymmetries have also become prominent between advanced economies. An example is the dissimilar socio-economic development of northern and southern European countries, in the aftermath of the financial crisis in 2008.

UNDERSTANDING THE MNC

An MNC may be broadly defined as a company which is *physically* active in more than one country (Hollinshead, 2009), it therefore possesses factors such as plants, technology, as well as expert knowledge of managers and workers in a country other than its country of origin. While, therefore, this definition embraces many household name MNCs, including Microsoft, Ford, or Mitsubishi, it would also include numerous internationally concerns, of varying sizes, which manifest a lower profile, for example an internationally based charitable or voluntary organization, estate agent, or finance house. As Steger (2013) points out, the number of MNCs increased dramatically from around 7,000 in 1970 to 80,000 in 2012. The top 2,000 MNCs now account for approximately half of global industrial output, and the headquarters of such enterprises are exclusively located in North America, Mexico, Europe, China, Japan, and South Korea (Steger, 2013).

The expanding, and fluctuating, pattern of MNC organization across the globe may be understood with reference to published data on flows of foreign direct investment (FDI) from region to region. FDI may be defined as 'an investment made to acquire lasting interest in enterprises operating outside the economy of the investor' (IMF, 1993). Recent statistics produced by UNCTAD (2014) reveals that, while the USA remains the largest provider of FDI outflow, (followed by Japan and China), as well as the largest recipient of inflow (followed by China and the Russian federation), the developed countries are actually losing ground to emerging countries (and particularly China) the latter becoming major providers and recipients of FDI. Nevertheless, in terms of FDI *outflow*, in 2013, the developed economies from within North America and Europe provided $857 billion of outward investment compared with $454 emanating from developing countries. It is also of interest to note that only two Chinese MNCs are in the 'top ten' MNC list, in terms of revenues, to date. Most of the listed MNCs still originate from Western capitalist countries, with companies based in the USA and the oil industry clearly being most prominent (see Table 25.1).

Table 25.1 Largest MNCs, Sectors, and Headquarters' Localities

Corporation	Industry/Headquarters
Royal Dutch Shell	Oil, Netherlands
Exxon Mobil	Oil, USA
Wal-Mart Stores	Retail, USA
Sinopec Corp	Oil, China
BP	Oil, UK
Vitol	Oil, Switzerland
China National Petroleum Corporation	Oil, China
Chevron Corporation	Oil, USA
Conoco Phillips	Oil, USA
Toyota Motors	Car, Japan

Adapted from Steger (2013).

Over the past thirty years, two 'rationalistic' approaches—the eclectic paradigm and the evolutionary model of the MNC—have not only dominated the field of IM but have also subdued more critical reflections and openness for alternative conceptual ideas. The *eclectic paradigm* was developed by the British economist Dunning (1977) and was subsequently further elaborated (e.g., by Hennart, 1991). Its key focus is on the question of how we explain the existence of MNCs in comparison to other forms of internationalization, for instance export or 'turnkey' projects. The decision of MNCs to integrate and (wholly) own its international ventures is mainly described in terms of transaction cost economics, as the most efficient response to the failure of market-like forms of organization, and because such organizational integration provides for locational and ownership advantages (Dunning, 1993). Scholars proposing the evolutionary model, on the other hand, based on evolutionary and contingency theories, stress the importance of effective MNC management. Effective managerial decisions are described as best strategic fit between organization structure and the economic and technological environmental pressures of more or less internationalized markets/industries (Bartlett and Ghoshal, 1989; see also Prahalad and Doz, 1999). This led to wider discussions in the IM field about how the MNC can be managed, given the dilemma that MNCs need to be simultaneously globally efficient and locally adaptive.

Motives for internationalization

The multinational enterprise has been in evidence for centuries, the earliest such corporations emerging as a product of colonialism, notably the two East India Companies originating from the British and the Dutch colonial empires (see also Cairns and As-Saber, 2017; Clegg, 2017). The modernist international configuration, however, gained increasing prominence after the Second World War, when Fordist production ideas travelled the world (see e.g., Djelic, 2001). In seeking to unravel the logics underlying the theory and practice of IM, it is initially instructive to reflect upon the fundamental question: *why do companies internationalize?* In a seminal response, Bartlett, Ghoshal, and Birkinshaw (2004) suggest that an evolutionary effect has been apparent in the key drivers impacting corporate internationalization strategy. Accordingly, for the early large modern MNCs, a premium was placed upon *accessing raw materials,* for example oil and aluminium, as well as *seeking new markets* and achieving *low cost production,* particularly in relation to labour inputs. The latter was one the main goals of the dominant Fordist production system. However, in more recent years, these authors (Bartlett, Ghoshal, and Birkinshaw, 2004) suggest that the corporate priorities driving internationalization have been subject to modification. Most notably, in highly competitive 'post-Fordist' global market circumstances, it is argued that unprecedented concentration is being placed on the acquiring of innovative capacity through extensive *investment into research and development (R&D) activity.* Also within a hyper-competitive market environment, considerable corporate attention is being devoted to

> **Table 25.2**
>
> **Reasons for Corporate Internationalization** (Bartlett, Ghoshal, and Birkinshaw, 2004)
>
> TRADITIONAL
>
> - Accessing raw materials
> - Market seeking
> - Low-cost production/labour cost arbitrage
>
> EMERGING
>
> - R&D investment/economies of scale/shortened product life cycles
> - Global scanning and learning
> - Competitive positioning

achieving *economies of scale* and *shortening product life cycles,* as well as gaining vital informational advantages through *global scanning and learning* alongside the accumulation of knowledge-based forms of capital (Burton-Jones, 2001; Bartlett, Ghoshal, and Birkinshaw, 2004). In sum, therefore, it is argued that a paradigm shift has been observable in the increasingly global mind-sets of managers of MNCs, which have been described as moving away from a primarily opportunistic managerial orientation towards internationalization towards one that embraces a more integrated strategic approach in a more transnational sense (Bartlett, Ghoshal, and Birkinshaw, 2004) (see Table 25.2).

In a complementary analysis, Dunning (1977, 1993, 2001) and Dunning and Lundan (2008), postulate that MNC investment decisions are influenced by *resource-seeking, market-seeking, strategic asset-seeking,* and *efficiency-seeking* behaviours (see Table 25.3). Implicit in such an exposition is that, while the market seeking goal driving MNC expansion remains critical, particularly in an era of global market liberalization, a parallel set of logics relating to the acquisition of world-wide assets, including knowledge, and the geographical spreading of production to reap the competitive reward of sourcing variable labour and other costs, remains equally compelling.

In drawing together various explanatory factors driving corporate internationalization Barrell and Pain (1997) suggest that the following factors are significant. First, the search for new markets is driven by restricted capacity in home markets, increasing competition in all markets, and growing opportunities overseas through the liberalization of transforming regions such as China, Russia, and India. Second, MNCs may be induced to physically locate productive facilities close to emerging markets in order to harvest indigenous supplies of knowledge and skill in the host country and to avoid import restrictions. Third, as Hollinshead and Hardy (2012) suggest, MNCs possess the strategic capability to undertake a 'cost-benefit' analysis of available physical and human resources on an international basis and to allocate productive processes accordingly. Salient factors are likely to

Table 25.3 Dunning's Resource-, Market-, Strategic Resource-, and Efficiency-Seeking Behaviours (adapted from Verbeke, 2009)

Resource-seeking behaviour involves the search for physical, financial, or human resources available in host countries leading to the possibility of higher value creation abroad than investment at home.

Market-seeking behaviour relates to the establishment of productive and sales activities in the foreign market in order to gain higher value than would be reaped at home.

Strategic resource-seeking behaviour concerns the aim of foreign investors to tap into distinctive knowledge, administrative, or reputational resources available overseas. Such intangible assets may only be acquired through joint ventures, international takeovers, etc.

Efficiency-seeking concerns the ability of international firms to capitalize on environmental factors or changes in the overseas locality. Examples could include technological or innovatory breakthroughs, economies of scale, shorter product life cycles or removal/ reduction of trade or tariff barriers in trade blocs.

include the cost of labour with reference to levels of skill and expertise, availability of raw materials, the quality of local suppliers, and the level of technological advancement. More generally, inward investors may be influenced by prevalent economic, political, social, environmental legal conditions prevailing in the host environment. Of course these factors may be subject to rapid change, with inward investors typically, subject to physical and other constraints, retaining the prerogative to switch capital from region to region, should a more favourable constellation of contextual phenomena appear elsewhere. Finally, in both developed and developing regions, host country governments and other indigenous stakeholders are frequently at pains to attract inflows of FDI through offering financial and other incentives. So, for example, 'economic processing zones' have been established by governments in various emerging and developing economies, typically close to ports, allowing MNCs to locate productive or manufacturing facilities in clusters benefiting from favourable taxation regimes. It is recognized in host countries that MNC investment can 'kick start' economic growth, as well as exerting a 'multiplier' effect on infrastructural development. As well as injecting much needed capital, MNCs can act as conduits for the flow of new technologies and ideas (Hollinshead, 2009).

INTERNATIONAL DIVISION OF LABOUR AND THE NEW DISPERSAL OF PRODUCTION

In following the logic of internationalization, and particularly that concerned with *resource* or *efficiency* seeking behaviour, it is instructive to consider why the dispersal of productive of service providing activities across various spaces or regions may offer cost or competitive advantages to the MNC. Edwards and Kuruvilla (2005) suggest a potentially fruitful, yet somewhat neglected, theoretical precept in IM and related disciplines is the *international division of labour*. This notion relates to the capability of the multinational concern, both in manufacturing and service provision, to stratify productive activities into discrete functional areas and to relocate each into appropriate geographical regions. As stated above, since their emergence on the global scene in the years following the Second World War, MNCs have recognized the competitive advantage that may be accrued through disaggregating and spatially relocating elements of their production or service delivery process. An archetypal example of this phenomenon would be the automobile manufacturing industry which, since the 1960s, has organized manufacture on the basis of a form of 'global production line'. Accordingly, taking a 'typical American' automobile, it has been discerned that at least eight countries are involved in aspects of its production including South Korea for assembly, Japan for components and advanced technology, Germany for design, Taiwan and Singapore for minor parts, the UK for marketing and advertising and Ireland and Barbados for Data Processing (Carlton Television, 2001).

In more recent years it has been observed that various contextual changes signifying an intensified global order have led to further fragmentation of productive or service delivery processes. Dicken (2011), referring to a *kaleidoscopic* picture of international production, highlights the following three factors as being of significance:

First, systems of mass production associated with heavy industry, with their fixed and static quality, have given way to computer-based flexible technological which may be replicated at various global locations.

Second, the shift towards knowledge or information-based society has been based on electronic and digital technologies which establish a form of instantaneous production and organization across national borders.

Third, profound changes have occurred in global financial systems, enabling the instantaneous flow of capital across financial centres. The ability to switch investment instantaneously from region to region not only serves to interconnect international economies, but also renders managers and workers within them susceptible to the volatilities of global financial markets.

It is within this novel global context that the process of 'slicing up' international 'value chains' has become intensified and has become an everyday facet of product or service delivery. The concept of *Global commodity chains (GCCs)* (Gereffi, 1999) or *global value chains (GVCs)* (Kaplinsky, 2013) provide valuable insight into why certain firms 'touchdown' in certain localities, and, more generally, how the internal functions of international organizations may be both disaggregated and coordinated.

According to Giddens (2006: 55) a GCC or, in his term for a closely associated phenomenon, the Global Production Network (GPN), represents 'the worldwide networks of labour and production processes which yield a finished product. These networks consist of all pivotal production activities that form a tightly interlocked 'chain' that extends from the raw materials needed to create the product to its final customer' (Gereffi, 1999; Hopkins and Wallerstein, 1996)

Following Taylor (2008), GCC analysis focuses upon first, the modularization of varied labour processes necessary for the creation of commodities or services and second, the subsequent distribution of related tasks between a network of firms. The GCC approach points to vitality of the social context of constituent actors in the international 'chain' of productive connections, and it suggests that power and control have an important role to play in the organization and coordination of dispersed economic activity. Lead firms within GCCs, which are invariably situated in advanced global regions, are typically well placed to assert market leadership or control, to configure the technology of production across the international network and to influence the distribution of costs across the stages of production (Taylor, 2008). Where the GCC is characterized by such a system of governance in which lead firms possess considerably superior financial and technological resources compared to suppliers, the former are able to control the appropriation of value across the chain as a whole (Taylor, 2008). In such a GCC configuration, a 'core' and 'periphery' model is likely to be apparent, with primary functions such a major R&D and branding being retained in headquarters, while low cost and labour intensive activities are devolved to suppliers in the developing world. A compelling strategic rationality for the construction of GCCs is therefore to enable the transnational enterprise to pursue indomitable market power through the construction of internationally configured and unique assets and capabilities.

Building on the resource-based view of the firm (RBV) (Barney, 1991; Grant, 1991; Amit and Shoemaker, 1993), and possessing considerable explanatory value in a global context in which international alliances and ventures across diverse cultural and institutional regions are becoming more commonplace, the *dynamic capabilities* perspective (Kogut and Zander, 1992; Teece, Pisano, and Shuen, 1997) refers to the processes used by companies to assemble and leverage knowledge assets rapidly and flexibly in response to environmental change. Central to the dynamic capabilities framework is the notion that fundamental competitive advantage may be derived from combining and synthesizing resources of knowledge and skill from a variety of geographically dispersed organizational sources (Kogut and Zander, 1992).

This new debate reflects a new meaning of the resource-seeking behaviour of MNCs. In comparison with Fordist MNCs, where low labour costs were a key asset for location decisions, research related to the dynamic capability framework suggests that the resource seeking bahaviour of post-Fordist 'high-tech' MNCs now necessitates a search for locations where expert knowledge and lower labour costs are available, for example in such as India or Ukraine. Our case study vignette (below) based on new research refers to the motives for and praxis of software development offshore outsourcing to Ukraine.

CASE STUDY VIGNETTE—THE OFFSHORE OUTSOURCING OF SOFTWARE DEVELOPMENT TO UKRAINE

Over the past decade or so, software 'capitalists' based in the UK or northern Europe have recognized the strategic and competitive advantages associated with outsourcing software development activity to highly skilled engineers in Ukraine, the former IT capital of the Soviet Union. As an alternative to such sourcing in India or perhaps China, Ukraine offers the advantage of geographic proximity, relative cultural consonance, and labour cost arbitrage. While the 'crown jewels', or primary design and R&D functions are invariably retained in the corporate headquarters, more routine developmental platforms have been devolved to Kiev or other major Ukrainian cities, with products being recycled into lucrative Western markets. While the Western software companies have sought to reap the competitive advantages associated with such international sourcing of such productive activity to low cost but highly skilled providers, certain risks have also been acknowledged. First, the Ukrainian political and institutional environment is notoriously volatile, thus demanding appropriate 'due diligence' and the consultation of third parties with finely tuned local knowledge when making the initial investment decision. Second, despite the apparently enthusiastic attachment of the local engineers to these enterprises, there is a persistent fear of intellectual property leakage, particularly into the informal economy. Third, despite the relative geographic proximity of Ukraine to the Western nerve centres, cultural differences sometimes render working relationships difficult. This particularly relates to the work ethic of the Ukrainian engineers who are prone to 'work to contract', or to take time off for family events. As a risk mitigation strategy, a number of the software companies are engaging in 'soft capitalist' techniques to engender employee commitment, for example distributing company 'mugs' or t-shirts to employees, or redesigning the interior of buildings to resemble 'silicon valley' facilities as a socializing effect. Ultimately, however, it should be recognized that such offshoring investments occur in a transient 'window', the software companies being prone to shift global sourcing locality if more favourable conditions emerge in another global region. Perhaps unsurprisingly, the Ukrainian engineers in their work orientation tend to mirror the instrumental approach manifested by the Western software capitalists, reserving the right to quit if perceived employment advantages diminish. (Source: Hollinshead and Hardy, 2012.)

Organizing the MNC

Having considered the rationale for the international spread of productive functions we now 'look inside' MNC organization to consider the dynamics of the pivotal relationship between 'parent' and 'subsidiary'. A key issue for the international concern is to combine being highly differentiated, so that there is sufficient flexibility to respond to local conditions, and particularly market requirements, with a level of global integration that will promote corporate coherence and economies of scale. Seminal contributors on this theme are Bartlett and Ghoshal (1989, 1993) who, on the basis of an extensive empirical study of MNCs straddling the USA, Europe, and Japan, posited an ideal typology as a reference point for future developments in MNC organization. These scholars took issue with prevailing 'images' of MNCs, which tended either to overemphasize the potency of managerial control from headquarters, envisaging MNCs as monolithic organizational entities, or to construe the structure and culture of the MNC almost entirely through the 'lens' of the subsidiary (Bélanger, Giles, and Grenier, 2003) or from a host country perspective. In reviewing 'traditional' constructs of MNC organization, Bartlett and Ghoshal expose the following typologies: (1) *multinationals*, which strive to build a strong local presence through sensitivity and responsiveness to local differences; (2) *global* companies, which maintain centralized global operations to gain cost advantages; and (3) *international* concerns, which take advantage of parent company knowledge and capabilities through worldwide dissemination and adaptation (Leong and Tan, 1993).

However, in aspiring to arrive at a new 'managerial theory of the firm' (Leong and Tan, 1993: 25) Bartlett and Ghoshal (1993) suggest that the traditional typologies of MNC organization, as inspired by authors such as Chandler (1962) and Cyert and March (1963), were losing explanatory purchase as the realities of conducting international business were becoming increasingly complex and dynamic. Consequently, they suggest that it is necessary for MNCs to aspire towards a 'transnational solution' which entailed being simultaneously locally adaptive and globally efficient. Holding a leading Swiss–Swedish headquartered electrical equipment manufacturer as an exemplary case, it was suggested that three major *processes* lay at the core of flexible, multi-domestic and transnational concern. Essentially, three strata of management assume responsibility for these processes, top-level managers defining organizational mission and purpose, middle managers integrating strategy and capabilities, and front-line managers acting as 'organizational entrepreneurs' (Bartlett and Ghoshal, 1989). A highly distinctive, and from the point of view of Bartlett and Ghoshal (1989), productive feature of this novel international configuration was the fragmenting of the global concern into 1,300 operating companies, further divided into 3,500 profit centres, rendering the corporation as a 'coalition of diverse interests' (Bartlett and Ghoshal, 1993: 36), within which entrepreneurialism is spawned. The transnational MNC (see box, Table 25.4) therefore, possesses the following characteristics which should serve to promote multinational flexibility

---

Table 25.4 (box) Bartlett and Ghoshal's Transnational Typology

The *transnational* MNC typology became a dominant model in the late 1970s when MNCs were seeking to tap into niche markets across national borders while seeking to maintain economies of scale in an increasingly competitive economic environment. There was a need to respond simultaneously to the conflicting strategic needs of global efficiency and local responsiveness. In these circumstances, while subsidiaries were 'empowered' with corporate responsibilities (such as research and development), a high degree of parent control remained through socializing subsidiary managers (and workers) into the corporate ethos, and through establishing interactive networks encompassing parent and subsidiaries. This form of MNC began to embody the notion of flexibility, using computer aided design and manufacturing, and formulating strategy in an incremental and adaptive fashion). Pharmaceutical and food MNCs approximate to the transnational model, which was also typical of some leading US, Dutch, and Swiss corporations.

and worldwide learning capability: (1) constituent units being interdependent, specialized and dispersed; (2) contributions being differentiated according to national units but towards integrated worldwide operations; and (3) joint development of knowledge across organizational units with worldwide sharing (Leong and Tan, 1993).

In a more recent study, which again focuses on the case of ABB, Bélanger, Giles, and Grenier (2003) offer a critique of the work of Bartlett and Ghoshal, essentially taking issue with the influential authors' perception of the Swiss–Swedish-owned MNC as an idealized form of transnational MNC. In an alternative and competing 'take' on the corporate anatomy of ABB, Bélanger, Giles, and Grenier (2003: 483), argue that, at the level of practice rather than managerial espousal, local subsidiaries do not constitute 'independent subsidiaries' but rather that they are 'monitored and constrained' by headquarters in a number of ways. In particular, local-level managers engage in a two-way political process with senior management with reference to broader interpretations of market constraints and opportunities impinging upon the enterprise. On the one hand, HQ acts as a 'rampart' against volatile market forces, shielding the subsidiary from excessive exposure to environmental factors. On the other, the 'parent' allows competition between various dispersed subsidiaries within the firm, invariably engaging in benchmarking or coercive comparisons. Subsidiaries within the MNC are therefore bound to deliver acceptable financial results and to interpret the local environment in an 'effective' fashion (Ferner, 2000). Through the exercise of politics and power, therefore, according to Bélanger, Giles, and Grenier (2003), the global corporation channels and mediates the most potentially detrimental effects of external market forces on subsidiaries.

Now turning briefly to two alternative conceptions of the global/ local dilemma, in a highly influential work originally published in 1969, and reiterated and rehearsed frequently in the domain of international management subsequently, Howard Perlmutter (1969) posits an evolutionary typology to cast light upon the 'tortuous' phases of evolution impinging upon the strategic relationship between 'parent' and 'subsidiary'. According to Perlmutter, in its first phase of development, the MNC tends to adhere to the *ethnocentric* 'state of mind' or paradigm. Here the corporate preference is to retain the 'reins of power', including R&D and other proprietary knowledge or functions in the country of origin. As Perlmutter suggests, however, while ethnocentricity may be accompanied by certain strategic advantages (see also Mayrhofer and Brewster, 1996), notably the ability of HQ to retain control and coordination over subsidiaries, there may be associated dysfunctions. From the position of the subsidiary, the ethnocentric profile may represent the imposition of 'alien' policies and practice emanating from the country of MNC origin, which will be subject to interpretation at local level, or even resistance. The occupying of the upper ranks of the corporation by home country nationals may also present a 'glass ceiling' constraining the promotion prospects of subsidiary managers and employees. From the perspective of HQ, the ethnocentric 'state of mind' runs the risk of neglecting or overlooking the wealth of resources, human and otherwise, embedded in host country environment, this constituting an opportunity cost as MNCs fail to capitalize on such precious intangible assets.

According to Perlmutter (1969), therefore, the next evolutionary stage of the MNC involves a move towards *polycentricity*, or the decentralization of managerial authority to subsidiaries. This phase of development is defined as 'tortuous' as the degree of trust evident between parent and subsidiary frequently lubricates the process of devolution. Accordingly, following screening, those regional subsidiaries which enjoy the greatest confidence of the parent will be ceded empowerment in advance of others. It should be noted also that divestment of decision-making authority to local-level management teams is invariably partial. While the parent company may be prepared to delegate aspects of the HRM or marketing functions, typically critical areas of financial management and R&D are retained in headquarters.

In the final stage of evolution, and reflecting Bartlett and Ghoshal's 'transnational' typology, MNCs are typically striving to strike an optimum balance between local responsiveness (differentiation) and international organizational coherence (integration). Perlmutter's *Geocentric* typology, therefore, captures the status of the advanced global concern, which simultaneously succeeds in combining local and international strategic resources. Salient features of the geocentric MNC would include flexible, as opposed to hierarchical, organizational structures, the devolution of responsibility to teams of staff across national and organizational boundaries depending on task, and the sharing of knowledge and learning throughout the organization. In a later study, Heenan and Perlmutter (1979) identified a fourth evolutionary profile for the MNC, termed *regiocentricity*. This orientation may be regarded as mid-way between ethnocentricity and a global profile. Regiocentricity implies the devolution of corporate responsibilities to headquarters at regional level, for example in Europe, East Asia, or North America.

The evolutionary tendencies of MNCs are also recognized by Adler and Ghadar (1990), who, in a theoretical contribution which in many senses parallels the highly influential work of Bartlett and Ghoshal, suggest that MNC strategies and structures relate to phases in its product life cycle. Drawing upon Vernon's product life cycle theory (1966), Adler and Ghadar identify successive phases of MNC development as follows: (1) Domestic: an emphasis is placed on home markets and exports, management operating from an ethnocentric perspective, with little attention given to foreign cultures. (2) International: involving a shift to local responsiveness and the transfer of learning. (3) Multinational: a focus is placed upon low cost and price competition. Foreign-based operations are significant as a means to obtain cost effectiveness on the basis of production factors differentials and economies of scale. (4) Global: emphasizing particular challenges in international competition and organization in the global era. This typology places a focus on both local responsiveness and global integration in seeking to combine cost advantages and low prices with high quality products or services, and adaptability to local tastes.

While the above theories provide valuable insights into the global/ local tendencies impacting MNC organization, to inherent tensions between parent and subsidiaries, and to evolutionary characteristics impacting their development, it should be recognized that such theories are based upon ideal typologies which do not always fit organizational reality. Taking Perlmutter's theory as an example, it is quite possible that an

MNC will straddle more than one typology, or even regress through the stages of development over periods of its life cycle.

Further insight and theoretical purchase is offered into vital and 'entrepreneurial' role of subsidiaries within the heterarchic fabric of the MNC as stressed by Hedlund (1986). The latter view abandons the top-down hierarchic view of MNCs which was dominant in earlier debates in IM and asserts that subsidiary managers may actually actively influence relations with HQ and with fellow subsidiaries, rather than being controlled by or just responding to HQ demands (e.g., Birkinshaw, 1996, 2000). In follow-up debates, the role and autonomy of subsidiary management is also stressed, suggesting that subsidiaries have, and develop, different roles in terms innovation, entrepreneurship, and mandate change within the MNC, which provide them with more or less *critical resources* to successfully bargain with the HQ. New research stresses that the importance of the subsidiaries' "issue-selling"-ability (see e.g., Dörrenbächer et al., 2014; Dörrenbächer and Geppert, 2014) when they are going to bargain about mandate changes imposed by the HQ or negotiate about support for entrepreneurial initiatives at subsidiary level.

INSTITUTIONALIST APPROACHES: HOME AND HOST COUNTRY EMBEDDEDNESS

There is growing recognition in critical IM literature that the expansion of MNCs across national and regional borders does not occur in a neutral, or disembodied, fashion, as has tended to have been envisaged by rational or economistic models. Instead, drawing upon the contribution of institutional, and comparative institutional, theorists, it is increasingly being acknowledged that the dispersed organizational sub-units which comprise the totality of MNC organization are respectively influenced by regulative, normative, and cognitive frames prevalent in their immediate surroundings (Powell and DiMaggio, 1991; Scott, 2001, Meyer and Rowan, 1977). *Organizational Institutionalism* therefore holds that, while MNC headquarters (HQs) are 'embedded' in the distinctive institutional and cultural contexts prevalent within their home locality, subsidiaries will be prone to internalize the socio-political, and related, rules and norms evident in their situated geographical positions (Geppert, Matten, and Walgenbach, 2006; Morgan and Kristensen, 2006; Harzing and Sorge, 2003; Powell and DiMaggio, 1991; Meyer and Rowan, 1977). Westney (1993) argues accordingly that the MNC management has to deal with two major institutional pulls (or institutional duality), where one is triggered by the firm's home country embeddedness and the other by the firm's host country embeddedness.

Following from such an analysis, it has been asserted that the nature of the 'business system' (Whitley, 1999) in the MNC's country of origin, including means of ownership, degrees of competition or collaboration between industrial and commercial concerns, and the quality of the relationship between management and workers or trade unions will critically determine the structural features of the internationally expanding concern. Consequently, 'policies, practices, national templates and routines of control' (Morgan and Kristensen, 2006: 1471) emanating from the home country will tend to be subject to diffusion and replication amongst subsidiaries. From the point of view of the subsidiary, problems of *institutional duality* might emerge. This means that local management is, on the one hand, subjected to regulatory, normative, and cognitive influences emanating from corporate HQ, and, on the other, conditioned to adopt practices associated with dominant host country conventions (see also Kostova and Roth, 2002; Kostova and Zaheer, 1999; Morgan and Kristensen, 2006). What is missing in these institutionalist debates is to consider the crucial role of the social agency, e.g., related on the different interests and identities of HQ and subsidiary managers, and ask questions about who is actually 'pulling', and how and why (see e.g., Geppert and Williams, 2006). Such questions are in the centre of debates about power and politics within MNCs, an issue we will return to in the following section.

In a parallel stream of literature, deriving particularly from the domain of industrial relations, the significance of a 'country of origin' or 'dominance' effect in the institutional make-up of the MNC has been increasingly acknowledged (Ferner, 1997). According to Edwards and Rees (2006), concepts of 'best practice' are most likely to flow from the home locality of the corporation, where they are associated with high levels of productivity and business success. So, for example, MNCs emanating from the US have served as conduits for the diffusion of managerial principles and practices to the far reaches of the globe, including 'Fordist' mass production systems in the 1940s to 1960s, 'Taylorist' job design and payment systems in the post-war period, and HRM-related innovations from the 1990s. Similarly, in the 1980s, Japanese MNCs were engaged in the global transposition of techniques such as 'lean production', 'just-in time' manufacturing, and 'total quality' management (Hollinshead, 2009; Edwards and Rees, 2006). Yet, in keeping with comparative institutional analysis, and the notion that different *business systems* (Whitley, 1999) or *varieties of capitalism* (Hall and Soskice, 2001) persist in different countries or regions, it may be predicted that managerial or organizational practices which are self-evidently rooted in one spatial domain may not be easily transposed across borders into institutionally contrasting environments. So, for example, in much of the continent of Europe the principles of 'social partnership' are adhered to as an industrial norm. Here, consensus arrangements between organizational stakeholders as manifested in codetermination arrangements at board level or works councils on the shop floor, or greater state intervention into factors such as pay or job security are commonplace. For a US MNC, therefore, seeking to transpose 'free market' orientated principles or practices (such as non-unionism, 'hiring and firing', or performance related pay) into, say, Germany, the 'co-ordinated' market institutional principles in evidence are invariably bound to represent a considerable structural obstruction and can lead to severe conflicts between key actors, in the HQ and locally (Hollinshead, 2009; Edwards and Rees, 2006). The latter issue leads us into a relatively new debate in IM to which we now turn.

Political Issues and Power Relations within the MNC

Accompanying the acknowledgement that the organizational sub-units of the MNC are 'embedded' in particular socio-economic contexts, there has been growing recognition amongst critical IM scholars that the scope exists, within the social fabric of the international organization, for pluralistic expression and the contestation of social space by internal factions or vested interests. Mainstream rationalistic and institutionalist approaches in IM fall short of understanding the dynamics of political processes and power relations within MNCs because most studies have systematically neglected the impact of social agency and political strategizing processes of powerful key actors. It has been shown that even in situations where power relations are asymmetrical and the HQ or a top manager have some authority to exercise power over other subunits and members of the multinational firm, subsidiaries and lower-level managers and employees are never really 'powerless' and can 'gain' influence in decision-making if they actively participate in political processes and micro-political games played in the firm (Bouquet and Birkinshaw, 2008). These games are based on formal and informal rules (Crozier and Friedberg, 1980), and actors can draw on different resources and skills to influence the setting of these rules. This is because 'the rules of the game' developed in the HQ or elsewhere always need to be contextualized and interpreted, which opens room for agency and political contestation (see e.g., Hardy and Clegg, 1996: 634). Thus, achieving local legitimacy across national borders, it has been argued, must be seen as a political process which sometimes leads to political conflicts. Power can be understood as a medium of "relations" in which subjectivity, as a complex, contradictory, shifting experience, is produced, transformed or reproduced through the social practices within which power is exercised (Knights and McCabe, 1999: 203). Thus, power in the MNC needs to be seen as a context-specific (institutional and culturally shaped but not determined) and interactively and discursively constituted social relationship.

Moreover, critical international business/IM approaches have highlighted that diverse institutions, identities, and interests come into play in MNC power relations and political processes (see also Geppert and Dörrenbächer, 2014; Geppert, Becker-Ritterspach, and Mudambi, 2016). In contrast to mainstream international business/ IM and institutionalist studies which largely concentrate on the macro-level (environmental economic or societal) and the meso-level (organizational and structural) it is evident that that newly emerging critical perspectives are offering a deeper understanding of political processes and power relations in the MNC through a more 'bottom-up' and actor-centred approach. The 'bottom-up' trajectory is prone to expose the MNC as a 'contested terrain' or political system characterized by political bargaining and negotiation (Morgan, 2001: 9–10). Accordingly, MNCs may be understood as being political systems socially constituted through political coalition-building (Whitford and Zirpoli, 2016). These coalitions can be more or less stable and fragmented 'not only between competing social forces but across national institutional domains, and along various "horizontal" cross-national organizational dimensions, leading to the pervasiveness of a micro-politics with distinct characteristics that reflect the international dimension of MNCs' operations' (Ferner and Tempel, 2006: 9).

CONCLUSION

Our chapter suggests studying the reality of MNCs as transnational social spaces and organizational entities, an approach which significantly differs from applied economics perspectives which see MNCs as disembodied or transcendent global phenomena. We have given attention to those factors which have driven the international dispersal of productive activities across global regions, most recently in the form of GCCs, invariably in the pursuit of extraordinary competitive advantage in highly volatile international market circumstances. In bringing to the fore the reality of MNC organization, it has been identified that asymmetry in terms of knowledge and power relations frequently characterizes the social relationship between 'parent' and 'subsidiary' and that reconciling global/ local organizational tensions remains a vital strategic area of concern. Accordingly, drawing upon contemporary theoretical departures in IM, we have taken issue within the notion that MNCs may be regarded as 'rationalistic' enterprises and have instead postulated that they may be regarded as fragmented sites for micro-political negotiation and contestation between dispersed organizational actors. In concluding, we highlight a number of desirable avenues for future research, especially when we see the MNC as a political system.

First, a closer examination of the wider national institutional and cultural context is essential, especially in order to gain enhanced understanding of how local embeddedness both constrains and enables key actors to build power resources and mobilize political support when negotiating or resisting the transfer and implementation of global best practices.

Second, research is needed to address how HQ-subsidiary power relations and political processes bring to light diverse identities and interests of actors. The classic question of HQ-subsidiary relations may be mutated into discussions concerning *interest* formation and political contestation, and whether local subsidiary managers *identify* more with the HQ or with their local company.

Third, there is a need to look into the issue of 'identity work' and identity politics within the local subsidiary itself, which can lead to political conflicts, stereotyping and sometimes misunderstandings, conflicts of interest, and political struggle. Here, not only are the power and political approaches of local managers and expatriates considered but also the role of identities and interests of employees in micro-political game playing and power struggles.

We would argue that future research should place more emphasis on *micro-level*, in-depth and case study-based analysis. Such a socio-political approach puts emphasis on the fact 'life is lively' in organizations (Ortmann, 1988: 7), meaning that power does not just play 'a role' in the MNC, but it also sheds light on the question of how power relations are actually socially constructed. A socio-political trajectory examines how actors with various interests and identities interact in MNCs across cultural and functional borders, leading to micro-political game playing or political battles when interests or identities conflict. Solving these conflicts requires skilful actors, able to negotiate and develop shared meanings.

References

Adler, N. J. and Ghadar, F. (1990). 'Strategic Human Resource Management: A Global Perspective', in R. Pieper (ed.), *Human Resource Management: An International Comparison*. Berlin: De Gruyter, 235–54.

Amit, R. and Shoemaker, P. (1993). 'Strategic Assets and Organizational Rent'. *Strategic Management Journal*, 14: 33–46.

Barney, J. (1991). 'Firm Resources and Sustained Competitive Advantage'. *Journal of Management*, 17: 31–46.

Barrell, R. and Pain, N. (1997). 'Foreign Direct Investment, Technological Change and Economic Growth within Europe'. *Economic Journal*, 107(445): 1770–86.

Bartlett, C. A. and Ghoshal, S. (1989). *Managing across Borders: The Transnational Solution*. Boston, MA: Harvard Business School Press.

Bartlett, C. A. and Ghoshal, S. (1993). 'Beyond the m-form: Toward a Managerial Theory of the Form'. *Strategic Management Journal*, 14(52): 23–46.

Bartlett, C. A., Ghoshal, S., and Birkinshaw, J. (2004). *Transnational Management: Text, Cases and Readings in Cross-Border Management*. New York: McGraw-Hill.

Bélanger, J., Giles, A., and Grenier, J. N. (2003). 'Patterns of Corporate Influence in the Host Country: A Study of ABB in China'. *International Journal of Human Resource Management*, 14(3): 469–85.

Birkinshaw, J. (1996). 'How Multinational Subsidiary Mandates are Gained and Lost'. *Journal of International Business Studies*, 27(3): 467–96.

Birkinshaw, J. M. (2000). *Entrepreneurship in the Global Firm*. London: SAGE.

Bouquet, C. and Birkinshaw, J. (2008). 'Managing Power in the Multinational Corporation: How Low-Power Actors Gain Influence'. *Journal of Management*, 34(3): 477–506.

Burton-Jones, A. (2001). *Knowledge Capitalism: Business, Work and Learning in the New Economy*. Oxford: Oxford University Press.

Cairns, G. and As-Saber, S. (2017). 'The Dark Side of MNCs', in C. Dörrenbächer and M. Geppert (eds.), *Multinational Corporations and Organization Theory: Post Millennium Perspectives, Research in the Sociology of Organizations*, Vol. 49. Bingley: Emerald, 425–43.

Carlton Television (2001). *The New Rulers of the World*.

Chandler, A. (1962). *Strategy and Structure: Chapters in the History of the Industrial Enterprise*. Eastford, CT: Martino.

Clegg, S. (2017). 'The East India Company: The First Modern Multinational?', in C. Dörrenbächer and M. Geppert (eds.), *Multinational Corporations and Organization Theory: Post Millennium Perspectives, Research in the Sociology of Organizations*, Vol. 49. Bingley: Emerald, 43–68.

Crozier, M. and Friedberg, E. (1980). *Actors and Systems: The Politics of Collective Action*. Chicago, IL: University of Chicago Press.

Cyert, R. and March, J. (1963). *A Behavioral Theory of the Firm*. Englewood Cliffs, NJ: Prentice Hall.
Dicken, P. (2011). *Global Shift: Mapping the Changing Contours of the World Economy*. London: SAGE.
Djelic, M.-L. (2001). *Exporting the American Model: The Postwar Transformation of European Business*. Oxford: Oxford University Press.
Dörrenbächer, C., Becker-Ritterspach, F., Gammelgaard, J., and Geppert, M. (2014). 'Subsidiary-initiative-taking in Multinational Corporations: The Role of Issue-Selling Tactics', in G. S. Drori, M. Höllerer, and P. Walgenbach (eds.), *Global Themes and Local Variations in Organization and Management*. New York and London: Routledge, 383–95.
Dörrenbächer, C. and Geppert, M. (2014). 'Power and Politics in Multinational Corporations: Towards more Effective Workers' Involvement'. *Transfer: European Review of Labour and Research*, 20(2): 295–303.
Dunning, J. H. (1977). 'Trade, Location of Economic Activity and the MNE: A Search for an Eclectic Approach', in B. Ohlin, P. O. Hesselbom, and P. M. Wijkmon (eds.), *The International Location of Economic Activity*. London: Macmillan, 395–418.
Dunning, J. H. (1993). *Multinational Enterprises and the Global Economy*, Wokingham: Addison-Wesley.
Dunning, J. H. (2001). 'The Eclectic (OLI) Paradigm of international Production: Past, Present and Future'. *International Journal of the Economics of Business*, 8(2): 173–90.
Dunning, J. H. and Lundan, S. M. (2008). *Multinational Enterprises and the Global Economy*, 2nd edn. Cheltenham: Edward Elgar.
Edwards, T. and Kuruvilla, S. (2005). 'International Human Resource Management, National Business Systems, Organizational Politics and the International Division of Labour in MNCs'. *International Journal of Human Resource Management*, 16(1): 1–21.
Edwards, T. and Rees, C. (eds.) (2006). *International Human Resource Management: Globalization, National Systems and MNCs*. Harlow: Pearson.
Ferner, A. (1997). 'Country of Origin Effects and HRM in Multinational Corporations'. *Human Resource Management Journal*, 7(1): 19–37.
Ferner, A. (2000). 'The Underpinnings of "Bureaucratic" Control Systems: HRM in European Multinationals'. *Journal of Management Studies*, 37(4): 521–39.
Ferner, A. and Tempel, A. (2006). 'Multinationals and National Business Systems: A Power and Institutions Perspective', in P. Almond and A. Ferner (eds.), *American Multinationals in Europe: Managing Employment Relations across National Borders*. Oxford: Oxford University Press, 10–33.
Friedman, T. L. (2007). *The World is Flat: The Globalized World in the Twenty-First Century*. London: Penguin.
Geppert, G. and Dörrenbächer, C. (2014). 'Politics and Power within the Multinational Corporation: Mainstream Studies, Emerging Critical Perspectives and Suggestions for Future Research'. *International Journal of Management Reviews*, 16(2): 226–44.
Geppert, M., Becker-Ritterspach, F., and Mudambi, R. (2016). 'Politics and Power in Multinational Companies: Integrating the International Business and Organization Studies Perspectives'. *Organization Studies*, 37(9): 1209–25.
Geppert, M., Matten, D., and Walgenbach, P. (2006). 'Transnational Institutional Building and the Multinational Corporation: An Emerging Field of Research'. *Human Relations*, 59(11): 807–38.

Geppert, M. and Williams, K. (2006). 'Global, National and Local Practices in Multinational Corporations: Towards a Socio-Political Framework'. *International Journal of Human Resource Management*, 17(1): 49–69.

Gereffi, G. (1999). 'International Trade and Industrial Upgrading in the Apparel Commodity Chain'. *Journal of International Economics*, 48(1): 37–70.

Giddens, A. (2006). *Sociology*, 5th edn. Cambridge: Polity Press.

Grant, R. (1991). 'The Resource-based Theory of Competitive Advantage: Implications for Strategy Formulation'. *California Management Review*, 33(3): 114–35.

Hall, P. and Soskice, D. (eds.) (2001). *Varieties of Capitalism. The Institutional Foundations of Comparative Advantages*. Oxford: Oxford University Press.

Hardy, C. and Clegg, S. R. (1996). 'Some Dare Call it Power', in S. R. Clegg, C. Hardy, and W. R. Nord (eds.), *Handbook of Organization Studies*. London: SAGE, 622–41.

Harzing, A.-W. and Sorge, A. (2003). 'The Relative Impact of Country of Origin And Universal Contingencies on Internationalization Strategies and Corporate Control in Multinational Enterprises: Worldwide and European Perspectives'. *Organization Studies*, 24(2): 187–214.

Hedlund, G. (1986). 'The Hypermodern MNC—a Heterarchy?'. *Human Resource Management*, 25(1): 9–35.

Heenan, D. A. and Perlmutter, H. V. (1979). *Multinational Organization Development*. Reading, MA: Addison-Wesley.

Hennart, J. F. (1991). 'The Transaction Costs Theory of Joint Ventures: An Empirical Study of Japanese Subsidiaries in the United States'. *Management Science INFORMS*, 37(4): 625–97.

Hollinshead, G. (2009). *International and Comparative Human Resource Management*. Basingstoke: McGraw-Hill.

Hollinshead, G. and Hardy, J. (2012). 'International Sourcing and Asymmetry: The Tapping and Decanting of Ukrainian Engineering Skills by Western Software Engineers'. *Work, Organization, Labour and Globalization*, 6(2): 58–76.

Hopkins, T. K. and Wallerstein, I. (1996). 'Commodity Chains in the World Economy prior to 1800'. *Review*, 10(1): 157–70.

IMF (International Monetary Fund) (1993). *Balance of Payments Manual*, 5th edn. Washington, DC: IMF.

Kaplinsky, R. (2013). 'Global Value Chains: Where They Came From, Where They Are Going and Why This Is Important'. *Innovation, Knowledge, Development Working Paper 68*, Milton Keynes: Open University.

Knights, D. and McCabe, D. (1999). '"Are There no Limits to Authority?": TQM and Organizational Power'. *Organization Studies*, 20(2): 197–224.

Kogut, B. and Zander, I. (1992). 'Knowledge of a Firm, Combinative Capabilities, and the Replication of Technology'. *Organization Science*, 3(3): 383–97.

Kostova, T. (1999). 'Transnational Transfer of Strategic Organizational Practices: A Contextual Perspective'. *Academy of Management Review*, 24(2): 308–24.

Kostova, T. and Roth, K. (2002). 'Adoption of Organizational Practice by Subsidiaries of Multinational Corporations: Institutions and Relational Effects'. *Academy of Management Journal*, 45(1): 215–33.

Kostova, T. and Zaheer, S. (1999). 'Organizational Legitimacy under Conditions of Complexity: The Case of the Multinational Enterprise'. *Academy of Management Journal*, 24(1): 64–81.

Leong, S. M. and Tan, C. T. (1993). 'Managing across Borders: An Empirical Test of the Bartlett and Ghoshal (1989) Organizational Typology'. *Journal of International Business Studies*, 24(3): 449–64.

Mayrhofer, W. and Brewster, C. (1996). 'In Praise of Ethnocentricity: Expatriate Policies in European Multinationals'. *Thunderbird International Business Review*, 38(6): 749–78.

Meyer, J. W. and Rowan, B. (1977). 'Institutionalized Organizations: Formal Structure as Myth and Ceremony'. *American Journal of Sociology*, 83(2): 340–63.

Morgan, G. (2001). 'The Multinational Firm: Organising across Institutional and National Divides', in G. Morgan, P. H. Kristensen, and R. Whitley (eds.), *The Multinational Firm: Organizing across Institutional and National Divides*. Oxford: Oxford University Press, 1–24.

Morgan, G. and Kristensen, P. H. (2006). 'The Contested Space of Multinationals: Varieties of Institutionalism, Varieties of Capitalism'. *Human Relations*, 59(11): 1467–90.

Ohmae, K. (1994). *The Borderless World: Power and Strategy in the Interlinked Economy*. London: Harper Collins.

Ortmann, G. (1988). 'Macht, Spiel, Konsens', in W. Küpper and G. Ortmann (eds.), *Mikropolitik*. Opladen: Westdeutscher Verlag, 13–26.

Perlmutter, H. (1969). 'The Tortuous Evolution of the Multi-National Corporation'. *Columbia Journal of World Business*, 4(1): 9–18.

Powell, W. W. and DiMaggio, P. J. (eds.) (1991). *The New Institutionalism in Organizational Analysis*. Chicago, IL: University of Chicago Press.

Prahalad, C. K. and Doz, Y. (1999). *The Multinational Mission: Balancing Local Demands and Global Vision*. New York: Free Press.

Rugman, A. (2001). *The End of Globalization: Why Global Strategy Is a Myth and How to Profit From the Realities of Regional Markets*. New York: Amacom.

Scott, W. R. (2001). *Institutions and Organizations*, 2nd edn. Thousand Oaks, CA: SAGE.

Steger, M. B. (2013). *Globalization: A Very Short Introduction*. Oxford: Oxford University Press.

Taylor, M. (ed.) (2008). *Global Economy Contested: Power and Conflict across the International Division of Labour*. London and New York: Routledge.

Teece, D., Pisano, G., and Shuen, A. (1997). 'Dynamic Capabilities and Strategic Management'. *Strategic Management Journal*, 18(7): 509–33.

UNCTAD (United Nations Conference on Trade and Investment) (2014). *World Investment Report*. Geneva: UNCTAD.

Verbeke, A. (2009). *International Business Strategy*. Cambridge: Cambridge University Press.

Vernon, R. (1966). 'International Investment and International Trade in the Product Cycle'. *Quarterly Journal of Economics*, 80(2): 190–207.

Westney, E. D. (1993). 'Institutionalization Theory and the Multinational Corporation', in S. Ghoshal and E. D. Westney (eds.), *Organization Theory and the Multinational Corporation*. London: Macmillan, 53–76.

Whitford, J. and Zirpoli, F. (2016). 'The Network Firm as a Political Coalition', *Organization Studies*, 37(9), 1227–48.

Whitley, R. (1999). *Divergent Capitalisms. The Social Structuring and Change of Business Systems*. Oxford: Oxford University Press.

CHAPTER 26

MANAGEMENT AND CONSULTANCY

Ambivalence, Complexity, and Change

ANDREW STURDY, CHRISTOPHER WRIGHT, AND NICK WYLIE

INTRODUCTION

> In place of the "organization man" of corporate hierarchies emerges a new stereotype: the brash ... high-flyer, adept with the language of MBA programmes and big league consultants, parachuting from one change assignment to the next ... For less senior managers, the new images available are ... managers as coaches, team-builders, facilitators and change agents. (Grey, 1999: 570 and 574).

THIS stereotype of the modern or '*post*-bureaucratic' *manager* at the turn of the last century bears a remarkable similarity with more established images of the management *consultant*. Have then, managers become more like management consultants, with an emphasis on change management, formal tools, project working, and facilitation preferred over explicit hierarchical control? In this chapter, we consider this question, but as part of a more specific focus on the wider relationship between management and consultancy in historical terms, as an activity and in relation to how managers interact with consultants. As we shall see, this is a difficult task because, if management is hard to pin down in definitional terms, the same is true of consultancy, if not more so. Both are diverse, contested, and subject to change. As Fincham and Clark (2002: 2) note in relation to consulting, 'no sooner are the limits of the industry identified or the composition of consultancy skills articulated than these factors (unique tasks, skills, and firms) become redundant'.

Nevertheless, most would concede that management and consultancy are closely related, with one shaping the other. First, as Kipping (2002) argues, the broad waves of consulting based upon scientific management, strategy, and information technology

(IT) emerged largely in response to the concerns of managers in large corporations. In the other direction, it also seems clear that consultancy has had some significant effects on management practice. One review for example (Sturdy, 2011), outlined a host of outcomes linked to the classic functions offered by consultants in projects—providing expertise, facilitation, extra resources, and/or legitimation. These combine with the effects of consulting activities outside of projects such as 'thought leadership', training future managers and as role models of management innovation such as with culture and knowledge management. These outcomes are not always positive for management in that consultancy can be a substitute for management and its success and legitimacy can serve to undermine the authority of other managers.

This chapter explores the relationship between management and management consultancy by drawing on a range of literature on the subject. This includes bringing together for the first time, some of our own research on managers acting as clients of consulting and as internal consultants or a new breed of 'consultant managers' (e.g. Sturdy, Wright, and Wylie, 2015; Sturdy and Wright, 2011; Wylie, Sturdy, and Wright, 2014). It is organized in the following way. In the next section, we explore the different ways of understanding the relationship between management and consulting, before analysing how relations have changed over time, up to the present. We then examine the relationship directly, in terms of how client managers interact with consultants in practice, before concluding with a brief discussion of the wider implications of our analysis and questions for further research.

A Confused and Ambivalent Relationship

We have already noted how both management and consulting have different and contested meanings. Some of this derives from differences over what management or consulting *should* be and, in particular, how inclusive or exclusive they are in membership (Grey, 1999). Such tensions are evident elsewhere such as in human resource management (HRM) (Guest, 1987) and project management (Hodgson, 2002), where exclusivity is typically associated with the professionalization projects of different occupational groups. Confusion and conflict also arise from the diversity of forms within an occupation and how these can provide the basis for different objects of personal identification. Internal diversity is quite normal in occupations (Fine, 1996), but is perhaps especially applicable to both management and consulting, given their openness and ambiguity (Harding, Lee, and Ford, 2014; Kitay and Wright, 2007). In management consulting, one can contrast, for example, the experienced sole practitioner providing niche or esoteric advice with the young 'blue chip' employee implementing standard models. But there are many other variations. A study by Kitay and Wright (2007) for example, found a wide range of activities and roles under the consulting label. These provided the basis for occupational identities categorized into the consultant as 'professional' (the most common), 'prophet' (elite), 'business person', and 'service worker'. Furthermore, they were drawn on by individuals selectively, according to the context such as a particular consulting sector or hierarchical level. Other identifications are also evident, including alternative occupations or disciplines such as HRM or OD, not least given the stigma sometimes attached to consulting (and management) (Brocklehurst, Grey, and Sturdy, 2010; Sturdy, 2009). Given such difficulties, analytically, we shall focus on dominant images of consultancy and management which relate mostly to those acting at the middle levels. Even here, we see three different positions on the relationship between management and consulting—as equivalent, different, and the same, only in some respects.

Management and Consulting as Equivalent

To many, there is little difference between management and consulting. Both often perform very similar types of activity, sometimes directly on behalf of the owners of organizations or, if not, consultants might simply legitimate management or act as a scapegoat for it (Sturdy, 2011). But consulting and management are seen as equivalent in two more specific senses, one more aspirational than the other. First, to those who subscribe to, or pursue a professional status for management, the roles are very close. For example, the early UK management pioneer, Lyndall Urwick, thought that management should be a third-party activity, independent from both capital and labour (Brech, Thomson, and Wilson, 2010; see also Shenhav, 1999). Variations of this view have persisted, albeit with limited success (Khurana, 2007; Poole, Mansfield, and Mendes, 2001), and are reflected in the fact that the professional body of consulting in the UK (the Institute of Consulting) is part of the broader Chartered Institute of *Management*.

Second and more significantly, management and consulting coincide in one of the two main definitions of consulting. This emphasizes the practice of providing assistance directed towards organizational improvement. Here, *we can all be consultants* in particular contexts, regardless of our main occupation: 'Thus a manager can also act as a consultant if he or she decides to give advice and help to a fellow manager, or even to subordinates rather than directing them or issuing orders to them' (Kubr, 1996: 3). This is a highly *inclusive* view of consulting, derived largely from humanistic and process consultancy traditions (Schein, 1987) where the emphasis is on facilitation or, more simply, helping (Schein, 2009). However, this tradition of consulting is declining in contexts where it was once significant, even if some of the activities (e.g., superficially non-directive styles of change intervention and coaching) are not.

Management and Consulting as Different

The second main view of consulting is an exclusive one, typically favoured by professional consulting associations (and shared by many consulting researchers). It presents consulting as a special service for managers which involves specific qualifications or skills and training, used to help identify and analyse problems and recommend solutions 'in an objective and independent manner' (Kubr, 1996: 3). As we shall see, this 'professional' and 'expert' model of consulting emerged in a particular way in the USA in the 1930s (David, Sine, and Haveman, 2013). It is not the only model, nor is it without internal tensions (e.g., over routes to professionalism), but it conforms to a broader, still dominant, image of consulting as a 'distinctive occupation' or profession compared to management (Kitay and Wright, 2007: 1615). This distinctiveness is evident in a number of respects, notably, in terms of knowledge, relationships, work and career patterns, and personal characteristics.

First, regardless of how 'objective' and 'independent' of managerial clients consultants actually are, they are seen as exempt from the day to day administration of organizations and as having no direct responsibility for decisions or hierarchical authority to instruct. This echoes wider, longstanding distinctions between managers and experts both within and beyond the organization (Brint, 1996). Given that, in most cases, there is no compulsion to use such experts, they have to rely strongly on persuasion and relationship building. *Within* organizations too, these 'staff professionals', as they were once known (Dalton, 1950; Daudigeos, 2013), were also considered distinctive from managers in terms of their lower organizational loyalty and greater commitment to specialist expertise and extra-organizational reference groups. They were more 'cosmopolitan' in their orientation or latent identity (Gouldner, 1957: 287).

With *external* experts, such as consultants, this distinction was reinforced by the short-term or project-based nature of assignments. Such a view of consultancy conforms to contemporary definitions used in the UK public sector for example, which distinguish consultancy from 'steady state' activities (and those of interim managers and outsourcing) (OGC, 2006). Likewise, a core area of expertise for consultants—change management—was long seen as being of only periodic concern to managers and even then, their focus would be on *implementation*, rather than planning and integrating functional groups (Armbrüster and Kipping, 2002). More generally, since the start of professional consulting, relatively abstract methods and models have been used which were quite alien to managers, at least until the rise of the Masters of Business Administration (MBA) (David, Sine, and Haveman, 2013; McDonald, 2013). Such approaches were deployed for a range of reasons such as ensuring consistency and quality (Werr, Stjernberg, and Docherty, 1997). This became especially important as consultancies grew in size and geographical coverage and adopted the approach, started by strategy firms such as McKinsey & Co., of recruiting large numbers of young, relatively inexperienced MBA graduates from elite universities and business schools (McKenna, 2006).

This shift in selection criteria, combined with the 'up or out' policy of many large consulting firms, generated an image and partial reality of consultants as quite distinct from their managerial clients in educational background, age, career dynamism and job security (Kipping, 2011). In countries like the UK for example, management careers traditionally would involve few, if any, changes of employer or function and formal management education has only taken off relatively recently (Poole, Mansfield, and Mendes, 2001).

Indeed, for some it would still be 'contentious' to include management as an expert group (Fincham, 2012: 209). Rather, in keeping with the UK's standard occupational classification for example, management is, once again, associated more with hierarchical levels and a control function than a specific occupational group. However, others do include management and its sub-disciplines in classifications of expertise. Reed (1996) for instance, in an influential study of expert labour, separates consultancy from management. Consultancy is classified (along with IT and financial consultants) under 'entrepreneurial professions' or knowledge workers who may subject managers to control on behalf of capital. By contrast, Fincham (2012) focuses only on specific management occupations, with consultancy again paired with IT as a 'business service', while HRM and project management are placed in a 'quasi-professions' group (also Muzio et al., 2011).

Such contrasting classifications of expert groups serve to highlight the contested nature of occupational boundaries, but they can be useful for specific analytical purposes—as ideal types. Indeed, while the distinctions outlined above are effectively stereotypes in that they are not presented as being especially sensitive to context or variation, they serve to highlight a central theme in our analysis—that the traditional, expert or professional view of the management consultant compares well with contemporary images of post- or, more specifically, the hybrid or *neo*-bureaucratic manager (Sturdy, Wright, and Wylie, 2015). As outlined in Table 26.1, this contrasts with images of the manager in bureaucracies in terms of work activities, occupational and career dynamics and identities (see also Donnelly, 2009, on contrasting employment relations between knowledge work, such as consulting and bureaucracy).

Table 26.1 Traditional (stereotypical) distinctions between managers and consultants (adapted from Sturdy, Wright, and Wylie, 2015)

	Bureaucratic managers	'Professional' consultants
Activities	Day to day; experience-based and sector-specific knowledge; change rare and has implementation focus. Relationships based on hierarchy and function; internally focused; and high accountability (masculine).	Short-term, change/project-based and integrative; use of qualification-based and abstract methods to advise. Formally independent of (client) hierarchy; reliance on persuasion (feminine); externally networked.
Occupation/Career	Little management education; single firm career by seniority; relative job security.	Specialized training/education (e.g. MBA); high job/employer mobility/insecurity ('up or out').
Identities	Bureaucratic/hierarchical and organization-based (locals).	Professional, qualification/occupation-based; externally and change oriented and distinct from (middle) managers (cosmopolitans).

Management and Consulting: the Same and Different

So, depending on one's perspective on in-/exclusivity and empirical focus, consulting and management can be seen either as very similar or quite distinct. This suggests that a more realistic position might be to see them as *both* the same *and* different. Indeed, others do implicitly adopt this position. In the prescriptive literature for example, Wickham (1999: 3) sees consulting as a 'special form of management'. More concretely, Fincham (2012: 215) sees it as the 'expert arm of management' or, by focusing on its agency role for managerial clients, as 'extruded management'—the 'agent's agent' (also Fincham, 2003)—or as competing directly with management groups. These are helpful from a structural perspective, but are also reflected in studies exploring identity. For example, Sturdy et al. (2009) show how consultants seek to identify *both* with their managerial clients (as 'insiders') *and* as separate from them, according to the specific context such as the phase of a project (also Kitay and Wright, 2003). Indeed, it is important to highlight that, for all but the self-employed, *external* consultants are simultaneously employees themselves, often in bureaucratic organizations, and sometimes acting as managers (see Donnelly, 2009, for a study of this tension). For example, in stark contrast to the often elite, even glamorous image of consulting, those who are consultants as a result of redundancy from a managerial position can see *consulting as failed management*. And even those in seemingly elite consulting positions can regard them as merely stepping stones to (senior) management (also McGinn, 2013). Such observations contribute to a more complex 'both/and' view of consulting and management (see Table 26.2), but also reiterate the importance of being more explicit about contexts. So, for example, the idealized contrast set out above might best be seen in terms of middle managers in bureaucratic organizations in the UK up to the 1980s, compared with middle and junior ranking consultants in large strategy or general consulting firms at the same time.

Table 26.2 The relationship between management and consulting (adapted from Sturdy, Wright, and Wylie, 2015)

Same	Consulting as management work—owners' agents or management scapegoats (Sturdy, 2011).
	Process consulting (facilitation) as integral to management (Schein, 1987, 2009).
	Management as an independent, professional, role (Khurana, 2007).
Different	Consulting as advisory (cosmopolitans) and management as a hierarchical level with day to day operational responsibility (locals).
	Consulting as knowledge work or an entrepreneurial profession; management as comprising organizational professions (Reed, 1996).
Both	Special, expert, and externalized management—the agents' agent or competitor (Fincham, 1999, 2012; Ruef, 2002).
	Identify variably with managers and consulting (Sturdy et al., 2009).
	Both are expert labour of different kinds (Fincham, 2012; Reed, 1996).

However, specification also highlights how forms of consulting and management, and therefore the relationships between them, are subject to change, to which we now turn.

Waves of Change and Convergence? The Ambivalent Historical Relationship of Management and Consultancy

A close but ambivalent relationship between consulting and management is also evident historically, where each party has stimulated changes in the other. A useful overview of this process is provided by Kipping (2002), who characterizes the long-term historical development of consultancy as occurring in a series of waves of different consultant offerings, expertise and models based in large part upon changes in managerial demand, that is, consulting as management-led. As he argues, 'consultancy can be understood as a kind of reflection of prevailing managerial problems and definitions. Thus, when there was a major shift in the role of managers and in the focus of their attention, the kind of consultancy they used also changed' (Kipping, 2002: 29).

The first wave of management consultancy evolved during the early twentieth century as the owners of large manufacturers struggled with the complexities of shop-floor efficiency, production control, and cost accounting. In response, a new breed of efficiency experts emerged and formed the first management consultancies, linked to the methods of scientific management (Wright and Kipping, 2012). During the 1920s and 1930s, the first international management consulting firm, the Bedaux Company, established a presence extending from the industrial heartland of the United States, to Canada, Europe, and Australia, working for major multinational corporations such as Eastman Kodak, General Electric, DuPont, and B. F. Goodrich (Kipping, 2002). Importantly, these early efficiency experts not only provided advice, but were actively involved in the implementation of work redesign, work measurement (time and motion study), and wage incentive schemes (Wright, 2000). Between the 1940s and the 1960s, scientific management continued to be a core area of management consulting services, as manufacturing industry expanded globally during the post-war economic boom. Here, external consultants often played a central role in not only disseminating new techniques and methods of production engineering and operational efficiency, but were also involved in the training of managers in production techniques, human relations, marketing, and cost accounting, and were also involved in early moves towards the professionalization of management as an occupational group (Wright, 1995, 2000).

However, the interrelationship of management and consultancy is not only evident in scientific management. A second and quite different wave of management consultancy began in the 1930s in the United States and reached international prominence during the 1960s (McKenna, 2006). Focused on working with the top executives of the largest corporations, these structure and strategy consultants emerged at the time when the largest US corporations were evolving into multi-divisional structures controlled by a corporate head office; companies like General Motors, US Steel, and DuPont (Chandler, 1962; Drucker, 1946). The most famous of the new elite consultancies was McKinsey & Co. (Kipping, 1999; McKenna, 2006), but competitors also emerged during the 1960s and 1970s such as Boston Consulting Group (BCG) and Bain and Co. Here, we can see perhaps the closest parallels with the traditional *professional* conception of consultancy as quite different from management, in these firms' emphasis upon their role as external advisors on new corporate structures and strategies (David, Sine, and Haveman, 2013; Kitay and Wright, 2007). Importantly however, they also had a powerful influence in shaping management education, specifically the emergence of the professional business school and the MBA programs that have now come to dominate global management education (Engwall, 2012; McKenna, 2006).

Changes in markets, technology and business needs further drove changes in consulting in the third wave. Here, the dominant driver was technological, most notably the rapid development of computers and the reorganization of business activities this precipitated (Kipping, 2002). First harnessed by the large accounting majors, computerization of businesses drove not only financial activities, but the very way in which corporations operated and interacted across supply chains. An early mover here was the accounting firm Arthur Andersen, which established its own consulting division, Andersen Consulting, to advise and help clients implement the new information technologies (Wright, 2002). Andersen was soon followed by the other large accounting firms, and as these consulting divisions grew in size and revenues they increasingly were spun-off as independent consulting firms (e.g., Deloittes, Coopers & Lybrand, Price Waterhouse, Ernst & Young) (O'Shea and Madigan, 1997). New information technologies also facilitated a focus on organizational restructuring, delayering, and downsizing, and during the 1990s and 2000s, management consultancies grew dramatically on the back of growing corporate demand for these services (Galal, Richter, and Wendlandt, 2012). One of the best-known examples of this trend was the vogue for Business Process Reengineering (BPR) (Fincham and Evans, 1999; Hammer and Champy, 1993). Indeed, consultancy increasingly became a form of 'externalized management' (Ruef, 2002), offering to take on many previous in-house management functions as outsourced providers (Galal, Richter, and Wendlandt, 2012).

Hence, rather than simple competitors, management consultants and managers have essentially existed in a symbiotic relationship, with consultants dependent on changing managerial needs and managers utilizing consultants to not only provide advice, but also assist in the implementation of organizational change and the training of managers in new techniques and methods of management. As we shall see, this symbiotic relationship has continued as consultancies have become an accepted part of managerial careers in the movement from MBA to a management position in industry (Lemann, 1999; Sturdy and Wright, 2008).

Consultancy becomes Management and Management becomes Consultancy?

We have seen how the form of external consulting and its relationship to management has changed, especially with the rise of the strategy or 'professional' model and then, of accounting and IT firms. Change continues such as through the offshoring and automating of *consulting* expertise (Christensen, Wang, and van Bever, 2013), but also more generally. In this section, we point to two particular developments whereby consulting and management seem to be moving together or becoming de-differentiated. First, for some time now, the consulting industry has shifted towards carrying out what were once considered management activities. This is most evident in the move towards consultancy being involved in change *implementation* rather than restricting itself to advice or facilitation (Morris, 2000). As we noted earlier, implementation was part of early forms of consulting, but re-emerged as a response to client manager criticisms of advice-based consulting as well as through consulting firms' own efforts to expand revenue streams (Sturdy, 1997). The shift is also reflected in the wider expansion of consulting firms' services such as outsourced IT-related activities discussed above, but also providing an extra resource as a 'body shop', even if these do not always come under the label of consulting per se. Thus, as O'Mahoney and Markham state, if one were to restrict the definition of consulting to providing expert management advice, about 50% of people who describe themselves as consultants would be excluded (O'Mahoney and Markham, 2013: 11) and this does not even consider various other groups such as internal consultants or 'consultant managers'. The final way in which consulting is becoming more like management is also, in part, a response to client managers' concerns. Here, some large firms have shifted away from appointing young MBA graduates with limited business experience towards seeking out more experienced managers (Sturdy, 2011).

While external consulting may have shifted towards activities and personnel, once more strongly associated with line management, probably the biggest shift has been in the other direction as we hinted with the quote at the start of the chapter. Here, as part of a broad shift towards *neo*-bureaucracy, managers have changed their form and become: more concerned with change, integrative project working and abstract tools and knowledge; more flexible/insecure in their careers; and less hierarchical and more market oriented in their style of interaction (Farrell and Morris, 2013; Reed, 2011). Such developments are neither wholesale nor necessarily widespread (Bolin and Härenstam, 2008; Johnson et al., 2009), but even sceptics agree on some form of change in management along these lines (Clegg, 2012; Hales, 2002). This has been driven by numerous factors, including the role of management education and financialization (see Sturdy, Wright, and Wylie, 2015). However, what is most relevant for our purposes is that the shift in management towards consultancy has been partly fuelled by consultancy itself. Consultancy is both a medium and an example of neo-bureaucracy.

Most conventionally, consultancy has been heavily involved in spreading management ideas to organizations, including those based around critiques of bureaucracy (Boltanski and Chiapello, 2005). This occurs either directly, through client projects or promotional activities such as 'thought leadership', or indirectly, as a role model in organizational innovation based on the success of the industry as whole (McKenna, 2006). But neo-bureaucracy is also being introduced in the *form* of consultancy, as management explicitly takes on or internalises consultancy practices. As we argue below, this is happening in three main ways: (1) changing occupational identities; (2) recruitment of ex-consultants; and (3) establishing consulting units.

First, the transformation of management occupations such as HRM or *internal* auditing has involved the adoption of consultancy as an inherent and explicit part of their work activity (Selim, Woodward, and Allegrini, 2009; Wright, 2008). This relates both to a more general move into change management and the pursuit of a more 'strategic', less hierarchical, advisory or partner role (Caldwell, 2001). The case of HRM is particularly illustrative of this shift. Historically the HRM function has always experienced a credibility gap given ambiguities around its contribution and whether it is a specialist or generalist activity (Legge, 1978). To address this, a frequent assertion has been that the HRM profession should focus on strategic rather than administrative work requiring HRM practitioners to operate as consultants or 'change agents' (Caldwell, 2001; Ulrich, 1997). Working in this way is therefore directly related to enhancing HRM's professional status, yet realizing these benefits can be more difficult. For example, change agency is typically associated with other professional groups such as OD specialists or those with expertise in change methodologies such as Lean/Six Sigma (Worren, Ruddle, and Moore, 1999). Consequently, HRM is entering what is already a congested domain in which a number of groups may be competing for jurisdiction (Wright, 2008). Successful claims rely on HR managers demonstrating how their role as change agents/consultants is distinct from other more established groups. This requires HR practitioners to overcome existing (and often negative) assumptions about their occupational background, as well as to ensure that they have sufficient personal credibility in their organization to support a consultancy role (Sturdy, Wright, and Wylie, 2015), problems HRM has tangled with for many years (Wylie, Sturdy, and Wright, 2014).

This again demonstrates the complex relationship between management and consultancy, as well as the different positions outlined above. For example, it is possible to see management and consultancy as equivalent if 'service' functions such as HRM regard offering advisory support and guidance as inherent to their role. Alternatively, the desire to explicitly identify consultancy as an added dimension to HRM work suggests a view of management and consultancy as mutually exclusive activities. As such the third position outlined above, that management and consultancy are both the same *and* different, may also apply. Here management occupations seek a dual identity in which they seek to retain their separate professional associations, but take advantage of the prestige and independence associated with consultancy. Although this would seem to combine the advantages of both being part of management and of consultancy, such dual identities can lead to insecurities (Sturdy, Wright, and Wylie, 2015).

The second mechanism by which management becomes more like consultancy is through the recruitment of ex-consultants. While consultancy practice is recruited into management by default, with the appointment of those trained by consulting firms, such importation is also proactively pursued by some recruiters. This 'consulting diaspora' (Sturdy and Wright, 2008) comprises those who are seen as highly change and market-oriented and skilled in relationship and project management techniques. One practitioner-expert described this phenomenon, coining the term '*consultant managers*', and saw their appointment as a threat to the business of *external* consultants (Czerniawska, 2011). Likewise, in a 2013 *Harvard Business Review* article on the consulting industry, it was claimed that 'precise data are not publicly available, but we know that many companies have hired small armies of former consultants' (Christensen, Wang, and van Bever, 2013: 110). This group not only brings consultancy practices with it, but is especially likely to maintain and develop informal relationships with external consultants (including former colleagues) outside of specific consulting projects. Indeed, as we shall see, working closely with or 'partnering' consultants in this way is an established practice for many externally-oriented managers, in order to keep up to date with management developments (on both sides) (Kitay and Wright, 2004). Again, this is a route through which consulting can be brought into management more or less informally.

The third mechanism involves the development of variously labelled consulting groups or units within large organizations to assist in the management of change projects and programmes. Internal consulting has, of course, existed for some time, but was typically only seen in relation to its external counterpart and, as a result, as rather unfashionable (Armbrüster, 2006; Lacey, 1995). Currently therefore, combined with the fact that management consulting as a whole sometimes has a stigma associated with it, the title 'consultant' or 'consulting' may be absent in internal units, even if many, if not all, of the core characteristics are evident. Indeed, it has been argued that 'internal consultancies have become major players; there are large numbers of managers who are, in fact, working as consultants (…) without even realizing it' (Law, 2009: 63; Visscher, 2006). These units, and the individuals who work in them, exemplify many of the characteristics of *neo*-bureaucracy. For example, they are often insecure, depending heavily on executive sponsorship, and adopt 'non-hierarchical' styles of interaction within hierarchical structures; use consulting methods of change and project management; and play a cross-functional integrating role, including through various forms of pseudo-market 'relationship management' (Sturdy, Wright, and Wylie, 2015).

Together, the developments reflected in these three routes to internalizing consulting have the potential to undermine or cloud the distinctions between consulting and management. One possible view of this de-differentiation is that, much as managerialism became so successful and widespread that the special status of management and of the manager declined (Grey, 1999), so too consultancy is becoming pervasive such that the consultant identity loses distinctiveness and prestige.

Managerial Use of Consultancy— the Active and Passive Client

We have seen how consulting and management have a complex, diverse, and changing relationship, both conceptually and historically. In this final section, we explore how such a pattern is reflected in the way in which they interact in practice. Here, the diversity of roles and positions as well as relations of power, resistance, and interdependence are more evident. These complexities crucially shape the nature of the relationship between managerial clients and consultants. As one senior manager quoted in Sturdy (1997) stated, 'I like working with consultants so long as they report to me and not my boss'. In particular, how active or passive a manager is in relations with consultants is especially important. However, despite a cultural value often being placed on action or 'pro-activity', neither being active or passive necessarily implies success or failure in achieving objectives (Hislop, 2002). We use the term 'active' as seeking to assert control or affect the environment—*deliberate action* (Bohart and Tallman, 1996) while being 'passive' implies an acceptance of the environment, of others' intentions, actions and their consequences.

The first problem is identifying what or who 'the client' is. This is not a new challenge. Schein, for example, described it as an 'ambiguous and problematical' process (1997: 202), rejecting a unitary view of the client as being the organization. He drew distinctions between the first '*contact*' for the consultant and '*primary*' owner of the problem, both of whom are likely to be managers, and other '*intermediate*' individuals or groups directly, *unwittingly* or *indirectly* involved in a project. To these, we might add the *potential* and *former* client, that is, those actors who engage with consultants in between formal projects and/or in relation to various forms of consultancy sales initiatives. In other words, manager-consultant relations are by no means restricted to projects.

The second problem concerns the object and motives of client activity. This arises from a degree of variability in focus in the literature where emphasis can be given to exerting control over (i.e. actively managing) *the consultants*, and/or *the ideas* associated with consulting interventions. For example, a client might actively seek out and select consultants for a project, but passively accept the management ideas involved without much criticism or adaptation (see Figure 26.1) (Hislop, 2002; Sturdy and Wright, 2011).

	Passive clients	Active clients
Controlling consultants	A Victims of the sales pitch	C Purchaser, competitor, or partner
Controlling ideas	B Followers of fashion	D Co-producers

FIGURE 26.1 Images of the Passive and Active Managerial Client

(adapted from Sturdy and Wright, 2011).

Passive Managers

The first of the two images of the passive managerial client (low assertion of control over consultants—quadrant A) is quite common in the literature. Here, managers are seen as highly dependent; lacking in knowledge or experience of consultancy use; doing little to manage or evaluate consultants; and being vulnerable, even gullible, with regard to their sales techniques and political manoeuvring (Ernst and Kieser, 2002). Furthermore, the passive client is implied in the many accounts of active *consultants*—doing things *to* clients as technical experts, rhetoricians, and 'catalysts' for example (Blake and Mouton, 1983). This also applies to the second image of the passive client, but with respect to management ideas (quadrant B). Here, the critical consulting literature, with its broader concern with management knowledge, emphasises the apparently uncritical adoption of management ideas and models by clients (Huczynski, 1993; Kieser, 2002).

Active Managers

The active user of consultants (quadrant C) involves images of managers as purchasers and partners acting at the organizational boundary (Karantinou and Hogg, 2009). The purchaser deploys resource power and project management skills to be controlling and systematic and even sceptical in the selection, management, and evaluation of consultants (Deelmann and Mohe, 2006). Such views of the active managerial client are reinforced by the few available images of consultants as subordinate, outsourced 'grey' labour (Alvesson and Johansson, 2002; Höner and Mohe, 2009). At the same time, managers can also be active in using the signalling function of consultants to legitimate their own or organizational ends (Armbrüster, 2006). Similarly, *potential* and *intermediate* clients may actively resist the use of consultants because of the personal, occupational, or organizational threat they pose or on the basis of consultants' outsider status—acting as gatekeepers (Sturdy, 1997). Such direct competition or conflict between managers and consultants remains relatively neglected in the literature although is widely recognized in practice (Sturdy and Wright, 2011). This position is also countered by the other dominant image of the active managerial user of consultants—as a 'partner' or trusted colleague. Here, emphasis is placed on establishing and maintaining shared objectives through negotiation and dialogue where parties co-habit a liminal space in between organizational boundaries as part of the same project team (Czarniawska and Mazza, 2003).

The partner image has a direct parallel with that of the final category—the active managerial client with respect to management ideas or the co-producer of knowledge (quadrant D). There are variations within this category between developing and adapting ideas into new knowledge—exploration—and managers actively seeking an off-the-shelf 'best practice'—exploitation (cf. Antal and Krebsbach-Gnath, 2001; March, 1991). Finally, as already noted, managers can be active with respect to the symbolic, signalling, and political role of management ideas for organizations, groups, and individuals (Staw and Epstein, 2000). Likewise, potential and indirect clients may actively resist new ideas from the outside because of their 'foreignness' or the other threats they pose (Kipping and Armbrüster, 2002).

Conditions for the Active Managerial Use of Consultancy

Images of the managerial user of consultancy in the literature continue to alternate between passivity and activity, depending in part, on the research focus and perspective. However, as Fincham (1999) pointed out some time ago, power, knowledge, and dependency relations vary according to context. So, we can ask the question, when are managers more likely to be active in relation to consulting use? The first thing to consider is the nature of the project itself. For example, Lippitt and Lippitt (1986) distinguished between *directive* projects, where solutions are recommended or imposed by consultants on managerial clients as 'patients', and *non-directive* projects such as those involving process consulting. Similarly, Markham (1997: 72) outlines different conditions associated with 'client-centred' projects:

- Client wants independence; to learn; and to take decisions
- Consultant wants to prevent dependency and the client to grow
- Little empathy in the relationship; consultant not totally acceptable to management
- High risk project or dynamic/long term problem

Implicit in these factors are the managerial client's ability/knowledge and power/dependency. Hence, we might expect to find the active use of consultants greater amongst managers with prior experience of consultancy (Sturdy and Wright, 2008), and in high risk and critical organizational changes (Abrahamson, 1996). Likewise, even highly dependent managers may pursue an active approach given sufficient levels of knowledge and individual self-confidence (Fincham, 1999). This might also be guided by formal training and governance mechanisms for the management of consultancy projects, or a culture of professional purchasing or project management (Werr and Pemer, 2007).

Pointing to likely general conditions of managerial activity can be helpful, but in keeping with the study of innovation more generally, patterns need to be identified within their specific contexts (Tidd, 2001). Furthermore, this approach to the concept of activity remains rather static. For example, Nachum (1999) points out how it is not so much that dependency relations shape how active managers might be, but that active participation itself creates interdependency over time. More conventionally, a number of accounts in the business services field point to variations in the level of client activity between phases of an engagement (Mills and Morris, 1986). Similarly, one of the few studies of consultancy to focus on the active managerial client identified variations over the course of the consulting project (Hislop, 2002). For example, in one case, a client was active in selecting a consultant, but then chose to define the consultant as the dominant actor in the subsequent phases—a form of 'active passivity' perhaps.

Conclusion

In this chapter, we have explored an otherwise neglected feature of management—its relationship with consulting. We have done so by examining how this has been perceived in different contexts, notably the contrasting dominant definitions of consulting as inclusive of management—'we are all consultants'—or exclusive and 'professional'. Our position of seeing management and management consulting as both the same *and* different was then developed through a brief historical account of the emergence of consulting in relation to changes in management, including recent patterns of convergence towards 'consultancy as management' and 'management as consultancy'. Finally, we looked at the relationship in terms of how managerial clients and their consultants actually work together. Here, power, resistance, and dependency came to the fore as well as the diversity of positions and contexts managers and consultants can occupy, with differing implications for their relationship as well as for the use of management ideas. In taking this perspective, we can see how although managers and consultants can share skills, orientations, identities, and interests, there are also zones of competition and conflict, even within the same project.

Our approach has sought to broaden the analysis of management away from traditional concerns with managerial functions, roles, and activities within organizations towards looking at a particular, extreme case of management that often spans organizational boundaries. Here, consultants are either: the 'shock troops' of management, helping to introduce ideas and practices onto other management groups; 'grey labour' serving their managerial client masters for expertise and legitimation; or seemingly innovative role models for managers to emulate or to emerge from on a career trajectory.

This analysis is helpful in extending the view of management in terms of its form, constituency, and effects and placing this in historical or dynamic perspective. However, it also raises questions which might be addressed in further research. In particular, in focusing on the relationship between management and consultancy, other expert groups are side-lined. For example, the few comparative historical analyses of consultancy that exist, highlight that there are often alternatives to consultancy, within and beyond management ranks, such as various industry and government bodies as well as universities, which provide management ideas and resources (Kipping and Wright, 2012). How then does consultancy come to assume dominance in some management, historical, geographical, and sectoral contexts and not others? Is this likely to continue or is contemporary management better served by other sources or channels of expertise? Finally, whether in the form of facilitative, process techniques or the more dominant, mechanistic tool-based approaches, consulting reflects a particular form of organizing. What alternatives are there to these and to management more generally as a form of organizing? In considering management as an activity, occupation, and identity, it behoves us as critical researchers to also imagine other forms of organizing beyond the current neo-liberal templates of market fundamentalism and 'rational' management.

References

Abrahamson, E. (1996). 'Management Fashion', *Academy of Management Review*, 21(1): 254–85.

Alvesson, M. and Johansson, A. (2002). 'Professionalism and Politics in Management Consultancy Work', in T. Clark and R. Fincham (eds.), *Critical Consulting: New Perspectives on the Management Advice Industry*. Oxford: Blackwell, 228–46.

Antal, A. B. and Krebsbach-Gnath, C. (2001). 'Consultants as Agents of Organisational Learning', in M. Dierkes, A. B. Antal, J. Child, and I. Nonaka (eds.), *Handbook of Organizational Learning and Knowledge*. Oxford: Oxford University Press, 462–83.

Armbrüster, T. (2006). *The Economics and Sociology of Management Consulting*. Cambridge: Cambridge University Press.

Armbrüster, T. and Kipping, M. (2002). 'Types of Knowledge and the Client–Consultant Interaction', in K. Sahlin-Andersson and L. Engwall (eds.), *The Expansion of Management Knowledge: Carriers, Flows and Sources*. Stanford: CA: Stanford University Press, 96–110.

Blake, R. and Mouton, J. (1983). *Consultation: A Handbook for Individual and Organizational Development*. Reading, MA: Addison-Wesley.

Bohart, A. C. and Tallman, K. (1996). 'The Active Client: Therapy as Self-Help'. *Journal of Humanistic Psychology*, 36(3): 7–30.

Bolin, M. and Härenstam, A. (2008). 'An Empirical Study of Bureaucratic and Post-Bureaucratic Characteristics in 90 Workplaces'. *Economic and Industrial Democracy*, 29(4): 541–64.

Boltanski, L. and Chiapello, E. (2005). *The New Spirit of Capitalism*. London: Verso.

Brech, E., Thomson, A., and Wilson, J. F. (2010). *Lyndall Urwick, Management Pioneer: A Biography*. Oxford: Oxford University Press.

Brint, S. (1996). *In an Age of Experts: The Changing Role of Professionals in Politics and Public Life*. Princeton, NJ: Princeton University Press.

Brocklehurst, M., Grey, C., and Sturdy, A. (2010). 'Management: The Work that Dares not Speak its Name', *Management Learning*, 41(1): 7–19.

Caldwell, R. (2001). 'Champions, Adapters, Consultants and Synergists: The New Change Agents in HRM'. *Human Resource Management Journal*, 11(3): 39–52.

Chandler, A. (1962). *Strategy and Structure*. Cambridge, MA: MIT Press.

Christensen, C. M., Wang, D., and van Bever, D. (2013). 'Consulting on the Cusp of Disruption'. *Harvard Business Review*, 91(10): 106–14.

Clegg, S. (2012). 'The End of Bureaucracy?'. *Research in the Sociology of Organizations*, 35: 59–84.

Czarniawska, B. and Mazza, C. (2003). 'Consulting as a Liminal Space'. *Human Relations*, 56(3): 267–90.

Czerniawska, F. (2011). 'Consultant-Managers: Something Else to Worry About'. *The Source Blog*, 3 May. Available at: <http://www.sourceforconsulting.com/blog/2011/05/03/consultant-managers-something-else-to-worry-about/> (accessed 26 July 2016).

Dalton, M. (1950). 'Conflicts between Staff and Line Managerial Officers'. *American Sociological Review*, 15(3): 342–51.

Daudigeos, T. (2013). 'In \Their Profession's Service: How Staff Professionals Exert Influence in Their Organization'. *Journal of Management Studies*, 50(5): 722–49.

David, R. J., Sine, W. D., and Haveman, H. A. (2013). 'Seizing Opportunity in Emerging Fields: How Institutional Entrepreneurs Legitimated the Professional Form of Management Consulting'. *Organization Science*, 24(2): 356–77.

Deelmann, T. and Mohe, M. (eds.) (2006). *Selection and Evaluation of Consultants*. Munich: Rainer Hampp Verlag.

Donnelly, R. (2009). 'The Knowledge Economy and the Restructuring of Employment: The Case of Consultants'. *Work, Employment and Society*, 23(2): 323–41.

Drucker, P. (1946). *The Concept of the Corporation*. New York: John Day.

Engwall, L. (2012). 'Business Schools and Consultancies: The Blurring of Boundaries', in M. Kipping and T. Clark (eds.), *The Oxford Handbook of Management Consulting*. Oxford: Oxford University Press, 365–85.

Ernst, B. and Kieser, A. (2002). 'In Search of Explanations for the Consulting Explosion', in K. Sahlin-Andersson and L. Engwall (eds.), *The Expansion of Management Knowledge: Carriers, Flows, and Sources*. Stanford, CA: Stanford University Press, 47–73.

Farrell, C. and Morris, J. (2013). 'Managing the Neo-bureaucratic Organisation: Lessons from the UK's Prosaic Sector'. *The International Journal of Human Resource Management*, 24(7): 1376–92.

Fincham, R. (1999). 'The Consultant-Client Relationship: Critical Perspectives on the Management of Organizational Change'. *Journal of Management Studies*, 36(3): 335–51.

Fincham, R. (2003). 'The Agent's Agent: Power, Knowledge, and Uncertainty in Management Consultancy'. *International Studies of Management and Organization*, 32(4): 67–86.

Fincham, R. (2012). 'Expert Labour as a Differentiated Category: Power, Knowledge and Organisation'. *New Technology, Work and Employment*, 27(3): 208–23.

Fincham, R. and Clark, T. (2002). 'Introduction: The Emergence of Critical Perspectives on Consulting', in T. Clark and R. Fincham (eds.), *Critical Consulting: New Perspectives on the Management Advice Industry*. Oxford: Blackwell, 1–18.

Fincham, R. and Evans, M. (1999). 'The Consultants' Offensive: Reengineering – from Fad to Technique'. *New Technology, Work & Employment*, 14(1): 32–44.

Fine, G. (1996). 'Justifying work: Occupational Rhetorics as Resources in Restaurant Kitchens'. *Administrative Science Quarterly*, 41(1): 90–116.

Galal, K., Richter, A., and Wendlandt, V. (2012). 'IT Consulting and Outsourcing Firms: Evolution, Business Models and Future Prospects', in M. Kipping and T. Clark (eds.), *The Oxford Handbook of Management Consulting*. Oxford: Oxford Univrsity Press, 117–36.

Gouldner, A. W. (1957). 'Cosmopolitans and Locals: Towards an Analysis of Latent Social Roles I'. *Administrative Science Quarterly*, 2(3): 281–306.

Grey, C. (1999). '"We Are all Managers Now"; "We Always Were": On the Development and Demise of Management'. *Journal of Management Studies*, 36(5): 561–85.

Guest, D. E. (1987). 'Human Resource Management and Industrial Relations'. *Journal of Management Studies*, 24(5): 503–21.

Hales, C. (2002). '"Bureaucracy-lite" and Continuities in Managerial Work'. *British Journal of Management*, 13(1): 51–66.

Hammer, M. and Champy, J. (1993). *Reengineering the Corporation: A Manifesto for Business Revolution*. New York: Harper Business.

Harding, N., Lee, H., and Ford, J. (2014). 'Who is "the Middle Manager"?'. *Human Relations*, 67(10): 1213–37.

Hislop, D. (2002). 'The Client Role in Consultancy Relations During the Appropriation of Technological Innovations'. *Research Policy*, 31(5): 657–71.

Hodgson, D. (2002). 'Disciplining the Professional: The Case of Project Management'. *Journal of Management Studies*, 39(6): 803–21.

Höner, D. and Mohe, M. (2009). 'Behind Clients' Doors: What Hinders Client Firms from "Professionally" Dealing with Consultancy?'. *Scandinavian Journal of Management*, 25(3): 299–312.

Huczynski, A. (1993). 'Explaining the Succession of Management Fads'. *International Journal of Human Resource Management*, 4(2): 443–63.

Johnson, P., Wood, G., Brewster, C., and Brookes, M. (2009). 'The Rise of Post-Bureaucracy: Theorists' Fancy or Organizational Praxis?'. *International Sociology*, 24(1): 37–61.

Karantinou, K. M. and Hogg, M. K. (2009). 'An Empirical Investigation of Relationship Development in Professional Business Services'. *Journal of Services Marketing*, 23(4): 249–60.

Khurana, R. (2007). *From Higher Aims to Hired Hands: The Social Transformation of American Business Schools and the Unfulfilled Promise of Management as a Profession*. Princeton, NJ: Princeton University Press.

Kieser, A. (2002). 'Managers as Marionettes? Using Fashion Theory to Explain the Success of Consultancies', in M. Kipping and L. Engwall (eds.), *Management Consulting: Emergence and Dynamics of a Knowledge Industry*. Oxford: Oxford University Press, 167–83.

Kipping, M. (1999). 'American Management Consulting Companies in Western Europe, 1910s to 1990s: Products, Reputation, and Relationships'. *Business History Review*, 73(2): 190–220.

Kipping, M. (2002). 'Trapped in Their Wave: The Evolution of Management Consultancies', in T. Clark and R. Fincham (eds.), *Critical Consulting: New Perspectives on the Management Advice Industry*. Oxford: Blackwell, 28–49.

Kipping, M. (2011). 'Hollow from the Start? Image Professionalism in Management Consulting', *Current Sociology*, 59(4): 530–50.

Kipping, M. and Armbrüster, T. (2002). 'The Burden of Otherness: Limits of Consultancy Interventions in Historical Case Studies', in M. Kipping and L. Engwall (eds.), *Management Consulting: Emergence and Dynamics of a Knowledge Industry*. Oxford: Oxford University Press, 203–21.

Kipping, M. and Wright, C. (2012). 'Consultants in Context: Global Dominance, Societal Effect and the Capitalist System', in M. Kipping and T. Clark (eds.), *The Oxford Handbook of Management Consulting*. Oxford: Oxford University Press, 165–185.

Kitay, J. and Wright, C. (2003). 'Expertise and Organizational Boundaries: The Varying Roles of Australian Management Consultants'. *Asia Pacific Business Review*, 9(3): 21–40.

Kitay, J. and Wright, C. (2004). 'Take the Money and Run? Organisational Boundaries and Consultants' Roles'. *The Service Industries Journal*, 24(3): 1–18.

Kitay, J. and Wright, C. (2007). 'From Prophets to Profits: The Occupational Rhetoric of Management Consultants', *Human Relations*, 60(11): 1613–40.

Kubr, M. (1996). *Management Consulting: A Guide to the Profession*. Geneva: ILO.

Lacey, M. Y. (1995). 'Internal Consulting: Perspectives on the Process of Planned Change'. *Journal of Organizational Change Management*, 8(3): 75–84.

Law, M. (2009). 'Managing Consultants'. *Business Strategy Review*, 20(1): 62–6.

Legge, K. (1978). *Power, Innovation, and Problem-Solving in Personnel Management*. London: McGraw-Hill.

Lemann, N. (1999). 'The Kids in the Conference Room'. *The New Yorker*, 75(31): 209–16.

Lippitt, G. and Lippitt, R. (1986). *The Consulting Process in Action*. San Diego, CA: University Associates Inc.

McDonald, D. (2013). *The Firm: The Story of McKinsey and Its Secret Influence on American Business*. New York: Simon and Schuster.

McGinn, D. (2013). 'Inside Consulting's Black Box'. *Harvard Business Review*, 91(9): 126–7.

McKenna, C. D. (2006). *The World's Newest Profession: Management Consulting in the Twentieth Century*. Cambridge: Cambridge University Press.

March, J. (1991). 'Exploration and Exploitation in Organizational Learning'. *Organization Science*, 2(1): 71–87.

Markham, C. (1997). *Practical Management Consultancy*. London: Accountancy Books.

Mills, P. K. and Morris, J. H. (1986). 'Clients as "Partial" Employees of Service Organizations: Role Development in Client Participation', *Academy of Management Review*, 11(4): 726–35.

Morris, T. (2000). 'From Key Advice To Execution? Consulting Firms and the Implementation of Strategic Decisions', in P. Flood, T. Dromgoole, S. Carroll, and L. Gorman (eds.), *Managing Strategic Implementation: An Organizational Behaviour Perspective*. Oxford: Blackwell, 125–37.

Muzio, D., Hodgson, D., Faulconbridge, J., Beaverstock, J., and Hall, S. (2011). 'Towards Corporate Professionalization: The Case of Project Management, Management Consultancy and Executive Search'. *Current Sociology*, 59(4): 443–64.

Nachum, L. (1999). 'Measurement of Productivity of Professional Services: An Illustration on Swedish Management Consulting Firms'. *International Journal of Operations & Production Management*, 19(9): 922–49.

O'Mahoney, J. and Markham, C. (2013). *Management Consultancy*. Oxford: Oxford University Press.

O'Shea, J. and Madigan, C. (1997). *Dangerous Company: The Consulting Powerhouses and the Businesses They Save and Ruin*. New York: Times Business.

OGC (2006). *Delivering Value from Consultancy*. London: Office of Government Commerce.

Poole, M., Mansfield, R., and Mendes, P. (2001). *Two Decades of Management*. London: The (UK) Institute of Management.

Reed, M. (1996). 'Expert Power and Control in Late Modernity: An Empirical Review and Theoretical Synthesis'. *Organization Studies*, 17(4): 573–97.

Reed, M. (2011). 'The Post-Bureaucratic Organization and the Control Revolution', in S. Clegg, M. Harris, and H. Höpfl (eds.), *Managing Modernity: Beyond Bureaucracy?* Oxford: Oxford University Press, 230–56.

Ruef, M. (2002). 'The Interstices of Organizations: The Expansion of the Management Consulting Profession, 1933–1997', in K. Sahlin-Andersson and L. Engwall (eds.), *The Expansion of Management Knowledge: Carriers, Flows, and Sources*. Stanford, CA: Stanford University Press, 74–95.

Schein, E. (1987). *Process Consultation: Lessons for Managers and Consultants*. Reading, MA: Addison-Wesley.

Schein, E. (1997). 'The Concept of "Client" from a Process Consultation Perspective: A Guide for Change Agents'. *Journal of Organizational Change Management*, 10(3): 202–16.

Schein, E. (2009). *Helping: How to Offer, Give and Receive Help*. San Francisco, CA: Berrett-Koehler.

Selim, G., Woodward, S., and Allegrini, M. (2009). 'Internal Auditing and Consulting Practice: A Comparison between UK/Ireland and Italy'. *International Journal of Auditing*, 13(1): 9–25.

Shenhav, Y. A. (1999). *Manufacturing Rationality: The Engineering Foundations of the Managerial Revolution*. Oxford: Oxford University Press.

Staw, B. M. and Epstein, L. D. (2000). 'What Bandwagons Bring: Effects of Popular Management Techniques on Corporate Performance, Reputation, and CEO Pay'. *Administrative Science Quarterly*, 45(3): 523–56.

Sturdy, A. (1997). 'The Consultancy Process – an Insecure Business?'. *Journal of Management Studies*, 34(3): 389–413.
Sturdy, A. (2009). 'Popular Critiques of Consultancy and a Politics of Management Learning?'. *Management Learning*, 40(4): 457–63.
Sturdy, A. (2011). 'Consultancy's Consequences? A Critical Assessment of Management Consultancy's Impact on Management'. *British Journal of Management*, 22(3): 517–30.
Sturdy, A., Handley, K., Clark, T., and Fincham, R. (2009). *Management Consultancy: Boundaries and Knowledge in Action*. Oxford: Oxford University Press.
Sturdy, A. and Wright, C. (2008). 'A Consulting Aiaspora? Enterprising Selves as Agents of Enterprise'. *Organization*, 15(3): 427–44.
Sturdy, A. and Wright, C. (2011). 'The Active Client: The Boundary-Spanning Roles of Internal Consultants as Gatekeepers, Brokers and Partners of Their External Counterparts'. *Management Learning*, 42(5): 485–503.
Sturdy, A., Wright, C., and Wylie, N. (2015). *Management as Consultancy: Neo-Bureaucracy and the Consultant Manager*. Cambridge: Cambridge University Press.
Tidd, J. (2001). 'Innovation Management in Context: Environment, Organization and Performance'. *International Journal of Management Reviews*, 3(3): 169–83.
Ulrich, D. (1997). *Human Resource Champions*. Boston, MA: Harvard University Press.
Visscher, K. (2006). 'Capturing the Competence of Management Consulting Work'. *Journal of Workplace Learning*, 18(4): 248–60.
Werr, A. and Pemer, F. (2007). 'Purchasing Management Consulting Services: From Management Autonomy to Purchasing Involvement'. *Journal of Purchasing and Supply Management*, 13(2): 98–112.
Werr, A., Stjernberg, T., and Docherty, P. (1997). 'The Functions of Methods of Change in Management Consulting'. *Journal of Organizational Change Management*, 10(4): 288–307.
Wickham, P. A. (1999). *Management Consulting*. London: Financial Times/Pitman.
Worren, N. A. M., Ruddle, K., and Moore, K. (1999). 'From Organizational Development to Change Management: The Emergence of a New Profession'. *Journal of Applied Behavioral Science*, 35(3): 273–86.
Wright, C. (1995). *The Management of Labour: A History of Australian Employers*. Melbourne: Oxford University Press.
Wright, C. (2000). 'From Shopfloor to Boardroom: The Historical Evolution of Australian Management Consulting, 1940s to 1980s'. *Business History*, 42(1): 86–106.
Wright, C. (2002). 'Promoting Demand, Gaining Legitimacy and Broadening Expertise: The Evolution of Consultancy-Client Relationships in Australia', in M. Kipping and L. Engwall (eds.), *Management Consulting: Emergence and Dynamics of a Knowledge Industry*. Oxford: Oxford University Press, 184–202.
Wright, C. (2008). 'Reinventing Human Resource Management: Business Partners, Internal Consultants and the Limits to Professionalisation'. *Human Relations*, 61(8): 1063–86.
Wright, C. and Kipping, M. (2012). 'The Engineering Origins of Consulting – and Their Long Shadow', in T. Clark and M. Kipping (eds.), *The Oxford Handbook of Management Consulting*. Oxford: Oxford University Press, 29–49.
Wylie, N., Sturdy, A., and Wright, C. (2014). 'Change Agencyin Occupational Context: Lessons for HRM'. *Human Resource Management Journal*, 24(1): 95–110.

Author Index

Aaker, D. 265
Abend, G. 387–8, 394, 396
Abrahamson, E. 95, 353, 485, 531
Adams, M. B. 154, 165, 463
Addison, J. T. 163
Adler, N. J. 411, 482, 509
Ahmad, R. 447, 449
Aiken, M. 133, 137
Ailon-Souday, G. 110, 112
Aitken, H. 404
Aitkin, H. G. J. 26
Al Arkoubi, K. 149
Alavi, M. 446–8
Albert, S. 261, 389
Aldrich, H. 140, 257, 265
Alford, R. 259, 409
Allegrini, M. 527
Alliger, G. M. 277
Allison, G. 304
Amit, R. 505
Amundson, S. D. 69
Anderson, J. C. 67, 266, 381
Andrews, K. R. 74
Andriopoulos, C. 350–352
Ang, J. S. K. 490
Angrave, D. 195
Ansari, S. 268
Ansell, C. K. 162
Antaki, C. 110
Antal, A. B. 530
Antonakis, J. 287
Apfelroth, D. S. 90
Appelbaum, E. 181–2, 188
Appelrouth, S. 372
Appleby, R. 92
Appleyard, M. 188
Apud, S. 490
Araujo, L. 66, 74

Arbaugh, J. B. 446–9
Archibald, T. 421
Argyris, C. 109
Aristotle 156
Arman, R. 334, 338
Armbrüster, T. 521, 528, 530–531
Armenakis, A. A. 344
Arnold, J. 429
Arthur, J. 182, 188
Ashby, W. R. 128
Ashcraft, K. 110, 389
Ashford, S. 283
Ashforth, B. 265
Ashkenas, R. N. 145
As-Saber, S. 501
Atwater, L. E. 286, 451
Augé, M. 468
Avey, J. B. 286
Avolio, B. J. 281–2, 286

Baden-Fuller, C. 263–4, 266
Badham, R. 351, 357
Baehr, P. 402, 411–12
Bailey, J. 152, 286
Balakrishnan, J. 74
Balogun, J. 344, 349
Bamberger, K. A. 249
Bamforth, K. 129
Bansal, P. 268
Baradel, A. 164
Baratz, M. S. 369
Barends, E. G. 420, 422, 424–5, 427
Bargh, J. A. 485
Barham, A. 154
Barker, J. R. 370, 406–7, 411
Barley, S. R. 1, 104–6, 373
Barnard, C. 129, 307–8, 310
Barnett, M. L. 302

Barney, J. B. 68, 139, 505
Barnwell, N. 27
Barr, P. S. 257, 484–7
Barratt, M. 68
Barrett, M. 249
Bartel, C. A. 262, 389
Barth, F. 401
Bartlett, C. A. 501–2, 506–7, 509
Bartunek, J. M. 452
Bascle, G. 303
Bass, B. M. 280–282
Bates, K. A. 57, 65, 134, 201
Batt, R. 180–182, 188
Battilana, J. 136
Baum, J. A. C. 299
Bauman, Z. 401–2, 407, 411, 413
Baumeister, R. F. 257–8
Baumeler, C. 151
Baxter, R. 412
Bearden, W. O. 67
Beatty, J. 445–6
Becerra, M. 264, 266
Bechky, B. A. 376
Beck, T. E. 413
Becker, D. L. 463
Becker-Ritterspach, F. 512
Bedeian, A. G. 403
Beer, S. 58, 180–181
Beeson, J. 357
Bélanger, J. 507–8
Bell, M. 451
Bendix, R. 1, 20, 373
Benjamin, R. I. 238, 462, 475
Bennett, A. A. 426
Bennis, W. G. 5, 146, 276, 447
Berger, P. 410
Berman, S. 165
Berry, W. 61, 492
Besanko, D. 307
Bettis, R. 305
Bhakoo, V. 69
Biais, B. 247
Bicheno, J. 207
Bidwell, A. 440
Biggart, N. W. 397
Billington, C. 69
Birkinshaw, J. 501–2, 510, 512

Bisognano, M. 346
Bitran, G. R. 66
Blackbourn, D. 164
Blader, S. L. 389
Blake, R. R. 285, 530
Blanchard, K. H. 278
Blau, P. 132, 137, 405
Blom, M. 115
Bloom, N. 182, 187–8
Bloor, D. 409–10, 466
Blum, A. F. 462
Blumenberg, H. 406
Blumer, H. 259
Boaden, R. 205, 211
Boddewyn, J. 44
Boggs, C. 20–22, 33
Bohart, A. C. 529
Boje, D. M. 149, 162, 405
Boland, R. J. 262–3
Bolin, M. 526
Boltanski, L. 527
Bonaparte, T. H. 94, 96
Bonss, W. 413
Borden, D. 286
Boreham, P. 160
Borgerson, J. 147
Borges, J. L. 145, 467, 470
Borys, B. 411
Boudreau, J. 194
Bougon, M. G. 258, 261
Bouie, E. L. Jr 32
Boulding, K. 128, 131
Bouquet, C. 512
Bourdieu, P. 151, 248, 268, 381, 409
Bourke, S. 337
Bourne, M. 69
Bowden, B. 2
Bowen, H. K. 209, 490
Boyett, I. 344
Brand, C. 212
Brandeis, D. 23, 48
Branson, N. 466
Braverman, H. 20, 468
Bray, D. 242
Brech, E. F. L. 25, 93, 520
Breen, W. J. 47, 49
Breeze, J. D. 403

Brett, J. F. 286
Brewer, C. S. 431
Brewster, C. 508
Brexler, J. 210
Briner, R. B. 422, 425, 427
Brint, S. 521
Brock, D. 297, 309–10
Brocklehurst, M. 520
Brodbeck, F. C. 288
Brody, B. 30
Broms, H. 110
Brooks, J. S. 21, 27, 31–2
Broström, A. 165
Brough, I. 380
Brower, H. H. 454
Brown, F. D. 86
Bruch, H. 353–4
Bruner, J. S. 257
Bruns, A. 269
Bruzelius, N. 157, 231
Bucci, G. 205, 208–10, 212
Buckingham, M. 464
Budd, J. W. 164, 430
Buehler, R. 231
Buffa, E. 57, 59–60, 63–5, 69–74
Bulmer, M. 40–41
Burns, P. 45
Burns, T. 134–6, 331
Burrell, G. 12, 111, 156, 404–8, 468
Burris, B. 376
Burton-Jones, A. 502
Butler, J. 110, 147, 475
Byrnes, K. 442
Byun, H. 110

Cadbury, E. 24, 466
Cahill, D. 161
Cairns, G. 501
Caldwell, R. 179, 186, 527
Calipha, R. 297, 309–10
Caliskan, K. 250
Callahan, R. E. 21, 23, 27, 31–2
Callon, M. 75, 248, 250
Calvo, G. 248
Cameron, K. S. 350, 409
Canato, A. 107
Canguilhem, G. 371

Cannella, A. A. 310, 485
Cannon-Brookes, M. 485
Cappelli, P. 182
Carasso, H. 476
Carey, A. 43
Carley, M. 164
Carli, L. L. 287
Carlson, S. 326–9
Carroll, S. J. 90, 92
Carsten, M. K. 287
Carter, C. R. 67, 152
Cartwright, D. 419
Cascio, W. 194
Castells, M. 151
Cauldwell, C. 210
Caza, A. 454
Cederström, C. 113
Chaboud, A. P. 247
Chalcraft, D. 411
Chaleff, I. 282
Chambers, S. 57
Champy, J. 145, 525
Chan, A 397
Chandler, A. 88, 307–8, 314, 387, 465–7, 507, 525
Chang, Y.-C. 165
Charlier, S. D. 427–8, 449
Chartrand, T. L. 485
Chase, R. 65
Chemers, M. M. 279
Chen, M. 293–9, 312, 320
Chew, C. 214
Chhokar, J. S. 288
Chia, R. 5, 147, 150–151, 156–7, 159
Chiapello, E. 527
Child, J. 137, 139–40, 162–3, 308–9, 375, 465–7, 475
Chin, J. L. 287
Chittipeddi, K. 257–8, 262
Choi, T. Y. 63, 68–9
Christensen, C. M. 238, 313, 344, 526, 528
Church, A. T. 491
Cialdini, R. B. 485
Clancey, W. J. 484
Clemons, E. K. 249
Cleveland, G. 67
Cloke, K. 1

Cocchiara, F. 451
Coff, R. W. & D. 454
Coffman, C. 464
Cohen, J. 402, 405
Cole, S. 423
Coleman, D. 94
Coleman, J. S. 410
Collini, S. 476
Collinson, D. L. 110, 283
Colville, I. 257
Combs, J. 182
Comte, A. 405
Conger, J. A. 280, 286
Conklin, B. 183
Connerley, M. 451
Contardo, I. 264, 266
Conway, N. 181
Cooke, M. L. 21, 24, 29, 31, 45, 48, 473
Coons, A. E. 278
Cooper, R. 405
Copley, F. B. 23–4, 26, 31–2
Cordiner, R. 85
Corley, K. G. 108, 110, 257, 261, 268
Cornelissen, J. P. 259–60, 266, 269
Coser, L. 373
Costas, J. 112, 301
Covey, S. 464–5
Craighead, C. W. 67
Crainer, S. 4
Cray, D. 482
Cremin, C. 374
Crosby, P. B. 62
Crossan, M. M. 268
Crotty, M. 260
Crouch, C. H. 448, 450
Crozier, M. 367–9, 376, 512
Crutzen, P. J. 462
Cukier, K. 247
Cullen, P. G. 396, 437, 439, 443–4, 451
Cyert, R. 139, 259, 304, 306, 507
Czarniawska, B. 75, 147, 157, 471, 528, 530

Dacin, M. T. 103, 107–8, 267, 306
Daday, G. 376
Dahl, R. 368–9, 378–80
Dahlgren, G. 145
Dale, B. 62

Dalpiaz, E. 108, 262, 266–8
Dalton, M. 331–3, 387, 391–2, 467, 521
Damast, A. 441–2
Dandridge, T. C. 261
Daniel, E. 345
Dansereau, F. 280
Darbishire, O. 192
Datar, S. M. 396, 437, 439, 443–4, 451
Daudigeos, T. 521
Davenport, T. H. 242
David, R. J. 521, 525
Davidson, S. L. 357
Davies, H. T. O. 419
Davis, G. F. 1, 129, 132, 152, 160, 286
Dawson, P. 350–352
Day, D. V. 112, 280, 285, 287, 522
De Menezes, L. 181
Deakin, S. 193
Dearlove, D. 4
Deeg, R. 163
Deelmann, T. 530
Deetz, S. 50–51, 122, 150
DeFillipi, R. 445
Delbridge, R. 188
Delery, J. 182
Deleuze, G. 470, 476
Dellve, L. 334, 338
Dembour, M.-B. 163
Deming, W. E. 62, 96, 98–9
den Hond, F. 462, 476
Denis, J 355
Denison, D. R. 211
Dennison, H. 44
Denyer, D. 360, 421, 426, 433
Deroy, X. 156
Derrida, J. 462, 476
DeRue, S. 283
Descartes, R. 156
DeSoucey, M. 269
Devine, D. J. 286
Dholakia, U. 262
Dicken, P. 504
Dickson, W. J. 42–3, 46
Diefenbach, T. 1
Dierdorff, E. C. 437, 443–4, 450–453
Dierickx, I. 301
Dietz, W. 47–8

DiMaggio, P. J. 148, 183, 186, 259, 408–10, 484–5, 492, 510
Dipboye, R. L. 284
Dobbin, F. 299, 397, 410
Docherty, P. 521
Dochy, F. 455
Dodd, S. D. 266
Dodge, J. M. 24
Dombret, A. 246
Dombroski, R. 28
Donaldson, L 135, 138, 145
Dong, Y. 67
Donnellon, A. 146, 258, 261, 368, 375, 381
Dooley, C. R. 47–8
Doray, B. 20, 24
Dörrenbächer, C. 510, 512
Dosi, G. 151
Doty, D. 182
Douglas, M. 408, 410
Doumpos, M. 249
Dow, G. 160, 165
Doz, Y. 501
Drazin, R. 309
Drucker, P. 7, 19, 81–91, 93–9, 276–7, 335, 525
Drury, H. B. 26, 29, 32
du Gay, P. 1, 12, 378, 405, 407–8, 411
du Pont, P. 86–7, 99
Dubrin, A. J. 230
Dukerich, J. M. 282
Dumdum, U. R. 282
Duncan, W. J. 39, 44
Duneier, M. 397
Dunford, R. W. 19, 33
Dunkerley, D. 20, 27–8
Dunlop, J. 192
Dunne, J. 110
Dunning, J. H. 501–3
Dunphy, D. 348, 352
Durand, R. 267
Durkheim, E. 12, 168, 386–8, 405, 407–10
Dutton, J. E. 262

Eagly, A. H. 287
Earl, M. J. 238, 241
Earley, P. C. 297, 300, 490, 492
Eastvold, R. 454
Eatwell, R. 408

Eberle, E. J. 164
Ebert, R. J. 67
Edwards, P. 193, 373, 468–9, 498, 503, 511
Ehrlich, S. B. 282
Eisenhardt, K. M. 266, 312
Eisenman, M. 267
Ekman, S. 50
Elliott, D. 360
Ellram, L. M. 69
Elsbach, K. D. 484–7
Emery, F. 132
Emirbayer, M. 312–15
Emory, F. 53
Engwall, L. 4, 525
Epstein, G. 239, 243, 530
Ernst, B. 530
Estryn-Behar, M. 431
Evans, C. 22, 525

Faems, D. 183
Faramarz Nazerzadeh, A. 89
Farber, H. 185, 193
Farjoun, M. 451
Farndale, E. 186
Farrell, C. 526
Fayol, H. 129, 158–9, 403–4, 464
Fazzini, D. 280
Feeny, D. 237
Feldman, M. S. 150, 249, 454
Feldmann, H. 193
Felin, T. 132, 137, 139–41
Ferguson, M. 93
Ferguson, N. 68
Ferner, A. 508, 511, 513
Ferraro, F. 451
Ferris, G. R. 357
Feyerabend, P. 476
Fiedler, F. E. 279, 286
Fillingham, D. 205
Fincham, R. 518, 522–3, 525, 531
Finkelstein, S. 310, 485
Fiol, C. M. 257, 261, 265
Fioretos, K. O. 164
Fish, L. 82, 200
Fisher, D. 41, 64
Fiske, S. T. 258–9
Fiss, P. C. 262

Flaherty, J. E. 94, 96, 98
Fleming, P. 11, 112–13, 367–70, 373–4, 376, 379, 381
Fletcher, C. 286
Fligstein, N. 3, 248, 308, 466
Flint, A. 429
Florén, H. 334, 337
Flower, L. 260
Flynn, B. B. 67
Flyvbjerg, B. 152–4, 157, 231–2, 382
Follett, M. P. 44, 130, 159–63, 166, 277, 404
Fombrun, C. J. 257, 264–5
Fones-Wolf, E. 48–9
Fong, C. 4, 447, 451
Ford, H. 371
Fornaciari, C. J. 446, 448
Forrester, J. 59–60, 63–4, 71
Foucault, M. 13, 22, 26, 29, 31, 51, 155, 247, 367, 371, 405, 463, 469–72, 476
Fox, A. 23
Francis, D. 223
Frankl, V. 52
Fraser, S. 47, 49
Freeden, M. 109
Freeman, J. 139, 191
Fricke, S. E. 233
Friedberg, E. 376, 512
Friedland, R. 259, 409
Friedman, M. 304, 498
Friesen, P. 138
Frijters, P. 431
Frohlich, M. 64
Fromm, E. 52
Frost, P. 105
Froud, J. 191
Fry, L. W. 282
Fukami, C. 6, 445
Funk, R. J. 246, 248

Gable, R. 28
Gabriel, Y. 114
Gadamer, H.-G. 147
Gahmberg, H. 110
Galal, K. 525
Galambos, L. 151
Galbraith, J. R. 145
Galliers, R. D. 237, 239

Ganco, M. 130, 134, 138–9, 141
Gantt, H. L. 29–31
Garbuio, M. 231
Garsten, C. 335
Gartrell, C. D. & A. W. 423–5
Garud, R. 257, 262, 266
Garvin, D. A. 396, 437, 439, 443–4, 451
Gash, D. C. 105
Gavetti, G. 139–40, 259
Gawande, A. 201
Gee, J. 258
Geertz, C. 109
Gehrke, T. S. 482
Gell, A. 406
Gemino, A. 235
Gentile, M. C. 439
Gereffi, G. 504
Gersick, C. 228
Gerstner, C. R. 280
Gerth, H. H. 130
Ghadar, F. 509
Ghemawat, P. 488
Gherardi, S. 157
Ghoshal, S. 152, 428, 447, 450–451, 501–2, 506–9
Giacolone, R. A. 437, 451
Gianpiero, P. 387
Gibbert, M. 304
Gibbs, B. W. 265, 447
Gibson, C. B. 481
Giddens, A. 110, 148, 151, 409, 504
Gilbreth, F. B. 24–6, 29
Gilbreth, L. 27
Giles, A. 507–8
Gillem, T. 210
Gillespie, R. 41–3
Gilson, M. 44, 46–7
Ginsburg, R. B. 164
Gioia, D. A. 110, 257–8, 261–2, 268
Giorgi, S. 267
Girard, M. 375
Gitelman, H. 41
Giuliani, A. P. 257
Given, W. B. 96
Glossner, C. L. 163
Glynn, M. A. 257, 265–9, 389
Godfrey, H. 24

Goffman, E. 259, 469
Golan, P. 430
Golden-Biddle, K. 261
Goldsmith, J. 1
Goldstein, M. 247
Goldstone, J. A. 350, 360
Golsorkhi, D. 367, 378, 380
Gomber, P. 247
Gomes-Casseres, B. 297, 309
Gopalan, S. 486
Gorman, L. 447
Gouldner, A. W. 105, 130, 132, 369, 377, 387, 407, 521
Graen, G. 280
Graff, H. J. 28
Gragg, C. I. 396
Graham, J. L. 482
Gramsci, A. 20–22, 27–8, 33
Granovetter, M. 248
Graves, F. 247
Gray, B. 258, 261
Greenleaf, R. 282
Greeno, J. G. 485
Grenier, J. N. 507–8
Griffin, D. 231
Grindley, K. 93
Gronn, P. 355
Gronroos, C. 66, 214
Groves, A. 91, 98
Grugulis, I. 3, 22
Guadalupe, M. 311, 317
Guerras-Martin, L. A. 293, 295–9, 312, 320
Guest, D. 181–2, 327, 519
Guillén, M. F. 1
Gulick, L. 130
Gulledge, T. R. Jr 210
Gupta, A. K. 238, 257, 266
Guthrie, J. 183, 205, 210, 403

Haas, M. R. 240
Haber, S. 24
Habermas, J. 122, 149, 152, 405
Hacking, I. 410
Haga, B. 280
Hage, J. 133, 137
Haigh, G. 21
Halachmi, A. 211

Hales, C. 23, 334–5, 526
Hall, P. 406, 511
Hall, R. H. 137
Hallett, T. 103
Halpern, D. 85
Halpin, A. W. 287
Hambrick, D. C. 293–9, 310–312, 320, 461, 485
Hamel, G. 304, 380
Hamilton, B. H. 302–3, 313
Hammer, M. 145, 525
Hampden-Turner, C. 482, 488
Hampton, D. 27
Hancock, P. 117, 475
Handel, M. 104
Handy, C. 335
Hannan, M. 139, 268
Hardie, J. 419
Harding, N. 422, 427–8, 519
Hardy, C. 155, 260, 409, 462, 476, 502, 506, 512
Härenstam, A. 526
Hargadon, A. B. 484–7
Hargreaves, R. 97
Harland, C. 63
Harris, H. 59
Harris, H. J. 48–9
Hartley, J. L. 63, 109
Harvey, C. E. 41
Harzing, A.-W. 446, 510
Hassard, J. 39, 41, 44
Hatch, M. J. 257, 261, 265–6
Haugaard, M. 157, 382
Haveman, H. A. 521, 525
Haveri, A. 213
Hayes, R. H. 62–3, 68, 74–5
Hayward, M. L. 257, 266–7
Hazelrigg, L. E. 402, 405
Heckscher, C. C. 146, 368, 375, 381
Hedberg, B. 145
Hedlund, G. 510
Heenan, D. A. 509
Heinemann, M. 466
Heinze, K. L. 269
Helfat, C. E. 268, 300, 309
Hendry, C. 490
Hendry, L. 74
Hennart, J. F. 501
Hennis, W. 402

Heracleous, L. 426
Hernandez, S. 377
Herrmann, P. 293
Hersey, P. 278
Herzberg, F. 52
Hesterley, W. 139
Hickson, D. J. 66, 134-5, 138
Higgins, W. 165
Hill, T. 60, 62, 70
Hillman, S. 47
Hines, P. 207-8
Hirokawa, R. Y. 228
Hirotaka, T. 242
Hirsch, P. M. 410
Hirschheim, R. 237
Hirschman, D. 246, 248
Hislop, D. 529, 531
Hitlin, S. 387, 397
Hjorth, D. 382
Ho, K. Z. 388, 390, 393-5
Hoare, Q. 22, 27, 33
Hobson, J. A. 30
Hochschild, A. R. 150
Hodgkinson, G. P. 461
Hodgson, G. M. 408, 519
Hofer, C. 294, 308
Hofstede, G. 481-2, 488
Hogan, R. 280
Hogg, M. A. 283, 530
Holden, P. 82
Hollenbeck, G. P. 283, 357
Hollis, I. N. 31
Holloway, S.S. 299
Holm, P. 409
Holmes, L. 22, 422
Holstein, W. J. 437
Holt, R. 59, 159, 265, 462, 476
Holtom, B. 437, 439-40, 443-4, 453
Holweg, M. 204, 206-7, 209, 211-12
Höner, D. 530
Hoopes, J. 41, 50, 90-91
Hope Hailey, V. 186, 349
Hopf, H. 89
Hopkins, T. K. 504
Houser, T. 390
Howard, A. 283-4
Howard-Grenville, J. 108

Hoxie, R. F. 26, 30
Hsieh, N. 396
Hsu, G. 268
Huczynski, A. 464, 530
Huff, A. S. 263-4
Humble, J. W. 84, 93-5, 98
Hung, S. C. 485
Hurley-Hanson, A. E. 19
Huselid, M. 182
Husserl, E. 151
Huy, Q. N. 267, 462, 476
Hwang, A. 1, 446, 448
Hyman, R. 380, 468

Iacono, C. S. 249
Ichniowski, C. 182, 188
Iewwongcharoen, B. 229
Illouz, E. 151
Inderrieden, E. 453
Inkson, K. 490
Irvine, R. F. 24
Islei, G. 237
Ives, B. 28, 447, 449

Jackall, R. 110, 121, 333-4, 388-95, 397
Jackson, J. P. 31
Jackson, S. E. 262
Jacoby, S. M. 45, 48
Jarvenpaa, S. L. 234, 446-8
Jarzabkowski, P. 293, 303, 320
Javidan, M. 490
Jeanes, E. L. 461
Jenkins, H. 269
Jensen, M. C. 163, 228
Jepperson, R. 410
Jesuthasan, R. 194
Jimmieson, N. L. 344
Joel, G. 387
Johansson, A. 530
Johnson, G. 303
Johnson, J. P. 490
Johnson, P. 526
Johnson, S. K. 283-4, 287
Johnston, R. 57, 65, 69, 211, 214
Jones, C. 145, 156-7, 475
Jones, D. T. 206
Jordan, K. 442

Josserand, E. 146
Joyce, W. F. 261
Judt, T. 161
Juran, J. M. 96–9
Jurkiewicz, C. L. 160

Kahn, R. 132–3, 278
Kahneman, D. 231
Kamsteeg, F. 121–2
Kanigel, R. 19–20, 27, 403
Kanter, R. M. 332, 335
Kantrow, A. M. 237
Kanungo, R. N. 280
Kaplan, R. S. 83–4, 93, 99, 257, 266, 314
Kaplinsky, R. 504
Karantinou, K. M. 530
Karwan, K. R. 205
Katz, D. 132–3, 192, 278, 447
Kaufman, B. 20, 39, 44, 163, 183–5
Kaulingfreks, R. 153, 157
Kavadias, S. 220
Kay, R. H. 448
Kayworth, T. 233
Keller, S. 347, 359
Kellerman, B. 285
Kelley, M. 223, 282
Kellogg, D. 65, 108, 375
Kelly, M. 160
Kemp, L. J. 23, 32–3
Kent, W. 31
Kepes, F. 426
Kerr, S. 192
Kersley, B. 186
Ketchen, D. J. 298, 321
Kharbanda, O. P. 223
Khurana, R. 5, 27, 149, 152, 293, 387, 450–451, 520, 523
Kickul, J. R. 74
Kiechel, W. 320
Kieser, A. 530
Kilburg, R. R. 286
King, B. 132, 137, 139–41, 447
Kinnie, N. 182
Kipping, M. 518, 521, 524–5, 531–2
Kirby, M. W. 58
Kirkman, B. L. 481–2, 492
Kirsch, D. 135

Kirschner, P. A. 449
Kitay, J. 519, 521, 523, 525, 528
Klein, H. K. 237, 280
Knauth, O. 82
Knights, D. 149, 468–9, 512
Knoll, K. 234
Knorr Cetina, K. 238, 248
Kocak, O. 268
Koch, J. 360
Kocka, J. 164
Kogut, B. 505
Kommers, D. P. 164
Kornberger, M. 150, 152
Koschmann, T. 157
Koslowski, P. 156
Kostova, T. 306, 511
Kotha, S. 257, 375
Kotter, J. P. 329–30, 333, 344, 346–7, 352–3, 355–6
Krajewski, L. 70–71
Kraljic, P. 63
Krebsbach-Gnath, C. 530
Krings, D. 205
Krippner, G. R. 243–4
Kristensen, P. H. 165, 510–511
Kubr, M. 520–521
Kuhlmann, M. 377
Kuhn, T. S. 152
Kumar, M. 247
Kunda, G. 1, 104–5, 109–12, 370, 373
Kuruvilla, S. 503
Kuutti, K. 157

Lacey, M. Y. 528
Ladkin, D. 159
Lagadec, P. 360
Laloux, F. 160
Lamming, R. 63, 68
Lamond, D. 2
Lamont, M. 387
Landman, T. 157
Landsberger, H. A. 41
Langley, A. 141, 350, 355, 358
Langton, J. 377
Lant, T. K. 266, 483–5, 488
Laporte, G. 423
Larson, S. M. 27

Lash, S. 12, 400, 402, 411–12
Latham, G. 427–8
Lather, P. 421
Latour, B. 151, 401
Lau, C 413
Lawler, E. 180–182, 359
Lawrence, T. 128, 134, 136–7, 262, 370, 409
Le Breton-Miller, I. 131
Lears, T. J. 21, 28
Lee, H. 519
Lee, M. 136
Lee, T. W. 429
Legge, K. 181, 420, 527
Leidner, D. E. 233–4, 446–8
Leigh, J. S. A. 445–6
Leister, A. 286
Lemann, N. 526
Lenartowicz, T. 490
Leonardi, P. M. 108
Leong, S. M. 507–8
LeSage, A. 448
Lester, R. H. 131
Leung, K. 482
Levenhagen, M. 266
Levine, D. 205
Levinthal, D. 140, 259
Levitt, T. 65, 94–5
Lewin, K. 11, 52, 346
Lewis, M. 57, 65, 73, 201, 381, 476
Leys, F. 356
Li, M. 68, 311, 317
Liden, R. C. 282
Lieberman, S. 487
Lilford, R. J. 205
Lilja, K. 165
Linda, K. 387
Linkletter, K. 162
Linstead, A. 110
Lippitt, G. 531
Lipset, S. M. 408
Lister, S. 212
Littler, C. R. 19, 21, 465
Lloyd, C. 22
Loan-Clarke, J. 429
Loch, C. 220
Locke, E. 44, 164
Lockwood, C. 267

Logue, D. 163
Lojo, M. 450
Lorange, P. 32, 304, 306
Lorsch, J. 128, 133–4, 136–7, 146
Louise, J. 387
Lovallo, D. 231
Lowe, J. 282, 481
Lozano, J. M. 455
Luce, S. 381
Lucey, J. 208
Luckmann, T. 410
Lukes, S. 368–70, 380
Lundan, S. M. 502
Lundin, R. A. 228
Luo, Y. 482, 486, 491
Lusch, R. F 66
Luthans, F. 333

McAdam, D. 248
Macbeth, D. 68
McCabe, D. 512
McCall, M. W. 357
McCann, L. 187
McCanse, A. A. 285
McCarthy, S. 451
McCloskey, J. F. 58
McCune, D. 165
McDaniel, M. A. 426
McDonald, D. 93, 521
MacDuffie, J. 182, 188, 192
McFarlan, F. W. 238
McGahan, A. M. 306
McGinn, D. 523
McGrath, R. G. 163, 375
Maciariello, J. A. 162
McKelvey, J. T. 45, 138, 287
McKenna, D. D. 286, 521, 525, 527
MacKenzie, D. 238, 245–7, 249
McKibbin, L. E. 13, 437–8, 443, 455–6
McLaughlin, K. 214
McNulty, T. 210
Macpherson, A. 265
Madigan, C. 525
Magat, R. 41
Maguire, S. 260, 409
Mahoney, J. 360
Maitlis, S. 258, 260, 262

Malhotra, D. 451, 453
Mallory, G. 482
Mann, R. D. 277
Mansfield, R. 520–521
Marcuse, H. 373
Marglin, S. 465
Margolis, J. D. 395
Marion, R. 287
Markham, C. 526, 531
Markland, R. E. 205
Marshall, G. 22
Martin, J. 105–6, 118, 261, 309
Marx, K. 12, 86, 402, 405
Maslow, A. 52
Maslyn, J. M. 280
Mason, P. A. 311, 332
Massey, L. 210
Mather, W. 466
Matsatsinis, N. F. 249
Matten, D. 510
Matthaei, E. 334, 336
Maurer, C. C. 268
Mauss, M. 387
Mautner, T. 425
Mayer, R. R. 65, 160, 264
Mayer-Schönberger, V. 247
Mayhrofer, W. 508
Mayo, G. E. 6–7, 39–51, 53, 145, 372, 404
Mazur, E. 448, 450
Mazza, C. 530
Mead, G. H. 259
Meaney, M. 347, 359
Megill, A. 470
Meindl, J. R. 282
Melé, D. 162
Mendenhall, M. 490–491
Mendes, P. 520–521
Mendoza, E. 248
Menges, J. I. 353–4
Menkveld, A. J. 247
Meredith, J. 57–8, 61–2, 67, 70
Merkle, J. A. 19–21, 23, 26–7
Merton, R. K. 132, 155, 369
Messersmith, J. 182
Meyer, J. W. 105, 138–9, 163, 410, 510
Meyerson, D. 118
Michel, A. 374

Michels, R. 379
Miller, D. 131, 138, 321, 404
Miller, P. 50–51
Miller, R. A. 164
Miller, V. 237
Milliken, F. J. 485
Millo, Y. 250
Mills, C. W. 389–93
Milosevic, D. Z. 229, 233
Mintzberg, H. 4–6, 74, 138, 146, 159, 304, 318–19, 326, 328–30, 335–7, 339, 344, 355, 387, 444, 451, 467–8
Mische, A. 312–15
Mitchell, T. R. 429
Mitchell, W. N. 60
Mitroff, I. 261
Mitsuhashi, H. 135
Mitukiewicz, A., A. 185–6
Mizruchi, M. S. 389–91, 395
Modigliani, F. 59
Mohe, M. 530
Moher, D. 432
Mohr, L. B. 358
Mohrman, S. A. 359
Moinas, S. 247
Monin, P. 267
Montgomery, D. 29
Mooney, J. 130
Moore, C. 344, 485, 527
Morgeson, F. P. 444–5, 451
Morrell, K. 419, 422–3, 425–7, 429, 431
Morrill, C. 387–8, 392–4
Morris, P 219, 226–7, 526, 531
Morrison, J. 466
Mortensen, M. 194
Mosakowski, E. 297, 300, 490
Moschella, D. C. 237
Mouritsen, J. 75
Mouton, J. S. 285, 530
Mouzelis, N. P. 128, 130, 132
Moxham, A. 86, 99
Moxham, C. 211
Mudambi, R. 512
Mueller, D. C. 302
Mukhi, S. 27
Mullins, L. 464
Mulrine, A. 223

Mumby, D. K. 377
Mumford, M. D. 287
Münch, R. 402
Muniesa, F. 249–50
Munsterberg, H. 27
Murnieks, C. 490
Murnighan, J. K. 451, 453
Murphy, S. E. 287
Murray, J. A. 337
Murray, P. 45–6, 48
Muth, J. 59
Muzio, D. 522
Mwasalwiba, E. S. 446

Nachum, L. 531
Nader, L. 387
Nadkarni, S. 264
Nadworny, M. 26–7
Nag, R. 293–9, 312, 320
Narayanan, V. K. 264
Naum, L. 59
Navis, C. 266, 269
Nazerzadeh, A. F. 89
Nelson, R. 300, 306, 313, 486
Netemeyer, R. G. 67
Neumark, D. 182
New, C. 63
Newman, W. H. 352
Nicholls, A. J. 163
Nicholson, L. 266
Nickerson, J. A. 302–3, 313
Nie, W. 65
Nietzsche, F. 468–70
Nisbet, R. A. 168
Nixon, J. 166
Noble, D. F. 21
Nonaka, I. 159, 242
Nonthaleerak, P. 74
Normann, R. 118, 214
Norton, D. P. 83–4, 93, 99
Novak, M. 280, 446
Numerof, R. E. 282
Nutley, S. M. 419

Oakland, J. S. 208
Ocasio, W. 140, 257–9, 410, 485–7
O'Connor, E. S. 39, 41, 43, 45, 51, 154, 437

Oddou, G. 490–491
Odiorne, G. S. 85–7, 99
O'Farrell, C. 470
Ogburn, W. F. 343
Ogden, C. 257, 259
Øgland, P. 22
O'Gorman, C. 337
Ohmae, K. 498
Olcese, R. 90
O'Leary, T. 51
Oliver, N. 306
Olsen, R. 65
Olve, N.-G. 145
O'Mahoney, J. 526
Orlicky, J. 61
Orlikowski, W. J. 249–50, 314, 375
Ormsby, J. G. 90
Ortmann, G. 513
Osborne, S. 206–7, 211–14
O'Shea, J. 525
Osofsky, S. 85
Oswick, C. 370
Otley, D. 464
O'Toole, J. 5, 146, 447
Ouchi, W. G. 146

Pache, A. C. 475
Pagnotta, E. 247
Paine, L. S. 396
Palley, T. I. 244
Palmer, T. B. 298
Park, C. L. 257, 259, 449
Parker, M. 28, 104, 149, 152, 188
Parkhurst, F. A. 29
Parmigiani, A. 299
Parsons, T. 128–9, 152, 380, 402
Patel, P. 183
Pathak, S. D. 69
Paul, K. 12, 405, 407
Pauwe, J. 193
Payne, S. C. 23, 321
Pearson, C. M. 381
Peaucelle, J.-L. 403
Peltokorpi, V. 242
Pemer, F. 531
Pendleton, A. 191, 193
Penrose, E. 299, 308, 313

Pentland, A. 240
Perlmutter, H. V. 508–9
Perrewé, P. L. 357
Perrow, C. 1, 133, 389
Peteraf, M. 300, 306
Peters, T. 27, 91, 93, 335
Peterson, S. J. 482, 492
Petkova, A. P. 257, 266–7, 447
Pettigrew, A. 205, 257, 306, 313, 350–351
Pfeffer, J. 4, 9, 139–40, 180–182, 256, 260, 266, 367, 369, 447, 451, 461
Pheysey, D.C. 66
Philippon, T. 247
Phillips, N. 107, 155, 161, 166, 367, 370
Piccoli, G. 447, 449
Pierson, F. C. 389
Piketty, T. 160
Pilkington, A. 61–2, 67
Pisano, G. P. 63, 68, 505
Pitesa, M. 475
Platts, K. 69
Plowman, D. A. 351–2
Plumer, B. 437
Pollack, J. 96, 98, 235
Pollard, S. 2, 465, 467
Pollock, T. G. 257, 266
Polodny, J. M. 437
Pontusson, J. 164
Poole, M. 228, 520–521
Porac, J. F. 263–4, 266
Porter, L. 13, 237, 306, 310, 372, 437–40, 443, 445, 455–6
Powell, W. W. 1, 148, 179, 183, 186, 408, 510
Prahalad, C. 304, 501
Pratt, M. 389
Preda, A. 238, 248
Pritchard, K. 189–90
Pritchett, H. S. 31
Proudlove, N. 211
Pugh, D. S. 27, 66, 133–5, 137–8, 346
Pung, C. 347, 359
Purcell, J. 182
Puschmann, A. R. 245
Pye, A. 258

Quinn, J. 304, 409
Quisenberry, D. 286

Rafferty, A. E. 343–4
Raghu, G. 387
Ramstad, P. 194
Rao, H. 267
Rashman, L. 204
Raskin, R. 280
Rasmussen, T. 195
Rast, D. E. 283
Ratcliffe, R. 440
Raubitschek, R. S. 268
Ravasi, D. 107–8, 257, 261–3, 267–8
Raveh, A. 451
Raven, B. 367
Ravenscraft, D. 310
Ray, C. A. 373
Raynard, M. 131
Reed, M. 3, 376, 522–3, 526
Reger, R. K. 263–4, 266
Reich, B. H. 235
Reiger, K. M. 27
Reilly, R. R. 285
Reinecke, J. 268
Reno, R. R. 485
Renold, C. 24, 466
Rhodes, C. 150
Rice, A. M. 129
Richards, G. 205, 257, 259
Richter, A. 525
Riesman, D. 389, 391
Rivera, L. A. 393
Roberts, J. 52–3, 149, 174, 321
Roberts, P 96–7
Robertson, M. 107, 112
Roethlisberger, F. J. 42–3, 46, 48, 50
Rogers, C. 52
Rogow, G. 247
Romanelli, E. 352–3
Ronda-Pupo, G. A. 293, 295–9, 312, 320
Roos, D. 145
Rosile, G. A. 162
Ross, M. 231
Ross-Smith, A. 152, 161
Roth, A. V. 67, 306, 511
Rothengatter, W. 157, 231
Rouleau, L. 344
Rousseau, D. M. 420, 422, 425–6, 433, 451, 461
Rövik, K. A. 117

Rowan, B. 139, 510
Rowe, K. H. 463
Rubery, J. 193
Ruddle, K. 527
Ruef, M. 523, 525
Rueschemeyer, D. 360
Rugman, A. 498
Ruigrok, W. 304
Rumelt, R. P. 294
Rundall, T. G. 419–20, 433
Rupp, D. E. 284
Rutherford, J. 163
Rylander, A. 112
Rynes, S. L. 420, 440, 445, 452–3

Sabine, W. C. 23
Sackett, D. L. 419, 422
Salaman, G. 3
Salancik, G. 139–40, 367, 369
Salipante, P. F. 482
Sallaz, J. 378, 380
Salmon, M. A. 66, 74
Salomon, R. M. 302
Sanchez, R. 242
Sanchez-Runde, C. J. 163
Sandberg, J. 146, 149, 157, 239
Sanders, N. R. 67
Sanderson, G. 21
Santos, F. M. 266, 475
Sarkar, P. 193
Sass, S. A. 4
Sasser, W. E. 65
Sauer, C. 235, 240
Schein, E. 261, 520, 523, 529
Schendel, D. E. 294, 308
Scherer, F. 310
Schiffer, S. 257
Schildt, H. A. 266
Schlesinger, L. A. 344, 352
Schmenner, R. W. 68–9
Schmitt, J. 185–6
Schoenherr, P. 137
Schön, D. 109
Schonberger, R. J. 62–3
Schram, S. 157
Schreyögg, G. 360
Schroeder, R. G. 66–7

Schultz, M. 257, 260–261, 265–6, 268
Schulz, M. 110, 163
Schumann, M. 377
Schumpeter, J. A. 26, 94
Schütz, A. 148
Schwyzer, P. 150
Scott, W. R. 1, 66, 128–9, 132, 249, 408, 510
Sebeok, T. A. 154
Seddon, J. 210–212, 245, 248
Segev, E. 451
Sejersted, F. 165
Selim, G. 527
Sels, L. 183
Seltzer, J. 282
Selznick, P. 132, 146–7, 336, 369
Senge, P. M. 145
Sennett, R. 110, 294, 315–18
Seo, M.-G. 409
Sergi, V. 355
Shah, R. 209
Shanley, M. 306
Sheehy, K. 439
Shenhar, A. J. 233
Shenhav, Y. A. 520
Shenkar, O. 482, 486, 491
Sherman, S. 85
Sheth, J. 32
Shields, M. A. 431
Shils, E. 375, 378–9
Shingo, S. 22, 62
Shoemaker, P. 505
Shotter, J. 110
Shuen, A. 505
Sideri, S. 190
Siehl, C. 106
Silveira, G. J. C. D. 74
Silvester, K. 205, 211–12
Silvia, S. J. 163–4
Simon, H. 59, 134, 158, 259, 302, 304, 487
Sine, W. 135, 521, 525
Singh, J. V. 280
Singhal, K. 57, 59, 70–71
Sirower, M. 310
Sitzmann, T. 449
Sivasubramaniam, N. 282
Skinner, W. 62–3, 73
Skyrme, D. J. 241

Slack, N. 57, 65, 73, 201
Sloan, A. Jr 87, 98
Smart, P. 421, 426, 433
Smiddy, H. 59, 84–5, 87, 89
Smircich, L. 105, 257, 261, 263, 488
Smith, A. 277, 388
Smither, J. W. 285
Snider, B. 74
Snow, C. C. 321
Söderholm, A. 228
Somers, M. R. 110, 160
Sommerkamp, P. 280
Sommers, R. A. 210, 483, 485
Sonenshein, S. 262
Sorge, A. 510
Soskice, G. 406, 511
Souitaris, V. 475
Sparrow, P. 188
Spear, S. 208–9
Spender, J. C. 164
Spicer, A. 1, 11, 119, 367–70, 381
Spicka, M. E. 163
Spoelstra, S. 156
Sprague, L. G. 57, 60
Stace, D. 348, 352
Stalker, G. M. 134–6, 331
Stark, D. 20, 375
Starkey, K. 239, 387, 469
Starr, M. K. 57, 59, 61, 66, 73
Statler, M. 159
Staw, B. M. 530
Steers, R. M. 163, 490
Steger, M. B. 500
Stephens, R. 451
Stewart, M. 30
Stewart, R. 327–9
Steyn, R. 211–12
Stigliani, I. 263
Stimpert, J. L. 257
Stivers, R. 406
Stjernberg, T. 521
Stockhammer, E. 160
Stogdill, R. M. 277–8
Storey, J. 179, 186, 490
Stout, L. A. 160
Streeck, W. 164
Stubbart, C. 257, 261, 263, 488

Styhre, A. 243
Sucher, S. J. 396
Suchman, M. C. 265
Suddaby, R. 370, 409, 462, 476
Sutton, R. I. 444, 451
Sveningsson, S. 107, 110–111, 121
Svoboda, S. 440
Swamidass, P. M. 67
Swedberg, R. 410
Sweller, J. 449
Swidler, A. 108–10, 112, 267, 412–13, 483, 492
Swink, M. L. 68
Sydow, J. 360

Takamiya, S. 96
Tallman, K. 529
Tamangani, Z. 335
Tan, C. T. 507–8
Taneja, S. 22
Tanner, S. J. 208
Taras, D. G. 163, 482, 492
Tarba, S. 309–10
Tarrant, J. J. 87
Tate, W. L. 69
Taylor, F.W. 6–7, 19–33, 44–5, 49, 51, 85, 112–13, 130, 145–6, 159, 183–4, 258–9, 277, 371, 403, 464, 473, 505
Tead, O. 44, 49
Teece, D. J. 294, 505
Tempel, A. 513
ten Bos, R. 156–7
Tenkasi, R. V. 262–3
Tennant, C. 93, 96–7
Teo, S. 146
Thau, S. 475
Thelen, K. 161
Thoenig, J. C. 377
Thomas, D. 490
Thomas, H. 32, 263–4, 266
Thomas, J. C. 213
Thomas, R. 110, 389
Thompson, C. B. 25, 29
Thompson, E. P. 473
Thompson, H. 31
Thompson, J. D. 132–4
Thompson, P. 115, 191, 380, 469
Thomson, A. W. J. 466–7, 471, 520

Thornborrow, T. 112, 370
Thornton, P. H. 257–9, 283–4, 410
Tichy, N. M. 85
Tidd, J. 531
Tiratsoo, N. 4, 387
Tiryakian, E. A. 411–12
Ton, Z. 195
Tonn, J. C. 162
Törnström, L. 334
Tosi, H. L. 90, 92
Townley, B. 51, 370
Trahair, R. 40–43, 48
Tranfield, D. 421, 426, 433
Trank, C. Q. 440
Treviño, L. K. 282, 396
Triandis, H. C. 486
Trist, E. 53, 129, 132
Trompenaars, F. 481–2, 488
Truss, C. 186
Tsang, E. W. K. 304
Tsoukas, H. 147, 149–50, 156–7, 159
Tsui, A. 138
Tsutsui, W. M. 19
Tuck, E. 4
Tuden, A. 134
Tung, R. L. 490
Turbeville, W. 244
Turner, A. N. 327
Turner, B. 256
Turner, B. A. 261
Turner, B. S. 401–2
Turner, V. 110
Tushman, M. L. 352–3, 451
Tversky, A. 231
Tyler, G. R. 160, 475
Tyson, L. D. A. 159

Udehn, L. 410
Uhl-Bien, M. 280, 282–3, 287
Ulrich, D. 187, 189–90, 195, 527
Urwick, L. 24–5, 89, 93, 95, 130, 464, 520

Vaisey, S. 387, 397
Vallas, S. P. 318, 377, 397
van Bever, D. 526, 528
Van Buren, M. 453

Van de Ven, A. 130, 134, 138–9, 141, 306, 309, 461
Van Hulst, M. 121
van Kleeck, M. 44
van Knippenberg, D. 283
Van Maanen, J. 106, 122, 387, 461
Van Marrewijk, A. 157
Van Wanrooy, B. 181
van Wyck, P. 153, 155
Vancil, R. 304, 306
Vargo, S. 66
Vaughan, D. 397
Vecchio, R. P. 286
Venkatraman, N. 309
Verbeke, A. 503
Verona, G. 268
Visscher, K. 528
Vollmann, T. 61
Von Bertalanffy, L. 128, 133
Vroom, V. 52, 278
Vurdubakis, T. 469

Waddock, S. 455
Wagner, P. 400, 410
Waldman, D. 286
Walgenbach, P. 510
Walker, C. 327
Walker, H. 201–2
Walker, M. 164
Walley, P. 208, 211–12
Walsh, J. P. 259, 395
Walshe, K. 419–20, 433
Walter, I. C. 419
Walton, R. 180–181
Walumbwa, F. O. 282
Wälz, C. 164
Wang, L. 451, 453, 526, 528
Wankel, C. 445
Ward, P. T. 209, 345
Wargo, D. T. 437
Waring, J. 204, 206–7, 209, 211–12
Warner, M. 22
Wasmeier, O. 163
Watrous, K. M. 23
Watson, T. 3, 110–111, 334
Watson, T. Snr 98

Weber, M. 1, 12, 103, 107–8, 130–131, 137–8, 147–8, 155, 249, 264, 267, 269, 277, 280, 367, 369, 373, 377, 380, 402–5, 407, 411–12, 464, 474
Webster, J. 429, 447
Wehmeier, S. 260, 266
Weick, K. E. 108, 150, 258, 263, 405, 488
Weisinger, J. Y. 482
Welch, J. 85, 91, 98
Wensley, R. 71
Werner, M. D. 259–60
Wernerfelt, B. 68
Werr, A. 521, 531
Westbrook, R. 64
Westney, E. D. 510
Westphal, J. D. 266
Westwood, R. 461
Wheeler, D. W. 282, 447
Wheelwright, S. C. 62, 74
Whetten, D. 132, 137, 139–41, 261, 389
Whitford, J. 512
Whitley, R. 461, 475, 510–511
Whybark, D. 61
Whyte, W. H. 131, 389, 391, 397
Wickham, P. A. 523
Wicki, B. 304
Widdicombe, S. 110
Wiener, N. 128
Wigforss, E. 165
Wikström, E. 334, 338
Williams, G. A. 21
Williams, R. 28
Williams, S. 210
Williams, W. 44
Williamson, O. E. 68, 447, 466
Willman, P. 3–4, 6
Willmott, H. 111, 149–50, 373–4, 410, 468
Wilson, S. 238, 242–3, 359, 445, 466–7, 471–2, 520
Wiltbank, R. 304
Winter, S. 300, 306, 313
Wisman, J. D. 160
Witt, J. F. 21, 27
Wittgenstein, L. 147, 264
Wittkower, M. & R. 316
Womack, J. P. 145, 206

Wood, J. C. 96, 163, 181
Woodard, T. D. 210
Woodman, R. W. 350
Woodward, J. 66, 133–6, 527
Woolagoodja, D. 154
Worley, C. G. 359
Worren, N. A. M. 527
Woywode, M. 192–3
Wrege, C. 43
Wren, D. A. 2, 19, 39, 43–4, 87, 90, 403
Wright Mills, C. 389, 392
Wry, T. 266, 268
Wrzesniewski, A. 389
Wuthnow, R. 387
Wyckoff, D. 65

Xin, K. 286

Yaconi, L. L. 487
Yammarino, F. J. 287
Yanow, D. 103, 105, 121
Yates, J. 375
Yeheskel, O. 482, 486, 491
Yetton, P. W. 278
Youndt, M. 182
Youngcourt, S. S. 23
Yun, K. A. 450
Yurov, K. 306

Zacher, H. F. 163
Zagelmeyer, S. 164
Zaheer, S. 511
Zajac, E. J. 262, 266
Zald, M. N. 379
Zander, A. 505
Zelizer, V. A. R. 387, 397
Zerzan, J. 23
Zhao, H. 447
Zilber, T. B. 257, 266
Zirpoli, F. 512
Zoican, M. A. 247
Zopounidis, C. 249
Zott, C. 267
Zuboff, S. 335
Zyphur, M. J. 405

Subject Index

Introductory Note
References such as '178–9' indicate (not necessarily continuous) discussion of a topic across a range of pages. Because the whole of this work is about 'management', use of this term (and certain others which occur throughout) as an entry point has been restricted. Please look under the appropriate detailed entries. Wherever possible in the case of topics with many references, these have either been divided into sub-topics or only the most significant discussions of the topic are listed.

AACSB (Association to Advance Collegiate Schools of Business) 4, 23, 32–3, 439–41, 443–4, 451
Abrahamsson, B. 165
academic rigour 5, 43, 450–451, 461
Academy of Management Learning and Education (AMLE) 420, 427, 445–7, 450
accountability 3, 32–3, 348, 371, 376, 454, 476
acquisitions 297, 301, 306, 310, 313, 391, 502
action learning 286
adaptability, cultural 490–492
agency 3, 103, 151, 249–50, 311–12, 406, 408–10, 512
  organizational 10, 294
agents 13, 248, 250, 402, 465, 485, 523
  change 11, 349, 351, 353, 355, 409, 518, 527
algorithmic trading 245–7, 249, 251
algorithms, computerized 9, 246–7
ALT (Authentic Leadership Theory) 10, 282
ambiguity 109, 111, 118, 262–3, 315–16, 332–4, 393, 403
ambivalence 12, 119, 376, 400–401, 411, 518
American Production and Inventory Control Society (APICS) 59, 62–3
American Society of Mechanical Engineers, see ASME
AMLE, see Academy of Management Learning and Education
APICS (American Production and Inventory Control Society) 59, 62–3
applied science 23, 25, 60, 70

appraisals 194, 258, 330, 463–4
appropriateness 133–4, 419
artefacts 9, 28, 238, 246, 249–50, 252, 473, 485
ASME (American Society of Mechanical Engineers) 30
assessment 40, 209, 283–5, 357, 402–3
Association to Advance Collegiate Schools of Business, see AACSB
assumptions 138, 140, 294, 304, 313, 315, 423–4, 450–451
  basic 8, 62–3, 146, 315, 450
  craftsman 316–17
Australia 40, 348, 524
Authentic Leadership Theory, see ALT
authority 131, 168–9, 229–30, 276–7, 335, 337, 377–9, 403–4
autonomy 181, 184, 188, 191, 223–4, 373–5, 400, 410

behaviours 13–14, 108–9, 230, 277–9, 284, 345–6, 481–7, 489–92
  individual 249, 481–2
  leadership 225, 278, 284
  managerial/leadership 10, 284, 325–6, 481–93
  organizational 23, 40, 50, 53, 239, 358, 413, 438–9
  relationship-oriented 278
beliefs 46, 106, 108–9, 257, 259–60, 262, 406–7, 453
biases, optimism 9, 154, 230–232

SUBJECT INDEX

boards 20, 163–4, 186, 222, 307, 317, 336, 344
boundaries, organizational 14, 256, 267, 509, 530, 532
branding 104, 115, 117
bureaucracy 128, 130–131, 133, 135, 137–9, 377–8, 401–3, 522
  mechanistic 392
  new bureaucracies 375–8
  study of 130, 132, 137
bureaucratic organizations 137, 158, 523–4
business climate 391–2
business education 4, 32, 149, 151–2, 156, 159, 163, 389; *see also* management education
business functions 5, 240, 439
business models 245, 263, 344
business morals 386–91
business schools 4–5, 13, 164, 166, 388, 437–56, 472, 474–6; *see also* management education
  critiques of 446–7, 450–453
  curricula 160, 166–7, 180, 237, 293, 438
business strategies 189, 405, 497

capabilities 296–7, 299–300, 306–10, 315, 356–7, 359–60, 504–5, 507
  organizational 267–8, 356, 359
capacity 63–4, 108, 110–111, 155–6, 354, 367–8, 377–8, 380
capital 13, 191, 465, 468, 499, 502–4, 506, 520
  social 309, 453
  symbolic 268
capitalism 160–161, 166, 191, 388, 412, 464, 475, 511
  managerial 388, 466
  welfare 44, 184–5
CDSR (Cochrane Database of Systematic Reviews) 429, 432
CED (Committee on Economic Development) 390, 395
central powers 376–8
centralization 137–8, 189
CEOs (Chief Executive Officers) 83, 85, 92, 114, 117, 164, 310–311, 313
change agents 11, 349, 351, 353, 355, 409, 518, 527
change initiatives 11, 210, 346, 356
change leaders 11, 347, 349–52, 355–8

change management 11, 14, 61, 343–60, 409, 518, 521, 527
  change leaders 11, 347, 349–52, 355–8
  pace of change 352–5
  post-crisis 11, 360
  problem definition 343–6
  processual perspectives 11, 350–352, 354, 358, 360
  recipes 346–9
  research agenda 358–60
  strategies 11
change processes 11, 309, 348, 350, 352, 357, 360
chaos 146, 151, 334, 340
charisma 10, 131, 281, 283
charismatic leadership 280
Chief Executive Officers, *see* CEOs
China 191, 440, 491, 499–500, 502, 506
choices 302, 305, 310, 312, 314, 339–40, 345, 352
  endogenous 302–3
  strategic 139–40, 192, 257, 298, 302–3, 313–14
CIM (Computer-Integrated Manufacturing) 66
circularity 466–7
clients 95, 220, 230, 316–17, 519, 522, 525, 529–31
closed systems 44, 128, 130
Cochrane Database of Systematic Reviews (CDSR) 429, 432
codetermination 45, 49, 149, 160, 163–4, 166
coercion 11, 169, 344, 368, 380
  power as 369
cognition 51, 150, 256–7, 259, 370, 411, 484–6, 489
  situated 484–6
cognitive processes 13, 263, 483–6, 492
coherence 131, 138, 150, 154, 159, 166, 262, 304
collective bargaining 184–6, 192, 468
Committee on Economic Development (CED) 390, 395
communication, with external stakeholder audiences 265–6
communication technologies 233–4, 446
communications management 225
competence 115, 119–20, 286, 474
competencies 8, 10, 179–80, 194, 233, 284–5, 452
competency frameworks 356–7

competitors 114, 117, 222, 300, 306, 523, 525, 529
complex firms 298-9, 308, 311-12
complex organizations 111, 316, 387
complexity 62, 134, 239, 293, 298-9, 306, 311-12, 489-90
Computer-Integrated Manufacturing (CIM) 66
computerization 9, 237-8, 246-7, 249, 252, 525
computerized algorithms 9, 246-7
computers 91, 240-241, 247, 251, 507, 525
conceptualization 10, 136, 151, 220, 226, 260, 325-6, 381
configuration approaches 321
conflict 162, 210, 234, 317, 392-3, 511, 513-14, 530
  constructive 162
  management 392, 481
consensus 193, 296, 309, 314, 380, 388, 422-3, 426
consent 20, 28, 351, 377, 380
constructive conflict 162
consultancy/consulting 14, 23, 30, 118-19, 278, 344, 393, 518-33
  active clients 530-531
  ambivalent historical relationship with management 524-8
  and management as different 520-522
  and management as equivalent 520
  and management as same and different 523-4
  managerial use of 529-31
  passive clients 530
  relationship with management 519-20
consultants
  external 401, 523-4, 528
  internal 519, 526
  management 11, 14, 85, 344, 348, 518, 522, 525
consumers 113, 117, 161, 167, 206, 211, 466, 473
contestation 14, 368, 498, 512-13
  political 512-13
context 481-5, 487-93
  cultural 21, 120, 482-4, 510, 513
  cultural and institutional 483, 486
  dynamic nature 486-9
  foreign 487-8, 490, 493

organizational 28, 311, 320, 344, 391, 413, 482-6, 490
  role 13-14, 483, 489, 493
  situational 483-4, 486-7, 489
contextual variables 13, 192, 482, 493
contingencies 138-9, 152, 309, 314, 411, 470
Contingency Model of Leadership 10, 279
contingency models 348-50
contingency theory 8, 10, 66, 71, 127-8, 132, 134, 136-41
continuity 131, 146, 299, 310, 317-18, 337, 344, 349
control 105-7, 129-30, 132-4, 190-193, 304-6, 372, 376-80, 505
  lateral 376-7
  managerial 401, 507
  neo-normative 7, 50, 112-14, 374
  normative 112, 114, 120
  organizational 111
  systems 135, 304, 308
cooperation 20, 31, 129, 315-16, 374, 378, 382, 404
coordination 129, 133, 162, 164, 299, 307, 310, 316
core processes of management 162
corporate culturalism 11, 373-5
corporate cultures 43, 111, 370, 387-8
corporate morality 393-4
corporate morals 12, 386-97
  contents of 387-8, 391, 395-6
  flavours 391-7
corporate social responsibility (CSR) 117, 163, 390, 452
cosmopolitans 521-3
costs 62, 187, 189, 205-7, 224-7, 230-232, 345, 502-3
  management 224
craftsman assumptions 316-17
craftsmanship 305, 315-16
  as agency assumption 315-17
  and strategy 317-18
craftsmen 47, 315-19
credentials 393, 442, 475
cross-cultural collaboration 107
CSR, *see* corporate social responsibility
cues 258-9, 388, 454, 492
cultural adaptability 490-492

cultural analysis 107–8, 112, 121
cultural change 107, 121, 242, 343
cultural contexts 21, 120, 482–4, 510, 513
cultural differences 14, 491, 493, 506
cultural distance 490–491
cultural processes 107, 268
cultural toolkits 122, 410
cultural trajectory 21–2, 27–8, 33
culturalism, corporate 11, 373–5
culture 28, 193, 256–7, 263–5, 267, 481–3,
    487–9, 491–3
  corporate 43, 111, 370, 387–8
  and managerial behaviour 481–2
  organizational 7, 9, 103–7, 114, 120–122, 261,
    265, 267–8
  in organizations 103–23
culture management 103–4, 106, 111–13,
    120–121
  possible return to 112–14

data 9, 67–8, 194–5, 237–43, 247, 251–2, 295–8,
    430–432
  management 237, 240–241, 251
  processing, see DP
decentralization 85–6, 89, 335, 509
decision processes 304–5, 317
decision rules 71–3
Decision-Making Model 10, 278–9
decision-making processes 241, 452
defamiliarization 7, 120–123
delivery 211, 214, 226, 230
  model 225, 230, 232
democracy 49, 98, 161–3, 165, 167–8, 360
  workplace 6, 41, 45, 50, 52; see also
    codetermination
demographics 88, 94, 234
dependencies 11, 338, 367, 531–2
deregulation of financial markets 243–5
descriptions, thick 104, 120–121, 299
design 129–30, 134, 148, 150–151, 155, 298,
    355–6, 429–30
deskilling 22, 47–8
differentiation 73, 136–7, 139, 401, 509
disciplinary power 29, 51–2
disciplinary procedures 468
discretion 131
  managerial 485

disparity, organizational 14, 497
disruptive innovation 344–5
distance, cultural 490–491
distribution 25, 45, 63–4, 192, 225, 241,
    367, 504–5
division of labour, international 14, 503–4
doctors 51, 427–8
dominant actors 498–9, 531
domination 5, 11, 28–9, 107, 169, 368, 370,
    400–401
  power as 370
DP (data processing) 237, 240–242, 504
dual identities 338, 527–8
duality, institutional 510–511

EBP, see evidence-based practice
ecology, organizational 1, 146
economics 245, 248, 250, 252, 293, 295–6,
    439, 453–4
  education 445, 451, 453
education
  business 4, 32, 149, 151–2, 156, 159, 163, 389
  economics 445, 451, 453
  management, see management education
  reform 30–33
edX 442
effective leadership 261, 277–80, 283–5
effective management 230, 277
effectiveness 4, 10, 86, 188–9, 193, 204–5,
    207, 268
efficiency 23, 25, 28, 32, 205, 209, 211, 235
  national 24–5, 371
EFMD (European Foundation for
    Management Development) 438–9
elites 22, 45, 50, 114, 167–8, 520, 523
  managerial 51, 379, 403
elitist management systems 6, 45
emotions 45, 51, 105–6, 150, 280, 331–2,
    370, 373
empirical objects 147, 151–2, 157
employees 112–14, 117–18, 163–4, 188, 191–3,
    353–4, 372–3, 389–90
  turnover 420, 429, 431
employers 23, 39–40, 48–50, 184–6, 429, 431,
    452–3, 455
employment 47, 86, 160, 179, 184–5, 192,
    318, 393–4

relationships 184, 186, 430
  security 180–181
empowerment 115, 188, 334, 377, 509
endogeneity 301–3
end-users 210–212
engagement 13, 98, 122, 207, 347–8, 359, 454, 531
entrepreneurs 112, 265, 267, 329, 466
environmental changes 300–301, 505
environmental demands 10, 138, 294, 305, 309
environmental enactment 9, 263–4
environmental uncertainty 133–4, 136, 138, 187
equilibrium, punctuated 228, 352
ethics 5, 10, 12, 394–6, 419, 422, 426, 445; *see also* morality
  normative 388, 396
ethnocentricity 508–9
European Foundation for Management Development (EFMD) 438–9
everyday life 115, 147, 405, 475, 482
everyday management 10, 277, 325
evidence-based management 12, 419–33
  medicalizing management 429–33
  paradigm shift 420–423
  as profession 426–9
  as science 423–6
evidence-based medicine 419, 422, 425, 427
evidence-based practice (EBP) 420–421
evolutionary model 501
execution-based project management model 9, 223
exit interviews 429–32
expansion 112, 117, 164, 184, 317, 437, 472, 475
expatriates 490–491, 513
expert knowledge 14, 500, 505
expertise 189–90, 376–8, 474–5, 519, 521–2, 524, 527, 532
  specialist 356–7, 521
  technical 20, 241, 389
experts 26, 153–4, 163, 357, 425, 472, 476, 521–3
external consultants 401, 523–4, 528
externalized management 523, 525

facilitation 14, 344, 356, 518–20, 523, 526
fads 7, 90, 93, 95, 99
FDI (foreign direct investment) 500, 503
feasibility 226–7

finance 31–2, 210, 237–41, 243, 245–7, 249–50, 439, 441
  sociology of 9, 238, 246, 248–50, 252
financial crisis 159–60, 163–5, 239, 244, 247, 249, 344, 437
financial market technology, *see* FinTech
financial markets 187, 190–191, 238–9, 243–52, 352
  computerization 246–7, 249
  deregulation 243–5
  models of financial trading 246–8
  sociology of finance 9, 238, 246, 248–50, 252
financial technology 245, 248–50
financial trading 238–9, 243, 245–7, 249–50, 252
financialization 9, 186–7, 190–191, 195, 238–9, 243–5, 252, 379
FinTech (financial market technology) 245–6, 248, 252
fit approaches 308–9
followers 10, 21–2, 24, 44, 276–7, 279–83, 285, 287
  and leaders 10, 276, 279–80, 283, 285, 287
force-field diagrams 466
Fordism 113, 180, 184, 187, 371–2
foreign direct investment, *see* FDI
foremen 327
formal structures 28, 117, 130, 151
fragmentation 293–8, 303–5, 313, 319–21, 327–9, 337, 461, 468
  intellectual 10, 293, 305
freedom 49, 51, 53, 84, 98, 112, 466, 470
front-line managers 337, 507
functional managers 190, 229
functional rationality 405–6

game playing, micro-political 513–14
GCCs (Global commodity chains) 504–5, 513
gender 120, 287, 332
general managers 295, 327, 329–30
general systems theory 8, 128, 130, 132
generalizability 320, 451
Germany 4, 163–4, 166, 183, 186, 191, 193, 504
GFC, *see* global financial crisis
Global commodity chains, *see* GCCs

global financial crisis (GFC) 159–60, 163–5, 437
global managers, role 14, 492–3
global value chains (GVCs) 504
global work 483–4, 488
globalization 8, 180, 186–7, 190–191, 195, 319, 335, 498–9
GMAT (Graduate Management Admissions Test) 440
goals 148–9, 219–20, 232–3, 259, 277–8, 306–7, 315–18, 347–8
  organizational 39, 52, 131, 181, 220, 389
Google 11, 113, 346, 371, 373–4
government 50, 53, 185, 192, 213–14, 239, 243–5, 421
Graduate Management Admissions Test (GMAT) 440
grandiosity 114–18, 120, 463
grievances 179, 194, 370, 392–3, 468
group performance 278, 286
growth 2–4, 9, 13, 194, 238, 244–5, 307–8, 438
GVCs (global value chains) 504

habits 28, 30–31, 108–9, 167, 248, 327, 408
Harvard Business School (HBS) 4, 6, 32, 41, 43–4, 65, 396, 442
Hawthorne studies 6, 39–44, 46–7, 372
HBS, *see* Harvard Business School
HBX 442–3
headquarters 299, 376, 489–90, 498, 500, 505, 507–9
healthcare 152, 201, 203, 207, 210–211, 213–14, 337–8, 430–431
healthcare management 419–20, 431
hegemonic ideology 6, 20–22, 33
  cultural trajectory 27–8
  scientific management as 21–3
hegemony 21–2, 27, 33
  cultural 28
heterogeneity 65, 133–4, 430
HFT (high frequency trading) 9, 246–52
HFT strategies 247, 249–51
hierarchy 113, 130, 380, 388, 390, 423, 425–6, 522
  managerial 307, 332
  organizational 195, 380

high commitment models 8, 179–83, 186–7, 190–191, 193–5
high frequency trading, *see* HFT
historical models 6, 8, 11, 17–69
historical research 469, 471–2
Hoshin Kanri 96–9
HRM, *see* human resources management
human relations 14, 39–53, 129, 185, 277, 466, 498, 524
  historical myth 45–50
  infrastructure 11, 372–3
  problematization of received wisdom 43–5
  school 39–40, 43–6, 48–53
human resources management 7–8, 50–53, 179–82, 187–8, 190–193, 420, 519–20, 527
  analytics and future 193–5
  globalization and financialization 190–191
  history 183–6
  institutional isomorphism 186–7
  national systems 191–3
  normative models 180–182
  and performance debate 182–3
human rights 163, 166
hybrid organizations 136

ideal types 64, 137–8, 147–8, 158, 211, 522
identities 110–112, 150–151, 157–8, 259, 261, 264–8, 370–373, 511–14
  dual 338, 527–8
  managerial 334
identity regulation 109, 111–12
identity work 14, 109–10, 513
ideologies 1–2, 14, 19–21, 109, 111, 245, 332, 421
  hegemonic 6, 20–22, 27, 33
IMF (International Monetary Fund) 499–500
immersion 7, 120–121, 123
incoherence 13, 379, 462, 464, 466
India 4, 95, 189, 191, 499, 502, 505–6
industrial psychologists 27, 43, 49
industrial relations 26, 161, 192, 468, 471, 511
industrial revolution 2–3, 24, 277, 465
industrial sociology 327, 469
inequality 331, 471, 476
informal curriculum 13, 454
information 9, 194, 237–43, 245–7, 251–2, 329, 448, 492–3

management 237-8, 241-2, 251
processing 485, 487, 489, 491-2
systems 61, 64, 307, 314, 441
technology 9, 147, 219, 237-43, 245-6, 249, 251, 335
infrastructures 219, 252, 368, 370-371, 374
organizational 371
of power 11, 368, 370-371
taylorist 371
innovation 8-9, 145, 153, 181, 262-3, 306, 308, 320
disruptive 344-5
sustaining 262, 344-5
Institute for Healthcare Improvement (IHI) 346-7
institutional context 190, 268, 483-4, 486, 498
institutional duality 510-511
institutional entrepreneurs 409-10
institutional environment 486, 491, 506
institutional isomorphism 8, 179, 186-7
institutional theory 12, 66, 69, 71, 139-40, 402, 408, 410
institutionalism 14, 408-9, 510, 512
integration 64, 66, 89, 136, 162, 226-7, 296-7, 304-5
management 224
theoretical 306, 319
total 84-5, 88-9
intellectual fragmentation 10, 293, 305
interconnectedness 306-8
interdependence 128-9, 133, 167, 529
pooled 133
interdependency management 233
internal consultants 519, 526
internal organization 132, 497
internal processes 139-41
internal systems 134-5, 352
international division of labour 14, 503-4
international management 14, 107, 483, 493, 497-514
global context 498-9, 505
institutionalist approaches 510-511
international division of labour and dispersal of production 503-5
motives for internationalization 501-3
offshore outsourcing 505-6

organizing MNCs 506-10
political issues and power relations within MNCs 512-13
understanding MNCs 499-501
International Monetary Fund, *see* IMF
internationalization 14, 501-3
motives for 501-3
internet 237-8, 245
intertemporal linkages 294, 300, 306, 308-10
interviews 46, 95-8, 119, 121, 284, 327, 330, 430-431
exit 429-32
intra-organizational management 213
intuition 72-3, 82, 309, 319
inventory 59-60, 64, 67
investors 243-5, 301-2, 500
iron cage 12, 150, 402, 411
isomorphic pressures 189-91
isomorphism, institutional 8, 179, 186-7
IT artefacts 9, 238, 246, 249-50

Japan 4, 7, 93, 96-8, 185, 499-500, 504, 506
Japanese contexts 7, 81, 85, 96
Japanese management styles 96, 98, 104-6
Japanese manufacturing 62, 71, 201
JIT (Just-in-Time) 62, 66-7, 69
Just-in-Time, *see* JIT

kanbans 67
knowledge 5-6, 9-10, 152-4, 224-5, 237-43, 251, 470-472, 530-531
expert 14, 500, 505
management 235, 238, 242-52, 519
rule-of-thumb 25, 29
social 426
work 9, 33, 115, 238, 315, 522-3
workers 22, 471, 522

labour 160-162, 165, 401, 403-4, 407, 468, 499, 503-5
markets 75, 161, 192, 442
language 28, 94-5, 140, 147, 149, 257, 260-261, 264
games 8, 147-9, 154, 158, 264
lateral control 376-7
layered interpretation 104, 120-121, 123

leaders 10, 22, 26, 114–16, 131, 257, 261–2, 276–87
  assessing, selecting, and developing 283–6
  change 11, 347, 349–52, 355–8
  charisma 280
  effective 277–8, 283–5
  and followers 10, 276, 279–80, 283, 285, 287
  selection 284, 287
  transformational 281–2
leadership 10, 106–7, 260–261, 276–88, 347–8, 355, 438–9, 452
  assessing, selecting, and developing leaders 283–6
  behaviours 225, 278, 284
  capacity 281–2, 285–6
  contemporary theories 279–83
  definitions, distinctions and early theories 276–9
  development 285, 444
  effective 261, 277–80, 283–5
  future of management and leadership studies 286–8
  organizational 167, 287
  roles 261, 283, 330, 355
  study of 283, 287–8
  traits 277–8
  transformational 106, 280–282
lean implementation 207–10
lean initiatives 188, 210
lean principles/production 8, 64, 73, 180–181, 187–8, 193, 200–201, 204–14
  definition 206–8
  in public services 208–13
lean thinking 204–6
learning processes 242, 300, 449
legitimacy 52, 116, 131, 265–6, 377, 379, 382, 426
  social 187, 191–2, 372
liaison 328
liberalism, neo-economic 161, 165
life cycles 93, 220–221, 226, 228, 233, 510
linkages 302, 307, 313, 315
  intertemporal 294, 300, 306, 308–9
literature 10, 12–14, 201–3, 238–9, 248–50, 258, 510–511, 529–31
LMX Theory 280, 286

McKinsey & Co 347–8, 521, 525
MAMM (management-as-medicine-motif) 12, 420, 423, 426–7, 433
management, see also Introductory Note
  as academic discipline 461–77
  as practice of power 367–82
management accounting 75, 194
Management by Objectives, see MbO
management consultants 11, 14, 85, 344, 348, 518, 522, 525; see also consultancy/consulting
management education 2, 4–5, 13, 90, 241–2, 251, 437–56, 526
  academic literature 445–53
  course demand 440–441
  critiques of business schools 446–7, 450, 453
  definition 438–9
  financial pressures 439–40
  forces for change 439–43
  formative studies on 443–5
  future research 449–50, 453–5
  online teaching and learning 446–9
  student characteristics 440
  and technology 441–2
management functions 82, 130, 183, 240–241, 403
management information systems, see MIS
management of meaning 9, 11, 21, 106, 256–69
  future research directions 266–7
  internal and external 260–261
  as managerial v organizational capability 267–8
  organizational and strategic change 262
Management of Projects (MoP) 9, 223, 225–7, 230; see also project management
management power 368, 374, 381
management practice 7, 10–11, 13–14, 81–2, 85, 91, 325–40, 467–8
  ethnographic stream 331–4
  functionalist stream 326–31
  gender 332
  management as work practice 330–331
  managerial identity 334
  middle management behaviour 331
  morality of management 333–4

nature of managerial work 328–9
networking 328, 333, 356
rationality of work fragmentation 329–30
recent research 334–40
research 326–40
in small companies and in public health care 337–8
stability and change 335–7
theses of managerial work 338–40
unofficial aspects of managerial work 331–2
variation in managerial work 327–8
management theory 53, 75, 98, 105, 195, 202–3, 461, 464
management-as-medicine-motif, see MAMM
managerial behaviour 10, 284, 325–6, 481–93
and context of global work 483–4
cultural and institutional context 483, 486
and culture 481–2
dynamic nature of context 487–9
organizational context 486
physical setting 487
situational context 486–7
socio-dynamics 487
and structural position 487, 490–491
theoretical implications and future research agenda 489–92
managerial capitalism 388, 466
managerial hierarchy 307, 332
managerial identity 334
managerial work 115, 327–40, 452
theses of 338–40
unofficial aspects 331–2
variation in 327–8
managerialism 149, 332, 391, 528
managerialization 462, 468, 475–6
manipulation 11, 28, 169, 245, 344, 368
power as 369
manufacturing 60, 62–6, 94–5, 149, 184, 200, 213, 379–80
strategy 62–3, 66–7, 73
marketing 5, 25, 30, 66–7, 75, 240–241, 439, 441
markets 135, 137, 244–8, 250, 266, 268, 502–3, 525–6
material properties 249–50, 252
Materials Requirements Planning, see MRP

mathematical models 59–60, 74
matrix structures 145, 229
MBAs (Master's degree in Business Administration) 4–5, 237, 241, 437–8, 440, 442, 452–4, 521–2
students 50, 201–2, 446
MbO (Management by Objectives) 7, 81–99
American view 85–92
Japanese view 96–9
outcome 85–99
setting of objectives 82–4
total integration 84–5
UK view 92–6
meaning
concept 257–60
construction/creation 259, 269, 488–9
shared 107, 118, 159, 260–261, 264, 386, 514
meaning-making 103, 105, 107, 123, 257–67, 492
mechanistic bureaucracy 392
medicalization 12–13, 429–33
medicine 5, 12, 344, 422–8, 433, 474
evidence-based 419, 422, 425, 427
mental revolution 20, 27, 31, 51
mergers 63, 191, 297, 301, 306, 310, 313
metaethics 388, 396
metaphors 108, 128, 344, 412, 469
root 103–5, 122
micro-political game playing 513–14
middle management 90, 331
middle managers 310, 331, 334–5, 337, 344, 507, 524
MIS (management information systems) 9, 61, 237–52
and financialization 243
mismanagement 223, 358
misrepresentation, strategic 231–2
Mitbestimmung 163
MNCs (multinational corporations) 14, 497–514, 524
home and host country embeddedness 510–511
organization 506–10
political issues and power relations within 512–13
understanding 499–501

models 7–12, 59–61, 182–3, 189–90, 207, 246–9, 346–7, 419–20
  contingency 348–50
  delivery 225, 230, 232
  high commitment 8, 179–83, 186–7, 190–191, 193, 195
  mathematical 59–60, 74
  normative 180–182, 188–9
  Ulrich 187, 189–90
modern organizations 154, 219, 229, 234, 402, 406, 462
Modernity 12, 154, 400–413, 469
  institutions and managers 408–11
  management in pursuit of progress 402–4
  reassessment of management in postmodern world 404–8
  reflexive 411–13
MOOCs 442, 448
MoP, *see* Management of Projects
moral infrastructure 371
moral silence 388, 394
morality 12, 121, 168, 333, 386–97, 412, 453
  corporate 393–4
  of management 333–4
  organizational 391, 395
morals 12, 28, 386–8, 391, 394–7, 470
  business 386–8, 391
  corporate 12, 386–97
motivation 50, 277, 280–281, 286, 373, 449
MRP (Materials Requirements Planning) 7, 61–3, 66, 74
multinational corporations, *see* MNCs
multiple stakeholders 266, 301–2, 318, 320
myths 104, 119, 154, 261, 265, 406–7

Nasdaq 246–7
national efficiency 24–5, 371
natural order 50, 403–4
Nazism 407–8
neo-bureaucracies 11, 375–7, 526–8
neo-economic liberalism 161, 165
neo-normative control 7, 50, 112–14, 374
Netherlands 192–3, 500
networking 328, 333, 356
networks 11, 248, 250, 258, 330, 332, 338, 504
new bureaucracies 375–8

new technologies 234, 240, 242, 335, 337, 343–4, 380–381, 449–50
normative control 112, 114, 120
normative models 180–182, 188–9
norms 28, 30, 191–3, 234, 265, 267, 408–9, 486
n-step recipes 346

objectives 1, 7, 81–91, 93–5, 97, 99, 146–7, 429; *see also* MbO
  organizational 81, 338, 379
objects
  empirical 147, 151–2, 157
  legitimate 150, 475
oil 222, 500–501
OM, *see* operations management
one best way 24, 134, 136, 139, 404
online teaching and learning 446–9
open systems 127, 131, 134–8, 140
  theory/models 7–8, 127, 132–3, 139–40, 444–5
operational processes 46, 206, 301
operations management 7–8, 57–75, 200–214, 423
  definition 57–8
  emergence 59–61
  incidencen of terms 58
  public services 204–6, 213
  relation between theory and practice 69–71
  research publication profile 201–4
  rise of theory 68
operations research 22, 58, 60, 71, 83, 88
operative work 117–18
optimism bias 9, 154, 230–232
organization charts 130, 166, 390
organization studies 49, 105, 148, 151, 156, 158, 421
organization theory (OT) 103, 127–41, 147, 167
organizational activities 9, 107, 243, 263, 266, 335, 368
organizational analysis 105, 109, 112, 137
organizational behaviour 23, 40, 50, 53, 239, 358, 413, 438–9
organizational boundaries 14, 256, 267, 509, 530, 532
organizational capability 267–8, 356, 359
organizational change 11, 107, 135, 343, 346, 350, 352, 359–60

organizational context 28, 311, 320, 344, 391, 413, 482–6, 490
organizational culture 7, 9, 103–4, 106–7, 114, 120–122, 261, 267–8
  culture toolkit and identity formation 108–11
  fall 105–7
  possible return 107–8
  rise 104–5
  and societal culture 268–9
organizational design 127, 130, 134, 136–9, 155, 189, 469
organizational ecology 1, 146
organizational forms 22, 131, 138, 148, 368, 370, 374, 392
organizational goals 39, 52, 131, 181, 220, 389
organizational life 103–5, 107, 110, 122–3, 195, 250, 258, 264
organizational objectives 81, 338, 379
organizational politics 332, 367
organizational power 352, 370, 373, 380
organizational researchers 157, 230, 268
organizational strategies 182, 220, 257, 262, 393, 467
organizational systems 22, 128–9, 140, 226
organizations
  bureaucratic 137, 158, 523–4
  contemporary 11, 110, 118, 120, 151, 370, 375, 382
  international 498, 504, 512
  modern 154, 219, 229, 234, 402, 406, 462
  studying culture in 103–23
organizing 145–7, 150–154, 156, 158–9, 161–2, 165–7, 405–8, 532
organizing principles 1, 22, 149, 158, 166, 168
OT, see organization theory
outputs 30, 45, 132–3, 219, 371, 444–5, 465
outsourcing, offshore 505–6
owner-managers 334, 337

paradigm shifts 6, 345, 391, 419–20, 502
participation 51–3, 92, 158–66, 340, 344, 348–9, 379
path dependence 8, 11, 179, 183, 313, 360
perceptions 28, 86, 264–5, 283, 285, 343, 351, 370

performance 82–6, 179–80, 194–5, 280–282, 307–8, 312–13, 317–18, 346–7
  expectations 301–2, 307, 310
  goals 92, 302, 353
  group 278, 286
  management 129, 181, 194, 202, 354, 360
  and strategic management 301–3
performativity 33, 149, 248, 250
personnel function 180, 184–6
personnel management, see human resources management
philosophy 20–21, 23, 25–7, 40, 86–7, 153, 156–8, 161
planning 7, 24–6, 30–31, 62, 129, 224–5, 230, 304
  fallacy 231–2
  processes 231, 304
  strategic 71, 304, 306
politics 11, 120–121, 165, 184, 350–351, 498, 508, 511
pooled interdependence 133
population ecology 139–40
positivism 13, 422–5, 433
post-bureaucracies 10, 146, 151, 335, 368, 375
post-crisis change management 11, 360
post-disciplinarity 13, 463, 468–74
power 11, 155, 160–162, 167–9, 229–30, 276–7, 470–472, 511–13
  central v peripheral 375–80
  as coercion 369
  consent and resistance in new bureaucracies 377–8
  dimensions of 11, 369–70
  as domination 370
  elite 389, 392
  future developments 380–381
  inequities 160–161
  infrastructures of 11, 368, 370–371
  management as practice of 367–82
  as manipulation 369
  organizational 352, 370, 373, 380
  relationships 276, 338, 367, 369, 375
  servants of 49, 51
  as subjectification 370
  theories of 369–70
prejudices 8, 28, 71, 146–7, 473
problematization 7, 120–123, 157

problem-solving 6, 206, 209, 452, 455
process improvements 188, 210, 234
process issues 10, 294, 312, 320
process mapping 207, 209
process theories 305, 321, 350, 352, 358
processual perspectives 11, 350–352, 354, 358, 360
procurement 226–7
procurement management 225
product markets 192, 306–7
production, *see also* manufacturing
    management 58–63
    planning 61, 66
    processes 23, 49, 60, 75, 83, 264, 504
productivity 41–2, 52, 65, 83, 180, 187–8, 277, 285
products 53, 133, 135, 206, 222–3, 244–5, 298–9, 504
profit accumulation 48–9
profitability 50, 302, 308, 318
project delivery 221, 226–7, 230–231
project life cycles 221, 223, 228–9, 234
project management 9, 118, 219–35, 356, 519, 522, 528, 531
    body of knowledge 224–5
    challenges 227–9
    managers of multiple projects 232–3
    paradigm 225–7
    planning and optimism bias 230–232
    responsibility and authority 229–30
    skills 9, 222, 530
    virtual project teams 9, 233–4
project success 223, 229, 234
project teams 220, 222, 225, 228–9, 233–4, 314, 393, 530
project-based work 9, 219–20, 222, 235
projects 119, 155, 219–34, 314, 316–17, 518–19, 529, 531–2
    life cycles 93, 220–221, 226, 228, 233, 510
    ubiquity 219–24
psychology 40, 50, 53, 277–8, 293, 296, 424, 426
public sector 90, 92, 94, 164, 187, 200, 203–5, 213
public services 8, 200–201, 203–8, 210–214, 466
    fitness for purpose of lean principles 212–13
    implementation of lean principles 208–12
    operations management 204–6, 213
punctuated equilibrium 228, 352

QESs (quasi-experimental studies) 429, 431
quality 62, 205–6, 220, 226–7, 280, 316–17, 430, 443–4
    management 62, 96, 200, 225
    revolution 62
    standards 315–16
quasi-experimental studies, *see* QESs

randomized controlled trials (RCTs) 422, 429–31
rapid improvement events, *see* RIEs
rational actors 409–10
rationality, functional 405–6
rationalization 24, 116, 152, 401–2, 406–7
RBV, *see* resource-based view
RCTs (randomized controlled trials) 422, 429–31
R&D 219, 222, 379, 501, 505, 508–9
realism 423–4
recession 205, 358–9
recipes 116, 165, 346, 348–9, 351, 358–9
reductionism 13, 425–7, 429, 432–3
regiocentricity 509
reification 147, 149–50, 153–6
relationships 9–12, 14, 132–3, 279–80, 374–6, 490–491, 518–24, 531–2
reliability 115, 234, 284–5
reorganization 31, 343, 525
reputation 41, 257, 266–8, 300, 345, 393, 445
research agendas 158, 256, 266, 320, 358–60, 489
research approaches 202, 313, 332
research designs 296–8, 303, 320
resistance 11, 313, 315, 343–4, 349–52, 367–8, 376–8, 381–2
resource holders 257, 264–5
resource-based view (RBV) 63, 68–9, 314, 505
resources 107, 109–10, 128–30, 132–3, 229–30, 260–261, 268, 295–7
    symbolic 114, 261, 265
responsibility 3, 53, 224–5, 227–30, 233–4, 375–6, 378–9, 407
responsiveness, local 507, 509

revenues 243-4, 440, 442, 500, 525
RIEs (rapid improvement events) 208-9
right to manage 48-9
rights 49, 51, 118, 163, 165-6, 168, 419
rigidity 106, 402-3
risk 223, 225-7, 244, 356, 358, 411, 506, 508
  management 225
risk ratios (RR) 430
role models 14, 281, 348, 354, 519, 527
RR (risk ratios) 430
rule-of-thumb knowledge 25, 29
rules 130-131, 192, 335, 372, 379-80, 408-9,
    411, 486
  managerial 380, 404
rules-in-use 388, 394

samples, large 298-9, 302, 310, 327
scheduled meetings 336-8
schedules 220-221, 339, 468
science of management 7, 59, 71, 74, 461
scientific management 19-33, 41, 44, 180,
    183-4, 188, 403-4, 524-5
  cultural trajectory of a hegemonic
    ideology 27-8
  educational reform 30-33
  as hegemonic ideology 21-3
  loci of diffusion 29-33
  methods and principles 25-7
  philosophy 23-5
  workplace reform 29-30
scope management 224
self-control 7, 81-99
self-efficacy 449, 453
self-esteem 114-15
self-fulfilment 52-3
self-management 53, 356
self-presentation 103-4
self-understanding 400
senior management 208, 224, 354, 508
senior managers 116, 119, 240, 518, 529
sensegiving 258, 262
sensemaking 107, 258, 261, 263, 484
servants of power 49, 51
service delivery 191-2, 195, 209
service delivery processes 209, 498, 504
service management 66, 204, 214
service processes 65-6, 208, 211, 213

service quality 104, 204
service users 205, 207-8, 210-212
services 60, 64-6, 205-7, 209-11, 213-14, 243,
    245, 524-6
shared meanings 107, 118, 159, 260-261, 264,
    386, 514
shared understandings 295, 386, 397
shareholder value 160, 395
shareholders 187, 189, 191, 243, 318, 338, 390,
    450-451
single-project managers 233
situated cognitions 484-6
  perspective of 13, 481, 483, 493
situational context 483-4, 486-7, 489
Situational Leadership Theory (SLT) 10,
    278-9, 285
skills 13-14, 108, 190, 193-4, 315, 452-3,
    455-6, 492-3
SLT (Situational Leadership Theory) 10,
    278-9, 285
SM, *see* scientific management
social capital 309, 453
social change 343, 408-9
social democracy 165-6, 168
social knowledge 426
social legitimacy 187, 191-2, 372
social order 168, 316, 368
social partnership 164, 511
social processes 160, 163, 330
social relations 21, 111, 169, 405-6, 408
social sciences 109, 147, 156, 422-4, 426, 431,
    472, 477
social structure 42, 248, 316, 386
social studies of technology 9, 246,
    249-50, 252
social systems 42-3, 128-9, 136, 338
social theory 312, 400, 402, 407-8
social world 401, 405, 423-4
socialization 22, 29, 113, 258, 260, 344, 397, 474
socio-cultural perspective 259, 269
socio-dynamics 487
sociology 50, 129, 131-2, 248, 252, 257,
    293, 295-6
  cultural 267
  of finance 9, 238, 246, 248-50, 252
  of financial markets 248
  industrial 327, 469

socio-technical systems 129, 132, 248
software 238, 241–2, 245, 251, 446, 505
solidarity 161, 376, 381
stability 12, 39, 135, 138, 394, 400–401, 409, 411
stakeholders 164, 224–7, 230, 232, 262, 264–5,
    301–2, 444
  management 225, 351
  multiple 266, 301–2, 318, 320
standardization 25, 28, 32, 130, 137–8, 189, 420
Stanford 4, 442, 444
statistical analysis 71, 424–5
status quo 280, 346–8, 408
strategic actors 298, 301, 303, 306, 312–13
strategic change 9, 262, 303, 345, 349
strategic choices 139–40, 192, 257, 298,
    302–3, 313–14
strategic decisions 148, 165, 293, 297–301,
    311, 317–18
strategic information systems 9, 237
strategic management 10, 238, 264,
    293–321, 498
  agency, strategy, and craft 311–13
  complexity 298–9
  craftsmanship and strategy 317–18
  craftsmanship as agency assumption 315–17
  and interconnectedness 306–8
  and inter-relational linkages 310–311
  and intertemporal linkages 294, 300,
    306, 308–10
  Mintzberg, strategy, and craft 318–19
  and performance 301–3
  process theories and craft
    perspectives 303–6
  recent studies of fragmentation 294–8
  strategy and agency construct 313–15
  theories 298–9, 302
  time 299–301
strategic misrepresentation 231–2
strategic partners 189–90
strategic planning 71, 304, 306
strategic thinking 302, 339, 356
strategies, organizational 182, 220, 257, 262,
    393, 467
strategy theories 10, 294, 299–300, 302, 308
structural position 487, 490–491
structures
  formal 28, 117, 130, 151

market 306, 467
matrix 145, 229
subjectification 11, 368, 370, 470
  power as 370
subordinates 91–2, 130–131, 278–9, 284–5, 328,
    330, 335–7, 390–392
subsidiaries 14, 299, 498, 506–13
subsidiary managers 119, 508, 510–511
subunits 136, 299, 307, 311, 313, 315, 320, 512
supervisors 82, 115, 130, 284–5, 327, 372
supervisory boards 163
supervisory work 327
suppliers 63–4, 71, 206, 225, 301, 306–7, 505
supply chain management 61, 63–4, 67, 70, 194
supply chains 63–4, 71, 225, 525
sustainability 71, 205–6, 210
Sweden 4, 119, 161, 163–6, 439
symbolic actions 9, 256, 266–7, 339, 351
symbolic resources 114, 261, 265
symbolism 105, 107, 261, 488
symbols 28, 118, 259–60, 262, 267, 269,
    485, 488
systematic review 421, 429, 431–3
systems, open 127, 131, 134–8, 140
systems approach/thinking 8, 60, 66, 128, 132,
    136, 455
systems theory 128–9, 133, 136, 140, 146, 152
  general 8, 128, 130, 132
  open 7–8

tautology 463, 466–7, 471–2
Taylorism 3, 6, 19–20, 50–51, 371, 382
Taylorist democrats 46, 48–9
teaching 29, 31, 62, 65, 438, 443–4, 448, 455–6
technical expertise 20, 241, 389
technological change 190, 192, 195, 238
technology 133–5, 137–8, 192, 238–40, 245–52,
    439–43, 446, 448–50
  management 242, 252
  social studies of 9, 246, 249–50, 252
temporal orientation 301, 314–15
terminology 7, 211, 336, 355
thick descriptions 104, 120–121, 299
time management 224, 356
total quality management 7, 22, 62, 97, 193,
    205, 334, 511
Total Quality Management, see TQM

TQM (Total Quality Management) 7, 22, 62, 66, 70, 73–4, 97, 99
trade schools 5
trade unions 42, 45, 47–8, 164, 184, 193, 468, 510
trading
   algorithmic 245–7, 249, 251
   financial 238–9, 243, 245–7, 249–50, 252
training 29–30, 45, 47–8, 180, 192–4, 349, 351, 519; *see also* management education
Training within Industry (TWI) 47–8
transaction cost economics 68, 501
transformational change 11, 343–4, 346–8, 359–60; *see also* change management
transformational leaders 281–2
transformational leadership 106, 280–282
Transformational Leadership Theory 10, 280–281, 286
trust 71, 163, 181, 234, 281, 335, 509
turnover 211, 310, 314, 372, 431–2
TWI (Training within Industry) 47–8

Udacity 442
Ulrich Model 187, 189–90
uncertainty 134–7, 263–4, 330, 333–4, 338, 360, 367, 369
   environmental 133–4, 136, 138, 187

unions 45–9, 163, 168, 181, 184–6, 193
users, service 205, 207–8, 210–212

value stream mapping 209
violence 12, 381, 466
virtual project teams 9, 233–4
visual management 207, 209

Wall Street 160, 393–5
welfare capitalism 44, 184–5
Western Electric, *see* Hawthorne studies
Wharton 4, 40–41, 442
women 42, 48, 165, 287, 332, 392, 440, 482
work fragmentation 336, 339
   rationality 329–30
work organizations 6, 148, 163, 187–8, 192, 276, 397, 468–9
work practices 46, 238, 248, 326–7, 329–30
   management as 330–331
workers 22–7, 29–30, 39–53, 181, 183–5, 191–4, 372–4, 376–7
workforce 47–8, 59, 105, 183–4, 186, 190, 193, 372
workplace democracy 6, 41, 45, 50, 52
workplace reform 29–30
workshops 31, 93, 208, 246, 285–6, 316–17, 356, 371

Lightning Source UK Ltd.
Milton Keynes UK
UKHW031023290920
370729UK00002B/2